FESTIVAL & SPECIAL EVENT MANAGEMENT

FIFTH EDITION

WILEY AUSTRALIA TOURISM SERIES

FESTIVAL & SPECIAL EVENT MANAGEMENT

FIFTH EDITION

JOHNNY ALLEN | WILLIAM O'TOOLE
ROBERT HARRIS | IAN McDONNELL

WILEY
John Wiley & Sons Australia, Ltd

Fifth edition published 2011 by
John Wiley & Sons Australia, Ltd
42 McDougall Street, Milton, Qld 4064

First edition published 1999

Second edition published 2002

Third edition published 2005

Fourth edition published 2008

Typeset in Berkeley LT Book 10/12

National Library of Australia Cataloguing-in-Publication entry

Title:	Festival and special event management/ Johnny Allen . . . [et al.].
Edition:	5th ed.
ISBN:	9781742164618 (pbk.)
Notes:	Includes index.
Subjects:	Festivals — Management. Special events — Management.
Other Authors/ Contributors:	Allen, Johnny.
Dewey Number:	394.26068

Typeset in India by diacriTech

Printed in Singapore by
Markono Print Media Pte Ltd

10 9 8 7 6

ABOUT THE AUTHORS

JOHNNY ALLEN

Johnny Allen was the foundation director of the Australian Centre for Event Management (ACEM) at the University of Technology, Sydney where he is now associate director, business development. He was event manager for the Darling Harbour Authority from 1989 to 1996, and has an extensive career in event planning. Prior to his position at the ACEM, he was the special event manager for Tourism New South Wales. Johnny is now semi-retired but continues his involvement with event management and event education.

WILLIAM O'TOOLE

William O'Toole is an international events development specialist. He assists councils, cities, regions, countries and companies to grow their events portfolio and write their strategies. For five years he advised the Supreme Commission for Tourism in the Kingdom of Saudi Arabia on the development of their tourism event program in the thirteen provinces. Bill trains and assists the United Nations event organisers in places such as the Sudan and Uganda and is facilitating the development of the event industry in Kenya. He is a founding director of the Event Management Body of Knowledge and key adviser to the International Event Management Competency Standard. From Scotland to Johannesburg, he has trained events staff in the application of project and risk management to their events. Bill has been involved in events innovation, creation, operations, management and strategy in over 30 countries. He is currently writing a textbook on events feasibility and development.

ROB HARRIS

Rob Harris has been involved in event management, education and research for over 10 years and has developed undergraduate, postgraduate and TAFE programs in the area. Rob teaches programs in event management in a number of countries around the world including England, Scotland, Singapore, China, Malaysia and New Zealand. He is a founding Director of the New South Wales Festivals and Events Association and is a member of the editorial board of the journals *Event Management* and *International Journal of Event Management Research*. He is currently completing his doctoral studies in the use of events as tools in driving the ecologically sustainable development agenda of the places where they take place.

IAN McDONNELL

Ian McDonnell is a senior lecturer in the Faculty of Business's School of Leisure, Sport and Tourism at the University of Technology, Sydney (UTS) where he teaches management and marketing of leisure and tourism services. He, along with Johnny Allen, constructed the very first academic course in event management in Australia and perhaps the world – the Executive Certificate in Event Management held at UTS in 1996. He soon discovered that there was no useful text book for a course of this type, hence the origin of the this text, now in its fifth edition. He continues to research in event management, particularly the sponsorship of events.

STEVE BROWN

Steve Brown is Head of the Tourism Department at Flinders University, South Australia, where he teaches festival and event design and management. Steve works as both an academic and event industry practitioner, working in most states of Australia designing and producing a wide range of large-scale outdoor festivals and events. He is a member of the International Festival and Events Association and the Event Education and Research Network Australasia, an Associate Fellow of Meetings Events Australia (MEA), and a founding member of the international Event Design Research Network. Steve is also a member of the Editorial Advisory Board of the *International Journal of Event and Festival Management* and has written chapters for a number of international event texts. In 2009, Steve was appointed to the judging panel for the Australian Event Awards for the Best Achievement in the Design category.

MEEGAN JONES

Meegan Jones is the author of *Sustainable event management: a practical guide*. She is an events professional focusing her work on developing sustainable management solutions for live events. She worked as Sustainability Co-ordinator for Festival Republic (Reading, Leeds, Latitude & Glastonbury Festivals UK), developed sustainability solutions at Peats Ridge Festival in Australia, and worked on greening for Live Earth India and the London Marathon. She is on the working group for Global Reporting Initiative's (GRI) events industry sector supplement, is a global greening consultant for Live Earth, and is festivals consultant for UK music industry climate impact organisation Julie's Bicycle. She consults on the UN Music & Environment Initiative and is on the working group for ISO 20121, a standard for events sustainability. She is Managing Director of GreenShoot Pacific in Australia, which works with events, screen and music touring industries to provide sustainable production solutions, workshops and consultancy services.

CONTENTS

Preface xvii
Acknowledgements xviii
Examples at a glance xxi

PART 1: EVENT CONTEXT 1

CHAPTER 1 An overview of the event field 3

Introduction 5
Special events as benchmarks for our lives 5
The modern Australian tradition of celebrations 6
The birth of an event industry 8
Challenges face the new industry 10
Events on the world stage 11
What are special events? 11
Types of event 12
Size 12
Form or content 15
The structure of the event industry 17
Event organisations 17
Event management companies 17
Event industry suppliers 17
Venues 17
Industry associations 18
External regulatory bodies 20
Event management, education and training 20
Identifying the knowledge and skills required by event managers 20
Training delivery 22
Career opportunities in events 23
Event profile: Australian Centre for Event Management (www.acem.uts.edu.au) 24
Summary 25
Questions 25
Case study: RSVP: The event for the events industry 26
References 28

CHAPTER 2 Perspectives on events 31

Introduction 32
The government perspective 32
National government 32
State government 33
Local government 33
The role of government in events 33
Event strategies 35
Creating celebration spaces and precincts 39
Events and urban development 40
The corporate perspective 43
Corporate use of events 44
Association conferences 45
Return on investment 46

The community perspective 47
Community events 47
Event profile: Mulga Bill Festival, Yeoval 47
Regional festivals as community builders 48
The individual perspective 48
Major events and the community 48
Strategies for community engagement 49
Summary 51
Questions 52
Case study: Townsville City Council: creating an events strategy for Queensland's biggest regional city council 52
References 57

CHAPTER 3 Event impacts and legacies 59

Introduction 60
Balancing the impact of events 60
Social and cultural impacts 61
Event profile: Schoolies Week 64
Political impacts 65
Environmental impacts 66
Tourism and economic impacts 68
Economic impacts and the role of government 70
Economic impact studies 71
Example of government use of economic impact studies 71
Community perceptions of event impacts 73
The legacy of events 76
Event profile: Sydney 2009 World Masters Games 76
Summary 77
Questions 77
Case study: The Australian Formula One Grand Prix 78
References 84

PART 2: PLANNING 87

CHAPTER 4 The strategic planning function 89

Introduction 90
What is strategic planning? 90
The strategic planning process and event organisations 91
Concept or intent to bid 92
Feasibility analysis 92
Decision to proceed or cease 92
Formation of a bidding body and bid preparation 92
Establishment of an organisational structure 95
Event profile: The Montana World of WearableArt Event 99
Strategic plan 102
Legacy 114
Strategic planning for existing events 114
Summary 114
Questions 115

Case study: Operational planning and the Rugby World Cup 115
References 124

CHAPTER 5 Conceptualising the event 125

Introduction 126
Stakeholders in events 126
The host organisation 127
  Types of host organisation 128
The host community 129
  Involving the host community 130
Sponsors 131
  Sponsors as partners in events 132
Media 132
Co-workers 134
Participants and spectators 134
Event profile: Identifying stakeholders and their roles 135
Sourcing events 136
  In-house events 136
  Pitching and tendering for events 136
  Bidding for events 137
  Franchising events 138
Creating the event concept 138
  Defining the purpose of the event 138
  Identifying the event audience 139
  Deciding the timing of the event 139
  Choosing the event venue 139
  Choosing the event concept 140
  Summarising the process of creating the event concept 141
  Designing the event experience 141
Event profile: The National Event Summit 2009 142
Evaluating the event concept 143
  The marketing screen 143
  The operations screen 143
  The financial screen 144
Event profile: Sony PlayStation 10th Anniversary Party 144
Summary 146
Questions 146
Case study: Seven Deadly Sins corporate event 147
References 151

CHAPTER 6 Project management for events 153

Introduction 154
Project management 154
Event profile: Applying project management to event planning 156
Phases of the project management of events 157
  Initiation 158
  Planning 158
  Implementation 158
  The event 159
  Shutdown 159

Knowledge areas 159
Role of the project manager 161
Key competencies of a project manager in events 161
Project management techniques 162
Defining the project and scope of work 163
Creating a work breakdown structure 164
Analysing the resources 165
Identifying tasks and responsibilities 166
Scheduling 166
Responsibilities — from documents to deliverables 170
Payback period and return on investment 171
Monitoring the project 172
Delegation and self-control 173
Quality 173
Work in progress report 173
Project evaluation 174
Project management systems and software 176
Limitations of the project management approach to event management 177
Convergence 178
Summary 179
Questions 179
Case study: Using spreadsheets to plan an event 179
Case study: Ha'il Desert Festival 183
References 186

CHAPTER 7 Financial management and events 187

Introduction 188
Forecasting finance and ROI 190
The budget 192
Constructing the budget 192
Control and financial ratios 197
The break-even chart 197
Ratio analysis 198
Cash flow 199
Costing and estimating 201
Tips on reducing costs 204
Revenue 205
Tips for increasing projected income 207
Financial reporting 208
Event profile: Cost blow-out forced Fringe action 209
Summary 210
Questions 210
Case study: Pricing event management service 210
References 214
Further reading 214

CHAPTER 8 Human resource management and events 215

Introduction 216
Considerations associated with human resource planning for events 216

The human resource planning process for events ... 216
Event profile: Cherry Creek Arts Festival volunteer program 217
Human resource strategy and objectives 218
Policies and procedures 224
Recruitment, selection and induction 226
Training and professional development 237
Supervision and evaluation 238
Termination, outplacement and re-enlistment 240
Evaluation of process and outcomes 241
Motivating staff and volunteers ... 243
Content theories 243
Process theories 245
Building effective staff and volunteer teams ... 246
Legal obligations ... 248
Summary 249
Questions 250
Case study: The people matrix of the Woodford Folk Festival 250
References 254

CHAPTER 9 Marketing planning for events 257

Introduction ... 258
What is marketing? ... 258
The need for marketing 259
Events as 'service experiences' 260
The connection between event marketing and management 261
The role of strategic marketing planning 261
Event marketing research ... 263
Analysing event environments 265
Event profile: The re-branding of Sydney's Royal Easter Show 266
The event consumer's decision-making process 271
Event satisfaction, service quality, repeat visits 275
Steps in the marketing planning process ... 277
Segmenting and targeting the event market 278
Positioning the event 280
Developing event marketing objectives 281
Choosing generic marketing strategies and tactics for events 282
Selecting the event's 'services marketing' mix 283
Planning event 'product' experiences ... 284
Developing the event 284
Programming the event 286
Packaging the event 287
People and partnerships ... 288
Pricing ... 289
Event 'place', physical setting and processes ... 291
Event profile: Manly Musical Society 293
The marketing plan ... 294
Summary 294
Questions 295
Case study: LAN Brazilian Festa at the ME Bank Starlight Cinema 295

Case study: The Growth and Development of the Middle East International Film Festival, Abu Dhabi. 299
References 304

CHAPTER 10 Promotion: integrated marketing communication for events 307

Introduction 308
Application of IMC 309
Establishing the IMC budget 311
What the event can afford 311
Percentage of sales method 312
Competitive parity method 312
Objective and task method 312
Elements of IMC 313
Event profile: Scotland Island Festival 314
Advertising 315
Public relations (publicity) 316
Sales promotion 316
Personal selling 320
Summary 322
Questions 322
Case study: Sydney's Royal Easter Show 322
References 324

CHAPTER 11 Sponsorship of special events 327

Introduction 328
What is sponsorship? 328
Trends influencing the growth of sponsorship 329
Sponsorship benefits for events and sponsors 332
How events can benefit from sponsorship 332
Sponsors' benefits — links with the consumer response 333
Event profile: Fujitsu and V8 336
Sponsorship leveraging — adding value to the investment 337
The fit between sponsor and sponsee 338
The value of sponsorship policy 339
Stages in developing the event sponsorship strategy 340
Profiling the event audience 340
Establishing what the event can offer potential sponsors 340
Building the event sponsorship list 341
Matching event benefits with potential sponsors 342
The sponsorship pitch 343
Managing sponsorships 347
Techniques for effective sponsorship management 348
Sponsorship management plans to service sponsors 349
Measuring and evaluating the sponsorship 351
Summary 352
Questions 352
Case study: NSW Fire Brigades and McDonald's 353
References 355
Further reading 357

CHAPTER 12 Sustainable event management 359

Introduction 360
The environmental impacts of event production 360
Sustainable purchasing in event planning 361
Sustainable energy use in event production 362
Sustainable waste management in event production 364
Event profile: Splendour In the Grass 2009 369
Sustainable transport solutions in event production 371
Sustainable water and sanitation for event production 372
Sustainability policy for events management 374
Best practice, certification, measurement 374
Measuring environmental impacts of event production 375
Sustainable event industry organisations 375
Green event certification and guidelines 376
Sustainable events 377
Summary 381
Questions 381
Case study: WOMADelaide 2005 381
References 384

CHAPTER 13 Event tourism planning 387

Introduction 388
Developing destination-based event tourism strategies 388
The event tourism strategic planning process 388
Situational analysis 389
Event profile: South Australian festivals: twice the impact or half the audience? 390
Development of event tourism goals 394
Leveraging events for economic gain 394
Geographic dispersal of economic benefits flowing from tourism 394
Destination branding 394
Destination marketing 395
Creating off-season demand for tourism industry services 396
Enhancing visitor experiences 396
Catalyst for expansion and/or improvement of infrastructure 398
Progression of a destination's social, cultural and/or environmental agenda 398
Measuring progress towards event tourism goals 398
Creation of an event tourism organisational structure 399
Development of an event tourism strategy 401
Existing event development 401
Event bidding 401
New event creation 402
General considerations in event tourism strategy selection 402
Implementation of an event tourism strategy 403
Financial support 403
Ownership 405
Bid development and bid support services 405
Event sector development services 405

Coordination 406
Event/destination promotion services 407
Other 410
Evaluation of an event tourism strategy 411
Tourism events and regional development 412
Summary 412
Questions 413
Case study: Barossa Under The Stars music concert 413
References 415

PART 3: EVENT OPERATIONS AND EVALUATION 419

CHAPTER 14 Staging events 421

Introduction 422
Theming and event design 422
Programming 423
Choice of venue 424
Audience and guests 426
The stage 427
Power 430
Lights 430
Event profile: Innovation and flexibility in staging 431
Sound 432
Audiovisual and special effects 434
Props and decoration 435
Catering 435
Performers 437
The crew 438
Hospitality 438
The production schedule 440
Recording the event 441
Contingencies 441
Summary 442
Questions 442
Case study: Festival of the Olive 443
Case study: Al Mahabba Awards Festival 2008 Abu Dhabi, UAE 447
References 449

CHAPTER 15 Logistics 451

Introduction 452
What is logistics? 452
The elements of event logistics 453
Supply of the customer 454
Links with marketing and promotion 454
Ticketing 455
Queuing 458
Customer transport 458
Supply of product — product portfolio 461

Transport 461
Accommodation 462
Artists' needs on site 462
Supply of facilities 462
On-site logistics 464
Flow 464
Communication 465
Amenities and solid waste management 467
Consumables — food and beverage 470
VIP and media requirements 471
Emergency procedures 473
Shutdown 474
Event profile: Clean-up 476
Techniques of logistics management 477
The event logistics manager 477
Site or venue map 482
Negotiation and assessment 483
Control of events logistics 484
Evaluation of logistics 484
The logistics or operations plan 485
Summary 485
Questions 486
Case study: Breakfast on the Bridge: on-the-day logistics 486
References 489

CHAPTER 16 Event evaluation and research 491

Introduction 492
What is event evaluation? 492
Event impacts and evaluation 492
Post-event evaluation 494
Measurement of event outcomes 494
Creation of a demographic profile of the event audience 494
Identification of how the event can be improved 494
Enhancement of event reputation 495
Evaluation of event management processes 495
Knowledge management 495
The event evaluation process 496
Planning and identification of event data required 496
Data collection 497
Data analysis 503
Reporting 504
Dissemination 504
Event profile: Floriade 504
Encore Festival and Event Evaluation Kit 507
Summary 510
Questions 510
Case study: Triple-bottom-line event evaluation and the 2010 CountryLink Parkes Elvis Festival 511
References 514

PART 4: LEGAL, RISK AND OHS MANAGEMENT AND EVALUATION 517

CHAPTER 17 Legal issues of event management 519

Introduction ... 520
Contracts ... 521
Contract management 523
Entertainment 524
Venue 525
Sponsor 525
Broadcast 525
Suppliers 526
Constructing a contract ... 527
Trademarks and logos ... 528
Duty of care ... 528
Legal issues with marketing events ... 530
Insurance ... 531
Event profile: So you think you have insurance! 533
Regulations, licences and permits ... 533
Summary 536
Questions 537
Case study: South Australian Brewing Company Pty Ltd v Carlton & United Breweries Ltd (2001) 537
References 541

CHAPTER 18 Risk management 543

Introduction ... 544
Risk management process ... 544
Understanding context 547
Identifying risks 549
Analysis and evaluation of the risk 552
Control 553
Mitigating actions 554
Further risk management methodologies 555
Specific event risks 558
Event profile: Crowd control at the Chinese Olympics 561
Review 562
Occupational health and safety (OHS) and events ... 562
Consultation 562
Summary 565
Questions 565
Case study: The Hajj of 2009 and the H1N1 virus 566
References 568

Index 570

PREFACE

In the past two decades, event management has shifted from being a field of dedicated and resourceful amateurs to being one of trained and skilled professionals. There are several reasons for this shift.

First, event management has emerged as the umbrella profession for a diverse range of activities that were previously viewed as discrete areas. These activities include festivals, sporting events, conferences, tourism and corporate events. This change has led to the need for a methodology broad enough to service this wide range of event types, but also flexible enough to encompass their individual needs and differences.

Second, the environments in which events operate and the range of stakeholder expectations have become much more complex and demanding. This change has led to the need for a robust methodology that is responsive to change and able to manage and encompass risk.

Third, corporate and government involvement in events has increased dramatically, in terms of both companies mounting events for their own purposes, and companies and governments investing in events through sponsorship and grants. This change has led to the need for management systems that are accountable and able to measure and deliver return on investment.

Fourth, the challenge of climate change has provided the imperative and the inspiration for finding ways of reducing the environmental impact and carbon footprint of events, leading to green event strategies across the broad spectrum of event management.

In response to these challenges, the event industry has relatively quickly developed a body of knowledge of industry best practice, supported by training and accreditation. To do so, it has borrowed much from other disciplines and adapted this knowledge to the event context.

This textbook attempts to capture and refine this emerging body of knowledge, and to document it in a useful form for both researchers and practitioners in the field. As authors, we each bring to the textbook the benefits of our own discipline and perspective, reflecting the many facets of event management. In developing this body of knowledge, we have also relied on colleagues in academia and industry — in fields as diverse as marketing, tourism, project management, business studies, law and accounting — who have assisted us in applying these disciplines in the event context.

Teaching event management throughout Australia, and in locations as diverse as London, Edinburgh, Kuala Lumpur, Singapore, Beijing, Auckland and Cape Town, has helped us to develop a global perspective on events, which is reflected in the range and diversity of case studies and examples in this textbook.

Compared with the early years when event management was still emerging as a discipline, there now exists a much greater body of research, and a larger number of academic conferences, courses and texts in the field. More is known about events and how they behave, and how they can be enhanced, leveraged and evaluated. This edition aims to embrace and extend this growing body of knowledge, and to track many of the recent changes and developments in the field.

Event management is still evolving as an industry and as a profession; hopefully, the fifth edition of *Festival and Special Event Management* will contribute to this evolution and to a better understanding of how events enrich our lives.

Johnny Allen
Bill O'Toole
Ian McDonnell
Rob Harris
July 2010

ACKNOWLEDGEMENTS

The authors and publisher would like to thank the following copyright holders, organisations and individuals for their permission to reproduce copyright material in this book.

IMAGES

© Julia Silvers, 21 (bottom) /Julia Rutherford Silvers. • © Commonwealth Games Federation, 96 /supplied courtesy of the Commonwealth Games Federation, London. • Roskilde Festival 97 /Source: Roskilde Festival 2010. • © Jim Sloman, 101 (middle) /Sloman, J 2006, Project Management (course notes), Major Event Management Program 9–14 June, Sports Knowledge Australia, Sydney. • © Ian Alker, 116 /Ian Alker.; 119 (top) /Ian Alker.; 120 /Ian Alker.; 121 /Ian Alker.; 122 /Ian Alker. • © EPMS, 157 (middle) /Event Project Management System Pty Ltd.; 165 (top) /Event Project Management System Pty Ltd.; 175 /www.epms.net. • © Department of Premier & Cabinet, 196 /Arts Victoria Do-It-Yourself Economic Impact Kit for Festivals & Events © State of Victoria. • © John Wiley & Sons UK, 200 (bottom) /*Project management: planning and control*, John Wiley & Sons Chichester 2nd Edn, © John Wiley & Sons Limited. Reproduced with permission. • © Cognizant Communication Corp., 217 (middle) /Getz, D 1997, *Event Management and Event Tourism*, Cognizant Communication Corporation, New York. • John Wiley & Sons Australia, 239 (middle) /from *Human Resource Management* 4th edition by Raymond J Stone, p. 291, 2002, John Wiley & Sons Australia.; 244 (top) /*Organisational behaviour: a global perspective* 3rd ed. Wood, Chapman, Fromholz, Morrison, Wallace, Zeffane, Schermerhorn, Hunt, Osborn. • © John Wiley & Sons, Inc, 243 (bottom) /*The volunteer management handbook*, p. 223 T Connors, John Wiley & Sons New York. This material is used by permission of John Wiley & Sons. Inc.; 334 (top) /*Psychology & Marketing*, vol. 18, no. 2. Feb 2001, pp. 95–122. T Meenaghan, John Wiley Inc. This material is used by permission of John Wiley & Sons, Inc.; 524 (top) /Corporate Event Project Management, O'Toole, 2002 John Wiley & Sons Inc. This material is used by permission of John Wiley & Sons, Inc. • © Harvard Bus. School Publishing, 245 (top) /Adapted and Reprinted by permission of *Harvard Business Review*, from One More Time How Do You Motivate Employees? by F Herzberg, 01/03 p. 90, Copyright 2003 by the Harvard Business School Publishing Corporation; 283 (top) /*Harvard Business Review*. 'Ansoff Matrix', Strategies for Diversification, F Brassington & S Pettitt, 1957. Copyright © by the Harvard Business School Publishing Corporation; all rights reserved. • © Simon & Schuster, Inc., 267 (middle) /Adapted with permissoin of The Free Press, Division of Simon & Schuster Adult Publishing Group, *Competitive Strategy: Techniques for Analyzing Industries & Competitors* M Porter. Copyright © 1980, 1998, by The Free Press All rights reserved. • © Pearson Education UK, 276 (bottom) /*Marketing for Leisure and Tourism*, Morgan, Pearson Education Limited. • © Pearson Education Australia, 285 (top) /Adapted from Lovelock, Patterson and Walker, *Services Marketing*, 4th edition © Pearson Education Australia, 2007, p. 258. • © Fit Sponsorship, 329 (bottom) /Fit Sponsorship - www.fitsponsorship.com. • © Kevin Gwinner, 338 (middle) /K Gwinner & G Bennet 2007, 'The impact of brand cohesiveness and sport identification on brand fit in a sponsorship context'. • © The Global Protection Agency, 370 (top) /© Mat Morris. • © Events Tasmania, 403 (top) /Events Tasmania. • © Getty Images, 431 (middle) /Sergio Dionisio/Stringer • © Historic Houses Trust, 446 (middle) /Historic Houses Trust. • © Advanced Soil Mapping, 468 /Advanced Soil Mapping; 469 /Advanced Soil Mapping. • © Leo Jago, Dr, 509 /L Jago, 2006, Encore

Festival and Event Evaluation Kit, Draft document prepared for CRC for Sustainable Tourism, Melbourne. • © Commonwealth Copyright Admin, 529 (bottom) /National OHS Strategy 2002–2012. Australian Safety and Compesation Council. Copyright Commonwealth of Australia, reproduced by permission.; 557 /The Guidance on the Principles of Safe Design for Work. Australian Safety and Compensation Council. Canberra, May 2006. Copyright Commonwealth of Australia, reproduced by permission. • © Ministry of Civil Defence NZ, 564 (top) /Ministry of Civil Defence & Emergency Management, New Zealand.

TEXT

© International Special Events, 18–19 /Reprinted with permission from the International Special Events Society; May 2007; All rights reserved. • © EventScotland, 38–9 /From 'Scotland: The Perfect Stage. A Strategy for the Events Industry in Scotland 2009–2010' © EventScotland 2009. • © Chris Gibson, 48 /From 'Reinventing rural places: The extent and impact of festivals in rural and regional Australia' by Chris Gibson and Anna Stewart, p. 7, 2009; 70 /From 'Reinventing rural places: The extent and impact of festivals in rural and regional Australia' by Chris Gibson and Anna Stewart, p. 20, 2009; • © IAP2, 49–50 /Copyright IAP2 — International Association for Public Participation. Reproduced with permission. • © UK Sport, 72 /'The economic impact of six major sporting events' from p. 2 of 'Measuring Success 3', UK Sport, 2007, www.uksport.gov.uk. Reproduced with permission. • © ACT Festival Fund, 93–4 /From the ACT Festival Fund Information Booklet 2010, pp. 3 & 20–22 © ACT Government. • © Local Government Association, 94–5 /Local Government Association of NSW. • © Wolfe Island Scene of the, 104 /Wolfe Island Scene of the Crime Festival, Inc. • © Oregon Shakespeare Festival, 104–5 /Reproduced with permission from the Oregon Shakespeare Festival. • © Trinidad and Tobago Cultural, 106 /Reproduced with permission from the Trinidad and Tobago Cultural Society of British Columbia. • © National Folk Festival, 112–3 /Reproduced with permission from the National Folk Festival, ACT; 229–30 /Reproduced with permission from the National Folk Festival, ACT; • © TP Events, 144–5 /TP Events. • © *Canberra Times*, 209 /'Cost blow-out forced Fringe action: Stanhope' by Diana Streak, © *Canberra Times* 21/8/09. • © Great Lakes Folk Festival, 222–3 /Reproduced with permission from Michigan State University Museum. • © John Wiley & Sons Australia, 223–4 /Source: American Liver Foundation 2009. • © Sport and Recreation Victoria, 225–6 /Mebourne 2006 Commonwealth Games. • © Midsumma Festival, 233–5 /Reproduced with permission from the Midsumma Festival. • © Volunteering Qld, 236 /Template reproduced with the permission of Volunteering Qld. • © Australian Centre for Event, 238 /Reproduced with permission from the Australian Centre for Event Management, University of Technology, Sydney.; 74–5 /L Fredline, M Deery & LK Jago 2005, 'Testing of a compressed generic instrument to assess host community perceptions of events'. A Case Study of the Australian Open Tennis Tournament. • © NSW Dept of Commerce, 249 /© State of New South Wales through the Office of Industrial Relations. • © Intermountain, 242 /Reproduced with permission from Intermountain www.intermountain.org. • © Pearson Education UK, 279 /*Marketing for Leisure and Tourism*, Morgan, Pearson Education Limited. • © Elsevier, 288 /from 'Innovative Marketing Communications' by G Masterman & E Wood 2006. Copyright Elsevier, Oxford, 2006. • © Pearson Education Australia, 290–1 /Adapted from Lovelock, Patterson and Walker, *Services Marketing*, 4th edition © Pearson Education Australia, 2007, p. 258. • © Seat Advisor, 293 /Product overview, Seat Advisor Australia 2009, from www.seatadvisor.com.au/product.htm. • © Dr Cristina Roche, 296 /From 'The Brazilians in

Sydney' by Cristina Roche, *Sydney Journal*, 1(2) June 2008. Reproduced with the permission of Dr Cristina Roche. •© *Manly Daily* Newspaper, 315 /*Manly Daily*, 11 August 2006, p. 27. • © Financial Review Case Studies, 336–7 /Australian Business Case Studies project, The Australian Financial Review Case Studies with business news.; 336–7 /Excerpt from The Australian Financial Review Case Studies with Business News. Permission given by Australian Business Case Studies Pty Ltd. • © Bruce McKaskill 353–5 • © Sustainable Living Foundation 365–6 /The Sustainable Events Planner has been developed to satisfy the demand from the events community for access to resources to help promote sustainable event practice.The Sustainable Events Planner has been developed by Sustainable Living Foundation (SLF). SLF is a community based not-for-profit organisation committed to helping accelerate the uptake of sustainable living. • © Greenpeace Australia Pacific, 376–7 /Greenpeace Olympic Environmental Guidelines, 2003. • © Zero Waste SA, 381–3 /Zero Waste, SA. • © Tourism WA, 396–7 /Reproduced with permission from eventscorp Western Australia, a Division of Tourism Western Australia. • © Auckland City Council, 407 /From the 'Auckland City Events Strategy, 2005'. Reproduced with permission from Auckland City Council. • © Melbourne Convention + Visitors Bureau, 407–8 /Melbourne Convention + Visitors Bureau www.mcvb.com.au. • © Tourism Australia, 411–2 /ICCA Data, Statistics Report — International Association Meetings Market 1996–2005, Released: June 2006. • © Northern Rivers Folk Festival, 467 /Peter Monley, Northern Rivers Folk Festival. • © FSANZ, 472 /Fact Sheet for Charities and Community Organisations on the Food Safety Standards, May 2002, © Food Standards Australia New Zealand, reproduced with permission of Food Standards Australia New Zealand. • © State Government of Victoria, 473 /State Government of Victoria. • © Dennis Wheeler, 476 / Dennis Wheeler, Snr Transport Planner Roads and Traffic Authority NSW. • © Rugby New Zealand 2011 Ltd, 479–82 /Reproduced with permission from Rugby New Zealand 2011 Ltd. • © Australian Capital Tourism, 504–7 /Extracts from 'Floriade 2007 Event Report' © Australian Capital Tourism, part of the ACT Government. • © Folk Federation of SA, 521–3 /Folk Federation of South Australia. • © Sport and Recreation Tasmania, 533 /Sport and Recreation Tasmania. • © *Sydney Morning Herald*, 549 /*Sydney Morning Herald*, 1 November 2005 by Nick O'Malley. • © AFP, 561–2 /'Crowd nightmare haunts Beijing Olympics organisers' by Talek Harris, 4/7/08 © AFP.

Every effort has been made to trace the ownership of copyright material. Information that will enable the publisher to rectify any error or omission in subsequent editions will be welcome. In such cases, please contact the Permissions Section of John Wiley & Sons Australia, Ltd.

EXAMPLES AT A GLANCE

Chapter	Event profile	Case study
1	• Australian Centre for Event Management	• RSVP: The event for the events industry
2	• Mulga Bill Festival, Yeoval	• Townsville City Council: creating an events strategy for Queensland's biggest regional city council
3	• Schoolies Week • Sydney 2009 World Masters Games	• The Australian Formula One Grand Prix
4	• The Montana World of WearableArt Event	• Operational planning and the Rugby World Cup
5	• Identifying stakeholders and their roles • The National Event Summit 2009 • Sony PlayStation 10th Anniversary Party	• Seven Deadly Sins corporate event
6	• Applying project management to event planning	• Using spreadsheets to plan an event • Ha'il Desert Festival
7	• Cost blow-out forced Fringe action	• Pricing event management service
8	• Cherry Creek Arts Festival volunteer program	• The people matrix of the Woodford Folk Festival
9	• The re-branding of Sydney's Royal Easter Show • Manly Musical Society	• LAN Brazilian Festa at the ME Bank Starlight Cinema • The Growth and Development of the Middle East International Film Festival, Abu Dhabi
10	• Scotland Island Festival	• Sydney's Royal Easter Show
11	• Fujitsu and V8	• NSW Fire Brigades and McDonald's
12	• Splendour In the Grass 2009	• WOMADelaide
13	• South Australian festivals: twice the impact or half the audience?	• Barossa Under The Stars music concert
14	• Innovation and flexibility in staging	• Festival of the Olive • Al Mahabba Awards Festival 2008 Abu Dhabi, UAE
15	• Clean-up	• Breakfast on the Bridge: on-the-day logistics
16	• Floriade	• Triple-bottom-line event evaluation and the 2010 CountryLink Parkes Elvis Festival
17	• So you think you have insurance!	• South Australian Brewing Company Pty Ltd v Carlton & United Breweries Ltd (2001)
18	• Crowd control at the Chinese Olympics	• The Hajj of 2009 and the H1N1 virus

PART 1

EVENT CONTEXT

The first part of this book looks at the history and development of events, and the emergence of the event industry in Australia. It examines the impacts of events, including their social/cultural, physical/environmental, political and tourism/economic impacts.

1 AN OVERVIEW OF THE EVENT FIELD

LEARNING OBJECTIVES

After studying this chapter, you should be able to:

1. define special events
2. demonstrate an awareness of why special events have evolved in human society
3. describe the role of special events in Australia and the Australian tradition of special events
4. discuss the growth of state event corporations and the emergence of an event industry
5. distinguish between different types of special events
6. list and describe the components of the event industry
7. list and describe the main professional associations in the event industry
8. discuss the attributes and knowledge requirements of a special event manager
9. list the types of organisation involved in the delivery of event management training.

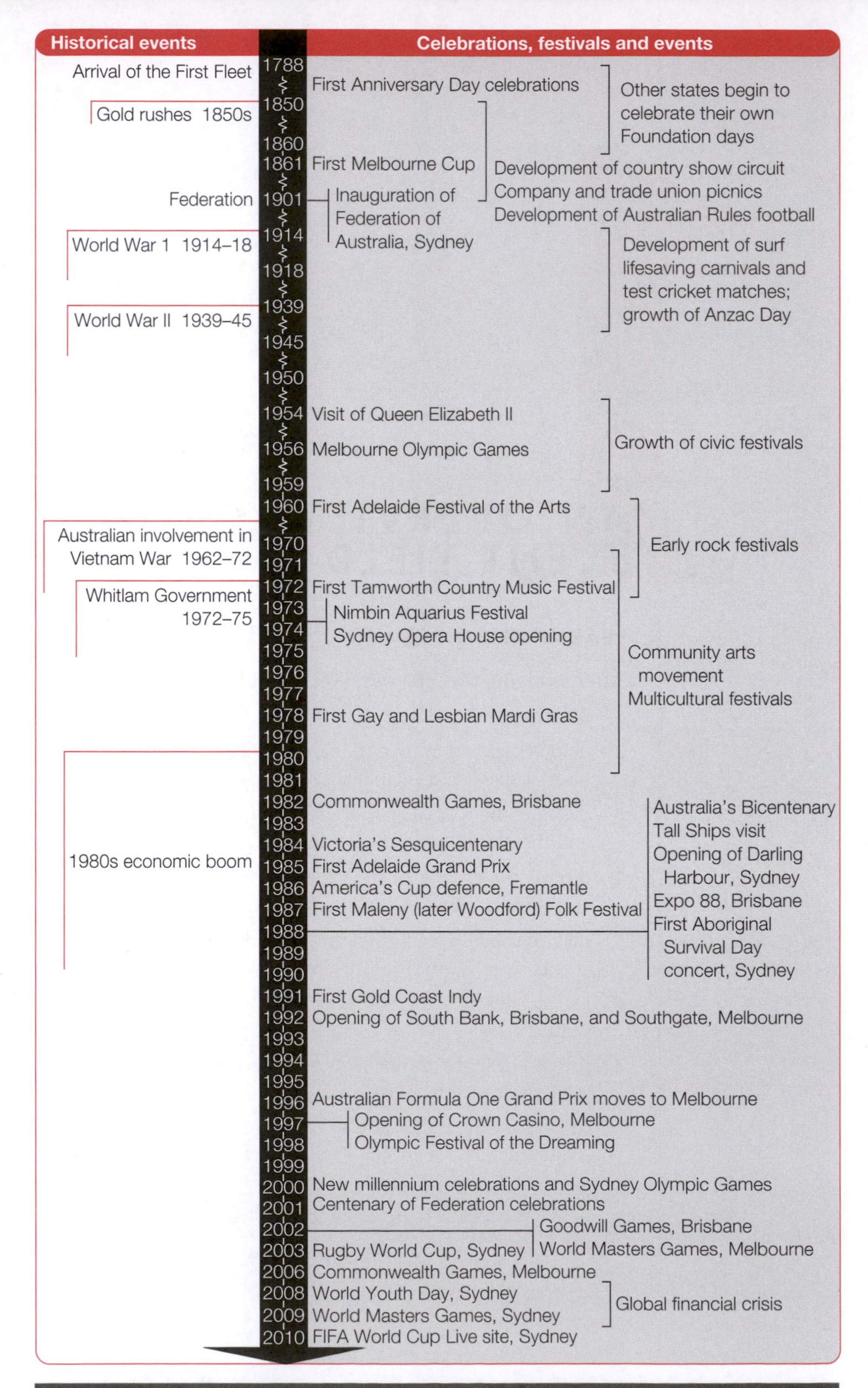

FIGURE 1.1 Australian event timeline

INTRODUCTION

Today, events are central to our culture as perhaps never before. Increases in leisure time and discretionary spending have led to a proliferation of public events, celebrations and entertainment. Governments now support and promote events as part of their strategies for economic development, nation building and destination marketing. Corporations and businesses embrace events as key elements in their marketing strategies and image promotion. The enthusiasm of community groups and individuals for their own interests and passions gives rise to a marvellous array of events on almost every subject and theme imaginable. Events spill out of our newspapers and television screens, occupy much of our time, and enrich our lives.

As we study the phenomenon of events, it is worth examining where the event tradition in Australia has come from, and what forces are likely to shape its future growth and development. As events emerge as an industry in their own right, it is also worth considering what elements characterise such an industry, and how the Australian event industry might chart its future directions in an increasingly complex and demanding environment.

SPECIAL EVENTS AS BENCHMARKS FOR OUR LIVES

Since the dawn of time, human beings have found ways to mark important events in their lives: the changing of the seasons, the phases of the moon, and the renewal of life each spring. From the Aboriginal corroboree and Chinese New Year to the Dionysian rites of ancient Greece and the European carnival tradition of the Middle Ages, myths and rituals have been created to interpret cosmic happenings. To the present day, behind well-known figures such as Old Father Time and Santa Claus lie old myths, archetypes and ancient celebrations.

The first Australians used storytelling, dance and song to transmit their culture from generation to generation. Their ceremonies were, and continue to be, important occasions in the life of the community, where cultural meaning is shared and affirmed. Similarly, in most agrarian societies, rituals were developed that marked the coming of the seasons and the sowing and harvesting of crops.

Both in private and in public, people feel the need to mark the important occasions in their lives, and to celebrate milestones. Coming of age, for example, is often marked by a rite of passage, as illustrated by the tribal initiation ceremony, the Jewish bar and bat mitzvahs and the suburban twenty-first birthday.

At the public level, momentous events become the milestones by which people measure their private lives. We may talk about things happening 'before the new millennium', in the same way that an earlier generation spoke of marrying 'before the Depression' or being born 'after the War'. Occasional events — Australia's Bicentenary, the Sydney Olympics and the new millennium — help to mark eras and define milestones.

Even in the high-tech era of global media, when many people have lost touch with the common religious beliefs and social norms of the past, we still need larger social events to mark the local and domestic details of our lives.

THE MODERN AUSTRALIAN TRADITION OF CELEBRATIONS

Australian Aboriginal culture had a rich tradition of rituals and ceremonies prior to the arrival of the first Europeans. This rich tradition continues to this day. There has also been a continuing protest at what many see as the invasion of Australia by Europeans in 1788, with an Aboriginal boycott of the centenary celebrations of the arrival of the First Fleet in 1888, and a Day of Mourning protest and conference at the sesquicentenary celebrations in Sydney in 1938. This protest continued at the Australian Bicentenary celebrations on 26 January 1988, when 40 000 people participated in the March for Freedom, Justice and Hope in Sydney, and the first national Sorry Day held on 26 May 1998. Corroboree 2000 took place in Sydney during Reconciliation Week in May 2000 to mark the end of the ten-year official reconciliation process, and, in an overwhelming show of endorsement for Aboriginal people, approximately 250 000 people marched across the Harbour Bridge in support of reconciliation (City of Sydney 2006). Finally, after a long wait, one of the first acts of the newly elected Rudd Labor Government in 2008 was an official apology to the Aboriginal people for the perceived injustices of the past.

In the cultural collision between Aboriginal people and the first Europeans, new traditions were formed alongside the old. Probably the first 'event' in Australia after the arrival of the First Fleet was a bush party to celebrate the coming ashore of the women convicts in 1788:

> Meanwhile, most of the sailors on *Lady Penrhyn* applied to her master, Captain William Sever, for an extra ration of rum 'to make merry with upon the women quitting the ship'. Out came the pannikins, down went the rum, and before long the drunken tars went off to join the convicts in pursuit of the women, so that, Bowes remarked, 'it is beyond my abilities to give a just description of the scene of debauchery and riot that ensued during the night'. It was the first bush party in Australia, with 'some swearing, others quarrelling, others singing' (Hughes 1987, pp. 88–9).

From these inauspicious beginnings, the early colonists slowly started to evolve celebrations that were tailored to their new environment, so far from Georgian Britain. Hull (1984) traces the history of these early celebrations, noting the beginnings of a national day some 30 years later:

> Governor Macquarie declared the 26th of January 1818 a public holiday — convicts were given the day off, a ration of one pound of fresh meat was made for each of them, there was a military review, a salute of 30 guns, a dinner for the officers and a ball for the colony society.

This may have been the first festival celebrated by the new inhabitants of Australia. Although 'Anniversary Day', as it was known, was not to become a public holiday for another 20 years, the official celebration of the founding of the colony had begun with the direct involvement and patronage of the government that exists to this day. In contrast to government-organised celebrations, settlers during the nineteenth century entertained themselves with balls, shows and travelling entertainments as a diversion from the serious business of work and survival. The rich tradition of agricultural shows such as the Sydney Royal Easter Show and race meetings such as the Melbourne Cup still survive as major events in their respective cities to this day.

At the turn of the century, the celebration of Australia's Federation captured the prevailing mood of optimistic patriotism:

> At the turn of the year 1900–1 the city of Sydney went mad with joy. For a few days hope ran so high that poets and prophets declared Australia to be on the threshold of a new

> golden age . . . from early morning on 1 January 1901 trams, trains and ferry boats carried thousands of people into the city for the greatest day in their history: the inauguration of the Commonwealth of Australia. It was to be a people's festival (Clark 1981, p. 177).

At the beginning of the twentieth century, the new inhabitants had come to terms with the landscape of Australia, and the democratic ritual of the picnic had gained mass popularity. This extended to guilds, unions and company workers, as demonstrated by the following description of the annual picnic of the employees of Sydney boot and shoe manufacturers McMurtie and Company, at Clontarf in 1906:

> The sweet strains of piano, violin and cornet . . . added zest and enjoyment to the festive occasion', said the Advisor. 'Laughter producers were also in evidence, several of the company wearing comical-looking hats and false noses so that even at the commencement of the day's proceedings hilarity and enjoyment was assured.' The enjoyment continued as the party disembarked to the strain of bagpipes, and the sporting programme began . . . The 'little ones' were provided with 'toys, spades, balls and lollies'. The shooting gallery was well patronised, and when darkness fell dancing went on in the beautiful dancing hall. Baby Houston danced a Scotch reel to the music of bagpipes. Miss Robinson sang *Underneath the Watermelon Vine*, and little Ruth Bailey danced a jig.
>
> At 8 pm, the whistle blew and the homeward journey commenced with 'music up till the last' and a final rendering of *Auld Lang Syne* as the *Erina* arrived at the Quay (Pearl 1974).

However, Australians had to wait until after World War II before a home-grown form of celebration took hold across the nation. In the 1940s and 1950s, city and town festivals were established, which created a common and enduring format. Even today, it is a safe assumption that any festival with an Aboriginal or floral name, and that includes a 'Festival Queen' competition, street parade, outdoor art exhibition and sporting event, dates to this period. Sydney's Waratah Festival (later replaced by the Sydney Festival), Melbourne's Moomba, Ballarat's Begonia Festival, Young's Cherry Festival, Bowral's Tulip Time, Newcastle's Mattara Festival and Toowoomba's Carnival of Flowers all date to the prolific era of local pride and involvement after World War II. Moomba and Mattara both adopted Aboriginal names, the latter word meaning 'hand of friendship'.

Holding such a festival became a badge of civic pride, in the way that building a School of Arts hall had done in an earlier era, or constructing an Olympic swimming pool would do in the 1950s and 1960s. These festivals gave the cities and towns a sense of identity and distinction, and became a focus for community groups and charity fundraising. It is a tribute to their importance to their communities that many of these festivals still continue after more than half a century.

Alongside this movement of community festivals was another very powerful model. In 1947 the Edinburgh Festival was founded as part of the post-war spirit of reconstruction and renewal. In Australia, the Festival of Perth (founded in 1953) and the Adelaide Festival of the Arts (founded in 1960) were based on this inspiring model. The influence of the Edinburgh Festival proved to be enduring, as shown by the resurgence of arts festivals in Sydney, Melbourne and Brisbane in the 1980s and 1990s. By the 1970s, however, with the coming to power of the Whitlam Government and the formation of the Australia Council, new cultural directions were unleashed that were to change the face of festivals in Australia.

The Community Arts Board of the Australia Council, under the leadership of Ros Bower, developed a strategy aimed at giving a voice to the voiceless, and taking arts and festivals into the suburbs and towns of Australia. Often for the first time, migrants, workers and Aboriginal people were encouraged to participate in a new cultural pluralism that broke down the elitism that had governed the arts in much of rural and suburban Australia. Sensing the unique cultural challenge faced by Australia, Bower (1981) wrote:

> In terms of our national cultural objectives, the re-integration of the artist into the community is of crucial importance. Australia lacks a coherent cultural background. The artist needs to become the spokesman, the interpreter, the image-maker and the prophet. He cannot do it in isolation or from an ivory tower. He must do it by working with the people. He must help them to piece together their local history, their local traditions, their folk-lore, the drama and the visual imagery of their lives. And in doing this he will enrich and give identity to his work as an artist. The arts will cease to be imitative, or pre-occupied with making big splashes in little 'cultured' pools. They will be integrated more closely with our lives, our history, our unique environment. They will be experimental and exploring forces within the broader cultural framework.

The 1970s involved not only the emergence of multiculturalism and the 'new age' movement, but also the forging of the community arts movement and a new and diverse range of festivals across Australia. Examples of the rich diversity spawned by this period are the Aquarius Festival staged by the Australian Union of Students at Nimbin in northern New South Wales, the Lygon Street Festa in Melbourne's Carlton, the Come Out young people's festival held in alternate years to the Adelaide Festival, the Carnivale celebration of multiculturalism across Sydney and New South Wales, and Sydney's Gay and Lesbian Mardi Gras. Festivals became part of the cultural landscape and connected again to people's needs and lives. Every community, it seemed, had something to celebrate, and the tools with which to create its own festival.

THE BIRTH OF AN EVENT INDUSTRY

Through the 1980s and 1990s, certain seminal events set the pattern for the contemporary event industry as we know it today. The Commonwealth Games in Brisbane in 1982 ushered in a new era of maturity and prominence for that city and a new breed of sporting events. It also initiated a career in ceremonies and celebrations for former ABC rock show producer, Ric Birch, which led to his taking a key role in the opening and closing ceremonies at the Los Angeles, Barcelona and Sydney Summer Olympics and the Turin Winter Olympics.

The Olympic Games in Los Angeles in 1984 demonstrated that major events could be economically viable. The organisers managed to combine a Hollywood-style spectacle with a sporting event in a manner that had not been done before, and that would set a standard for all similar events in future. The production and marketing skills of the television industry brought the Olympics to an audience wider than ever before. Television also demonstrated the power of a major sporting event to bring increased profile and economic benefits to a city and to an entire country.

The entrepreneurs of the 1980s economic boom in Australia soon picked up on this potential, and the America's Cup defence in Perth and Fremantle in 1986–87 was treated as an opportunity to put Perth on the map and to attract major economic and tourism benefits to Western Australia. By 1988 there was a boom in special events, with Australia's Bicentenary perceived by many as a major commemorative program and vehicle for tourism. This boom was matched by governments setting up state event corporations, thereby giving public sector support to special events as never before. In Brisbane the success of Expo 88 rivalled the Bicentennial activities in Sydney, and Adelaide managed a coup by staging the first Australian Formula One Grand Prix.

The Bicentenary caused Australians to pause and reflect on the Australian identity. It also changed forever the nature of our public celebrations:

> I would argue that the remarkable legacy of 1988 is the public event. It is now a regular feature of Australian life. We gather for fireworks, for welcome-home marches for athletes and other Australians who have achieved success. We go to large urban spaces like the Domain for opera, rock and symphonic music in our hundreds of thousands. The Sydney Festival attracts record numbers. The Gay Mardi Gras is an international phenomenon . . . Whatever the nature of debate about values, identity and imagery, one certainty is that Australians are in love with high-quality public events that are fun and offer to extend the range and experience of being Australian (McCarthy 1998).

The Bicentenary also left a legacy of public spaces dedicated to celebrations and special events, and of governments supporting events for their perceived social and economic benefits. Sydney's Darling Harbour opened to welcome the Tall Ships on 16 January 1988 and provided the city with a major leisure centre. Darling Harbour incorporates dedicated celebrations areas, tourist attractions, a festival marketplace, the Sydney Convention and Exhibition Centre and the Sydney Entertainment Centre, all adjacent to the Powerhouse and National Maritime Museums. Likewise, Brisbane's riverside Expo 88 site was converted into the South Bank Parklands, and Melbourne followed suit with the Southbank development on the Yarra River.

Whatever its economic causes, the recession of the late 1980s and early 1990s put a dampener on the party mood and the seemingly endless growth of events — that is, until 4.27 am on 24 September 1993 when International Olympic Committee President Juan Antonio Samaranch spoke those memorable words: 'And the winner is . . . Sydney!'

Many said that the late 1980s recession ended the day Sydney was awarded the Olympic Games of the new millennium. Certainly, it meant the event industry could once more look forward with optimism, as though the recession had been a mere pause for breath. Event corporations formed in the late 1980s and early 1990s started to demonstrate that special events could generate economic benefits. This led to competition between the states for major events, which became weapons in an event war fuelled by the media. Australia approached the end of the century with a competitive events climate dominated by the Sydney Olympics, the new millennium and the Centenary of Federation celebrations in 2001. This enthusiasm for events has continued well into the first decade of the new century, with the staging of the Goodwill Games in Brisbane in 2001, the World Masters Games in Melbourne and the International Gay Games in Sydney in 2002, the World Rugby Cup in venues around Australia in 2003, the Commonwealth Games in Melbourne in 2006, the World Swimming Championships in Melbourne and the World Police and Fire Games in Adelaide in 2007, World Youth Day in Sydney in 2008, and the World Masters Games in Sydney in 2009.

The corporate world was quick to discover the marketing and image-making power of events, and events became established through the 1990s and the early 2000s as an important element of the corporate marketing mix. Companies and corporations began to partner major events, such as AMP's links with the Olympic Torch Relay in 2000 and the Centenary of Federation Journey of a Nation in 2001. Other corporations created events as vehicles for their own marketing, an example being One Summer of Sport presented by Uncle Tobys, St.George Bank and the 10 Network, which toured nationally in 1999–2000. By the early 2000s, corporate involvement in events had become the norm, so that sponsorship was perceived as an integral part of staging major events. Companies became increasingly aware of the role that events could play in promoting their image and increasing their market share, but they also became more focused on event outcomes and return on investment. It became common for large companies to have an in-house event team, focused not only on the company's involvement in public events, but also on the internal role of events in company and product promotions, staff training and morale building. Events became not only a significant part of the corporate vocabulary, but also a viable career option with employment opportunities and career paths.

Challenges face the new industry

However, the path of the modern event industry has not always been smooth, and it has faced many challenges in its short history. These include the September 11 terrorist attack on New York; the SARS crisis; and a major upheaval in the global insurance industry, resulting in escalating insurance costs and in the need for the industry to adopt strategies for managing the risks to events.

As we entered the mid 2000s, the spectre of climate change began to affect the industry as the world became increasingly aware of the threat of global warming. Environmental sustainability became a key event management concept, with green initiatives adopted to reduce the environmental impact and the carbon footprint of events. Many events were created as models to impart awareness of climate change, and to encourage participants to change their habits and lifestyle. Indicating the development of public awareness of the issue is the remarkable growth of Earth Hour, an initiative of the World Wildlife Fund to switch off the lights in major cities to encourage awareness of climate change, starting in Sydney in 2007 with 2.2 million participants. In 2008, 50 million people participated across 35 countries. For the March 2009 event in the lead-up to the Climate Change Summit in Copenhagen, hundreds of millions of people participated from 88 countries and 4000 cities and towns (Earth Hour 2010).

Much of the rapid expansion of events was fuelled by the longest economic boom in living memory, and, by the end of the first decade of the 2000s, a reality check was long overdue. This came with the global financial crisis sparked by the US sub-prime mortgage affair in 2008, continuing worldwide into 2009. As the economy worsened, many corporate clients cancelled events, and those that continued them tightened their budgets. The mood switched swiftly to one of austerity, and the events that continued were required to exhibit modesty and thrift — virtues that the event industry now had to practise in order to survive.

Jon Hutchison, the CEO of Business Events Sydney, travelled to North America in January 2009 and consulted widely with industry associations and corporate clients in order to assess the impact of the financial climate on Sydney's prospects for success in attracting international business events. He found the move to protectionism a strong factor, with large international associations likely to continue to travel overseas, but with smaller associations either cancelling conferences or falling back on US destinations. His conclusions led to three areas of action perceived as necessary for his organisation to pursue in the current financial climate:

1. Working to maintain events that have already booked in
2. Focussing on the ability to win and breakthrough
3. Maintaining delegate attendance (Hutchison 2009).

Although the global financial crisis had a considerable impact on the event industry, events, now established as an integral part of modern business practice, tended to survive the economic downturn, as they have survived other challenges in the past.

A lasting legacy is that event managers have been called upon to deliver more with less, and to tread a thin and careful line between the twin challenges of economic and environmental sustainability.

Events on the world stage

This brief outline of the history of modern events relates primarily to the Australian situation, but a similar story has been replicated in most post-industrial societies. The balance between more traditional festivals and contemporary corporate events changes according to the nature of the society in a given geographic area.

Nevertheless, there is ample anecdotal evidence to suggest that both the growth of events and the twin challenges of economic and environmental sustainability are worldwide phenomena. The results of a survey of 700, mainly European, meeting industry professionals was presented at EIBTM, the global Meetings and Incentives Exhibition held in Barcelona in December 2008. Sixty-four per cent of respondents stated that the economic climate and pressure to reduce costs were the factors most likely to influence the coming year. However, 25 per cent expected to organise more international events in 2009, 9 per cent to organise more national events, and 35 per cent to organise roughly the same number of events as in the previous year. Thirty-nine per cent expected a decrease in budgets for 2009, although 61 per cent expected their budgets to either increase (20 per cent) or to stay the same (41 per cent). Despite the economic pressures, 86 per cent stated that corporate social responsibility (CSR) and environmental policies would remain highly influential over the next decade, with 46 per cent believing that their CSR policies impacted on all aspects of event organisation.

The author of the report, Sally Greenhill, added:

> Recession and economic slowdowns are nothing new; the meetings industry has weathered such storms before and can do so again. The report shows that organisers have a positive outlook for 2009 on the whole, but will be looking more closely than ever at quality of service, no-frills destinations and real ROI from their events. The key to success in this environment will be for venues and destinations to work closely together to ensure an end-to-end package that exceeds buyer expectation and delivers real value at every opportunity (Greenhill 2008).

Meanwhile in Asia, the staging of World Expo in Shanghai and the Asian Games in Guangzhou in 2010 and the Commonwealth Games in Delhi in 2010 will see these cities use major events to showcase their emerging prominence to the world. This increasing interest in events in Asia is reflected in the establishment of International Festivals and Events Association affiliates in Beijing and Singapore (International Festivals and Events Association 2006).

Australia still retains a degree of prominence in the international events field, with state governments' event corporations and the staging of the Sydney Olympics, the Rugby World Cup and the Melbourne Commonwealth Games being regarded as international benchmarks for best practice in the field.

WHAT ARE SPECIAL EVENTS?

The term 'special events' has been coined to describe specific rituals, presentations, performances or celebrations that are consciously planned and created to mark special occasions or achieve particular social, cultural or corporate goals and objectives. Special events can include national days and celebrations, important civic occasions, unique cultural performances, major sporting fixtures, corporate functions, trade promotions and product launches. It seems at times that special events are everywhere; they have become a growth industry. The field of special events is now so vast that it is impossible to provide a definition that includes all varieties and shades of events. In his groundbreaking work on the typology of events, Getz (2005, p. 16) suggests special events are best defined by their context. He offers two definitions, one from the point of view of the event organiser and the other from that of the customer or guest:

1. A special event is a one-time, or infrequently occurring event outside the normal program or activities of the sponsoring or organizing body.
2. To the customer or guest, a special event is an opportunity for an experience outside the normal range of choices or beyond everyday experience.

Among the attributes that he believes create the special atmosphere are festive spirit, uniqueness, quality, authenticity, tradition, hospitality, theme and symbolism.

TYPES OF EVENT

There are many different ways of categorising or grouping events, including by size, form and content, as discussed in the following sections. This text examines the full range of events that the event industry produces, using the term 'event' to cover all of the following categories.

Size

Special events are often characterised according to their size or scale (figure 1.2). Common categories are mega-events, hallmark events, major events and local/community events, although definitions are not exact and distinctions can be blurred.

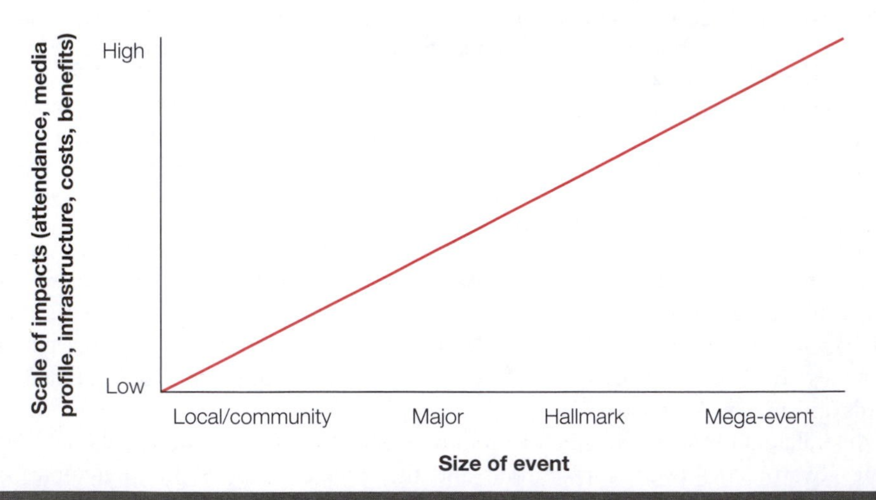

FIGURE 1.2 Categorisation of events

Mega-events

Mega-events are those events that are so large that they affect whole economies and reverberate in the global media. They include Olympic Games, the FIFA World Cup and World Fairs, but it is difficult for many other events to lay claim to this category. Marris in Getz (2005, p. 18) defines mega-events in the following way:

> Their volume should exceed 1 million visits, their capital cost should be at least $500 million, and their reputation should be that of a 'must see' event.

Getz (2005, p. 6) goes on to say:

> Mega-events, by way of their size or significance, are those that yield extraordinarily high levels of tourism, media coverage, prestige, or economic impact for the host community, venue or organization.

Hall (1992, p. 5), another researcher in the field of events and tourism, offers this definition:

> Mega-events such as World Fairs and Expositions, the World Soccer Cup final, or the Olympic Games, are events which are expressly targeted at the international tourism market and may be suitably described as 'mega' by virtue of their size in terms of attendance, target market, level of public financial involvement, political effects, extent of television coverage, construction of facilities, and impact on economic and social fabric of the host community.

By these definitions, the Sydney Olympic Games in 2000 was perhaps Australia's first true mega-event. The Melbourne Olympics in 1956 belonged to an earlier era of far less extensive media coverage and smaller television audiences, although in relative terms it may qualify as a mega-event of its era. Even Brisbane's Expo 88 was officially a 'B' class World Expo, and events such as the Commonwealth Games in Brisbane in 1982 and the America's Cup defence in Perth and Fremantle in 1986–87 would struggle to meet Marris's criterion of exceeding 1 million visits. More recently, the Rugby World Cup in 2003, the Commonwealth Games in Melbourne in 2006 and World Youth Day in Sydney in 2008 may qualify in terms of media coverage and profile.

Hallmark events

The term 'hallmark events' refers to those events that become so identified with the spirit or ethos of a town, city or region that they become synonymous with the name of the place, and gain widespread recognition and awareness. Tourism researcher Ritchie (1984, p. 2) defines them as:

> Major one-time or recurring events of limited duration, developed primarily to enhance awareness, appeal and profitability of a tourism destination in the short term and/or long term. Such events rely for their success on uniqueness, status, or timely significance to create interest and attract attention.

Classic examples of hallmark events are the Carnival in Rio de Janeiro, known throughout the world as an expression of the vitality and exuberance of that city, the Kentucky Derby in the USA, the Chelsea Flower Show in Britain, the Oktoberfest in Munich, Germany, and the Edinburgh Festival in Scotland. Hallmark events may even relate to whole countries rather than just cities or regions, with some examples being the Tour de France and Mexico's Day of the Dead celebrations. Such events, which are identified with the very character of these places and their citizens, bring huge tourist dollars, a strong sense of local pride and international recognition. Getz (2005, pp. 16–17) describes them in terms of their ability to provide a competitive advantage for their host communities:

> In other words, 'hallmark' describes an event that possesses such significance, in terms of tradition, attractiveness, quality, or publicity, that the event provides the host venue, community, or destination with a competitive advantage. Over time, the event and destination can become inextricably linked, such as Mardi Gras and New Orleans.

Examples in Australia might include the Sydney Gay and Lesbian Mardi Gras, the Australasian Country Music Festival at Tamworth, the Melbourne Cup and the Adelaide Festival, all of which have a degree of international recognition and help to identify the ethos of their host cities. Hallmark events are an important component of destination marketing, which will be discussed further in chapter 13, 'Event tourism planning'.

Major events

Major events are events that are capable, by their scale and media interest, of attracting significant visitor numbers, media coverage and economic benefits. Melbourne has developed the Australian Open tennis tournament and the Australian Formula One Grand Prix into significant annual major events, and hosted the Commonwealth Games in 2006 and the World Cup Swimming in 2007. Perth has staged significant major events, including the Hyundai Hopman Cup in tennis and the Johnnie Walker Classic golf tournament. Cultural events can also be contenders, such as the Adelaide, Sydney and Melbourne arts festivals, and regional festivals such as 10 Days on the Island in Tasmania, the Queensland Music Festival, and the Margaret River concerts in Western Australia.

Local or community events

Most communities produce a host of festivals and events that are targeted mainly at local audiences and staged primarily for their social, fun and entertainment value. Such events can be found in almost every city and town in Australia. Some examples deserving of attention because of their unusual nature or unique setting include the Birdsville Races in outback Queensland, the Henley-On-Todd Dry River Boat Regatta in Alice Springs, and the Nymagee Outback Music Festival in central New South Wales. These events often produce a range of benefits, including engendering pride in the community, strengthening a feeling of belonging and creating a sense of place. They can also help to expose people to new ideas and experiences, encourage participation in sports and arts activities, and encourage tolerance and diversity. For these reasons, local governments often support such events as part of their community and cultural development strategies.

Janiskee (1996, p. 404) defines them as:

> ... family-fun events that are considered 'owned' by a community because they use volunteer services from the host community, employ public venues such as streets, parks and schools and are produced at the direction of local government agencies or non-government organizations (NGOs) such as service clubs, public safety organisations or business associations.

Janiskee also comments that community festivals can become hallmark events and attract a large number of visitors to a community. Janiskee estimates that community celebrations in the USA have been increasing at an annual rate of 5 per cent since the 1930s, and it is reasonable to assume that they have increased at a similar rate in Australia.

Another growing subsection of community events is charity fundraising events, which seek to increase the profile and raise funds for their respective charities. Well-known examples include Community Aid Abroad's Walk Against Want, SIDS' Red Nose Day and Movember, a moustache growing charity event held during November each year that raises funds and awareness for men's health (Movember 2010). Although these events often have key financial objectives, they are generally seen as part of the not-for-profit community sector.

Form or content

Another common means of classifying events is by their form or content. Festivals are a universal form of event that pre-date the contemporary event industry and exist in most times and most societies. Sports events have grown out of similar roots to become a sizable and growing sector of the event industry. Business events, sometimes called MICE (Meetings, Incentives, Conventions and Exhibitions) events, are an established arm of the event industry, and generate considerable income for their host cities and, increasingly, for regional centres.

Festivals

Festivals are an important expression of human activity that contributes much to our social and cultural life. They are also increasingly linked with tourism to generate business activity and income for their host communities.

The most common type of festival is the arts festival, which can encompass mixed art forms and multiple venues — such as the capital city arts festivals — or single art forms such as the Queensland Music Festival, the Sydney Biennale or the Melbourne Writers Festival. The most popular form of arts festival is the music festival. Music festivals can range from classical music festivals such as the International Music Festival in Canberra, to jazz festivals such as the Melbourne International Jazz Festival, to folk and blues festivals such as the East Coast Blues and Roots Music Festival at Byron Bay and the Woodford Folk Festival in Queensland, to rock festivals such as the Big Day Out and Homebake.

Another type of festival that has become universally popular is the food and wine festival. These range from large festivals in the capital cities to local festivals showcasing regional cuisine. Other festivals such as the Tropfest short film festival and the Big Day Out have become multi-state festivals, while festivals such as Floriade in Canberra and the Sydney Gay and Lesbian Mardi Gras approach hallmark status in their respective cities. Regional festivals, too, are a growing phenomenon, with many large and small towns expressing their unique character and distinctiveness through well-honed festivals and community celebrations. Some examples of the tremendous variety and array of regional festivals include the Mount Isa Rodeo in Queensland, the Wangaratta Jazz Festival in Victoria and the Parkes Elvis Festival in New South Wales. Festivals have become a pervasive feature of our cultural landscape and constitute a vital and growing component of the event industry.

Sports events

The testing of sporting prowess through competition is one of the oldest and most enduring of human activities, with a rich tradition going back to the ancient Greek Olympics and beyond. Sports events are an important and growing part of the event industry, encompassing the full spectrum of individual sports and multi-sport events such as the Olympic, Commonwealth and Masters Games. Their ability to attract tourist visitors and to generate media coverage and economic impacts has placed them at the fore of most government event strategies and destination marketing programs. Sports events not only bring benefits to their host governments and sports organisations, but also benefit participants such as players, coaches and officials, and bring entertainment and enjoyment to spectators. Examples of sports events can be readily identified in each of the size categories listed earlier.

Business events

Another long-established component of the event industry is business events, also known as the meetings industry or the MICE (Meetings, Incentives, Conventions and Exhibitions) industry. This sector is largely characterised by its business and trade focus, although there is a strong public and tourism aspect to many of its activities. Meetings can be very diverse, as revealed by the definition of the Commonwealth Department of Tourism (1995, p. 3):

> . . . all off-site gatherings, including conventions, congresses, conferences, seminars, workshops and symposiums, which bring together people for a common purpose — the sharing of information.

The International Congress and Convention Association (ICCA), based in Amsterdam, releases annual data on meetings organised by international associations, which take place on a regular basis, and which rotate between a minimum of three countries. In the latest available data, their researchers identified over 7475 events that took place in 2008, a rise of approximately 800 over 2007. The top ten countries, ranked in order of the number of meetings hosted, were USA, Germany, Spain, France, United Kingdom, Italy, Brazil, Japan, Canada and Netherlands, with Australia ranked fourteenth (International Congress and Convention Association 2010).

The National Business Events Study (NBES) conducted by the Sustainable Tourism CRC, based on data gathered in 2003, identified 316 000 events in Australia with 22.8 million participants, a total expenditure of $17.3 billion, and a contribution to total national employment of 214 000 jobs (Meetings and Events Australia 2006). Average expenditure of international delegates was $3526 per total trip and $554 per day — six times that of the average tourist.

Business events bring considerable exposure, visitors and economic benefits to the host city. The Lions Club International Convention hosted in Sydney in 2010 was expected to attract 25 000 people from more than 100 countries, and to generate more than $91 million for the city (Nori 2003). The Rotary International Convention to be hosted in Sydney in 2014 is expected to attract 22 000 delegates and to inject an estimated $63.8 million into the local economy (Sydney Convention and Visitors Bureau, 2006). Melbourne secured a total of 127 business events in 2008–09, representing 81 879 delegates. Recent wins include the 4th World Congress of Asian Psychiatry in 2011, which is expected to attract 1000 delegates with an economic impact of over $4 million, and the International Symposium on Hepatitis C Virus and Related Viruses in 2011, which is expected to attract 1000 delegates with an economic impact of over $5 million (Melbourne Convention and Visitors Bureau, 2010).

Another lucrative aspect of the business events industry is incentive travel, defined by the Society of Incentive Travel Executives (1997) (cited in Rogers 1998, p. 47) as 'a global management tool that uses an exceptional travel experience to motivate and/or recognise participants for increased levels of performance in support of organisational goals'. Australia's colourful and unique locations and international popularity as a tourism destination make it a leading player in the incentive travel market.

Last, but not least, exhibitions are a considerable and growing part of the business events industry. Exhibitions bring suppliers of goods and services together with buyers, usually in a particular industry sector. They can be restricted to industry members — in which case they are referred to as trade shows — or open to the general public. The

International Motor Show, the Home Show and the Boat Show are three of the largest exhibitions in Sydney, each generating tens of thousands of visitors. Major convention centres in most Australian cities and many regional centres now vie for their share of the thriving business events industry market.

THE STRUCTURE OF THE EVENT INDUSTRY

The rapid growth of events in the past decade led to the formation of an identifiable event industry, with its own practitioners, suppliers and professional associations. The emergence of the industry has involved the identification and refinement of a discrete body of knowledge of industry best practice, accompanied by the development of training programs and career paths. The industry's formation has also been accompanied by a period of rapid globalisation of markets and communication, which has affected the nature of, and trends within, the industry. Further, it has been accompanied by an era of increasing government regulation, which has resulted in a complex and demanding operational environment. The following sections describe the key components of the event industry.

Event organisations

Events are often staged or hosted by event organisations, which may be event-specific bodies such as the Sydney Festival, the Adelaide Festival, or the Australian Open tennis tournament organisers in Melbourne. Other events are run by special teams within larger organisations, such as the City to Surf fun run organised by *The Sun-Herald* newspaper in Sydney, the Sydney to Hobart Yacht Race organised by the Cruising Yacht Club of Australia, or the Taste of Tasmania organised as part of the Hobart Summer Festival by Hobart City Council. Corporate events are often organised by in-house event teams or by project teams within the companies that are putting on the event.

Event management companies

Event management companies are professional groups or individuals that organise events on a contract basis on behalf of their clients. The Australia Day Council, for example, may contract an event management company to stage an Australia Day ceremony, or Mercedes Benz may contract an event manager to stage the launch of a new Mercedes car model. The specialist companies often organise a number of events concurrently, and develop long-term relationships with their clients and suppliers.

Event industry suppliers

The growth of a large and complex industry has led to the formation of a wide range of specialist suppliers. These suppliers may work in direct event-related areas, such as staging, sound production, lighting, audiovisual production, entertainment and catering, or they may work in associated areas, such as transport, communications, security, legal services and accounting services. This network of suppliers is an integral part of the industry, and their increasing specialisation and expertise assist the production of professional and high-calibre events.

Venues

Venue management often includes an event management component, whether as part of the marketing of the venue or as part of the servicing of event clients. Many venues, such as historical houses, galleries, museums, theatres, universities and libraries, create additional revenue by hiring their facilities for functions and corporate events. Sydney's Unique Venues Association (2006) encompasses a wide range of venues including Taronga Park Zoo, Luna Park, Oceanworld at Manly and Sydney Olympic Park. Types of venues that commonly include an event management component include hotels, resorts, convention and exhibition centres, sports and fitness centres, sports stadiums, performing arts centres, heritage sites, theme parks, shopping centres and markets.

Industry associations

The emergence of the industry has also led to the formation of professional associations providing networking, communications and liaison within the industry, training and accreditation programs, codes of ethical practice, and lobbying on behalf of their members. Because the industry is so diverse, multiple associations have arisen to cater for specific sectors of the industry. Some are international associations with affiliated groups in countries such as Australia; others are specific to their region or country. Some key industry associations relevant to the interests of event managers are described below.

- *The International Special Events Society (ISES) (www.ises.com)*
  The International Special Events Society (ISES) is an international organisation with Australian chapters in Sydney, Melbourne and Queensland. It is comprised of more than 4000 professionals in over 35 countries representing special event producers (from festivals to trade shows), caterers, decorators, florists, destination management companies, rental companies, special effects experts, tent suppliers, audiovisual technicians, party and convention coordinators, balloon artists, educators, journalists, hotel sales managers, specialty entertainers, convention centre managers, and many more.

  The mission of ISES is to educate, advance and promote the special events industry and its network of professionals along with related industries. To that end, it strives to:
  - uphold the integrity of the special events profession to the general public through its principles of professional conduct and ethics (see figure 1.3)
  - acquire and disseminate useful business information
  - foster a spirit of cooperation among its members and other special events professionals
  - cultivate high standards of business practices.

  ISES runs professional development and certification programs. The designation Certified Special Events Professional (CSEP) is earned through education, performance, experience, and service to the industry, and reflects a commitment to professional conduct and ethics.
- *Meetings & Events Australia (MEA) (www.meetingsevents.com.au)*
  Meetings & Events Australia (MEA) is a national organisation dedicated to fostering professionalism and excellence in all aspects of meetings management.
  The aims of MEA are to:
  - create business opportunities and facilitating [sic] business to business relationships
  - encourage better business practice
  - promote professional development
  - provide information, forums and advice that lead to improved business performance
  - promote the value of meetings, events and our industry
  - advocate issues pertinent to industry
  - manage a sustainable association.

EACH MEMBER OF ISES SHALL AGREE TO ADHERE TO THE FOLLOWING:

- Promote and encourage the highest level of ethics within the profession of the special events industry while maintaining the highest standards of professional conduct.
- Strive for excellence in all aspects of our profession by performing consistently at or above acceptable industry standards.
- Use only legal and ethical means in all industry negotiations and activities.
- Protect the public against fraud and unfair practices, and promote all practices which bring respect and credit to the profession.
- Provide truthful and accurate information with respect to the performance of duties. Use a written contract clearly stating all charges, services, products, performance expectations and other essential information.
- Maintain industry accepted standards of safety and sanitation.
- Maintain adequate and appropriate insurance coverage for all business activities.
- Commit to increase professional growth and knowledge, to attend educational programs and to personally contribute expertise to meetings and journals.
- Strive to cooperate with colleagues, suppliers, employees, employers and all persons supervised, in order to provide the highest quality service at every level.
- Subscribe to the ISES Principles of Professional Conduct and Ethics, and abide by the ISES Bylaws and policies.

FIGURE 1.3 ISES Principles of Professional Conduct and Ethics

Source: International Special Events Society 2006, 'ISES Principles of Professional Conduct and Ethics', www.ises.com. Reprinted with permission from the International Special Events Society, May 2007.

MEA offers professional development programs and accreditation, disseminates information, provides a forum for its members to discuss current issues, represents the industry to government and creates a business-to-business (B2B) community. Its members agree to subscribe to a professional code of ethics. The accreditation program includes Accredited Meetings Manager (AMM), Accredited In-House Meetings Manager (AIMM), Accredited Meetings Management Company (AMMC) and Associate-Fellow of MEA (AFMEA). The status of Associate-Fellow of MEA is open to all MEA members and indicates the member has proven dedication to the industry and its association and to ensuring their skills and knowledge remain current through ongoing professional development.

MEA has a student membership category for full-time or part-time students not currently employed in the industry. It also offers young professional and student scholarships, which provide registration to the MEA Annual Conference, air travel and accommodation.

- *The Exhibition and Event Association of Australasia (EEAA) (www.eeaa.com.au)*

The Exhibition and Event Association of Australasia (EEAA) is a not-for-profit organisation whose primary objective is facilitating the growth of the exhibition and event industry. The EEAA achieves this through promoting the professionalism of its members and the unique benefits offered by exhibitions.

It has a number of working committees that focus on special areas of interest to members. These committees have specific functions including market research, public relations, training and education, venue liaison, fundraising and recruiting new members. Each committee is chaired by a member of the committee of management and is comprised of association members.

The EEAA commits itself to continual improvement within the industry, and sees the industry-wide development of an understanding and awareness of risk management as a key issue.

External regulatory bodies

As noted, contemporary events take place in an increasingly regulated and complex environment. A series of government and statutory bodies are responsible for overseeing the conduct and safe staging of events, and these bodies have an integral relationship with the industry. For example, many local councils now require a development application for the staging of outdoor events. This application may cover regulations governing the erection of temporary structures, traffic plans, noise restrictions and so on. Councils also often oversee the application of state laws governing the preparation and sale of food, and by-laws regarding street closures, waste management and removal. In addition, event organisers have a legal responsibility to provide a safe workplace and to obey all laws and statutes relating to employment, contracts, taxation and so on. The professional event manager needs to be familiar with the regulations governing events and to maintain contact with the public authorities that have a vested interest in the industry.

EVENT MANAGEMENT, EDUCATION AND TRAINING

As the size and needs of the event industry have grown, event management training has started to emerge as a discrete discipline. In the early years of the industry, leading up to the mid 1990s, the field was characterised by a large number of volunteers. Those few event managers who obtained paid positions came from a variety of related disciplines, drawing on their knowledge gained from that discipline and skills learnt on the job. Many came from allied areas such as theatre and entertainment, audiovisual production and film, and adapted their skills to events. Others came from working for event suppliers such as staging, lighting and sound production companies, having discovered that they could expand and build on their existing skills to undertake the overall management of events. However, as the use of events by government and industry has grown, event budgets have increased, and the logistics of events have become more complex, the need has emerged for skilled event professionals who can meet the industry's specific requirements. Education and training at both vocational and tertiary levels have arisen to meet this need.

Identifying the knowledge and skills required by event managers

In addition to generic management skills, Getz and Wicks (1994, pp. 108–9) specify the following event-specific areas of knowledge as appropriate for inclusion in event management training:

- history and meanings of festivals, celebrations, rituals and other events
- historical evolution; types of events

- trends in demand and supply
- motivations and benefits sought from events
- roles and impacts of events in society, the economy, environment and culture
- who is producing events, and why?
- program concepts and styles
- event settings
- operations unique to events
- management unique to events
- marketing unique to events

Studies by Perry, Foley and Rumpf (1996), Harris and Griffin (1997), Royal and Jago (1998), Harris and Jago (1999) and Arcodia and Barker (2002) largely confirm the importance of these knowledge/skill areas. Silvers (2006), as part of the Event Management Body of Knowledge (EMBOK) program, has further defined four event management knowledge domains, each with its own requirement for specialisation (see figure 1.4). Despite occasional differing emphases and nuances, therefore, the field generally agrees on the specific body of knowledge of best practice appropriate to the training of professional event managers.

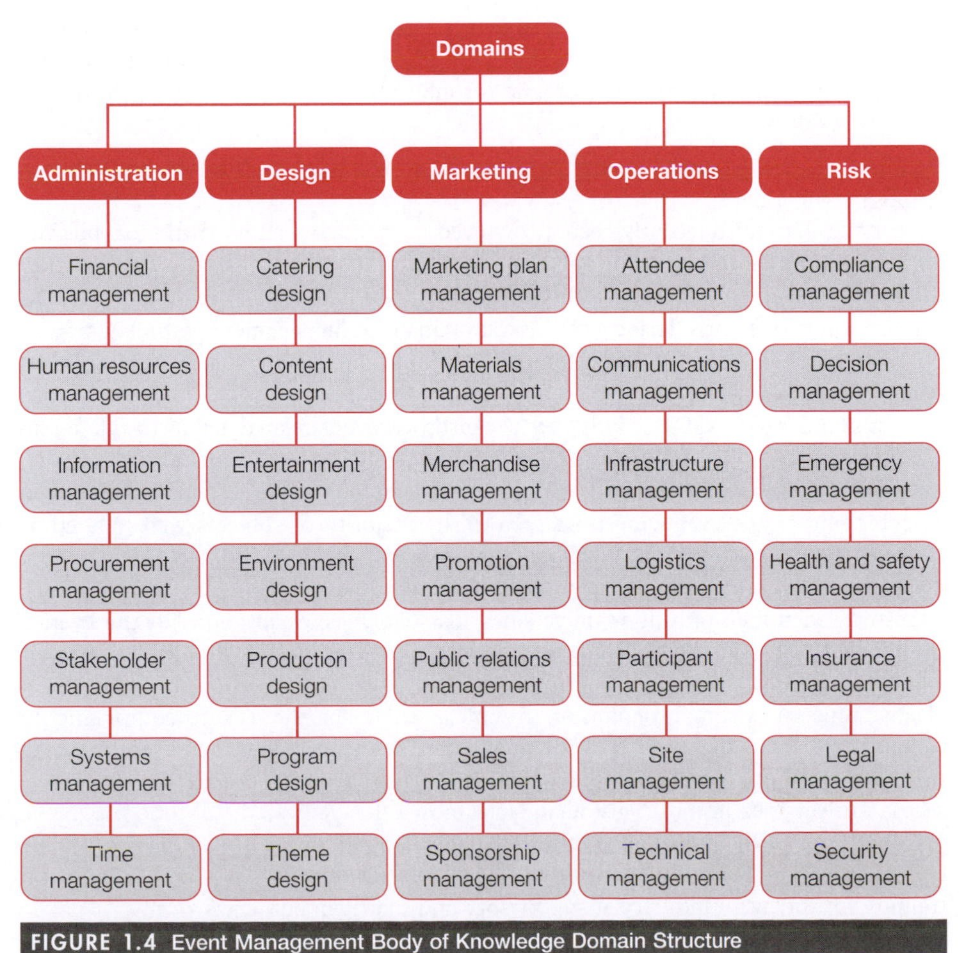

FIGURE 1.4 Event Management Body of Knowledge Domain Structure

Source: Silvers, J 2006, Event Management Body of Knowledge Domain Structure, www.juliasilvers.com/embok/update.

The content and organisation of this book parallels closely the knowledge domains identified by Silvers and other researchers in the field. Part 1, event context, provides a general background to the event industry, the range of perspectives on events and event impacts. Part 2, planning, deals with the knowledge areas of administration and marketing. Part 3, event operations and evaluation, deals with the knowledge area of operations, while part 4, legal, risk and occupational health and safety management, deals with the knowledge areas of risk management and associated issues.

Training delivery

As training has become needed, it has been delivered in a range of formats by a variety of institutions.

Industry associations

The major event industry associations have all been involved in the delivery of training and certification programs. These programs typically involve a points system whereby accreditation can be gained from a mix of dedicated training programs, participation in the association, contribution to the industry, attendance at conferences and seminars, and often a written paper or examination. Prerequisites often include membership of the association, industry experience and allegiance to a written code of conduct or ethics. Accreditation programs are usually supported by educational provisions such as seminar training programs, online training courses and self-directed learning resources.

Universities and other tertiary education institutions

Universities have also recently become involved in event education, with most offering event management or marketing subjects as part of tourism, hospitality, recreation and/or sport management programs. The George Washington University in Washington DC was an early pioneer in offering a concentration in event management within a graduate program. In 1994 it commenced a complete certification program in event management (Getz and Wicks 1994).

Harris and Jago (1999) conducted a census of event-related subjects offered in Australian universities by assessing the courses listed on each university's website. Of the 29 universities examined, 17 offered at least one subject that was identified as belonging to the events/meetings sector. The majority of subjects were offered as electives within tourism, hospitality, sport management and human development programs, with others offered in marketing, communication and fine art programs. The study identified only four universities that offered specialisations in the events/meetings sector. The study also found that the offering of the tertiary and further education (TAFE) and private college sector was similarly limited to the inclusion of elective units in existing programs or, in some cases, to specific streams comprising up to four units. Since the study, the growth and development of dedicated event management courses has continued apace across the full spectrum of the tertiary education sector. Universities in most Australian states now offer dedicated full-time programs, and, with the development of a national qualifications framework, TAFE and private colleges are now able to offer diploma and certificate qualifications with a focus on training for the event industry at supervisory and management levels.

In the UK, where the successful bid to stage the London Olympics in 2012 has placed great emphasis on public events, WorldofEvents.net emanating from Leeds Metropolitan University lists over 50 universities that offer event-related courses, with the majority of these in the UK, USA and Australia (World of Events 2009). Given the increasing proliferation of such courses, their actual number is likely to be much higher.

CAREER OPPORTUNITIES IN EVENTS

As demonstrated, events are an expanding industry, providing new and challenging job opportunities for people entering the field. Roles, titles, salaries and job descriptions are not yet standardised in the industry, and details vary from city to city and between countries. However, the International Special Events Society has been consulting with its members and the industry in order to achieve some degree of general agreement on these issues. Landey (2006) lists the following roles as having some degree of general acceptance among event management companies (see table 1.1).

TABLE 1.1 Roles in the event industry

Role	Qualifications
Event professional	Certified professional
Event producer	Five years experience Major role in at least 10 events
Event manager	Three to five years experience Major role in at least five events
Event coordinator	Up to three years experience
Event support	Entry level into industry

However, a career in the event industry is not limited to just these roles or to event management companies. There is a vast array of event positions available in different sectors of the industry, including in corporate and government institutions, public relations companies, the media, arts and sports organisations, not-for-profit groups and charities, non-government and community organisations, to name just a few. Inside these and the companies that supply them there is a variety of roles to suit all interests and backgrounds, including project managers, stage managers, technicians, graphic artists, set designers, costume makers, make-up artists, marketers, publicists, photographers, entertainers, comperes, caterers, pyrotechnicians — again, the list is seemingly endless. It is in the nature of the industry that much of this work is free-lance and spasmodic, with many event staff working on a short-term contract basis for a series of employers and events.

A successful career in events depends on applicants identifying their own skills and interests, and then matching these carefully with the needs of prospective employers. Areas of expanding activity — such as corporate events, conferences, local government and tourism — may be fruitful areas to examine. Employers often look for a mix of qualifications and experience, so intending job seekers may be advised to consider volunteering and/or taking entry-level positions in order to build their resumes and to gain a foothold in the industry. A satisfying and rewarding career awaits those who apply themselves with vision, passion and perseverance.

event profile

AUSTRALIAN CENTRE FOR EVENT MANAGEMENT (WWW.ACEM.UTS.EDU.AU)

The Australian Centre for Event Management (ACEM) was established at the University of Technology, Sydney, in 1999. It aims to provide research and training services to the event industry. It also aims to position Sydney and Australia as centres of excellence in the development of skills and knowledge associated with the creation, conduct and evaluation of events.

Following are some of the education and training programs provided by ACEM.

- Executive Certificate in Event Management — a six-day intensive course tailored to the needs of people working in or wanting to enter the event industry.
- Event management seminars — a series of short seminars on current topics and issues in event management delivered by industry practitioners.
- Master of Management in Event Management — a masters program in event management, delivered by the university's Faculty of Business. The program covers all aspects of event management and may be taken at the graduate certificate and graduate diploma levels, as well as the full masters level.
- Event management short courses — short courses in event management, delivered by the centre in association with university partners around Australia and overseas. Such courses have been delivered in Melbourne, Brisbane, Perth, Hobart, London, Edinburgh, Auckland, Singapore, Macau and Kuala Lumpur.
- In-house training — training programs in event management tailored to the needs of specific government and industry clients. Clients have included Tourism New South Wales, the New South Wales Department of State and Regional Development, the New South Wales Attorney-General's Department, the ACT Chief Minister's Department, artsACT, Canberra Arts Marketing and Casula Powerhouse.
- Research — ACEM conducts research on core issues in event management, and provides a research service to clients in government and industry. Clients have included the City of Sydney, Sydney Olympic Park Authority, Playbill Venues at Fox Studios in Sydney and artsACT.
- Event Research Conference — a biennial international research conference in event management held since 2000. Conferences have included:
  2000 — Events Beyond 2000: Setting the Agenda
  2002 — Events and Place Making
  2005 — The Impacts of Events
  2007 — Re-eventing the City: Events as Catalysts for Change (staged in association with Victoria University)
  2009 — Meeting the Challenge of Sustainable Development (staged in association with Griffith University).
- Publications — a range of event management resources published on the centre's website (www.acem.uts.edu.au), including full conference proceedings of the above conferences and a complete Australian and international bibliography of event management publications. The website also provides details of current ACEM research and training programs and activities.
- Event and Olympic Studies online collection — an online resource collection of research papers, documents and templates relating to the event industry.

SUMMARY

Special events perform a powerful role in society, and they have existed throughout human history in all times and all cultures. Prior to the arrival of the Europeans, the Australian Aboriginal culture had a rich tradition of rituals and ceremonies. The event tradition in modern Australia began in a primitive way with the arrival of the First Fleet, and developed through the late eighteenth and nineteenth centuries as the colony prospered and the new inhabitants came to terms with their environment. The ruling elite often decided the form and content of public celebrations, but an alternative tradition of popular celebrations arose from the interests and pursuits of ordinary people. During the twentieth century, changes in society were mirrored by changes in the style of public events. The post-war wave of civic festivals and arts festivals was strongly influenced by the community arts movement in the 1970s, along with multiculturalism and the 'new age' movement. Notions of high culture were challenged by a more pluralistic popular culture, which reinvigorated festivals and community events.

With the coming of the 1980s, governments and the corporate sector began to recognise the economic and promotional value of special events, and state events corporations spearheaded a new level of funding, profile and professionalism. With the advent of the global financial crisis in 2008, event managers faced a new challenge in balancing the economic and environmental sustainability of events.

Events can be classified by size — including mega-events, hallmark events, major events and local or community events — and by form or content — including festivals, sporting events and business events. With increasing expansion and corporate involvement, events have emerged as a new growth industry, capable of generating economic benefits and employment.

Significant components of this industry include event organisations, event management companies, event industry suppliers, venues, industry associations and external regulatory bodies. In response to the requirement for professional event management training, industry associations, universities and other tertiary institutions have developed programs. Intending entrants to the industry are advised to study the industry carefully to match their own interests and skills with those required by prospective employers.

QUESTIONS

1. Why are special events created? What purpose do they serve in society?
2. Why have special events emerged so strongly in recent years in Australia?
3. What are the key political, cultural and social trends that determine the current climate of events in Australia?
4. What do you perceive as the major challenges currently facing event managers in Australia?
5. Identify an event in your city or region that has the capacity to be a hallmark event. Give your reasons for placing it in this category.
6. Examine the structure of the event industry in your area and identify local examples of the components outlined in this chapter.
7. Do you agree with the attributes and knowledge areas required by event managers identified by the studies in this chapter? Create a list of your own attributes and skills based on these listings.

case study

RSVP: *THE EVENT FOR THE EVENTS INDUSTRY*

RSVP is a trade event (business to business or B2B event) dedicated to the special events and corporate party industry. First conducted in London in 2001, RSVP has expanded to be held annually in London, Sydney, Melbourne and Manchester. RSVP is owned by Exhibitions and Trade Fairs (ETF), an Australian based exhibition organiser.

The Sydney event has been conducted since 2005 and is currently held at the Sydney Convention and Exhibition Centre (SCEC). Typically, more than two hundred companies exhibit and a total of 5000 people attend. The event also includes an entertainment stage, food tasting sessions, educational presentations, roving entertainment and networking functions.

While trade events and exhibitions have the same basic structure and procedures common to many events, a trade exhibition's commercial purpose is to provide a sales and marketing opportunity for sellers (exhibitors) and buyers (visitors or attendees). This is in contrast to conferences where the key purpose is knowledge and information exchange.

Most trade exhibitions compete less against other exhibitions and more against alternative sales and marketing techniques that are employed by companies such as sales teams, direct marketing (mail, email), advertising, promotions, and product launches. To be competitive against these sales and marketing alternatives, a trade exhibition must add value to the sell-buy process for both the exhibitor and attendee.

The main unique selling point (USP) for an exhibition is that it is the only place a buyer (attendee) can 'see, discuss and compare' the products and ideas they are looking for. Other unique features include the fact that attendees are 'volunteer customers' — that is, active participants who have taken the trouble to attend, allowing face-to-face time with customers — and that it is a platform for effective industry networking. As most people in modern society are time poor, attending a trade exhibition is also a time-effective buying process as many potential suppliers can be seen over a few hours.

Trade exhibitions in Australia usually generate most revenue from the sale of exhibition space. There is generally no or low revenue from charging visitors to attend. However, attracting both quality and a high quantity of visitors underpins the on-going revenue stream of successful trade exhibitions.

Profile of RSVP

At RSVP the exhibitors are mainly from the areas of entertainment, decoration and theming, party planning, production, sound, lighting, equipment hire, corporate entertainment, floristry, catering, event management, coach hire, and team building. The exhibitors, primarily from the service industry, are predominantly based in Sydney. The attendees include corporate event managers, executive assistants, marketing managers, function organisers, professional conference organisers (PCOs), and party planners. Most attendees come from Sydney.

RSVP serves as an effective way for buyers to see, discuss and compare their event planning requirements. Key reasons for attending include:

- Discovering 'what's new'. People are looking for ideas to make their next event 'the best ever', including new venue ideas, different theming ideas, alternative ideas for entertainment, and innovations in menus and catering.

- Networking with their peers and suppliers to discuss ideas and trends, find out what the competition is up to, and even look for a new job.
- Participating in and finding out about educational and training opportunities covering creative and logistical topics.

RSVP does not charge visitors to attend the event and, as the target audience is Sydney-based, most people incur only incidental travel costs. The main factor affecting attendance, especially for the corporate sector, is securing time away from the office. Surveys of those who register to attend show that 'intention to attend' does not always translate into actual attendance. This issue is common to many trade exhibitions, and the rule of thumb is that up to 50 per cent of the people who pre-register do not attend.

Strategic development

In 2007 ETF purchased the Business Events Expo, a Sydney-based trade exhibition. Previously called Sydney on Sale, the event was targeted at that section of the events industry that covered the business events sector.

Exhibitors at the Business Events Expo came from such areas as destinations, venues, accommodation, travel and event services. There was an approximate crossover of 30 per cent between RSVP and Business Events Expo exhibitors. Visitors comprised mainly corporates, associations, not-for profit groups and professional conference organisers (PCO), with approximately 10 per cent of attendees visiting both exhibitions. However, further research showed that upward of 70 per cent of the two events' target visitor audience said they 'intended' to visit both. This was because many organisations that were buyers of special event and corporate party products were also buyers of business events sector products. One of the main factors that led to the large gap between *intention* to attend both events and *actual* attendance was lack of time. Also, for some potential visitors, one event was more important to attend than the other.

A strategic decision was made in 2009 that the two events would co-locate at the Sydney Convention and Exhibition Centre. The Business Events Expo was also re-launched as the Australian Business Events Expo to better reflect its national exhibitor profile. The objectives were to grow the total visitor attendance and increase exhibitor participation by adding value to all the stakeholders involved in the two events. The key benefits to the industries served by the exhibition are as follows.

- Exhibitors — Thirty per cent of the exhibitors participated in both RSVP and ABEE. For these companies, co-location can significantly reduce their total exhibiting costs. For companies who did not already exhibit in either event, co-location offers greater incentive to participate.
- Attendees — Co-location means attendees have now only to attend one event per year, which reduces non-attendance due to being 'time poor'. Also, a larger, more comprehensive event should attract new buyers to attend.
- Events, Media and Industry Associations — ETF's ownership and subsequent co-location of the two events means that these stakeholders are no longer torn between which event to support, and can focus on one major annual event in the Sydney marketplace.

A changing world

Not long after the co-location launch in mid 2008, the economic turndown hit the events industry very hard. As well as an immediate reduction in the number of

events due to reduced budgets, certain types of events, such as lavish social events, were seen to be inappropriate.

Also, as is often the case in a turndown, businesses used the opportunity to reset their staff's and clients' expectations as to the size and number of events they might conduct. The UK, which was much harder hit by the economic downturn than Australia, saw a significant drop in exhibitor and visitor attendance at RSVP London.

In Sydney, co-location, originally a strategy to increase attendance, now became instrumental to minimising a reduction in participation, because only one event, rather than two, needed to be organised. Had co-location not occurred, it is likely both events would have seen a significant reduction in attendance, as the pressures of being 'time poor' became an even greater factor preventing people from leaving the office. As it was, attendance was in line with previous years.

It is worth noting that, for a well-organised trade exhibition, a lower attendance rate in difficult economic times reflects a decline in the number of buyers, not necessarily the effectiveness of the exhibition. In fact, in tougher economic times an exhibition is an important way of identifying those companies that are still in the buying cycle, as the effort of attendance is an active indicator of buying intention.

A return to economic growth should see an increase in participation. However, the size and nature of events is likely to change for the next few years, with a greater focus on events that involve training and education.

Rodney Cox, Business Development Director, Exhibitions and Trade Fairs

Questions

1 What are the two main stakeholder groups in an exhibition? Identify a large exhibition in your city, and describe the two major stakeholder groups for this exhibition.

2 Summarise the main reasons for the co-location of the two exhibitions in the case study.

3 What was the overall outcome of co-locating the two exhibitions during an economic downturn in the market?

REFERENCES

Arcodia, C & Barker, T 2002, 'A review of web-based job advertisements for Australian event management positions', in *Events and place making: proceedings of International Research Conference held in Sydney 2002*, eds L Jago, M Deery, R Harris, A Hede & J Allen, Australian Centre for Event Management, Sydney.

Australian Centre for Event Management 2009, www.acem.uts.edu.au.

Bower, R 1981, 'Community arts — what is it?', *Caper*, vol. 10, Community Arts Board, Australia Council, Sydney.

City of Sydney 2006, 'Significant Aboriginal Events in Sydney', Indigenous History of Sydney, www.cityofsydney.nsw.gov.au.

Clark, M 1981, *A History of Australia*, vol. 5, Melbourne University Press, Melbourne.

Commonwealth Department of Tourism 1995, *A national strategy for the meetings, incentives, conventions and exhibitions industry*, Australian Government Publishing Service, Canberra.
Earth Hour 2010, *Voice of the people crucial in fight against climate change, UN Chief of Staff tells world*, www.earthhour.org
Exhibition and Event Association of Australasia 2006, www.eeaa.com.au.
Getz, D 2005, *Event management and event tourism*, Cognizant Communication Corporation, New York, p. 6.
Getz, D & Wicks, B 1994, 'Professionalism and certification for festival and event practitioners: trends and issues', *Festival Management and Event Tourism*, vol. 2, no. 2, pp. 108–9.
Greenhill, S 2008, 'EIBTM Reveals Mood of the Market', press release, 6 December, www.eibtm.com.
Hall, CM 1992, *Hallmark tourist events: impacts, management and planning*, Belhaven Press, London.
Harris, R & Griffin, T 1997, *Tourism events training audit*, Prepared for Tourism New South Wales Events Unit, Sydney.
Harris, R & Jago, L 1999, 'Event education and training in Australia: the current state of play', *Australian Journal of Hospitality Management*, vol. 6, no. 1, pp. 45–51.
Hughes, R 1987, *The fatal shore*, Collins Harvill, London.
Hull, A 1984, 'Feasting on festas and festivals', Paper delivered to the Association of Festivals Conference at the Caulfield Arts Centre, Victoria.
Hutchison, J. 2009, pers. comm. 13 February 2009.
International Congress and Convention Association 2010, 'ICCA country and city rankings 2007', www.iccaworld.com.
International Festivals and Events Association 2006, Regions and affiliated chapters, www.ifea.com.
International Special Events Society 2006, ISES principles of professional conduct and ethics, www.ises.com.
Janiskee, R 1996, 'Historic houses and special events', *Annals of Leisure Research*, vol. 23, no. 2, pp. 398–414.
Landey, J 2006, 'Representation of a selection of disciplines required for the successful implementation of events', www.juliasilvers.com/embok/.
McCarthy, W 1998, 'Day we came of age', *The Sun-Herald*, 25 January, p. 46.
Meetings & Events Australia 2006, National Business Events Study (NBES) — Key Findings, www.meetingsevents.com.au.
Melbourne Convention and Visitors Bureau 2010, 'Melbourne Convention + Visitors Bureau Business Events — 2008/2009', Business Events data, www.mcvb.com.au
Movember 2010, au.movemberfoundation.com.
Nori, S 2003, 'The lion's roar — Sydney to host $91 million conference', Media release of Sydney Convention & Visitors Bureau, Sydney, 15 April.
Pearl, C 1974, *Australia's yesterdays*, Reader's Digest, Sydney.
Perry, M, Foley, P & Rumpf, P 1996, 'Event management: an emerging challenge in Australian education', *Festival Management and Event Tourism*, vol. 4, pp. 85–93.
Ritchie, JRB 1984, 'Assessing the impact of hallmark events: conceptual and research issues', *Journal of Travel Research*, vol. 23, no. 1, pp. 2–11.
Rogers, T 1998, *Conferences: a twenty-first century industry*, Addison-Wesley Longman, Harlow.
Royal, CG & Jago, LK 1998, 'Special events accreditation: the practitioner's perspective', *Festival Management and Event Tourism*, no. 5, pp. 221–30.

Silvers, J 2006, Event management body of knowledge domain structure, www.juliasilvers.com/embok/.

Sydney Convention and Visitors Bureau 2006, 'Sydney wins $63.8 million Rotary International convention', Media release, www.scvb.com.au.

Sydney's Unique Venues Association 2006, List of venues, www.suva.com.au.

World of Events 2009, Education & Training — University/College Courses, www.worldofevents.net.

2

PERSPECTIVES ON EVENTS

LEARNING OBJECTIVES

After studying this chapter, you should be able to:

1. list the range of roles that governments play in events
2. describe the nature and function of government event strategies
3. discuss the use of events by governments as tools for economic regeneration and development
4. discuss the use of events by the corporate sector
5. describe the role that events play in integrated marketing strategies
6. list and describe methods used by the corporate sector in measuring the return on investment (ROI) of events
7. discuss the benefits that can result to communities from the staging of events
8. list the range of strategies available to event managers to promote community engagement in events
9. discuss the implications for event managers of differing perspectives on events in the event planning process.

INTRODUCTION

As we have seen in chapter 1, events take place across the full spectrum of society, leading to differing contexts, goals and objectives. In this chapter we will look at events from the perspectives of the three major sectors — government, corporate and community — and examine how these perspectives vary and the implications of this for event managers.

Governments play a leading role in events, and increasingly employ event strategies in order to guide their involvement, priorities and decision-making. In recent years, many governments have created dedicated celebration spaces for the staging of public events, and some have consciously used events in tandem with other policies and strategies as tools for urban regeneration and development.

The corporate sector is a major player in events, using them regularly in the course of business administration, staff motivation and training, and as a significant element of the integrated marketing mix in the sale and promotion of goods and services. Companies also sponsor public events in order to demonstrate product attributes, build brand awareness and reach target markets effectively.

Events have long played a universal and enduring role in communities, whose prime focus is on their direct entertainment, social, cultural and sporting benefits. In planning events, event managers need to devise and incorporate appropriate strategies for community ownership, participation and engagement.

THE GOVERNMENT PERSPECTIVE

All levels of government, national, state and local, make frequent use of events both in conducting the affairs of government and as part of their service delivery. Executive offices of all three levels of government — for example, the departments of the Prime Minister and Premier, or the office of the Mayor — are often involved in the conduct of civic events such as official visits, national days and citizenship ceremonies. They will often combine in the celebration of significant national anniversaries and events, as was seen in Australia with the nation's bicentenary in 1988 and the centenary of Federation in 2001.

National government

However, it is the national or federal government that usually has the prime carriage of these major celebrations of national significance. It will then work closely with other levels of government to augment related programs at state and local levels.

National governments are also increasingly involved with hosting and organising major international political and economic gatherings; for example, the Copenhagen Climate Change Summit, the G20 Summit, the Commonwealth Heads of Government Meeting (CHOGM) and the Asia–Pacific Economic Cooperation forum (APEC). Such events present increasing logistic and security challenges, but confer significant prestige on their host governments. National governments also make significant use of cultural events in the promotion of trade through their foreign affairs departments, as was seen in the lead-up to the Beijing Olympics by the Year of Paris in Beijing and the corresponding Year of Beijing in Paris.

The staging of major sporting and cultural events on home soil is more the province of state and city governments, though, interestingly, the International Olympic Committee has stated that the Olympic Games will not be awarded in future to cities that do not have the express underwriting and support of their national governments.

State government

State governments play a major role in bidding for and staging major events of economic and tourism significance, often setting up event corporations and convention and visitor bureaus for this purpose, as we saw in chapter 1. Most state government departments are involved in staging or assisting events as part of their portfolio — for example, arts ministries with major festivals, sports ministries with major sporting competitions, ethnic affairs ministries with events celebrating ethnic diversity, or tourism ministries with flagship tourism events. They may sponsor or be involved in events that carry messages relevant to their charters. For example, the Victorian Health Ministry, in partnership with the Transport Accident Commission (TAC), sponsors the Wangaratta Festival of Jazz in order to promote 'don't drink and drive' messages (www.wangaratta-jazz.org.au). Almost all government departments make extensive internal use of events in order to train staff, develop networks and communicate with the public.

Local government

Local governments are also increasingly involved with events, seeing them as an important means of creating quality of life for their constituents, and attracting tourism and economic benefits to their regions. Local government in Australia is now one of the biggest players in the event field, with almost every local government body employing an event manager or team, and with most providing funding and support for a wide range of local events. These may include events specifically designed to support tourism visitation and expenditure, and to increase the profile of the destination as an attractive place to visit or to do business. They may also include events whose primary focus is the local community, thus increasing their entertainment, cultural, leisure or sporting options. Increasingly, local governments aim to support and encourage business events such as conferences, meetings and exhibitions that attract visitors from the business sector.

The role of government in events

Governments commonly perform a wide and complex variety of roles in events, particularly in the arena of public outdoor events and festivals. The extent and scale of these roles will vary according to the size and level of governments, and to the degree of their resources and commitment. However, the roles listed below and the issues that arise from them are common to most governments, and provide the impetus for them to form event departments and create strategies in order to delineate and implement their role in events.

Venue owner/manager

Governments are often the owners of parks, playing fields, streets, town halls, stadiums, and sports and community centres where events are staged. They are responsible for the development and maintenance of these assets, as well as managing them on a day-to-day basis. They therefore need to employ staff to run them, and set and administer policies and charges for their use.

Consent authority and regulatory body

Governments also set and administer many of the laws and policies that govern the staging of events in matters such as the creation of temporary structures, the sale of food, noise restrictions, street closures and traffic and parking requirements. Local councils often work closely with other government agencies such as road and traffic authorities, health departments and police in the drafting, implementation and monitoring of rules and regulations governing these areas. For large events, councils may require a formal development application addressing issues such as environmental impact, traffic management and safety, while smaller events may simply require the issue of a licence or permit.

Service provider

Many of the services required by events are provided by governments on a cost recovery basis. These can include cleaning, waste removal and traffic management. For larger events with the involvement of state governments, these services can extend to the provision of public transport, police and emergency services. In the case of major events, central government may play a coordinating role across a range of government-related services and agencies (see figure 2.1, Central Sydney Operations Group). In some cases, government services may be provided gratis in lieu of the perceived value of the event to the local economy. For example, in Sydney, events defined as having hallmark status may be provided free government services such as police and traffic assistance.

The Central Sydney Operations Group (CSOG) is a best practice example of the coordination of major events across a wide range of government departments and agencies. It sits inside the Office of Protocol and Special Events of the New South Wales Premier's Department, which provides coordination services for the Premier in special events, official visits and awards. Special events are defined as those events that involve investment of government resources and require specialist central agency coordination; for example, New Year's Eve and the City to Surf fun run.

CSOG meets monthly and is attended by government agencies and managers of upcoming approved events. Participating agencies include:

- the City of Sydney
- Botanic Gardens
- Sydney Opera House
- Sydney Harbour Foreshores Authority
- Roads and Traffic Authority
- Sydney Ferries
- Sydney Buses
- Railcorp
- Ministry of Transport
- Sydney Ports
- New South Wales Police
- ambulance
- fire brigades.

At its meetings, CSOG coordinates the planning of upcoming major events, identifies issues and reviews recent events. CSOG was a legacy of the Sydney Olympic Games, and remains an ongoing asset for New South Wales and the City of Sydney in the government coordination and servicing of major events.

FIGURE 2.1 Central Sydney Operations Group

Source: Willard 2005.

Funding body

Governments often establish funding programs that aim to develop and assist events. This may be at a community level, where assisting events is seen as part of the overall provision of services to the community. In such cases, the scale of funding is likely to be modest, and guidelines are likely to focus on community/cultural services and outcomes. In other cases, governments may support events because of their perceived economic and tourism benefits, and will seek to fund and develop events that match this agenda. Clear funding criteria and guidelines need to be established, and procedures put in place for the monitoring of event implementation and the reporting and measurement of event outcomes.

Event organiser

Governments may also themselves be event producers or host organisations. This may involve the organisation and protocol of official visits and ceremonial events, or the celebration of national days and important anniversaries such as Anzac Day and Australia Day. Governments may also choose to mount a program of local events and celebrations in order to animate civic spaces, to enhance the quality of life of residents or to attract visitors.

Event/destination marketer

Governments may assume some responsibility for the compilation and promotion of an annual calendar of events, both as a service to residents and as part of the overall tourism promotion of the city or destination. Such event calendars may be supported by a communications strategy, with highlight events the subject of individual campaigns. The use of events as part of destination marketing strategies will be discussed further in chapter 13.

Event strategies

Increasingly governments are developing event strategies in order to coordinate their overall involvement in events, to plan the use of resources and to improve and measure the outcomes of programs and services. Such strategies ideally dovetail with other policies and strategies in the areas of urban planning, community and cultural services, economic development and tourism. They also establish strong links with agencies at other levels of government, and the private sector.

Event strategies seek to delineate government objectives in the events area, and to identify the appropriate policies, infrastructure, resources, staffing and programs needed to achieve them. They often include the development of a portfolio or annual program of events designed to reflect the particular characteristics and needs of a city or region. Such a portfolio may include a broad range of events, including signature or flagship events that are intended to promote the destination, and other events designed to serve particular cultural, sporting, economic or tourism goals and objectives. Event portfolios may involve both existing events, and the sourcing of new events by bidding for suitable event properties or by developing events from the ground up. Event strategies provide a framework for the appraisal of proposed new events in order to determine their fit with strategic objectives.

An event strategy will often include the creation of a 'one stop shop' for event organisers in order to bring together and coordinate various government departments and services related to events. This will greatly assist in the efficient planning and delivery of events, and create an 'event friendly' culture and working environment that will strengthen the role of events and the outcomes of the strategy.

Scotland Events Strategy

In 2009 EventScotland produced 'Scotland the Perfect Stage: A Strategy for the Events Industry in Scotland 2009–2020' (EventScotland 2009). Building on an earlier event strategy created in 2002, this document addresses the changed events landscape in Scotland due to the securing of the Commonwealth Games and the Ryder Cup in 2014, and the advent of Homecoming Scotland in 2009. It will be reviewed in 2014, and its timeframe extended to 2025, after which it will be reviewed every five years.

The vision contained in the strategy is: 'To establish Scotland as the perfect stage for events'. Flowing from this, the mission is: 'To develop a portfolio of events that delivers impact and international profile for Scotland' (EventScotland 2009).

Strategy for Scotland

In order to fulfill this mission, the strategy aims to utilise assets that make Scotland 'The Perfect Stage' for events. Assets identified in the strategy include:

- *Cultural identity and heritage* — including Scotland's rich history, its food and drink, its reputation in the fields of education and innovation, and its iconic poets, artists, writers, musicians and vibrant contemporary culture
- *People* — including a strong business community with good international links and large numbers of people across the world who have an affinity for Scotland
- *Natural environment* — including dramatic landscapes ranging from mountains to lochs, beaches and islands
- *Built facilities* — Scotland has a long architectural history and tradition, including castles, public buildings and cityscapes, as well as iconic buildings, in which to stage events, and quality facilities being designed to house the Glasgow 2014 Commonwealth Games
- *Signature events* — Scotland already has a range of iconic signature events to build upon, including Edinburgh's Festivals, the Glasgow Commonwealth Games, the Ryder Cup in 2014 and Homecoming Scotland in 2009.

The strategy plans to further develop its events portfolio by adding new events on a major scale, and by developing Scotland's own events to stand alongside these.

Rationale

The strategy identifies seven areas of event impacts that can be used to evaluate the level of impact of new events, and to determine whether they should receive public sector support, and whether this should be at a national or local level. The impact areas are:

- tourism
- business
- image and identity as a nation
- media and profile
- participation and development
- environment
- social and cultural benefits.

These key areas can also be used in post event assessment, and in defining return on investment of public funds.

Priorities

In investing its allocated budget in events, EventScotland will give priority to:

- those events whose estimated economic impacts demonstrate a return on investment of at least 8:1

- for events where media is the prime driver for investment, a media index of 8, 9 or 10/10
- demonstrated levels of funding by other partners of at least 1:1.

Its main emphasis is on economic and media benefits, with a focus on events of national and international significance, complemented by other events that are supported at the local level.

Principles

Three core principles will guide the work of EventScotland:

- EventScotland will work in partnership with event organisers, deliverers and funding partners.
- EventScotland will support work that has national significance in terms of the seven impacts, and will aim to support events in every local authority area over each four-year period, ensuring that the benefit reaches all of Scotland.
- EventScotland's input will bring additionality by using funding to add value to existing events, or by securing an event that would not otherwise come to Scotland.

Operational functions

EventScotland will play a leadership role in events in Scotland in the following areas:

- developing strategy
- developing and measuring impact and methodology
- gathering best practice examples and information
- evaluating and sharing the impact of events on other key policy areas
- building international reputation and expertise in events
- capitalising on opportunities, including the development of new and upgraded facilities offered by events such as Homecoming Scotland 2009, The Commonwealth Games and the Ryder Cup in 2014
- coordinating public sector support
- identifying and maximising event legacies
- assessing which events should be supported and at what levels
- monitoring and evaluating supported events
- establishing partnerships to ensure high quality delivery of events.

Operational practice

EventScotland will assess all events supported or considered for support using the seven impact areas previously listed, including a pre-event assessment of potential economic and media benefits. It will operate support programs to deliver against 'The Perfect Stage', and the range and scope of these programs will be reviewed regularly to ensure maximum outcomes. EventScotland will also coordinate input from other public agencies, and seek to engage the business community in events.

It will not normally consider support for conferences, as this function is undertaken by the Business Tourism Unit of VisitScotland. Exhibitions may be considered, using the event evaluation framework.

In the area of sports events, EventScotland aims to balance three categories:

- fixed events held annually in the same location in perpetuity
- recurring events held annually in the same location for a number of years
- one-off events, usually subject to the bid process for a single staging.

One-off events selected must fit the UK and Scottish priorities for the sport, be winnable, and be able to be delivered in existing facilities with available resources.

The approach to cultural events will differ somewhat, as few cultural events are subject to the one-off international bid process. Many fixed cultural events will be treated in the same way as sports events, by providing additionality in order to help them grow. Specific events that have growth potential, and where the ambition to grow is shared by event organisers and other partners, will be the subject of a long-term and proactive approach by EventScotland. It will also research and seek cultural events that can be attracted to Scotland or bid for.

In both sports and cultural events, a key role of EventScotland will be to gather international intelligence and engage proactively with the copyright holders of international events prior to the bid process. EventScotland will also take a proactive role in the training, development and networking of the event industry, including the staging of a national events conference.

Legacy

The strategy places strong emphasis on delivering both long-term and short-term benefits from events. It acknowledges the importance not only of resourcing events, but also of core funding for the building of event facilities, and the need for allocating resources for developing event legacies. It further acknowledges the importance of planning for legacy at the outset of events, of government agencies agreeing on common objectives, and of developing methods of evaluating legacy. Event legacy might include economic benefit, facilities, and an increase in personal and community capacity. Legacy goals and results should be explicit, and will be communicated to the wider Scottish community as a key aim of 'The Perfect Stage'.

What will make Scotland 'The Perfect Stage'?

The strategy envisions the events scene in Scotland in 2020 will be characterised as following:

- Scotland will be recognised as a leader in the development of events.
- Events will take place in Scotland across the calendar year and throughout the country.
- The events industry will be a significant contributor to the Scottish economy.
- An events portfolio of core events unique to Scotland, covering all aspects of Scottish culture, will be delivered annually.
- The portfolio will be complemented by a range of high profile one-off and recurring events attracted by Scotland's unique appeal and international event reputation.
- The roles of public, private and voluntary agencies will be clearly identified and working in partnership will be a recurring theme.

In order to achieve this, it identifies several critical factors:

- successful delivery of the identified event impacts
- the ability and credibility of EventScotland to lead the implementation of the strategy, and the expertise and network of key contacts of its staff
- the credibility and capacity of Scottish and UK event partner agencies and their staff
- the engagement and support of the business community
- a high level of political support for events
- positive national and international media coverage delivering the desired messages
- the vision to anticipate market changes, and the ability to adapt plans and practices
- resources that match the level of ambition
- a well-trained and motivated volunteer workforce

- a successful track record at international, national and local levels
- international standard venues
- the ability to identify, develop and utilise Scotland's unique selling points.

These critical success factors will be reviewed and reported on by EventScotland in its annual report (EventScotland 2009).

The Scotland event strategy can be considered a best practice example of the strategic planning of events at government level. It illustrates the complexity of factors that must be taken into account, and the unique circumstances that each event strategy needs to address. It also demonstrates that a clear vision, accompanied by the right skills and resources, can contribute greatly to the successful event outcomes of both cities and nations.

Creating celebration spaces and precincts

The relationship between entertainment and commerce has a long history that dates back at least to medieval times, when town markets and fairs attracted not only traders and their customers, but also a colourful bevy of minstrels, jugglers and acrobats. Indeed, the origins of the street theatre of today can be traced back to the bazaars and marketplaces of the ancient world.

Many cities and towns now consciously set out to create civic areas and public celebration spaces that perform much the same function as the traditional city square or village green. A seminal example in the 1960s was the development of the Inner Harbor of Baltimore in Maryland, USA. Initially a community celebration was held in order to promote cultural diversity in a derelict downtown area that had been the site of riots in the city. This ultimately inspired the regeneration of the Inner Harbor shores, with a festival marketplace, museums and hotels transforming the rundown area into a lively urban precinct. This in turn became the model for similar waterfront precincts in other parts of the world, including Darling Harbour in Sydney, Cape Town in South Africa, Yokohama in Japan, Fisherman's Wharf in San Francisco and the Singapore riverfront.

In Sydney, the celebration of Australia's Bicentenary in 1988 became the catalyst to transform the derelict railway goods yards adjacent to the city into the modern tourism precinct of Darling Harbour. A combination of festivals, community events and street theatre was used to attract visitors to the precinct, and to position it as 'Where Sydney Celebrates'.

The Bicentennial celebrations were also the catalyst for the Newcastle Foreshore Development, again transforming a disused rail yard on the city's edge into a prime harbourside recreation space for the city and its visitors. In Brisbane, the Expo 88 site across the river from the city would eventually become South Bank Parklands, a popular urban leisure park and centre for festivals and events. In Melbourne, the Southbank precinct along the Yarra River began a transformation of the city that has continued with the construction of Federation Square to mark Australia's centenary of Federation in 2001.

Town councils and urban planners everywhere were influenced by these ideas, with waterside areas at Kiama, Nelson Bay and The Entrance in New South Wales serving as just a few examples of the creation of public recreation and celebration spaces that have become widespread in Australia and other Western nations. Festivals, concerts, markets, public art programs and street theatre are tools commonly used to animate these spaces, and to make them congenial spaces for people to congregate in and enjoy.

Events and urban development

Governments have increasingly come to see events as potential tools for urban regeneration and renewal. They can provide the impetus for development, and become catalysts for the commitment of public funds and the investment of private capital needed to secure it. Integrated with other strategies such as town planning, commercial development, arts and cultural development and tourism, they can become powerful drivers in changing the image of destinations and in bringing new life and prosperity to communities.

An early example in Australia was the hosting of the America's Cup by Fremantle, Western Australia, in 1986–87. An icon of the sport of yachting with one of the world's oldest sporting trophies, the race had been dominated for most of its long history by North American yachting teams. When in a surprise coup a West Australian syndicate led by Perth entrepreneur Alan Bond snatched victory, tradition decreed that the team's home city would host the next event.

The port city of Fremantle, which had suffered a long economic downturn due to the slow decline of the shipping industry, had been the subject of various government regeneration and improvement proposals. The momentum of hosting the America's Cup was used to fast-track these proposals, and to attract finance and the will to transform the city. Motivated by the promise of a tourism bonanza and the stimulus that 'the eyes of the world will be on Fremantle', an enthusiastic wave of refurbishment and new building transformed the sleepy working class port into a popular tourism destination. While some of the visitor predictions ultimately proved an exaggeration, the city of Fremantle emerged with a greatly improved image and higher self-esteem, though arguably at the expense of its original working class character and values (Hall and Selwood 1995).

The spell of the Americans having been broken, the America's Cup was hosted by Auckland, New Zealand, in 1999–2000 and 2002–03. The somewhat dilapidated Auckland harbourside was transformed into an upmarket restaurant precinct, with positive urban redevelopment and tourism outcomes for the city.

The UK example

Perhaps nowhere has the use of events as tools for urban regeneration been as striking as in the United Kingdom. From having been the leader of the industrial revolution, by the mid-twentieth century many of the UK's major industrial cities, particularly in the north of England and in Scotland, were in an advanced state of decay. Typically, the inner-city urban areas where industrial plants had congregated were subject to high levels of unemployment, high rates of crime, substandard housing and low self-esteem.

With strong initiative and ingenuity, the UK tackled this problem to become a pioneer in urban regeneration and the use of event-based strategies. A series of five National Garden Festivals during the 1980s and early 1990s in Liverpool, Stoke-on-Trent, Glasgow, Gateshead and Ebbw Vale were used to transform derelict sites into attractive housing estates and parkland (Shone 2001). The Glasgow site now houses the Glasgow Science Centre and a digital media village on the banks of the River Clyde. Glasgow went on to use the accolade of European City of Culture in 1990 and the UK City of Architecture and Design in 1999 to transform its image from that of a decaying industrial city into that of a dynamic centre with a strong arts and tourism base.

Probably the most outstanding example of the use of events in urban regeneration in the UK is that of the Manchester 2002 Commonwealth Games.

Background: Manchester in decay

By the 1990s Manchester, once known as 'the workshop of the world' during the industrial revolution, had been in a period of steady decline for several decades (Commonwealth Games Legacy Manchester 2002, Hughes 1993). With the economic recessions of the 1970s and 1980s, it lost 60 per cent of its employment base. Between 1981 and 1991 the resident population fell by 11.5 per cent, leaving a demographically unbalanced population with heavy concentrations of the old, the young, ethnic minorities and the economically disadvantaged. By August 1992, unemployment had risen to 17.5 per cent (compared with a UK average of 9.9 per cent), and more than a third of the population received income from social security. An IRA bomb explosion in 1996 led to the further demoralisation of the city.

Government strategies for urban renewal

In the 1990s a comprehensive and integrated approach was established to regenerate the city (Manchester City Council 2005). The area was identified as one of 17 national pathfinders under the New Deal for Communities (NDC) Initiative in 1998. The East Manchester Plan, Beacons for a Brighter Future, was the first successful NDC scheme in the country, securing funding of £51.7m. Its key themes were tackling crime and the fear of crime; improvements to housing and neighbourhood management; the provision of positive open space; an emphasis on education, skills and training to help local people take advantage of employment opportunities; capacity building within the community to increase confidence and promote sustainability; and projects aimed at promoting the health and wellbeing of the community. Subsequently, complementary UK government funding from the Single Regeneration Budget of £25m enabled the activity and benefits from the NDC to be rolled out across the wider area.

East Manchester was also identified as one of three pilot urban regeneration companies in the UK, with New East Manchester Limited set up by the government in 1999 to provide an integrated and coordinated approach to regeneration. Formed as a partnership between the City Council, English Partnerships, the North West Development Agency and the local communities covering the wider East Manchester area, its charter was to prepare and implement a strategic framework for the area, secure additional funding, take the lead on particular development projects, secure inward investment and coordinate the range of initiatives in East Manchester.

The Commonwealth Games serve as a catalyst

An important strategic initiative of the regeneration program was to utilise the hosting of major events as a tool for urban regeneration and economic development. The City of Manchester bid unsuccessfully for the 1996 and 2000 Olympic Games, and was finally awarded the 2002 Commonwealth Games in 1995. The staging of the Games became a catalyst to inspire commitment and fast-track much of the planned regeneration and development. The building of venues was used to rejuvenate East Manchester, and to upgrade the transport and accommodation infrastructure of the city. The successful hosting of the Games not only brought visitors and media attention to the city, but also attracted further business investment and support. The final Games report (Commonwealth Games Legacy Manchester 2002) stated that over the following 15 years New East Manchester was expected to secure more than $2 billion in public and private funding, with the New Business Park development expected to create more than 6000 jobs, and a new retail centre, four star hotel and new housing developments expected to create 3800 jobs for the people of East Manchester.

The legacy continues

Manchester has continued to pursue a major events strategy, with a Five Year Regional Events Strategy drawn up by the North West Development Agency in 2004. Manchester City Football Club, as the new resident in the City of Manchester stadium, draws 40 000 people to the streets of East Manchester for each of its home games. Concerts by U2 and Oasis in the summer of 2005 attracted 360 000 music fans. In 2005 Manchester Event Volunteers, an outgrowth of the Games, had a database of over 2000 volunteers taking part in a wide range of events including the Salford Triathlon, the Great Manchester Run and the World Paralympics event.

The final Games report (Commonwealth Games Legacy Manchester 2002) concludes that:

> This event had to be about more than municipal ego. More than an opportunity to bathe in the reflected glory of a world event successfully staged. Manchester was always explicit in its intention. In bidding for the Commonwealth Games its aim was not only to deliver a world-class event but also to create a lasting legacy for Manchester and the region. A unique and innovative approach was taken to the legacy of the Manchester Games. Any city or organisation would expect the successful delivery of such a huge event to deliver benefits to tourism, sporting infrastructure and measurable commercial gains. Manchester went further.
>
> The aim was for the hosting of the Games to provide the catalyst for the whole scale regeneration of a large area of the city.

London Olympics 2012: The Regeneration Games

The notion of using major sporting events as catalysts for urban regeneration has been carried over from the Manchester Commonwealth Games in 2002 to the London Olympic and Paralympic Games in 2012.

The regeneration of the East End of London was established by The London Olympic Board as one of five key priorities for the legacy of the London Games (London 2012 2007):

- Making the UK a world-leading sporting nation.
- Transforming the heart of east London.
- Inspiring a new generation of young people to take part in volunteering, cultural and physical activity.
- Making the Olympic Park a blueprint for sustainable living.
- Demonstrating the UK is a creative, inclusive and welcoming place to live in, visit and for business.

East London is an area of over 300 square kilometres encompassing seven London boroughs, with a population in 2004 of 1.5 million. It suffered badly as a result of deindustrialisation when the Docklands area was unable to compete with new container ports in the 1960s and 1970s. The Docklands area underwent a major transformation that was completed in 1998, including the establishment of a secondary financial district, the Docklands Light Railway and the City Airport.

The Thames Gateway project is now extending the regeneration further east to a 64 km segment of the Thames estuary. It has a focus on sustainability, using existing Brownfield sites and regenerating deprived populations in 'linked communities' with affordable housing. London's successful bid to host the 2012 Olympic Games has helped to kickstart regeneration programs in the area.

The Lower Lea Valley in the Newham Borough has been chosen as the Olympic Park site. When completed, it will host the Olympic Stadium with a capacity of

80 000 spectators, the Olympic Village accommodation for athletes, the Aquatics Centre and the Hockey Centre. The project is expected to create around 12 000 new permanent jobs as well as thousands of temporary jobs. The Docklands Light Railway will be extended to the site, and much of the Olympic Village will be converted into affordable housing after the Games, with a total of 9000 new homes to be built in the vicinity. Five of the new sports venues will remain for use by the local community, and will be available to all people, irrespective or age or disability (Geography Teaching Today 2009).

The creation of Olympic Park will involve a massive rejuvenation of the Lower Lea Valley's waterways, after years of contamination and neglect. The project has been described as:

> The creation of one of the largest new urban parks in Europe in 150 years . . . The parklands will restore and enhance the recreational and ecological role of this important river valley. It will become part of London's famed network of green spaces — connecting the 26 km of the Lea Valley Regional Park in the north to the canal networks and river corridors that connect with the River Thames in the south (Public Service UK 2008).

The sheer scale of the project has led the Olympic Delivery Authority to describe the London Olympics as the 'Regeneration Games' (Armitt 2008).

However, not everyone agrees with the approach or the likely success of the project:

> The Games, then, are not really about the force of international competition in sport — the setting of new peaks of achievement in human skills, strength, speed or stamina. They're about economic, environmental and social regeneration . . . In place of the idealism of the Greek founders of the Games, we have cost/benefit analysis. It is the kind of analysis which imagines not just that the Games are an investment that will pay for itself, but also that they can be a 'catalyst' for the regeneration of east London. That is an error. A true geographical rebalancing of London from west to east is a feat too historic even for the Olympics to begin to bring about. The regeneration of east London is not a chemical reaction just waiting for a catalyst to show up and set it off (Woudhuysen 2008).

No doubt the debate will rage up to and beyond the London Olympics in 2012. What is not debatable, however, is that urban regeneration has been made central to their philosophy, planning and implementation, and that a valuable legacy will be the regeneration of the Lower Lea Valley.

THE CORPORATE PERSPECTIVE

Events have a unique ability to bring people physically together, and to inspire and communicate with them in ways that cannot be easily duplicated by other means and media. This has been recognised by the corporate sector, which, as we saw in chapter 1, increased its use of events rapidly in the 1990s, establishing a trend that continued into the first decade of the new millennium. This trend reflects the recognition of the power of events by the corporate sector, and its increasing use of events as tools both to improve company morale and business procedures, and to increase profitability and income.

Kline (2005) summarises this trend:

> We have seen a significant shift in the way companies are allocating funds — moving their dollars from extensive advertising toward the development of event-focused integrated marketing programs. Corporations are investing money in their events and in their people. Special events are seen as opportunities to motivate and educate their work force in an effort to be more successful at reaching their audience and goals. Consumer

lifestyle events are created that bring relevance, influence behaviour and present new choices to the public.

Corporate use of events

Silvers (2007) describes corporate and business events as 'any event that supports business objectives, including management functions, corporate communications, training, marketing, incentives, employee relations, and customer relations, scheduled alone or in conjunction with other events.'

The use of events by companies and businesses may be focused internally, aimed at their own business practices and staff, or may be focused externally, aimed at their customers and clients (see table 2.1). The common thread is the demonstrated ability of events to deliver results in terms of business objectives, and therefore to provide a return on investment.

TABLE 2.1 Corporate use of events

Internal	External
Annual General Meetings (AGMs)	Grand openings
Corporate retreats	Product launches
Board meetings	Sales promotions
Management meetings	Media conferences
Staff training	Publicity events
Team building	Photo opportunities
Staff social events	Exhibitions
Incentive events	Trade missions
Award nights	Trade shows
Sales conferences	Client hospitality
Dealer network seminars	Event sponsorship

Internal events

Internally, companies make significant use of events such as management meetings and staff training in the day-to-day conduct of their business. Given the modern corporate environment, major internal company events such as Annual General Meetings (AGMs), corporate retreats and board meetings are often treated as significant occasions deserving of dedicated organisation and meticulous attention to detail. Other internal events such as staff social events, team building, incentives and award nights are seen as valuable tools to inspire and motivate staff, and as contributing to the development of a successful corporate culture. Sales conferences and product seminars are used to extend this culture further to company representatives and dealer networks. Many companies contribute considerable resources towards ensuring that such events are perceived as part of their corporate identity and style, and that they are conducted with high standards of professionalism and presentation.

A prime example of the internal use of events is that of Herbalife's 25th Anniversary Extravaganza (Kline 2005). This three-day event for more than 35 000 dignitaries and distributors from all over the world included a one-of-a-kind product launch, executive keynote addresses, sales training symposiums and an exclusive performance by Sir Elton John, leaving attendees motivated, educated and rejuvenated.

External events

Externally, events are highly valued for their ability to communicate corporate and sales messages, and to cut through the clutter of advertising and media to reach customers and clients directly and effectively. As detailed in table 2.1, grand openings, product launches, sales promotions, media conferences, publicity events and photo opportunities are just some of the wide variety of events that are used to gain the attention of potential customers, and to create a 'buzz' around new products and services. Companies also use exhibitions, trade missions and trade shows to reach distribution networks, and to maintain a company presence in selected markets.

An example of the use of events to promote a corporate image and launch new products is provided by the official midnight launch of the PlayStation 3 (PS3) console by Sony Computer Entertainment Australia (SCEA) in March 2007. Teaming up with SCEA for the event, the department store Myer set up a big viewing space outside its store with a free screening of *Casino Royale*. The film was played directly from a PS3, and gamers were given the chance to play the PS3 on the big screen and to win PlayStation-themed giveaways (Ramsay 2007).

Another growing corporate use of events is the entertaining of clients in order to build and nourish business relationships with them. This can take the form of hosted cocktail parties, dinners or receptions, or hospitality at company sponsored public events. Often the sponsorship of events can bring many of these aspects together, enabling companies to reach event attendees and demonstrate product attributes through associating their product with the event, while at the same time hosting clients in a convivial atmosphere.

Association conferences

Another corporate-related use of events touched on in chapter 1 is that of conferences and business meetings. A large and growing number of professional, academic and industry associations use meetings, congresses and conferences to communicate with their members, to explore relevant issues and to disseminate information to their respective audiences. These can be local, national or international in scope, with many international associations maintaining a structure and bidding process similar to that of major sporting bodies. An important aspect of these events is the opportunity provided by participants to keep abreast of developments in their professional fields, and to network with colleagues and associates. There has been recent speculation in the industry that the fragile economic climate, increasing environmental impacts, travel costs and security issues, coupled with the increasing technological capacity for online meetings and video conferencing, will slow the growth of the industry. However, the advantages of direct networking and face-to-face contact still provide a powerful incentive for live meetings, and association conferences continue to be held worldwide albeit with reduced budgets and, in some cases, declining numbers.

Return on investment

The growth in the use of events by the corporate sector has been accompanied by an increasing desire and need to evaluate their outcomes. With the increasing amount spent on events, companies understandably want to know what their events are achieving, and their effectiveness and return on investment (ROI) compared with other marketing tools and strategies. This has led to a greater emphasis on the establishment of measures, or metrics, to benchmark events and to quantify their outcomes.

However, many of the benefits and outcomes of events are difficult to quantify in monetary terms, and different companies will use different measures and yardsticks. Myhill (2006) maintains that the ROI for meetings and training events can be calculated by the use of careful data planning and analysis, using the Phillips ROI methodology developed in the 1970s. The methodology uses five levels of evaluation, leading to the full numerical calculation of return on investment.

- Reaction and planned action — measures attendee satisfaction, usually by the use of generic questionnaires. While important, attendee satisfaction does not in itself guarantee the acquisition of new skills, knowledge or professional contacts.
- Learning — uses tests, skill practices, group evaluations and other assessment tools to ensure that attendees have absorbed the meeting material and know how to use it properly. However, it does not guarantee that what has been learnt will be used on the job.
- Job applications — used to determine whether attendees applied what they learnt from the meeting on the job. While a good gauge of the meeting's success, it still does not guarantee a positive business impact for the organisation.
- Business results — focuses on the results achieved by attendees as they successfully apply what they learnt from the meeting. Typical measures include output, sales, quality, costs, time, and customer satisfaction. However, this still does not provide a measure of the financial value of the meeting or event.
- Return on investment — compares the monetary benefits gained from the meeting with the costs. A numerical ROI percentage can be obtained using the formula:

$$\frac{\text{Meeting benefits} - \text{meeting costs}}{\text{Meeting costs}} \times 100$$

This formula can be used to compare the ROI of meetings and events with alternative events and strategies. However, Myhill suggests that it is not appropriate to conduct such a study on all meetings and events. She recommends that only five to 10 per cent of events should be taken to ROI, with the most suitable being those linked to the operational goals and/or strategic objectives of the organisation, and which incur significant costs and staff/participant time.

Events aimed at external stakeholders are typically measured by attendance numbers, sales leads obtained, or changes in attitude or perception. It is often as much about brand awareness and enhancement as it is about actual sales or measurable outcomes. Kline (2005) comments:

> ROI is very important, but it is measured differently by each client. The return could be measured by the number of people attending the event, how the event looked and was perceived, or how each attendee felt as they left the event. We believe that ROI of events can be somewhat intangible, but the true value resides in that moment when the brand achieves relevance and preference to the audience, and that is what we focus on.

THE COMMUNITY PERSPECTIVE

Most public events are either community events, or major events that take place in host communities that have a particular interest in and attitude toward the event. Thus the community is a major stakeholder in events, and it is incumbent on event managers to consider the community perspective and to include this in the event planning process.

Community events

As discussed in chapter 1, some form of festivals and events can be identified in every human society and in every age. They are part of how we interact as humans, and form part of the social fabric that binds our communities together. This can be seen in many country town and regional festivals, where the main social event of the year is often the town festival. The myriad social interactions that go into creating the festival — the committee meetings, the approaches to local businesses for support, the involvement of local arts and sports groups, the contacting of service groups and volunteers — all help to create social capital and community wellbeing. In many cases, these festivals provide an annual opportunity for local clubs and societies to fundraise and recruit new members, which is crucial to their survival. Communities, of course, are not always heterogeneous, and festivals can provide the stimulation for healthy disagreement and debate about their priorities and identity. In many very real ways, therefore, these festivals help to create and strengthen a sense of community and belonging. For this and related reasons, they are often supported by local governments and other government agencies concerned with maintaining and supporting healthy communities.

event profile

MULGA BILL FESTIVAL, YEOVAL

Many country towns build an annual festival around unique elements such as local produce, geographical features, historical events or famous citizens, in order to theme the celebration and to inspire local involvement.

One such example is the Mulga Bill Festival in Yeoval, a small village with a population of 400, in central western New South Wales. The festival celebrates the life and work of Banjo Paterson, one of nineteenth century Australia's greatest bush poets and the town's most famous son.

The 2009 festival, held 24–26 July, featured themed activities including 'A Night with Banjo Paterson' bush poetry performance; 'Poetry in the Park'; camp-oven cooking; displays of vintage engines, tractors, trucks and motor bikes; a 'quick shear' competition; model flying aircraft; Mulga Bill golf and bowls days; the Buckinbah Art Show; and culminated with a family bike ride.

The festival also incorporates themed activities held throughout the year including the Banjo Paterson Birthday Bash, a luncheon with music, song and a guest speaker; the Yeoval Family History Museum; and a cultural project recording local history.

The festival's theme and activities saluting the town's most famous resident provide a unique tourism attraction, as well as a strong framework for the townsfolk to showcase their local heritage.

Source: Based on New South Wales Department of State and Regional Development 2009 and Mulga Bill Festival 2009.

Regional festivals as community builders

Gibson and Stewart (2009) surveyed 480 regional festivals and events from a database of 2856 festivals in New South Wales, Victoria and Tasmania. They found that the most common types were sporting, community, agricultural and music festivals, which together made up three quarters of the festivals surveyed. Country, jazz, folk and blues festivals accounted for over half of the music festivals, despite the popularity of styles such as rock in the wider recorded music retail market. Sixty-seven festivals (15 per cent) had been running before 1900 — mostly gardening and flower festivals and agricultural shows; 24 per cent were established between 1900 and 1980; and 61 per cent after 1980, with music, food and wine festivals the most common in this group,

The average attendance of the festivals surveyed was 7000, although there was a wide variation in attendance, and 11 festivals (2 per cent) had an attendance of more than 50 000. Attendees across all festivals were 58 per cent local, 11 per cent from the state capital, 21 per cent other intrastate, 8 per cent interstate and 1 per cent international.

The average duration of the festivals was 3.3 days, and the average number of stalls including food, clothing and merchandise was 67. Seventy-four per cent of the festivals were run by non-profit organisations, with only 3 per cent run by profit-seeking private companies. The majority of festivals were linked to the interests and passions of the organising committee, or had cultural goals, such as building community, rather than income generation. Nevertheless, the researchers concluded that regional festivals were a sizeable industry in a cumulative sense, with the surveyed festivals generating total ticket sales of $550 million annually, as well as considerable related economic activity.

The researchers noted the community building aspect of regional festivals:

> It is a truism to say that festivals build community — but it is worth highlighting the extent and functions of festivals in local communities, and especially in small places ... Festivals are pivotal dates on the annual calendars of towns and villages, they support charities and provide opportunities for high schools and Rotary clubs to raise funds; they bring together scattered farm-folk, young and old and disparate subcultures; they blend attitudes, expand social networks and encourage improvements in social cohesion ... Festivals provide rural communities with coping mechanisms at times of drought and economic hardship, and catalyse community in the name of fun.

The individual perspective

From the perspective of community members, their requirements and expectations of community events are often very simple and direct. They want to participate and be entertained — to have a social and enriching experience beyond their everyday reality. They may want to participate as a family, so that they can enjoy the experience together and so that children are provided a special treat at an affordable cost. They may want to showcase their creative talents in the case of arts or cultural festivals, or to enjoy friendly competition in the case of sporting events. In some cases they may want the satisfaction and achievement of being involved as organisers, or the social contact and recognition of being involved as volunteers. They may have some awareness of the larger role of the event in their community, but are likely to be more interested in the social and cultural benefits than the business and economic outcomes of the event.

Major events and the community

The community perspective changes when we examine major events within the community that attract many visitors. Community members may still look forward to enjoying the event as participants or spectators. However, as the event organisation becomes larger and more professional, much of the event planning is often taken out of the hands of members of the host community. They are now more likely to be concerned with the wider impacts of the event, which may include a sense of pride in their community, economic and job creation benefits, and physical impacts such as traffic restrictions and crowd congestion. Their relationship with the event is likely to be less direct, and the media may become the main source of information on the planning of the event and predictions of visitor numbers, media coverage, economic benefits and job creation. Under such circumstances, it is easy for members of the community to become distanced from the event, and to fluctuate in their perceptions and expectations of the event experience and outcomes.

For the event organisers, keeping the host community informed and on side becomes a vital task in the event planning process. Not only is it important to keep the community engaged with the event, but if it becomes disaffected then this attitude is likely to affect the experience and enjoyment of visitors to the event. The protest by Albert Park residents over the alienation of parklands by the Australian Grand Prix in Melbourne and the backlash against Schoolies Week on the Gold Coast are just two examples of the negative impact of community disengagement with events. Event organisers therefore need to develop strategies to involve the host community in the planning of the event, to maintain good community relations, and to monitor the community's perceptions of and attitudes to the event.

The Henry Lawson Festival of Arts at Grenfell, NSW, used a mix of public meetings and local newspaper articles in 2009 to involve the community in a re-evaluation of the festival's priorities and future. Many events use social media such as facebook, Twitter, Flickr and YouTube to stay in touch with their audiences and to invite feedback from the local community. Federation Square in Melbourne, for example, uses a live twitter feed on screens at outdoor events to incorporate feedback from their audience (Dunbar 2009). A more detailed description of strategies for community engagement follows.

Strategies for community engagement

Community perceptions of an event will depend to a large extent on the levels of community engagement, and on the efforts made by event organisers to involve the community in the planning, implementation and evaluation of the event. Appropriate liaison with stakeholders will ensure that the event represents the true values of the community, and will often serve to resolve many of the potential community conflicts and disruptions in relation to the event.

Harris and Allen (2006), in a study for artsACT, examined 22 medium to large-scale public events in Australia and overseas in order to identify strategies employed by event managers to facilitate community engagement. They posited core values for public engagement and participation based on those of the International Association for Public Participation (IAP2):

1. Public participation is based on the belief that those who are affected by a decision have a right to be involved in the decision-making process.
2. Public participation includes the promise that the public's contribution will influence the decison.
3. Public participation promotes sustainable decisions by recognizing and communicating the needs and interests of all participants, including decision makers.
4. Public participation seeks out and facilitates the involvement of those potentially affected by or interested in a decision.

5. Public participation seeks input from participants in designing how they participate.
6. Public participation provides participants with the information they need to participate in a meaningful way.
7. Public participation communicates to participants how their input affected the decision.

In practice, the study found that the extent and type of community engagement varied widely in the events that they studied, with some events much more proactive than others in seeking to involve and engage the community. Mechanisms for community engagement in the events examined by the study included:

Participation facilitation
- Free or discounted transport provision
- Provision of on-site facilities and services for specific groups, such as marquees for elderly people and creches for young families
- Radio broadcasts for community members who are housebound
- Free access to aspects of an event's program
- Discount ticket prices for selected groups, such as the unemployed, pensioners and students and access to free tickets for selected groups
- Provision of specific services and facilities for people with a disability
- Embracing a variety of geographic locations within a community when delivering the event program, or when engaged in outreach activities.

Community input and feedback facilitation
- Public meetings
- Community based 'whole of event' strategic reviews
- Festival workshops designed to seek input with regard to event design and programming
- Open calls for membership of an event organising committee
- Dedicated local radio talkback sessions with event organisers
- Community advisory committees or consultation groups that serve to provide input into the event, or the inclusion of community representatives on the organising committee
- Inclusion of a feedback or contact facility on the event website.

Inclusive programming
- Targeting of specific community groups to deliver, or assist with, one or more aspects of the event program. Such groups included the unemployed, at-risk youth and special interest groups such as environmental organisations.
- Designing program elements with the needs of specific groups in mind (for example, the participation of schools by incorporating an 'education day').

Incentives
- The provision of free stall space to non-profit organisations and charities to raise funds, attract new members, or raise awareness of a particular issue or cause
- Competitions and contests that serve to encourage involvement by particular community groups such as school children, local artists and sporting groups.

Outreach
- Profits from the event used to engage in extension activities to specific, often disadvantaged groups in the community
- Shop fronts that provide an ongoing connection between the event and its community
- Involvement of schools by seeking inclusion in school curriculum activities or by creating lesson plans for use by teachers that deal with various aspects of events in general

- Access to event websites for non-profit organisations so that they may enhance their community presence
- The use of symbolism to reach out to communities on an ongoing basis (for example, a public installation or sculpture to remind local people of the ongoing connection between the town and the event)
- Broadening the local community by expanding the footprint of the event into nearby areas.

Community development and capacity building

- Internships, traineeships and work experience programs that provide opportunities for young people to learn new skills and knowledge that can in turn be used within their communities on a paid or voluntary basis
- Provision of volunteering opportunities, training sessions and volunteer social events that facilitate the creation of new networks within the community, and may result in new business and other opportunities for volunteers
- Enhancement of the community's capacity to deal with a specific issue or problem
- Channelling financial resources from an event into the development of various non-profit community organisations in order to progress a community's development efforts.

Friends of the event/event alumni associations

- The creation of 'friends' or 'alumni' groups to integrate an event further with its community.

Local business engagement

- Encouragement of attendee expenditure at local businesses through the creation of special incentives tied in with the event
- Giving preference to local businesses for the supply of services.

This study is primarily an exploratory one, and more research needs to be devoted to identifying community engagement mechanisms, and their relative effectiveness. Nevertheless, for the event manager it indicates that there is a broad range of initiatives available to engage the involvement and participation of host communities in events. However, considerable care must be taken to ensure that the particular strategies chosen are best suited to the particular community and its needs, and are most likely to achieve results. This in turn will reap rewards in terms of a greater sense of community ownership of the event, and a more positive perception of its benefits and impacts.

SUMMARY

This chapter examined a number of important perspectives that have implications for event managers in the planning and delivery of events. From the government perspective, a number of disparate roles and functions in events are often integrated through the use of event strategies, as illustrated by the Scotland events strategy. Governments may also create dedicated celebration spaces, and use events as tools for urban renewal. Event managers need to be aware of government regulations and requirements, and to see governments as key stakeholders and potential partners in events. The corporate sector uses events to achieve both internal and external goals and objectives, as well as sponsoring public events in order to obtain commercial benefits. Event managers need to be aware of corporate objectives, and of the increasing need of companies to identify the return on investment (ROI) of events. From the community perspective, community members are often focused on the direct impacts and benefits of events on them personally and on the community in general. Managers of public events need to carefully choose and implement appropriate mechanisms for communication and engagement with the community.

QUESTIONS

1. Does local government in your area have an event strategy? Analyse the roles that your local government plays in the regulation and coordination of events.
2. Can you identify a dedicated celebration space in your city or region? How is the space managed, and what role does it play in the life of the community?
3. Identify a corporate event in your city or region. What were the objectives of the event, and how did it fit with the overall marketing strategy of the company?
4. Analyse the corporate sponsorship of an event and identify the main benefits that were obtained.
5. Choose a community event with which you are familiar, and identify the benefits to individuals and to the community from the staging of the event.
6. Identify a local community event that you are familiar with. Analyse and describe any strategies that the event has for engagement with the local community, and how it contributes to community building.
7. Discuss the implications for event managers that arise from the analysis of the government, corporate and community perspectives on events.

case study

TOWNSVILLE CITY COUNCIL: CREATING AN EVENTS STRATEGY FOR QUEENSLAND'S BIGGEST REGIONAL CITY COUNCIL

Scope

Townsville is Queensland's largest regional city since it merged with Thuringowa City in 2008. In 2008 Queensland State Government introduced local government reform that merged many of Queensland's local councils to produce more efficiency for local regions throughout the state. Upon that merger, Townsville took a new direction in delivery of event programs, event strategies and event management principles for the region.

History

Townsville City Council had a population base of 120 000 pre-amalgamation, while Thuringowa City Council had a population base of 60 000 pre-amalgamation. Both Councils had an events program, but delivered in vastly different management structures. Only Thuringowa City Council had an events strategy document.

Event delivery pre-amalgamation

Townsville City Council produced many events through its different departments; that is, Community, Environmental, Planning and Parks Services, Strand Office and Public Relations. Excluding Public Relations, no individual department had any event managers or trained event staff to deliver their individual program of events. Public Relations had some event-trained staff, but tended to use event management contractors to deliver their large scale events. There was little strategic planning of

event calendars between departments, and event management processes were not consistent over the individual events.

Thuringowa City Council had two full-time event staff who were responsible for the direct delivery of the city's event program, developing a city event strategy, and to ensure project management principles were applied to all events delivered by Council.

Post-amalgamation event structure

Management team

The new Townsville City Council reconfigured its event delivery structure to enable a more focused event delivery model. This was centred on the development of a professional event management team that had specific skills in the delivery of events, event programs and the ability to develop events strategically for the region.

This team also played a role in:

- advising on funding applications for externally run events for the city
- consulting with external groups on event management, scheduling and delivery of events across the city
- developing relationships across the region in relation to tourism, economic development and event industry identities.

The Events and Protocol Unit was formed in July 2008 and was given the following responsibilities:

- to produce all events for Council that attracted an audience in excess of 500 people or that had a high profile or high protocol focus
- to produce a balanced events program that took into consideration internal and external events supported by Council in some way
- to develop and implement an Events Strategy for the city
- to set up a management system for event delivery of Council-run events, including a client producer relationship between Council's different departments that had a need to produce events to deliver their programs, activities and policies.

FIGURE 2.2 The Events and Protocol Unit structure

Strategy

To ensure the needs of the city were met at internal, external and holistic levels, one of the first tasks of the Events and Protocol Unit was the implementation of an Events Strategy.

The strategy initially identified and established:

- a definition of events
- an events continuum
- the key stakeholders
- a methodology
- the history of Townsville and Thuringowa Councils' event coordination
- the challenges facing Council in relation to events and event programs
- the aim of events in the Townsville region
- the gaps and opportunities in the region's event program
- a best practice event management structure.

This strategy would define the city event program objectives, and the delivery and management processes, by establishing a series of goals, and actions to achieve those goals.

- Goal 1: To centrally coordinate and plan Council's program of events, and ensure that they are of the highest possible standard.
- Goal 2: To develop a program of events that is responsive to and inclusive of community needs, funded efficiently, strategically scheduled, and meets Council's Corporate Plan.
- Goal 3: Improve the environmental outcomes for all Council run events.
- Goal 4: Promote and market Townsville events in an effective and innovative manner.
- Goal 5: Encourage community groups, and private enterprise groups to hold events in Townsville in a well-managed, structured and scheduled manner.
- Goal 6: Ensure Townsville City Council events are safe and responsive to contemporary threats of Workplace Health and Safety issues and external issues (i.e. terrorism, natural disasters).
- Goal 7: Improve inclusion and accessibility outcomes for all Council-run events in relation to disadvantaged and isolated groups.

Challenges in delivering the Events Strategy

Some challenges faced the successful implementation of the new Events Strategy, which can be identified within several vital areas.

Program

Combining two cities' events programs during a time of extreme budgetary pressure created many challenges. Some events were easily merged due to both cities having to celebrate the same events. Events such as Australia Day, New Year's Eve celebrations, Pioneer's Lunch, and Carols by Candlelight were easily merged so that one event for each occasion, rather than two, now served the whole of the new city.

However, some events were not easily merged nor suited the new city. For example:

1. *Anzac Day Services*. This involved two separate sub-branches of the Returned Services League who both wished to continue with separate Dawn and Morning Services. The Townsville East services involved in excess of 12 000 people for the Dawn Service and in excess of 14 000 people for the Morning Service and

parade. The new Townsville West service involved in excess of 2000 people for the Dawn Service and around 5000 people for the Morning Service and parade. The Townsville East services have strong support from the military, while the Townsville West services, since amalgamation, have dwindling military support. Logistically and financially it would be far simpler to stage one set of Anzac Day Services for the city. However, politically, this was unachievable.

2. *Neighbourhood Fun Days program*. Delivered by the former Townsville City Council, this program involved small fair style events throughout the city's suburbs. The former Thuringowa City Council had phased these events out of their program due to high cost versus community benefit analysis.
3. *Three environmental festivals*. These festivals, delivered between the two former city councils, required merging to produce one substantial event for the city.

Budget

Community and Council expected that, by amalgamating two city councils, substantial cost savings would be achieved in all areas of council business, including event delivery. The Townsville community also had an expectation that the quality of events would increase as costs come down. This was simply unachievable without major changes to the event program and its delivery method.

Culture

Both previous Councils had differing cultures, management structures, policies and processes. Upon amalgamation, new relationships and trust between the Events and Protocol Unit and different Council departments had to be developed.

Delivering large scale events directly, as opposed to contracting event management companies, was a clear change in direction. Smaller events, normally delivered by Council departments, were handed over to the Events and Protocol Unit to project manage in partnership with those departments. These changes, like all change, were met with some resistance by some, and welcomed by others.

Delivery

Event delivery procedures had to be studied so that project management principles and practices were utilised for all internally managed events. Particular emphasis was placed upon stakeholder analysis, risk management, milestones, budget control, and run sheets to ensure all aspects of all events were properly managed and assessed.

Further to this practice, a high emphasis was placed upon researching other similar events, staff training and reviewing of all events, inclusive of stakeholder input. Documentation via council systems and full event reports were delivered post-event, and several committees/groups outside of the Events and Protocol Unit were given the opportunity to comment on program and delivery of all council events.

Outcomes and conclusions

Eighteen months after the amalgamation of Townsville and Thuringowa City Councils, the Events and Protocol Unit has successfully merged programs, established high-end management structures and has delivered a vast array of events for the city of Townsville.

The city has developed its reputation as a regional leader for staging events, and project management has become the tool of use for delivery of events for the Council.

The transition is considered a success, with continued effort being injected into ensuring the city's event program is:

- balanced
- responsive to community needs and expectations
- financially responsible
- an example of 'best practice' standards in event management.

Through the merging of the councils, the following was achieved:

Program

- Townsville City Council now has an eighteen-month events program responsive to and inclusive of externally run events for the city. This program is reviewed and added to every six months, ensuring a program with events scheduled a minimum of twelve months in advance is confirmed and active.

Budget

- The Council has achieved budget savings on the event program of 15 per cent in 2008–09 financial year, and 10 per cent in 2009–10 financial year.
- Budget reviews ensure that adequate funds are available for large-scale events of a high-profile nature, as required.
- Council has established a more competitive quotation process for suppliers.

Culture

- There is now a high level of trust between departments and the Events and Protocol Unit based on the delivery of a large number of high quality Council events, with increased public and corporate participation.

Delivery

- The Council can now boast the effective delivery of over 100 events per year, including civic receptions, citizenship ceremonies, markets, festivals, and commemorative and special events.
- The successful delivery of these events has resulted in expanding positive relationships with all stakeholders.
- Townsville is now recognised as an 'events city' in regional Australia.
- There is now an increased interest in external events coming to the region.

Events of significance that were delivered in 2009 include:

- Dunlop Townsville 400 Supercars — audience 160 000
- Townsville 400 Festival — audience 30 000
- Townsville Air Display and Family Fireworks Spectacular — audience 80 000
- Townsville Carols By Candlelight — audience 18 000.

Tom Aubrey, Events and Protocol Manager, Corporate Communications, Townsville City Council

Questions

1 From the description of the Event Strategy outlined in the case study, list the roles that Townsville City Council plays in events.

2 What do you think were the main outcomes of merging the event teams of the two Council areas?

3 What were the main challenges in merging the event teams, and how were they resolved?

REFERENCES

Armitt, J 2008, London 2012 on track to be the 'Regeneration Games', media release, www.london2012.com.

Commonwealth Games Legacy Manchester 2002, The XVII Commonwealth Games 2002 Manchester: Regeneration/Legacy, www.gameslegacy.com

Dunbar, P 2009, 'Using Social Media for Events Promotion', address given to Australian Events Master Class on Social Media Marketing for the Events Industry in Sydney on 8 October 2009.

EventScotland 2009, *Scotland The Perfect Stage*, www.eventscotland.org.

Geography Teaching Today 2009, Urban Regeneration in East London — 'geography explained' fact sheet, www.geographyteachingtoday.org.uk.

Gibson, C & Stewart, A 2009, *Reinventing Rural Places: The extent and impact of festivals in rural and regional Australia*, Australian Centre for Cultural Environmental Research, Wollongong.

Hall, CM & Selwood, JH 1995, 'Event tourism and the creation of a postindustrial portscape: the case of Fremantle and the 1987 America's Cup', in *Recreation and tourism as a catalyst for urban waterfront development: an international survey,* eds SJ Craig-Smith & M Fagence, Praeger Publishers, Westport, Connecticut.

Harris, R and Allen, J 2006, Community engagement and events: a study for artsACT, unpublished report by the Australian Centre for Event Management, Sydney.

Hughes, H 1993. 'Olympic tourism and urban regeneration', *Festival Management and Event Tourism*, vol. 1, no. 4, pp. 157–62.

International Association for Public Participation 2010, 'IAP2 Core Values', www.iap2.org.

Kline, J 2005, 'Jeff Kline, Guest Room: Jeff Kline on TBA Going Global', www.specialevents.com.

London 2012 2007, 'London 2012 legacy vision presented to IOC', press release, 12 June, www.london2012.com.

Manchester City Council 2005, Regeneration in Manchester statement: regeneration initiatives — East Manchester, www.manchester.gov.uk.

Mulga Bill Festival 2009, www.mulgabillfestival.com.au.

Myhill, M 2006, Return on investment: the bottom line, www.meetingsnet.com.

New South Wales Department of State and Regional Development 2009, Mulga Bill Festival, www.business.nsw.gov.au.

Public Service UK 2008, 'Constructing a green and beneficial Olympics', 4 Nov., www.publicservice.co.uk.

Ramsay, R 2007, 'Sony unveils official Aussie PS3 midnight launch event', www.cnet.com.au.

Shone, A 2001, *Successful event management*, Continuum, London.

Silvers, J 2007, www.juliasilvers.com.

Wangaratta Jazz Festival 2009, www.wangaratta-jazz.org.au.

Willard, J 2005, 'Central Sydney Operations Group — a best practice model', unpublished keynote address delivered to The Impacts of Events, Event Management Research Conference convened by the Australian Centre for Event Management in Sydney, July 2005.

Woudhuysen, J 2008, The 'Regeneration Games', London 2012, www.culturewars.org.uk.

EVENT IMPACTS AND LEGACIES

LEARNING OBJECTIVES

After studying this chapter, you should be able to:

1. explain the role of the event manager in balancing the impacts of events
2. identify the major impacts that events have on their stakeholders and host communities
3. describe the social and cultural impacts of events and plan for positive outcomes
4. discuss the political context of events
5. describe the environmental impacts of events
6. discuss the tourism and economic impacts of events
7. discuss why governments become involved in events
8. describe the use of economic impact studies in measuring event outcomes
9. discuss methods for identifying community perceptions of the impacts of events.

INTRODUCTION

Events do not take place in a vacuum. They touch almost every aspect of our lives — social, cultural, economic, environmental and political. The benefits arising from such positive connections are a large part of the reason for the popularity and support of events. They are increasingly well documented and researched, with strategies formed to enhance event outcomes and optimise their benefits.

The recent explosion of events, along with the parallel increase in the involvement of governments and corporations, has led to an increasing emphasis on an economic analysis of event benefits. Understandably, governments considering the investment of substantial taxpayers' funds in events want to know what they are getting for their investment and how it compares with other investment options. This climate has given rise to detailed studies of event impacts by economists, and to the development and application of increasingly sophisticated techniques of economic analysis and evaluation. There is also increasing emphasis on both the social and environmental impacts of events. Governments often take a 'triple bottom line' approach that takes into account the social and environmental impacts, as well as the economic impacts, when deciding which events to support, or when evaluating the final outcomes of events.

However, events can also have unintended consequences that can result in their gaining public prominence and media attention for the wrong reasons. The cost of event failure can be disastrous, turning positive benefits into negative publicity, political embarrassment and costly lawsuits. An important core task in organising contemporary events is the identification, monitoring and management of event impacts. In this chapter, we examine some of the main areas affected by events, along with the strategies that event managers can employ to balance event impacts.

BALANCING THE IMPACT OF EVENTS

Events have a range of both positive and negative impacts on their host communities and stakeholders (table 3.1). It is the task of the event manager to identify and predict these impacts, then manage them to achieve the best outcomes for all parties, so that the overall impact of the event is positive. To achieve this, the event manager must develop and maximise all foreseeable positive impacts, and counter potential negative impacts. Often, negative impacts can be addressed through awareness and intervention, so good planning is always critical. Ultimately, the success of the event depends on the event manager achieving this positive balance sheet and communicating it to a range of stakeholders.

Great emphasis is often placed on the financial impacts of events, partly because employers and governments need to meet budget goals and justify expenditure, and partly because such impacts are most readily assessed. However, government policies commonly acknowledge the 'triple bottom line' of social, economic and environmental goals/yardsticks in relation to events. Event managers should not lose sight of the full range of an event's impacts and the need to identify, manage and document them. It is also important to realise that different impacts require different means of assessment. Social and cultural benefits, for example, are vital contributors to the calculation of an event's overall impact, but describing them may require a narrative rather than a statistical approach. In this chapter, we discuss some of the complex factors that need to be taken into account when assessing the impacts of events.

TABLE 3.1 The impacts of events

Impacts of events	Positive impacts	Negative impacts
Social and cultural	• Shared experience • Revitalisation of traditions • Building of community pride • Validation of community groups • Increased community participation • Introduction of new and challenging ideas • Expansion of cultural perspectives	• Community alienation • Manipulation of community • Negative community image • Bad behaviour • Substance abuse • Social dislocation • Loss of amenity
Political	• International prestige • Improved profile • Promotion of investment • Social cohesion • Development of administrative skills	• Risk of event failure • Misallocation of funds • Lack of accountability • Propaganda • Loss of community ownership and control • Legitimation of ideology
Environmental	• Showcasing of the environment • Provision of models for best practice • Increased environmental awareness • Infrastructure legacy • Improved transport and communications • Urban transformation and renewal	• Environmental damage • Pollution • Destruction of heritage • Noise disturbance • Traffic congestion
Tourism and economic	• Destinational promotion and increased tourist visits • Extended length of stay • Higher yield • Increased tax revenue • Business opportunities • Commercial activity • Job creation	• Community resistance to tourism • Loss of authenticity • Damage to reputation • Exploitation • Inflated prices • Opportunity costs • Financial mismanagement • Financial loss

Source: Adapted from Hall 1989.

Social and cultural impacts

All events have a direct social and cultural impact on their participants and sometimes on their wider host communities, as outlined by Hall (1989) and Getz (2005). This impact may be as simple as a shared entertainment experience, as created by a sports event or concert. Events can also result in intense community pride, as demonstated by the citizens of Geelong on winning the 2009 AFL Premiership.

Events also have the power to challenge the imagination and explore possibilities. A series of reconciliation marches around Australia in 2000 as part of the national Sorry Day initiative served to express community support for reconciliation with Aboriginal Australians, and to bring this issue powerfully to the attention of the media. In Sydney, the march took the unprecedented step of closing the Sydney Harbour Bridge, providing a powerful symbolic statement of bridging the Aboriginal and wider Australian communities. A further example is the Weipa Crocodile Festival in northern Queensland. This youth festival, bringing Aboriginal and white Australian youths together, has contributed to the reconciliation process and served as a model for similar festivals in Alice Springs and other outback areas (Jago et al. 2002, Croc Festival 2009).

As part of the 2010 Sydney Festival, a special concert in Parramatta Park by A. H. Rahman, a Bollywood composer best known in the west for his music for the film *Slumdog Millionaire*, aimed to ease tension between the Australian and Indian communities arising from recent the attacks and murders of Indians in Australia. The composer expressed his belief in the role of music in healing the tensions: 'This concert is about reaffirming the friendship and interest of both people, and I hope this concert brings that' (Rahman 2010).

Events can also contribute to the political debate and help to change history, as demonstrated by the watershed United Nations Conference on Environment and Development ('The Earth Summit') in Rio de Janeiro in 1992. Further, they can promote healing in the community, as demonstrated by events dedicated to the victims and survivors of the terrorist attack in New York on 11 September 2001, the Bali nightclub bombing in October 2002, the Canberra bushfires in January 2003, the Asian tsunami in December 2004, the Chinese earthquake in Sichuan Province in May 2008, and the Victorian bushfires in February 2009.

Research suggests local communities often value the 'feel good' aspects of hallmark events and are prepared to put up with temporary inconvenience and disruption because such events generate excitement and the long-term expectation of improved facilities and profile. Researchers, for example, identified the Australian Formula One Grand Prix in Adelaide as being popular among residents: 'The Grand Prix in 1985 set Adelaide alive ... The spirit infected all of us, including large numbers of people who in "normal" times might be expected to be against the notion of this garish, noisy, polluting advertising circus' (Arnold et al. 1989, p. 187). This 'feel good' factor is often a feature of the hosting of major events, seen more recently in the immense sense of pride demonstrated by the people of China in hosting the Beijing Olympic Games in 2008.

However, such events can have negative social impacts too. Arnold et al. (1989) identified 'the hoon effect' in relation to the 1985 Australian Formula One Grand Prix in Adelaide, when the number of road accident casualties in the five weeks around the event rose by 34 per cent compared with the number in the same period for the previous five years. Accounting for the rising trend of road accident casualties over those years, the researchers calculated that about 15 per cent of these casualties were unexplained, and suggested these casualties could be due to people's off-track emulation of Grand Prix race driving.

The larger the event and the higher its profile, the greater is the potential for things to go wrong, thus generating negative impacts. Consider the tragic drownings during the Sydney to Hobart Yacht Race in 1998, the death of a young rock fan in the mosh pit at the Big Day Out music festival in Sydney in 2001, the death of a race marshal at the Melbourne Grand Prix in 2001 and the death of a competitor in the Finke Desert Race south of Alice Springs in 2008. All of these incidents have had far-reaching negative impacts on the event participants, stakeholders and host communities. In a less serious, but still damaging, example, chaos broke out and police were forced to send extra highway patrol officers to a Hunter Valley winery in 2009 when 1000 people were turned away from a Smokey Robinson concert because promoters gave away too many free tickets (O'Neill 2009). The incident created negative headlines and damaged the reputation of the event.

Managing crowd behaviour

Major events can have unintended social consequences such as substance abuse, bad behaviour by crowds and an increase in criminal activity (Getz 2005). If not managed properly, these unintended consequences can hijack the agenda and determine the public perception of the event. Events as diverse as the Australasian Country Music Festival at Tamworth in New South Wales, the Australian Motorcycle Grand Prix at Phillip Island in Victoria, the Woodford Folk Festival in Queensland and Schoolies Week on the Queensland Gold Coast (see event profile on page 64) have had to develop strategies to handle alcohol-related bad crowd behaviour to protect their reputation and future.

Crowd behaviour can be modified with careful planning. Sometimes, this is an evolutionary process. The management of New Year's Eve in Sydney, for example, has led to a series of modifications and adjustments over successive years. In the early 1990s, teenage alcohol abuse resulted in bad crowd behaviour at Darling Harbour, including confrontations with police, injuries and arrests. The Darling Harbour Authority subsequently had its regulations changed to allow it to prevent alcohol from being brought to the venue. It also modified its program and marketing strategies to create the expectation of a family-oriented celebration. The result was a turnaround in crowd behaviour and a dramatic decrease in injuries and arrests. In the lead-up to the New Year's Eve of the new millennium, the celebrations were spread around different locations in the city, facilitating better crowd management and a reduction in behaviour problems. In more recent years, the celebrations on Sydney Harbour have featured two fireworks displays — one early in the evening allowing families with young children to depart early, and a second display at midnight to mark the start of the New Year.

Another example of using the event structure and program to assist in crowd control is the Party held at the conclusion of the Sydney Gay and Lesbian Mardi Gras Parade. Originally suggested by the police in 1979 as a form of crowd control, the Mardi Gras Party has become a main attraction and financial mainstay of the event, attracting 18 000 people over seven venues in 2009 (McInerney 2009).

Since the terrorist attack in New York on 11 September 2001, the threat of terrorism has resulted in increased security at major events worldwide. However, due to appropriate precautions, events such as the Rugby World Cup in Australia in 2003, the Commonwealth Games in Melbourne in 2006 and the FIFA World Cup in Germany in that same year were conducted safely without major incidents. Security for the Olympics was increased from 11 500 (including 4500 police officers) for the Sydney Games in 2000 to 45 000 (including 25 000 from the police force) for the Athens Games in 2004 (Kyriakopoulos and Benns 2004). Land forces of the Peoples Liberation Army were used to help safeguard the Beijing Games in 2008, with an anti-terrorist force of nearly 100 000 commandos, police and troops placed on high alert (China Daily 2008).

Community ownership and control of events

Events can also have wider effects on the social life and structure of communities. Some Byron Bay residents have complained about car traffic to the East Coast Blues and Roots Music Festival impeding access to their homes, and some residents of Sydney's north shore and northern suburbs complained of traffic jams caused by the closing of the Sydney Harbour Bridge in 2009 for the Breakfast on the Bridge event. Other impacts may include a loss of amenities due to excessive noise or crowds, the resentment of inequitable distribution of costs and benefits, and the cost inflation of goods and services, which can upset housing markets and has the most severe impact on low-income groups, as outlined by Getz (2005). Communities should thus have a major say in the planning and management of events. However, Hall (1989) concludes that the role of communities is often marginalised and that governments often make the crucial decision of whether to host the event without adequate community consultation. Public participation then becomes a form of placation designed to legitimise the decisions of government and developers, rather than a full and open discussion of the advantages and disadvantages of hosting events.

It is therefore all the more important for governments to be accountable, through the political process, for the allocation of resources to events. Hall (1992) maintains that political analysis is an important tool in regaining community control over hallmark events and ensuring the objectives of these events focus on maximising returns to the community. The Tibetan protests during certain stages of the 2008 Beijing Olympic Games Torch Relay, and the opposition by some sections of the community in the Northern Rivers region of NSW to the Repco Rally Australia in 2009, are indications of the political fallout that can occur for governments when sections of the community are alienated by aspects of the conduct of major events.

event profile

SCHOOLIES WEEK

Schoolies Week began at Surfers Paradise on the Queensland Gold Coast in the 1970s as a celebration marking the end of high school, and a 'rite of passage' for young people entering the adult world. It has since become an Australian tradition, and expanded to include other major holiday destinations in most Australian states, as well as Bali, Fiji and Vanuatu.

As Schoolies Week grew, significant problems arose because of the nature of the event and the behaviour of its participants. Major issues listed on the Schoolies website include alcohol and drug abuse, sexual health, sexual assault, drug spiking, cults and evangelists, suicide and other deaths, and negative community impacts including 'taking over the town', noise, litter, vandalism and damage to hotel and other property.

Schoolies Week has a long history of organised support groups working with young people involved in the celebrations to counter the negative impacts of the event. Following significant incidents of violence at Schoolies Week on the Gold Coast in 2002, the Queensland Government took over the running of the event from the Gold Coast City Council in 2003 and 2004. Council returned to a significant management role in 2005 (National Schoolies Website 2010).

Although it does not promote participation in Schoolies Week, the Queensland Government has responded to the influx of tens of thousands of young people with the Safer Schools Initiative, a partnership with other agencies, community organisations and councils to minimise disruption to communities and to encourage the safe and responsible behaviour of school leavers. Activities under this initiative include a highly visible police presence; additional emergency services;

improved coordination of councils, volunteers and community organisations; a centralised hotline for complaints and feedback; an official Schoolies website; and educational awareness programs in schools. Funding is available for organisations coordinating safety responses during Schoolies Week for targeted responses to minimise local risks, issues and problems. Funding covers measures such as registration and wrist banding to identify schoolies, the recruitment and training of volunteers to give advice and support, free transport, and schoolies-only activities in alcohol and drug-free environments (Queensland Department of Communities 2010).

Political impacts

Politics and politicians are an important part of the equation that is contemporary event management. Ever since the Roman emperors discovered the power of the circus to deflect criticism and shore up popularity, shrewd politicians have had an eye for events that will keep the population happy and themselves in power. No less an authority than Count Niccolo Machiavelli (1515), adviser to the Medicis in the sixteenth century, had this to say on the subject:

> A prince must also show himself a lover of merit, give preferment to the able and honour those who excel in every art . . . Besides this, he ought, at convenient seasons of the year, to keep the people occupied with festivals and shows; and as every city is divided into guilds or into classes, he ought to pay attention to all these groups, mingle with them from time to time, and give them an example of his humanity and munificence, always upholding, however, the majesty of his dignity, which must never be allowed to fail in anything whatever.

The British Royal House of Windsor took this advice to heart, providing some of the most popular public events of the past century, with the coronation of Queen Elizabeth II and the fairytale-like wedding of Prince Charles and Princess Diana. Former Australian prime minister Robert Menzies made good use of the public affection for the British royal family, with royal tours to Australia providing a boost to the popularity of his government. Successive Australian politicians have continued to use the spotlight offered by different events to build their personal profiles and gain political advantage. Former South Australian premier Don Dunstan used the Adelaide Festival to create an image of Adelaide as the 'Athens of the South' and of himself as a visionary and enlightened leader. Former New South Wales premier Neville Wran and colleague Laurie Brereton used the building of Darling Harbour to create an image of New South Wales as a go-ahead state, but critics at the time accused them of creating a monument to themselves. Former prime minister Bob Hawke bathed in the glory of Alan Bond's America's Cup victory in Fremantle. Continuing in the grand tradition, former Victorian premier Jeff Kennett used events such as the Australian Formula One Grand Prix to create an image of himself as a winner — and former New South Wales premier Bob Carr as the loser — in the race for events. Announcing in 2006 an extra $52.2 million over four years to maintain and build Victoria's major events calendar, then Victorian minister for tourism and major events John Pandazopoulos was quoted as saying 'We are the best in the world at winning and staging major events and this additional funding will keep us ahead of the competition' (Pandazopoulos 2006). More recently, Prime Minister Kevin Rudd demonstrated an understanding of the power of symbolism in politics by staging a formal apology to the stolen generations of Indigenous Australians, and by taking a strong role in the lead-up and conduct of the G20 Summit in London and the International Climate Change Summit in Copenhagen in 2009. On the international stage, the swearing in of US President Barack Obama on the same Bible as that used by president Abraham Lincoln was part of a powerful symbolic statement that reverberated around the world in 2009.

Arnold et al. (1989, pp. 191–2) leave no doubt about the role of events in the political process.

> Governments in power will continue to use hallmark events to punctuate the ends of their periods in office, to arouse nationalism, enthusiasm and finally, votes. They are cheaper than wars or the preparation for them. In this regard, hallmark events do not hide political realities, they are the political reality.

Governments around the world have realised the ability of events to raise the profile of politicians and the cities and states that they govern. Events gain media coverage and notoriety, and at the same time they attract visitors and therefore create economic benefits and jobs. This potent mixture has prompted governments to become major players in bidding for, hosting and staging major events. This increasing involvement of governments in events has politicised the events landscape, as recognised by Hall (1989):

> Politics are paramount in hallmark events. It is either naïve or dupli[citous] to pretend otherwise. Events alter the time frame in which planning occurs and they become opportunities to do something new and better than before. In this context, events may change or legitimate [sic] political priorities in the short term and political ideologies and sociocultural reality in the longer term. Hallmark events represent the tournaments of old, fulfilling psychological and political needs through the winning of hosting over other locations and the winning of events themselves. Following a hallmark event some places will never be the same again, physically, economically, socially and, perhaps most importantly of all, politically.

Events can promote international cooperation, as in the co-hosting of the Soccer World Cup by Japan and Korea in 2002. They can showcase emerging nations and economies, as in the hosting of the Olympic Games by Beijing in 2008 and the Commonwealth Games by Delhi in 2010. However, events can take on a more sinister political overtone, as with the use of the Nuremberg Rallies by Hitler in Nazi Germany, and of rallies in Russia, China and North Korea by their leaders, to stir nationalism and promote aggression. The emotive power of events to mesmerise crowds and provoke deep emotions has, it seems, the potential for both political good and evil.

Environmental impacts

An event is an excellent way in which to showcase the unique characteristics of the host environment. Hall (1989) points out that selling the image of a hallmark event includes marketing the intrinsic properties of the destination. He quotes the use of images of Perth's beaches, the Swan River and historic Fremantle in advertisements for the America's Cup defence in 1987, and the emphasis on the creation of an aesthetically pleasing environment in the promotion of Sydney's Darling Harbour. Governments and tourist bodies regularly use major events to promote destinations through their television coverage, as was demonstrated by the partnership between Tourism Australia and the Sydney Olympic Games to promote Australia to the world in 2000, and that between Tourism Victoria and the Melbourne Commonwealth Games to promote Victoria in 2006.

However, host environments may be extremely delicate, and great care should be taken to protect them. A major event may require an environmental impact assessment before council permission is granted for it to proceed. Even if a formal study is not required, the event manager should carefully consider the likely impact of the event on the environment. This impact will be fairly contained if the event is to be held in a suitable purpose-built venue — for example, a stadium, sportsground, showground or entertainment centre — but may be much greater if the event is to be held in a public space not ordinarily reserved for events — for example, a park, town square or street. Crowd movement and control, noise levels, access and parking will often be important considerations. Other major issues may include the impact on the natural and physical environment, heritage protection issues and disruption of the local community.

Effective communication and consultation with local authorities can often resolve some of these issues. In addition, careful management planning may be required to modify impacts. In Sydney, the Manly Jazz Festival worked for several years to reduce progressively the traffic impact of visitors to the festival, by developing a 'park and ride' system of fringe parking with shuttle buses to the event area. Many food and wine events have reduced their impact on the environment by using biodegradable containers and utensils instead of plastic, and by selling wine-tasting souvenir glasses that patrons can take home after the event. Computer applications now exist to measure the carbon footprint of events, and to take steps to reduce their impacts or purchase carbon credits to offset them. Many event managers are discovering that such measures make good financial as well as environmental sense.

In the staging of large events, the provision of infrastructure is often a costly budget component, but this expenditure usually results in an improved environment and facilities for the host community, and provides a strong incentive for the community to act as host. Brisbane profited from the transformation of the Expo 88 site into the South Bank leisure and entertainment precinct. Sydney's public space was enhanced by the redevelopment of derelict railway goods yards to create the Darling Harbour leisure precinct for Australia's Bicentenary in 1988. The Sydney Olympic Games in 2000 left a legacy of major state-of-the-art sporting venues and associated transport and communications facilities. The America's Cup in Auckland in 2000 and 2003 resulted in the transformation of the Auckland waterfront into an up-market restaurant precinct. All these examples illustrate the lasting benefits that can result from the hosting of large-scale events.

Waste management and recycling

Governments are increasingly using public education programs and legislation to promote the recycling of waste materials and reduce the amount of waste going to landfill. Events are targeted as opportunities to demonstrate best practice models in waste management and to change public attitudes and habits. The NSW Department of Environment and Climate Change promotes a fully integrated event waste management and recycling program, with detailed instructions on what to do before, during and after an event. It includes information on public area recycling equipment such as bin caps and colour-coded wheelie bins, and service area equipment such as a bale and frame, skip bins and portable compactors to assist in forming an effective waste management program. Their website provides a range of case studies on event waste management, and quotes research that shows that 89 per cent of people surveyed at special events in New South Wales consider recycling at events to be a very important issue (NSW Department of Environment and Climate Change 2009).

For the event manager, incorporating a waste management plan into the overall event plan has become increasingly good policy. Community expectations and the health of the environment require that events demonstrate good waste management principles and provide models for recycling. The waste-wise event manager will reap not only economic benefits, but also the approval of an increasingly environmentally aware public.

A more detailed discussion of the environmental aspects of events is provided in chapter 12.

Tourism and economic impacts

A primary concern of an event entrepreneur or host organisation is whether an event is within budget and, hopefully, results in a surplus or profit. This is a simple matter of whether the income from sponsorship, merchandise and ticket sales exceeds the costs of conducting and marketing the event. However, from the perspectives of the host communities and governments, a wider range of economic impacts is often of equal or greater significance.

One of the most important impacts is the tourism revenue generated by an event. In addition to their spending at the event, external visitors are likely to spend money on travel, accommodation, and goods and services in the host city or region. This expenditure can have a considerable impact as it circulates through the local economy. Effective tourism promotion can result in visitors to the event extending their length of stay and visiting other regional tourism destinations and attractions. In addition to the tourism generated during the event, events may attract media coverage and exposure that enhance the profile of the host town or city, resulting in improved long-term tourism image and visitation. Chapter 13 discusses these and other aspects of the tourism impact of events.

Business opportunities

Events can provide their host communities with a strong platform for showcasing their expertise, hosting potential investors and promoting new business opportunities.

During the Sydney Olympics, the New South Wales Government spent $3.6 million on a trade and investment drive coinciding with the event (Humphries 2000). This effort led to more than 60 business-related events, board meetings of international companies, briefings and trade presentations being held in Sydney at the time of the Olympics. Forty-six international chambers of commerce were briefed on business opportunities, and more than 500 world business leaders, Olympic sponsors and New South Wales corporate executives attended four promotional events. State treasurer Michael Egan was quoted as saying, 'We'll be benefiting from the Games well after we think the benefits have worn off and in ways that will never show up in statistics' (Humphries 2000).

Similar business development strategies accompanied the staging of the World Rugby Cup in 2003, the Melbourne Commonwealth Games in 2006 and the World Swimming Championships in Melbourne in 2007. However, little research has been done on analysing such strategies, and quantifying the amount of business that they generate. More work needs to be done so event enhancement frameworks are better understood and their outcomes can be assessed.

Leveraging the business outcomes of events

Many of the anticipated economic impacts of events are predicated on the benefits to local businesses, and through them to the community as a whole. However, without appropriate strategies in place to leverage the economic benefits of events, such benefits may not eventuate or may be less than anticipated.

Chalip and Leyns (2002) conducted a study of local business leveraging of the Gold Coast Honda Indy motor race held on the Queensland Gold Coast in Australia in October 1999. The researchers interviewed the managers of 22 small local businesses in the accommodation, retail and restaurants categories. Of these businesses, the majority (64 per cent) did little or nothing to leverage the event, and in five of the eight instances where some leveraging was attempted, their efforts were seen as minimal. However, in the cases of the three businesses that engaged in more aggressive leveraging — one retailer and two restaurant managers — their efforts paid substantial dividends.

These three cases were examined in more detail in order to determine the nature and success of the strategies employed. The retailer had extended her trading hours and placed a sales table of selected merchandise in front of her store in order to attract Indy patrons. One large restaurant, directly adjacent to the race precinct, had implemented a multi-faceted promotions and advertising campaign designed to position itself as 'the place to be' for race enthusiasts. Another restaurant, this time outside the racing precinct, participated in an auto-racing theming strategy implemented jointly by all licensed businesses and traders in the neighbourhood. Although unable or unwilling to provide exact figures, all three businesses maintained that their strategies had achieved positive results.

A task force of nine experts was then assembled to consider further the potentials and challenges of leveraging the Indy. The task force concluded that small businesses need some assistance in leveraging the event, and that strategies would best be formulated and implemented through alliances of core businesses. They recommended that a central coordinating body should be established, with adequate staff and funding to assist. They also recommended that demographic information be collected, and different strategies be developed for locals and visitors to the event.

The findings of the task force were then tested against the response of local businesses. All interviewees agreed with the leveraging objectives of the task force, but were skeptical about the formation of a central coordinating body, and favoured achieving these objectives through an existing business organisation or network.

Employment creation

By stimulating activity in the economy, expenditure on events can have a positive effect on employment. Employment multipliers measure how many full-time equivalent job opportunities are supported in the community as a result of visitor expenditure. However, it is easy to overestimate the number of jobs created by major events in the short term. Because the demand for additional services is short lived, employers tend to meet this demand by using their existing staff more, rather than employing new staff members. Existing employees may be released from other duties to accommodate the temporary demand or requested to work overtime.

However, major events can generate substantial employment in the construction phase, as well as during the staging of the event. The America's Cup in Auckland in 2000 was estimated to generate 1470 new jobs in construction, accommodation, marine and related activities (Scott 2003). The World Masters Games in Sydney in 2009 generated the equivalent of about 78 full-time, year-long jobs through the 2847 full-time jobs created over the ten days of the event, (see the 'Sydney 2009 World Masters Games' event profile on page 76) (Department of State and Regional Development 2009).

Keeping business local

The economic impacts of major events on their host cities are well documented, but what benefits, if any, to smaller and regional communities accrue from the hosting of local events?

Gibson and Stewart (2009), in their major study of regional festivals in New South Wales, Victoria and Tasmania (see page 48), found that although festival organisers themselves may make little or no direct profit, festivals benefit many functionally related local small businesses such as cafes and restaurants, hotels and motels, pubs, sound and lighting suppliers, printers, advertising agencies, legal services, catering companies and petrol stations.

They found that certain inputs, such as staff, catering and staging, were primarily sourced locally, while stall holders and talent, including musicians, performers and contestants, were sourced from a wider geographical base, though with a substantial local component (see table 3.2). They concluded that festivals are strongly connected to local economies, with a strong priority for festival organisers being to keep business in the local community.

TABLE 3.2 Sources of festival inputs

	Local %	Capital %	State %	Interstate %	International %
Talent	56.5	11.6	20.2	9.6	2
Staff	90.6	4.4	3.2	1.5	0.1
Catering	90.4	2.3	6.5	1.1	0
Stalls	64	6.1	23.9	6	0.3
Staging	84.3	5.7	7.6	2.3	0

Source: Gibson, C, Waitt, G, Walmsley, J and O'Connell, J 2010, 'Cultural festivals and economic development in regional Australia', *Journal of Planning Education and Research*, vol. 29, no. 3, pp. 280–93.

ECONOMIC IMPACTS AND THE ROLE OF GOVERNMENT

The strong growth of the festival and special event sector is part of a general economic trend away from an industrial product base to a more service-based economy. Traditionally, communities and governments have staged events for their perceived social, cultural and/or sporting benefits and value. This situation began to change dramatically in the early 1980s when major events in many parts of the world began to be regarded as desirable commodities for their perceived ability to deliver economic benefits through the promotion of tourism, increased visitor expenditure and job creation.

Mules (1999) dates this change in attitude in Australia to around 1982–86, with the staging of the Commonwealth Games in Brisbane (1982), the Formula One Grand Prix in Adelaide (1985) and the America's Cup defence in Perth (1986–87). He notes that state governments began around this time to be aware of the economic significance of events, aided by studies such as that of the Formula One Grand Prix (Burns, Hatch and Mules, cited in Mules 1999), which established that the income generated by the event exceeded the cost to the South Australian Government of staging it.

As outlined in chapter 1, various state governments in Australia have pursued vigorous event strategies since the 1980s, building strong portfolios of annual events and aggressively bidding for the right for their state to host major one-off events. Apart from interstate rivalry and political kudos, what motivates and justifies this level of government involvement in what otherwise might be seen as largely commercial enterprises? According to Mules (1999), the answer lies in what he terms the 'spillover effects' of events. While many major events might make an operational loss, they produce benefits for related industry sectors such as travel, accommodation, restaurants, hirers and suppliers of equipment and so on. They may also produce long-term benefits such as destination promotion resulting in increased tourism spending. However, a single organisation cannot capture this wide range of benefits. Governments thus sometimes play a role in funding or underwriting events so these generalised benefits might be obtained.

ECONOMIC IMPACT STUDIES

In deciding what events should be funded and what levels of funding are appropriate, governments need to obtain a full picture of the events' costs and the anticipated return on investment. To do so, they sometimes undertake economic impact studies, which seek to identify all of the expenditure involved in the staging of events, and to determine their impacts on the wider economy.

The impacts of an event derive from three main sources (Jago and Dwyer 2006):

1. expenditure by visitors from outside the region
2. capital expenditure on facilities required to conduct the event
3. expenditure incurred by event organisers and sponsors to stage the event.

However, this expenditure has flow-on effects that need to be taken into account in calculating the economic impact of an event. Money spent on a meal by a visitor to an event, for example, will flow on to businesses that supply the restaurant with food and beverage items. The money spent on the meal is direct expenditure, while the flow-on effect to suppliers is indirect expenditure. The event may also stimulate additional activity in the economy, resulting in increased wages and consumer spending. This is referred to as induced expenditure.

The aggregated impact on the economy of all of the expenditure is expressed as a multiplier ratio, a concept used widely by economists. Multipliers reflect the impact of the event expenditure as it ripples through the economy, and they vary according to the particular mix of industries in a given geographic location. The use of multipliers is controversial, and some studies prefer to concentrate on the direct expenditure of an event as being more reliable, although this does not give a true picture of the complex impact on the economy of the event expenditure.

Conducting economic impact studies that account for all of the myriad factors of the event expenditure and environment is quite complex and usually undertaken by specialist researchers with an economic background. However, a considerable body of literature is available to provide an insight for event managers into the process of conducting economic impact studies on events (see Burgan and Mules 2000; Crompton and McKay 1994; Giddings 1997; Hunn and Mangan 1999; Mules 1999; Mules and McDonald 1994; Jago and Dwyer 2006, Dwyer and Forsyth 2009).

Example of government use of economic impact studies

A good example of government use of event impact studies to evaluate the outcomes of a funding program is the research conducted by UK Sport.

Building on the evaluation of 16 events conducted between 1999 and 2003 (UK Sport 2004), in 2005 UK Sport commissioned the Sport Industry Research Centre at Sheffield Hallam University to conduct economic impact studies of six major sports events that had been supported by its World Class Events Programme (UK Sport 2007).

The standard UK Sport evaluation methodology based on direct expenditure of non-residents and event organisers was used to calculate the additional expenditure in the host economy resulting from each of the following events:

2005

- Bearing Point Rowing World Cup, held at Dorney Lake, Eton, 26–28 May
- UEFA Under 19 Football Championships held in Northern Island, 18–29 July
- UCI Women's World Cup Cycling Grand Prix of Wales, held at Celtic Manor, 20 August
- FEI Blenheim Pet Plan European Eventing Championships, held at Blenheim, 8–11 September

2006

- Volvo ISAF World Youth Sailing Championships, held in Weymouth/Portland, 13–20 July
- World Rowing World Championships, held at Dorney Lake, Eton, 20–27 August.

Key findings of the research are summarised in table 3.3.

TABLE 3.3 Economic impact of six major sports events

	Rowing World Cup	UEFA U19 Football	Women's Cycling	Euro Eventing	ISAF World Youth Sailing	World Rowing Championships
Event days	3	12	1	4	7	8
Commercial bed-nights	4 867	6 160	673	25 744	5 585	29 072
Visitor spend	£466 088	£560 131	£49 877	£1 914 498	£274 845	£2 680 070
Organisational spend	£117 811	£192 645	£6 537	£202 201	£74 529	£588 633
Overall impact	£583 899	£752 776	£56 413	£2 116 699	£349 374	£3 268 703
Impact per event day	£194 633	£62 731	£56 413	£529 175	£49 911	£408 588
Visitor impact/ event day	£155 363	£46 678	£49 877	£478 624	£39 264	£335 009
Pre-event forecast	£763 865	£632 005	£132 235	£1 608 800	£533 800	£2 841 866

Source: UK Sport 2007.

Conclusions that were able to be drawn from the research included:

- The average return on the £2.2 million funding of the World Class Events Programme across the six events was £7.1 million, or £3.20 for every £1 spent.
- The most significant event in terms of economic impact was the World Rowing Championships in 2006, which generated nearly £3.27 for every £1 spent for the host economy. The expenditure was comprised of 82 per cent external visitor spend and 18 per cent organisational spend on the event's infrastructure.
- However, based on per day visitor expenditure, the European Eventing event had the most significant impact with £479 000 per day.

- The smallest economic impact was that of the Women's Cycling event (£56 413). This was partly explained by the event duration of one day (three hours), and by the fact that the major aim of funding the event had been to promote women's cycling in the UK, rather than economic benefit.
- Visitor expenditure is the major source of economic impact, at least 74 per cent for each of the six events.
- Delegations and spectators have the largest economic impact because they are the groups with the highest volume of people attending the event.
- Of the four major groups (spectators, delegations, officials and the media) connected with the six events, the average daily spend of spectators was the lowest (£38 pounds), and that of officials the highest (£87 pounds). This was because a relatively smaller proportion of spectators stayed in commercial accommodation than the three other groups.
- Accommodation, food and drink were together the main item of expenditure across all events.
- The forecasting model achieved an accuracy rate of 87 per cent at the World Rowing Championships and 84 per cent at the UEFA U19 Football. In general, the model was more accurate at predicting the daily expenditure of each of the four groups than the volume of attendance. This emphasised the variations of the model across the six events, and the importance of primary data collection.
- Expenditure by overseas visitors, representing 'new' money to the UK economy, was £2.7 million across the four events hosted in England, with the World Rowing Championships generating nearly £2 million in additional visitor expenditure from overseas attendance, with more than three quarters of this attributable to the 60 nations taking part.

The six-event study confirmed that significant economic impact of events is inextricably linked to:

- the ability of the event to attract people from outside the host economy
- the duration of the event, combined with the ability of the host economy's ability to serve the needs of an influx of visitors
- the desire and support of local partners to make the event a commercial success.

It is worth noting that UK Sport considers economic impact as just one measure of the success of an event, quoting also sport development, home advantage, place making and public profile effects. For the events surveyed, a number of other factors were taken into account, including preparation for the London 2012 Olympic venues with the rowing and sailing events, the encouragement of youth participation with the sailing event, and the promotion of women's cycling with the cycling event.

Research such as this enables governments to make informed decisions on what events to fund, and to evaluate the overall outcomes and effectiveness of event support programs. However, as the above study illustrates, a wide variety of factors influence event economic impacts, making their accurate assessment both complex and challenging.

COMMUNITY PERCEPTIONS OF EVENT IMPACTS

For annual events, surveys of the host community's perceptions of an event can provide valuable tools for identifying and addressing community concerns in the planning of the next event. A number of researchers have sought to establish a generic survey instrument capable of accurately and reliably measuring such perceptions, and to track changes in them over time.

A study funded by Australia's Sustainable Tourism Cooperative Research Centre (Fredline, Deery and Jago 2005) surveyed attitudes of the Melbourne community to the Australian Open Tennis Tournament in 2003. For the study they developed a survey instrument using 12 items compressed from a 42-item scale that had been previously tested in a range of case studies. This survey was administered four to five weeks after the event via a telephone interview to 300 subjects chosen at random from the Melbourne telephone directory. For each of the 12 items, the respondents were asked whether they agreed or disagreed with the statements, then whether the impact affected their personal quality of life and the community as a whole. If they perceived an impact, they were asked to rate this in terms of its direction (positive or negative) and intensity on a scale ranging from −3 to +3. The summary of responses to these specific impacts is illustrated in table 3.4.

The most strongly perceived positive impacts at a personal level were entertainment, pride, the showcase effect, economic impact and maintenance of facilities, while the same five impacts were most highly rated at the community level in a slightly different order.

TABLE 3.4 Summary of responses to specific impacts

	Part A			Part B	Part C
	Agree	Disagree	Don't know	Personal impact mean	Community impact mean
Entertainment: The Australian Open gave Melbourne residents an opportunity to attend an interesting event, have fun with their family and friends, and interact with new people.	94.0%	3.3%	2.7%	0.92	1.53
Public money: The Australian Open was a waste of public money; that is, too much public money was spent on the event that would be better spent on other public activities.	6.7%	80.3%	13.0%	−0.12	−0.04
Economic benefits: The Australian Open is good for the economy because the money that visitors spend when they come for the event helps to stimulate the economy, stimulates employment opportunities, and is good for local business.	95.3%	2.3%	2.3%	0.38	1.52
Disruption to local residents: The Australian Open disrupted the lives of local residents and created inconvenience. While the event was on, problems like traffic congestion, parking difficulties and excessive noise were worse than usual.	20.6%	66.9%	12.5%	0.02	−0.10
Maintenance of public facilities: The Australian Open promoted development and better maintenance of public facilities such as roads, parks, sporting facilities, and/or public transport.	56.0%	15.1%	28.9%	0.38	0.97

	Part A			Part B	Part C
	Agree	Disagree	Don't know	Personal impact mean	Community impact mean
Bad behaviour: The Australian Open was associated with some people behaving inappropriately, perhaps in a rowdy and delinquent way, or engaging in excessive drinking or drug use or other criminal behaviour.	11.4%	78.3%	10.4%	−0.03	−0.03
Community pride: The Australian Open made local residents feel more proud of their city and made them feel good about themselves and their community.	80.3%	5.3%	14.3%	0.70	1.45
Environmental impact: The Australian Open had a negative impact on the environment through excessive litter and/or pollution and/or damage to natural areas.	3.3%	89.0%	7.7%	0	−0.01
Regional showcase: The Australian Open showcased Melbourne in a positive light. This helps to promote a better opinion of our region and encourages future tourism and/or business investment.	97.7%	1.0%	1.3%	0.48	1.53
Prices: The Australian Open Tennis 2003 led to increases in the price of some things such as some goods and services and property values and/or rental costs.	29.0%	27.0%	44.0%	−0.02	−0.06
Community injustice: The Australian Open was unfair to ordinary residents, and the costs and benefits were distributed unfairly across the community.	6.7%	68.7%	24.7%	−0.02	0
Loss of use of public facilities: The Australian Open denied local residents access to public facilities, that is, roads, parks, sporting facilities, public transport and/or other facilities were less available to local residents because of closure or overcrowding.	15.1%	66.2%	18.7%	0	−0.10

Source: Fredline, Deery and Jago 2005.

The survey went on to identify groups within the community with differing perceptions of the Australian Open, and to seek qualitative data through the use of open questions. The overall results demonstrate a high level of support among Melbourne residents for the Australian Open, with a perception of substantial benefits and few costs associated with the event.

In order to ascertain the effectiveness of the survey instrument, the researchers went on to compare the results of this survey with the results of similar previous surveys that they had conducted of other events. They noted that differences observed among the ratings appeared to be associated with the variation in the contexts of the case studies rather than in the measurement properties of the scale, suggesting that the scale is an effective indicator of the impact of events on the quality of life of local residents.

Test instruments such as these are valuable tools for event managers to assess community perceptions of the impacts of events, enabling them to develop strategies to manage these impacts in line with the expectations of the community.

The legacy of events

In recent years the emphasis of government evaluation of events has shifted from short-term to long-term impacts (often referred to as the *legacy* of events). Thus an event whose short-term balance sheet reflects a loss — that is, its costs outweigh its income — may be perceived as having a long-term positive legacy of improved infrastructure, transport and communication facilities, urban regeneration, and increased awareness of the host destination, resulting in greater business activity and tourism visitation. The hosting of mega-events, such as the Olympics, World Cup Soccer and World Expositions, as well as a range of second tier regional major events such as the Commonwealth Games, the Asian Games and the Pan American Games, can be seen as an exercise in strengthening the brand and awareness of host cities.

As yet there are very few longitudinal studies that are able to trace the long-term benefits of mega-events, and over time, the influence of other mitigating factors obscures them, making such benefits difficult to trace. For example, tracing the long-term tourism impacts of the Sydney Olympics would involve separating out the negative counter impacts of events such as 9/11, the SARS epidemic and the 2008–09 global financial crisis — a difficult, if not impossible, task.

Nevertheless, the legacy of events has become a significant factor in event evaluation and planning, influencing the thinking of governments, and the philosophy and approach of organisations such as the International Olympic Committee (IOC). 'The Legacy of the Olympic Games: 1984–2000', an International Symposium held by the IOC at Lausanne in 2002, examined the nature of legacy from a number of international perspectives and topic areas, and made a significant contribution to the thinking and literature of event legacy.

Thomson, Schlenker and Schulenkorf (2009) examined the definitions and key considerations inherent to legacy as found in the event evaluations of seven sport events, over a period from 1991–2007. They concluded that it is important that a strategic management approach be taken to legacy promises and planning, and that leveraging strategies need to be put in place around an event to ensure the desired outcomes are achieved.

event profile

SYDNEY 2009 WORLD MASTERS GAMES

Sydney hosted the seventh World Masters Games from 10–18 October 2009. Over 28 000 competitors from 95 countries participated — more than three times the number of athletes who competed in the Sydney 2000 Olympic Games. The World Masters Games is the world's largest multi-sport event, with 15 'core sports' — including archery, athletics, badminton, basketball, canoe/kayak, cycling, football (soccer), hockey, orienteering, rowing, shooting, softball, squash, table tennis and weight lifting — and an additional 13 'optional sports'. It was staged in over 70 venues in Sydney, capitalising on the many fine sites created for the 2000 Olympic Games.

The term 'Masters' does not denote the level of proficiency or achievement, but instead refers to the minimum age requirement, (generally 30 or 35, depending on the sport) for the mature-aged sports men and women who participate in the Games. Three-quarters of all participants of the Games are under 55 years of age. Participants compete as individuals or teams, and do not officially represent countries. The event is a combination of sport and entertainment, and is a social celebration of like-minded people.

The World Masters Games is coordinated globally by the International Masters Games Association (IMGA) and has been held approximately every four years since 1985. In addition to the 2009 Games in Sydney, other state capitals have played host, including Brisbane in 1994 and Melbourne in 2002.

The 2009 Sydney Games was organised by the Sydney 2009 World Masters Games Organising Committee (SWMGOC), a statutory corporation of the NSW Government. A Games Advisory Committee (GAC) consisting of eight leaders from the sports and business fields was recommended by the Minister for Sport and approved by Cabinet.

World Masters Games participants generally stay in the host country for a period before or after the Games, and tend to have high disposable incomes. The NSW Department of State and Regional Development estimated that the economic impact of the event was A$48 million, generating 2847 full-time jobs over the ten days of the event, or the equivalent of 78 full-time, year-long jobs.

Sydney 2009 World Masters Games, 2009; McKay J. 2009.

SUMMARY

All events produce both positive and negative impacts, which it is the task of the event manager to assess and balance. Social and cultural impacts may involve a shared experience and may give rise to local pride, validation and/or the widening of cultural horizons. However, social problems arising from events may result in social dislocation if not properly managed. Governments have long recognised the political impacts that often include an increased profile and benefits to the host community. However, the emotive power of events can also be subject to manipulation and abuse. Events are an excellent opportunity to showcase the physical characteristics of a destination, but event environments may be very delicate and care should be taken to safeguard and protect them. Event managers are increasingly aware of the value and importance of incorporating environmental strategies into their events. Tourism and economic impacts include the expenditure of visitors to an event, the promotion of business opportunities, the creation of commercial activity and the generation of employment.

Since the 1980s, governments in Australia have become increasingly aware of the potential tourism and economic benefits of events, and bid competitively for the right to host and stage them. In considering appropriate levels of funding for events, governments use economic impact studies to predict the likely impacts of events and then determine the wider outcomes. Methodologies are also available to identify community perceptions of event impacts, so that strategies can be developed to incorporate community participation and feedback in the planning of events.

QUESTIONS

1 Describe an example of an event whose needs have been perceived to conflict with those of the host community. As the event manager, how would you have resolved these conflicting needs?

2 Identify an event that you know has been marred by social problems or bad crowd behaviour. As the event manager, what would you have done to manage the situation and improve the outcomes of the event? In your answer, discuss both the planning of the event and possible on-the-spot responses.
3 Describe an event that you believe was not sufficiently responsive to community attitudes and values. What steps could the community take to improve the situation?
4 Select a major event that has been held in your region. Identify and describe the environmental strategies that were employed by the event, and evaluate the overall outcome of these strategies.
5 Select an event that you have been involved in as a participant or close observer. Identify as many impacts of the event as you can, both positive and negative, and then answer the following questions.
   (a) Did the positive impacts outweigh the negative?
   (b) What measures did the organisers have in place to maximise positive impacts and minimise negative impacts?
   (c) As the event manager, what other steps could you have taken to balance the impacts and improve the outcomes of the event?
6 List and describe what you consider to be the main reasons why governments support events.
7 Obtain three event reports that have been compiled on events in your area or state. Compare and contrast these reports in terms of (a) the methods used to compile them and (b) how they have been used to communicate and promote the outcomes of the event.

case study

THE AUSTRALIAN FORMULA ONE GRAND PRIX

Background on the Australian Formula One Grand Prix

The Australian Grand Prix was first held at Phillip Island in 1928, and then at various locations in Victoria, South Australia and NSW until 1984. In 1985 it became part of the Formula One World Championship, and was thereafter held on a street circuit in Adelaide until 1995. The Australian Formula One Grand Prix moved from Adelaide to Melbourne in 1996, where it remains today.

For the decade until the early 1990s, Victoria was seen to be the 'rust bucket' of Australia, and its capital city, Melbourne, suffering serious decline in comparison to Sydney. Melbourne is Australia's 'second city' after Sydney and was struggling to find a unique selling proposition. It did not have iconic natural landmarks like the Great Barrier Reef in Queensland or Uluru in Northern Territory, nor architectural icons such as the Harbour Bridge or Opera House in Sydney. With the election of a Liberal Government in October 1993, under the leadership of Jeff Kennett, a decision was made to use Melbourne's well-known interest and expertise in events, sporting in particular, to underpin a major event strategy that would become Melbourne's unique selling proposition.

As Melbourne had been unsuccessful in its bid to host the 1996 Summer Olympics, there was substantial pressure to obtain the rights to host another international sporting event, and the Australian Grand Prix was seen to provide such an opportunity. The Kennett government spent a large, but undisclosed, sum to lure

the Australian Grand Prix from Adelaide, and the event moved to Melbourne in 1996. As the race in Melbourne was to be run on a street circuit based around the lake at Albert Park, there was substantial controversy about stopping the public from accessing parklands for a couple of weeks each year. A protest group called the 'Save Albert Park' group was formed, to try to prevent the race from being held in Albert Park, arguing that a dedicated racing circuit was a more appropriate venue.

The Kennett government invested heavily in the upgrade of the natural and man-made facilities of Albert Park as the region had slipped into serious decay over the previous decades. The government argued that there were substantial benefits for Melbourne in having the Australian Grand Prix on a street circuit in Albert Park, as the race attracts enormous international television coverage and the City of Melbourne skyline would provide an ideal backdrop to the race at Albert Park. This was seen to be very important to help promote Melbourne internationally and to attract increased numbers of international tourists.

In support of its case to prevent the Australian Grand Prix from being staged in Albert Park, the 'Save Albert Park' group challenged the fact that the government was paying a large sum to an international promoter in order to win the rights to stage the event in Melbourne, and that there was so much secrecy surrounding the amount paid. They claimed that this money would be better spent on areas such as education and public health. The group also challenged the economic benefits of the race that were claimed by the government, believing them to be grossly overstated.

As part of the strategy to position Melbourne as a leading sporting city on the international stage, the promotional theme for the 1996 Australian Grand Prix was 'Melbourne — What a Great Place for the Race'. The first event attracted 401 000 attendees, which has been the highest attendance figure at Albert Park, as the following table shows.

Year	Attendance figure
2009	287 000
2008	303 000
2007	301 000
2006	302 000
2005	359 000
1996	401 000

While there is generally strong community support for major events in Melbourne, motor racing events do tend to polarise the community, particularly when run on public streets. The same result has been found in other destinations where street circuits have been used, such as the V8 car racing series in Canberra that used the parliamentary triangle and caused substantial community backlash against the event.

Not only do motor racing events on street circuits inconvenience the local community by blocking streets and access to parks within the track precinct, they also involve substantial noise that proves very disruptive to those with an aversion to the sport. The sound from motor car racing drifts across the entire city, depending on wind conditions, and has been a factor in many local residents seeking to move out of the city for the duration of the event.

The inconvenience factors as outlined, coupled with the fact that substantial state government funds are provided to underwrite the event, have prompted controversy as to the true economic value of the event to Melbourne and whether there is an acceptable return to the community from this government investment of funds. Some members of the community, not just members of groups such as 'Save Albert Park', believe that government funds should not be used to support private sector activity such as events, and should be used instead for mainstream public sector activities such as education and health. The fact that the government funds supplied to underwrite the staging of the Formula One Grand Prix in Melbourne actually go to an international promoter of the sport to purchase the right to stage, acts like a 'red rag to a bull' for many in the community.

Economic evaluations of the Australian Formula One Grand Prix

Economic evaluations of a number of the Australian Grand Prix events staged in Melbourne have been undertaken, and the figures published in the media, to highlight the good returns that the government is getting from its investments. Most of these evaluations have been performed by the National Institute of Economic and Industry Research (NIEIR) (NIEIR 2010), which is a long-established company specialising in economic consultancy and research. Despite these evaluations, a growing number of people are now questioning whether the evaluations have been undertaken objectively and whether they represent a true return for the state compared to other activities. Some media have become quite vocal in their condemnation of the event and thus raised the profile of the objections to the event.

NIEIR had undertaken evaluations of the Australian Formula One Grand Prix in 1996 and 2000 for the Department of State and Regional Development, and was commissioned by the Australian Grand Prix Corporation to evaluate the 2005 Grand Prix. The key focus of these evaluations was the economic contribution that the event made to the state. NIEIR employed a range of questionnaires to collect the data needed for the economic assessment of the event. Samples of visitors, media, racing teams and local businesses were surveyed during the event to capture data on their expenditure profiles, as well as a range of other demographic and behavioural dimensions.

In collecting expenditure data from interstate and international visitors to the event, NIEIR was careful to identify only those visitors whose visit to Melbourne was motivated by the event and who would not have visited if the Grand Prix had not been staged. This approach excludes those visitors who were already in Melbourne and those who simply changed the timing of their trip to coincide with the staging of the Grand Prix. If these existing visitors and time-switchers extended the duration of their trip in order to attend the Grand Prix, then the expenditure on the additional nights was counted in the calculation of inscope expenditure.

NIEIR included a 'retained expenditure' component in its calculation of inscope expenditure. This is the expenditure made by Victorian residents at the Grand Prix that would have otherwise been spent outside the state if the Grand Prix was held in another state. While this is an economically sound approach, it is very difficult to estimate what would happen in such situations and, as a consequence, this form of expenditure is usually left out of evaluations. Expenditure made by local residents can be included in evaluations if the expenditure is funded from a draw down of long-term savings rather than from normal discretionary income. In the questionnaires that were administered to local event visitors, a question was included that

asked respondents about the source of the funds used to purchase tickets to the Grand Prix. NIEIR included the expenditure made by local residents who indicated that their tickets were purchased using long-term savings. NIEIR also included an induced tourism effect as a result of the international exposure of Melbourne that was generated by coverage of the Grand Prix being staged in Melbourne. This represents the economic benefit for Melbourne as a result of tourist visitation prompted by the Grand Prix that occurs in the years after the event. Table 3.5 provides an overview of the key outcomes of the 2005 Australian Formula One Grand Prix based on the NIEIR evaluation, using data presented in the 2007 Victorian Auditor-General's Report.

TABLE 3.5 Key outcomes of the 2005 Australian Formula One Grand Prix

Variable	Impact
Increase in gross state product (GSP)	$174.8m
Private consumption expenditure	$78.6m
Business investment	$54.0m
Employment (FTE)	3670
State government tax receipts	$15.2m
Visitor nights	194 994

Source: NIEIR cited in Victorian Auditor-General's Office 2007, *State Investment in Major Events,* p. 128.

After winning the rights to host the Australian Formula One Grand Prix, Melbourne was highly successful in its mission to build an international calendar of events based on a mix of annual events such as the Grand Prix, Australian Open Tennis and the Spring Racing Carnival, coupled with one-off type events such as the Masters Games. Internationally, Melbourne became recognised as an events capital and many other cities both in Australia and overseas sought to emulate Melbourne's performance in this area. In order to ensure that Melbourne's position as a leading event city was secure, the state government continued to invest substantial funds in attracting and managing events.

> In 2006–07, it [state government] increased its [major event] appropriation by $50.4 million over 4 years and the 2007–08 Budget provides an additional $34.2 million from 2007–08 through to 2010–11 (Victorian Auditor-General's Office 2007, *State Investment in Major Events*, p. v).

Auditor-general review of the evaluations of the Australian Formula One Grand Prix

As a result of the substantial investment that the state government was making in order to attract events to the state, the auditor-general felt that it was important to audit the event evaluations that were being undertaken. This would enable the auditor-general to verify whether the state was getting an appropriate return on its investment in events. According to the auditor-general, the objectives for the audit into major events were as follows.

- To examine:
  - the soundness of pre-event assessments leading to the recommendation to financially support a major event;

- the management of funding agreements and contractual requirements with major event organisers;
- the post-event evaluations of the economic value derived from major events;

- To provide independent assessments of the level of economic value derived by Victoria from the 2005 Australian Formula 1 Grand Prix (Victorian Auditor-General's Office 2007, p. 15).

The auditor-general decided that the most expedient method for doing an assessment of how the Australian Formula One Grand Prix had been evaluated was to independently evaluate the event using the raw data that had been collected in the original evaluation. It was decided that the 2005 event should be the case study for the audit for two reasons:

- the 2005 event had been subjected to a comprehensive evaluation by NIEIR on behalf of the Australian Grand Prix Corporation
- Melbourne had hosted the Commonwealth Games around the same time as the 2006 Australian Formula One Grand Prix and this may have distorted the findings for that year. (Victorian Auditor-General's Office 2007, pp. 81–2).

It was decided that two methodologies would be used to assess the contribution of the 2005 Australian Formula One Grand Prix, namely, cost benefit analysis (CBA) and computable general equilibrium (CGE) modelling. These methods were adopted for the following two reasons:

> A CBA approach is a robust methodology that addresses the extent of net social benefit to Victoria from the Grand Prix itself however it cannot measure the level of economic activity generated from the event or the wider flow-on effects;
>
> CGE provides a sophisticated and comprehensive modelling of the Victorian and national economies to measure the level of economic activity. CGE analysis cannot address the issue of whether a project is worth proceeding with; hence the need for a CBA approach (Victorian Auditor-General's Office 2007, *State Investment in Major Events*, p. 39).

For the purposes of this case study, only the results of the CGE modelling are included. The reader is encouraged to access the full report of the auditor-general for discussion on the results of the CBA.

As the auditor-general had concerns about a number of the assumptions that had been used by NIEIR in its evaluation of the 2005 Australian Formula One Grand Prix, it was decided to adopt two scenarios in the CGE analysis of the data so that the impact of these assumptions could be tested. The first scenario included all of the assumptions that had been used in the NIEIR analysis, while the second scenario excluded a number of assumptions, the most important being:

- the induced tourism effect
- retained expenditure (includes an estimate of the expenditure that would have occurred outside the state caused by locals going to the Grand Prix interstate if it was not held in Victoria)
- enhanced resident expenditure effect (counting local expenditure because it is assumed to have come from long term savings) (Victorian Auditor-General's Office 2007, p. 44).

The auditor-general used the raw data collected by NIEIR in its evaluation of the 2005 Australian Formula One Grand Prix so that data collection techniques would not be a cause for differences in the outcomes.

The results of the CGE analysis for the two scenarios undertaken by the auditor-general compared to the NIEIR evaluation are presented in table 3.6. It can be seen

that the NIEIR results are considerably higher than the outcomes obtained using CGE modelling as part of the audit, either with the same assumptions as NIEIR or with more conservative assumptions. This result confirmed concerns regarding the approach that had previously been used to evaluate the economic contribution of the Australian Formula One Grand Prix, as well as some of the overly optimistic assumptions that had been included.

TABLE 3.6 Comparison of key outputs from the audit compared to NIEIR

Output	Scenario 1 (CGE with NIEIR assumptions)	Scenario 2 (CGE with stricter assumptions)	NIEIR
GSP	$110.9m	$62.4m	$174.8m
Private investment	$24.1m	$12.7m	$54.0m
Private consumption	$56.8m	$16.1m	$78.6m
State tax receipts	$11.9m	$3.5m	$15.2m
Employment	600	400	3650

Source: Victorian Auditor-General's Office 2007, *State Investment in Major Events,* p. 128.

The key recommendations coming out of the 'Auditor-General's Report' (2007, p. 3) in relation to post event evaluation included:

- evaluations should move towards a triple bottom line approach embracing not only economic but social and environmental factors
- cost benefit analysis should be used at the pre-event stage for all events to determine the net benefits of the funding sought
- computable general equilibrium modelling should be used for larger events at the post-event stage to assess their impact on the economy
- for events other than the very largest, a range of key performance indicators based on expenditure of interstate and international visitors should be used to evaluate the performance of the event.

Whilst the auditor-general accepted that their may well be an induced tourism effect from major events, this could only be included if its effect could be quantified. It was recommended, therefore, that research be undertaken to quantify induced tourism.

Professor Leo Jago PhD, Christel DeHaan Tourism and Travel Research Institute, University of Nottingham.

Questions

1. Why was the Victorian 'Auditor-General's Report' undertaken, and what did it set out to achieve?
2. From the information provided in the case study, what are the comparative advantages and disadvantages of cost–benefit analysis and computable general equilibrium (CGE) modelling?
3. What are the implications of the Victorian 'Auditor-General's Report' for the evaluation of other major events in Australia?

REFERENCES

Arnold, A, Fischer, A, Hatch, J & Paix, B 1989, 'The Grand Prix, road accidents and the philosophy of hallmark events', in *The planning and evaluation of hallmark events*, eds GJ Syme, BJ Shaw, DM Fenton & WS Mueller, Avebury, Aldershot.

Burgan, B & Mules, T 2000, 'Event analysis — understanding the divide between cost benefit and economic impact assessment', in *Events beyond 2000: setting the agenda — event evaluation, research and education conference proceedings*, eds J Allen, R Harris, LK Jago & AJ Veal, Australian Centre for Event Management, Sydney.

Chalip L & Leyns, A 2002, 'Local business leveraging of a sports event: managing an event for economic benefit', in *Journal of Sport Management*, vol. 16, no. 2, pp. 132–58.

China Daily 2008, 'Security beefed up in Beijing to ensure safe Olympics', *China Daily*, www.chinadaily.com.cn.

Croc Festival 2009, www.crocfestival.org.au.

Crompton, JL & McKay, SL 1994, 'Measuring the impact of festivals and events: some myths, misapplications and ethical dilemmas', *Festival management and event tourism*, vol. 2, no. 1, pp. 33–43.

Department of State and Regional Development 2009, quoted in *Sydney 2009 World Masters Games Background Information Paper*, Sydney.

Dwyer, L & Forsyth, P 2009, 'Public sector support for special events: reconciling economic impacts with costs and benefits', in *The Proceedings of The International Event Management Summit* held in Surfers Paradise in July 2009, ed J Allen, Australian Centre for Event Management, Sydney.

Fredline, L, Deery, M & Jago, L K 2005, 'Testing of a compressed generic instrument to assess host community perceptions of events: a case study of the Australian Open Tennis Tournament', in *The impacts of events: proceedings of International Event Research Conference held in Sydney in July 2005*, ed J Allen, Australian Centre for Event Management, Sydney.

Getz, D 2005, *Event management and event tourism*, Cognizant Communication Corporation, New York.

Gibson, C & Stewart, A 2009, *Reinventing rural places: the extent and impact of festivals in rural and regional Australia*, Australian Centre for Cultural Environmental Research, Wollongong.

Gibson, C, Waitt, G, Walmsley, J & Connell, J 2010, 'Cultural festivals and economic development in regional Australia', *Journal of Planning Education and Research*, vol. 29, no. 3, pp. 280–93.

Giddings, C 1997, *Measuring the impact of festivals — guidelines for conducting an economic impact study*, National Centre for Culture and Recreation Studies, Australian Bureau of Statistics, Canberra.

Hall, CM 1989, 'Hallmark events and the planning process', in *The planning and evaluation of hallmark events*, eds GJ Syme, BJ Shaw, DM Fenton & WS Mueller, Avebury, Aldershot.

Hall, CM 1992, *Hallmark tourist events — impacts management and planning*, Belhaven Press, London.

Humphries, D 2000, 'Benefit to economy is unseen', *The Sydney Morning Herald*, 23 August, p. 8.

Hunn, C & Mangan, J 1999, 'Estimating the economic impact of tourism at the local, regional, state or territorial level, including consideration of the multiplier effect', in *Valuing tourism: methods and techniques*, eds K Corcoran, A Allcock, T Frost & L Johnson, Bureau of Tourism Research, Canberra.

Jago, L, Chalip, L, Brown, G, Mules, T & Ali, S 2002, 'The role of events in helping to brand a destination' in *Events and place making: proceedings of International Research Conference held in Sydney 2002*, eds L Jago, M Deery, R Harris, A Hede, & J Allen, Australian Centre for Event Management, Sydney.

Jago, L & Dwyer, 2006, *Economic evaluation of special events: a practitioner's guide*, Common Ground Publishing, Altona, Victoria.

Kyriakopoulos, V & Benns, M 2004, 'Passing the torch to Athens', *The Sun-Herald*, 22 February.

Machiavelli, N 1962 (1515), *The Prince*, trans. L Ricci, Mentor Books, New York.

McInerney, A 2009, pers. comm. in presentation to The Event Creation Workshop at the University of Technology, Sydney, 1 May 2009.

McKay J 2009, 'Closing Ceremony Brings Down Curtain', Media release, www.2009worldmasters.com.

Mules, T 1999, 'Estimating the economic impact of an event on a local government area, region, state or territory', in *Valuing tourism: methods and techniques*, eds K Corcoran, A Allcock, T Frost & L Johnson, Bureau of Tourism Research, Canberra.

Mules, T & McDonald, S 1994, 'The economic impact of special events: the use of forecasts', *Festival Management and Event Tourism*, vol. 2, no. 1, pp. 45–53.

National Institute of Economic and Industry Research (NIEIR) 2010, www.nieir.com.au.

National Schoolies Week 2010, 'Schoolies History', www.schoolies.org.au.

NSW Department of Environment and Climate Change 2009, www.environment.nsw.gov.au.

O'Neill, M 2009, 'Concert in Chaos', *Sunday Telegraph,* 13 December, p. 23.

Pandazopoulos, J 2006, '$73 Million for Tourism Support and Major Events', Media release, www.dpc.vic.gov.au.

Queensland Department of Communities 2010, 'Safer Schoolies Initiative', www.communityservices.qld.gov.au.

Rahman, A R 2010, 'Musical manna will rain down from a Sufi heaven', *The Sydney Morning Herald,* 15 January, p. 3.

Scott, E 2003, 'On the waterfront', *Australian Leisure Management*, February–March 2003.

Sydney 2009 World Masters Games 2009, *Sydney 2009 World Masters Games Background Information,* paper prepared by 2009 World Masters Games, Sydney.

Thomson, A, Schlenker, K & Schulenkorf, N 2009, 'The legacy-factor: towards conceptual clarification in the sport event context', in *The Proceedings of The International Event Management Summit* held in Surfers Paradise in July 2009, ed J Allen, Australian Centre for Event Management, Sydney.

UK Sport 2004, 'Measuring Success 2 — the economic impact of major sports events', www.uksport.gov.uk.

UK Sport 2007, 'Measuring Success 3 — the economic impact of major sports events', www.uksport.gov.uk

Victorian Auditor-General's Office 2007, *State Investment in Major Events*, Victorian Government Printer, Melbourne, http://archive.audit.vic.gov.au.

PART 2

PLANNING

Conceptualising events that will inspire, impart knowledge, or achieve any of a myriad of other objectives is a perpetual challenge for the practising event manager. Whatever concept that is decided upon then needs to be subjected to a range of planning processes if it is to successfully meet the expectations of its various shareholder groups, such as the attendees, community, sponsors and the event 'owner'.

In this section of the book, the areas of event conceptualisation and planning are discussed, with specific chapters dealing with strategic, financial, human resource, project, marketing and sponsorship planning, and event concept development. Additionally, this section includes a chapter on sustainable development, an increasingly significant factor influencing overall event planning.

4

THE STRATEGIC PLANNING FUNCTION

LEARNING OBJECTIVES

After studying this chapter, you should be able to:

1 discuss the nature of the strategic planning process
2 describe the various stages in the strategic planning process within an event context
3 undertake a SWOT or situational analysis and identify the appropriate strategy option for a given event
4 identify an appropriate organisational structure through which to conduct a given event
5 identify a basic strategic plan for a given event.

INTRODUCTION

This chapter provides an overview of strategic planning as it applies to the conduct of events. It begins by discussing the importance of planning to the overall success of an event and then moves on to describe the strategic event planning process. This process comprises a number of sequential and interrelated steps, beginning with the development of an event concept and/or intent to bid, and ending with event shutdown, evaluation and reporting. The potential for legacy related outcomes flowing from the application of this process is also acknowledged and briefly discussed here.

WHAT IS STRATEGIC PLANNING?

In its simplest form, the strategic planning process involves determining where an organisation is at present, deciding where it should be positioned in the market place in order to maximise its chances of progressing its mission, and creating strategies and tactics to achieve that position. In other words, the strategic planning process is concerned with end results and the means to achieve those results.

The value of strategic planning is evident in the following conversation between the Cat and Alice in Lewis Carroll's famous children's story *Alice's Adventures in Wonderland* (1865):

> 'Cheshire Puss, . . . Would you tell me, please, which way I ought to go from here?'
>
> 'That depends a good deal on where you want to get to,' said the Cat.
>
> 'I don't much care where —,' said Alice.
>
> 'Then it doesn't matter which way you go,' said the Cat.
>
> '— so long as I get SOMEWHERE,' Alice added as an explanation.
>
> 'Oh, you're sure to do that,' said the Cat, 'if you only walk long enough.' (p. 87)

This quotation, in a somewhat humorous way, makes the point that if you haven't thought about where you wish to go (in our case, your strategic direction), you could end up anywhere. To avoid this situation, an event organisation needs to think through its vision, mission or purpose, concepts that will be discussed later in this chapter.

While the power of strategic planning in facilitating an organisation's progress towards its vision and mission has been acknowledged by many writers (see Grant 2009; Hill, Jones, Galvin and Haidar 2007; Pitts and Lei 2006; and Pearce and Robinson 2005), actually engaging in it involves a measure of discipline on behalf of the event organisation. As Sir John Harvey-Jones, a past chairman of ICI in the United Kingdom, notes, 'Planning is an unnatural process: it is much more fun to do nothing. The nicest thing about not planning is that failure comes as a complete surprise, rather than being preceded by a period of worry and depression' (Focused Performance, 2006).

Event organisations need to be mindful that strategic plans, as Pitts and Lei (2006) note, need to be adapted to changing circumstances. Additionally, they need to be conscious of not falling foul of planning 'pitfalls', including:

- overplanning and becoming obsessed with detail as opposed to overall strategic considerations
- viewing plans as one-off exercises rather than active documents to be regularly consulted and adapted
- seeing plans as conclusive rather than directional in nature (Johnson and Scholes 2001).

Event organisations should also be alert to the fact that occasionally successful strategies might emerge without prior planning (Hill et al. 2007). Such 'emergent' strategies may be a result of unforeseen circumstances, or might flow from actions taken for non-strategic reasons. For example, a community fair may decide to include a brief music program at its conclusion as a way of encouraging people to leave the event site progressively in order to reduce the big departure rush and subsequent traffic congestion. If this dimension of the program were to meet with a strong unexpected positive response from attendees, the event organisers might be prompted to consider changing the event's format to embrace a stronger music component.

THE STRATEGIC PLANNING PROCESS AND EVENT ORGANISATIONS

The process of strategic planning in an event context involves an event manager moving through a number of sequential and interrelated steps (see figure 4.1). In this section, each of these steps is identified and briefly overviewed.

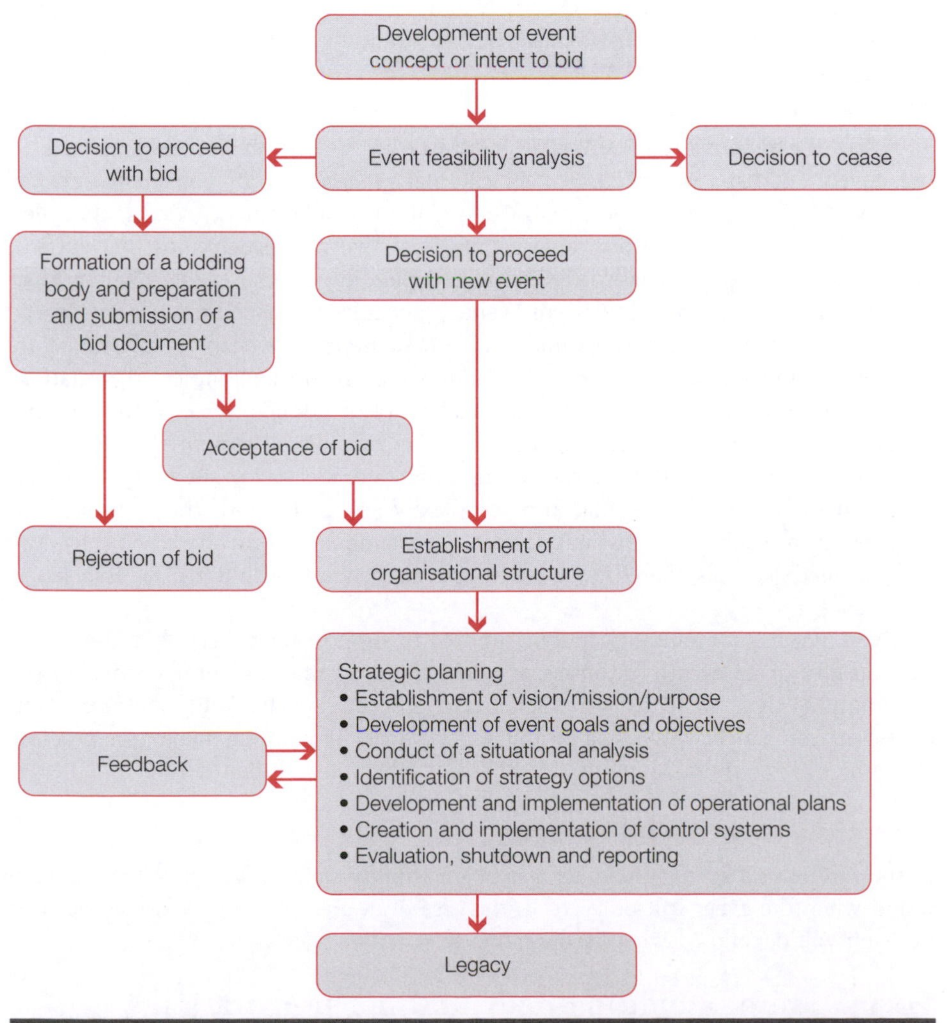

FIGURE 4.1 The strategic event planning process

Source: Grant 2009.

Concept or intent to bid

In the context of proposed new events, this preliminary stage in the strategic event management process involves making decisions (often after consultation with potential stakeholder groups such as sponsors, telecasters, potential attendees and government departments) that act to refine the initial event concept. These decisions will centre on matters such as the final type/form of the event; duration; location/venue; timing; and key program elements that will serve to make the event unique or special. Once the event concept is sufficiently developed, it can then be subjected to more detailed analysis.

In instances where bidding is involved, events for which bids can be made need to be firstly identified. Organisations involved in the identification process may include convention and visitors' bureaus, major event agencies, tourism bodies, or local chapters of national or international associations. Once identified, a preliminary assessment can be made as to their 'fit' with the capabilities of the potential event organising body and the hosting destination. Events deemed worthy of further investigation may then be the subject of more detailed scrutiny via a feasibility analysis (see chapter 13 for a discussion of organisations involved in the event bidding process).

Feasibility analysis

To assess the potential an individual event has for success, it is sound practice to objectively (perhaps via the use of an external organisation or consultant) engage in a formal analysis of this potential. Conducting this assessment, commonly called a feasibility study or situational analysis, involves many considerations that need to be taken into account. These may include (depending on the event) likely budget requirements; managerial skill needs; venue capacities; host community and destination area impacts (both economic and non-economic); availability of volunteers and supporting services (for example, equipment hire firms); projected visitation/attendance; infrastructure requirements; availability of public/private sector financial support (for example, grants, sponsorship); level of political support for the event; and the track record of the event in terms of matters such as profitability. It should be noted that the level of detail and complexity associated with these studies will vary. An event such as an Olympic Games, for example, will involve a more lengthy and detailed analysis than, say, a state sporting championship or an association conference.

Given that many events seek public funding to support their creation and delivery, the capacity of an event's organisers to convince government granting bodies of the 'feasibility' of their event is often crucial to its proceeding. This being the case, event organisers can benefit from using the criteria employed by granting bodies (see example in figure 4.2) when evaluating the feasibility, or otherwise, of their event.

Decision to proceed or cease

In the case of new events, the outcomes of a feasibility analysis will directly determine if and when the event will proceed. In the case of events involving a formal bid, this decision will depend on whether the bid is accepted or rejected.

Formation of a bidding body and bid preparation

Once it has been decided to proceed with a bid, a body will need to be established to prepare a formal bid document. Often established organisations, such as those noted in connection with intent to bid, will play the central role in this process. Such bids, as noted previously, should only proceed after a formal feasibility analysis.

The bidding process commonly involves a number of steps:

- developing a timeline for the preparation and presentation of a bid document to the owners of the event
- responding to each of the bid criteria set by the event owners (see figure 4.3)
- identifying the key elements of past successful bids to ensure these elements are dealt with fully in the bid document
- preparing a bid document
- presenting and/or submitting a bid to the owners of the event
- lobbying in support of the bid
- evaluating reasons for bid failure (if necessary).

It should be kept in mind that the bidding process is likely to commence a number of years out from the date an event is scheduled to take place. It is also not uncommon for organisations seeking to host an event to go through the bidding process on several occasions before they are successful, if indeed they do succeed.

FIGURE 4.2 Australian Capital Territory new festival funding criteria

FESTIVAL FUND GUIDELINES

To achieve the aims of the ACT Festival Fund, the ACT Government will support new and existing festivals that:

- reflect the wide range of our community interests and activities
- enrich our community's experience of living in Canberra
- actively engage our community as participants and audiences
- are innovative and of high quality
- are well planned, well managed and viable.

The emphasis is on supporting innovative celebrations that link to Canberra's identity, that stimulate community engagement and that complement and do not duplicate existing festivals. All applications for funding to the ACT Festival Fund will be considered and assessed in this context.

ASSESSMENT CRITERIA — NEW FESTIVALS

All applicants are considered against the assessment criteria and relative to the other applications received for the Festival Program Funding round.

Applicants must clearly and separately address each of the following assessment criteria and are strongly encouraged to use separate headings for each criterion.

1. **Describe your project/festival fully including:**
   - an overview of the concept of the proposed festival
   - the objectives of the festival
   - the size and scope of your project/festival
   - the proposed timing and venue of the festival, including a demonstration of how the festival complements and not competes with existing festivals on the ACT calendar
   - the proposed draft program that includes details of performers and artists
   - any other relevant background information.
2. **Describe fully how the activity will specifically address the following criteria:**
   - demonstrate how the festival will reflect Canberra's community and how it links to Canberra's identity
   - identify proposed community participation and engagement in the festival activity

FIGURE 4.2 *(continued)*

- demonstrate quality in festival concepts, including originality, progress and development, and how the festival may evolve over the next three years to enhance the Centenary of Canberra celebrations in 2013.

3 **Demonstrate that the proposal is well planned and achievable including:**
- the proposed management structure
- the proposed marketing plan that identifies the target audience and demonstrates how you will reach them
- possible risk issues and limitations that could affect the success of the festival and demonstrate how these will be overcome
- a comparison of the proposed festival with other festival and event models
- details of proposed revenue including participation fees, ticket sales, sponsorship and funding sources. Where possible, claims of sponsorship, either cash or in-kind, should be evidenced by letters of support
- a proposed planning timeline that demonstrates the current planning stage and identifies the next step in planning.

4 **Demonstrate fully the ability of the people involved to deliver the stated outcome including:**
- key personnel involved and their qualifications
- experience and skills
- past event management, artistic and administrative performance
- viability of the group or organisation.

5 **Demonstrated need for ACT Government funding for an activity that would not otherwise occur**

6 **Realistic, sound and substantiated budget. Applicants must use the budget template provided in the application form to ensure consistency across applications. Applicants may also attach additional information on their budgets or additional self generated detailed budgets. Significant revenue or expenditure items in the budget should be evidenced in writing.**

7 **Identify any fallback options if full funding is not provided. If you consider that any reduction in funding would make the activity impossible to proceed with, please make this clear in the application. It is important to identify a dollar amount as a fallback or it maymean your activity is not funded at all.**

8 **If your activity is dependent on other funding, then provide an explanation of how the activity will proceed if other funding is not secured.**

Source: Australian Capital Territory 2010.

FIGURE 4.3 Essential criteria for bids submitted to host the New South Wales 2008 Local Government Association Conference

ESSENTIAL CRITERIA

1. **Accommodation: at least 650–700 rooms with private facilities.**
Note: A bidding council MUST be able to guarantee a minimum of 70 hotel rooms per night for the duration of the conference (Saturday through to Tuesday or Wednesday) for Association use only as part of the overall number or rooms, preferably within the one location.

The accommodation for the Association must be of a minimum of 3–4 star standard and must be connected to or within close proximity (**maximum five minutes walk**) to the conference venue. A map should be provided as part of the application outlining where the 700 rooms lie.

FIGURE 4.3 *(continued)*

2. **Auditorium: must hold up to 700 people seated theatre style**
   The facilities must have a minimum of:
   - Disabled access and amenities (access, egress and toilets)
   - A raised stage large enough to hold a top table for 12 people
   - Air conditioning
   - Adequate lighting
   - Public address and audiovisual facilities.
3. **Mobile telephone & wireless internet reception**
   All facilities must have mobile telephone reception and free wireless internet access for delegates.
4. **Conference support facilities**
   The facilities must have:
   - A large space suitable for use as a polling place, preferably onsite
   - A large secure (lockable) space for use as offices for LGA staff, must be onsite
   - A large secure (lockable) space for use as a breakout area for LGA staff and Executives, must be onsite
   - A large space suitable for use as a media room (this space must be enabled for internet and telephone access)
   - A large space adjoining the conference venue to be used as a trade display area, capacity up to 40 booths.
5. **LGA office**
   The LGA office must contain:
   - 3 desks or benches
   - 1 high speed laser printer, capable of printing a minimum of 10 pages per minute
   - A high speed photocopier capable of copying a minimum 25 copies per minute
   - A fax machine capable of faxing a minimum of 6 pages per minute
   - 6 fully adjustable ergonomic office chairs
   - 2 telephone handsets
   - Telephone and data facilities
6. **Dinner venue for 650–700 persons**
   A bidding council must be able to provide a suitable venue to host the main conference dinner a maximum of 15 minutes drive from the main conference venue.
7. **Childcare facilities**
   Childcare facilities must be made available during conference sessions and functions (including nightly dinner functions).
8. **Motor vehicles and drivers**
   A bidding council must be in a position to supply two motor vehicles (of minimum Holden Berlina standard) and two drivers for Association use for the duration of the conference. The vehicles and drivers must be available or on call from 8.00 am until 11.00 pm each day.
9. **Ecological Sustainable Development Principles and the conference**
   The 1999 Local Government Association Conference resolved that '… councils hosting future LGA Conferences to show a commitment to ESD principles by ensuring the planning and running of conferences consider:
   (i) energy efficiency
   (ii) water conservation
   (iii) waste minimisation
   (iv) pollution control
   That delegates, as part of the Conference background papers, be provided with a statement of where those principles impacted upon that Conference.' This statement is on our website under events. The Association reserves the right to amend and instruct on the sustainability practices for the conference.

Source: Local Government Association of New South Wales 2009.

Establishment of an organisational structure

Once a decision is made to conduct an event, an organisational structure will need to be established through which the event can be delivered. Such structures serve to assign people to tasks, and connect the activities of different people and functions so that an event can be conducted in an efficient and effective way. They also distribute decision-making power, and define lines of communication and reporting (Hill et al. 2007).

There are a number of organisational structures through which events are commonly conducted, with the decision as to which structure is best depending on the characteristics of the event itself.

Functional structures

As the name suggests, a functional structure is based upon the main tasks or functions that an organisation needs to perform in order to fulfil its mission. Such tasks commonly emerge from the work breakdown structure process discussed in chapter 6, and will vary from event to event. The Port Fairy Folk Festival (Victoria), for example, has identified some 15 key task areas central to its successful conduct, specifically: sponsorship, finance, security, stalls and markets, concessions, catering, community liaison, artist accommodation, council liaison, ticketing, bars, construction, volunteers, programming and administration. The committee responsible for this event has allocated individuals from within its own ranks to each of these functions (Port Fairy Folk Festival 2010). By way of contrast, and to highlight the fact that each event will customise its functional breakdown of tasks to meet its own specific needs, the Roskilde Festival (a large Danish music festival) has broken its organisational structure into eight functional areas, each with its two manager(s) (see figure 4.4). Note that there are eight functional areas with two managers but the festival's structure is an unusual one in that under 'Management' there are five other functional areas with one manager; namely administration, production, development (sponsorship), music and market research.

The more complex an event the greater the number of tasks there will be that will need to be embraced within a function-based organisational structure. By way of example, figure 4.5 shows the complex organisational structure used to deliver the 2006 Melbourne Commonwealth Games.

This structure also serves to highlight the diversity of tasks associated with large-scale events. In this instance, tasks extend from those of a commercial nature, to construction, risk management, overall project management, venue, financial, sport and human resource management, ceremonies and broadcasting.

A number of benefits can be attributed to the use of a function-based organisational structure within an event context. Central among these is that people are able to specialise, and so make use of their pre-existing expertise in a specific area and/or further develop such expertise. This is particularly the case when individuals are placed into functional teams where they can learn from others (Lynch 2006).

Additionally, when task areas are identified and responsibility given to groups/individuals to carry them out, consideration can be given to the amount of work involved within each task such that it can be realistically performed within the time available. The Philadelphia Folk Festival, for example, uses an organisational structure comprising 30 task-based committees (Philadelphia Folksong Society 2006). The use of such a large number of committees, it can reasonably be assumed, is in acknowledgement of the event being entirely run by time-constrained volunteers. By breaking down an event into task areas, functional structures also reduce the possibility of inefficiencies resulting from overlapping areas of responsibility.

Finally, as events tend to build their organisational structures quickly, and to tear them down even faster, this structure offers event organisations the ability to quickly add, subtract or expand the number of functional areas based on their needs. This capacity is particularly useful when it is necessary to functionally 'evolve' event organisational structures as an event moves from its planning phase through to its delivery (see the case study on the 2003 Rugby World Cup on pages 115–123).

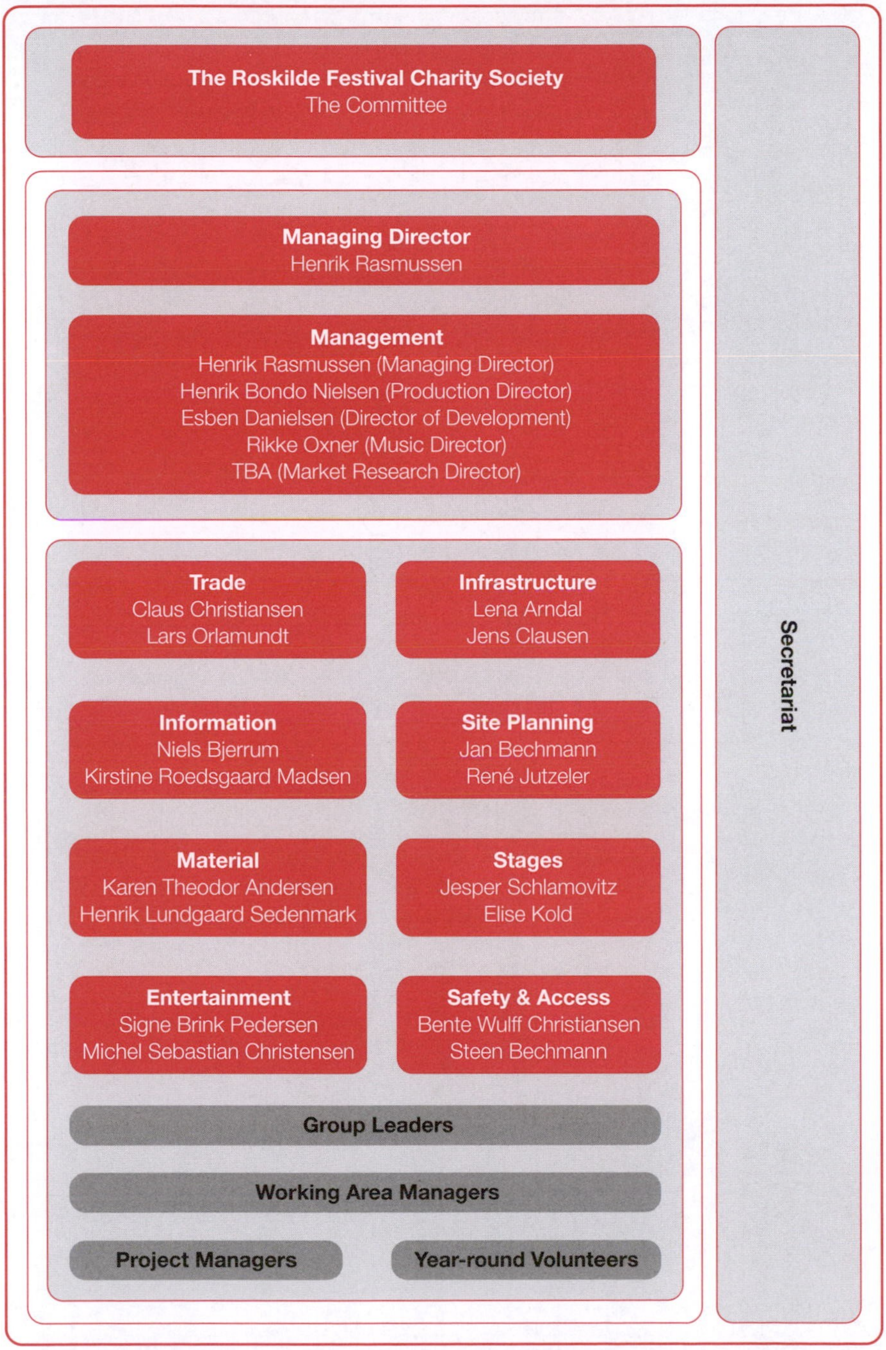

The Roskilde Festival Charity Society
The Committee

Managing Director
Henrik Rasmussen

Management
Henrik Rasmussen (Managing Director)
Henrik Bondo Nielsen (Production Director)
Esben Danielsen (Director of Development)
Rikke Oxner (Music Director)
TBA (Market Research Director)

Trade
Claus Christiansen
Lars Orlamundt

Infrastructure
Lena Arndal
Jens Clausen

Information
Niels Bjerrum
Kirstine Roedsgaard Madsen

Site Planning
Jan Bechmann
René Jutzeler

Material
Karen Theodor Andersen
Henrik Lundgaard Sedenmark

Stages
Jesper Schlamovitz
Elise Kold

Entertainment
Signe Brink Pedersen
Michel Sebastian Christensen

Safety & Access
Bente Wulff Christiansen
Steen Bechmann

Group Leaders

Working Area Managers

Project Managers

Year-round Volunteers

Secretariat

FIGURE 4.4 The functional organisational structure of the Roskilde Festival

Source: Roskilde Festival 2010.

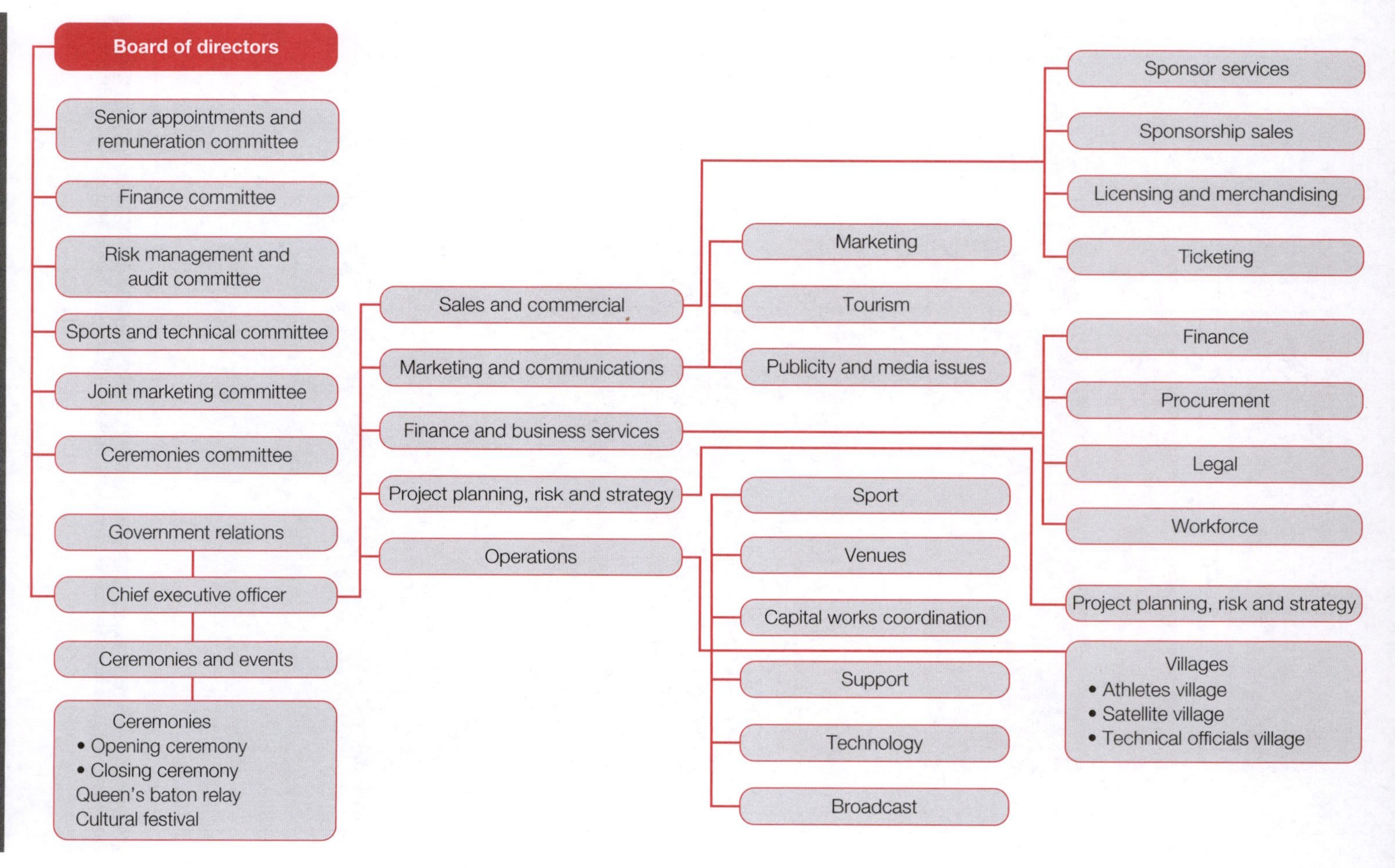

FIGURE 4.5 2006 Commonwealth Games organisational structure

Source: Office of Commonwealth Games Coordination 2006.

While a widely used approach to structuring the organisation of an event, there are nonetheless potential limitations to this method. These include problems of coordination due partly to a lack of understanding by staff in individual functional areas of the responsibilities of people in other task areas, and the possibility of conflict between functional areas as each seeks to protect what it considers its interests (Hill et al. 2007). Various techniques can be identified that go some way to preventing these problems. These comprise employing multi-skilling strategies that require the rotation of staff through different functional areas, regular meetings between the managers/chairs of all functional areas, general staff meetings, and communications (such as newsletters) that aim to keep those engaged on the event aware of matters associated with its current status (for example, budgetary situations or the passing of milestones).

event profile

THE MONTANA WORLD OF WEARABLEART EVENT

Background

The WOW (World of WearableArt) event began as a small community arts event in the town of Nelson, New Zealand, in 1987. The event is based around designers and artists who produce pieces that are part costume, part artwork, or wearable art. The pieces compete for prizes in a number of categories and are then showcased in a two-hour performance that combines fashion, theatre, music, dance, comedy and more.

From modest beginnings, the event has grown into one of New Zealand's major cultural attractions with international entrants from Australia, Hong Kong, United Arab Emirates, USA, India, Japan, Canada, Netherlands, Israel, Germany, Thailand and Fiji. The event runs over ten nights in the TSB Bank Arena in Wellington, New Zealand's cultural capital, and features strong production values and spectacular staging, set design, lighting, dance, soundscapes, and audio-visual elements.

Planning the timeline

November

- Floor plan for the next show established
- Design brief given to set, stage, lighting and sound designers

December

- Base script for the show developed

February

- Tickets go on sale
- Three to four sections of the themed sections of the show are creatively developed (these sections change each year)
- Work on the design of technical production for the event begins
- Competition entries open

March

- Final script completed

April

- Show tickets are usually sold out

May

- Entries close

June

- The competition entry garments arrive

July

- Entries are judged for the various competition award categories

August

- Artistic director matches each entry with performers and the script, music and basic staging already developed
- Week 2 — Children's and models' rehearsals underway

September

- Week 1 — Dancers' rehearsals underway
- Week 2 — Judging completed

October

- Production weeks
- Performances commence

Production weeks

- Production work is undertaken over 11 days prior to the first performance. The initial bump-in includes all rigging of sound, lighting, staging and audio-visual elements as well as decoration and branding of the venue, installation of seating, and the establishment of catering and merchandise outlets within the venue.
- In the final production week the backstage areas are set up and finalised and the lighting is focused and plotted with the artistic director. Sound is balanced for the venue and plotted, along with any set design and staging elements.
- Technical rehearsals commence four days out from the first performance, with a full dress rehearsal occurring one day out.

Performance weeks

- On the first day of the 11-day season (ten paid performances and one paid preview performance), any technical work required is undertaken from 0900 followed by an Awards Ceremony rehearsal (1200), a short break and then other rehearsals as required (1500). The cast call is at 1800 and doors open at 1830. The show call is 1930 and the event commences at 2000.
- Pre-show entertainment outside and inside the venue, and various merchandise and catering outlets, commences upon the doors opening. Sponsors, media and VIPs are met and hosted at various entertainments and functions within the venue until the show commences.
- Subsequent performances have rehearsals and technical work as required and follow the same cast call and show times.

Shutdown

- The bumpout commences after the final performance on the Sunday night and continues until 2300 on the Monday.
- Data about the event, including attendance numbers, is captured through the box office and audience surveys, and analysed and evaluated to contribute to the planning of the next year's event.

Outcomes

WOW continually revisits its objectives and analyses its situational environment. It has a functional organisational structure, employs a growth strategy and, as a consequence, has proven to be a particularly successful event. WOW attracts close to 40 000 attendees to the event with audiences spending more than NZ$15 million as a result of the event.

Gabrielle Hervey, Managing Director, WOW® Ltd. www.worldofwearableart.com.

Program-based matrix structures

Matrix structures group activities by function as well as by project (Hill et al. 2007). What this means is that people working within such a structure commonly have two bosses: a functional boss who is responsible for the particular function to which they have been assigned; and a project boss who is responsible for the specific project on which they are working. In an event context, these structures can be seen in operation in large scale multi-venue events, such as an Olympic Games. Toohey and Halbwirth (2001) note that the organisational structure of the 2000 Sydney Olympic Games, for example, moved from a purely functional structure to that of a venue-based matrix structure as the event approached (see figure 4.6). The reason for this movement lay in the need to 'push' functional expertise (for example, security, ticketing), which had been developed centrally, out to venues where these tasks needed to be actually undertaken. Additionally, by acting in this way, decision-making bottlenecks and communication problems that might have occurred under a centralised functional structure were able to be largely avoided. While there is much to recommend this structure in large multi-venue events, if the event is to be presented as a unified whole, a high value must be placed on coordination across the various venues by senior management. Additionally, as staff located in venues effectively have two bosses, issues can arise around communication, reporting and lines of authority.

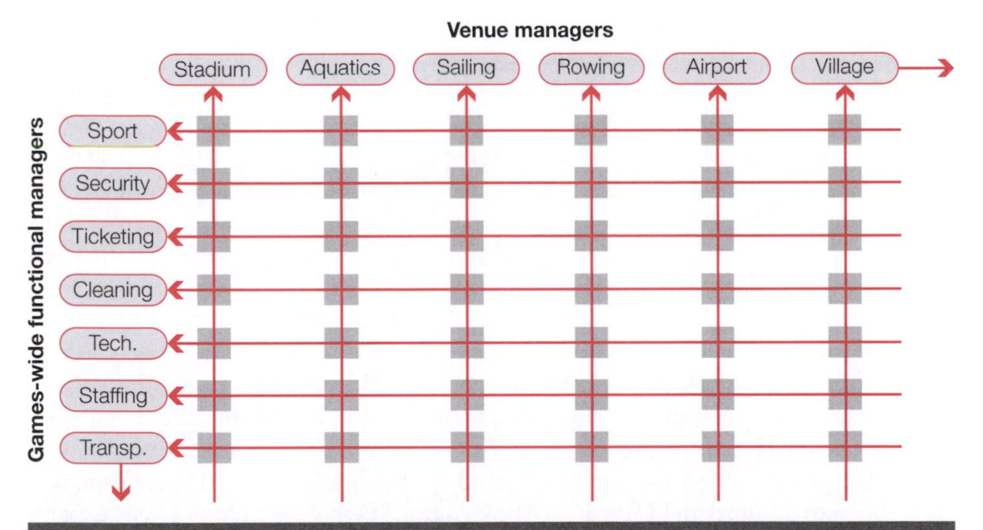

FIGURE 4.6 Sydney 2000 Olympic Games matrix organisational structure

Source: Sloman 2006.

Multi-organisational or network structures

Most specialist event management companies are relatively small in size (fewer than 20 people), yet many conduct quite large and complex events. This is possible because these organisations enlist the services of a variety of other firms (see figure 4.7). In effect, they create 'virtual' organisations that come together quickly and are disbanded shortly after an event is concluded. Central among the benefits of employing this structure is its ability to allow the event management firm to specialise in the 'management' function and so become increasingly capable in this area. This structure also avoids the need to maintain a large staff with multiple skills, which for periods between events would have little or nothing to do.

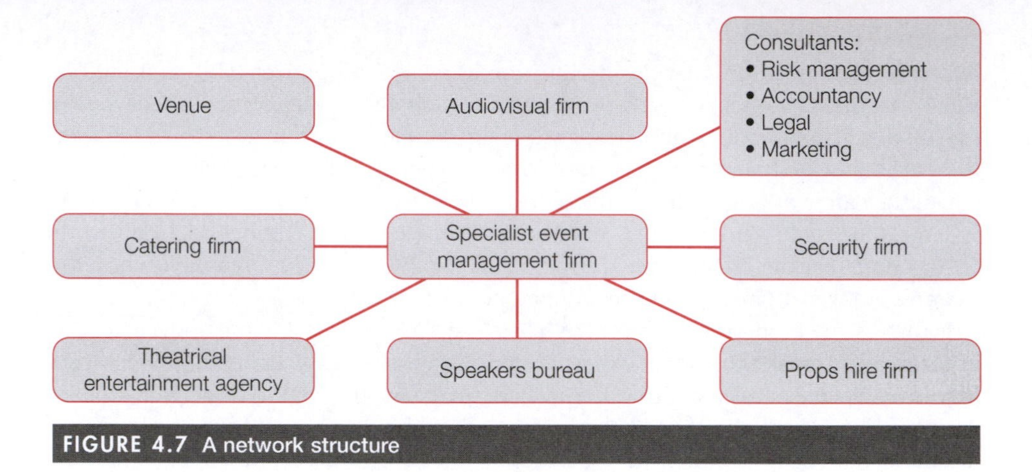

FIGURE 4.7 A network structure

Other advantages of the network structure include the ability to contract specialist businesses with current expertise and experience; greater accuracy in the event costing process as supplier expenses can be established via the contracting process; and quick decision making as the 'core' management group is made up of only a few people or one individual.

As with the other structures previously discussed, there are also possible disadvantages to be considered. These include concern over quality control and reliability that arise from the use of outside contractors, and the associated potential difficulties involved in developing an integrated event 'team' to deliver the event. Nevertheless, the concept of the network structure is supported by contemporary management thinking on downsizing, sticking to core activities and outsourcing, and can be very effective for certain kinds of events. Whatever the structure decided upon it must first meet the needs of the event, and enable the event to achieve its stated aims and objectives.

It should also be noted that often a single event may have a number of different organisational structures. For example, as large scale events move through their strategic planning process they will need to continuously adapt their organisational structure to the evolving needs of the event (see the Rugby World Cup case study at the conclusion of this chapter). This will mean that additional people with different types of skills/experience will need to be employed as the event moves ever closer to its final delivery date. The addition of these employees will expand the organisational structure, creating new lines of authority and communication. The structure will be at its most developed at the time of event delivery, shrinking to a handful of people charged with the responsibility of finalising various tasks (for example, preparation of the final event report) a few months after the event has concluded.

Strategic plan

Once established, an event organisation's first task is to engage in the formal strategic planning process.

The strategy process, as noted previously, is essentially about identifying the purpose or vision/mission an event organisation is seeking to fulfil or process through conducting a specific event, and creating plans and undertaking actions, to achieve that purpose or vision/mission (Lynch 2006, p. 5). It is a staged process involving an event organisation determining the current situation it faces (strategic awareness), the strategic options available to it (strategic choices) and the mechanisms for implementing, monitoring and evaluating whatever strategy(ies) it selects (strategic implementation) (Thompson 1997, p. 51). Additionally, in the case (particularly) of large-scale events where the creation of legacy outcomes (such as new infrastructure developments) are an aspect of an event's overall strategy, event organisations will need to consider how they will drive this aspect of the overall event program.

In this section each of the steps associated with strategic planning in an event organisational context are overviewed.

Purpose, vision and mission statements

At a minimum, a clear statement of purpose should underpin every event. This statement, in turn, will be conditioned by the needs of its various stakeholder groups. Such groups may include client organisations, the local community, government at various levels, potential attendees and participants, media partners, sponsors and volunteers.

In the case of events with relatively few stakeholders and/or those which are relatively straightforward in nature, a considered statement as to its purpose is all that is really required to provide adequate strategic direction. For example, Brain Awareness Week, an annual international event conducted by the Dana Alliance, a private philanthropic organisation that seeks to provide information about the personal and public benefits of brain research, has as its stated purpose:

> Brain Awareness Week is an international effort organized by the Dana Alliance for Brain Initiatives to advance public awareness about the progress and benefits of brain research (Dana 2006).

For events that are more complex in nature (such as large public events) and/or that involve a number of stakeholder groups, it can be beneficial to reflect more deeply on the matter of purpose. It is evident that many events are now doing this and, as a result, are creating vision and/or mission statements to guide their development and conduct.

A vision statement can be separate from an event's mission, or the two may be combined (Pearce and Robinson 2005). Vision statements describe what an event organisation is seeking to achieve in the longer term through the conduct of an event (Viljoen and Dann 2000 p. 31). They are often brief, precise and motivational in nature, as can be seen from the following examples:

- San Jose Jewish Film Festival — 'Expanding the world of Jewish culture through film' (San Jose Jewish Film Festival 2010)
- Fort Armstrong Folk Festival — 'A fine arts and crafts festival held along the tree lined banks of the beautiful Allegheny River that uplifts the community's spirit and pays tribute to Armstrong County's heritage' (Fort Armstrong Folk Festival 2010)
- Oregon Shakespeare Festival — 'Inspired by Shakespeare's work and the cultural richness of the United States, we reveal our collective humanity through illuminating interpretations of new and classic plays, deepened by the kaleidoscope of rotating repertory' (Oregon Shakespeare Festival 2010).

Some events use more expansive vision statements, which are really a combination of the event organisation's vision, mission and, sometimes, goals. The Wolfe Island Scene of the Crime Festival is one such example.

Its vision is stated as:

> The Wolfe Island Scene of the Crime Festival is committed to:
> - raising awareness of Wolfe Island's important cultural and historical legacy as the birthplace of Grant Allen, Canada's first crime writer
> - strengthening Wolfe Island's cultural life and encouraging a healthy arts community by embracing and celebrating the Island's unique literary heritage
> - increasing knowledge and fostering public appreciation of Canadian crime writing by providing a public forum for and interactive access with authors, aspiring writers, readers, and interested parties
> - benefiting the community of Wolfe Island by bringing visitors to the Island in a way that honours the Island's heritage, enhances its cultural, artistic, and economic life, while being sensitive to the environment
> - enhancing Wolfe Island's role and participation in the southeastern Ontario region's cultural landscape
> - developing and promoting initiatives to increase voluntarism in the Island's cultural sector (Wolfe Island Scene of the Crime Festival 2010).

While such combined statements are not uncommon, and while acknowledging that they do provide direction for an event, an argument can nonetheless be made that this approach is not as effective as dealing with vision, mission and goals separately.

It should be noted that vision statements do not necessarily need to be written down (although it is often useful to do so), providing they are shared and understood by those involved with an event. It would be fair to say, for example, that while no formal vision statement existed at the time the Sydney Gay and Lesbian Mardi Gras began, those involved with it understood clearly that its ultimate intent was about achieving equality and social acceptance.

A mission statement describes in the broadest terms the task that the event organisation has set for itself. If the event has also established a vision statement, then the mission needs to be viewed in terms of fulfilling this vision. Such statements, at their most advanced, seek to define an event's purpose; identify its major beneficiaries and customer groups; indicate the broad nature/characteristics of the event; and state the overall operating philosophy, or values, of the organisation conducting it (for example, to conform to best business practice; to operate within a context of equal opportunity; to adopt environmentally sustainable practices). For an example of such values, see figure 4.8.

FIGURE 4.8 Oregon Shakespeare Festival values

Excellence

We believe in constantly seeking to present work of the highest quality, expecting excellence from all company members.

Inclusion

We believe the inclusion of a diversity of people, ideas and cultures enriches both our insights into the work we present on stage and our relationships with each other.

Learning

We believe in offering company members, audiences, teachers and students the richest possible learning experiences.

Financial health

We believe in continuing our long history of financial stability, making wise and efficient use of all the resources entrusted to us.

FIGURE 4.8 *(continued)*

Heritage

We believe that the Festival's history of almost seventy-five years gives us a heritage of thoughtful change and evolution to guide us as we face the future.

Environmental responsibility

We believe in making responsible choices that support a sustainable future for our planet.

Company

We believe in sustaining a safe and supportive workplace where we rely on our fellow company members to work together with trust, respect and compassion. We believe that the collaborative process is intrinsic to theatre and is the bedrock of our working relationships; we are committed to the Festival's Communication Credo. We encourage and support a balance between our lives inside and outside the Festival.

Source: Oregon Shakespeare Festival 2010.

Once established, a mission statement acts as the basis upon which goals and objectives can be set and strategies established. It also serves to provide a shorthand means of conveying to staff (either paid or voluntary) an understanding of the event and what it is trying to achieve.

Several event mission statements that, to varying degrees, fulfil the previously stated criteria are provided in table 4.1.

TABLE 4.1 Sample event mission statements

Event	Mission statement
Services for Australian Rural and Remote Allied Health (SARRAH), Conference, 2006	The conference provided a forum for the rural and remote allied health workforce to: • demonstrate allied health leadership for the future delivery of health services to meet the needs of an ageing population • drive the development and look of the future health professional workforce • have input and influence from the 'grass roots' into national and state health policy and service delivery • promote continuing education and professional development activities • promote good health and wellbeing through the delivery of allied health services to and by Indigenous and non-Indigenous people in rural communities.
Greek Orthodox Folk Dance Festival, San Francisco	The Greek Orthodox Folk Dance and Choral Festival Ministry is dedicated, through Orthodox Christian Fellowship and committed leadership, to promoting, encouraging and perpetuating Greek heritage and culture among individuals, families and communities expressed in folk dance, folk art, music and language.
National Folk Festival, Canberra	To preserve, nurture and promote folk culture as an essential element in Australian life.

(continued)

TABLE 4.1 *(continued)*

Event	Mission statement
Caribbean Days Festival, North Vancouver	The TTCS of BC is an organisation dedicated to providing cross cultural understanding, acceptance and interaction between peoples of diverse nationalities and heritage through their art, their music and their respective talents and abilities. Three of the main purposes of the Society as set out in our Constitution are: • to foster among members of the community mutual understanding, appreciation and awareness of the multicultural nature of Trinidad & Tobago. • to generate interest and participation in activities that would provide for better cooperation and understanding among members of the community, nationals of Trinidad & Tobago, and the wider Canadian community, and with other organizations with similar aims and objectives. • to promote amicable relations between the people and Government of Trinidad & Tobago and the people of Canada, especially those resident in British Columbia.
Edinburgh Festival	To be the most exciting, innovative and accessible festival of the performing arts in the world, and thus promote the cultural, educational and economic well-being of the people of Edinburgh and Scotland. By: • presenting arts of the highest possible international standard to the widest possible audience • reflecting international culture to audiences from Scotland, the rest of the UK and the world • offering an international showcase for Scottish culture • presenting events which cannot easily be achieved by any other UK arts organisation through innovative programming and a commitment to new work • actively ensuring equal opportunities for all sections of the Scottish and wider public to experience and enjoy the Festival • encouraging public participation in the arts throughout the year by collaborating with other arts and festival organisations. • ensuring the Festival has adequate core funding to fulfil its mission and address its sustainability

Source: National Rural Health Alliance, www.ruralhealth.org.au; Greek Orthodox Folk Dance and Choral Festival, www.yourfdf.org; National Folk Festival, www.folkfestival.asn.au; Caribbean Days Festival, www.caribbeandays.ca; Edinburgh International Festival, www.eif.co.uk.

Goals and objectives

Once an event's mission has been decided, the event organisation needs then to establish its goals and objectives. It should be noted that while the terms 'goals' and 'objectives' are often used interchangeably, they are really distinct concepts. Goals are broad statements that seek to provide direction to those engaged in the organisation of the event, as can be seen in table 4.2. They are particularly useful when events are complex in nature and have a number of stakeholders. In such instances, they serve a useful role in expanding on an event's mission statement in order to provide more detailed direction to those involved in its creation and delivery.

TABLE 4.2 Stated goals for selected events

Event	Goals
Northern Lights Festival Boreal (NLFB), Sudbury, Ontario	• NLFB is committed to operating in a professional, fiscally responsible manner with the goal of financial self-sufficiency. • NLFB is committed to reflecting the cultural diversity of Northern Ontario in its operations and programming. • NLFB is committed to treating all performers and artists and their work professionally, with dignity, respect and fairness. • NLFB is committed to developing, promoting and advocating for local artists and performers. • NLFB is committed to developing, supporting and honouring the work of its volunteers, Board and staff. • NLFB is committed to the accountability of the Board of Directors. • NLFB is committed to developing, supporting and acknowledging the interests of its audiences. • NLFB is committed to cultivating relationships with the community, other arts and cultural organisations, umbrella groups, sponsors and other community groups. • To be an internationally acclaimed open access event for artists of all art forms.
Adelaide Fringe	This will be achieved through encouraging participation by artists, presenters and audiences and nurturing and stimulating innovative and leading edge art forms. We shall aim to increase patronage to the event by local, interstate and international audiences and continue to stimulate growth in economic and social well being and be a major contribution to the cultural life of South Australia.

Source: Northern Lights Festival Boreal, www.nlfbsudbury.com; Adelaide Fringe, www.adelaidefringe.com.au.

Objectives are used to quantify progress towards an event's goals and as such set performance benchmarks, so allowing event organisations to assess what aspects of their planning have succeeded or failed. Useful criteria that can be applied to the establishment of objectives are summed up by the acronym SMART, which refers to the fact that objectives should be:

- *specific* — focused on achieving an event goal (or, if no goals have been developed, its purpose)
- *measurable* — expressed in a way that is quantifiable (when at all possible)
- *agreeable* — agreed on by those responsible for achieving them
- *realistic* — in terms of the event organisation having the human, financial and physical resources to achieve them
- *time specific* — to be achieved by a particular time (ChangingMinds.org 2006).

Each event will obviously vary in terms of the objectives it establishes. However, common areas, along with selected specific examples, where an event organisation might set objectives include the following.

- *Economic*
  - percentage return on monies invested or overall gross/net profit sought
  - dollar value of sponsorship attracted
  - percentage of income to be raised from fundraising activities
  - percentage increase in market share (if the event is competing directly with other similar events).
- *Attendance/participation*
  - total attendance/attendance by specific groups (for example, people from outside the area, individuals from within specific age groups)

  - size of event in terms of stallholders/exhibitors/performers/attendees/registrants
  - number of local versus international artists/speakers in an event's program
  - percentage of an area's cultural groups represented in a program
  - number of community groups involved with the event.
- *Quality*
  - level of attendee/exhibitor/sponsor/volunteer satisfaction (as a percentage)
  - number of complaints from attendees/exhibitors/volunteers
  - number of injuries.
- *Awareness/knowledge/attitudes*
  - percentage of attendees or others that have changed levels of awareness/knowledge as a result of the event
  - percentage of attendees or others who have altered their attitudes as a result of attending the event.
- *Human resources*
  - percentage of staff/volunteer turnover during event operational cycle
  - percentage of volunteers retained from previous year.

Situation analysis

Before moving to establish specific strategies for an event, its organisers are well advised to undertake an assessment of its internal environment (for example, financial situation, staff expertise, quality/number of venues, market perception of event) and external environment (for example, the number/type of competing events, legislative changes, community attitude to event or events in general, impact of climate change). One common way of undertaking this task is by employing a strengths, weaknesses, opportunities and threats (SWOT) analysis. Such an analysis will likely involve referring to a range of existing information sources, including data collected previously by the event, census data and general reports/studies on relevant matters such as trends in leisure behaviour. On occasions it may be necessary to commission studies in order to fill information gaps, or to update an event organisation on particular matters. A deeper understanding of the needs, wants, motives and perceptions of current or potential customer groups, for example, may be deemed necessary before dramatically altering an event's program in an effort to increase attendance. For a more detailed discussion of this aspect of strategic planning, see chapter 9.

Identification of strategy options

The environmental scanning process gathers crucial information that can be used by an event organisation to achieve its vision/mission or purpose. Strategies must use strengths, minimise weaknesses, avoid threats and take advantage of opportunities that have been identified. A SWOT analysis is a wasted effort if the material gathered by this analytic process is not used in strategy formulation.

Before examining several generic business strategies that might be adopted by an event organisation, it needs to be noted that some events, specifically those of a public nature, have goals that do not link strongly to concerns such as market share, competitiveness and profit. Goals, for events of this nature, may be set in any number of areas, such as community building, environmental enhancement and community awareness raising around specific issues. Because of the wide range of potential goals public events might pursue, it is difficult to comment specifically on their strategic choices. Nonetheless, whatever choices they do make must, as with other events, progress their vision and associated mission.

Growth strategy

Many event organisations have a fixation on event size and, as such, seek to make their events bigger than previous ones or larger than similar events. Bigger is often thought to be better, particularly by ambitious event managers. Growth can be expressed as more revenue, more event components, more participants or delegates, or a bigger market share. It is worth pointing out that bigger is not necessarily better, as some event managers have discovered. An example of this is the Sydney Festival (a cultural festival that takes place each year in Sydney in January). It adopted a growth strategy by absorbing other events taking place in Sydney in January and describing them as 'umbrella' events. Some critics observed that by doing this the festival lost its focus. A subsequent festival director responded by concentrating the festival around Sydney Harbour foreshore areas and decreasing the number of event components, but increasing their quality.

It is important to recognise that an event does not necessarily have to grow in size for its participants to feel that it is better than its predecessors — this can be achieved by dedicating attention to quality activities, careful positioning and improved planning. However, a growth strategy may be appropriate if historical data suggest there is a growing demand for the type of event planned, or a financial imperative necessitates increasing revenue. The annual Woodford Folk Festival in Queensland, for example, expanded the focus of its program by including contemporary rock acts in an attempt to appeal to a market segment with a strong propensity to attend music events. Increased revenue gained in this way was directed at repaying the festival's debt.

Consolidation or stability strategy

In certain circumstances it may be appropriate to adopt a consolidation strategy — that is, maintaining attendance at a given level. Strong demand for tickets to the Port Fairy Folk Festival, an annual event in Victoria, for example, has allowed this event to sell tickets well in advance, cap attendance numbers and further enhance the quality of its program. By capping ticket sales in a climate of high demand, this event has also created a situation in which it has greater pricing freedom.

Retrenchment strategy

An event's situational analysis may suggest that an appropriate strategy is to reduce the scale of an event, but add value to its existing components. This strategy can be applicable when the operating environment of an event changes. Retrenchment can seem a defeatist or negative strategy, particularly to long-standing members of an event committee, but it can be a necessary response to an unfavourable economic environment or major change in the sociocultural environment. The management of a community festival, for example, may decide to delete those festival elements that were poorly patronised and focus only on those that have proven to be popular with its target market. Likewise, an exhibition company, which had previously conducted a conference in association with one of its major exhibitions, may cease to do so due to falling registrations. Resources freed in this way could then be used to add value to its exhibition by, for example, offering a free seminar series and introducing a limited entertainment program.

Combination strategy

As the name suggests, a combination strategy includes elements from more than one of these generic strategies. An event manager could, for example, decide to cut back or even delete some aspects of an event that no longer appeal to their event target market(s), while concurrently growing other aspects.

It should be noted that various marketing strategies (discussed in chapter 9), are integral to the pursuit of these broad strategies.

Strategy evaluation and selection

In order to determine which strategic option, or options, is likely to be most successful in progressing an event organisation's vision/mission, some form of analysis is necessary. In this regard, Lynch (2006), while acknowledging that each organisation will approach this task in their own way, identifies six general criteria that can be used for this purpose:

1. *Consistency with mission and objectives*. If a strategic option does not meet an organisation's mission and objectives there is a strong case for dismissing it.
2. *Suitability*. A strategy, when viewed within the context of the environment in which an organisation is operating and its available resources, needs to be viewed as appropriate.
3. *Validity*. The assumptions (for example, likely future demand for an event) upon which a strategy is based need to be well supported by appropriate research.
4. *Feasibility of options*. A proposed strategy must be able to be carried out. Several areas where possible constraints might arise need to be taken into account.
   (a) *Organisational culture, skills and resources*. Will an event organisation have the financial capacity or expertise necessary to pursue a particular strategy?
   (b) *Constraints external to an organisation*. Will an event's customer base be accepting of a particular strategy? Will competing events adapt quickly and restrict the ability of an event organisation to pursue a particular strategy? Will government or other regulatory bodies allow the strategy to be progressed?
   (c) *Lack of commitment from management and employees*. While more a potential issue with large-scale events, it is nonetheless the case that there must be an acceptance of whatever strategy is selected by staff if it is to have a reasonable chance of success.
5. *Business risk*. Strategic options bring with them various levels of risk. Such risks need to be identified and assessed in terms of how acceptable they are to an organisation. For example, an exhibition company that is thinking of doubling the size of one of its major exhibitions would need to establish what potential impact such a growth strategy would have on its cash flow and borrowing requirements. As part of this analysis it is likely it would also work through various scenarios around different cost structures, levels of demand, and exhibitor and entry fees.
6. *Attractiveness to stakeholders*. Whatever strategy is chosen needs to have some appeal to an event organisation's major stakeholders. This may be difficult to achieve at times. For example, the organisers of a major city-based festival may wish to pursue a retrenchment strategy due to overcrowding and associated traffic congestion that they view as compromising the experience of attendees, as well as creating problems for residents around the event site. Major sponsors, on the other hand, may be against such a strategy as it might reduce the number of people exposed to their promotional efforts.

Operational planning

Once a strategy(ies) has been agreed upon, the event organisation needs to develop a series of operational plans in support of it. The application of project management practices and techniques (see chapter 6) is particularly useful at this point in the strategic planning process.

Operational plans will be needed for all areas central to the achievement of an event's objectives and the implementation of its strategy. Areas for operational planning will vary, therefore, across events. It would be common, however, for plans to be developed in areas such as finance, marketing, administration, staging, research and evaluation, security and risk management, sponsorship, environmental management, programming, transportation, merchandising and staffing (paid and volunteer).

Each area for which an operational plan is developed will require a set of objectives that are linked to the achievement of the overall event organisation's strategy; action plans and schedules; monitoring and control systems, including a budget; and an allocation of resources (financial, human and supporting equipment/services).

Given that many festivals, exhibitions and events are not one-off, but occur at regular intervals — yearly, biennially or, in the case of some major sporting events, every four years — standing plans can be used in a number of operational areas. Standing plans are made up of policies, rules and standard procedures and serve to reduce decision-making time by ensuring similar situations are handled in a predetermined and consistent way.

Policies can be thought of as guidelines for decision making. An event may, for example, have a policy of only engaging caterers that meet particular criteria. These criteria may be based on licensing and insurance. Policies in turn are implemented by following established detailed instructions known as procedures. In the case of the previous example, procedures may require the person responsible for hiring caterers to inspect their licence and insurance certificates, check that they are current, and obtain copies for the event's records. Rules are statements governing conduct or action in a particular situation. An event may establish rules, for example, regarding what caterers can and cannot do with the waste they generate on site, or on what they can or cannot sell.

In some instances, particularly in the context of large-scale sporting events, the implementation phase may also involve the conduct of test events as a way of identifying any shortcomings in event delivery systems. Test events also provide a 'real world' training opportunity for staff, and assist in the development of greater coordination between the various 'teams' involved in event delivery.

Control systems

Once operational plans are implemented, mechanisms are required to ensure that actions conform to plans, and that adjustments are made for changing circumstances. These mechanisms take the form of systems that allow performance to constantly be compared to operational objectives. Performance benchmarks and milestones that indicate progress towards these objectives are particularly useful in this regard. Meetings and reports are generally central to the control process, as are budgets. Budgets allow actual costs and expenditure to be compared with those projected for the various operational areas. A detailed discussion of the budgeting processes appears in chapter 7.

Event evaluation, shutdown and reporting

For many events, evaluation remains a neglected aspect of their strategic event planning; yet, it is only through evaluation that event organisations can determine how successful or otherwise their efforts have been in achieving whatever goals and/or objectives they have set. In figure 4.9, an example is given of how one event (the National Folk Festival, Canberra) has used evaluation practices to determine how successful it has been in achieving its stated goals.

As a result of the evaluation process, information is captured and reports prepared for major event stakeholders such as granting agencies and sponsors. Additionally, problems and shortcomings in current event planning and delivery processes are identified and recommendations made for change. A complex area of the strategic event management process, event evaluation, is explored further in chapter 16.

FIGURE 4.9 Evaluation of progress towards selected National Folk Festival (Canberra) goals

Goal 1

To be accepted as the national folk event with strong attendance from around the country. In 1998, 69 per cent of patrons were visitors from interstate or overseas. Overall interstate and overseas visitation has increased steadily each year.

Goal 2

To achieve a high level of self-sufficiency. In 1998, 77 per cent of income was Festival generated, from ticket sales, camping fees, stall fees, bar sales, shop sales and program sales.

Goal 3

To achieve 30 per cent growth in attendance per annum (1993–97). An average growth of 36.5 per cent p.a. was achieved: from 8000 (1992) to 38 000 (1997). Targets for growth in attendance have since been revised to 20 per cent per annum. Growth in attendance was 21 per cent in 1997 and 11 per cent in 1998.

Goal 4

To develop an established loyal base of support. In 1998, 56 per cent of visitors had attended the Festival the previous year; 73 per cent said they would come the following year and 25 per cent said they might do so.

Goal 5

To develop healthy participation and attendance by young people, thereby stimulating the creation of a new generation of people involved in folk culture. In 1998 the proportion of visitors less than 30 years old was 35 per cent and less than 20 years old was 23 per cent.

Goal 6

To attract a strong sponsorship base for the event. In 1998 the Festival was sponsored by the Canberra Tourism and Events Corporation; Construction, Forestry, Mining and Energy Union; Guinness Australia; Prime Television; Radio 2CC and Ridges Canberra.

Goal 7

To develop a strong sense of shared ownership in the event. This has been achieved in two main ways: through the strength of the volunteer team, which has grown from 200 (1993) to 700 (1998), and through the Featured State strategy.

Goal 8

To develop a strong volunteer team. The volunteer team in 1998 numbered 700, with 400 of these each working a rostered 16 hours (or more) for the Festival. A strong team of volunteers staffed the office throughout the year. The volunteer survey carried out in 1997 revealed that the Festival retained 50 per cent of volunteers from previous years. Of those who had previously participated, 77 per cent had volunteered in 1996. Volunteers were either very satisfied or satisfied (96 per cent) with their volunteering experience; 92 per cent said they would like to volunteer in 1998. The Festival has a strong team of 30–40 volunteer co-ordinators who manage volunteers in different areas of the event, such as bar, child-care, garbage, stage management and ticket office.

Goal 9

To incorporate a strong educational element to the Festival. The Easter School was established in 1996 with an attendance of about 120. The 1998 Festival program included 126 workshops teaching dancing, singing and instrument playing.

FIGURE 4.9 *(continued)*

Goal 10

To keep the Festival accessible by keeping ticket prices down. Ticket prices in 1998 were:

Adult Season Ticket $85

Adult Day Ticket (9 am to midnight) $25

These prices are generally below those of other major folk festivals in Australia and compare very well with theatre, cinema tickets or events such as the WOMAdelaide festival ($49 per day). The cost of a season ticket for a similar event in the United Kingdom would be in the order of A$250.

Goal 11

To pre-sell as many tickets as possible before the event to allow for the risk of bad weather and resultant possible low day attendance. In 1998, 52 per cent of ticket income was pre-sold.

Goal 12

To be a truly multicultural event by presenting a comprehensive view of folk culture including traditions, belief systems, folklore, crafts and food, in addition to the music, song, dance and spoken word of the many cultures that make up our population. The 1998 Festival program presented works from over 30 cultures. There were over 1000 performers in 255 acts with 740 hours of performance. These included: 142 concerts; 14 social dances and balls; 40 dance displays; 126 workshops in singing, playing instruments and dance; 59 children's activities; and numerous unprogrammed concerts, sessions and street shows. Some of the cultures represented were Aboriginal, African, Australian, Breton, Bulgarian, Canadian, Caribbean, Celtic, Central American, Chinese, Dutch, Ecuadorian, English, Finnish, German, Greek, Indian, Irish, Israeli, Italian, Macedonian, Middle Eastern, North American, Pacific Islander, Russian, Scottish, South American, Slovenian, Spanish, Tibetan, Torres Strait Islander and Welsh.

Goal 13

To establish the Festival as an environmentally responsible event. In 1998 the Festival extended its commitment to waste minimisation, asking all food-stall holders to minimise their use of plastics. All food is now served in paper containers or washable plates. Styrofoam cups have largely been eliminated by the provision of a Festival washing-up service. Stalls and venues have collection points for washable cups and plates. The Festival recycles all plastics, glass, paper, cardboard and aluminium cans throughout the site.

Goal 14

To encourage the recording and preservation of traditional folk arts and culture. The National Folk Festival works with the National Library of Australia to record much of the material presented at the Festival for archive purposes, to provide a permanent record and to help preserve our culture. In addition, the Festival assists collectors of folk heritage to prepare and present their work at the Festival.

Source: National Folk Festival, www.folkfestival.asn.au.

Once an event is concluded, a range of tasks remain that must be undertaken in order to complete the 'shutdown' phase. The previously cited reporting task is but one of these. To this task can be added a range of others, including returning the site/venue to its original condition; paying suppliers; selling off equipment; grant acquittal (if required); thanking suppliers, government agencies (such as the police), volunteers and other groups associated with event delivery; winding up, or in the case of recurring events, dramatically reducing in size, the event organisation itself; and managing the knowledge associated with the event. This last point is significant, particularly in the case of recurring events, as capturing the systems and processes used in planning and delivery, along with information flowing from the evaluation process, provides a sound base for an event's future conduct. Indeed, the owners of some large-scale events, such as the Olympic Games, have created specific bodies (Olympic Knowledge Services) for this purpose (International Olympic Committee 2002).

Legacy

For some events, particularly large-scale public events, the issue of legacy has become central to the decision to host or create them. Legacy outcomes can span a wide range of areas including infrastructure improvements, increases in tourism visitation, enhanced industry capacities and workforce skills, environmental improvement and improved economic conditions (see chapter 3).

In order to secure event legacies some writers (such as Kearney 2006) suggest that a separate legacy program be created as part of the overall strategic planning process, and that a senior level management position be built into the organisational structure of events with this specific responsibility. While few events have yet to act in this way, the issue of legacy is nonetheless a major consideration with many event organisations. The 2007 World Swimming Championships Corporation (WSCC), for example, identified sporting and community legacy as one of its six 'principles for success'. These principles in turn act to 'provide a framework for the planning and conduct of the Championships' (WSCC 2006).

STRATEGIC PLANNING FOR EXISTING EVENTS

In addition to events that are attracted through the bidding process and those that are created as 'clean sheet' exercises, some event organisations will be responsible for the conduct of recurring events such as annual festivals or conferences. In such situations, the event organisation concerned would begin with an appraisal of the current situation faced by the event, and then move on to review its organisational structure and previous strategic plan. This process is likely to result in minor changes or refinements in its structure, vision/mission statements, goals, objectives and/or strategies, as well as the development of revised operational plans in areas such as marketing, human resources and finance. On occasions, however, such reviews may result in major changes to an existing strategy. Indeed, event managers need to keep in mind, as Mintzberg, Quinn and Voyer (1995) point out, that the strategic planning process tends to encourage incremental change, when what may be needed is a complete rethink of the current strategy.

SUMMARY

The strategic planning process provides an event organisation with a systematic approach to the challenge of planning and delivering successful events. Its preliminary stages involve the decision to proceed or not to proceed with an event, with this choice being dependent upon the outcome of a feasibility analysis. If an event proceeds, an appropriate organisational structure is needed. The most common of such structures in an event context are function, network or matrix based. Once established, an event organisation following the strategic planning model proposed here would then progress to establish a strategic plan. This plan begins with the creation of a vision, mission or statement of purpose, and then proceeds through a cascading series of steps to event evaluation, shutdown and reporting. Flowing from the implementation of this plan, and depending on its mission or purpose, will potentially be a range of legacies.

QUESTIONS

1. Briefly discuss the value of setting vision/mission/purpose statements for events.
2. Choose a particular event type (for example, festivals), identify four events that have established mission statements and compare these to the criteria given in this chapter.
3. Conduct an interview with the manager of a particular event with a view to identifying the key external environmental factors that are impacting on their event.
4. When might an event employ a retrenchment strategy *or* a growth strategy? Can you identify any specific event where one of these strategies is in evidence?
5. Select a hallmark or mega-event and discuss the ways in which the event plans for legacy outcomes.
6. Select an event with a functional organisation structure and another with a network structure. Describe each of these structures and discuss why you believe each event chose the organisational structure it used.
7. Explain the differences between a strategic plan and an operational plan, and between a policy and a procedure.
8. What control systems can be established for an operational plan? What response should there be if the key objectives are not met?
9. Explain why stakeholders are significant from the perspective of establishing vision and mission statements.
10. Critically examine the strategic planning process of a particular event in the light of the process discussed in this chapter.

case study

OPERATIONAL PLANNING AND THE RUGBY WORLD CUP

Introduction

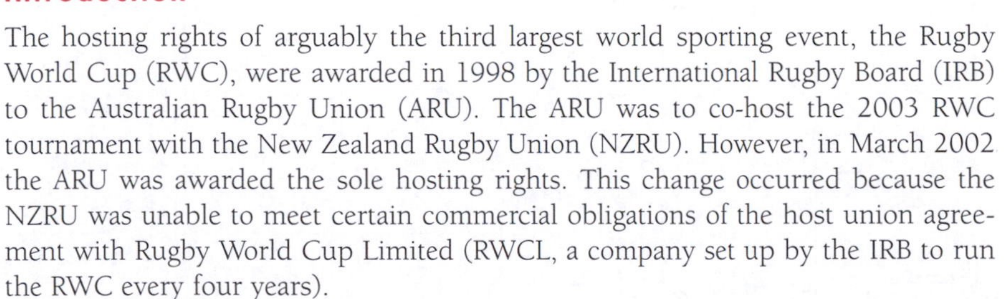

The hosting rights of arguably the third largest world sporting event, the Rugby World Cup (RWC), were awarded in 1998 by the International Rugby Board (IRB) to the Australian Rugby Union (ARU). The ARU was to co-host the 2003 RWC tournament with the New Zealand Rugby Union (NZRU). However, in March 2002 the ARU was awarded the sole hosting rights. This change occurred because the NZRU was unable to meet certain commercial obligations of the host union agreement with Rugby World Cup Limited (RWCL, a company set up by the IRB to run the RWC every four years).

The Rugby World Cup 2003 involved the planning and ultimate delivery of 48 matches across 11 venues, in six states and one territory in a six-week period. In undertaking this task the ARU began 'ramping up' its organisational capacity from January 2001, more than two and a half years prior to the event, which took place from 10 October to 22 November 2003.

Integral to the ramping-up process was the establishment of an RWC unit with responsibility for delivering the event. It is this unit, and, more specifically, the events and operations component of this unit, that is the subject of this case study.

The Rugby World Cup unit

The RWC unit was established in 2001. It reported through the General Manager 2003 RWC, who in turn reported to the ARU managing director and CEO (see figure 4.10). A tournament organisation committee was also established to

provide input into the operational planning aspects of the event. As the event approached, two additional decision-making bodies were created, a tournament commission and a tournament coordination committee. The function of the tournament commission was to meet as required to deal with major issues that arose in regard to the event, both operational and public affairs related. The tournament coordination committee met daily through the tournament and dealt with the day-to-day matters arising. If required, issues were passed by this body to the tournament commission for final decision making.

Within the RWC unit was located the events and operations department. This department had responsibility for designing and implementing a venue and precinct operational planning strategy designed to ensure the professional delivery of operations supporting the RWC 2003.

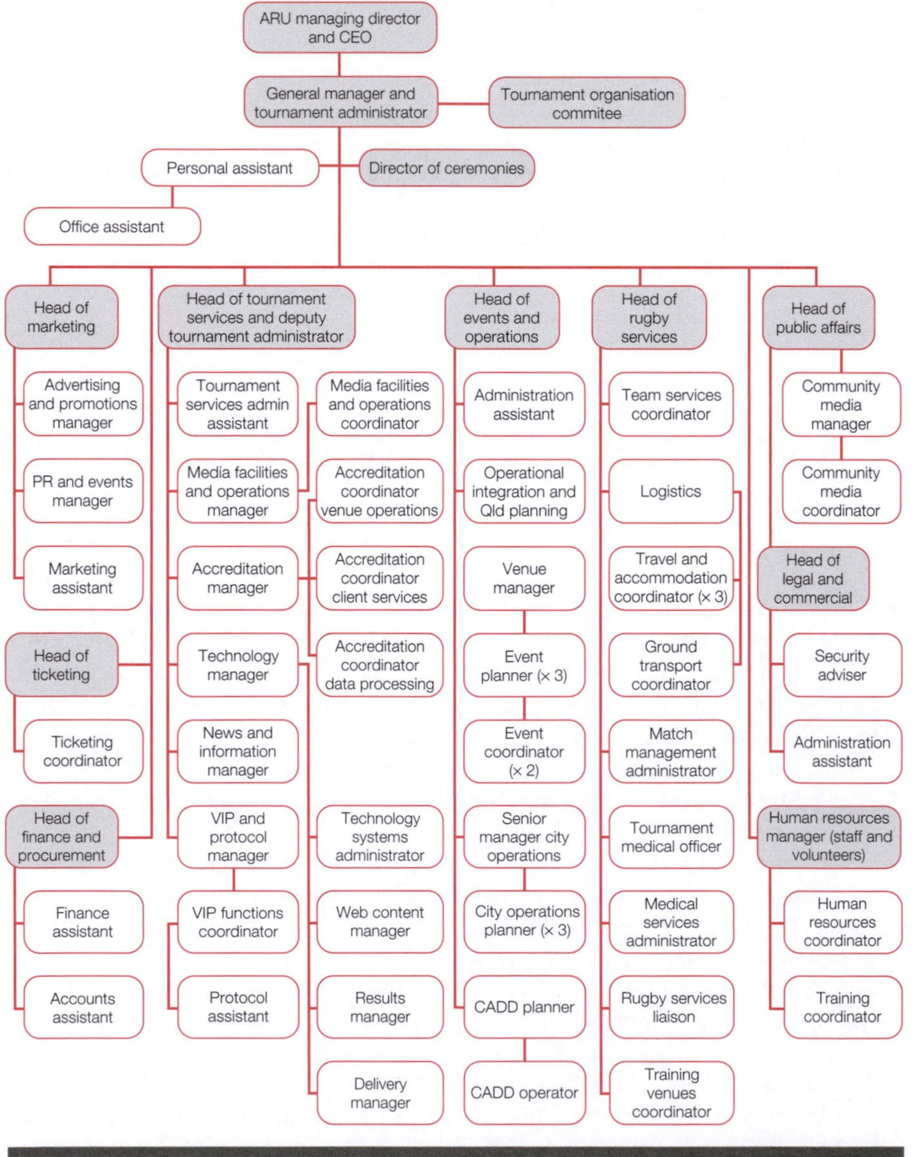

FIGURE 4.10 Rugby World Cup unit organisational structure

Tasks of the events and operations department

The events and operations department was charged with a range of tasks, specifically:

- coordination and integration of all operational planning and delivery by the various departments of the ARU and associated third-party service providers for operations delivered in tournament venues. This included developing planning mechanisms on a month-by-month basis that all departments were to follow to ensure necessary planning tasks were completed.
- procurement of match and training venues, city office spaces and the commercial rights to the 500-metre radius around each venue on favourable commercial terms
- scoping and delivery of match and training venue specific overlay, including the field of play (such as signage, seating and camera positions)
- development of a computer aided design and drafting (CADD) facility in-house for the preparation of detailed venue drawings and plans
- delivery of appropriate levels of venue services (for example, catering, cleaning and waste, security) as required under contractual arrangements with each venue
- ensuring all events and operations team members (paid, volunteer and contractor) were appropriately skilled, experienced and able to receive appropriate training to carry out their assigned roles efficiently and effectively
- ensuring the event teams were operationally ready to deliver the tournament. This included third party service providers who were part of the team.
- providing venue operational management in all tournament match venues
- providing the key liaison and coordination point for television and radio broadcast elements of the tournament
- management of the media operations and accreditation functions during tournament operations
- providing a key liaison and coordination point for commercial operations associated with tournament operations as they related to venues and precinct activities
  - acting as the primary operational contact for International Marketing Group (IMG, RWCL's commercial agent for the tournament)
  - coordinating commercial in-stadia activities such as pourage, hospitality requirements including space allocations, signage and imaging implementation
  - coordinating sponsor activities in match venues and precincts
- ensuring the overall budget for the events and operations department was appropriately managed and controlled
- facilitating reporting and issue resolution from tournament locations to World Cup headquarters during operations.

In addition to these largely venue and precinct related tasks, the events and operations department was also charged during the planning stage of the event with what was titled the City Operations Program. This program was moved to report to a different manager (head of tournament services) two months prior to commencement of the tournament. Broadly, the scope of this program included:

- facilitating the relationships between government agencies and the ARU with respect to the delivery of services by those agencies to the tournament
- establishment of key planning meeting frameworks/committees
- facilitating, where appropriate, the effective flow of information and communication between the ARU, state and local government agencies regarding the provision of government land and/or services to support the Rugby World Cup. This included the creation of key management planning forums incorporating major government service agencies.

- working with all stakeholders (such as marketing, sponsorship, RWCL commercial partners and the government) to develop a strategy and facilitate city festivities/activities
- facilitating and/or coordinating the implementation of local marketing, public affairs and promotional initiatives associated with the RWC in host cities
- coordinating the planning and delivery of precinct activities with landholders and subsequently with IMG in their capacity as coordinator of RWC partners and sponsors.

Integrating planning and operations

As the department responsible for ensuring successful operational delivery across all tournament venues, events and operations coordinated a program of planning designed to ensure information was shared between departments at appropriate times and that planning was undertaken such that services would be delivered according to agreed scope. An overarching planning framework was documented and it sets out the approach that was undertaken to achieve a coordinated planning effort. Importantly, wherever possible, venue owners and operators, as well as key third party service providers, were included in planning discussions. Under the program, the events and operations team led initiatives such as:

- developing *A concept of operations for a match venue*, which set out how RWC venues were to be operated, including the role of events and operations. This document was reviewed by all functional departments and represented the common understanding within the host union regarding how tournament match venues would operate.
- undertaking a detailed analysis of venue resource requirements, including those to be provided by the venue operator. This analysis initially resulted in the creation of generic tools in the form of room data sheets, venue overlay and equipment lists, which were later customised by specific venue.
- conducting operational planning group meetings or 'hubs'. These were convened on a needs basis, with targeted subject matter based on the detailed planning activities to be undertaken.
- facilitation of workshop sessions to address operational issues
- leading scenario planning exercises, designed to address operational procedure in both ordinary operations and extraordinary situations. This included detailed tabletop exercises carried out in each venue just prior to the commencement of tournament operations.
- leading a process to develop and communicate detailed policies covering all aspects of tournament operations. This ensured a level of consistency of operations across the tournament.
- creation of a detailed venue operations plan for each venue. This was a substantial document in each case and set out the key dimensions of all aspects of the operations at the venue, including venue and event profiles and an outline of the operations of each organisational area.

Progression by the events and operations department through these, as well as other, planning and operational tasks is shown in figure 4.11.

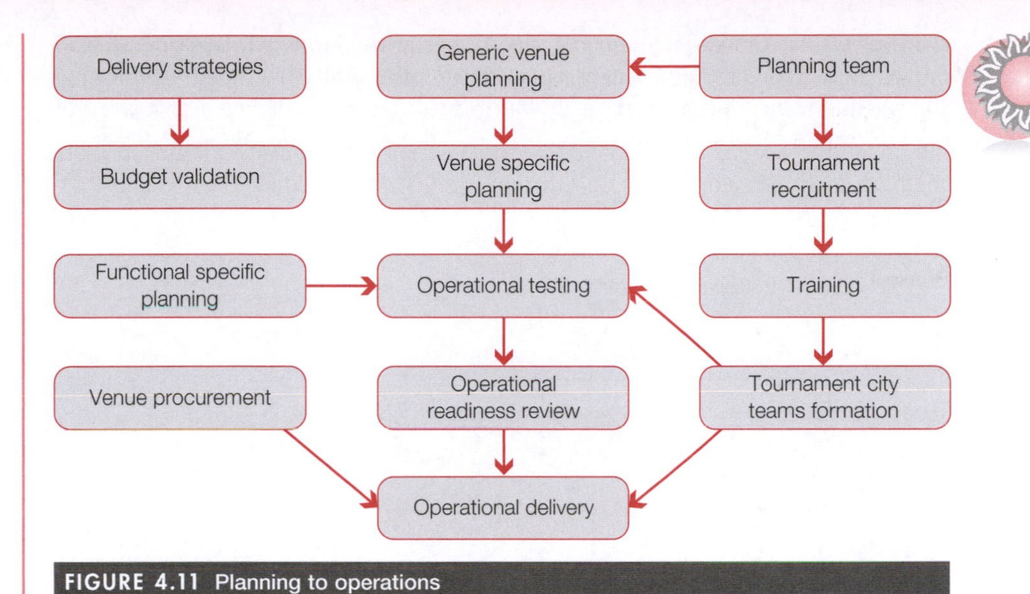

FIGURE 4.11 Planning to operations

Staffing and organisational structure evolution

The staffing model adopted by the events and operations department involved creating a core team of staff who would undertake the planning and coordination task centrally in 2001–02. This group later moved (from early to mid 2003) to become key venue management and geographic area personnel controlling their own teams. Making this task easier was the fact that a number of senior team members were existing ARU employees and as such possessed a sound understanding of what was required to plan and create operational venue overlays for rugby-based sporting events.

Volunteers were a major component of the RWC 2003 workforce, filling a number of match day staff positions and providing the 'arms and legs' on event day. To assist volunteers in gaining familiarity with their venue and its procedures, they were, where possible, given roles at scheduled Rugby test matches in 2003. These 'test' events also allowed management to gauge the suitability of each volunteer to their RWC 2003 position.

The 2003 annual domestic test season not only provided an opportunity to further develop the skills of the RWC 2003's volunteer workforce, but also allowed the testing of proposed RWC 2003 policies and procedures. It also enabled some RWC staff to fill operational roles similar to those that they would hold at tournament time. To formalise this latter opportunity, a program was developed whereby a significant portion of the planning and delivery of annual test events was undertaken by the RWC staff. The evolution of the staffing structure of the events and operations department is shown in figure 4.12.

The growth in staff from 2002 to 2003 reflected the movement from overall planning to operations, where much greater detailed work was required, including operational testing. Operational integration between departments was also a major concern over this period as the detailed components of each venue were planned, reviewed and confirmed. Additionally, city operations planning was also key at this time, as city operations planners sought to assist state host unions and their respective state governments in their efforts to maximise benefits from the conduct of RWC matches.

As the tournament date approached, the events and operations department moved to its final tournament time structure (see figure 4.13), reflecting the expanded

range of tasks required for event delivery. It was at this time that department staff moved into their key tournament operational roles, which included establishing eight venue teams. Management staff within these teams participated in a week of intense briefing and training two months out from the event. A detailed manual covering all planning carried out to date was produced for each match venue and this formed the basis of a job-specific training week.

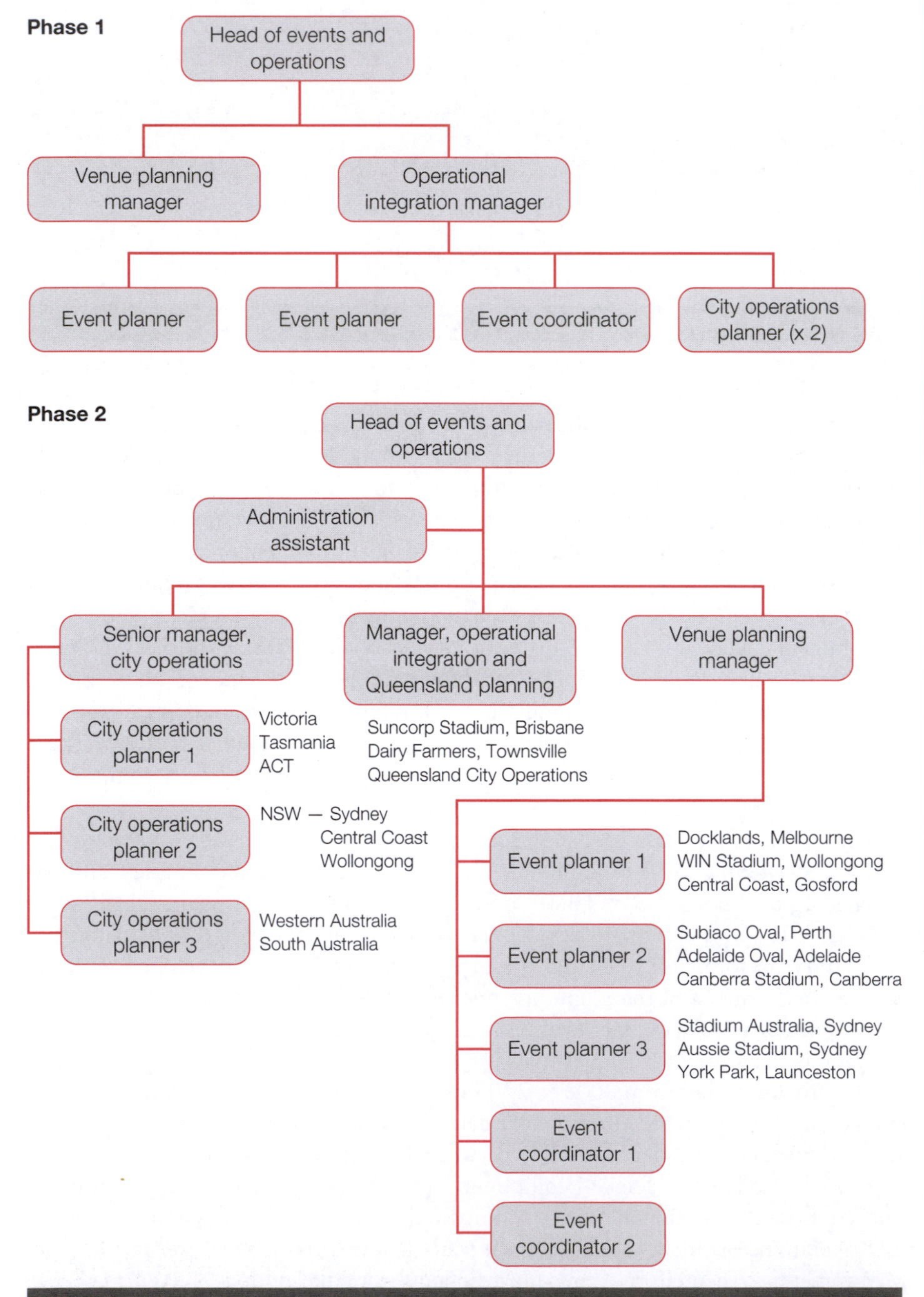

FIGURE 4.12 Evolution of the staffing structure of the event and operations department 2002–03

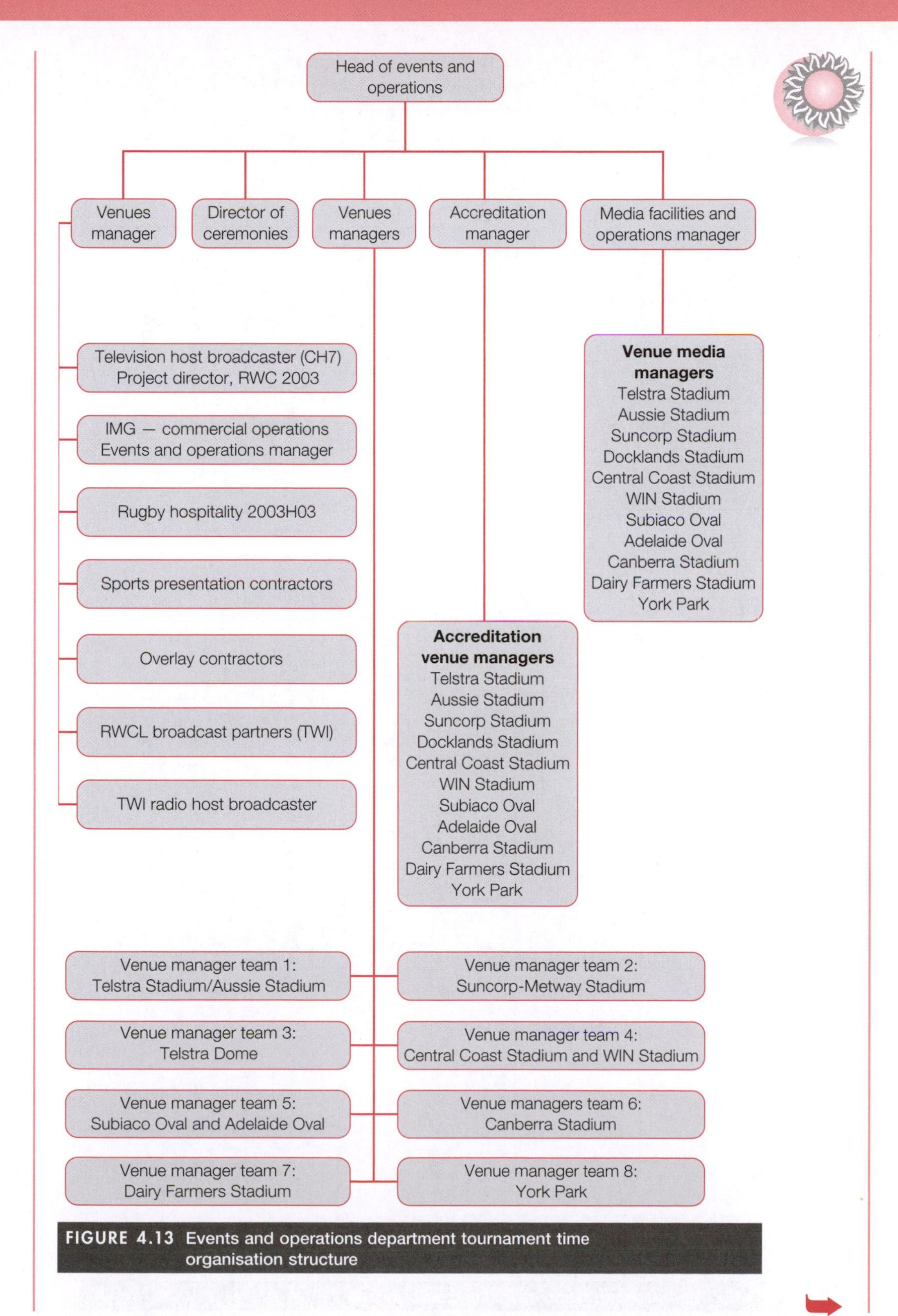

FIGURE 4.13 Events and operations department tournament time organisation structure

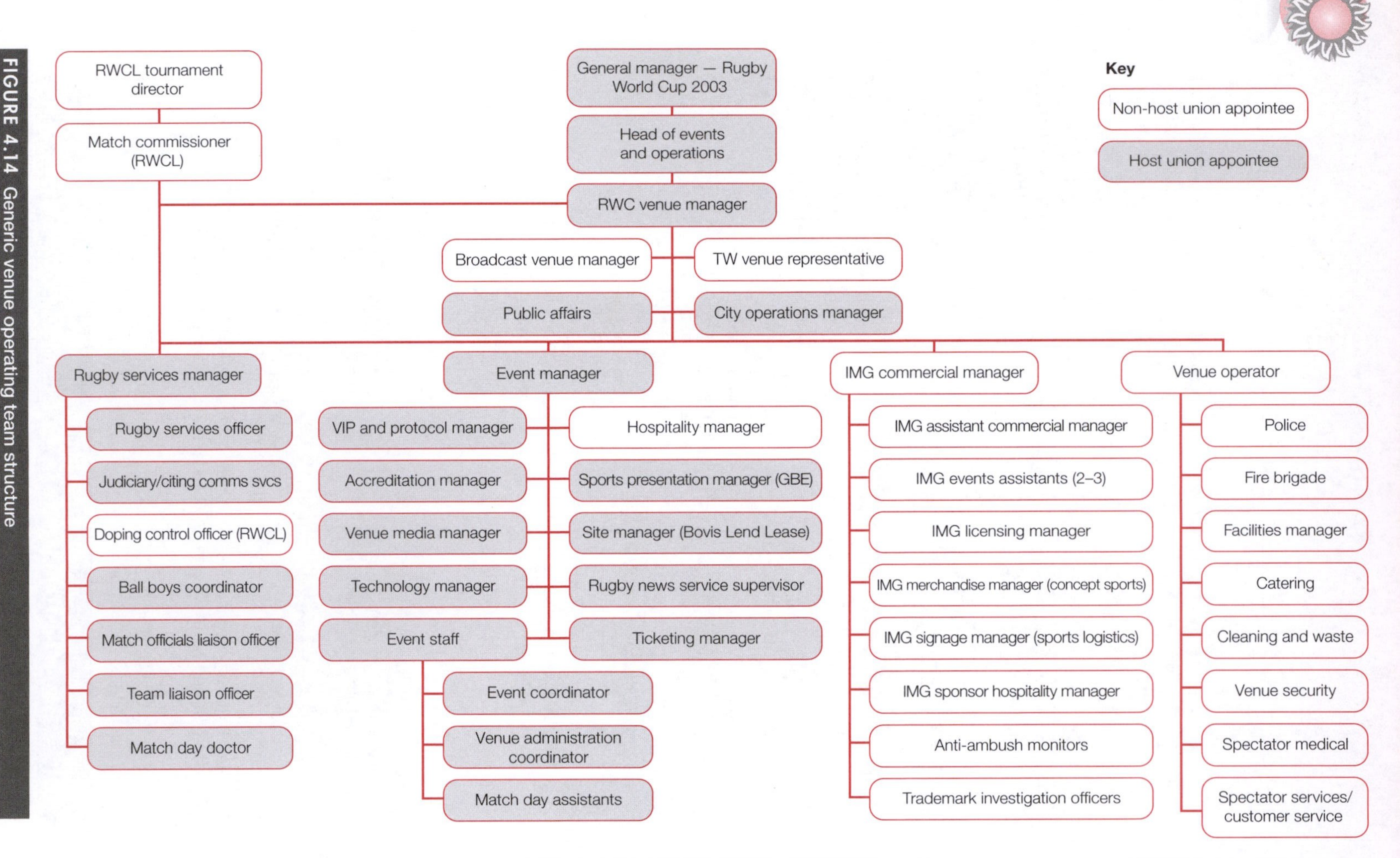

FIGURE 4.14 Generic venue operating team structure

The job-specific training week was essential to the overall success of the event as it ensured that all venue and event managers went into their venues with a consistent and common understanding of how the ARU was going to stage the tournament. The manual itself was also a valuable resource, enabling the teams to take away documented details of their venue operations planning to date, together with key policies, procedures and operational schedules.

Following the week of training, the venue teams were deployed to their venues/city offices to finalise preparations for their respective matches and further develop their own operational relationships with key external and internal organisations. The tasks they were charged with at this time included:

- overlay implementation/management
- final review of detailed planning, deployment of venue staff, security and access control and timings
- documentation of a detailed event plan specific to the individual matches and which was complementary to the venue operations plan
- development of detailed (minute by minute) run sheets for each match
- operations meetings, held weekly to the day prior to each match
- transition planning, including development of detailed bump in and bump out schedules.

At each match venue an organisational structure was required to deliver the event as planned (see figure 4.14). At each venue the events and operations venue manager, guided by their respective run sheets, was ultimately responsible for the delivery of the event on match day, acting to support and direct their respective teams as required. They were also required to escalate issues as applicable to the head of events and operations who was part of the tournament coordination committee.

Conclusion

This case study shows how the tasks, structure and staffing requirements of one department within a large-scale sporting event evolved over a three-year period. In doing so it highlights how events move from their planning phase into their operational and delivery phases. Accompanying this movement is a range of challenges, including the need to build workable, but increasingly complex organisational structures; deal with an expanded and increasingly complex range of tasks; and establish and train integrated 'teams' capable of employing various operational systems and processes.

Ian Alker, head of events and venues, Australian Rugby Union

Questions

1 Why do event organisational structures evolve over time?

2 What issues arise as event organisational structures develop?

3 What benefits are there in developing centrally a core team of staff that is later deployed in key venue management and other roles?

4 What function do 'test' events play from an event operations perspective?

5 What function can computer aided design and drafting software play in event operations?

6 What role does staff training play in event operations? What types of training are evident in this case study?

7 What issues might have arisen if the ARU had decided to try to use a centralised organisational structure to conduct the RWC 2003 rather than devolve responsibility to individual venues?

REFERENCES

Adelaide Fringe 2010, 'About us', www.adelaidefringe.com.au.

Australian Capital Territory 2010, *ACT Festival fund information booklet 2010*, www.events.act.gov.au, pp. 20–22.

Caribbean Days Festival 2010, 'About the society', www.caribbeandays.ca.

Carroll, L 1977 (first published 1865), *Alice's Adventures in Wonderland*, Puffin Books.

ChangingMinds.org 2006, 'SMART objectives', www.changingminds.org.

Dana Alliance for Brain Initiatives 2006, 'Brain awareness week', www.dana.org/brainweek.

Edinburgh International Festival 2010, 'Our mission', www.eif.co.uk.

Focused Performance 2006, 'Unconstrained quotes', www.focusedperformance.com.

Fort Armstrong Folk Festival 2010, 'Home', www.armstrongfestival.com.

Grant, R 2009, *Contemporary strategy analysis*, Malden, Blackwell, Melbourne.

Greek Orthodox Folk Dance and Choral Festival 2010, 'About us', www.yourfdf.org.

Hill, C, Jones, G, Galvin, P & Haidar, A 2007, *Strategic management*, 2nd edn, John Wiley & Sons, Brisbane.

International Olympic Committee, *The Olympic Games knowledge services*.

Johnson, G & Scholes, K 2001, *Exploring corporate strategy*, 6th edn, Prentice Hall Europe, Hemel Hempstead.

Kearney, A 2006, *Building a legacy — sports mega events should last a lifetime*, Kearney Inc., www.atkearney.com.

Local Government Association of New South Wales 2009, 'Hosting the 2011 Annual Conference', www.lgsa.org.au, pp. 1–3.

Lynch, R 2006, *Corporate strategy*, 4th edn, Prentice Hall, Harlow.

Mintzberg, H, Quinn, J & Voyer, J 1995, *The strategy process*, Prentice Hall, New Jersey.

National Folk Festival 2010, 'Management' and 'History', www.folkfestival.asn.au.

National Rural Health Alliance, Services for Australian Rural and Remote Allied Health (SARRAH) Conference 2006, 'Conference mission statement', www.ruralhealth.org.au.

Northern Lights Festival Boreal 2006, 'Mission statement', www.nlfbsudbury.com.

Office of Commonwealth Games Coordination 2006, internal document.

Oregon Shakespeare Festival 2010, 'Our mission', www.osfashland.org.

Pearce, J & Robinson, R 2005, *Strategic management*, 9th edn, McGraw-Hill Irwin, New York.

Philadelphia Folksong Society 2006, 'Volunteers', www.pfs.org.

Pitts, R & Lei, D 2006, *Strategic management*, Thomson, Mason.

Port Fairy Folk Festival 2010, 'The committee', www.portfairyfolkfestival.com.

Roskilde Festival 2010, 'Roskilde Festival's organizational structure', www.roskilde-festival.dk.

San Jose Jewish Film Festival 2010, 'About SJJFF', www.sjjff.org.

Sloman, J 2006, Project management (course notes), Major Event Management Program 9–14 June, Sport Knowledge Australia, Sydney.

Thompson, JL 1997, *Strategic management: awareness and change*, 3rd edn, International Thompson Business Press, London.

Toohey, K & Halbwirth, S 2001, *The Sydney Organising Committee of the Olympic Games and knowledge management: learning from experience*, www.sprig.org.uk, p. 4.

Viljoen, J & Dann, S 2000, *Strategic management*, 3rd edn, Longman, Sydney.

Wolfe Island Scene of the Crime Festival 2010, 'Vision statement', www.sceneofthecrime.ca.

World Swimming Championship Corporation 2006, 'Principles for success', www.melbourne2007.com.au.

CONCEPTUALISING THE EVENT

LEARNING OBJECTIVES

After studying this chapter, you should be able to:

1. identify the range of stakeholders in an event
2. describe and balance the overlapping and sometimes conflicting needs of stakeholders
3. describe the different types of host organisations for events
4. discuss trends and issues in Australian society that affect events
5. understand how to engage sponsors as partners in events
6. understand the role of the media in events
7. identify the unique elements and resources of an event
8. understand the process of developing an event concept
9. understand the importance of designing the event experience
10. apply the screening process to evaluate the feasibility of an event concept.

INTRODUCTION

A crucial element in the creation of an event is the understanding of the event environment. The context in which the event is to take place will play a major role in determining the event concept. In order to understand this environment, the event manager must first identify the major players — the stakeholders who are the people and organisations likely to be affected by it. The event manager must then examine the objectives of these major players — what each of them expects to gain from the event, and what forces acting on them are likely to affect their response to the event. Once this environment is understood, the event manager is then in the best position to marshal the creative elements of the event, and to shape and manage them to achieve the best outcomes for the event. Here, design will play a key role in shaping the experience to be provided for event participants. This chapter examines the key stakeholders in events, and outlines some of the processes that event managers can use to devise creative and successful event concepts.

STAKEHOLDERS IN EVENTS

As discussed in the previous chapters, events have rapidly become professionalised and are increasingly attracting the involvement and support of governments and the corporate sector. One aspect of this growth is that events are now required to serve a multitude of agenda. It is no longer sufficient for an event to meet just the needs of its audience. It must also embrace a plethora of other requirements, including government objectives and regulations, media requirements, sponsors' needs and community expectations.

People and organisations with a legitimate interest in the outcomes of an event are known as stakeholders. The successful event manager must be able to identify the range of stakeholders in an event and manage their individual needs, which will sometimes overlap and conflict (figure 5.1). As with event impacts, the event will be judged by its success in balancing the competing needs, expectations and interests of a diverse range of stakeholders. For example, the media organisation doing a live broadcast of an event may require it to be held in prime time, which may not be suitable for participants and attendees. When questioned on the reasons for the success of the Sydney Olympic Games, chief executive of SOCOG Sandy Hollway attributed the effective coordination and management of a large and diverse range of stakeholders (Hollway 2002).

Mal Hemmerling (1997), architect of the Australian Formula One Grand Prix in Adelaide and former chief executive of SOCOG, describes the task of the contemporary event manager as follows:

> So when asked the question 'what makes an event successful', there are now numerous shareholders that are key components of modern major events that are looking at a whole range of different measures of success. What may have been a simple measure for the event organiser of the past, which involved the bottom line, market share, and successful staging of the event are now only basic criteria as the measures by other investors are more aligned with increased tourism, economic activity, tax revenues, promotional success, sustained economic growth, television reach, audience profiles, customer focus, brand image, hospitality, new business opportunities and investment to name but a few.

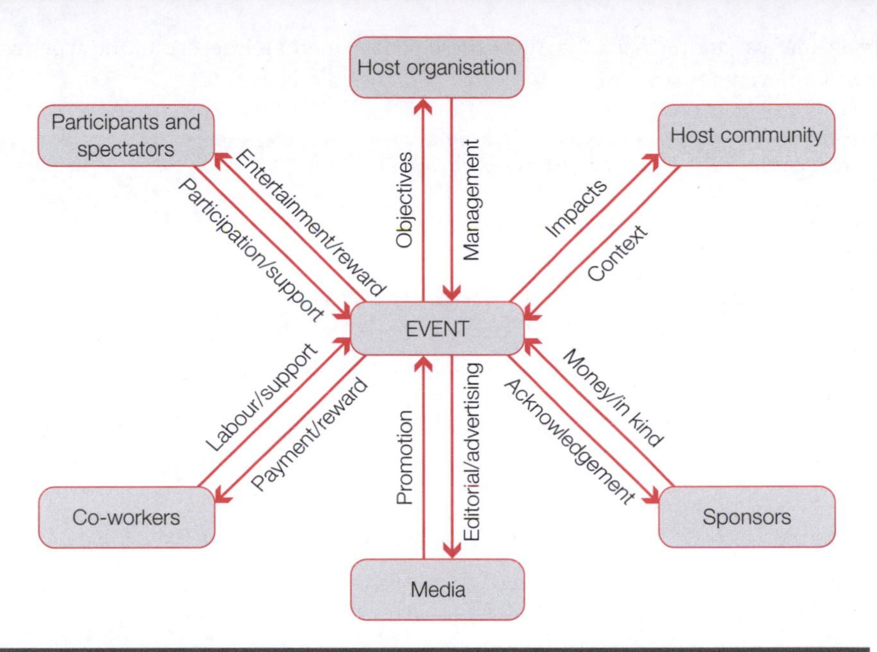

FIGURE 5.1 The relationship of stakeholders to events

THE HOST ORGANISATION

As we saw in chapter 3, events have become so much a part of our cultural milieu that they can be generated by almost any part of the government, corporate and community sectors (see table 5.1). Governments create events for a range of reasons, including the social, cultural, tourism and economic benefits generated by events. These events are often characterised by free entry and wide accessibility, and form part of the public culture. Government bodies often have a mixed role including not only the generation of events, but also their regulation and coordination, as was discussed in detail in chapter 2. The corporate sector is involved in events at a number of levels, including staging their own events, sponsoring events in order to promote their goods and services in the marketplace, and partnering with other events that have a common agenda. These events, although they may still offer free entry, are often targeted at specific market segments rather than at the general public.

These sectors often interact, with public events providing opportunities for corporate sponsorships and hosting.

Within the corporate sector, there are also entrepreneurs whose business is the staging or selling of events. These include sports or concert promoters who present ticketed events for profit, and conference organisers or industry associations who mount conferences or exhibitions for the trade or public — for example, wine shows, equipment exhibitions or medical conferences. Media organisations often become partners in events organised by other groups, but also stage events for their own promotional purposes or to create program content. Examples are radio stations promoting their identity through concerts, newspapers promoting fun runs, or television networks presenting Christmas carol programs live to air.

Other events emanate from the community sector, serving a wide variety of needs and interests. These may include local sporting events, service club fundraisers, car club gatherings, local art and craft shows — the spectrum is as wide as the field of human interest and endeavour. All of these sources combine to create the wonderful tapestry of events that fill our leisure time and enrich our lives.

TABLE 5.1 Event typology

Event generators	Types of event
Government sector	
Central government	Civic celebrations and commemorations — for example, Australia Day, Anzac Day
Event corporations	Major events — focus on sporting and cultural events
Public space authorities	Public entertainment, leisure and recreation events
Tourism	Festivals, special interest and lifestyle events, destinational promotions
Convention bureaus	Meetings, incentives, conventions, exhibitions
Arts	Arts festivals, cultural events, touring programs, themed art exhibitions
Ethnic affairs	Ethnic and multicultural events
Sport and recreation	Sporting events, hosting of state, national and international championships
Economic development	Focus on events with industry development and job creation benefits
Education	Training and educational events, academic conferences
Local government	Community events, local festivals and fairs
Corporate sector	
Companies and corporations	Promotions, product launches, image-building sponsorships, staff training and incentive events
Industry associations	Industry promotions, trade fairs, conferences
Entrepreneurs	Ticketed sporting events, concerts and exhibitions
Media	Media promotions — for example, concerts, fun runs, appeals
Community sector	
Clubs and societies	Special interest group events
Charities	Fundraising and profile-building events
Sports organisations	Local sporting events

Types of host organisation

Whether events emanate from the corporate, government or community sectors will determine the nature of the host organisation. If the host is from the corporate sector, it is likely to be a company, corporation or industry association. The event manager may be employed directly by the host organisation, or on a contract basis with the organisation as the client. If the host is from the government sector, the host organisation is likely to be a government or council department. Again the event manager may be a direct employee, or a contractor if the event is outsourced. If the host is from the community sector, the host organisation is more likely to be a club, society or committee, with a higher volunteer component in the organisation.

Whatever the host organisation, it is a key stakeholder in the event, and the event manager should seek to clarify its goals in staging the event. These goals will often be presented in a written brief as part of the event manager's job description or contract. Where they are not, it will be worthwhile spending some time to clarify these goals and put them in written form as a reference point for the organisation of the event, and a guideline for the evaluation of its eventual success.

THE HOST COMMUNITY

Event managers need to have a good grasp and understanding of the broad trends and forces acting on the wider community, as these will determine the operating environment of their events. The mood, needs and aspirations of the community will determine its receptiveness to event styles and fashions. Accurately gauging and interpreting these are basic factors in the conceptualising of successful events.

A major factor currently impacting on events is climate change, and the resulting worldwide interest and commitment to sustainability and the protection of the environment. This has given rise to specific events that aim to galvanise public opinion and action, such as Earth Hour, which was celebrated in 4000 cities in 88 countries in 2009, encouraging people to turn out their lights for an hour in order to show their support for the environment (Earth Hour 2009). The sustainability issue has also given rise to a wide range of initiatives to green events and reduce their carbon footprint, such as the use of environmentally sustainable products and services, the use of green electrical power, and catering with food sourced from the local district. An example of an event using a wide range of initiatives to address this issue is provided in the 'The National Event Summit' event profile later in this chapter. Other significant forces currently acting on the community are globalisation and technology, which are combining to make the world seem both smaller and more complex. These forces affect almost every aspect of our lives, including events. As international travel, trade and communications increase, national boundaries and local differences are increasingly subsumed into the global marketplace.

This process is accelerated by technology and the media, which have the power to bring significant local events to a worldwide audience, overcoming the barriers of geographic boundaries and cultural differences. This is exemplified by the global television coverage of major sporting events. World championships and mega-events such as the Olympics and World Cup Soccer are beamed instantly to live audiences throughout the world, giving them previously unimagined coverage and immediacy.

As global networks increasingly bring the world into our lounge rooms, the question arises of how local cultures can maintain their own uniqueness and identity in the face of global homogenisation. International arts festivals increasingly draw from the same pool of touring companies to produce similar programs. Local festivals and celebrations must increasingly compete with international products and the raised expectations of audiences accustomed to streamlined television production. The challenge for many events is how to function in this increasingly global environment while expressing the uniqueness of local communities and addressing their specific interests and concerns.

Globalisation also influences corporate events as companies increasingly plan their marketing strategies, including their event components, with potential global audiences in mind. This has resulted in some local Australian event companies being bought out by overseas companies in an attempt to create networks that can serve the international needs of their clients. This approach sometimes comes unstuck as different markets in, say, New York, Sydney and Hong Kong reflect different event needs and audience responses. However, the forces of globalisation are likely to lead to an increasing standardisation of the corporate event product and market.

Simultaneously, the all-pervasive internet and advances in information technology are increasing the availability and technological sophistication of events. Event participants now use the internet and mobile phone technology to research events prior to their attendance, to augment the event experience, and to relive the highlights after the event. During the Beijing Olympics, online broadcasts in China far exceeded conventional television broadcasts in terms of total hours. CCTV.com broadcast the Games in cooperation with eight domestic websites, with 6.329 billion page views and 138 million unique visitors per day, greatly outnumbering the 65 million television viewers per day. The general manager of CCTV.com (Wang 2008) commented:

> Different types of media have their own strengths in presenting the Olympic experience: television highlights the feeling of being present at the scene; newspapers and magazines provide in-depth coverage that lasts over time; the Internet delivers instant information and interactivity; mobile TV is portable and is regarded by users as a kind of companion. People select different combinations of media according to their preferences and changing demands.

Technology had impacted not just on how audiences receive events, but also on how they are created and delivered. Event managers must be aware of this trend and learn to operate in the new global environment. Event software programs and templates can reduce the planning time of events, and enable event managers to work on several events simultaneously. Social media such as Twitter can be used to track popular trends in the 'Twitter Universe', which can then be incorporated into the theming and content of events. However, despite the increasing technological sophistication, the opportunity that events provide to mix and interact with other people in a live situation remains one of their enduring strengths. Paradoxically, live events may increasingly become the means by which communities affirm their own sense of place, individuality and cultural uniqueness.

Involving the host community

In addition to the wider general community, events have a specific host community that impacts greatly on the success or failure of the event. This can be the geographical community where the event is located, or a community of interest from which the event draws its participants and spectators. Many researchers (Getz 2005; Goldblatt and Perry 2002; Jago et al. 2002) have recognised the importance of the host community being involved in and 'owning' the event, which in turn emits positive messages to visitors. An example quoted by Jago et al. (2002) is the Gold Coast's Indy Carnival during the lead-up to the Indy 300 race day, where community events helped to create a local atmosphere that contributed to the destination's brand. In another example, a 'My Family's Olympics' competition conducted in China during the Beijing Olympics included a group of children from a mountainous area who organised their own torch relay using sticks of corn as torches, which was filmed by an internet user and broadcast on CCTV.com (Wang 2008).

Many community members actively participate in events in their communities, and act as advocates on behalf of the event to potential participants. The Sydney Gay and Lesbian Mardi Gras and Nimbin's Mardi Grass are examples of events that are fuelled by social activists committed to the goals of the event. Local participation and ownership of events is perhaps most visible in the many local and regional events that continue to exist only because of the committed input of dedicated volunteers.

The host community may also include residents, traders, lobby groups and public authorities such as council, transport, police, ambulance and fire brigades. The event manager should aim to identify and involve representatives of these groups, and to consult them in the planning of the event. As discussed in chapter 3, councils may have certain requirements, such as parade and catering permits. Often police and councils will combine to form a 'one stop shop' for such matters as street closures, special access and parking arrangements. If the event is large enough to impact significantly beyond the boundaries of the venue, a public authorities' briefing may identify innovative ways to minimise the impact and manage the situation. The Australia Day fireworks spectacular at Sydney's Darling Harbour, for example, regularly attracts 300 000 spectators, most of whom used to depart immediately after the end of the fireworks, causing an hour-long traffic jam on the surrounding freeways. By stepping down the entertainment in stages, working with point duty police and implementing one-way traffic in some areas, the delay was reduced to less than half that time.

In addition to formal contact with authorities, the event manager should be aware of the all-important local rumour mill that can often make or break the host community's attitude to the event.

Music festival organisers know only too well the power and impact of word of mouth on festival attendances. The success of music festivals such as the Big Day Out and V Festival in recent years has largely been driven by their reputations, making it imperative for the organisers to keep their programs current and in tune with their audiences. The Port Fairy Folk Festival in Victoria and the Woodford Folk Festival in Queensland both sell out with minimal expenditure on publicity, but only because their organisers jealously guard and protect the reputations of their festivals. The effort and cost of maintaining the quality of these events is rewarded by exceptional word of mouth.

SPONSORS

In recent decades, there has been an enormous increase in sponsorship, and a corresponding change in how events are perceived by sponsors. There has been a shift by many large companies from viewing sponsorship largely as a public relations tool generating community goodwill, to regarding it as a primary promotional tool in the marketing mix. Successful major events are now perceived as desirable properties, capable of increasing brand awareness and driving sales. They also provide important opportunities for relationship building through hosting partners and clients. Corporations invest large amounts in event sponsorship, and devote additional resources to supporting their sponsorships, to achieve corporate objectives and sales goals.

In order to attract sponsorships, event managers must offer tangible benefits to sponsors, and effective programs to deliver them. Large corporations such as Coca-Cola and Telstra receive hundreds of sponsorship applications each week, and only consider those events that have a close fit with corporate objectives and a demonstrable ability to deliver benefits.

Sponsors as partners in events

It is important for event managers to identify exactly what sponsors want from an event and what the event can deliver for them. Their needs may be different from those of the host organisation or the event manager. Attendance numbers at the event, for example, may not be as important to them as the media coverage that it generates. It may be important for their chief executive to officiate or to gain access to public officials in a relaxed atmosphere. They may be seeking mechanisms to drive sales, or want to strengthen client relationships through hosting activities. The event manager should take the opportunity to go beyond the formal sponsorship agreement and to treat the sponsors as partners in the event. Some of the best ideas for events can arise from such partnerships. Common agendas may be identified that support the sponsorship and deliver additional benefits to the event.

Countrylink, which runs country rail services to regional New South Wales, sponsors the Parkes Elvis Festival each January by running an Elvis Express train between Sydney and Parkes for the festival. Elvis impersonators entertain passengers on the journey, and the mayor and councillors greet the train in Elvis costumes. The opening of ticket bookings is awaited eagerly each year by Elvis fans, and the available tickets sell out within hours. As a quirky news item, the Elvis Express generates enormous publicity for the festival, and promotes Countrylink as supportive of the local community.

For the FIFA World Cup in Germany in 2006, German Railways provided free domestic rail travel for 6000 overseas media representatives for the duration of the tournament. The selection of the Escort Kids (McDonalds), the Ball Crew (Coca-Cola) and the Flag Bearers (adidas) provided further evidence of the commitment of the official partners and suppliers to staging attractive promotions in partnership with the event (Niersbach 2006).

The role of sponsors in events, along with techniques for identifying, sourcing and managing sponsorships, is treated in more detail in chapter 11.

MEDIA

The expansion of the media, and the proliferation of delivery systems such as cable, satellite television and the internet, have created a hunger for media product as never before. The global networking of media organisations and the instant electronic transmission of media images and data have made the global village a media reality. When television was introduced to Australia in time to cover the Melbourne Olympic Games in 1956, the world still relied largely on the physical transfer of film footage to disseminate the images of the Games interstate and overseas. Australia's Bicentennial celebrations in 1988 featured an Australia-wide multidirectional television link-up, which enabled Australians to experience the celebrations simultaneously from a diverse range of locations and perspectives, seeing themselves as a nation through the media as never before. The opening ceremony of the Winter Olympic Games in Nagano in 1998 featured a thousand-member world choir singing together from five different locations on five continents, including the forecourt of the Sydney Opera House. Global television networks followed New Year's Eve of the new millennium around the world, making the world seem smaller and more immediate. When the 2000 Olympics began, a simultaneous global audience estimated at two and a half billion people was able to watch the event tailored to their own national perspectives, with a variety of cameras covering every possible angle. As might be expected, the Beijing Olympic Games attracted the largest global television audience ever, with 4.7 billion viewers — or 70 per cent of the world's population — tuning in over the period of the Games (Nielsenwire 2008).

A good example of how technology can expand exponentially the audience for a local event is Tropfest, which began with a small local audience at a Sydney coffee shop in 1993, and is now screened simultaneously to a crowd of 150 000 people in

Sydney, Melbourne, Canberra, Perth, Brisbane, Hobart and Adelaide (Conroy 2009). Mobile phone applications such as the Optus Festival Buddy (Sydney Festival 2010) allow festival audiences to plan their attendance, purchase tickets, read event descriptions and reviews, access directions and public transport details, and interact with each event on their favourite social networks. Other specialised applications enable sports fans to access the latest results and news as it happens for a range of sports events from their mobile phones.

The social media, including Facebook, Twitter, YouTube, Flickr and LinkedIn, have made events more personalised in their communication and more interactive. Many events now incorporate social media into their websites, enabling patrons to feed back their comments and opinions, exchange views with other event participants, and even participate in the design and programming of events.

This revolution in the media has in turn revolutionised the conduct of events. Media innovations such as YouTube have created new forms of virtual events, such as the YouTube Symphony Orchestra, with musicians from 30 countries selected from 3000 musicians by open audition on YouTube, leading to a live performance in Carnegie Hall in April 2009 and available for viewing on YouTube (Nichols 2009). The Portable Film Festival enables phone owners to participate in a short film festival with selected films downloaded to their phones (Portable Film Festival 2010).

Events now have a virtual existence in the media at least as powerful, sometimes more so, than in reality. The live audience for a sports event or concert may be dwarfed by the television audience. Indeed, the event may be created primarily for the consumption of the television audience. Events have much to gain from this development, including media sponsorships and the payment of media rights. Their value to commercial sponsors is greatly increased by their media coverage and profile. However, the media often directly affect the way events are conceptualised and presented, as in the case of One Day Cricket and Super League, where the competition formats have been modified in order to create more appealing television product. So far, sports events have been the main winners (and losers) from this increased media attention.

The available media technology influences the way that live spectators experience an event. The wiring of the modern stadium allows for digital television and enables every spectator to have a unique seat with personalised communication services. Increasingly, spectators' viewing capabilities are technologically enhanced to parallel those of people watching at home.

Media interest in events continues to grow as their ability to provide saleable product and to attract commercial sponsors is realised. Sporting events, parades, spectacles, concerts and major public celebrations are areas of strong interest to the media, where the imperatives of television production are likely to continue to influence the direction and marketing of events. The role of the media can vary from that of media sponsors to becoming full partners — or even producers — of the event.

Whatever the role of the media, it is important for the event manager to consider the needs of different media groups, and to consult with them as important stakeholders in the event. Once the media are treated as potential partners, they have much to offer the event. The good media representative, like the event manager, is in search of the good idea or unusual angle. Together they might just dream up the unique approach that increases the profile of the event and, in turn, provides value to the media organisation. The print media might agree to publish the event program as editorial or as a special insert, or might run a series of lead-in stories, competitions or special promotions in tandem with sponsors. Radio or television stations might provide an outside broadcast, or might involve their on-air presenters as comperes or special participants in the event. Mobile phone companies and internet providers might integrate their products with the promotion and delivery of the event. This integration of the event with the media provides greater reach and exposure to the event, and in turn gives the media organisation a branded association with the event. New media developments and increasingly innovative technologies continue to expand the media dimension of events, and to provide additional opportunities for collaboration between event organisers and the media.

CO-WORKERS

The event team that is assembled to implement the event represents another of the key stakeholders. For any event to be truly effective, the vision and philosophy of the event must be shared by all of the team, from key managers, talent and publicist, right through to the stage manager, crew, gatekeepers and cleaners. No matter how big or small, the event team is the face of the event, and each member a contributor to its success or failure.

Goldblatt (1997, p. 129) describes the role of the event manager in this process:

> The most effective event managers are not merely managers, rather, they are dynamic leaders whose ability to motivate, inspire others, and achieve their goals are admired by their followers. The difference between management and leadership is perhaps best characterised by this simple but effective definition: *managers control problems, whereas leaders motivate others to find ways to achieve goals.*

Most people have experienced events that went well overall, but were marred by some annoying detail or shortcoming. There are different ways of addressing such problems, but good teamwork and management are always crucial factors in handling them. The Disney organisation, for example, has a system in which roles, such as performer, cleaner and security, are merged so that staff consider themselves to be one team looking after the space. The roles tend to ride with the needs of the moment — when the parade comes through the theme park, it is all hands on deck. The daily bulletin issued to all staff members reminds them that customers may visit Disneyland only once in their lives, and their impressions will depend forever on what they experience that day. This is a very positive philosophy that can be applied to all events.

PARTICIPANTS AND SPECTATORS

Last but not least are the 'punters' on the day — the participants and spectators for whom the event is intended and who ultimately vote with their feet for the success or failure of the event. The event manager must be mindful of the needs of the audience. These include their physical needs, as well as their needs for comfort, safety and security. Over and above these basic requirements is the need to make the event special — to connect with the emotions of the participants. A skilled event manager strives to make events meaningful, magical and memorable. Hemmerling (1997) describes the criteria by which spectators judge an event:

> Their main focus is on the content, location, substance and operation of the event itself. For them the ease with which they can see the event activities, the program content, their access to food and drinks, amenities, access and egress etc., are the keys to their enjoyment. Simple factors such as whether or not their team won or lost, or whether they had a good experience at the event will sometimes influence their success measures. Secondary issues, such as mixing with the stars of the show, social opportunities,

corporate hospitality and capacity to move up the seating chain from general admission to premium seating are all part of the evaluation of spectator success.

Current technologies can assist the event manager in involving and servicing event participants, as was discussed earlier with the use of contemporary stadium technologies to enhance the audience experience, and the use of the internet to extend the reach and access to events.

By understanding how the nature and make-up of the event audience influence the event concept, event managers can tailor their events more adequately to meet the needs of participants. As discussed in greater detail in chapter 9, this understanding also helps to accurately direct the marketing efforts by using channels specific to the audience — for example, the marketing of Schoolies' Week on the Gold Coast through secondary schools in New South Wales, Victoria and Queensland.

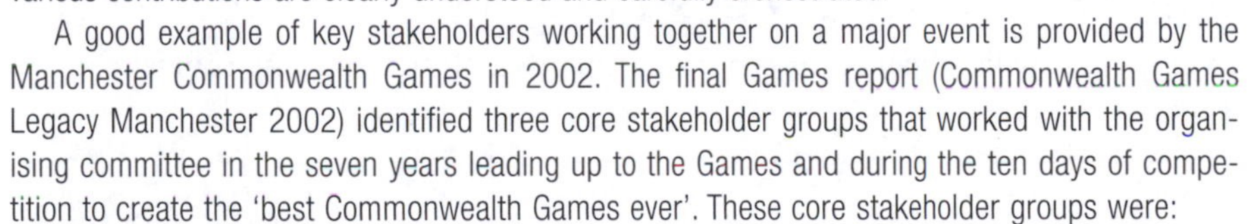

IDENTIFYING STAKEHOLDERS AND THEIR ROLES

It is essential that the roles of all stakeholders in an event are clearly delineated, and that their various contributions are clearly understood and carefully orchestrated.

A good example of key stakeholders working together on a major event is provided by the Manchester Commonwealth Games in 2002. The final Games report (Commonwealth Games Legacy Manchester 2002) identified three core stakeholder groups that worked with the organising committee in the seven years leading up to the Games and during the ten days of competition to create the 'best Commonwealth Games ever'. These core stakeholder groups were:

- strategic and funding stakeholders
- operational stakeholders
- regional stakeholders.

Strategic and funding stakeholders

When Manchester City Council and the Commonwealth Games Council for England submitted the bid to host the 2002 Commonwealth Games, they were supported by two powerful organisations that stayed true to the vision and the partnership right to the end — The Sports Council (revamped into Sport England in 1997) and the British government. Funding and support were provided for different elements of the games through this partnership.

Roles and responsibilities

The key roles of the strategic and funding stakeholders were:

- *Manchester City Council* — to be the host city; to design and procure the venues; and to secure the legacy of the city image and venues, and the economic, social and sporting legacy to the region
- *Sport England* — to ensure that the sporting facilities were of world standard; and to provide a legacy for elite athletes and the venues after the Games
- *Department for Culture, Media and Sport* — to promote the UK's ability to provide world class venues and to stage major events; and to ensure that the facilities became part of the English Institute of Sport network of facilities and services after the Games (Manchester 2002).

Operational partnerships

A great many partnerships formed with other organisations assisted the Games to run smoothly. The Manchester City Management Group, business groups and local community groups worked together to create a community spirit such as had not been seen in the city for many years. The close relationship between the Games organisers and the Manchester City Police meant that issues were mitigated and dealt with quickly and efficiently, and that the Games and associated events ran smoothly and safely. Through the efforts of the Greater Manchester Passenger Transport Executive and their partners, the Manchester transport system worked effectively to transport thousands of spectators to venues, with more than 75 per cent of all spectators at Sportcity using public transport. Partnerships with the BBC as host broadcaster, and with sponsors and partners, ensured the smooth running of many facilities, and provided operationally vital valuable in-kind services.

Regional partnerships

Regional partnerships helped Manchester to secure over £600 million of public and private investment. Nearly 30 million people now consider Manchester or the North West as a possible business and visitor destination because of their improved image, and an estimated 300 000 extra visitors are expected to visit the city and the region each year.

The Games generated more than 6000 permanent jobs in the region, as well as long-term cultural programs such as a regional cultural festival, Cultureshock, and an annual Commonwealth film festival that hopes to continue in the region after its inaugural success as part of the Commonwealth Games Spirit of Friendship Festival.

SOURCING EVENTS

Events are usually obtained or generated from one of the following sources:

- in-house events
- pitching and tendering for events
- bidding for events
- franchising events.

In-house events

Many events are conducted in-house by corporate, government, education, charity and community organisations. In such cases, the management of the event may be a part of the job description and responsibilities of a staff member. For example, the event manager of a company may be responsible for its annual conference, Christmas party or client function. An event manager working in local government may be given the responsibility of organising a local festival, tourism event or school holiday program. In each case, the event manager may inherit existing events, each with their own history and established venues and formats. Alternatively, they may be given the task of initiating new events, which have to be created from scratch with no previous history of precedents.

In some instances companies are set up whose entire function is the conduct of an event; for example, The Australian Tennis Open or the Sydney Festival. Other companies are set up whose business is the staging of events for profit. This is common in the entertainment industry, with specialist companies staging theatrical shows and touring concert performers and bands.

Pitching and tendering for events

Many corporate events are subject to the process known as pitching for events. In this instance, the company or organisation intending to stage the event will invite a number of event management companies to present or 'pitch' their creative concepts for the event. Prior to formulating their ideas, a company pitching for an event will usually research thoroughly the aims of the client and the context of the event. They will then brainstorm a creative concept for the event, and prepare a presentation including a detailed description of the event, often supported by sketches, story boards and a detailed breakdown of the event costs including the event management fee. The pitch will usually involve a live presentation providing an opportunity for the event management company to 'sell' their event concept, and to strike a rapport with the client. Often the detail involved in the presentation is such that, should the pitch be successful, much of the basic planning and costing of the event will already have taken place.

The tender process is similar to pitching in that a formal public invitation is issued seeking proposals from companies or individuals interested in managing an event. The tender is often advertised, and tender documents issued outlining the terms of the tender and the parameters of the event. Companies intending to respond may be given the opportunity to meet with and question the client in order to clarify any aspects of the tender. Formal tenders are then lodged, and the successful company appointed to manage the event. The tender process is often employed by government organisations where an open and transparent selection process is required.

Bidding for events

There are many existing events that are 'footloose' in the sense that they are seeking cities or organisations to host them, and that may be obtained through the competitive bidding process. This is particularly true of major sporting events and conferences, which typically move between cities on a regular, often annual basis. These events are usually controlled by a national or international body that is the 'owner', or copyright holder of the event. Permission to stage the event locally must be obtained by successfully bidding for the right to host the event.

There are usually three parties involved in the bid process:

1. the local chapter of the event owning body; for example, a sporting or industry association
2. a government body that backs and supports the bid; for example, an event agency such as the Victorian Major Events Company, Events NSW, Queensland Events Corporation or EventsCorp Western Australia, or a convention bureau such as the Melbourne Convention and Visitors Bureau or Business Events Sydney
3. tourism and event industry suppliers, such as event management companies, hotels and airlines, whose involvement is often coordinated through the event corporation or convention bureau.

Considerable research, effort and, often, cost need to be committed to the bid process, which is described in more detail in chapter 4.

Although the basic format of the sporting event or conference will usually already be established, the host city or organisation will contribute greatly to giving the event a local context and creative flair. No two events are ever exactly the same. The Commonwealth Games, for example, will take on a different image and flavour according to whether it is hosted by Manchester, Melbourne, Delhi or Glasgow. The same industry conference in, say, Brisbane will vary greatly if it is staged in Cairns, Hobart or Adelaide, or for that matter in Shanghai, Singapore, Kuala Lumpur or Hong Kong.

Once the bid has been won and the event obtained, the successful sporting or industry association will appoint a committee and event management team to develop a creative concept and plan the event.

Franchising events

A variation on bidding for events is franchising, where the core concept of the event is developed by an organisation that then permits or sells the rights for the event to be developed in other locations. An outstanding example is the Rock Eisteddfod Challenge, which began in 1980 as a New South Wales Arts Council sponsored event featuring a handful of Sydney high schools. In 1988, the New South Wales Health Department came on board, seeing the Rock Eisteddfod as an opportunity for delivering their 'Quit for Life' anti-smoking message to secondary school students in New South Wales. The event spread rapidly, so that in 2009, nearly 300 Australian schools and 25 000 students took part in shows in 17 regions across Australia. More than 1 million students have now performed on stages from Belfast to Albany, Johannesburg to Thursday Island, and Aberdeen to Auckland as part of Global Rock Challenge. (Rock Eisteddfod Challenge 2009).

A successful offshoot in 1988 was the Croc Festival, a series of three-day festivals for indigenous and non-indigenous students in rural and remote areas of Australia. The celebration embraces health, education, employment and performing arts in the spirit of reconciliation. By 2005 more than 18 000 students from 416 schools participated in eight Croc Festival events.

In each of these instances the creative format and template of the event is supplied to local event organisers, and applied by them to create the event under a franchise agreement.

CREATING THE EVENT CONCEPT

In all of the above instances, a core task of the event manager or team will be to create a strong concept for the event, or to update an existing concept and apply it to the particular context and circumstances of the event. Deciding on the basic idea or concept of an event creates the foundation on which the whole event creation process will later be built. It is crucial therefore to identify a sound and robust concept, based on a good understanding of the full context of the event and its stakeholders. The concept must be capable of achieving the event's purpose, flexible enough to serve the full range of stakeholders, and achievable within the available resources.

Identifying an appropriate event concept will require considerable research, insight and creativity. However, getting the concept right will greatly increase the potential for a successful event outcome.

Defining the purpose of the event

The first step in creating the event concept is to define the purpose of the event, which ideally should be outlined in the event brief supplied by the host organisation. For corporate events, this is sometimes known as the business case, or the justification for holding the event. This in turn will drive the major decisions regarding the development of the event, including the choice of theme and elements and the key corporate messages that the event needs to deliver.

If the purpose of the event is not clearly expressed in the event brief, then the event manager will need to interact with the client in order to clarify and articulate it. Likewise, for public events, the event manager should clarify with the host organisation the purpose for holding the event. The purpose may be multi-faceted — for example, to provide a leisure activity for residents, to attract visitors and to create economic benefit. Identifying the purpose fully and accurately will provide a sound starting point for determining the event concept.

Identifying the event audience

The next important question to clarify is who will be attending the event. For corporate events, knowledge of factors such as the age and gender of attendees, their levels of seniority in the participating organisation, and their experiences and tastes will be of great assistance in tailoring the event concept to the needs of the audience. The event needs and expectations of a group of senior executives and clients will differ greatly from those of younger staff members or middle management. Often, the audience will encompass a wide range of ages and backgrounds, which, in turn, will influence decisions about the event concept. It will be useful to inquire what previous events the company has conducted, and what concepts worked for them. This will provide insights into their corporate culture, and help to avoid repeating ideas or themes they have experienced previously.

For public events, it is important to know whether the event is directed at the whole community, or to one or more segments within it; for example, teenagers, young singles, couples, families with children or seniors. Their age range, income levels and lifestyle interests will all help to determine the event concept. Studying the history of a repeat event may reveal what has been done before, what was successful and what could be improved. For new events, it may be worth searching the internet to identify other events that are similar in style or content.

Deciding the timing of the event

Important decisions need to be made about the duration of the event, and about the season/time of year, day/s and time/s when the event will be held. For corporate events, the business cycle may influence the timing; for example, the avoidance of a particularly busy time of the year for the company, or to coincide with the launch of a new product. A similar logic will determine an appropriate day of the week and time of the day; for example, a product launch may best be held on a week day when clients and the media are available to attend, or a company celebration may best be held on a Friday night isolated from the business week and providing time for recovery.

The timing of public events may be determined by favourable seasons — for example, spring and autumn are likely to provide temperate weather for outdoor events, though this may lead to increased competition with other events in the marketplace. A family event may best be held on the weekend when all family members are available, or a seniors' event may best be held on a weekday morning to suit the needs of participants.

Choosing the event venue

The location of the event will be another important factor in developing the event concept. The venue must meet the needs of the event, not only catering for the number of attendees, but also contributing to the desired style and atmosphere. A formal event, such as an awards night or a black tie ball, will have different needs to an informal event, such as an office party or a rock concert. The venue must be able to meet the operational needs of the event in terms of access, catering, staging and facilities. It will need to fit inside the budget, including the costs of decoration, theming, and the provision of adequate power, water and staging facilities if these are not provided.

Lastly, it will need to meet the needs of participants including transport, parking and convenience.

Choosing the event concept

Once the basic parameters of the event have been identified, the task is to choose an event concept that best meets the needs of the event. Firstly, a decision will need to be made about the overall format of the event. If it is a corporate event, should it be a product launch, a training seminar or a media conference? Is a cocktail party appropriate, or is a formal sit-down dinner required? For a public event, it may be a concert, a festival, an exhibition or a parade. Should it be indoors or outdoors? How large should it be?

A widely used and rewarding technique employed by many event managers for developing event concepts is brainstorming (see figure 5.2). This involves first bringing a group of people together that may include stakeholders, other work colleagues and interested people. The group should then be briefed on the context and parameters of the event, and encouraged to participate in a free and associative flow of suggestions and ideas for the event concept. The only rule is that 'there are no rules', with participants invited to express whatever enters their minds, no matter how outrageous or impractical it may seem. It is useful to record ideas as they are expressed on a whiteboard or butchers' paper. Often the ideas tend to come in waves, with one person stimulated and inspired by the ideas of another until that particular wave is exhausted. Then, after a pause, another idea will start the process again. The brainstorm should be allowed to continue until the waves have subsided and the process is exhausted. Then the ideas can be reviewed and evaluated. At this stage, some ideas may be dismissed as marginal or impractical. Elements of some may be combined with others to form a single concept. If good fortune prevails, one idea may resonate so strongly that it emerges as the chosen event concept. Otherwise the ideas should be prioritised and carried forward for further consideration and development. In some instances the brainstorming process can be conducted over several sessions, or a single session can be used as the basis for identifying ideas that the event manager or team will continue to develop and refine.

- Define the parameters of the event
- Form a group of event stakeholders and colleagues
- Brief them on the event context and the parameters of the event
- Brainstorm a wide range of event concepts and ideas
- Identify the ideas that best serve the needs of the event
- Evaluate and prioritise these ideas
- Choose and refine an event concept

FIGURE 5.2 The brainstorming process

Another issue closely related to the event concept is that of the theme. For a corporate event, this may simply be the corporate colours of the company, or a smart contemporary look and feel. The message that the event is required to deliver may suggest a theme that amplifies and supports the message. A theme taken from popular culture, such as a current film or musical era, might help to strengthen the event and to unify and provide inspiration for the other creative elements and program. Whatever theme is chosen, it is essential that it matches the purpose and needs of the event.

Remember that the event concept is only the basic idea for the event, which will be fleshed out and elaborated later in the event creation process. However, the identification of the event concept is a crucial decision on which the ultimate success of the event will depend.

Summarising the process of creating the event concept

Goldblatt (1997) suggests that the process of creating an event concept can be summarised by asking five key questions that he terms the 'five Ws' of the event.

1. *Why* is the event being held? There must be compelling reasons that confirm the importance and viability of holding the event.
2. *Who* will be the stakeholders in the event? These include internal stakeholders, such as the board of directors, committee, staff and audience or guests, and external stakeholders such as media and politicians.
3. *When* will the event be held? Is there sufficient time to research and plan the event? Does the timing suit the needs of the audience, and if the event is outdoors, does it take the likely climatic conditions into account?
4. *Where* will the event be staged? The choice of venue must represent the best compromise between the organisational needs of the event, audience comfort, accessibility and cost.
5. *What* is the event content or product? This must match the needs, wants, desires and expectations of the audience, and must synergise with the why, who, when and where of the event.

Exploring these key questions thoughtfully and fully will go a long way towards identifying a strong event concept tailored to the specific context and needs of the event, which can then be built upon to create a unique and memorable experience. The elaboration of the event concept and its implications for theming, programming, performance, props and decoration, catering and staging will be discussed in detail in chapter 14.

Designing the event experience

Some writers (Silvers 2004; Berridge 2007) approach events as experiences, and note the role and importance of such experiences in contemporary lifestyles and the modern economy. People seek and embrace experiences that enrich their lives, and that resonate with their images of themselves and of their desired or imagined lifestyles. Thus lifestyle events that cater to people's tastes in music, fashion, leisure, food and wine become part of how they define themselves, and how they construct their identity and social networks. Companies also create events that enable their clients to experience the personality and attributes of their brands and products.

From an event manager's viewpoint, an event can be seen as a designed experience, consciously created in order to achieve a given purpose or objective. The task of the event manager is, then, to formulate a clear vision of the event experience, and to identify and design the elements needed for the experience to be realised. Seen from this perspective, the role of design in events involves much more than just the invitation, sets, costumes and table settings. The design process involves a myriad of decisions and choices that contribute to the overall experience of the event attendees. It includes elements such as the site layout, flow of guests, performance program, catering, security, site decoration and atmosphere. Berridge (2007) suggests that the design process can also be applied to the senses (sight, hearing, touch, smell and taste), interaction (such as trying out products and sampling services), the emotions and even the meaning and significance that participants take away from events. The total effect of these decisions will determine the nature of the event experience, and how it is received by individual participants or guests. Berridge (2007) emphasises the importance of this wider concept of the design process to events:

> The most important part of any understanding of design is to recognise that it is a planned process, and one that leads onto a pre-conceived outcome from an original idea and one that can be estimated and produced and that this applies to any number of applications. In an event there is a clear intention to firstly identify a set of features and then to see them translated into a (temporary) reality (or fantasy) that others can then experience, and therefore the role of design should be regarded as of fundamental and central significance to this process.

The application of the design process to all aspects of an event is illustrated in the following event profile.

event profile

THE NATIONAL EVENT SUMMIT 2009

The National Event Summit held on the Gold Coast in Queensland, Australia, in July 2009, had as its theme: 'Meeting the challenge of sustainable development: How do public and corporate events engage in the global agenda?'

The venue was chosen not only for its ability to accommodate the needs of the conference participants, but also for its adherence to sustainable policies. The use of spaces was designed to include a plenary auditorium and breakout rooms, a small exhibition of green suppliers and sponsors, an internet cafe where guests could check their email, and a green room for informal meetings and exchanges. Research papers were invited, and keynote speakers and case studies on Earth Hour, Clean Up Australia and Clean Up the World were chosen to enhance the theme. The Carbon Reduction Institute was engaged as a consultant to advise on sustainable event practices, and to calculate the carbon footprint of the conference. Carbon credits were purchased to offset the carbon footprint, and green energy was purchased to run the event. Slow Food Sydney was also engaged to work with the hotel chef to create food menus based on local produce, and to explain the environmental significance of this to participants. Paper wastage was minimised through the use of an online registration system, programs were printed in organic inks on recycled paper, and conference papers were distributed on USB sticks in bamboo containers. Artists were commissioned to decorate the venue with artworks created from recycled materials. Roving performers dressed as scientists 'measuring' the carbon footprint of participants were engaged to welcome guests and to lead them to the conference dinner at a nearby hotel by means of a 'walking bus'.

At the conclusion of the conference, the Carbon Reduction Institute reported on the environmental outcomes of the conference, and a free Carbon Calculator software application was launched for future use by the industry to help calculate and reduce the carbon impact of events.

Where possible in the design and implementation of the conference event plan and activities, choices were made to reinforce the environmental awareness of participants and to create a total event experience that exemplified and embodied the theme of the conference.

EVALUATING THE EVENT CONCEPT

Once the event concept has been decided and an initial scoping of the event completed, it is essential to examine whether the event can be delivered successfully within the available timeframe and resources. This process is known as a feasibility study, and may be conducted internally or, in the case of larger events, contracted to an external body (see also the section on feasability analysis in relation to bidding for events on page 92). On the basis of the feasibility study, a decision will be made as to whether or not the event will proceed. Shone and Parry (2004) describe what they refer to as the 'screening process' to examine the feasibility of the event. This involves using marketing, operations and financial screens to determine whether the event concept matches the needs and resources of the event. The three screens are:

1. the marketing screen
2. the operations screen
3. the financial screen.

The marketing screen

The marketing screen involves examining how the target audience of the event is likely to respond to the event concept. To determine this, an environmental scanning process needs to be conducted. This will help to determine whether the event concept resonates with current tastes and fashions, and whether it is likely to be perceived as innovative and popular or as boring and predictable. A good barometer will be the media response to the concept. If media representatives consider it to be of current interest, they are likely to become allies in the promotion of the event. If the media response is poor, then it will be difficult to promote interest and engage the audience.

For much of this assessment, event managers will need to rely on their own instincts and on testing the response of friends, co-workers and stakeholders to the concept. An alternative, particularly if a large investment is involved in the event, is to undertake some form of market research. This can be done within the resources of the event management company or by employing marketing professionals to conduct a market survey or focus group research. Such research may reveal not only the likely market acceptance of the concept, but also additional information, such as how much the target audience is prepared to pay for the event, or how the event concept may be adapted to meet market expectations or requirements.

A further factor in the environmental scan will be to examine the competition provided by other events in the market. This step will examine whether there are other events on a similar theme or in a similar timeframe, or major events and public holidays that are likely to impact on the target market. An investigation of the competition through a 'What's On' in the city listing, tourism event calendars and so on will assist the event manager to identify and hopefully avoid direct competition with other events in the marketplace.

The operations screen

The operations screen will consider the skills and resources needed to stage the event successfully, and whether the event manager has these skills and resources or can develop them or buy them in for the event. Specialised technical skills, for example, may be needed to implement the event concept. The event manager will need to consider whether event company staff members have these skills, or whether an external supplier needs to be engaged to provide them. Special licences, permits or insurance may be needed in order to implement the concept. If the event concept is highly innovative and challenging, the event manager may need to consider the degree of risk involved.

It may be desirable to deliver an innovative event, but costly and embarrassing if the event is a failure because the skills and resources available to stage it are inadequate.

Another major consideration, as part of the operations screen, is staffing. This step will examine whether the event company has sufficient staff available with the right mix of skills and at the right time, place and cost to deliver the event effectively. If the event needs to rely heavily on volunteers, the operations screen will examine whether sufficient numbers are likely to be available, and whether the right motivation, training and induction procedures are in place.

The financial screen

The final screen suggested by Shone and Parry (2004) is the financial screen. This screen examines whether the event organisation has sufficient financial commitment, sponsorship and revenue to undertake the event. The first step in this process is to decide whether the event needs only to break even, which may be the case if it is being staged as a company promotional event, or whether it is required to make a profit for the host organisation.

The next step will be to undertake a 'ballpark' budget of the anticipated costs and income of the event. Breaking the event down into its component parts will allow an estimate to be formed of the costs for each component. A generous contingency should be included on the cost side of the ledger, as at this stage of the event there are bound to be costs that have been underestimated or not yet identified. Calculating the income may require deciding on an appropriate pricing strategy and identifying the 'break-even' point of ticket sales. Other key revenue items to take into account may include potential government grants or subsidies, merchandising income and sponsorship support, both in cash and in-kind. It is important not to overestimate the sponsorship potential, and professional advice or a preliminary approach to the market may be required in order to arrive at a realistic estimate.

Cash flow is an important aspect of the financial screen often overlooked by inexperienced event managers. It is important not only to have sufficient funds to cover the expenses of the event, but to have them available when they are required. If, for example, a large part of the revenue is likely to be from ticket sales on the day, then it may be necessary to chart out the anticipated expenditure flow of the event, and to consider whether credit arrangements need to be made

Once the event concept has been screened and evaluated from the marketing, operations and financial aspects, the event manager is in a position to make an informed decision with regard to the conduct of the event. If the result is a 'go' decision, then the process of refining the event concept and developing the all-important event strategies and plans, the subject of later chapters of this book, can begin.

event profile

SONY PLAYSTATION 10TH ANNIVERSARY PARTY

'Expect the unexpected: we are like no other company and the events we put on must always stand out.'

This was the challenge Sony Computer Entertainment set TP Events when producing their tenth anniversary event in Sydney in 2005.

Retailers, corporate partners, employees and the general media were invited to celebrate this milestone in PlayStation's legendary history. With a brand that had experienced phenomenal growth and sales over ten years, TP Events had to produce an event that reflected PlayStation and its mark on the world of computer gaming.

Wharf 8 Industrial Hall was chosen as an urban setting that best suited the type of event envisaged. The concept was designed to immerse guests in a 'dark and surreal urban jungle' environment, spiced up with eclectic evolving entertainment.

However, with a same day bump-in, the event had to be meticulously planned. Teams and a crew of over one hundred were contracted to manage different aspects of the elaborate set up, along with TP Events' core production team. Riggers, audio-visual technicians, stylists and designers, light and sound crew, catering teams and 40 entertainers collaborated to create a futuristic urban city reflective of the gaming world and the Sony brand.

Guests arrived and were ushered into a red-draped room flanked with festoons, as a quirky music box played and tray sellers offered test tubes containing potent tequila shots. A Mr Whippy van served ice cones laced with colourful alcoholic shots and an eclectic mix of pre-show style food.

As the crowd swelled and the atmosphere built, guests who thought they were already at the event suddenly realised that everything was not going to be as expected. As a masterful soundscape sounded, the giant red curtains lifted to reveal Sony City — a futuristic and edgy world where anything goes and nothing is certain. Over the city a dazzling ceiling of lights and special effects formed a canopy of colour.

A wire-caged entertainment arena kept guests enthralled with a variety of freak-show style performances, including a world champion sword swallower, body piercers and punk roller derby rink skaters. A centre stage featured burlesque dancers and dramatic performances by a team of performance artists, including champion hula hoop dancers. Scattered around the city were ten years of Sony memorabilia, displayed for people to discover and marvel at.

A giant 60 foot projection screen covered the entire far end of the room, becoming a canvas for a visual montage of 'PlayStation 10 years in the making'. A retrospective montage of some of Sony's great television commercials was overlaid with high-end visual graphics and gaming footage, produced for the event by the TP studio.

Three giant, internally lit bars featured vodka luges (ice sculptures used as drinking vessels), bizarre cocktails and a living graffiti wall that evolved into a completed canvas at the end of the night. Wait staff in Sony PlayStation t-shirts, carrying custom-made perspex trays shaped like Sony PlayStation logos, passed pallets of delicious snacks. A 20-metre sushi train offered a moving selection of dishes that changed every hour. There was no certainty if the same dish would arrive on the next train, or if the train would de-rail mid delivery.

In the village area, smoking oil drums set the scene for an all-night noodle bar that served fresh portions, made to order. Satays, noodle boxes and stir fries became popular as the alcoholic creations started to work their magic.

DJ Steven Ferris played a fusion of modern and retrospective tunes to rouse the crowd between each act and during the performances. After short speeches by Sony's managing director and IBMS Intel director, a band played, along with 12 of Sydney's hand-picked leading session musicians, styled to rock the room.

The six hundred guests were still partying well into the morning and had to be ushered to a post-party venue to allow the TP team some time to dismantle the event.

Source: TP Events 2005.

SUMMARY

Events are required to serve a multitude of agenda, due to the increased involvement of governments and the corporate sector. The successful event manager needs to be able to identify and manage a diverse range of stakeholder expectations. Major stakeholders include the host organisation staging a particular event and the host community, as well as the various public authorities whose support will be needed. Both sponsors and media are significant partners, and can make important contributions to an event of support and resources beyond their formal sponsorship and media coverage. The members of the event team should share the same vision of the event and understand the philosophy behind it, and the contribution of the team members should be recognised. Ultimately, it is the spectators and participants who decide upon the success or failure of an event, and it is crucial to engage with them on an emotional level to create an entire event experience.

Events can be sourced or generated in a number of different ways. However, once the event has been obtained, the creation or updating of the event concept is a crucial step in the event management process. This begins with identifying the objectives of the event, and researching its history and participants. The next priority is to brainstorm ideas with stakeholders so that a shared vision for the event can be shaped and communicated. All aspects of events need to be designed, so that a total event experience is created, serving the needs of all stakeholders. The screening process then needs to be applied to the chosen concept to determine whether it is feasible given the limited resources available to the event. No event is created by one person, and success will depend on a collective team effort.

QUESTIONS

1 Who are the most important stakeholders in an event, and why?
2 Give examples of different events staged by government, corporate and community groups in your region and discuss their reasons for putting on these events.
3 Name a major event that you have attended or in which you have been involved, and identify the prime stakeholders and their objectives.
4 Focusing on an event that you have experienced first-hand, list the benefits that the event could offer a sponsor or partner.
5 Identify an event that uses social media to engage participants in the event. List the media that it uses, and describe how they are utilised in the event.
6 What are the means by which an event creates an emotional relationship with its participants and spectators?
7 What events can you think of that demonstrate a unique event concept or idea? What are the aspects or qualities that you consider to be unique?
8 Choose one of the events that you identified in the previous question, and discuss how the design process has been applied to choosing and implementing all aspects of the event.
9 Imagine you are planning a tourism event in the area where you live in order to promote the area as a tourism destination. What are the unique characteristics of the area, and how might these be expressed in the event?

case study

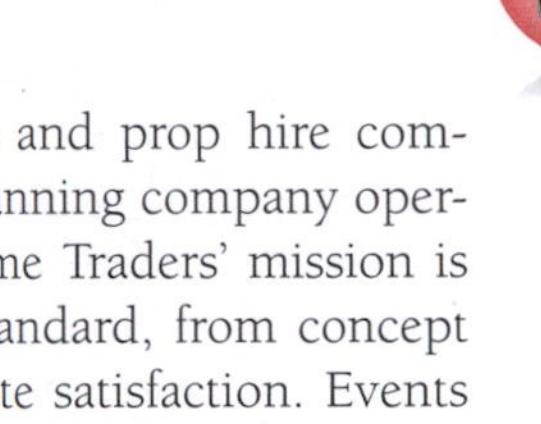

SEVEN DEADLY SINS CORPORATE EVENT

Theme Traders, London

Theme Traders, a London-based event management, props and prop hire company, was launched in 1989 as a creative events and party planning company operating worldwide. A vertically integrated one stop shop, Theme Traders' mission is to give a personal and professional service of the highest standard, from concept to completion, delivering creative solutions to ensure absolute satisfaction. Events organised by Theme Traders include weddings, bar and bat mitzvahs, corporate functions, children's parties, product launches, window dressing, set builds, exhibition stands, fashion shows, and public events. With a large number of high-profile clients, they have even worked for Her Majesty The Queen in Buckingham Palace.

At the end of 2005 Theme Traders was invited to pitch for a large event being held on 7 July 2007. The event was for a large shipping and distribution company that was celebrating their bicentenary throughout 2007. The company felt that a key element of their celebrations would be a huge party to thank their staff for all their hard work.

The brief

Theme Traders consider it essential that a brief is always read thoroughly by more than one staff member to ensure that nothing is missed or misunderstood. The brief in question outlined the following:

- The guest list would include directors, office-based staff, warehouse managers and lorry drivers. The party therefore had to appeal to all employees.
- The client wanted a linked event for up to 4000 people, to take place simultaneously at a number of locations/venues across the UK, on one memorable date — 07/07/07.
- The client wanted to introduce a theme that unified the locations of the parties; it was essential that employees enjoyed the same type of experience. Keywords included 'original', 'memorable', 'exciting', 'unique' and 'amazing'.
- Catering had to be considered although menus were not required at the pitch stage. The drink allowance had to be clearly stated in the pitch.
- Entertainment had to be described in the pitch.
- In order to reinforce a feeling of company unity, the company asked that the pitch consider the possibility of a live satellite link-up at some point during the evening.
- Everything had to be included in the budget — all project and event management, site visits, technical drawings, transport, crewing, health & safety (H&S) assessments and such.
- The budget equated to £100 per head + VAT (Value Added Tax)

Four companies were invited to pitch for the event. The pitch took place in front of 15 board members, including the managing director.

To pitch or not to pitch

Before Theme Traders agreed to enter the tendering process, they analysed the budget to assess whether it was feasible. They ascertained that if they looked at the

total budget — £100 × 4000 = £400,000 total — they would be able to achieve and exceed the client's expectations.

They then had a brainstorming session with members of their creative and project management departments. They knew that the theme was going to be a key factor in winning the job. The first idea that came out of the session was '007', but, being so obvious, they dismissed it. They decided it was highly likely that the other companies competing for the event may also suggest this concept and it was crucial to Theme Traders that they stand out from the crowd.

After considering the 'Seven Wonders of the World' as a concept, they finally settled on the 'Seven Deadly Sins'. They felt that this opened the door for fabulous décor and inspired entertainment. The brainstorming group became very excited about this theme and they hoped that the client would share their enthusiasm. They decided to create a PowerPoint presentation focussing heavily on visuals to stir the client's imagination.

The pitch

The presentation contained the following Theme Traders USPs (unique selling points).

Theme Traders knew that they were the best company for the job; they now had to persuade the client. It was critical that they communicate how they are different to the competing event management companies. The company USPs outlined in the pitch included the following:

- they are a vertically integrated company
- they own a fleet of 15 vehicles
- they have over 50 members or experienced creative staff
- they have in-house creatives, project management and logistic staff
- they own and make all of their stock and the client is welcome to view their showrooms and warehouses at any stage during the project
- their track record is excellent — they talked the group through some case studies of high-profile jobs, including the Queen's 80th birthday celebrations at Buckingham Palace.

Party locations

Following the introduction, Theme Traders explained the proposed locations for the parties. They had analysed the client's employee location map and chosen cities that had a high employee residency, and that were close to transport links for those that had to come from further afield. They decided upon six locations to stage the event:

1. London
2. Birmingham
3. Blackburn
4. Liverpool
5. Leeds
6. Edinburgh.

At this stage they did not suggest venues, rather Theme Traders nominated to take the client to see two suitable venues in each city, upon acceptance of their pitch.

Food and delivery

Theme Traders outlined a fork buffet with four complimentary drinks per head, which would be feasibly accommodated by the budget. Tastings would be arranged at the venues so the client could decide upon menus.

Design and entertainment

Theme Traders' creative department presented mood boards to communicate the look and atmosphere of the event. They also took the opportunity to describe the proposed entertainment. They talked the client through each sin:

- *Envy.* The entrance to each venue would be transformed into a 'Green with Envy' area, complete with green-painted stilt walkers.
- *Gluttony*. The buffet stations would pay homage to gluttony, with giant ice cream statues and chocolate fountains.
- *Greed*. A section of the venue would be glitzy and glamorous with gold palm trees and giant £ signs. Casino tables would provide entertainment in this area.
- *Pride*. Giant trophies, medals and winners' podiums combined with a giant Scalextric would make this a fun part of the event.
- *Lust and Sloth*. Decorated double beds, giant floor cushions and cherub statues would signpost areas guests could visit should they desire a head massage or a temporary tattoo.
- *Wrath*. This sin would be depicted over the dance floor, portrayed by moving lightening bolts and thunder sound effects.

At this stage of the pitch Theme Traders stressed that the venues would be identically decorated and would offer the same entertainment, to ensure that guests across each of the six venues would share the same experience.

Satellite link-up

The brief requested that Theme Traders explore the possibility of a live satellite link-up to connect the parties, at some stage during the proceedings. Having researched the concept, they recommended an alternative: a pre-recorded speech by the managing director that would be played simultaneously at each of the venues on large screens. The cost implications of a live link-up prohibited it as a viable option within the budget.

Budget

Finally, it was necessary that Theme Traders discuss the budget. They provided the client with a spreadsheet, breaking down how the £100 per head budget had been allocated, to demonstrate that the client would get value for money.

Waiting game

Two weeks after the pitch, Theme Traders was informed that they had won the contract. The client felt safe choosing them for such a large project because of their size and track record. Additionally, the client loved the 'Seven Deadly Sins' idea; they had discounted one company competing for the contract for pitching a '007' theme, thus validating earlier decisions about thinking outside the box and not choosing the obvious. (The client also disclosed that another company had presented a 'German Bierfest' concept, with girls in costume present throughout the pitch. The managing director asked this company to leave the room before they had finished. He found the idea offensive, particularly considering that they were pitching to both men and women. This indicates how important it is to know the audience to whom you are pitching. It also demonstrates that using props such as costumed performers during a pitch doesn't always work.)

Planning

- *Team structure*. As soon as the job was confirmed, the team was formed. The six events were organised by an executive event producer with two assistants. This core team took care of the entire planning process. They also allocated a core team of two to each party location — a senior project manager and a project manager. These sub teams would be responsible for the parties on the night.
- *Venues*. Theme Traders spent the next couple of months visiting venues in the proposed cities. Once the venues were selected, they would be able to concentrate on other elements.
- *Props*. The props team started making additional items for the parties; for example, they required 24 giant £ signs and had only 6 in stock, so 18 extra signs were constructed.
- *Entertainment*. Aware that 07/07/07 would be a popular day for events, they secured all entertainment months in advance.
- *Tastings*. The core team along with the sub team for each venue and the client attended tastings at each venue. Theme Traders advise to always photograph tastings and make notes, to ensure that the catering on the night matches the quality of the tasting.
- *Lighting/Sound/AV*. Some of the selected venues had in-house technicians and equipment; others were simply empty spaces that required them to bring in their own lighting and sound crews. This, again, involved site inspections at all venues.
- *Logistics*. The operations department was responsible for the vast undertaking of planning the trucking and crew for the job. On top of this, five other large events were scheduled on the same date, thus 11 events in total.
- *Health and safety*. Last, but definitely not least, the health and safety aspects of the event were addressed. Theme Traders carried out risk assessments and provided method statements for each venue. They also required these from all of their performers and suppliers. The health and safety paperwork alone for this job was enormous.

Showtime

The months of planning, the inclusion of contingency plans, and the attention to detail given to the planning process meant that each party took place without a hitch. The varied entertainment and the relaxed atmosphere at each venue meant that the employees socialised well and there was plenty for everyone to do.

From Theme Trader's point of view, the event was a great challenge and a fantastic project to be a part of.

Theme Traders, www.themetraders.com.

Questions

1. What do you think were some of the challenges in producing a similar event experience in six different event locations simultaneously? How did Theme Traders overcome these challenges?
2. What main elements were used to create and embellish the theme of the 'Seven Deadly Sins'?
3. Other than the theme elements referred to in question 2, what other major elements of the event would Theme Traders have had to design?

REFERENCES

Berridge, Graham 2007, *Events design and experience*, Butterworth-Heinemann, Oxford: Burlington, MA.

Commonwealth Games Legacy Manchester 2002, Post Games report, www.gameslegacy.com.

Conroy, S 2009, 'He who dares, wins' in Virgin Blue Voyeur July 2009 issue, Text Pacific Publishing, Sydney.

Earth Hour 2009, www.earthhour.org.

Getz, D 2005, *Event management and event tourism*, Cognizant Communication Corporation, New York.

Goldblatt, Dr JJ 1997, *Special events — best practices in modern event management*, Van Nostrand Reinhold, New York.

Goldblatt, J & Perry, J 2002, 'Re-building the community with fire, water and music: the WaterFire phenomenon', in *Events and place making: proceedings of international research conference held in Sydney 2002*, eds L Jago, M Deery, R Harris, A Hede & J Allen, Australian Centre for Event Management, Sydney.

Hemmerling, M 1997, 'What makes an event a success for a host city, sponsors and others?', Paper presented to The Big Event Tourism New South Wales Conference, Wollongong, New South Wales.

Hollway, S 2002, Keynote address delivered to Events and Place Making Conference, Australian Centre for Event Management, University of Technology, Sydney, 15–16 July 2002.

Jago, L, Chalip, L, Brown, G, Mules, T & Ali, S 2002, 'The role of events in helping to brand a destination', in *Events and place making: proceedings of International Research Conference held in Sydney 2002*, eds L Jago, M Deery, R Harris, A Hede & J Allen, Australian Centre for Event Management, Sydney.

Nichols, M 2009, 'YouTube orchestra prepares for Carnegie debut', http://uk.reuters.com

Nielsenwire 2008, 'Beijing Olympics Draws Largest Ever Global TV Audience', http://blog.nielsen.com.

Niersbach, W 2006, FIFA World Cup Germany 2006, News 15 An XXL World Cup for the media, www.fifaworldcup.com.

Portable Film Festival 2010, www.portablefilmfestival.com

Rock Eisteddfod Challenge 2009, www.rockchallenge.com.au.

Shone, A. with Parry, B. 2004, *Successful event management*, Thomson Learning, London.

Silvers, Julia Rutherford 2004, *Professional event coordination*, John Wiley and Sons, New Jersey USA.

Sydney Festival 2010, 'Optus Festival Buddy', www.sydneyfestival.org.au.

TP Events 2005, 'Sony PlayStation tenth anniversary party', www.tpevents.com.au.

Wang, W 2008, 'The Internet and the Beijing Olympic Games', www.china.org.cn.

PROJECT MANAGEMENT FOR EVENTS

LEARNING OBJECTIVES

After studying this chapter, you should be able to:

1. discuss project management as an approach to the management of festivals and events
2. describe the phases of event management
3. discuss the knowledge areas involved in conducting an event using project management techniques
4. describe the project manager's place in the event management structure and the competencies required
5. use the fundamental techniques of project management
6. comment on the limitations of the project management approach in event management.

INTRODUCTION

The production of a festival or event is a project. There are many advantages in using project management techniques to manage the event or festival. Project management oversees the initiation, planning and implementation of the event, in addition to monitoring the event and the shutdown. It aims to integrate management plans from different knowledge areas into a cohesive, workable plan for the entire project.

In this chapter, we will examine how the project manager fits into the event management structure. There are specific tools and techniques used by project managers and we overview the most common of these. We will then examine how evaluation of a project can build on the project management knowledge base to improve future project performance. We also look at some limitations of the project management approach to event management.

PROJECT MANAGEMENT

According to the leading textbooks on project management, world business is moving towards the accomplishment of business objectives through separate projects. Due to the changing nature of modern business, products and services now have to be managed as projects as a response to this change. A product in the modern world is continually evolving. Software upgrades are an example of this evolution and they create, in turn, an environment that is constantly evolving.

The event industry is expanding in response to this turmoil, and to the constant renewal of products and services. New events are needed to launch products, new conferences and seminars are needed to educate the market and new festivals are needed to reposition towns and regions in the marketplace as the national economy changes. Government departments are not immune. The Australian Taxation Office, for example, organised a number of events to explain the goods and services tax to the public and to tax agents. Events and festivals can, then, be seen as a response to a constantly changing business and cultural environment.

Just as new developments in business need to be project managed, events and festivals require managing using project management techniques. As projects, events and festivals employ an increasingly pervasive management methodology.

Special events and festivals are projects. They:

- are non-routine and occur at or over a specific period
- are limited by time, budget and scope
- produce an outcome designed to meet a client's need.

A project produces an asset such as a building, film, software system or even a man on the moon — or a special event or festival. The asset is the ultimate deliverable of the project. The management is the planning, organising, leading and controlling of the project.

The project management of events concentrates on the management process to create the event, not just what happens at the event. Many texts and articles confuse the event with its management. The event is the deliverable of a management process. A bridge, for example, is the deliverable of a series of processes called engineering and construction. An event may take place over a period of hours or days. The event management process may take place over many months or years. Project management is a system that describes the work before the event actually starts, the event itself and finally the shutdown of the event.

Project management is called the 'overlay', as it integrates all the tasks of management. Event management is made up of a number of management areas, including planning, leading, marketing, design, control and budgeting, risk management, logistics, staging and evaluation. Each of the areas continuously affect each other over the event project phases. Project management can be regarded as integrating all of these disciplines; thus it covers all the different areas of management and integrates them so they all work towards the event objectives.

O'Toole and Mikolaitis (2002, p. 23) describe the advantages of using project management for events:

1. It is a systematic approach that can be improved with every event. Project management describes the management system. Once something is described it can be improved. If it remains hidden there is nothing to improve.
2. It avoids the risk that the event's success relies on one person. By having a system with documentation, filing and manuals, as well as clear communication and teams, the event is understood by anyone with the right experience.
3. It uses a common terminology and therefore facilitates clear, timely communication.
4. It ensures accountability to the stakeholders. Stakeholder management is a fundamental knowledge area of project management.
5. It makes the management of the event apparent. Too often the management is hidden by the importance of the event.
6. It helps train staff in a common system and provides a competency framework by which they can measure their level of expertise. This identifies gaps in their knowledge and skill and provides a pathway for improvement.
7. It is used in all other areas of management, not just events. Management methodology used for the event can be transferred to any project. Once the event is over, staff will have learned a useful, transferable skill.
8. It is common to other businesses. Many of the event stakeholders will already be familiar with the terminology.

Points 4 and 5 are related to the event itself being mistaken for the management. Clear and timely accountability to numerous event stakeholders is a requirement for event managers. Accountability cannot wait until the event is delivered. Stakeholders, such as the police, sponsors and government, may want a series of reports on the progress of the management. It is too late to find out that the management company was incompetent during the event. Clients are demanding a work in progress (WIP) report. A project management system has this reporting facility as a part of the methodology.

To this list it can be added that project management knowledge and skills is regarded by many event courses, certificates and forthcoming standards as a core competency. Both the Event Management Body of Knowledge (EMBOK) and the International Event Management Standard (IEMS) list project management skills as essential to event management (CTHRC 2010).

Project management comprises basic concepts that are not necessarily found in ongoing management. A project has a specific completion date, budget and product. This product or deliverable cannot be improved. Unlike ongoing management, such as a company continually producing a product and adapting it, a project has to produce the best product the first time. There is no time for improvement. To borrow words from the music industry, 'you are only as good as your last gig'. This is particularly true for a one-off, special event. A yearly festival may grow and develop each year, but each festival, including the first, has to be great to ensure the festival's longevity.

The management of the project passes through phases. The management team has to be aware of the knowledge areas and the way they change over the project life cycle.

event profile

APPLYING PROJECT MANAGEMENT TO EVENT PLANNING

James Mackay is a highly experienced event coordinator in a major city in Australia. He organises events ranging from civic ceremonies to launches and public festivals. He started using project management to organise events about ten years ago. The following is based on an interview with James.

There are three advantages of using the project management approach to delivering an event:

1. systematic planning
2. clear communication
3. effective monitoring.

Project management enables the event manager to identify the stakeholders of an event, to call them to a meeting, and to agree upon the project definition, objectives and expectations in a planned way. Says James:

> We re-launched a historic site, for example, and we agreed that we needed to re-engage community ownership and create a spectacular event to give it prominence, and develop awareness [about it] as a tourism facility. We needed to have political representation at the highest level and to demonstrate the value of the events. At the same time, we needed to demonstrate intergovernmental cooperation.

Project management is an agreed upon methodology used by professionals across organisations. This methodology means that James can be precise with his communications, and engineers and trades people know exactly what is required. Many of the events James manages take place on government property; he is often talking to professionals with no event management experience, but who understand project management terminology. Project management therefore enables him to bridge this gap. For example, the concept of 'percentage of task completed' is understood by those with no event management experience.

James also works with professionals outside his organisation, such as the Department of Finance and Administration, military, police, Road Transport Authority, emergency services and various subcontractors. They understand the event framework of tasks and schedules, and the project management methodology. It is a common language. 'The use of milestones that are agreed upon by the stakeholders enable me to confidently monitor our progress.' The work breakdown structure and the schedule becomes the basis on which the event team's progress can be plotted.

For example, one Australia Day, James was organising a citizenship ceremony for 100 candidates, which would include participation by the Australia Day ambassador and a dance performance group, and which would conclude with a morning tea. This was to be followed 90 minutes later by a Volunteers Recognition Ceremony at the same outdoor (bare) venue. Both events were to have a different look and theme, which would involve a change of signage, seating plan, caterers and entertainment, plus different participants, guests and audiences. After referring to the project plan, the scope of work and the schedule, James realised that, while the other tasks could be achieved, it was not practical to use different caterers.

James Mackay, interview 2010.

PHASES OF THE PROJECT MANAGEMENT OF EVENTS

A project will pass through a series of phases or stages. Figure 6.1 illustrates these phases.

A project phase is a series of related tasks, performed over a period of time and under a particular configuration of management to produce a major deliverable. The end of a phase is often characterised by a major decision to begin the next phase. There are a number of different views on project phases. Some texts on project management for software development describe up to seven phases. Civil engineering texts have four phases of project management, described in *A guide to the project management body of knowledge 2008* (Project Management Institute 2008). According to the International Event Management Body of Knowledge (EMBOK 2006), event and festival management is accurately portrayed as having five domains: administration, marketing, design, operations and risk. These domains are subdivided into categories or classes.

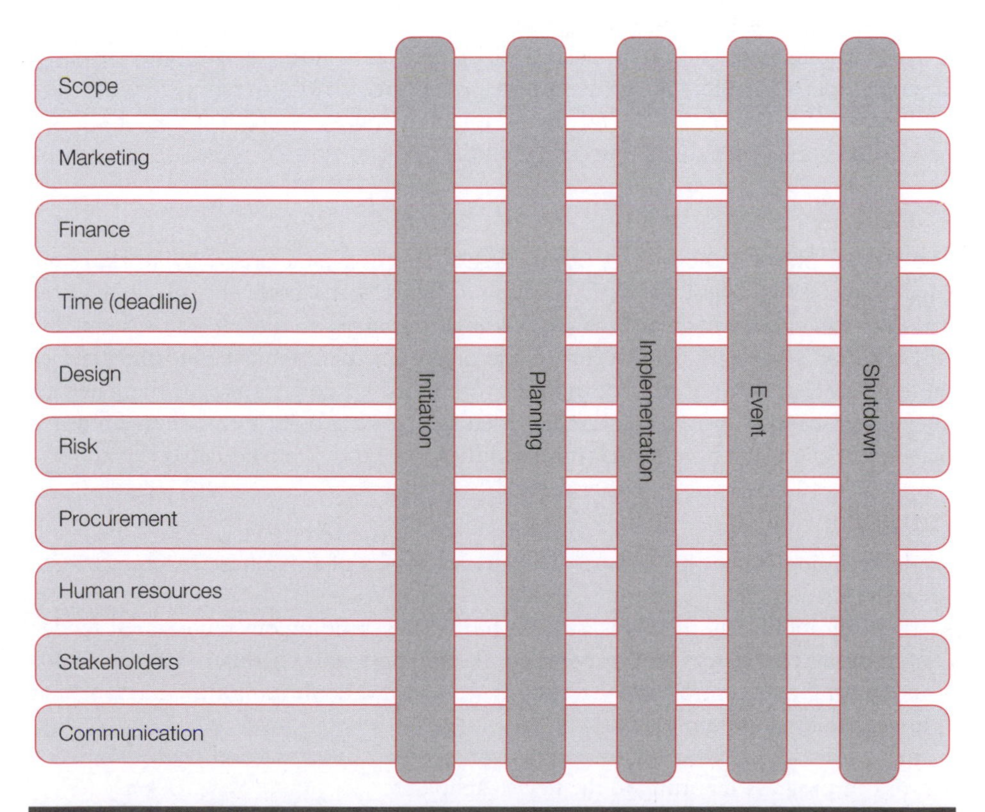

FIGURE 6.1 The phases of project management

Source: EPMS 2010.

The phase approach to describing the management of an event is purely descriptive — as with any description, it approximates reality. The aim is to provide clarity to the confusing tasks involved in event management. Some project phases overlap; planning and implementation can take place at the same time in different areas of management. The promotion schedule, for example, may be happening at the same time as aspects of the program are being redesigned. This chaos, however, does have a pattern and the five-phase approach is a useful tool to help the reader to understand it.

Initiation

The first phase of project management, initiation, is characterised by the idea of the event being developed and setting the objectives. It may be a vague idea, for example, that a town should organise a heritage festival, or a promoter decides to organise a rainforest concert. As well as this event concept, the initiation phase may include a feasibility study. The project feasibility study will report on the viability of the event and the management required to deliver it. It may include site and date suggestions, possible sponsors and supporters, a draft budget, possible risks, required management for the event and event logistics. The feasibility study may incorporate a number of alternative configurations of the event, so that the sponsor or client can choose the best options that will suit them. The initiation phase interfaces and overlaps with the strategic planning process as discussed in chapter 4 and with conceptualising the event as set out in chapter 5. The project objectives will relate to the objectives of the host in sponsoring the event.

The business case for the project is often used as a form of feasibility study. It describes the reason for the event in terms of the return on investment to the host community or company. The end of the initiation phase is characterised by a 'go/no-go' decision — whether to proceed with the event or not.

Planning

The second phase is the project planning. Planning is characterised by working out what is needed and how it will fit together. Chapter 4 discusses this phase in detail from a strategic point of view. Each of the knowledge areas on the left side of figure 6.1 will produce a separate plan. A major role of project management is to integrate all these plans; that is, to make sure they all work together. For this reason the plans are often called baseline plans. They are regarded as a starting point rather than a finished plan. Once the plans have been formulated they need to be implemented.

Implementation

Implementation is the third phase. The characteristics of this phase in project managing events are:

- the application of all the plans, such as hiring staff, sending out requests for tender, confirming contractors and carrying out the promotional schedule
- monitoring and controlling — testing the plans and confirming how relevant they are as the organising progresses
- making decisions based on the comparison between the plans and reality
- work in progress reporting to the key stakeholders
- active risk management.

The beginning of this phase is a time of high activity with meetings to discuss specific issues, decisions to be made and communication between various parties. Management may need to revisit the planning phase when there are major changes and the plans need to be revised. During the implementation phase the team has to be focused on the project scope and ensure all the plans are compatible with each other and with the overall objectives of the event.

In traditional project management, this third phase is the final phase and involves the handover of the deliverable. Events are not a tangible asset that can be handed over in the same way as a building. For this reason, it is wise to add an extra phase into the project phases and call this 'the event'.

The event

Unlike civil engineering project management, the project event manager is working during the deliverable; that is, the event. Although this is not seen as a separate phase by traditional texts on project management, it fits into the definition above. During the event, the tasks and responsibilities tend to roll on regardless of what the management wants to have happen. The staff numbers during the event, including volunteers, may increase dramatically. The short time period, attendance of the major stakeholders, the audience and the participants, mean that the management cannot rely on the same management techniques used during the lead-up to the event. This is recognised in all events, when the operations manager, artistic director or the stage manager takes over the running of the event. In the theatre, at an agreed time before the show, the stage manager is regarded as the ultimate authority. At a certain time before the event, the management team will move into 'operations mode', which might mean getting out of the office and into their costumes for the event. The monitoring and controlling at this point will be devolved to other teams and the management will run the event by looking for errors and making on-the-spot decisions. The tools and techniques used by management during this phase are found in chapter 14 on staging.

Shutdown

The event manager will be responsible for the shutdown of the event. It is the last phase and requires a separate series of tasks and responsibilities. Management will be scaled down and return to their pre-event formation. Chapter 15 describes the processes used in event shutdown. This phase includes the on-site shutdown and the management closure. The shutdown plans will be created during the planning phase and the shutdown ideally is the implementation of these plans. However, in an industry beset by major changes, the shutdown will rarely go exactly to plan. Monitoring and decision making from management will be needed. The shutdown phase can take the event from a seeming success to a failure if the management does not make the right decisions at this time. Shutdown includes preparation for the next event. On-site, this includes packing for the next event; off-site, the management will be archiving the documents and assessing their management. It is during this phase that the success of the management system is evaluated and the baseline plans or templates created for future events.

In summary, the best way to describe the event management process from a project management perspective is in terms of five phases: initiation, planning, implementation, the event and shutdown. These phases comprise the life cycle of the project. Each of the phases will require different management techniques and tools. Different areas of knowledge will be used. During the event, the event management team will be monitoring the event for any changes, rather than initiating any major new actions.

Knowledge areas

The management of any festival or special event will be concerned with the areas illustrated on the left side of figure 6.1. The relative importance of each of these management areas will change and evolve over the phases. From this figure, the event itself is seen as a small part of the whole management process.

As mentioned in the planning section, management will produce a number of deliverables in each of these knowledge areas. In the finance area, for example, management will produce a financial plan and a budget. The marketing area will produce a marketing plan and a promotion plan. The design area will produce the site plan and the actual event program. These deliverables are used throughout the management process to organise the event. They focus the staff in each individual area and become the documentation of the event. The areas correspond to the departments of an ongoing business organisation. The project management approach seeks to integrate the plans from each separate knowledge area into a cohesive, workable plan for the project.

PMBoK 2008^{TM} (the *Project management body of knowledge*) lists nine areas of knowledge for traditional project management areas: scope, cost, time, integration, procurement, quality, human resources, communication and risk. Event management is slightly different. It will also be concerned with marketing and designing the event. In the construction industry, the project manager would rarely be involved in designing the building, finding the money to build it or making decisions on the building's marketability. These are major concerns for the special event and festival manager. These areas of event project management knowledge can be explained as follows:

- *Scope* encompasses all the work, including all the plans, and is defined further in this chapter. The scope, therefore, helps to integrate the many plans. Controlling the scope is a fundamental responsibility of the project manager.
- *Marketing* is a combination of processes that help define the event and, therefore, the scope of the event. Marketing is described in chapter 9. Marketing the asset is not a traditional separate function of project management; however, some of the modern texts on civil engineering and software projects are teaching aspects of marketing. Marketing may be regarded as a feed-forward control mechanism for events and as a risk management tool to minimise uncertainty.
- *Finance* would be called 'cost' in traditional project management. In some industries, the project management would not be concerned with the source of funds. However, in events and festivals, the funding — or revenue — is often a basic responsibility of the event or festival management. These issues are dealt with in chapters 7, 10 and 11.
- *Time management* in the form of schedules and milestones is primary to all project management. For events and festivals the deadline takes on a higher significance. Project management has developed numerous techniques to manage time.
- *Design* and creation of the asset is found in the project management of software and product development. The event or festival may be changing design right up until the day it starts. Event project management, therefore, must incorporate design under its integration of the event planning. Chapters 5 and 14 describe the processes involved in event design. Within the design area of knowledge resides the PMBoK heading of 'quality'.
- *Risk management* is seen as one of the knowledge areas of project management. Although it is a recent phenomenon in event management, managing risk is a fundamental function of project management. It covers all the other areas of management, is constantly undertaken and produces up-to-date reports, which is why it has been adapted for the project management of many events. Projects do not see risk management as an arduous exercise. It is regarded as a way to improve the quality of the project and the deliverable. Chapter 18 describes event risk management in detail.

- *Procurement* includes the sourcing and managing of supplies and the management of contracts. This is described in chapter 17. It is closely linked to sponsorship, finance and risk management.
- *Human resources* could be seen as a part of procurement, but the special conditions of dealing with people, such as team building and leadership, are indispensable to all projects, and so human resources is considered a separate area of knowledge. Chapter 8 describes this aspect in relation to events in detail.
- *Stakeholder management* is an important responsibility of the event manager. Some large public events will have more than 70 stakeholders; therefore, it is an important area of management for the event team. Finding and servicing sponsors is one of the areas of stakeholder management. Sponsorship will be examined in detail in chapter 11.
- *Communication* includes external communication with the stakeholders and internal communication with the event team. It changes as event organising progresses. The external communication is linked to marketing and stakeholder management. On-site communication is linked to the staging and logistics of events as described in chapters 14 and 15.

Role of the project manager

Project management can be seen as a collection of skills and knowledge that allows the integration of various contractors to deliver the project. The old term for a project manager was a contract manager. What is the role of the event manager, given that they are also project managers? There are three solutions to this problem:

1. Expand the skill base of the event manager to include project management.
2. Reduce the responsibilities of the event manager and hire a project manager.
3. Train existing project managers in events management.

Each of these solutions is being undertaken for different events and festivals. Event managers are being trained in project management at a variety of courses around the world. Project management is now a core subject in these courses. Figure 6.1 illustrates all the areas of responsibility of the event manager trained in project management. Solution 2 is found in public events where the event management is split between the event director and the producer in charge of the creative aspects of the event, and the event project manager (who is in charge of the contracts, communication, compliance and other management areas). The event producer and event project manager have equal status in the organisation and report to the client. Originally, for large events, the roles would have been event director and operations or logistics manager; however, the operations manager could not take on the responsibilities of legal compliance, management integration and accountability, hence the pressure to create a new position of event project manager. In figure 6.1, the event director would be mostly concerned with the event design.

Solution 3 is used for very large events such as the Olympics and Grand Prix. The large project management companies, such as APP and GHD, are involved in events as diverse as the Asian Games and the Sydney Royal Easter Show. In this case, the event is planned and controlled by the project management company, which hires an event director as a contractor. In figure 6.1, the project company is responsible for all the areas of management. Their primary task is integration and contract management. Most of the areas, such as marketing and finance, would be outsourced.

Key competencies of a project manager in events

Education providers and project managers' employers are moving towards a competency approach to training and employment. Project managers employed by events and festivals are expected to prove their skills in the application of project management to events. This is often expressed in terms of key performance indicators, competency levels or education benchmarking.

An informal survey of recent project management job descriptions for events and festivals demonstrates the competencies or skills considered essential to the position by listing the following requirements or actions:

- develop and work in a team and provide leadership
- successfully define tasks and deliver on time and to quality
- integrate the project plan with the strategic, marketing and artistic plan of the event
- undertake risk management according to the standards of the industry
- use financial controls, indicators and reports effectively
- develop a procurement plan and manage contracts
- demonstrate high level communication skills in presentation and negotiation
- liaise with and manage a wide range of external stakeholders, including public and private organisations
- produce management progress reports for senior management and clients, including project evaluation and project closure
- possess knowledge of the event and similar events in this field
- have the ability to employ and assess project software and management systems related to events.

Other areas that may come under the responsibilities of the event project manager are:

- site design and management
- defining client requirements
- sponsorship management
- event concept development.

The three areas of event management often missing from the project management areas of responsibility are the event concept creation, sponsorship development and marketing. In the more traditional application of project management, the finance of the project and the design of the asset are not in the domain of the project manager. In civil engineering, for example, the client will provide the finance and the architect will provide the asset design. However, these are increasingly becoming the roles of project management. Software project management will have a large influence on the design of the product; therefore, an event project manager may be required to expand their competencies to include design, marketing and finance.

Most universities offer courses on project management and many event courses around the world have adopted modules on project management. The national competency standards in Australia for event management include competencies in project management. The International Event Management Competency Standard developed in Canada has project management as a core knowledge area.

PROJECT MANAGEMENT TECHNIQUES

Numerous techniques have evolved in project management through live testing in areas as diverse as information technology, product development and engineering. Many techniques originally come from other disciplines such as operations, research and logistics. Most of these techniques are useful to event management. The scope and work breakdown structure are used to delineate the event and provide a management framework for planning and control. The techniques are not used in isolation and they form a process or a series of tasks that overlap. The process is outlined as a cascade model in figure 6.2. The description of project management as a linear process is only an approximation, as each stage of the process will influence the early stages.

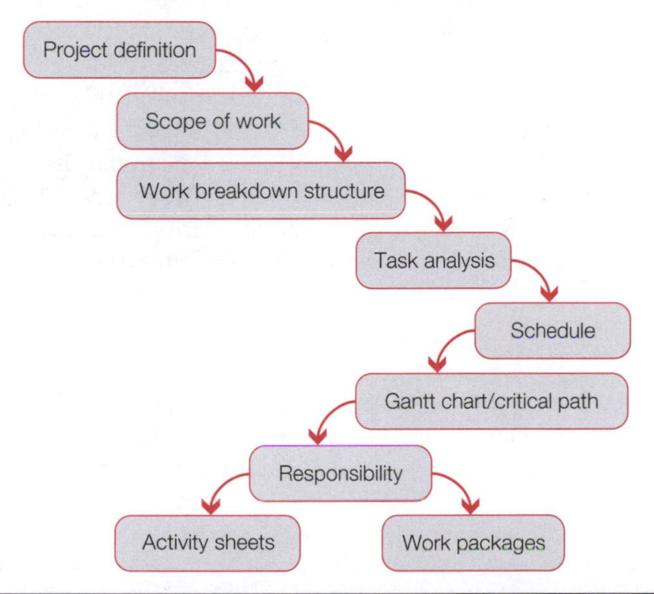

FIGURE 6.2 Project management cascade

Defining the project and scope of work

The indispensable technique in project management is defining the project and, therefore, defining the scope. Misunderstandings over what is involved in the management of an event are common. Most project management literature stresses that the time spent on clearly defining a project in the initiation phase is time well spent. What is involved in the management? Who will do what? What will be the responsibilities of the client and the event company? These are some of the questions that assist project definition. Note that project definition is not the same as defining the event. A simple event may still be a complex project.

The scope — or scope of work — refers to the amount of work required to get the event up and running and then to shut it down; it is all the work. To define the scope is to gain an understanding of the event and its management. Often the event is described in terms of what is happening at the event. The scope definition captures the work necessary to deliver the event, as well as what is going on at the event.

The scope definition may be contained in the brief from the client or primary event sponsor; however, the client brief may be too simple and eventually lead to misunderstandings. Often the brief will only describe the deliverable — that is, the event — and the work required to create it will be hidden. This has been a common problem in project management and the clarity and detail of the brief is identified as essential in the initiation period. For this reason, the event brief may be clarified by an addition of a statement of work (SOW). This is a document that summarises the key points of the project, such as a list of the stakeholders, event objectives, draft budget, schedule and responsibilities.

An important part of defining the scope is listing and understanding the requirements of the event stakeholders. In project management, a stakeholder is an organisation or an individual who has an interest in the project. Under this definition, the list will include negative stakeholders, such as competing events and organisations opposed to the event. The primary stakeholders will include sponsors and the organising committee. Secondary stakeholders include organisations that have an interest in the event if some action is not completed, or an unexpected incident occurs. For many events the police and emergency services are secondary stakeholders.

The deliverable of the stakeholder analysis is the stakeholder management plan. A good example of a stakeholder management plan in events is the sponsorship plan, as the sponsors are key stakeholders in events. The number of stakeholders in a simple event is large when compared to other projects. For this reason, figure 6.3 and figure 6.1 show stakeholder management as a major function of the event project manager.

Creating a work breakdown structure

The next step in the cascade is the 'work breakdown structure' (WBS). Once the scope has been decided and defined, it needs to be categorised, documented and communicated. The creation of the WBS is a technique that focuses management on the work required to deliver the event. The creation of a visual display of all the work that needs to be done can assist the staff in understanding the scope of the work.

To deliver the event there will be an extensive number of tasks that have to be completed. These tasks can be complex and a long list of them may not be very helpful. A way to get this under control is to 'aggregate' the tasks under headings. All the tasks concerning the venue, for example, could be grouped under the heading 'venue' or 'on-site'. The tasks that concern finding the money and working out the cost could be listed under the heading 'finance'. Deciding on task groups and headings should be completed during the initiation phase or at the beginning of the planning phase.

Alternatively, another way to describe task grouping is breaking down all the work required to deliver the event into manageable units. These management units will require common resources and skills. The work breakdown structure often parallels the folder system used on the computer or in the filing cabinet. For a public festival, the work breakdown structure may parallel the subcommittees set up to organise the event. A festival may have four systems: committee, file folders, email folders and paper folders. It makes sense to have them all integrated under the names of the headings in the work breakdown structure. The committee, the paper folder, the email folder and the file folder should all be called 'venue', for example. It is a simple procedure to standardise the names of folders, but often overlooked. A local festival, for example, may have the following subcommittees: finance, marketing (or promotion), legal or risk, human resources (such as volunteers) and administration. Note that each of these correspond to knowledge areas illustrated in figure 6.1. This is an example of the work breakdown structure where the subcommittees represent the work needed to organise the event.

Once the work breakdown structure is created it can be used for the next stage in planning the event. Figure 6.3 illustrates the plans and documents that can be created from the WBS. These plans and documents are often called the deliverables. They are proof that the tasks have been carried out and they are used by other areas of event management; that is, they are delivered to the event management team.

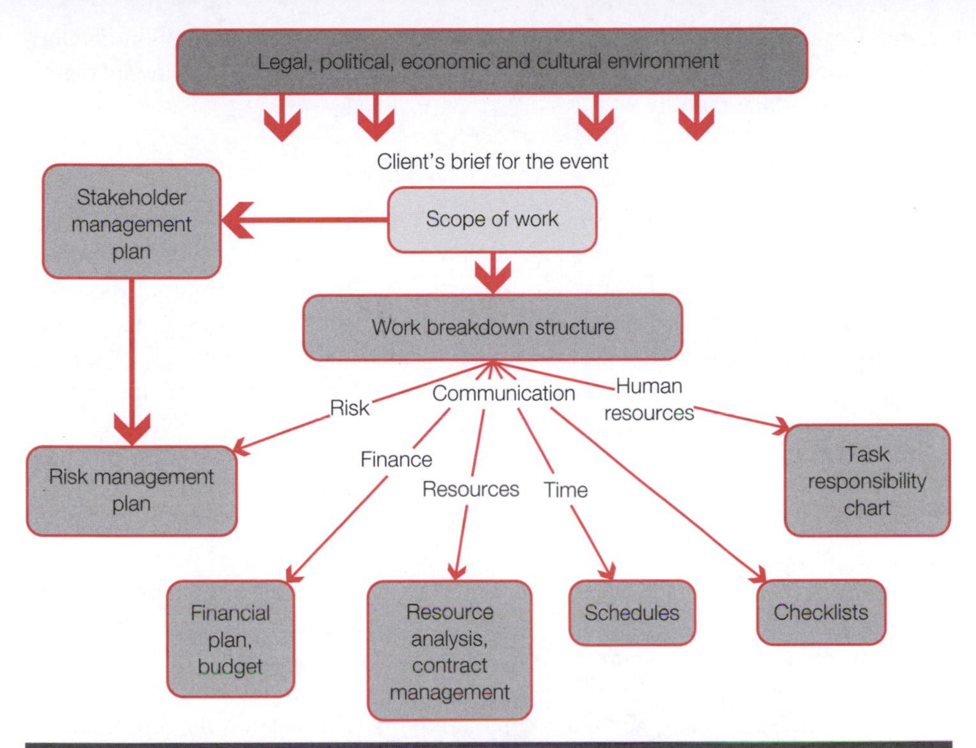

FIGURE 6.3 Plans and documents created from the work breakdown structure (WBS)

Source: EPMS 2010.

Analysing the resources

The resource list is developed from the WBS. The WBS is fundamental to resource analysis. The resources may be services, such as security, or goods, such as tents and chairs. Resources may also be a mixture of both, such as catering and sound. Resource analysis allows the event management to decide on what services and goods are:

- outsourced to suppliers
- sourced from the client or sponsor
- specially created or constructed for the event.

These are major decisions as they will impact on the budget. The resources may be grouped together and given to the one supplier. In project management this is called creating a work package. On large events, the supplier may need to submit a tender to supply these goods or services. An example of this is the supply of sound. A WBS may show that sound equipment will be needed in various areas of the event, including the different stages and the entrance. These requirements are grouped together and given to a number of sound companies to supply a quote for the work.

One of the outputs or deliverables of the resource analysis is a list of suppliers. This deliverable is the input into the contract management process. Chapter 18 on risk management explains this process in detail.

Perhaps the most important output of the resource analysis will be the human resource plan. This plan will be linked to the tasks and responsibilities described in the next section. In project management, the tasks are matched to the skills found in the pool of human resources available for the project. This process is outlined in chapter 8. A straightforward measurement of hours required for the event and the cost per hour can give the overall cost of this resource; however, many events use volunteers. A cost–benefit analysis of volunteers is difficult, as there are so many intangible benefits and hidden costs.

Identifying tasks and responsibilities

The breakdown of event management into the WBS may identify all the tasks that need to be completed to deliver the event; however, this is highly unlikely as there are myriad tasks for even the simplest of events. One only has to think of the many tasks involved in organising a wedding. The WBS will classify the tasks in manageable units. Each manageable unit will have groups of tasks associated with it. A WBS, for example, may have 'promotion' as a heading. Promoting the event will include the tasks of identifying the media, contacting the media, creating a schedule, creating a press release and many more. Each task has to be completed by a certain time and by a person or group of people, hence the task analysis is the beginning of assigning responsibilities. Chapter 8 on human resources goes into this area in more detail. In a special event and festival environment, a task analysis is deemed more suitable since the activities performed are usually too varied to be adequately captured by a job analysis. Job analyses don't address the question of what needs to be outsourced, and special events and festivals farm out most of the work (for example, catering, advertising and audiovisual).

In project management practice it is common to map the WBS on the organisational structure. Each organisational unit corresponds to an area of the WBS. The management structure of a community event, for example, will be made up of a number of subcommittees. Each will have a clearly defined group of tasks assigned to it.

An output of this process, often called task analysis, is the task responsibility chart or document. On this document are listed the tasks, who is responsible or what company, when the tasks should be completed and how the completion of tasks will be communicated. A task/responsibility list can also be put together at the end of meetings. Sometimes these are called action lists. Project managers prefer a task/responsibility list to the minutes of the meeting, because they are a 'call to action'. They are direct and the task is not hidden in other information that is not relevant to the required actions.

Scheduling

Project management can be loosely defined as planning the who, what, where and when. The schedule represents the when. Almost all events have a fixed date or a deadline. Completed tasks take on an importance not found in other types of management. The schedule is a vital control tool allowing the project to progress. A mistake in scheduling can have a widespread effect on the other areas of management — leading to blowouts in costs, thereby compromising quality. The deadline is so important that most event managers work back from the date of the event. The schedule can be clearly represented by a Gantt chart.

Gantt chart

Gantt charts are bar charts named in honour of the management science theorist Henry Gantt, who applied task analysis and scheduling to the construction of navy ships. The Gantt chart is simple to create and its ability to impart knowledge quickly and clearly has made it a popular tool in project management. The steps in creating a Gantt chart are described as follows:

- *Tasks* — break down the work involved in the area of event management into manageable tasks or activities. One of the tasks, for example, of the security team for the event is the erection of the perimeter fence around the site. This can be further broken down into the arrival of the fencing material, the arrival of volunteers and equipment, and the preparation of the ground. As discussed above, this work is usually done as part of identifying tasks and responsibilities.
- *Timelines* — set the time scale for each task. Factors to consider are the starting and completion times. Other considerations in constructing a time scale are availability, hiring costs, possible delivery and pick-up times and costs. A major factor in the arrival time and set-up of large tents, for example, is their hiring costs. These costs can depend on the day of the week on which they arrive, rather than the amount of time for which they are hired. Note that the schedule for many aspects of the event management will work back from the date of the event.
- *Priority* — set the priority of the task. What other tasks need to be completed before this task can start? Completing this priority list will create a hierarchy of tasks and identify the critical tasks.
- *Grid* — draw a grid with the days leading up to the event across the top and a list of the tasks down the left-hand side of the grid. A horizontal bar corresponding to each task is drawn across the grid. The task of preparing the ground for the fencing, for example, depends on the arrival of materials and labour at a certain time and takes one day to complete. The starting time will be when the prior tasks are completed and the length of the timeline will be one day. The horizontal bars, or timelines, are often colour coded so each task may be easily recognised when the chart is completed for all activities.
- *Milestones* — as the chart is used for monitoring the progress of the event, tasks that are of particular importance are designated as milestones and marked on the chart. The completion of the security fence, for example, is a milestone as it acts as a trigger for many of the other event preparation activities.

Figure 6.4 shows an example of a simplified Gantt chart. This chart is common to most small regional festivals.

Tasks	F	S	S	M	T	W	T	F	S	S	M	T	W	T	F	S	S
Clear and prepare site											Opening night						
Generators arrive																	
Lighting on site																	
Tents arrive																	
Stages arrive and set up																	
Site security																	
Sound system arrives																	

Milestone: start of festival

FIGURE 6.4 Simplified Gantt chart of a small festival

In his work on the human factors in project management, Dinsmore (1998) stressed that this display of project tasks and timelines has a high communication value to an event. It forestalls unnecessary explanations to the staff and sponsors and gives a visual representation of the event. Timelines are used in all events, regardless of their size. The on-time arrival of goods and services, even at a small event, can add significant value.

The advantages of a Gantt chart are that it:

- visually summarises the project or event schedule
- is an effective communication and control tool (particularly with volunteers)
- can point out problem areas or clashes of scheduling
- is readily adaptable to all event areas
- provides a summary of the history of the event.

For the Gantt chart to be an effective tool, the tasks must be arranged and estimated in the most practical and logical sequence. Underestimating the time needed (length of the timeline) can give rise to cost blow-out and render any scheduling ineffective. For example, if the time allocated to assess the competency of a contractor is short, the assessment will not be valid. This can result in huge problems on the day of the event that may only be solved by hiring another contractor at great expense. Overestimating the time needed to accomplish a task or extending the schedule can cause as just as many problems. Aside from the cost of the extra time to accomplish the task, this slackness can create complacency in the event staff.

Network analysis: critical path

One important aspect of any project is the relationship of tasks to each other. This can be difficult to show on a chart. With larger events, the Gantt chart can become very complex, and areas where there is a clash of scheduling may be obscured by the detail of bars and colours. A vital part of event management is giving tasks a priority.

Assigning a priority to a task is essential as the event must be delivered on time. The arrival and set-up of the main stage at an event, for example, is more important than finding an extra extension cord. However, on a Gantt chart all of the listed tasks are given equal importance (or weight). The network analysis tool was developed to overcome these problems.

Network analysis was created and developed during defence force projects in the USA and United Kingdom in the 1950s and now has widespread use in many project-based industries. The basis of network analysis is its critical path analysis, which uses circles to represent programmed events and arrows to illustrate the flow of activities, thus the precedence of programmed tasks is established and the diagram can be used to analyse a series of sub-tasks. The most efficient scheduling can be derived from the diagram; this is known as the critical path. Figure 6.5 illustrates a network derived from the Gantt chart shown in figure 6.4. The critical path is shown as an arrow. This means if the generator did not arrive on time, everything along the critical path would be directly affected. The lights would not be put up and, without evening light or electricity to run the pneumatic hammers, the tents could not be erected. Without the protective cover of the tents, the stage could not be constructed and so the sound system could not be set up. The critical path is indeed critical.

There are a number of software packages available to help create the Gantt chart and critical path. These are project management programs, which are usually used in the construction industry. Unfortunately, most of these packages are based on a variable completion time or completion within a certain time. In the event industry, the completion time (that is, when the event is on) is the most important factor and every task has to relate to this time. The event manager cannot ask for an extension of time to complete all of the tasks. Time charts and networks are very useful as a control and communication tool; however, like all project management techniques, they have their limitations. Graham, Goldblatt and Delpy (1995) describe how the Los Angeles Olympic Organising Committee gave up on the critical path chart as it became too unwieldy. There were 600 milestones. Rather than assisting with the communication and planning, it only created confusion. The solution was for the committee to return to a more traditional method of weekly meetings.

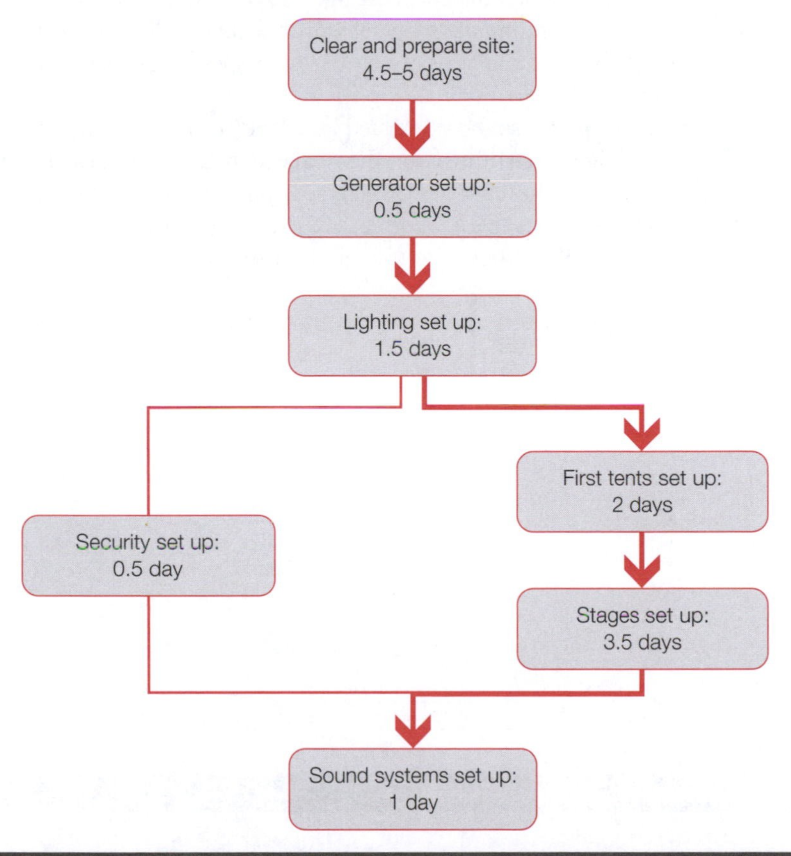

FIGURE 6.5 Gantt chart represented as a network

Project management triangle

A commonly used saying in the event industry is: 'Cheaper, faster or better. Pick two — you can't have all three'.

The project management triangle is a model to assist decision making in the project environment. As the project progresses, numerous decisions are made and contracts negotiated. There are three important constraints to be considered: time, cost and scope. The interdependence of these variables are such that their relationship is dynamic. Any change in one of these will affect one or both of the others. Many event decisions are a trade-off between the cost, time and scope. If, for example, the cost of an event is to be lowered, then the amount of time spent organising it will change and, possibly, the scope of the project will need to be readjusted. Likewise if the time for organising the event is extended then the scope of the event and/or the cost will change. The time variable includes the event duration as well as the time taken to organise it. The scope refers to the program of the event and the scope of work needed to deliver the event. The cost is both the cost of the event and the cost of the management of the event. These three variables also affect the quality of the event.

A wedding event can be used to illustrate this concept. In the planning of a wedding, the cost is often a fixed amount dictated by the budget. However, due to the sensitive nature of the event and the number of keenly interested stakeholders, there are almost always changes. When the client changes their mind about the venue or the wedding band, they are expanding the scope of work needed to deliver the event. This will have an affect on the cost and possibly on the time spent organising the event or the length of the booking.

The project triangle may also be expressed as: time/cost/quality and time/tasks/resources. Quality is often substituted for the scope constraint in describing event management decisions. As the client is directly concerned with the quality of the event, the time/cost/quality triangle is more easily explained to the client. The fixed deadline of most events affects how the triangle is used for decisions. As the event nears, the time component of the project triangle becomes the priority. Some events will need extra money and will need to expand the scope of work to make sure the events occur on the advertised dates.

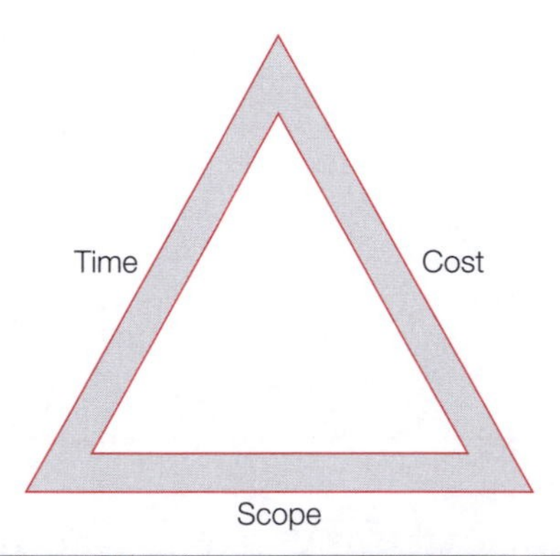

FIGURE 6.6 Project management triangle

Responsibilities — from documents to deliverables

In managing a large event, the staff will be made up of various teams, volunteers and subcontractors. If they are together only for a single event, they may not have a history of working together. This unfamiliarity with each other may lead to confusion in communication. There must be a way of communicating to the management team and stakeholders when tasks are completed, without creating unnecessary data. The concept of deliverables is one way to control this complexity.

The event itself is the major deliverable of all the tasks that make up the event management. A deliverable within the management of the event is the map of the site showing the layout of the event. To create this map the person responsible has to complete the design of the event and consider its logistics; therefore, the map is one of the outputs of the design process. The map is then delivered to other members of the event management team for use in her or his areas. A contract with a supplier is also a deliverable. It is proof that the negotiations have been completed. The deliverable of time planning is the schedule.

As seen from these examples, the deliverables are often documents or files. They are developed by one group and passed on to another. After the event, these documents are also used to evaluate the management and may be used to prove the competence of the management. Figure 6.3 shows some of the event documentation. Some project management theory suggests that the project should identify all the deliverables and work backwards from these to discover the tasks necessary to create them. This working back from the deliverables allows the construction of the project's WBS.

Deliverables include the following eight points:

1. *WBS* — a deliverable of the planning scope
2. *task responsibility chart* — a result of analysing all the tasks that need to be completed and assigning them to the relevant people
3. *checklists* — an indispensable tool for the event manager (these are created across all areas of the event)
4. *schedules* — these range from the Gantt charts to production schedules used on the day of the event
5. *resource analysis* — list all resources required and the contracts needed
6. *financial plan and budget* — an output of the financial planning process
7. *stakeholder management plan* — includes the sponsorship plan and the various communication plans, such as the promotion plan, as well as the reporting plan for the secondary stakeholders; for example, the local police
8. *risk management plan* — a deliverable of the risk management. It may take the form of a risk register and a procedure for updating the register.

The deliverables from points two to eight emanate from the WBS and they help to refine the WBS. There are other documents used in events, including the contact list and site or venue layout map. The event documents can be compiled into an event manual. The manual can then be used for future events, as these documents may be used as templates.

Payback period and return on investment

As mentioned in chapter 2, return on investment (ROI) is a term that is increasingly used in the event industry. It is a financial measure of the return to the event's key stakeholders as a result of its outcomes. The effects of the event can be multiple and include an increase in sales, community goodwill, increase in tourism, and a change of behaviour. These outcomes should relate to the event objectives — a reason that the objectives should be measurable. In project management, it is expressed as the payback period. The payback period is the length of time needed to pay all the costs of the event. After the payback period, the consequences of the event produce a surplus. A music concert payback period may occur during or before the concert, as the ticket sales will cover the event costs. The payback period for a local car rally may be measured in years after the event as the cost of the event to the community will not be met for quite a while.

There are a number of payback problems found only in events (and not other project-based industries). To establish the payback period, the real costs of the event have to be estimated. Some events, such as those that have in-kind sponsorship or use volunteers, will have difficulty achieving this. The benefits of many events are intangible and difficult to measure in financial terms; however, there are economic tools to assist this process. The most common tool for measuring the intangible benefit of community wellbeing is to establish the consumer surplus. The consumer surplus is the amount that the attendee would have paid to attend the event. Using this tool the cost/benefit of an event can be estimated and therefore so can the payback period.

Monitoring the project

Project management is not just a planning tool. It is a method of constructing the plan so that the project can be controlled as it progresses towards the event. This control is dynamic as the project may need to be tweaked or undergo large changes. It means that the event team is comparing the progress of the project to the project plan. The advantage of a project management system is that many of the gaps are visible to the management team. Comparing the Gantt chart to the actual progress enables the event team to identify problems. Any gaps that appear will encourage active management to remedy the situation. The budget is another control element as it enables the event team to identify any over-commitment of funds.

Controlling the project is an important responsibility of the event team. The formal process of control involves establishing standards of performance and ensuring that they are realised. This can be a complex process, but consists of three main steps:

1. *establishing standards of performance* — these can come from several sources, including standard practices within the event management industry; guidelines supplied by the board of management of the event; specific requirements of the client and sponsors; and audience or guest expectations. Standards must be measurable.
2. *identifying deviations from standards of performance* — this is done by measuring current performance and comparing it with the established standards. Since the event budget is expressed in measurable terms, it provides an important method of highlighting areas that are straying from the plan and that require attention.
3. *correcting deviations* — any performance that does not meet the established standards must be corrected. This can entail the use of many types of problem-solving strategies, including renegotiating contracts and delegating.

There are numerous informal methods of control that include talking to the staff and volunteers and establishing a conducive team atmosphere so that any gaps are brought to the attention of senior management.

Reports and meetings

Reports that evaluate the progress of an event are perhaps the most common control method. The reports are presented at management or committee meetings. The frequency of these meetings will depend on the proximity of the event date. Many event management companies hold weekly meetings with reports from the teams (or subcommittees) and individuals responsible for particular areas. The meetings are run using standard meeting rules with a time for subcommittee reports. The aim of these reports is to assist the meeting in making decisions. Typically, an annual community festival would have monthly meetings throughout the year leading up to the event, and increase these to weekly meetings two months before the festival is scheduled to begin. The Broome Shinju Matsuri Festival of the Pearl, for example, has weekly meetings that alternate between the festival committee and those of the general community (which discuss major decisions by the festival committee). In this way, the public has some control over the planning of the festival. At the committee meetings, the subcommittees dealing with publicity, sponsorship, entertainment, youth and community relations report their actions. The reports expose any gaps so the event coordinator can take action to close them. This is also called management by exception because it assumes everything is flowing well, that routine matters are handled by the subcommittee, and that the event coordinator need step in only when significant deviations from the plan demand it.

Delegation and self-control

The use of subcommittees at a festival is an example of delegating activities to specialist groups. Part of the responsibility of each subcommittee is to solve problems before they occur. Since it is impossible for the event manager to monitor all the areas of an event, this method is valuable because it allows delegated groups to control their own areas of specialisation. However, the subcommittee must confine its actions to its own event area and the event manager must be aware of possible problems arising across different subcommittees. Solving a problem in the entertainment part of an event, for example, could give rise to problems in the sponsorship areas. The entertainment committee may hire a performer who has a sponsorship deal. The performer's sponsor may be a competitor with the sponsor of part of the festival.

Quality

There are various systems to control the quality of an event and the event company itself. In particular, quality control depends on:

- gaining and responding to customer feedback
- the role played by event personnel in delivering quality service.

Integrating the practical aspects of controlling quality with the overall strategy of an event is called total quality management (TQM). TQM seeks to create an event company that continually improves the quality of its services. In other words, feedback, change and improvement are integral to the company's structure and operations.

Various techniques of TQM are used by event companies. One technique is finding and rewarding quality champions — volunteer programs often have awards for quality service at an event. Different professional organisations, such as the International Special Events Society (ISES) and the International Festivals and Events Association (IFEA), share the same aim: to strive to improve the quality of festivals and events. They do this by disseminating information and administering a system of event evaluation and awards for quality.

Work in progress report

The client or major sponsor of an event cannot afford to wait until the event to know if it will be a success. Often, they require a report on how well the management is doing. This status report, commonly known as WIP (work in progress) in the event industry, is a 'snapshot' of the progress of the project. The WIP report is one of the control mechanisms for event management. Using a project management methodology means that these reports are easily generated. The Gantt chart should give the client an idea of how the tasks are going. The headings often found in a WIP report for a large or complex event include:

- *work breakdown structure (WBS)* — areas filled in according to their progress
- *funds committed* — the commitment of funds may be informal (such as by verbal agreement), but will have an effect on the amount of funds available
- *risk register* — a list of the risks and the status of their treatment
- *variances or exceptions* — any changes to the original plans.

Part of the WIP report is the risk register (outlined in chapter 18). The register describes the risks that have been identified and the actions taken to treat them. Whereas the WIP is 'static', the actual risk register is a 'live' document regularly reviewed and updated.

Earned value

Earned value is a project technique that places a value on the percentage of the task completed. If the $10 000 promotion campaign for the event is 50 per cent complete at a certain date, for example, it is said to have an earned value of $5000.

PROJECT EVALUATION

The evaluation of an event is generally concerned with its impact and level of success. Chapter 16 goes into this matter in detail. Project evaluation concerns the evaluation of the management of the event. The term that is common in other areas of project management is the acronym 'PIER' (post implementation evaluation and review). This evaluation process is performed after the project is completed.

One of the attractions of using a project management system is that it enables this type of evaluation and subsequent improvement in management. By setting up a WBS, the management can assess the tasks, responsibilities, schedules and risk management systems and improve upon them.

Project evaluation includes comparing the actual progress of the project against the project plan. As a result, the evaluation can suggest areas for improvement in the management. This is different to evaluating the event. It may be part of an event evaluation process; however, it is often forgotten. Figure 6.7 illustrates the project management system used by various events. One essential part of this system is the evaluation and archiving. Whereas PIER occurs after the project is complete, the event plan, archive and review system is a description of the whole project management system from an evaluation point of view. Understanding the way a management system is evaluated creates a system that can be evaluated. The evaluation in this case is evaluating the validity of the system itself. As EPARS — the event, plan, archive and review system — in figure 6.7 illustrates, one event is used as the baseline plan for the next event.

Event project evaluation includes:

- comparing the task descriptions and planned timelines with their actual performance
- assessing the ability of the system to respond to change; that is, its flexibility
- evaluating the timeliness of reports
- assessing the effectiveness of management decisions
- comparing planned milestones with the reality.

Each of these areas should indicate a fault or success in the management system. This feedback system can be used for each event to improve the management of the events. In this way, the event or festival is far more than a temporary and intangible affair. It is a way to improve the management of events in general. The event or festival can be regarded as a test of the management system.

An interesting offshoot of using such a system as EPARS is that events can be used as a training model. By having a repeatable and improvable management system, a local festival can be used to train people in the skills of project management. Without a describable management system, the skill learned by working on a project cannot be assessed and, therefore, certified. Certification is basic to proving competency. A number of countries, such as South Africa, are assessing this as a way to train their unemployed youth in business and organisational skills. The EMBOK is an attempt by event practitioners and academics to produce an international model of event management that can be used to develop a competency system for training. As events progress towards a worldwide industry, governments need to assess the qualities of an event company. It is too late to find out during the event that the event company is incompetent. Competency standards go hand in hand with industry standards and provide a measure of ability. Standards provide a framework for all parties in the event industry to work within:

> The work of Janet Landey and her company, Party Design, in Johannesburg is revolutionising the role of events in a developing country. As part of the government's policy of Black Economic Empowerment, her company trains the unemployed through work at events. Even the cleaners become part of the entertainment at the events. Party Design assists in setting up event companies in places like Soweto and in the townships.

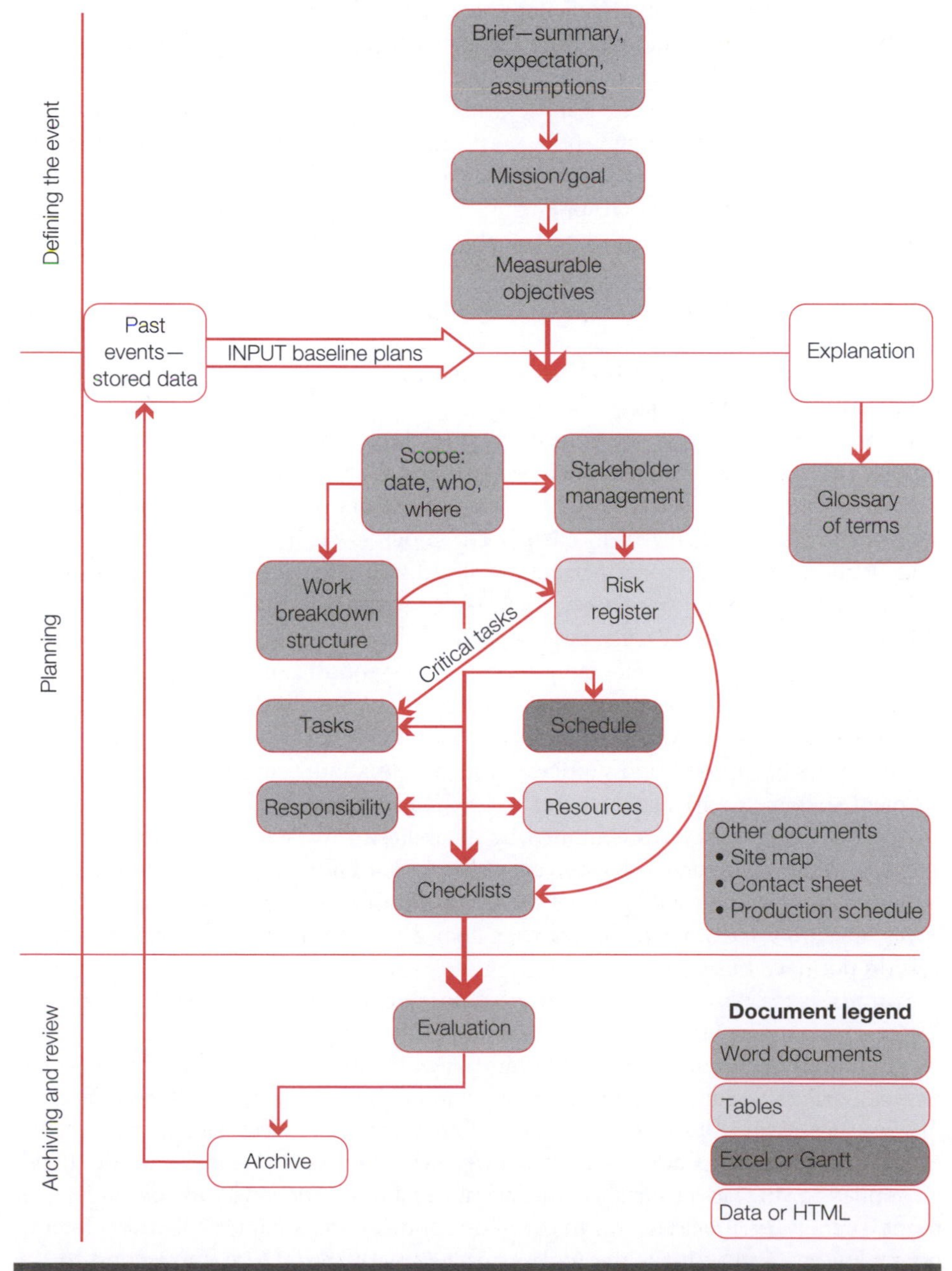

FIGURE 6.7 The event plan, archive and review system

Source: O'Toole 2010.

PROJECT MANAGEMENT SYSTEMS AND SOFTWARE

As project management is an integrated system, it appears to be easily translated into a software system. There are a number of project management software systems available to assist the practising project manager. Whether any of these can be directly and simply applied to events is a point for further discussion. Much of the project management software is excellent for planning the event management, as it imposes a discipline on the event team and demands a common language. Each of the systems is similar, but, due to the fluid nature of event management, is limited in its usefulness. The Kepner-tregoe, Project Cycle Management and Prince 2 are examples of highly developed and tested project management systems. The event plan, archive and review system, shown in figure 6.7, is a visual display of the project management system used to structure the management of the event and, at the same time, assist in knowledge management. By creating templates the company or organisation can save this information to be fed back into the next event. EPARS represents the adaptation of the traditional project management process, as illustrated in figure 6.2, to the event environment. The inclusion of the stakeholder management as a basic function of event management is an example of this. EPARS includes the use of checklists in the event management process. Checklists are used continually by event managers as they are easy to create and change.

Of the software systems, the most popular for event management is Microsoft Project and the open source alternative OpenProj (see OpenProj.org). They are easy to obtain and readily set up. They can construct a Gantt chart quickly and are useful tools for explaining the event to clients. The progress of the event management can be quickly ascertained by the percentage of tasks completed. The limitations of any project management software application to event management is a result of the variability of events themselves. Changes happen all the time. Venue changes, airline cancellations, different performers, more finance, new sponsors and new opportunities to promote the event are just some of the common changes in the event environment. In particular, a special event — that is, one not attempted before — will have a new configuration of suppliers and supplies. In such a situation, using current project management software to manage the event will be inadequate.

Using software for events is limited by its ability to work in a complex, changing and uncertain environment. Most event software currently employed is found in the more predictable and stable parts of the event industry — repeat exhibitions, conferences, meetings and seminars have a wide choice of software. Special events and festivals do not have this software choice.

Spreadsheet applications are perhaps the most common software used in developing the event plan. The first case study at the end of the chapter outlines a series of worksheets that are used to establish the framework for the event. In this case, it is the opening ceremony for an extensive property development. However, a similar layering of worksheets can be used for most events to develop the project plan.

An important aspect of the project management process is that it is scalable. It can be applied to small events or large festivals. It can also be applied to any one area of an event, such as the promotion, or to the whole of the event. Chapter 14, which focuses on staging an event, shows the tools associated with this. These correspond to the outputs of the project management process. The production schedule is a combination of task/schedule and responsibility documents. Project management software may be successfully applied to a part of the event; for example, a predictable section of the event, or a promotion schedule.

LIMITATIONS OF THE PROJECT MANAGEMENT APPROACH TO EVENT MANAGEMENT

The limitations of the direct application of traditional project management have been analysed by many authors and the development of the new PMBOK 4th edition shows how the profession is changing rapidly. Traditional project management depends on a solid definition of the asset during the initiation phase and on a stable management environment. All the management tasks can then be measured against the defined asset. Festivals and special events are not as clearly defined. Often they become more defined as the management of the project progresses, new marketing information comes to hand, and new promotion ideas and programming openings arise. A large part of event managing is taking advantage of new opportunities, which can mean that events can radically change, right up until the morning of the event. Project management, therefore, has to be flexible. Increased documentation, plans, written procedures and rules can easily lead to a management inertia unsuitable to this industry. It can destroy the core characteristic of special events and diminish the 'wow factor', the surprise, the vibe, or the theatre of events — essentially what makes the event 'special'. One solution to this problem used by major events (described in the previous section) is to appoint an artistic director and an event project manager. The former represents the innovative and creative aspects of the event content, while the project manager looks after the management responsibilities. Other areas that limit the use of project management are:

- *using volunteers* — the work of the volunteers is difficult to quantify and yet, as shown in chapter 8, they are vital to the success of many festivals. To measure key success factors is an imperative task in a traditional project management system.
- *stakeholders number* — more stakeholders mean more objectives the event has to meet. Given that some stakeholders will change during the lead-up to the event, there is more uncertainty in these objectives. This leads to a fluid management environment, with the event company continually keeping an eye on any change to the stakeholders. When this is combined with the intangible outcomes of an event, clearly defining stakeholder requirements can be almost impossible. In one sense, each individual audience member may have an array of expectations.
- *marketing* — the ability to respond to market changes is a fundamental principle of marketing. This is in opposition to a management system that relies on the definition of the deliverable to stay the same. In project management, thinking about marketing can be regarded as a risk management strategy. The aim of marketing from this point of view is to increase the predicability of management. Using marketing tools such as consumer decision profiling, marketing segmentation, promotion and optimising the market mix can reduce uncertainty.
- *finance* — finance may be found right up to the day of the event, during the event and after it is over. Extra sponsors may 'come on board', more tickets may be sold, or, for example, an auction may be a great success. This is another area of uncertainty that makes project planning difficult. Most project management theory assumes a fixed and defined source of funds, therefore it tends to concentrate on the control of costs.

- *event design* — many events are supposed to have a large element of surprise, called the 'wow factor'. This is not an easy element to quantify or describe. At many events and festivals the right 'wow' can be the difference between success and failure. Traditional project management depends on the asset or deliverable being defined during the initiation phase. The surprise aspect of the event is often difficult, if not impossible, to describe. For some events, describing the 'wow' or surprise (for example, the printing blocks coming to life at the opening ceremony of the Chinese Olympics) may lessen its value. It would be similar to describing the plot of a 'who-dunnit' mystery before reading the book.
- *infrastructure and resources* — usually of a temporary nature. Events and festivals can have notoriously short timelines. Other projects may take years to complete, whereas the event project may be over in a month. Short-term logistics, temporary structures and short-term contracts do not allow the luxury of detailed analysis that is recommended by many project management books. Overall, the event management is under the cloud of the deadline. Every aspect of the management, therefore, must be continually assessed according to its effect on the deadline.
- *creativity* — a core element of many events is the creativity of the event team. Special events, in particular, require creative thinking. Some event directors see project management as being at odds with creativity. A system can easily become an end unto itself. It can overpower the artistic basis of an event. Unless these formal tools and techniques are regarded as a support system for the event, they may make the creativity disappear. It is a risk and must be understood by anyone creating and developing an event.

CONVERGENCE

Both the event management theory and project management theory are converging. The traditional civic engineering project management is under pressure from the software development project management. In the latter case, software development project management requires softer skills and is considered more of an 'art' than a 'science'. Strict time/cost/quality considerations and tightly planned tasks are giving way to rolling plans and agile systems that are more responsive to change. A new approach to project management, Agile Project Management, attempts to create a different model. This is in response to the enormous number of projects that fail. The Agile approach stresses the human interaction involved in the project and the need to adapt the project and tasks as the situation demands. It emphasises progress through relatively small tasks, not large plans.

The Project Management Association of Japan describes this development as the second generation of project management. It is characterised by applications well outside the traditional engineering field and stresses organisation, communication and other soft processes. Their third generation project management is characterised by 'not analytical ability, but broad visions, value consciousness and rich insights' (PMAJ 2005, p. 8). Fortunately, event management is exactly at that position. Agility in planning, responsiveness to change, leadership, soft skills, understanding values and the art of management are all skills necessary for an event manager. The model for event management has developed independently from the model for software development and other second generation projects. It is in response to the need for accountability of management and the transferability of the skill across different events, all of which reflects a rapidly growing industry.

SUMMARY

An event or a festival has all the characteristics of a project. The traditional tools of project management can assist the event team integrating all the areas of management. Each of these areas of management produces deliverables. The deliverables are the result of a number of tasks (proof of good management) and are communicated to the event team. Project management can supply management structure of the event, and enable monitoring of the creation, development and organisation of the event. It concentrates on this management, whereas the event itself is often the focus of event studies. Event managers can benefit by using techniques such as scope definition, WBS, scheduling and critical path analysis. The WBS describes the work and generates other plans, such as the tasks, resource analysis and the risk register. By using project management, the event manager can easily produce the progress reports on the management. It provides a professional methodology and the language of modern business that can be adapted to the event management environment.

As events grow in scope, the project management becomes the most important aspect of the management. In such cases, an event project manager will be appointed. The event project manager's role is to integrate all the event plans and produce an accountable management system. Although project management is increasingly seen as a solution to compliance and management accountability, it has its limitations. These arise from the intangible nature of the event and the ever-changing event environment.

QUESTIONS

1 Construct a work breakdown structure for these events:
   (a) rose festival
   (b) computer gaming competition
   (c) wedding
   (d) product launch
   (e) graduation ceremony
   (f) welcome ceremony for a royal visit.
2 Construct a schedule of key tasks for the events listed in question 1.
3 List the milestones for the events listed in question 1.
4 What are examples of tasks that can clash? What techniques can be put in place to recognise these clashes in time to enable the event management to fix them?
5 List the types of events and their characteristics that would suit the project management approach.

case study

USING SPREADSHEETS TO PLAN AN EVENT

The simplicity of the spreadsheet is invaluable to the planning of an event. Using the project management tools and techniques and a series of linked worksheets enables the event team to construct an event plan quickly. The worksheets can then easily be expanded and cut and paste into other software as required.

The following plan is for a special event — the opening of a new major property development on the Red Sea. Integrated property developments have many dimensions — such as housing, hotels, offices, shops, malls and entertainment precincts.

The opening ceremony can be an important statement to potential buyers and to current property owners of the status and desirability of the development. It is an opportunity to invite VIPs and government officials to view the finished development at a time of celebration. At the same time, the developers are interested in heightening their reputation and their brand.

There will be many changes in the event plan from the time the client decides to have an opening ceremony to the actual event. It is therefore important to have a framework that enables the event management to start work on the planning of the event, but that does not inhibit the development of the event. Spreadsheets can capture the scope of work at the beginning of the planning and easily adapt to the inevitable changes.

The event plan is a spreadsheet made up of the worksheets that document the following:

- work breakdown structure
- schedule
  - milestones
  - timeline
  - production schedule
  - running sheet
- stakeholders
- contacts
- task responsibility
- resources
- budget
- program
- risk register
- site map
- checklists (for the many aspects of the event).

The order of these is not important as they are worksheets in a spreadsheet and the navigation is achieved by internal hyperlinks within the spreadsheet.

For this event, it was decided the scope of work could be subdivided into:

- *Venue or site*. The operational issues and the design of the event.
- *Administration*. The management of the event.
- *Program*. What is on at the event.
- *Logistics*. The coordination of the event. (The opening ceremony will be held at the site of the development, and a number of buyers are travelling from overseas for the event.)
- *Protocol*. The diplomacies and formalities of the event. (There will be a number of government officials attending the event.)
- *Catering*. The food and drink to be provided at the event. (As with many official events in the Middle East, the catering is very important.)
- *Design*. The design includes the event site design, the branding and general look of the event.
- *Entertainment*. The activities and performances that will take place at the event. (The client requested a Lebanese headline performer and fireworks.)
- *Communication marketing*. The promotion of the event. (The event is to be marketed to the buyers and owners, as well as the government and the media.)

Note that these categories will vary according to the event, the event team and the country. Protocol, for example, at this event is essential to its success. Inviting the right VIPs and government officials will ensure that the event has fewer problems.

The way they are greeted, seated and the order of introductions is very important. A lot of effort is spent on this aspect of the event planning. In this case, each member of the event team on the day of the event has a full list of the VIPs with their photos to make sure there are few protocol mistakes. Often, the level of importance of the guests is not indicated by their dress.

Within their spreadsheets, some event companies will include the program and entertainment under the heading 'design'. Others will use the term 'operations' rather than 'logistics'. 'Catering' may be placed under 'design' or 'site'. The headings often reflect the work history of the event team. The aim of the work breakdown structure is to effectively describe the scope of work. They can easily be expanded and categories can be added as the scope of work is defined.

Once the scope of work has been drafted, key dates are decided for the planning. These are the milestones. The key date for 'catering', for example, is the securing of the catering contract, although there are many other important dates in the catering component of the scope. The milestone allows the team to work backwards from that date and decide upon the other dates — such as when to 'sign off on menu'. The catering contract is a deliverable that can be the assigned responsibility of a subgroup in the team.

The two milestones in figure 6.8 are indicated by the term 'Key'. As the client insisted on a star performer, the securing of this contract was critical to the event. The other entertainment contracts — such as band, visual performers and fireworks — were secondary to this contract. Additionally, as protocol was vital to the event's success, the attendance of certain VIPs and government officials was considered extremely important. Hence, the 'Key VIP list' was a milestone. The guest list component can prove problematic (read 'risk') in the region as VIPs will often delay their acceptance until they know which other VIPs have agreed to attend.

Scope and Milestones

Code	Category		Milestones	Date
Site	Site	Site visit		
		Floor plan		
		Stage design	Site design/map	10 April
		Security		
		Cleaning		
		Power supply		
Cat	Catering	Sourcing supplier	Catering contract	15 May
		Menu		
		Hostesses		
		Table/access		
Ent	Entertainment	Sourcing suppliers	Key Ent contract	30 Jan.
		A/V		
		Guest speakers		
		Fireworks		
Log	Logistics	Booking/buy air ticket	OS Arrival sched.	30 June
		Signage		
		Transportation		
		Meet and Greet		
		Hotel bookings		
Pro	Protocol	Assign staff	Key VIP list	30 May
		Seating arrangement		
		CEO schedule		
		Welcome kits		
		VIP invites		

Jan. Feb. Mar. Apr. May June July

EVENT — 23 JULY

Scope / Resources / Risk Register / Production Schedule / Budget

Sheet 1 / 5 Default 100% STD * Sum=0

FIGURE 6.8 Show WBS

At the same time as the WBS framework is being produced, the other worksheets can be developed. The resource list uses the WBS list as the basis for deciding what resources are needed. The decisions made while the resource checklist is being compiled concern whether the resource is to be delivered in-house or outsourced. If the resources are to be outsourced, then a number of quotes may have to be obtained.

The decision to choose a particular supplier is then recorded and can be used to defend the action if there are any questions about the choice. The resource list can also help to identify any resources that may be clustered and hired from a single supplier.

	A	B	C	D	E	F	G	H
1				Resources				
2	WBS	Resources	Outsource Y/N	Companies	Quotes	Contract	Special Requirements	
3								
4	Admin.	Internet access	No – use provider					
5		Computer	Use in-house					
6		Couriers	Yes					
7		Personnel	Yes – extra staff – 5					
8		Legal rep	No					
9		Event office	No					
10		Printers	Yes – for badges					
11		Laptop	No					
12		Fax	No					
13		Insurance	Yes – ask client					
14		Security	Yes					
15		Recruitment agency	No					
16		Accountant	Ask client					
17		Sales team	Ask client					
18		Stationery	Yes – see design					
19		Media office	Yes					
20		Office space	On-site needed					
21	Design	Graphics	Yes					
22		Florists	Yes					
23		Name Badges	No					
24		Office stationery	Yes (with event logo)					
25		Designer	Yes					
26	Enter	MC						
27		Entertainers						
28		Fireworks						
29	Logistics	Shuttle bus						
30		Limo service						

FIGURE 6.9 Show resource list

As the WBS and resource worksheets are developed, work can commence on the risk register. Project risks will constantly be identified and negotiated over the entire planning and implementation cycle. Using the risk register facilitates discussion about the things that may go wrong. For example, the risk of a sandstorm in the region of the event is identified as likely. Some of the team members from other countries may not realise that this could be a risk. The risk register, then, serves to prepare the team to deal with potential risks.

All worksheets can be filled in concurrently as the project progresses. From the WBS comes the task responsibility worksheet. The work is further broken down to list the actual tasks and the people assigned to those tasks. In some cases there is no need to go into great detail; the milestone and the deliverable are sufficient information for experienced team members. The checklists and the risk register are used by all team members. For example, the contract with the key performer (or headline act) is a deliverable that may be delegated to specific team members. They should have sufficient experience in the field, but they can use the project plan and checklists to help them.

Once the overall cost limitations are agreed upon in consultation with the client (the developer, in this case), the WBS is used to create a detailed budget.

After the event, the spreadsheet becomes an asset and a resource to the event team as the worksheets can be used as a template for other events. It provides a framework that encourages event teams to plan in a structured way while allowing for changes in scope.

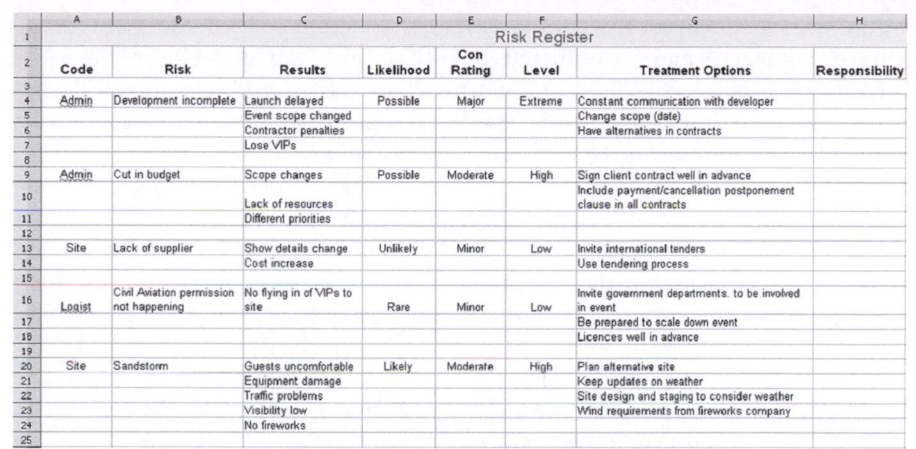

Risk Register

Code	Risk	Results	Likelihood	Con Rating	Level	Treatment Options	Responsibility
Admin	Development incomplete	Launch delayed	Possible	Major	Extreme	Constant communication with developer	
		Event scope changed				Change scope (date)	
		Contractor penalties				Have alternatives in contracts	
		Lose VIPs					
Admin	Cut in budget	Scope changes	Possible	Moderate	High	Sign client contract well in advance	
		Lack of resources				Include payment/cancellation postponement clause in all contracts	
		Different priorities					
Site	Lack of supplier	Show details change	Unlikely	Minor	Low	Invite international tenders	
		Cost increase				Use tendering process	
Logist	Civil Aviation permission not happening	No flying in of VIPs to site	Rare	Minor	Low	Invite government departments. to be involved in event	
						Be prepared to scale down event	
						Licences well in advance	
Site	Sandstorm	Guests uncomfortable	Likely	Moderate	High	Plan alternative site	
		Equipment damage				Keep updates on weather	
		Traffic problems				Site design and staging to consider weather	
		Visibility low				Wind requirements from fireworks company	
		No fireworks					

FIGURE 6.10 Show risk register

Questions

1 Considering the scope of work illustrated in this case, discuss the changes to this scope if the opening event took place in western Europe.

2 Estimate how many people would comprise the event team. Which tasks and responsibilities would be outsourced? What are the problems outsourcing poses?

3 How would you deal with the last minute cancellation of the main entertainment act?

case study

HA'IL DESERT FESTIVAL

The city of Ha'il, an oasis surrounded by deserts and mountain ranges, is in the north of the Kingdom of Saudi Arabia. It has been in the forefront of Arabian peninsular history for thousands of years as it lies on the main trade and camel caravan route. The population of the city is approximately 300 000. With the wealth of Saudi Arabia being invested in infrastructure throughout the country, the city is undergoing rapid expansion. The airport and the university, in particular, are being improved.

Desert life, trade, culture and agriculture are all important to Ha'il's history. As part of the tourism strategy, developed over the last ten years in Saudi Arabia, the provinces have been encouraged to develop unique festivals to attract internal tourism and visitors from the Gulf countries. The movement of people around the country is part of the general nation building of Saudi Arabia.

Governor of Ha'il, Prince Saud ibn Abdul Mohsen and the national tourism body, the Supreme Commission for Tourism (SCT), supported the idea of a festival that

would take advantage of the unique history and culture of Ha'il and demonstrate it to the country. A number of these types of festivals, such as the River Festival in Brisbane, Australia, were discussed and used as models for developing Ha'il's signature event. To develop a sustainable festival, it had to have a genuine connection with the desert heritage of the region.

The festival began in 2008 and fitted with the policies of the national tourism body and the concept of signature events. As a result it had the support of the government from the outset. However, it needed to be able to grow in both size and program. To facilitate this, the management team built upon their collective event experience by training their staff in risk and project management, in order to compare their skills with world best practice in event management.

Other considerations for future festivals included the fact that Ha'il was expanding rapidly, with major government investment in the infrastructure of the city. The university revealed a plan to expand to a new campus, nine square kilometres in size. It was important that the festival had university support and input into the program. Also, Ha'il is in the region of Saudi Arabia called the Nej, a traditional and conservative part of the Kingdom. The festival events needed to be suitable for the cultures of the region. The 2008 festival was used as the foundation for building the subsequent festivals.

To meet the conditions of government support for the event, as well as the benchmarks of best practice, the organisers needed to establish an evaluation system. In particular, measured tourism outcomes were necessary to justify the support from the SCT. From a study of similar events, it was obvious that the festival needed time to develop to produce measurable outcomes. In fact, since it may take up to three years before a solid program is established and as it is certain to have both failures and successes, the event team and the key stakeholders must view the festival as a work in progress, not a final product. For this reason a strategic approach was taken.

With all these factors in mind the organising committee created their vision and goals (note that these have been translated from Arabic):

The vision

Establish Ha'il as an international centre for desert-related sciences, cultures and investments by promoting its environmental, scientific and tourism status locally, regionally and internationally through an international annual event concerning the desert and all its tangible and intangible factors, employing the desert-related elements and components in Ha'il.

The vision was transformed into the following goals:

- Identify and develop the tangible and intangible factors contributing to making Ha'il an international destination for the desert researches and sciences.
- Attract and exchange the desert-related sciences, sports, and cultures from different parts of the world to Ha'il and invest them in tourism.
- Attract the largest number possible of visitors from inside and outside the Kingdom to Ha'il to enjoy its tourism attractions and the festival in order to draw economic and social benefits into the region.
- Encourage, direct and guide the investments in the environmental, tourism and economic products in a way to achieve the investment objectives.
- Gain the community partnership in the economic, scientific and tourism activities and benefit from them socially and economically.

Based on these goals and the existing program the festival organising structure was developed, as outlined in figure 6.11. The structure reflected a mix of functional units, such as safety and marketing, and program elements, such as scientific and cultural.

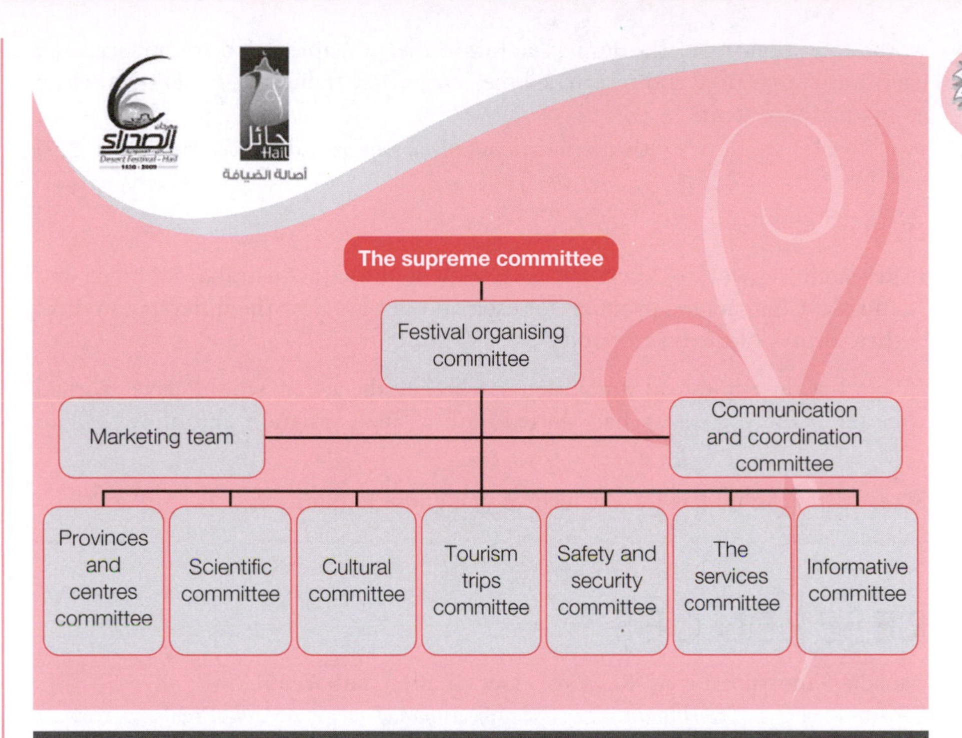

FIGURE 6.11 Festival organising structure

The festival events were highly varied, with the intention of progressively refining the festival program each year. The events included a scientific program, a cultural exhibition, cultural and folkloric demonstrations and sports events. A workshop was arranged in cooperation with the University of Ha'il under the title 'Desert and water: environment and growth'. The papers presented at the Ha'il university included such topics as the management of desert tourism, Bedouin culture and natural wildlife reserves. The festival provided further stimulus for the University of Ha'il to establish a department of tourism.

Some the events included:

- *Falconry exhibition and contest.* The Arabian peninsular is well known for the sport of falconry. This event included a falcon beauty contest.
- *Saluki Dogs contest.* The hunting hound dogs have an ancient lineage in the desert and are known for their speed, endurance and stamina.
- *Poetry evenings.*
- *Family traditional enterprises.* An exhibition and sale by local families of traditional arts, food and handicrafts of the region.
- *Al Hujaini.* A traditional camel calling contest.
- *Tata'ese.* A competition in which cars race up high and steep sand dunes.

To ensure the festival's ongoing improvement, the event team and the SCT established a measurement system. From this they were able to project future festival figures and set a number of indicators and targets including the number of visitors, tourists, events and activities, participants, and participating provinces. Additionally they projected the targeted countries, the budget and the revenue to the region.

The development of the festival followed the principles of best practice. The team was experienced and researched the event. They trained their staff and set up an evaluation system.

Based on interviews with the Supreme Commission for Tourism (SCT) and the Desert Festival organisers

Questions

1 Research the world's desert festivals, such as those in Australia, Morocco and Tunisia. Compare the program for each and discuss how the differences reflect the cultures of the host country.

2 Select a desert festival and discuss whether the event would have worked better if the organisers had started with a small program and allowed it to grow.

3 List the stakeholders for the festival you chose in question 2.

REFERENCES

Canadian Tourism Human Resource Council 2010, http://cthrc.ca.

Dinsmore, PC 1998, *Human factors in project management*, AMACOM, New York.

EMBOK 2006, www.embok.org.

Graham, S, Goldblatt, J & Delpy, L 1995, *The ultimate guide to sports event management and marketing*, Richard Irwin, Chicago.

O'Toole, W 2000, 'Towards the integration of event management best practice by the project management process', in *'Events beyond 2000: setting the agenda — event evaluation, research and education conference proceedings'*, eds J Allen, R Harris, LK Jago & AJ Veal, Australian Centre for Event Management, Sydney.

O'Toole, W 2010, *Event project management system (EPMS 2010)*, CD-ROM, www.epms.net, Sydney.

O'Toole, W & Mikolaitis, PJ 2002, *Corporate event project management*, John Wiley & Sons, New York.

Project Management Association of Japan 2005, *A guidebook of project and program management for enterprise innovation*, PMAJ, www.pmaj.or.jp.

Project Management Institute 2008, *Guide to the project management body of knowledge: PMboK guide 4th edition*. Project Management Institute, Inc., Newtown Square, PA.

FINANCIAL MANAGEMENT AND EVENTS

LEARNING OBJECTIVES

After studying this chapter, you should be able to:

1. understand the role of financial management in the overall management of an event
2. create an event budget
3. understand the methods of event costing and ticket pricing
4. monitor and control the event spending and incoming finances
5. identify the key elements of budgetary control and explain the relationship between them
6. understand the advantages and shortcomings of using a budget.

INTRODUCTION

Financial management is defined as decisions that concern the sourcing, planning, allocation, monitoring and evaluation of the money resource. In the event environment, financial decisions take place within the overall objectives of the event or festival. This chapter concerns the financial tools and techniques that are used in the process of delivering an event and the management of a portfolio of events. Many of these tools and techniques are taken from the financial management of ongoing companies and from project management. Although these tools are the same, the event environment will place a different emphasis and priority on their employment. As well as the well-known general financial management tools, tools and techniques have been developed specifically for the event industry.

Money is one of the resources of event management. If an event is run for profit, the sourcing and allocation of money will be very important. This is because the primary objective of the for-profit event is to have incoming dollars greater than outgoing dollars. Other events and festivals, however, regard profit as a lesser objective. They may have a combination of aims, such as community development, tourism, business networking and public awareness. For some events and festivals, a financial surplus can be a problem. Their aim is to break even. They may just want to meet their budget and no more. As Sounder (2004, p. 137) writes,

> Even if money is not the issue, your event will have to meet or exceed certain financial performance objectives. All events must have responsible financial management.

Mismanagement of finance can lead to unforeseen operational risk, such as safety, crowd control and legal problems. So it behoves all event managers to know about financial management. There are legal obligations on an event team to ensure the event finance is managed in a proper and correct manner. Tax obligations, such as GST, require an event to have systems to record all transactions. A client or major sponsor may want to see the financial statements. In some cases, if there is any problem, the client may want to audit the books of the event company.

It is therefore a necessity that the event organisation set up a management system that can control the flow of money to the various management areas, such as marketing, insurance, venue costs and design. At the same time, the event team may be looking for extra inflow by seeking new sponsors and re-examining contracts, while also looking for cost savings. Unforeseen costs can quickly arise. The client can also change their requirements; for example, the opening of the Burj, the tallest tower in the world in Dubai, was significantly changed due to the global financial crisis. The official opening was delayed and its name was changed from Burj Dubai to Burj Khalifa. External influences can impinge on finance, such as an airline strike or a supplier going bankrupt.

The fluidity of the event environment is illustrated by a quote from Ric Birch from his insightful book *Master of the Ceremonies* (2004, pp. 281–2). He describes the numerous meetings leading up to the 2000 Sydney Olympics:

> By late 1999, the content of the opening and closing ceremonies was more or less settled. There were still changes to come, but they could now be made within the framework of a budget that was much more accurate. The SOCOG group around the table, however, could only see that the budget had increased from A$43 to A$54 million.
>
> I pointed out that over a five-year period, the budget had increased only eight per cent from my original estimate, which was less than inflation. I also pointed out that SOCOG had made a windfall profit of more than $20 million from the extra seats that had become available when the athletes were removed from the stands for the opening ceremony . . . But no one around the table was interested.

In this quote Ric Birch illustrates a number of characteristics of financial management for events:

- Although there was a framework for the budget, its accuracy changed over time.
- Unexpected income and costs arise, even for a major event such as the Olympics.
- Financial management is a high-level responsibility.
- The event manager is expected to defend the spending.
- There are mutual dependencies between the areas of event management (in this case the finance, the operations and the program).

Even with all these changes, the event must go on. The cloud that hangs over every financial decision is the deadline. Figure 7.1 illustrates the financial management process from the project management point of view.

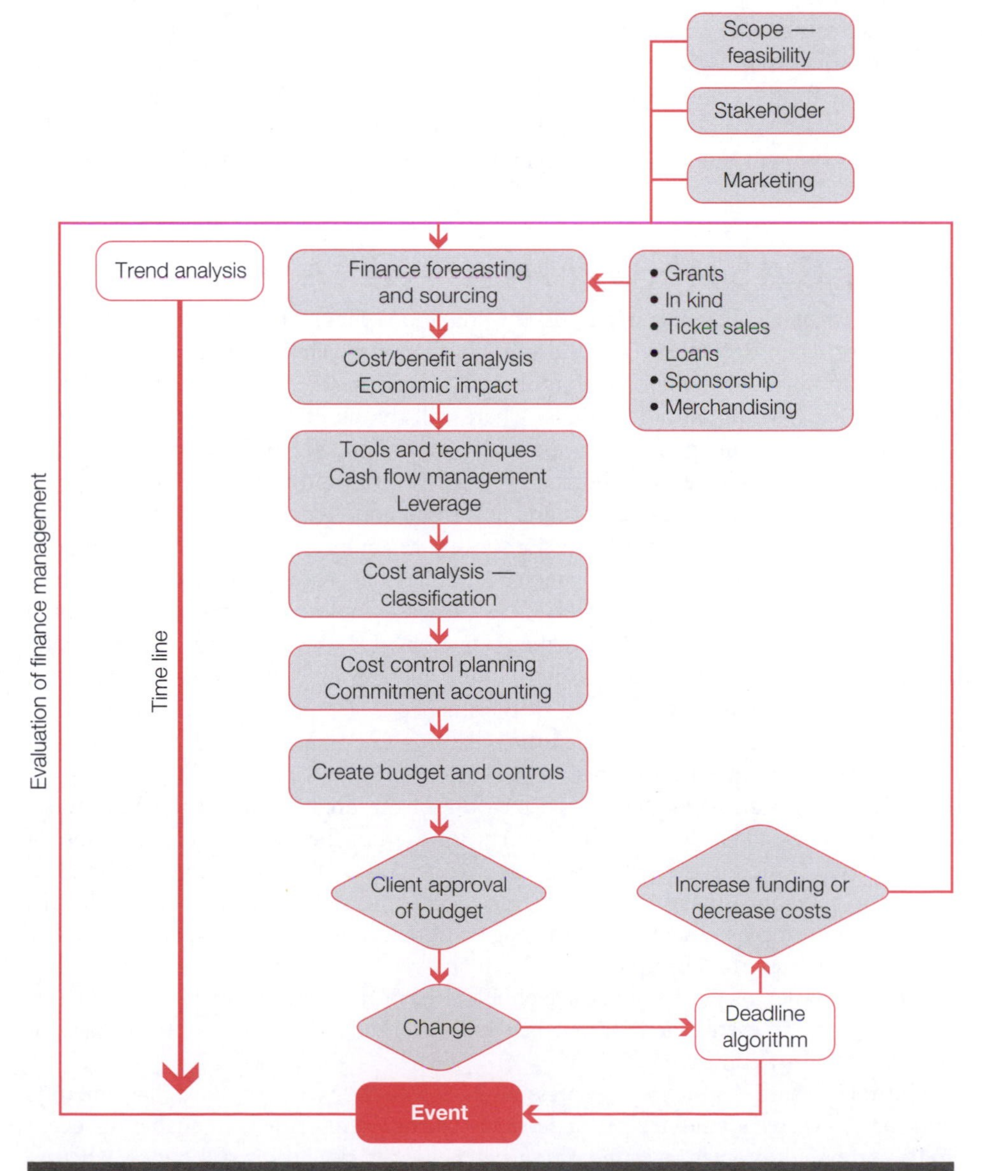

FIGURE 7.1 Financial management process from the project management point of view

Source: EPMS CD-ROM 2010.

The management of event finance is a process, a series of steps that starts with forecasting and setting up to monitor the event finances. As illustrated in figure 7.1, there are inputs to this process. The primary inputs come from the management areas of scope, stakeholder and marketing. Each of these management areas directly influences the finance. Stakeholders, for example, can increase funding through sponsorship, ticket sales or legislation. Although the process is illustrated as being step by step, the reality is many of the tools are used concurrently.

Cost benefit analysis and cost analysis go hand in hand. The budget can be developed as a draft budget and then refined as the cash flow management and the cost control planning becomes more detailed. At all times the event manager has to be aware of external trends that will affect the event finance. As with every aspect of special event and festival management, there will be developments. Management of finance is not just observing the flow of money according to how it is set out in the budget. It is active management. It is decision making that concerns the reallocation of funds, finding new sources of income and reducing new costs. All of these decisions sit under the cloud of the deadline. Every financial decision in the event environment must take into account the variable, time, and the constant, the deadline.

FORECASTING FINANCE AND ROI

Financial management begins during the initiation phase of event management. It takes place when deciding on the feasibility of the event. The question, 'Will it work?' generally implies, 'Are there enough funds?'. The case presented for the event will have 'finance' as a heading; in other words, where will the money come from. In this text there is a chapter on sponsorship and many events depend heavily on sponsorship for their finance. Other events, such as corporate events and council events, are given a fixed amount. Events such as concerts and some conferences will depend on ticket sales for their main source of income. Some event organisations will have all the money up-front and therefore have the financial certainty that many other event companies would envy. Other events are expected to earn the money over the period leading up to the event. Others may only make their money on the day of the event. Finally there are events that will make some of their income after the event has finished. In the case of product launches, all of the finance is generated post-event. Time — when the finance comes in and when the bills have to be paid — is an important part of financial management for events.

ROI or return on investment is the measure of the financial return for the investment in the event. The ROI will be different for each of the stakeholders. The host of a major event, such as the government or a large corporation, will expect a complex return on their investment. It may not easily be expressed in financial terms. In this context, the complexity stems from the degree of risk caused by a number of variables. An event such as the Olympics provides many returns on the government's investment. A number of the Olympic stakeholders have not agreed on the value of this return. For small events the ROI may be simply worked out in terms of ticket sales or incoming registration payments.

Currently there is a trend to express all of the complex returns in dollar amounts and therefore give a more realistic assessment of the event. This is to enable the event to be compared to other investment projects. However, the jury is still out on whether this can be achieved. How can 'community happiness', for example, be expressed in dollar terms? The ROI (or lack thereof) for many events may not actualise until years after the event. The 2010 Winter Olympics in Vancouver is an example of the need to employ numerous measures to ensure that the immediate and future intangible benefits are not overlooked. There is detailed analyses of the impact of the events on Canada with a series (126 in total) of socio-cultural, economic and environmental indicators. By setting these indicators, the Olympic movement hopes to measure the impact, assist cities in their application to host the Olympics and develop benchmarking for future games.

The measure of benefits and impacts are complex issues and involve cost–benefit analysis, input–output analysis and other economic tools (see economic impact studies in chapter 3). It should be noted that not all economists agree on the tools or the conclusions reached when applying them to events and festivals. As outlined in chapter 6, another measure of the financial success of a special event or festival is the time it takes the event to pay off its expenses, the payback period. The Victorian Auditor-General's 2007 report on major events illustrates this with the comparison of two very different economic benefit studies of the 2005 Melbourne Grand Prix (Victorian Auditor-General 2007).

The complexity of return on investment is illustrated by figure 7.2. Here, in plain speak, are the tips from the 'event frontline'. The importance of having or hiring financial expertise is said to underpin all the other aspects of the event.

FIGURE 7.2 Profit or perish

Successful events are big business, requiring leaders who understand the importance of profit making. Consumers demand innovation and quality. Innovation and quality cost big bucks. If you don't offer what your customers want then your competitor will. Profits mean success, confidence and influence. Leisure and the arts are not immune to such market trends.

Money will always get in the way, but the more money you have, the less painful your problem is! It's easier to manage the threat of compromising your artistic integrity for commercial imperatives than explaining to your investors that you've planned for their demise.

Producing events is a serious business. If your strength is about inspiring and creating, then you may find yourself too busy and (most probably) by nature unable to focus on maintaining the level of discipline, attention to detail and tough decision making that the business of events requires. Don't try to do it all, play to your strengths and weaknesses by developing the team around you. A call to the best accountancy firm in town may prove to be your best investment!

Step one of the business of any event is to appoint, befriend and learn to trust your chief financial officer or treasurer. Build a working relationship of respect that actively engages those with the discipline and expertise of money management in your decision making. Step two is to underpin your relationship with your financial adviser with the belief that one of the primary aims of operating a business is to make money, to make as large a profit as possible while balancing your need to achieve your event's primary goals. It is more than appropriate that you measure your event's overall success in terms of other less tangible goals, among which you may list the celebration of a moment, community development, attendee satisfaction, challenging your audience, delivering an intended message or the like. Such claims of success belong in the introductory section of your annual report to excite and engage your event constituents. However, these words will stand for little if your financial statement records an undisciplined budget result. When seeking sound financial advice, be sure to maintain the

FIGURE 7.2 *(continued)*

responsibility of making the final decisions on the artistic and strategic directions of your event. Such decisions can then be made with the confidence that you have proactively sought the financial implications and therefore clearly understand and can articulate the implications of these decisions. After all, you will ultimately be held accountable for the areas of your responsibility.

So long as you understand that profit equals success, continuity and strength, then you'll be on the right track. With money in the bank you have options and opportunities. The alternative of operating at a loss is that your event will struggle, your ability to influence your financiers will be eroded and if the problem persists, your position and your event, or both, will perish. Some of your peers may wish to challenge your decision making with cries of 'too commercial' or 'sold out for the almighty dollar', but at least you'll be around to take heed of such criticism and reassess the balance of your business, artistic and strategic intent.

No matter how engaging, wholesome and humanistic your ideology or creativity may be, if you don't possess a robust business plan centred on the discipline of good decision making and wise investment of your available resources — including meticulous assessment of the risk elements of your adventurous plan — then your position or your event will be short-lived. All that you stood for, sought to achieve, your artistic endeavour and uncompromised beliefs and, perhaps more tragically, the countless hours you and your loyal followers invested will result in nothing but heartache. You owe it to yourself, your investors, your followers and believers, including financial backers, staff, volunteers, sponsors and attending public, to make as much money as you can to enable the business of your event to grow and prosper.

Please disregard all of the above if money grows on trees in your neck of the eventing woods.

John Aitken, General Manager, Events and Marketing, Sydney Royal Easter Show.

THE BUDGET

A budget can be described as a quantified statement of plans (in other words, the plan is expressed in numerical terms). The budget process includes costing and estimating income and allocating financial resources. An event budget is used to compare actual costs and revenues with projected costs and revenues. In particular, maximum expenditure for each area of the event's operation is estimated. To achieve this efficiently, a budget can take many forms. It may be, for example, broken into sub-budgets that apply to specific areas of a complex or large event such as the staging, logistics, merchandising and human resources.

Budgets are of particular importance to the management of events because most aspects of the event incur costs requiring payment before the revenue is obtained. Cash flow needs special attention. Most funding or sponsorship bodies need to see a budget of the proposed event before they will commit their resources.

The second part of this chapter expands on these points and provides an example to illustrate them.

Constructing the budget

Two types of budget process can be used in event management. The line-item budget, as the name suggests, focuses on each cost and revenue item of the total event. The program budget is constructed for a specific program element. An example of the latter is a budget devised for a festival that concerns only the activities of one of the performance areas or stages. Such a budget effectively isolates this area of the event from the general festival finance. In this way, individual budgets can be used to compare all the performance areas or stages. The line items are performers' fees and so on.

The creation of a budget has the advantage of forcing management to establish a financial plan for the event and to allocate resources accordingly. It imposes a necessary financial discipline, regardless of how informally an event may be organised. In a similar way to the Gantt chart, it can be used for review long after the event is over.

Preparing a budget is illustrated by figure 7.3. The process begins by establishing the economic environment of the event. The economics of the region and the nation (and even world economics) may impinge on the event and significantly change the budget. An example of this is the effect of the global financial crisis on the availability of funding and sponsorship. The initial response of many companies was to cut their promotion and sponsorship budgets. The immediate result of this was the downsizing of many events and the cancellation of others. The product launch events in the automotive industry were savaged by the flow-on effects of the crisis. In cities highly exposed to international finance, such as Dubai, the crisis forced many event companies out of business and saw others trying to recoup their investments, having been engaged as event suppliers to the property industry. The indirect result of the September 11 terrorist attack on New York's World Trade Towers was the reduction in tourism to Europe and the United States from the Gulf states. In response, the European luxury brands, such as Gucci, set up outlets in Saudi Arabia. Therefore there was little need for the wealthy Saudis to travel outside the country to shop for luxury goods. Both of these factors — September 11 and the global financial crisis — produced major problems for the Dubai Shopping Festival, established in 1996, that depended on Saudi tourism.

To determine the economic environment for a proposed event, it is useful to ask the following questions:

- What similar events can be used as a model for the proposed event and its environment?
- Will changes in the local or state economy affect the budget in any way?
- If the event is to involve international performers or hiring equipment from overseas, will there be a change in the currency exchange rates?
- How exposed is the event to changes in world tourism patterns?

These questions underline the importance of understanding the event's target market. If a significant part of the event's finances depend on income from foreign visitors, an international crisis, such as swine flu or terrorism, will change the financial equation.

These and many more questions need to be answered before constructing a budget that will result in reasonable projections of costs and revenue.

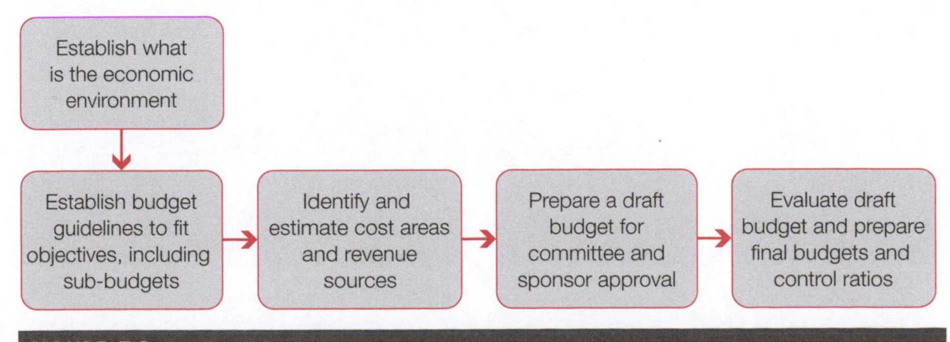

FIGURE 7.3 The budget process

The next step is to obtain the guidelines from the client, sponsors or event committee. A client may request, for instance, that only a certain percentage of their sponsorship be allocated to entertainment, with the rest to be allocated to hospitality. Guidelines must fit with the overall objectives of the event and may require constructing sub-budgets or program budgets. This is both an *instructive phase* — in that the committee, for example, will instruct the event manager on the content of the budget — and a *consultative phase*, because the event manager would ask the advice of other event specialists and the subcontractors.

The third step is to identify, categorise and estimate the cost areas and revenue sources. The categories become the line items in the budget. A sample of the categories is given in table 7.1. This is a summary, or a first-level budget, of the cost and revenue areas. The next level down expands each of these line items and is shown in tables 7.2 (see p. 202) and 7.3 (see p. 206). The use of a computer-generated spreadsheet enables a number of levels in the budget to be created on separate sheets and linked to the first-level budget. Cost items take up the most room on a budget and are described in the following pages.

TABLE 7.1 Generic budget — first level

Income	Amount	Expenditure	Amount
Grants		Administration	
Donations		Publicity	
Sponsorship		Venue costs	
Ticket sales		Equipment	
Fees		Salaries	
Special programs		Insurance	
Concessions		Permits	
TOTAL		Security	
		Accounting	
		Cleaning	
		Travel	
		Accommodation	
		Documentation	
		Hospitality	
		Community groups	
		Volunteers	
		Contingencies	
		TOTAL	

Once the costs and possible revenue sources and amounts are estimated, a *draft budget* is prepared and submitted for approval to the controlling committee. This may be, for example, the finance sub-committee of a large festival. The draft budget is also used in grant submissions and sponsorships. The federal government funding bodies, including the Australia Council and Festivals Australia, have budget guidelines and printed forms that need to be completed and included in the grant application. Figure 7.4 (see page 196) shows a software program from Arts Victoria to assist festivals in their budgeting.

A major problem associated with a budget, particularly for special events, may involve blind adherence to it. It is a tool of control and not an end in itself. The elegance of a well laid-out budget and its mathematical certainty can obscure the fact that it should be a slave to the event objectives, not their master. A budget is based on reasonable projections made within an economic framework. Small changes in the framework can cause large changes in the event's finances. For instance, extra sponsorship may be found if the right products are added to the event portfolio. A complicated, highly detailed budget may consume far more time than is necessary to make the event a success. However, this may be required by the client and the time and cost to create such a budget needs to be factored into the overall project plan.

Time is a crucial factor in special event management. Keeping rigidly within budgetary standards can take up too much time and energy of the event management, thus limiting time available for other areas.

Finally, a budget that is constructed by the event management may be imposed on staff without adequate consultation. This can lead to losing valuable specialist staff if they find themselves having to work to unreasonable budgetary standards. In particular, an innovative event requires the creative input of all the staff and subcontractors. At these events, informal financial control using a draft budget is often far more conducive to quality work than strict budgetary control.

It needs to be remembered that a budget is only an approximation of reality, it is a plan for what should be done, and not reality itself. It will need to be adjusted as the event changes and new information comes to hand. However, it is a vital part of the financial management of events.

The final step involves preparation of the budget and financial ratios that can indicate deviations from the initial plan. An operating business has a variety of budgets, including capital expenditure, sales, overheads and production. Most special events will require only an operations budget or cash budget.

Note the similarity between the classification system used for the budget (see table 7.1) and the WBS described in chapter 6, 'Project management for events'. The WBS is often used as a basis of a budget. The costs of the lower levels are added to give the overall costs; this is called 'rolling up'. This means many aspects of the event can be coded. A simple coding system can be used to link the WBS, the budget, the task sheets and risk analysis — for example, the artwork (A) and the publicity (P) can use the code PA. This can be cross-referenced to the company, person who is responsible, possible risks or the amount budgeted.

A wise event company sets up a system for coding during the initiation phase of planning an event. It can be derived for the WBS and extended to file names, used in the spreadsheets and in the communication subject lines. Data overload and the need to keep records can result in a company losing the ability to find information quickly and make competent decisions. A hierarchy in the coding is important as a way to control this overflow of management data.

FESTIVAL EXPENDITURE Menu Save

Press to go to different sections

- **Performers**
- **Visual arts**
- **Facilities/equipment**
- **Operating expenses**
- **Festival salaries**
- **Travel costs**
- **Administration**

Press to recalculate the total

Performers

Actual	Estimate	Item	$	% External
◉	○	Performers' fees		
◉	○	Music/stage director's fee		
◉	○	Other—performers		
Top of page		*Press to recalculate the total*		

Operating expenses

Actual	Estimate	Item	$	% External
◉	○	Marketing—publicist		
○	◉	Marketing—advertising		
◉	○	Marketing—printing		
○	◉	Marketing—other		
○	◉	Documentation		
◉	○	Materials		
◉	○	Royalties, prizes		
○	◉	Other—operating expenses		
Top of page		*Press to recalculate the total*		

Festival salaries

Actual	Estimate	Item	$	% External
◉	○	Festival director's fees		
○	◉	Coordinators		
◉	○	Administration		
○	◉	Other—festival salaries		
Top of page		*Press to recalculate the total*		

FIGURE 7.4 Festival expenditure template

Source: Arts Victoria's Festivals DIY Kit.

CONTROL AND FINANCIAL RATIOS

Once a plan has been developed and agreed to, the next step is to monitor and control its implementation. For large events, such as the Asian Games in Doha, the control mechanisms are set up when the management plan is created. The budget is a control mechanism as it enables the event management to identify when the organising of the event is drifting away from the forecast.

As described in chapter 6, the process of control involves the following steps:

- establishing standards of performance: this is the budget itself, indicator ratios, success factors and milestones.
- identifying deviations from standards of performance by comparing the budget to the actual spend. Often this can be difficult as the spend can be spread over time. Therefore the ratios and milestones become important as a method to indicate if there are problems.
- correcting deviations — this may involve cutting costs, finding more money or shifting resources.

The break-even chart

This simple graphic tool can highlight control problems by finding the intersection of costs and revenue. Figure 7.5 shows a simple but effective break-even chart for an event that is dependent on ticket sales. A concert, for example, would have fixed costs of stage, audio visual and administration. But the greater the attendance, the larger the cost of security, seating, cleaning, toilets and so forth. However, at one point the revenue from ticket sales exceeds the costs. At this point — the break-even point — the event starts making a profit.

If a fixed cost such as venue hire is increased, the extra number of people needed through the door can quickly be calculated. How would the organisers attract those extra people to the event? One means might be increased promotion. This would then increase the fixed costs. So, an optimal solution is needed so that the increase in people at some point covers the cost of increasing the promotion.

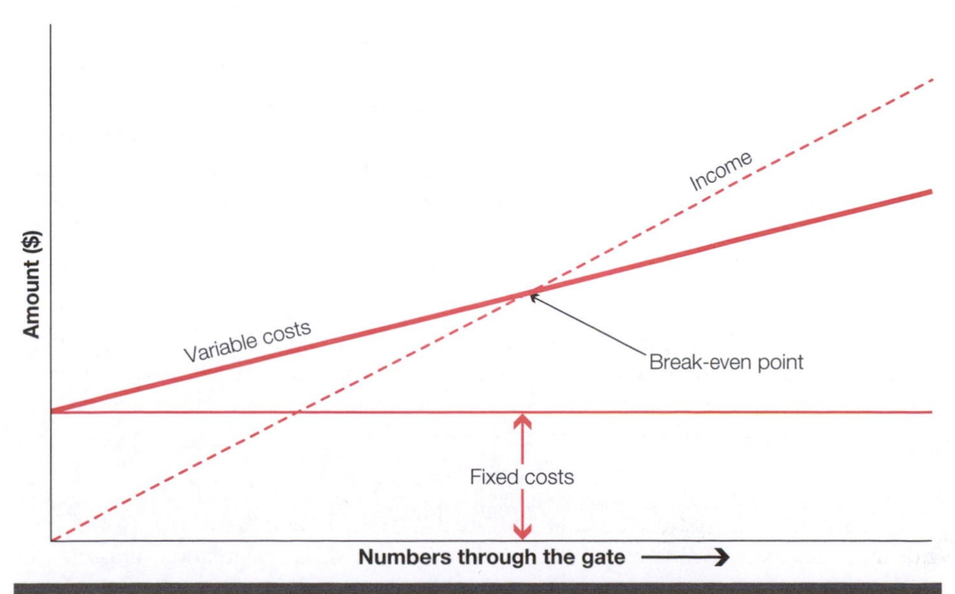

FIGURE 7.5 The break-even chart

Figure 7.6 illustrates the situation when more money is needed for promotion to ensure more ticket sales. It shows that, at a certain time out from the event, the tickets are not selling as well as expected. The event team decides to increase the advertising. This is shown as a step up in the fixed cost line on the graph. This is added to the overall cost of the event. The ticket prices stay the same, so the event team must sell more tickets to cover the added advertising cost. Consequently, the break-even point moves to the right of the graph and there is a new intersection between the event income and the variable costs. If the break-even point is not reached in time for the event, the event team must make more decisions about ways to increase the sales. The decisions about finance and the break-even point illustrate a general rule about event management: all decisions are affected by the deadline.

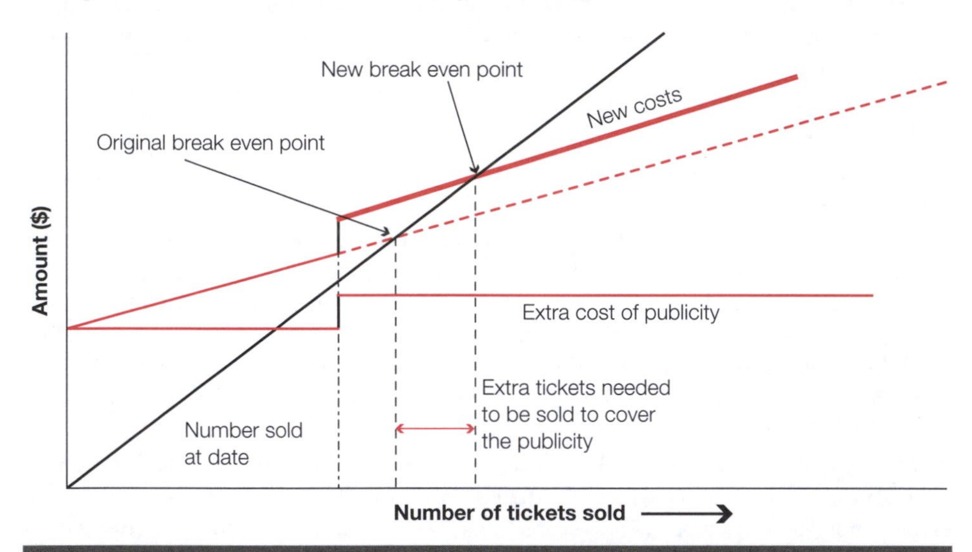

FIGURE 7.6 The event break-even chart

The importance of the factor of 'time' differentiates the normal break-even chart from the event break-even chart. It is *when* the extra money is spent on the promotion that will influence the cash flow and therefore the success of the event. The event break-even chart, in other words, has a third dimension of time. The event manager must always be aware of the time/cost/quality project triangle illustrated in chapter 6. For many events, the surplus or profit will be highly dependent on when the incoming and outgoing payments are made. This can lead to conflicts with the average order/invoice/payment cycle of key stakeholders.

Ratio analysis

There are several ratios that can be used to identify any problems in the financial management of an event or the event company. They can also be used to predict problems. Their main function is as indicators of the health of the event organisation. In particular the ratio of:

$$\frac{\text{Current assets}}{\text{Current liabilities}}$$

indicates the financial strength of the organisation. However, calculation of assets can be difficult, since special events, by their nature, have few current assets except those intangible qualities: goodwill and experience. In a similar way to a film production company, an event company may be formed to create and manage a one-off festival for which every asset is hired for the duration of the event.

Return on investment (ROI) is a significant ratio for any sponsors or investors in an event. This is expressed as:

$$\frac{\text{Net revenue}}{\text{Investment}}$$

The revenue for a sponsor may be expressed in advertising dollars. Print press exposure, for example, can be measured by column centimetres and approximated to the equivalent cost in advertising. This ratio is most often used for events that are staged solely for financial gain. An entrepreneur of a major concert performance must demonstrate a favourable ROI to potential investors to secure financial backing.

Other ratios can provide valuable data. The ratio between net and gross profit is important in deciding the efficiency of an event for fundraising, and provides a means to compare one event to another. This ratio is called the percentage of profit or the profit margin. Another useful ratio is free publicity to paid advertising, particularly for concert promoters.

By performing a series of appropriate ratio analyses, an event management company can obtain a clear picture of the viability of the organisation and identify areas requiring more stringent control.

Perceived value/cost pax

A ratio that is common to event financial management is the perceived value compared to the cost per head (pax). It is employed in corporate special events, festivals and conferences. The perceived value is an estimate of the value the attendees regard as gaining from attending the event. It is what they would expect to pay for the event, if they had to purchase a ticket. This is similar to the concept of consumer surplus used in the assessment of the economic value of public works, national parks and public events. The 'cost per head' is the total cost of the event divided by the number of attendees. A jazz festival, for example, may attract 5000 attendees. The total cost of the festival is estimated as $200 000. The cost per head is therefore $40. The question then becomes: does a member of the audience get $40 worth of value from the event? This ratio is particularly important at high-level corporate events. If the ratio is greater than one, the event management may consider if they are giving too much value for the cost. If it is less than one, the event management may be in trouble! To estimate the cost of a public event or festival, cost per head can be used. This can be averaged over a number of public events. For example, the cost of the 2009–10 New Year's Eve celebration on Sydney Harbour was estimated at $5 million dollars to the local council. The audience was estimated to be 1.5 million; therefore, the cost per head was around $3 to $4. A local council can cost all their free public events in the same way. Over a period of years the local council will have a good indicator of their free events and can estimate the cost of future public festivals.

Cash flow

The special nature of events and festivals requires close attention to the flow of cash. Goldblatt (2005), Getz (2005) and O'Toole and Mikolaitas (2002) all emphasise the importance of the control of cash to an event. Goldblatt (2005) stresses that it is imperative for the goodwill of suppliers. Without prompt payment the event company faces immediate difficulties. Payment terms and conditions have to be fully and equitably negotiated. These payment terms can ruin an event if they are not given careful consideration beforehand. To obtain the best terms from a supplier, Goldblatt suggests the following:

- Learn as much as possible about the suppliers and subcontractors and the nature of their business. Do they own the equipment? What are the normal payment terms in their business? Artists, for instance, expect to be paid immediately, whereas some information technology suppliers will wait for 60 days.
- Be flexible with what can be offered in exchange — including sponsorship.
- Try to negotiate a contract that stipulates a small deposit before the event and full payment after it is over.
- Suggest a line of credit, with payment at a set time in the future.
- Closely control the purchasing.
- Ensure all purchases are made through a purchase order that is authorised by the event manager or the appropriate finance personnel. A purchase order is a written record of the agreement to supply a product at a pre-arranged price. All suppliers, contractors and event staff should be informed that no purchase can be made without an authorised form. This ensures spending is confined to what is permitted by the budget.
- Obtain a full description of the product or service and the quantities required.
- Itemise the price to a per unit cost.
- Calculate any taxes or extra charges.
- Determine payment terms.
- Clarify delivery details.
- Consider imposing penalties if the product or service delivered is not as described.

As figure 7.7 shows, the ability of an event coordinator to effect any change diminishes rapidly as the event draws closer. The supply of goods and services may, of necessity, take place close to or on the actual date of the event. This does not allow organisers the luxury of reminding a supplier of the terms set out in the purchase order. Without a full written description of the goods, the event manager is open to all kinds of exploitation by suppliers and, because the event may be on that day, there may be no choice but to accept delivery.

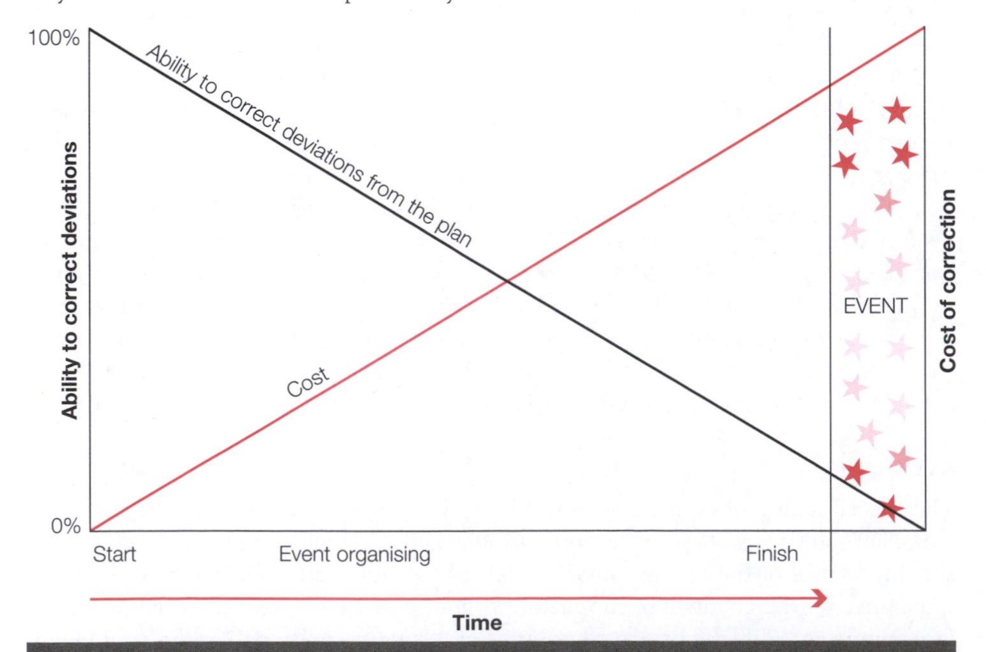

FIGURE 7.7 Control, cost and time

When considering cash flow, ticketing strategy advantages of events such as the Port Fairy Folk Festival are obvious. As tickets are sold months before the event, the management is able to concentrate on other areas of planning. A similar advantage is obtained by event companies that specialise in the corporate area — generally, they are paid up-front. This allows the event manager or producer the freedom to negotiate terms and conditions with the suppliers without having to worry about the cash flow. A cash flow timing chart similar to the Gantt chart is often helpful in planning events. This shows the names of the suppliers and their payment requirements. It includes deposit dates, payment stages, payment on purchase, monthly fixed cost payments and 30-, 60- or 90-day credit payments.

COSTING AND ESTIMATING

The cash flow at an event is heavily dependent on the cost of goods and services. These are estimated for the construction of the budget. The prediction, categorisation and allocation of costs is called the costing. In relation to the break-even chart (figure 7.5), two types of costs have been identified. These are described in the following text.

Fixed costs or overheads are costs associated with the event that occur regardless of how many people come to the event. They include the unchanging expenses concerned with the operation of the event management company; for example, rent, staff salaries, telephone and other office expenses. At a large festival these expenses may include rates, land tax and interest on loans. When deciding on a budget, these costs should be apportioned reasonably to the various event areas. This process is called absorption of the overheads by the cost centres. Cost centres, for example, include entertainment, catering, staging or travel. If the fixed costs are incorrectly absorbed the cost centre will be wrongly described. For a correct financial picture of a future event, the overheads have to be reasonably spread to all areas. The aim of an event company is to reduce the fixed costs without affecting the quality of the event.

Variable costs are expenses that pertain solely to the event and are directly related to the number of people who attend the event. Food and beverage costs are linked directly to the number of people attending an event. If more people attend an event, more tickets need to be printed, more staff may need to be hired and certainly more food provided.

This division of costs is not as clear-cut in the event industry as in other industries. It is sometimes clearer instead to talk in terms of direct costs (the costs directly associated with the event, whether variable or fixed) and overheads (costs associated with the running of the event company). In this case, the direct costs are the major costs — and the aim of the event company is to control these costs. Table 7.2 lists the detailed budgeted costs of a one-off event.

The advantage of a budget in table 7.2 is that it can be used as a template for future events. The use of a spreadsheet template allows the festival organiser to create a generic budget and apply it to each event. The items not needed are simply deleted.

As is demonstrated in the case study in chapter 6 on the use of spreadsheets to plan events, the template is essential to reducing the administration work. It acts as both a guide and a checklist for the budget. Once the WBS is drafted, it can be copied into another worksheet. Each of the cost of the items can be estimated to draft the budget.

TABLE 7.2 Projected costs — second level

Income		$
Administration	Office rental	
	Fax/photocopy	
	Computers	
	Printers	
	Telephone	
	Stationery	
	Postage	
	Office staff	
	SUBTOTAL	
Publicity	Artwork	
	Printing	
	Poster and leaflet distribution	
	Press kit	
	Press ads	
	Radio ads	
	Programs	
	SUBTOTAL	
Venue	Hire	
	Preparation	
	SUBTOTAL	
Equipment	Stage	
	Sound	
	Lights	
	Transport	
	Personnel	
	Toilets	
	Extra equipment	
	Communication	
	First aid	
	Tents	
	Tables and chairs	
	Wind breaks	
	Generators	
	Technicians	
	Parking needs	
	Uniforms	
	SUBTOTAL	
Salaries	Coordinator	
	Artists	
	Labourers	
	Consultants	
	Other	
	SUBTOTAL	

Income		$
Insurance	Public liability	
	Workers compensation	
	Rain	
	Other	
	SUBTOTAL	
Permits	Liquor	
	Food	
	Council	
	Parking	
	Childcare	
	SUBTOTAL	
Security	Security check	
	Equipment	
	Personnel	
	SUBTOTAL	
Accounting	Cash and cheque	
	Audit	
	SUBTOTAL	
Cleaning	Before	
	During	
	After	
	SUBTOTAL	
Travel	Artists	
	Freight	
	SUBTOTAL	
Accommodation		
	SUBTOTAL	
Documentation	Photo/video	
	SUBTOTAL	
Hospitality	Tent	
	Food	
	Beverage	
	Personnel	
	Invitations	
	SUBTOTAL	
Community	Donations	
	SUBTOTAL	
Volunteers	Food and drink	
	Party	
	Awards and prizes	
	SUBTOTAL	
Contingencies		
	SUBTOTAL	

Catherwood and Van Kirk (1992) divide the costs of an event into four main categories:

1. *operational or production costs*, including hiring of event staff, construction, insurance and administration
2. *venue/site rental*
3. *promotion* — advertising, public relations, sales promotion
4. *talent* — costs associated with the entertainment.

To obtain the correct cost of each of the elements contained in the budget categories (sometimes called cost centres) there is a common costing process involved. According to O'Toole and Mikolaitis (2002), the tools of project management can be used to estimate event costs. These include:

- *Top–down estimating*. The event management arrives at a figure based on their experience and a comparison to events of a similar type and size. It can also be called a conceptual estimate or 'ballpark figure'. It is used in the early development stage of the event to give management an idea of the costs involved. Generally this would have an accuracy of +/– 25 per cent.
- *Bottom–up estimating*. The event is divided into its components and the costs are estimated for each component. If the event company employs a project management approach, this is easily accomplished using the work breakdown structure as a guide. During the feasibility study only the major costs may be identified and estimated. The cost of headline speakers, for example, varies according to their popularity and type of career. Asking other event managers about current speaker fees gives the event producer a basis for negotiating a fair price and a more realistic budget estimation. A more accurate estimate is obtained by getting quotes from the suppliers. The larger festivals will put many of the elements of the event out to tender, including sound, lights and security. A near-correct estimate can be made on this basis. For small events, the quote may be obtained by phoning a selection of suppliers and comparing the costs. However, it is rarely the case that the costs are comparable, as there are so many unusual features or special conditions. Once an event company has built up a relationship with a supplier, it tends to stay with that supplier.
- *Parametric estimating*. Parametric estimating is where 'the overall cost of the event is assumed to be related to one element, a parameter of the event' (O'Toole and Mikolaitas 2002, p. 226). The cost of a single person at an event is one such parameter. If the cost of one person is multiplied by the number of people, the cost of the whole event can be estimated. Parametric estimating is common in conferences and exhibitions. The latter uses 'floor space' or 'cost per square metre' as the parameter. Note that this is related to the perceived value ratio explained earlier in this chapter.

Costing time

It would not be a complete chapter on finance without a mention of how the event company costs its time. A private event company will generally charge at least 20 per cent of the total amount to organise the event. It can be a percentage of the overall event budget, a fixed fee as a lump sum or a per hour rate, an incentive fee or a mixture of the three. If the event income is dependent on ticket sales or registrations and the event company owns the event, its fee will be the profit that is left after all expenses are paid. An event unit within a government or a major company may have to demonstrate it has produced a surplus. Most of these event units are a cost to the organisation. In this case the event unit will be expected to 'cost its time'.

The most common problem in an event is the cost blow-out. Special event planners often encounter unforeseen circumstances that can cost dearly. The subcontractor who supplies the sound system, for example, can go bankrupt; the replacement subcontractor may prove far more expensive. One of the unwritten laws of project management is that the closer the project is to completion, the more expensive any changes become. Appropriate remedial action may be to use cheaper catering services or to find extra funding. This could take the form of a raffle to cover the extra costs. Figure 7.7 graphically shows how the cost of any changes to the organisation of an event escalate as the event date nears.

Sensitivity analysis

The degree of influence the changes in the costs have on the event and its management is called sensitivity. It is almost certain that there will be changes over the time the event is organised. The change could be external, such as political or economic, or internal, such as staff or the event program. The wise event company is aware of the effect of any changes. The example of the opening of the Burj Khalifa and the Dubai Shopping Festival in this chapter provided two instances. Some costs will remain constant and others will vary. Some real examples of unpredictably changing costs are airline ticket prices, exchange rates, sponsor withdrawal and extraneous artists' expenses. There will be other changes that can be a result of the event being developed and responding to opportunities. The marketing team, for example, may find better promotional channels, causing an increase of interest in the event, which flows on to an increase in demand for the press release and complimentary tickets to the event.

The contingency amount is the expected change in the budget estimation. It reflects the uncertainty in event finance. This will be different according to how the budget is estimated, the expertise of the estimator and the type of event. However, the contingency can also be given by the client. Some event companies add a 10 to 15 per cent contingency in their budgets.

Tips on reducing costs

With careful and imaginative planning, costs can be reduced in a number of areas.

- *Publicity*. An innovative event may need a large publicity budget that is based on revenue from ticket sales. The event manager's aim should be to reduce this wherever possible. Established festivals may need very little publicity as word of mouth will do all the necessary work. The annual Woodford Folk Festival, with a budget of $2.3 million, spends very little on publicity because it has built up a strong reputation with its target audience. The more innovative the event, the greater the possibility for free publicity. The Tropfest, the world's largest short film festival, for example, gains enormous free publicity as it attracts film stars to the event. A major art event used a problem as a promotion. In this event, the sculptures were placed along a free public-accessed park. The event organisers found that, occasionally, sculptures were placed on the site without going through the normal process of selection. The event organisers used this to their advantage by staging a sculpture being secreted in the exhibition and having a press photographer take photos of the 'illegal' action. The next day the photo gained a half page in the newspaper, thereby indirectly promoting the exhibition.
- *Equipment and supplies*. Suppliers of products to events have down times during the year when their products may be hired cheaply. In particular, theatrical productions

at the end of their run are a ready source of decoration and scenery. Annual events like the Sydney Gay and Lesbian Mardi Gras often have equipment in storage that can be hired.

- *In-kind gifts*. Many organisations will assist events to achieve cross-promotional advantages. Entertainment can be inexpensive if there is a chance that an organisation can promote a performance or product at the event. For instance, a boutique wine company agreed to supply their wine freely to the pre-event party for the media and friends, in exchange for the rights to sell their product at the concert.
- *Hiring charges*. The hire costs of large infrastructure components, such as tents, generators and headline acts, can be reduced by offering work at other festivals and events. The large cultural festivals around Australia, for example, including the Melbourne International Festival and the Adelaide Festival of the Arts, can offer a festival circuit to any overseas performer. Costs are amortised over all the festivals.
- *Prioritise cost centres*. At some time it will be necessary to cut costs. You will need to anticipate the effect on the overall event if one area is significantly changed or eliminated. Estimates are made of the influence of cost changes on the event and the cost centres are placed in a priority list according to the significance of the effect. A sensitivity analysis, for example, could be applied to the effect of imposing a charge on a program that was previously free. While this could significantly increase revenue, it may produce a negative effect in sponsorship and audience satisfaction, which may well be translated into the reduction of revenue.
- *Volunteers*. Costs can be reduced by using volunteers instead of paid staff. It is important that all of the skills of the volunteers are fully utilised. These skills should be continually under review as new skills may be required as the event planning progresses. For charitable functions, volunteers will often absorb many of the costs as tax deductible donations.

Revenue

Anticipating potential sources of revenue should be given as much attention as projecting expenses. The source of the revenue will often define the type of event, the event objectives and the planning. A company product launch has only one source of revenue — the client. Company staff parties, for example, are paid for by the client with no other source of revenue. The budget then has only one entry on the left-hand side. A major festival, on the other hand, has to find and service a variety of revenue sources such as sponsors and participants. This constitutes a major part of festival planning.

Revenue can come from the following sources:

- ticket sales — most common in entrepreneurial events
- sponsorship — common in cultural and sports events
- merchandising
- advertising
- 'in-kind' arrangements
- broadcast rights — an increasingly important source of revenue in sport events
- grants — federal, state and local government
- fundraising — common in community events
- the client — the major source for corporate events.

Table 7.3 features an expanded list of revenue sources. For many events, admission fees and ticket prices need careful consideration. The revenue they generate will impact on the cash flow and the break-even point.

TABLE 7.3 Revenue sources — second level

Income		$
Grants	Local	
	State	
	Federal	
	Arts	
	Other	
	SUBTOTAL	
Donations	Foundations	
	Other	
	SUBTOTAL	
Sponsorship	In-kind	
	Cash	
	SUBTOTAL	
Individual contributions		
	SUBTOTAL	
Special programs	Raffle	
	Auction	
	Games	
	SUBTOTAL	

Income		$
Ticket sales	Box office	
	Retail outlets	
	Admissions	
	SUBTOTAL	
Merchandise	T-shirts	
	Programs	
	Posters	
	Badges	
	DVDs	
	SUBTOTAL	
Fees	Stalls	
	Licences	
	Broadcast	
	SUBTOTAL	
Advert sales	Program	
	Event site	
	SUBTOTAL	
Concessions		
	SUBTOTAL	

The ticket price can be decided by one or more of three methods.

1. *Covering costs.* All the costs are estimated and added to the projected profit. To give the ticket price, this figure is then divided by the expected number of people that will attend the event. The method is quick, simple and based on knowing the break-even point. It gives a 'rule of thumb' figure that can be used as a starting point for further investigations in setting the price.
2. *Market demand.* The ticket price is decided by the prevailing ticket prices for similar or competing events. In other words, it is the 'going rate' for an event. Concert ticket prices are decided in this way. In deciding on the ticket price, consider elasticity of demand. For instance, if the ticket price is increased slightly, will this affect the number of tickets sold?
3. *Perceived value.* The event may have special features that preclude a price comparison to other events. For an innovative event, for example, the ticket price must be carefully considered. By its nature this kind of event has no comparison. There can be variations in the ticket price for different entertainment packages at the event (at many multi-venued events the ticket will include admission only to certain events), for extra hospitality or for special seating. Knowing how to grade the tickets is an important skill in maximising revenue. There are market segments that will not tolerate differences in pricing, whereas others expect it. It can be a culturally based decision and may be part of the design of the event. As Gaur and Saggere succinctly write, 'will the event be able to make them (the customers) happy at (the) end?' (2004, p. 108).

Tips for increasing projected income

Ticket scaling

There are many ticketing strategies that strive to obtain the best value from ticket sales. The most common strategy is to vary the pricing, according to seat position, number of tickets sold and time of sale. Early-bird discounts and subscriptions series are two examples of the latter. Another strategy involves creating a special category of attendees. This could include patrons, special clubs, 'friends of the event', people for whom the theme of the event has a special meaning or those who have attended many similar events in the past. For a higher ticket price, for example, patrons are offered extra hospitality, such as a separate viewing area, valet parking and a cocktail party.

In-kind support and bartering

One way to increase income is to scrutinise the event cost centres for areas that could be covered by an exchange with the supplier or bartering. The advertising can be expanded for an event, for example, with a program of 'give-aways'. These are free tickets to the event given away through the press. Due to the amount of goodwill surrounding a fundraising event, bartering should be explored as a method of obtaining supplies. Bartering may have significant tax implications. It should not be undertaken without close scrutiny of this risk.

Merchandising

The staging of an event offers many opportunities for merchandising. The first consideration is 'Does the sale of goods enhance the theme of the event?'. The problems of cash flow at an event, as stated earlier in this chapter, can give the sale of goods an unrealistically high priority in event management. It is easy to cheapen a boutique special event with the sale of trinkets. However, the attendees may want to buy a souvenir. A large choir performing at a one-off spectacular event, for example, may welcome the opportunity to sell a video or DVD of its performance. This could be arranged with the choir beforehand and result in a guaranteed income. As a spin-off, the video or DVD could be incorporated into promotional material for use by the event management in bidding for future events.

Broadcast rights

An increasingly important source of revenue, particularly in sports events, is the payment for the right to broadcast. A live television broadcast of an event is a lucrative area for potential income — but it comes at a price. The broadcast and its requirements become master of the event, rather than the needs and expectations of the live audience. Often the live audience becomes merely one element in the televising process. At the ARIA (Australian Record Industry Association) Awards the audience includes 'fillers' — people who fill any empty seats so that the camera will always show a capacity audience.

If the entire event is recorded by high-quality video equipment, future broadcast rights should also be investigated. For instance, in many countries there is a constant demand for worthwhile content for pay television (cable or satellite). There have been a number of music and image broadcasts over the internet, but they are limited by the size of the bandwidth. There can be no doubt that this will become an important medium for the event industry. Podcasting is an interesting alternative to webcasting. Podcasting involves recording aspects of the event and uploading these to the event website. These can be downloaded at anytime and viewed or listened to on the computer or a portable digital device. Podcasts of literary discussions and debates at festivals have been used to generate interest in the next event.

Sponsorship leverage and activation

Leverage is the current term for using event sponsorship to gain further support from other sponsors. Very few companies or organisations want to be the first to sponsor a one-off event. However, once the event has one sponsor's support, sufficient credibility is gained to enable an approach to other sponsors. Gaining the support of a major newspaper or radio station, for example, allows the event manager to approach other sponsors. The sponsors realise that they can obtain free publicity. Activation refers to adding to the sponsor's benefits through extra services and innovative ideas. Innovation can create a deeper involvement by the sponsor in the event.

Special features

When an event is linked to a large population base, there are many opportunities for generating income. Raffles, for example, are frequently used to raise income. At a concert dance in England, all patrons brought along a prize for a raffle to be drawn on the night. Everyone received a ticket in the raffle as part of the entry fee to the event. The prizes ranged from old ties to overseas air tickets. Every person received a prize and the raffle became part of the entertainment of the evening.

Holding an auction at an event is also an entertaining way to increase income. Prior to the Broome Fringe Festival, the event manager organised an innovative auction. The items auctioned included haircuts, 'slave for a day', body work and massages. The sale of players' jerseys, complete with the mud stains, after a major football match has also proved a lucrative way of raising revenue.

Financial reporting

The budget report is a means of highlighting problems and suggesting solutions. It is an effective form of communication to the event committee and staff and should be readily understood. It is important that appropriate action is taken in response to the report's suggestions. Figure 7.8 is a list of guidelines for a straightforward report.

- The report should relate directly to the event management area to which it is addressed.
- It should not contain extraneous information that can only obscure its function. Brevity and clarity are key objectives.
- The figures in the report must be of the same magnitude and they should be comparable.
- The report should describe how to take remedial action if there is a significant problem.

FIGURE 7.8 Reporting guidelines

For many events financial reports may need to be sent to interested parties. In particular the taxation office will require GST reports. The client may need ongoing financial reports. The budget can be revisited with a new column called 'actuals'. This lists the actual amount spent. At the end of the event, a profit and loss statement may need to be prepared and sent to the host organisation. All these activities must be placed on the management timeline. If the event management opens a special bank account for the event, the reporting can be simplified as the bank will have an online statement of the account.

A tool used in project management and one that is common in the event industry is the commitment account. One of the problems met by events is that they are unlike most other continuous businesses. They have a short timeframe. Therefore the most common accounting methods can miss the financial action. An example will illustrate this statement. Consider an event with a budget of $200 000 and the event manager contacts a sound company and agrees over the phone to a fee of $50 000. This means that there is $150 000 left to spend. It is obvious. However, according to accounting rules, there is nothing to record. There have been no goods or services delivered. Therefore event and project managers often have a commitment account where they note these 'transactions' or commitments. The short timeframe for many events means that many of these decisions are made 'on the run' and based on trust. Having a record of commitments is a safe way to ensure that the trust between the event management and the suppliers is maintained.

event profile

COST BLOW-OUT FORCED FRINGE ACTION

Chief Minister Jon Stanhope said yesterday Fringe Festival director Jorian Gardner should have been included in a discussion to sever it from the Multicultural Festival, but a huge cost blow-out meant radical changes were necessary.

He said this was not a rebuke for Minister for Multicultural Affairs John Hargreaves, but he did have regrets over the lack of consultation with Mr Gardner about the decision to hand the Fringe over to the National Folk Festival, which will receive $30 000 to run it.

Mr Hargreaves announced this week the 10-day Multicultural Festival would be downgraded to three days and would be transferred from a government-delivered festival to a community-run festival, with the government as a 'platinum sponsor' providing $418 000.

The excessive cost, $100 000, of this year's Fringe Festival was part of the decision to cut it from the Multicultural Festival.

Mr Stanhope said the Multicultural Festival expenditure of $960 000 was more than double its agreed budget which made it unsustainable.

He said the Fringe was not 'necessarily a good fit' with the Multicultural Festival but it had happened organically.

ACT Greens Multicultural Affairs spokesperson, Amanda Bresnan, said the decision to give $30 000 to the National Folk Festival to run the Fringe appeared to be a 'creative use of multicultural funds'.

'The whole process just doesn't seem to make much sense. There's no clarity about why particular decisions have been made,' she said.

Source: Streak 2009.

SUMMARY

There is little point expending effort in creating a plan for an event if there is no way to closely monitor it. The event plan is a prerequisite for success. The control mechanisms to keep the project aligned to the plan need to be well thought out and easily understood by the management team. When the event strays from the plan there needs to be ways to bring it back into line or to change the plan.

An estimate of the costs and revenues of an event is called the budget and it acts as the master control of an event. With a well-reasoned budget in place, all sections of an event know their spending limits and can focus on working together. The cash flow of an event needs special considerations. When is the cash coming in? Moreover, when does it need to go out? An event that does not have control mechanisms, including a well-planned budget, is not going to satisfy its stakeholders. Not only will it fail, but organisers will never know the reason for its failure. A sound budget gives management a solid foundation on which to build a successful event.

QUESTIONS

1 The budget is often perceived as the most important part of event management. What are the limitations of running an event by the budget? Do many events, such as the arts festivals, always come in under budget? What can lead to drastic changes in the budget?

2 It is said that the cost of a public festival divided by the number of attendees is approximately the cost of a cinema ticket in that country. Is this true? Is this an example of the consumer comparing how they will spend their money? Using a local festival or sports event, test this hypothesis.

3 Identify the cost centres and revenue sources for:
   (a) a celebrity poetry reading for a charity
   (b) a rural car auction with antique cars
   (c) a corporate Christmas party
   (d) a hot-air balloon festival.

4 Why is cash flow of such importance to event management? Can an event be run on credit?

5 Using the event break-even chart in this chapter (figure 7.5 on page 197), explore other options to increase the ticket sales. Include the element of time, such as the timing of decisions and when the effects of decisions are felt. Discuss how problems of control and information of the ticket sales in the lead up to an event will affect the chart and therefore the decisions?

case study

PRICING EVENT MANAGEMENT SERVICE

The importance of 'pricing right'

Event firms sell a complex, intangible basket of skills and services of event infrastructure, design, event management experience, knowledge, project management skills, technical skills, processes, and vendor networks. Firms are often expected to include in their price the supply of the 'tangible' aspects of the events like props, decor, venue rental, food and beverages, performances and so on. Determining the

direct costs of an event is already challenging — many events are out of the ordinary in nature. The more 'special' the event is, the more unique the scope of work and the more extraordinary items there are. This complexity is compounded by long planning periods, which span months or even years, making it notoriously difficult to estimate costs.

Additionally, the event industry is maturing, resulting in greater competition, higher demands from clients, more sophisticated audiences and the increasing prevalence of procurement processes. This boils down to an immense downward pressure on price while expectations increase, adding further difficulties to an already challenging process. The temptation and danger of underpricing is thus very real.

According to Ronnie Lim, CEO of The Event Company, consistent underpricing could lead to a firm's 'extinction'. Underpricing is charging below the cost to deliver, which can result in a downward cyclical effect on the firm as illustrated in figure 7.9. He explains that underpricing puts a strain on resources; charging below cost to deliver per event requires the firm to increase the number of events delivered in order to compensate. The same amount of resources now needs to a deliver greater volume of work, affecting both client satisfaction and employee morale.

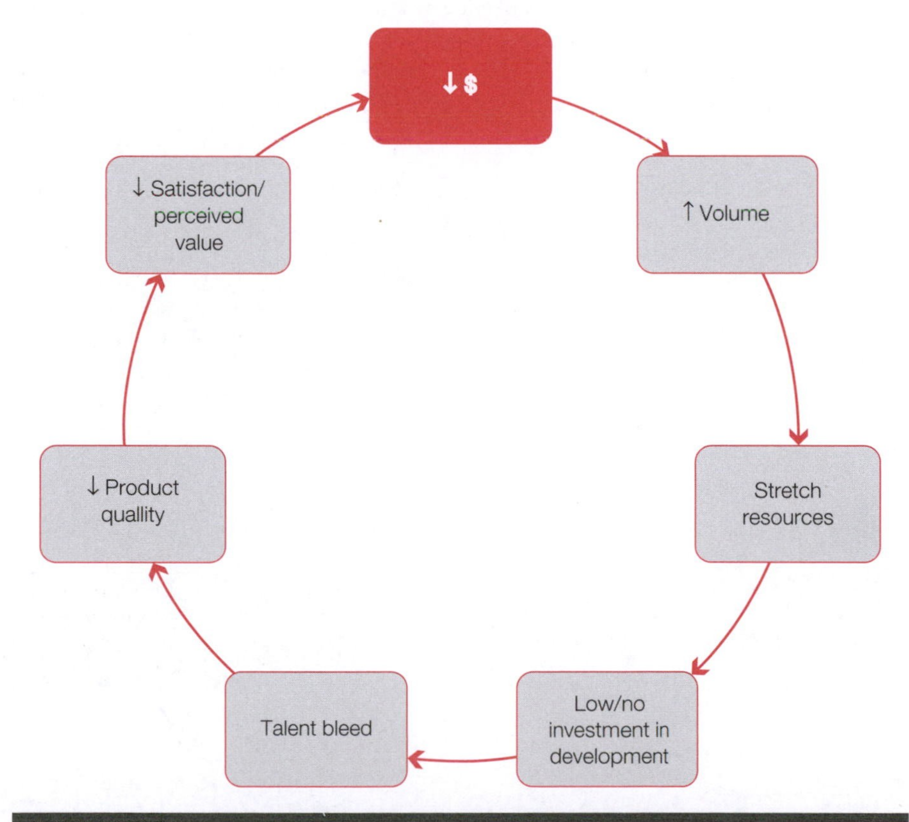

FIGURE 7.9 The cycle of under-pricing

Employees are the key resource of all event management firms and, on the employee front, there are short- and long-term impacts. In the short term, with resources spread too thinly, there is the immediate danger of poor event delivery leading to very unhappy clients.

In the long term, stretched resources, focused only on event delivery, working beyond sustainable levels, the threats of exhaustion and burn out all become very real. There will be no resources left to re-invest in staff and the firm. Staff exhaustion, lack of development and low product quality will lead to erosion of morale and dissatisfaction. The talented personnel will either burn out or simply leave for more rewarding and fulfilling jobs, leaving the firm with an inexperienced and, therefore, less effective team, further exacerbating product quality deterioration.

On the client front, a lower quality product reduces customer satisfaction and lowers perceived value. Dropping quality from overstretched resources culminates in poor event delivery and events that don't meet objectives — clients will cease to see value in outsourcing their events, making them even harder to price right. This downward spiral continues until the event planner is driven out of the market.

The solution, however, is not to charge as much as you can — overpricing is as detrimental to a firm's continued existence as underpricing. According to Ronnie Lim, the firm needs to find the model that allows them to *price right* — to find the balance allows the firm to acquire the right mix of work at the right volume. This positions the firm as an effective resource to clients, and enables personnel to get to know the firm and understand their brand sufficiently in order to value-add. It gives the event company the much needed resources to invest back into the business, be it in training, process improvement or research. The ultimate outcome: client satisfaction and a reinforced belief in the power of events, both of which are critical for the firm and the industry to evolve. Ronnie refers to this as the *cycle of evolution* (see figure 7.10).

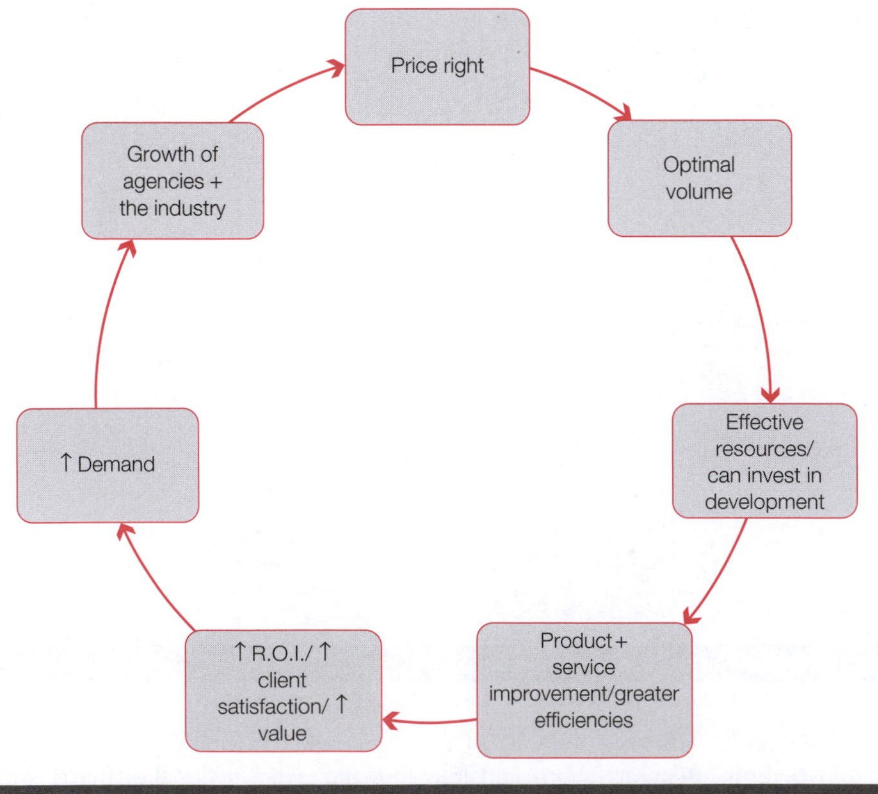

FIGURE 7.10 The cycle of evolution

Pricing — some models

There are several pricing models that a firm can undertake and, over the course of The Event Company's development, the following approaches have been used:

- *'Main-con' approach*. This is an approach that is adopted by young and smaller agencies. It essentially prices the event at third party cost plus a minimal fee. The underlying assumption is that the key service provided is one of event sourcing and coordination.
- *Value-added project manager approach*. This is similar to the 'Main-con' approach, and tends to be adopted by slightly more established companies. This approach imposes a higher event management fee on top of projected third party costs. Here, the services provided are more sophisticated and the agency plays a project management, rather than a simple coordination, role.
- *Value pricing or a fee+ approach*. In this approach, the agency charges a fee that reflects the value of services provided, and then passes through the third party costs of the event. The fee component is often developed based on an hourly rate, cost of resources and time spent on the project. It works on the premise that the agency works as a full partner to the client and is selling a complex set of services, ranging from experience and design to creative, project and event management.

A firm may need to adopt different approaches depending on the nature of the project, the market forces and the type of services required by each client. However, there still needs to be an underlying framework that guides the overall pricing strategy. In Ronnie's view, to build this framework, a firm needs to:

- *have clarity on what services they are selling*. For example, event supplies, event planning, project management, design and experience (i.e. a producer's role), or a combination of the above. Having clarity lends the firm the ability to not only price accordingly, but to articulate the value of the services.
- *recognise itself*. It's essential for the firm to understand their own strengths, where they stand with their clients, as well as their level of skill and experience. This allows them to identify the value they bring their competitors.
- *upgrade and educate*. Firms need to work closely with their clients to continually educate them and show them the value that an agency can bring. In addition, they need to spend sufficient time to train staff, improve processes and build infrastructure
- *embrace transparency*. The increasing focus on corporate governance is here to stay; firms need to embrace this and fully understand how it impacts their business.

There is no one stock solution to finding the right price. With all of the complexities involved and with prevalent market forces, a firm cannot underestimate the importance of spending the required time to develop their pricing strategy. They must determine the right balance that allows them to remain competitive, and yet reinvest for growth.

Prepared by Ronnie Lim, The Event Company.

Questions

1 Analyse the risk of underpricing.

2 Is there an ethical problem with overpricing? Discuss the long term implications of overcharging for the event industry and the event company.

3 Can there be a standard price for event management services? Could this be set by government? What would be the implications?

REFERENCES

Aitken, J 2006, General Manager, Events and Marketing, Sydney Royal Easter Show, Royal Agricultural Society of New South Wales, personal communication, June.

Arts Victoria, 'Festivals DIY Kit', www.arts.vic.gov.au.

Birch, R 2004, *Master of ceremonies*, Allen & Unwin, Sydney.

Catherwood, D & Van Kirk, R 1992, *The complete guide to special event management*, John Wiley & Sons, New York.

EPMS CD-ROM 2010, www.epms.net.

Gaur, S & Saggere, S 2004, *Event marketing and management*, Vikas, New Delhi.

Getz, D 2005, *Event management and event tourism*, 2nd edn, Cognizant Communications, New York.

Goldblatt, J 2005, *Special events*, 4th edn, John Wiley & Sons, New York.

O'Toole, W & Mikolaitas P 2002, *Corporate event project management*, John Wiley & Sons, New York.

Sounder, M 2004, *Event entertainment and production*, John Wiley & Sons, New York.

Streak, D 2009, 'Cost blow-out forced Fringe action: Stanhope', *Canberra Times* 21 Aug., www.canberratimes.com.au.

The OGI-UBC Research Team, 2009, Olympic Games Impact (OGI) Study for the 2010 Olympic and Paralympic Winter Games, University of Columbia.

Victorian Auditor-General 2007, *State investment in major events*, Victorian Auditor-General's Office, Melbourne.

FURTHER READING

Silvers, JR 2004, *Professional event coordination*, John Wiley & Sons, New York.

Tassiopoulis, D (ed.) 2010, *Event management: a developmental and managental approach*, 3rd edn, Juta Academic, South Africa.

Van Der Wagen, L 2005, *Event management for tourism, cultural, business and sporting events*, 2nd edn, Pearson, Australia.

HUMAN RESOURCE MANAGEMENT AND EVENTS

LEARNING OBJECTIVES

After studying this chapter, you should be able to:

1. describe the human resource management challenges posed by events
2. list and describe the key steps in the human resource planning process for events
3. discuss approaches that can be employed to motivate event staff and volunteers
4. describe techniques that can be used for event staff and volunteer team building
5. state general legal considerations associated with human resource management in an event context.

INTRODUCTION

Effective planning and management of human resources is at the core of any successful event. Ensuring an event is adequately staffed with the right people, who are appropriately trained and motivated to meet its objectives, is fundamental to the event management process. This chapter seeks to provide an overview of the key aspects of human resource planning and management with which an event manager should be familiar. It begins by examining considerations associated with human resource management in the context of events. It then moves on to propose a model of the event human resource management process and to discuss each of the major steps in this model. Selected theories associated with employee/volunteer motivation are then described, followed by a brief examination of techniques for staff and volunteer team building. The final part of this chapter overviews legal considerations associated with human resource management.

CONSIDERATIONS ASSOCIATED WITH HUMAN RESOURCE PLANNING FOR EVENTS

The context in which human resource planning takes place for events can be said to be unique for two major reasons. First, and perhaps most significantly, many events have a 'pulsating' organisational structure (Hanlon & Jago 2000; Hanlon & Cuskelly 2002). This means they grow rapidly in terms of personnel as an event approaches and contract even more quickly when it ends.

From a human resource perspective this creates a number of potential challenges. These include:

- obtaining paid staff given the short-term nature of the employment offered
- working to short timelines to hire and train staff
- attrition due to the pressure of working to tight deadlines
- shedding staff quickly once an event is over.

Secondly, as volunteers, as opposed to paid staff, can sometimes make up a significant proportion of an event's workforce, or indeed, on occasions, can comprise its entire workforce, matters specific to the management of this labour source need to be understood by the managers of many types of events.

THE HUMAN RESOURCE PLANNING PROCESS FOR EVENTS

Human resource planning for events should not be viewed simply in terms of a number of isolated tasks, but as a series of sequential interrelated processes and practices that take their lead from an event's vision/mission, objectives and strategy. If an event seeks to grow in size and attendance, for example, it will need a human resource strategy to support this growth through such means as increased staff recruitment (paid and/or volunteer) and expanded (and perhaps more sophisticated) training programs. If these supporting human resource management actions are not in place, problems such as high staff/volunteer turnover due to overwork, poor quality delivery and an associated declining marketplace image may result, jeopardising the event's future.

Events will obviously differ in terms of the level of sophistication they display in the human resources area. Contrast, for example, a local community festival that struggles to put together an organising committee and attract sufficient volunteers to a mega-event such as the Olympic Games. Nonetheless, it is appropriate that the 'ideal' situation is examined here — that is, the complete series of steps through which an event manager should proceed for human resource planning. By understanding these steps and their relationships to one another, event managers will give themselves the best possible chance of managing human resources in a way that will achieve their event's goals and objectives. The 'Cherry Creek Arts Festival volunteer program' event profile and 'The people matrix of the Woodford Folk Festival — building a passionate team' case study in this chapter introduce you to how various aspects of this process apply to events.

While a number of general models of the human resource management process can be identified, the one chosen to serve as the basis of discussion in this chapter is that proposed by Getz (2005), specifically for events (see figure 8.1).

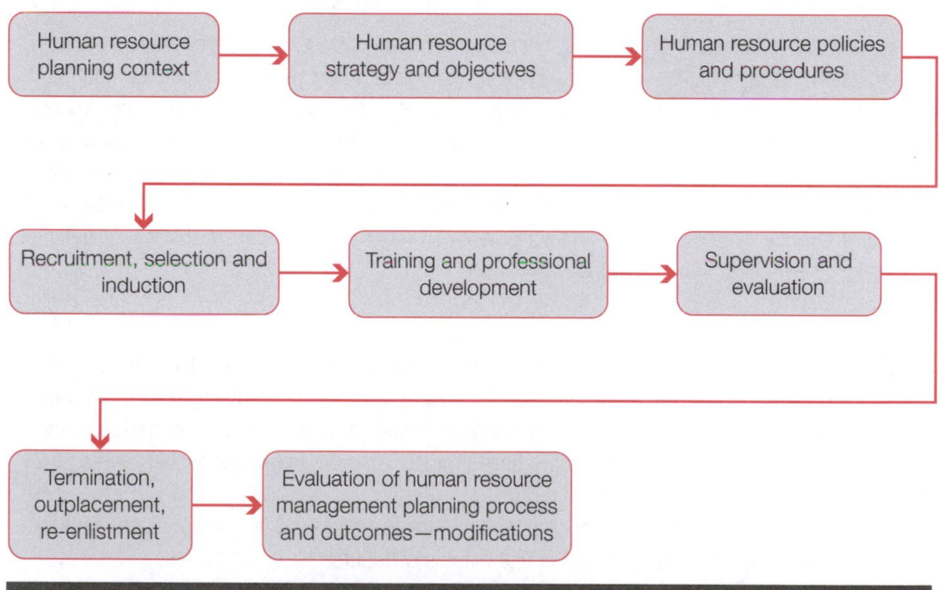

FIGURE 8.1 The human resource planning process for events

Source: Based on Getz 2005, p. 221.

event profile

CHERRY CREEK ARTS FESTIVAL VOLUNTEER PROGRAM

The Cherry Creek Arts Festival is Colorado's signature cultural event and one of America's most competitive outdoor juried arts festivals. The festival offers the opportunity for visitors to meet and talk with exhibiting artists, sample fine cuisine, visit special exhibits and create their own works of art.

Since its commencement in 1990, the Cherry Creek Arts Festival has made use of the services of more than 12 000 volunteers, who collectively have invested more than 200 000 hours of their time. The success of the festival's volunteer program has resulted from its focus on retention, recruitment, benefits and training, each of which is briefly discussed in this profile.

Retention

The festival encourages volunteers to remain 'connected' to the event throughout the year by involving them in a range of activities associated with preparing for it, such as mail-outs and weekly

pre-event administrative and operational activities. There is also a monthly emailed newsletter that updates volunteers on matters of interest.

Volunteers need to see there is room for upward movement in connection with their involvement with the event. To achieve this, the festival ensures each of the 20 committees (all of which are chaired by volunteers) have at least two assistant chairs. Assistant chairs must have at least two years experience on the committee and chairs must have had at least one year's experience as an assistant.

To ensure volunteers are effectively managed, a volunteer coordination committee has been created. This committee monitors volunteer food and beverage services, ensures volunteers are in the right place at the right time, and generally seeks to ensure the approximately 600 volunteers are looked after, resulting in a high rate of volunteer retention.

Recruitment

While efforts at volunteer retention have been very successful, there is still the need to replace approximately 30 per cent of volunteers. In order to replace these people, a volunteer information and registration form is emailed to a wide variety of businesses, organisations and groups each year. Additionally, a 'Get involved with art' volunteer recruitment postcard is mailed six weeks before the event. Details regarding the volunteer program are also included in the festival's annual newspaper supplement, which is published the weekend before the event. Another key recruitment method is the use of public service announcements on radio and television. Website registration also makes the process of becoming involved easier.

Volunteer training

Volunteers are the frontline of the event, so their performance is a key criterion by which patrons evaluate the festival. Event training is conducted for two groups: new volunteers (two hours) and returning volunteers (one hour). Once their training is completed, volunteers are required to spend time with the committees to which they have been allocated, in order to familiarise themselves with the committee's role and their respective tasks.

A training handbook, containing important information like contact details of key staff, parking directions and event rules, regulations and site map, is distributed to all volunteers.

Recognition and benefits

Recognition must be frequent, meaningful and from the heart to maintain and grow a volunteer program. Although T-shirts, food and beverages are nice (provided via partnerships with local businesses), they are not enough to keep volunteers coming back year after year. The recognition tools that the festival employs are:

- 'thank you' notes to each volunteer who assists pre-, post- and during the event
- formal acknowledgement of the important role performed by volunteers in many of the communications sent out to various stakeholders
- gifts of appreciation to volunteer chairs
- a volunteer 'thank you' party at the completion of the event
- a committee chair 'wrap up' dinner two weeks after the event
- publication of a complete listing of volunteer names in a full-page advertisement two weeks after the event.

Source: Cherry Creek Arts Festival 2009.

Human resource strategy and objectives

This stage in the human resource management process for events involves a variety of activities, including establishing guiding strategies and objectives, determining staffing needs (paid and volunteer), and undertaking a job analysis and producing job descriptions and specifications. Each of these tasks is discussed in turn in this section.

Strategy

An event's human resource strategy seeks to support its overall mission and objectives. This link can be demonstrated by reference to the following examples that identify a few selected areas in which an organisation might set objectives, and the implications of such objectives from a human resource management perspective:

- *cost containment* — improved staff/volunteer productivity, reduced absenteeism and decreased staff numbers
- *improved quality* — better recruitment and selection, expanded employee and volunteer training, increased staff and volunteer numbers, and improved financial rewards and volunteer benefits
- *improved organisational effectiveness* — better job design, changes to organisational structure and improved relations with employees and volunteers
- *enhanced performance regarding social and legal responsibilities* — improved compliance through training with relevant legislation, such as that relating to occupational health and safety, anti-discrimination and equal employment opportunity.

Staffing

Staffing is the main strategic decision area for event managers in the area of human resources, because without staff there is nothing really to 'strategise' about! Event managers need to make decisions concerning how many staff/volunteers are needed to deliver the event, what mix of skills/qualifications/experience is required, and when in the event planning process these staff and volunteers will be needed (for example, the event shutdown stage only). The starting point for these decisions should be an event's work breakdown structure (WBS) (see chapter 6). As an event's WBS serves to identify the tasks associated with its creation, delivery and shutdown, an event manager can use this document as the basis for: determining the number of people needed to deliver the event; identifying the skills and knowledge needed by them; and establishing the level of managerial/supervisory staff required in each task area. Additionally, once event tasks have been identified, decisions as to what work will be contracted out, or done in-house by event staff and/or volunteers can begin to be made. Also, by placing the tasks identified in the WBS into a Gantt chart (see chapter 6), the event manager is able to identify when various components of the event's workforce will be needed.

Perhaps the most difficult task in the previously outlined process is that of determining exactly how many people will be needed to perform the various identified tasks, particularly if the event is new. Armstrong (1999) claims that managerial judgement is by far the most common approach used in business to answer this question. Such an observation is also likely to apply to the world of events. That is, the event manager, or various functional managers if the event is large enough, will act to estimate how many, and what type, of human resources are needed to meet their objectives. In doing so, they are likely to base their decision on such factors as: their own experience; demand forecasts for the event; the number of venues/sites involved; skill/expertise requirements of the event workforce; previous instances of similar (or the same) events; the degree of outsourcing possible; the availability of volunteers; and the human resource strategies adopted by the event. It should be noted that it is not uncommon in the context of large-scale events for initial estimates of workforce size to grow as an event's delivery date draws closer. The Manchester Commonwealth Games, for example, first estimated (via a consultant's report) its core workforce requirements at 262. This number was revised upwards to 660 as the organising committee gained first-hand experience of other major sports events and their workforce requirements (Manchester Commonwealth Games 2003, p. 10).

In the case of some tasks associated with the conduct of events, it is possible to estimate staffing needs by engaging in some basic arithmetic. The number of people who can pass through a turnstile per hour, for example, can be easily calculated by dividing the processing time for an individual into 60 minutes. Assume the figure generated in this way is 240 — that is, 240 people can be processed in an hour through one turnstile. Next, an estimate of event attendance (including peaks and troughs in arrivals) is required. Now assume total attendance for the event has been fairly consistent at 5000 over the past three years, with 80 per cent (4000) of people arriving between 9.00 am and 11.00 am. If this number of people is to be processed over a two-hour period, about eight turnstiles would need to be open (4000 attendees divided by two hours [= 2000 per hour], divided by 240 transactions per hour per turnstile). Based on these calculations, eight turnstile operators would be required for the first two hours; after this time, the number of operators could be dramatically decreased. Calculations such as this could also be used in other areas of event delivery. For example, it should be possible to estimate with a fair degree of accuracy the number of staff required to prepare, plate and serve a given number of meals within a particular time period, or the number required to process a given number of on-site registrations at a conference/exhibition.

Job analysis

Job analysis is an important aspect of this stage of the human resource planning process. It involves defining a job in terms of specific tasks and responsibilities and identifying the abilities, skills and qualifications needed to perform that job successfully. According to Stone (2007), questions answered by this process include the following:

- What tasks should be grouped together to create a job or position?
- What should be looked for in individuals applying for identified jobs?
- What should an organisational structure look like and what interrelationships between jobs should exist?
- What tasks should form the basis of performance appraisal for an individual in a specific job?
- What training and development programs are required to ensure staff/volunteers possess the needed skills/knowledge?

The level of sophistication evident in the application of the job analysis process will differ between events. Some small-scale events that depend exclusively, or almost exclusively, on volunteers may simply attempt to match people to the tasks in which they have expressed an interest. Even under such circumstances, however, some consideration should be given to experience, skills and physical abilities.

Job descriptions

Job descriptions are an outcome of the job analysis process with which event managers need some measure of familiarity if they are to effectively match people (both employees and volunteers) to jobs. Specifically, a job description is a statement identifying why a job has come into existence, what the holder of the job will do, and under what conditions the job is to be conducted (Stone 2007).

Job descriptions commonly include the following information:

- *Job title and commitment required* — this information locates the paid or voluntary position within the organisation, indicates the functional area where the job is to be based (for example, marketing coordinator), and states the job duration/time commitment (for example, one-year part-time contract involving two days a week).
- *Salary/rewards/incentives* associated with position — for paid positions, a salary, wage or hourly rate needs to be stated, along with any other rewards such as bonuses. With regards to bonuses, it is not uncommon for large-scale events to make payments of this nature conditional on seeing their contract through to the end. In this way the number of staff, particularly senior staff, leaving at crucial times in the event's delivery cycle is reduced. In the case of voluntary positions, consideration should be given to identifying benefits such as free merchandise (for example, T-shirts and limited edition souvenir programs), free or discounted meals, free tickets and end-of-event parties, all of which can serve to increase interest in working at an event.
- *Job summary* — this brief statement describes the primary purpose of the job. The job summary for an event operations manager, for example, may read: 'Under the direction of the event director, prepare and implement detailed operational plans in all areas associated with the successful delivery of the event'.
- *Duties and responsibilities* — this information lists major tasks and responsibilities associated with the job. It should not be overly detailed, identifying only those duties/responsibilities that are central to the performance of the position. Additionally, it is useful to express these in terms of the most important outcomes of the work. For an event operations manager, for example, one key responsibility expressed in outcome terms would be the preparation of plans encompassing all operational dimensions of the event, such as site set-up and breakdown, security, parking, waste management, staging and risk management.
- *Relationships* with other positions within and outside the event organisation — what positions and service suppliers report to the job? (An event operations manager, for example, may have all site staff/volunteers/suppliers associated with security, parking, staging, waste management, utilities and so on reporting to him/her.) To what position(s) does the job report? (An event operations manager may report only to the event director/manager.) What outside organisations will the position need to liaise with to satisfactorily perform the job? (An event operations manager may need to liaise with, for example, local councils, police, road and traffic authorities, and local emergency service providers.)
- *Know-how/skills/knowledge/experience/qualifications/personal attributes* required by the position — in some instances, particularly with basic jobs, training may quickly overcome most deficiencies in these areas. However, for more complex jobs (voluntary or paid), such as those of a managerial or supervisory nature, individuals may need to possess experience, skills or knowledge before applying. Often, a distinction is drawn between these elements, with some being essential while others are desirable. Specific qualifications may also be required. Increasingly, job advertisements for event managers, for example, are listing formal qualifications in event management as desirable. Personal attributes — such as the ability to work as part of a team, to be creative, to work to deadlines and to represent the event positively to stakeholder groups — may also be relevant considerations.
- *Authority* vested in the position — what decisions can be made without reference to a superior? What are the expenditure limits on decision making?

- *Performance standards* associated with the position — criteria will be required by which performance in the position will be assessed. While such standards apply more to paid staff than to voluntary positions, they should still be considered for the latter. This is particularly the case if volunteers hold significant management or supervisory positions where substandard performance could jeopardise one or more aspects of the event. If duties and responsibilities have been written in output terms, then these can be used as the basis of evaluation.
- *Trade union/association membership* required with position.
- *Special circumstances* associated with the position — does the job require heavy, sustained lifting, for example?
- *Problem solving* — what types of problem will be commonly encountered on the job? Will they be routine and repetitive problems or complex and varied issues?

While job descriptions for paid positions often involve most, if not all, of the information noted previously, voluntary positions are often described in far more general terms. This is because they often (but not always) involve tasks of a less complex nature. This is evident from figure 8.2, which provides job descriptions for a number of voluntary positions at the Great Lakes Folk Festival, Michigan.

FIGURE 8.2 Great Lakes Folk Festival volunteer job descriptions

POSITION	DESCRIPTION
Bike Parking	'Free Guarded Bicycle Parking' volunteers will help check-in and check-out bicycles for festival goers.
Buddy	Greet and orient performers to festival site and East Lansing. Help transport performers from Marriott to performance stages. Buddies are assigned to one group and need to be available anytime during the entire festival.
Bucket Brigade	Spend your volunteer time near the Music Stages! Provide the opportunity for festival goers to support the festival with a donation as you pass through the crowd. Last year we raised over $27 000!
Children's Area	Facilitate children's activities (games, crafts and performances) by assisting and encouraging children's participation. Assist with visitor questions and safety.
JOATMON - (Jack-of-all-trades, master-of-none, formerly 'Floater')	Act as a fill-in at sites that need assistance during the festival. You never know where you'll be assigned with this one.
Folk Arts Marketplace	Work in the Folk Arts Marketplace (craft vending area). Provide general assistance and serve as booth sitters.
Green Room	Staff the green room where food and beverages are provided for performers, volunteers and staff. This is a good job for people who can't be on their feet too much or need to stay out of the sun.
Information Booth	Provide information to the general public, including performance times, restroom locations, transportation options, directions ...
Documentation Assistant (formerly 'Logger')	Accurately log live musical performances and demonstrations in sound booth. Record performances to DAT tapes.

FIGURE 8.2 *(continued)*

POSITION	DESCRIPTION
Operations	Assist in the operations office just before and during the festival. Job tasks could range from phone or radio duty to running supplies to stages. Must be able to walk from one end of the site to the other in 10 minutes or less, and be able to lift 25 lbs. Experience with golf cart driving and hand tool use a plus.
Set-up/Take down crew	Volunteers will set up and/or take down site signs, tent signs, banners (will use ladders and hand tools).
Site Coordinator	Oversee stage seating areas and resolve issues such as seating, crowd control, and lost children.
Sales, CD	Assist with performer CD sales and sales of shirts and other Festival souvenirs.
Seniors on the Go	Drive a golf cart around the Festival Site to help move people of all ages with mobility challenges. Must have valid Drivers' License.
Transportation	Transport performers, staff and equipment to music stages. Must be able to safely drive a golf cart.
Volunteer Registration	Check-in volunteers prior to each shift at the Marriott Hotel.

Source: Great Lakes Folk Festival 2008.

Job specification

A job specification is derived from the job description and seeks to identify the experience, qualifications, skills, abilities, knowledge and personal characteristics needed to perform a given job. (Crompton, Morrissey and Nankervis 2002). In essence, it identifies the types of people who should be recruited and how they should be appraised. The essential and desirable criteria shown in figure 8.3 provide an example of how job specifications are used in the recruitment process.

FIGURE 8.3 Job advertisement for an event manager

AMERICAN LIVER FOUNDATION HOUSTON EVENTS MANAGER JOB DESCRIPTION

The position description is a guide to the critical duties and essential function of the job, not an all-inclusive list of responsibilities, qualifications, physical demands and work environment conditions. Position descriptions are reviewed and revised to meet ALF's changing needs, at the sole discretion of management.

Primary function/purpose

Manage, coordinate and implement major fundraising projects annually to generate unrestricted funds for American Liver Foundation in the State of Texas. You must be a self-starter to complete projects on your own, willing to make cold calls, have the ability to handle multiple events while working out of your home.

FIGURE 8.3 *(continued)*

Major duties and responsibilities

- Coordinate and manage fundraising events (Liver Life Walk Houston, Flavours of Huston and Flavours of Dallas) and activities in assigned areas, to include the following:
  - cultivate and solicit new corporate and individual donors for all events
  - recruit, organise, orientate and train volunteers
  - assist with developing written communication and event materials
  - undertake public relations
  - monitor of each event/activity budget.
- Network in the community with new groups, organisations, and community resources to seek new sponsors, volunteers and committee members.
- Interact with members of the Metro Leadership Council in Houston and Event Committees.
- Perform administrative tasks necessary to the maintenance of the chapter office, such as answering telephone, handling or referring calls/emails as appropriate; maintaining office supplies; disseminating educational information as needed.
- Perform other duties as required to meet the needs of the American Liver Foundation.
- Report progress daily to the Division Vice President located in Phoenix, AZ.

Fiscal responsibility

Monitoring budget of each event/activity and maintaining accurate recordkeeping.

Position requirements

Education: Bachelor's Degree (or equivalent) required.
Experience: Three years work experience with not-for-profit organisations required.
Related Skills or Knowledge: Microsoft Office (Word, Excel, PowerPoint).
Work Environment: Must be willing to work a flexible schedule including some nights and weekends. Must be willing to work out of your home.
Salary range: $32 000–$36 000 DOE.

Source: Adapted from American Liver Foundation 2009.

Policies and procedures

Policies and procedures are needed to provide the framework in which the remaining tasks in the human resource planning process take place: recruitment and selection; training and professional development; supervision and evaluation; termination, outplacement, re-employment; and evaluation. According to Stone (2007), policies and practices serve to:

- reassure all staff that they will be treated fairly — for example, seniority will be the determining factor in requests by volunteers to fill job vacancies
- help managers make quick and consistent decisions — for example, rather than a manager having to think about the process of terminating the employment of a staff member or volunteer, they can simply follow the process already prescribed
- give managers the confidence to resolve problems and defend their positions — for example, an event manager who declines to consider an application from a brother of an existing employee may point to a policy on employing relatives of existing personnel if there is a dispute.

Human resource practices and procedures for events are often conditioned or determined by those public or private sector organisations with ultimate authority for them. A local council responsible for conducting an annual festival, for example, would probably already have in place a range of policies and procedures regarding the use of volunteers. These policies and procedures would then be applied to the event. Additionally, a range of laws influence the degree of freedom that the management of an event has in the human resource area. Laws regarding occupational health and safety, privacy (see figure 8.4), holiday and long service leave, discrimination, dismissal and compensation all need to become integrated into the practices and policies that an event adopts.

FIGURE 8.4 Melbourne Commonwealth Games Workforce Privacy Policy

Introduction

Melbourne 2006 Commonwealth Games Corporation has been appointed by the Commonwealth Games Federation to organise and stage the XVIII Commonwealth Games to be held in Melbourne and surrounding areas in March 2006.

Melbourne 2006 Commonwealth Games Corporation has created this workforce privacy policy in order to demonstrate our firm commitment to protecting the personal and health information (referred to collectively in this document as personal information) of job applicants and all members of the Melbourne 2006 Commonwealth Games Corporation workforce. We are bound by the *Privacy Act 1998* (Cwlth), the *Information Privacy Act 2000* (Vic) and the *Health Records Act 2001* (Vic).

We have adopted the Information Privacy Principles and Health Privacy Principles as minimum standards in relation to handling personal information.

What we collect and how

Personal information

Melbourne 2006 Commonwealth Games Corporation collects personal information about you when you apply for a position or during your employment. The personal information which may be collected includes your name; date of birth; address; referee names; tax file number; banking details; superannuation details; qualifications; performance appraisals; details of paid outside work/directorship; referee reports; and other information collected from various sources. This information can be voluntarily provided when you apply for employment or from information contained in Melbourne 2006 Commonwealth Games Corporation employment forms. Your supervisor and nominated referees will also provide Melbourne 2006 Commonwealth Games Corporation with information about yourself. If you are on secondment from another organisation the Melbourne 2006 Commonwealth Games Corporation may gather information from your employer.

Health information

Health information may be collected as part of the employment application process or when the candidate commences employment with Melbourne 2006 Commonwealth Games Corporation.

Use of personal information

Melbourne 2006 Commonwealth Games Corporation may collect your personal information for the purpose of processing and assessing your employment application. If you are employed by Melbourne 2006 Commonwealth Games Corporation, the primary purpose for collecting personal information is to maintain your records and to administer the employment contract, salary, superannuation and other related human resource policies. Your personal information may also be used in an aggregate (non-identifying) form to report on workforce profiles.

Disclosure of personal information

Melbourne 2006 Commonwealth Games Corporation does not use or disclose personal information about an individual for a purpose other than that for which it was collected, unless such use or

FIGURE 8.4 *(continued)*

disclosure would be reasonably expected or consent from you has been obtained. Please note that if at any time Melbourne 2006 Commonwealth Games Corporation is required by law to release information about you or your organisation, Melbourne 2006 Commonwealth Games Corporation must fully cooperate.

Information provided by you is used primarily for the purpose of recruitment. The information is disclosed only to our staff who are on the selection panel and any recruitment agency used in the recruitment process. Melbourne 2006 Commonwealth Games Corporation may keep an electronic copy of your application to be considered for future employment. This information is confidential.

Accuracy, security and storage of personal information

Melbourne 2006 Commonwealth Games Corporation stores personal information in computer and paper-based record management systems. Melbourne 2006 Commonwealth Games Corporation has designed security measures to protect against the loss, misuse and/or alteration of the information under its control. These security measures include restricted access, password protection on databases and clauses in employee agreements requiring confidentiality.

Melbourne 2006 Commonwealth Games Corporation takes reasonable steps to ensure the personal information it stores is accurate, complete and up to date. Where Melbourne 2006 Commonwealth Games Corporation shares your personal information with any third party (such as a recruitment agency), Melbourne 2006 Commonwealth Games Corporation seeks a commitment from such parties to protect the information in accordance with our policy.

Access to personal information

As is reasonable in the circumstances and subject to any limitation required by law, you may gain access to your personal information at any time. You can also contact us to update your details when necessary.

Updates to this policy

Melbourne 2006 Commonwealth Games Corporation will update the workforce privacy policy as required. Any changes will be posted on this website.

Source: Melbourne Commonwealth Games 2006.

If an event manager goes to the time and effort to develop policies and procedures, he or she also needs to ensure these are communicated to all staff and applied. Additionally, resources need to be allocated to this area so the 'paperwork' generated by those policies and procedures can be stored, accessed and updated or modified as required. Such paperwork may include various policy/procedure manuals and staff records such as performance evaluations and employment contracts.

Again, the larger (in terms of number of staff and volunteers) and more sophisticated (in terms of management) the event, the more likely it is that the event managers would have thought more deeply about policy and procedural concerns. Nonetheless, even smaller events will benefit in terms of the quality of their overall human resources management if some attempt is made to set basic policies and procedures to guide actions.

Recruitment, selection and induction

The recruitment of paid and volunteer employees is essentially about attracting the 'right' potential candidates to the 'right' job openings. Successful recruitment is based on how well previous stages in the human resource planning process have been conducted, and involves determining where qualified applicants can be found and how they can be attracted to the event organisation. It is a two-way process, in that the event is looking to meet its human resource needs at the same time as potential applicants are trying to assess whether they meet the job requirements, wish to apply for the position and perceive value in joining the organisation. Figure 8.5 represents the recruitment, selection and induction process in diagrammatic form.

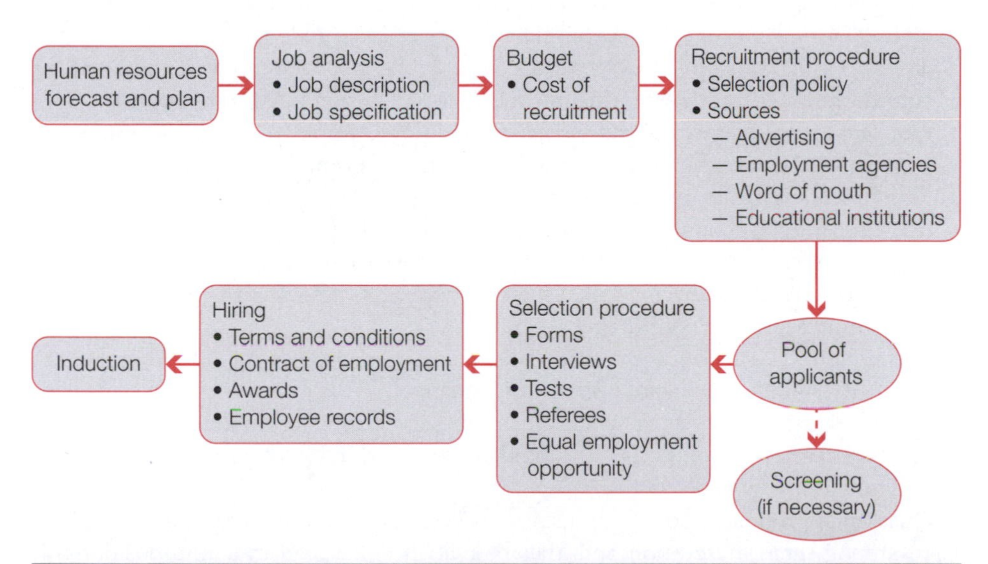

FIGURE 8.5 The recruitment, selection and induction process for paid and voluntary employees

Source: Based on Clark 2000.

How event managers approach the recruitment process depends on the financial resources they have available to them. With large events, a budget is likely to be set aside for this purpose, designed to cover costs such as recruitment agency fees (including online recruitment firms), advertising, the travel expenses of non-local applicants and search fees for executive placement companies. The reality for most events, however — particularly those relying heavily on volunteers — is that they will have few resources to allocate to the recruitment process. Nonetheless, they can still successfully engage in this process by:

- *using stakeholders* (for example, local councils, community groups, sponsors and event suppliers) to communicate the event's staffing needs (volunteer and paid) to their respective networks. McCurley and Lynch (1998), in the context of volunteers, call this approach 'concentric circle recruitment' because it involves starting with the groups of people who are already connected to the event or organisation and working outwards. It is based on the premise that volunteers are recruited by someone they know — for example, friends or family, clients or colleagues, staff, employers, neighbours or acquaintances such as members from the same clubs and societies.
- *negotiating sponsorship agreements* in a way that requires the sponsor, as part of their agreement with the event, to provide temporary workers with particular skills, such as marketing staff
- *identifying and liaising with potential sources of volunteers/casual staff*, including universities and colleges (projects and work placements/internships may be specially

created for these groups, particularly if they are studying festival, exhibition and event management or a related area such as film), job centres, religious groups, service clubs (such as Lions and Rotary), community service programs, senior citizen centres and retirement homes, chambers of commerce, and community centres. The International Festival and Events Association (www.ifea.com) and the Australian Centre for Event Management (www.acem.uts.edu.au) are examples of organisations that maintain an event-based internship/employment 'bank' on their websites.
- *seconding staff* from associated organisations, such as state and local government
- *utilising existing programs for the unemployed*
- *determining the make-up* (for example, age, sex, occupations) and motivations of existing volunteers, and using this information as the basis of further targeted recruitment
- *gaining the assistance of local and specialist media* (for example, radio, television, newspapers, specialist magazines) in communicating the event's human resource needs. This process is greatly assisted if one or more media organisations are in some way (such as through sponsorship) associated with the event.
- *targeting specific individuals within a community who have specialist skills* to sit on boards or undertake specific tasks, such as those tasks associated with the legal and accounting aspects of conducting an event
- *registering with volunteer agencies*. In Australia, these agencies include Volunteering NSW/ACT/South Australia/Queensland/Tasmania.
- *conducting social functions* at which, for example, existing volunteers or staff might be encouraged to bring potential candidates, or to which particular groups/targeted individuals are invited.

Once an appropriate pool of applicants has been identified, the next step is to select from among them those applicants that best fit the identified available positions. It is important to approach this process systematically, employing appropriate tools, to avoid the costs (financial and otherwise) that come from poor selection (increased training time, high turnover of staff/volunteers, absenteeism, job dissatisfaction and poor performance).

A useful starting point in the selection process is a selection policy. This policy should have been developed earlier in the policy and procedures stage of the human resource planning process. In constructing such a policy, thought needs to be given to:
- approaches to measuring the suitability of candidates — for example, simple rating scales based on set criteria
- sourcing people — for example, will the event organisation promote from within where possible?
- the decision makers — who will have the final decision on who to engage?
- selection techniques — for example, will tests be employed? Will decisions be made after one interview or several?
- the organisation's business objectives — for example, do the candidates selected have the qualities and qualifications to progress the event's objectives?
- how the event organisation intends to comply with equal employment opportunity legislation.

The application process will vary based on the needs of the position, the number of applications anticipated and the resources of the event organisation. In cases where a large number of applications are anticipated, it may be appropriate to consider screening applicants by telephone by asking a few key questions central to the position's requirements — for example, 'Do you have a qualification in event management?' Those individuals who answer these questions appropriately can then be sent an application. In the case of volunteers, applicants for positions in small-scale events may be asked to simply send in a brief note indicating what skills/qualifications they have, any relevant experience and the tasks they would be interested in doing. For larger events, volunteers may be asked to complete a registration form (increasingly online) such as that developed by the National Folk Festival in Australia (figure 8.6).

However basic, application forms for paid employees generally seek information on educational qualifications, previous employment and other details deemed relevant to the position by the applicant. The names and contact details of referees who can supply written and/or verbal references are also normally required. Additionally, a curriculum vitae (CV) is generally appended to these forms. Once received, applications allow unsuitable applicants to be culled; those applicants thought to be suitable for short-listing can be invited to attend an interview. It is often the case with volunteers that selection is based only on the information supplied on their application/registration form, with successful applicants being contacted and asked to attend a briefing session.

FIGURE 8.6 National Folk Festival volunteer registration form

National Folk Festival 2010

Step 1 - Volunteer Application Form

Contact Info

First Name *

Surname *

Postal Address *

Postal Town or Suburb *

Postal State * Select...

Postal Postcode *

Preferred Phone Number (Include Area Code) *

Type * Select...

Alternate Phone Number (Include Area Code)

Type Select...

Email *

Preferred Method of Contact * Select...

You must be 15 years of age, at the time of the Festival, to be considered for a voluntary position. If you are under 18 years at the time of the Festival, you will receive a permission slip that must be signed by a parent or guardian and returned to the National Folk Festival. This will be emailed to you after you complete your application.

Date ot birth (dd/mm/yyyy) *

/ /

Gender *

O Male O Female

Emergency Contact Details

Emergency Contact Name *

Relationship * Select...

Emergency Contact Phone *

(continued)

FIGURE 8.6 *(continued)*

Volunteer Period

You must select a period for which you are available. Volunteers are now required to do a minimum of 20 hours Volunteering, regardless of the period that they work. Please select more than one period if you would like to spread your 20 hours across a longer period of time, or would like to be more generous with your time.

☐ Setup 29 March – 1 April 2010

☐ Festival 1 April – 5 April 2010

☐ Packdown 6 April – 8 April 2010 Tickets must be purchased for this period and will be refunded after 20 hours work.

Volunteer Team Selection

Team - 1st Preference *

- Please Select -

How many years have you volunteered for the National Folk Festival? (0 for none)

If you are under 18 at the time of the Festival, you are not permitted to camp on site at EPIC, unless a responsible adult accompanies you. You will receive a permission slip that must be signed by a parent or guardian who is camping with you, and be returned to the National Folk Festival. This will be emailed to you after you complete your application.

Do you intend to camp at EPIC during the Festival? *

○ Yes ○ No

Additional information

Please include any special requirements you may have, skills you have or would like to learn, etc.

Licenses/Certificates you have:

☐ Security License

☐ Forklift License

☐ Current 1st Aid

☐ CPA

☐ Trade Qualifications

Special Requirements:

☐ Other

Do you have any additional comments?

I have read and agree to abide by the National Folk Festival Code of Conduct and to complete the required rostered hours during the Festival (this does not include training hours in the lead-up to the Festival). In exchange I will receive a season pass to the Festival, including camping, and access to volunteer facilities and benefits such as subsidised meals from the Volunteer Kitchen.

I understand that if I do not fulfil my part of the agreement (e.g. collect my pass but do not turn up to work my allocated shifts) I will be invoiced for a season pass with camping. I understand that if I breach the Code of Conduct I may be dismissed for misconduct, escorted from the site, and have future volunteer applications declined. In the event of an accident, misadventure or illness I will contact the Festival as early as possible so that a replacement can be found.

I accept these conditions and agree to abide by them

○ Yes ○ No

Source: National Folk Festival 2010.

When selecting applicants, Robertson and Makin (1986) (cited in Beardwell and Holden 2001) suggest taking into account the following factors:

- The use of *past behaviour* can be employed to predict future behaviour. That is, the manner in which a person completed a task in the past is the best predictor of the way that person will complete a task in the future. Biographical data (obtained from the curriculum vitae or application form), references and supervisor/peer group ratings are commonly the major sources of such information.
- A range of techniques can be used to assess *present behaviour*, including:
  - tests, which may be designed to measure aptitude, intelligence, personality and basic core skill levels (for example, typing speeds)
  - interviews (see later discussion)
  - assessment centres, which conduct a series of tests, exercises and feedback sessions over a one- to five-day period to assess individual strengths and weaknesses
  - portfolios/examples of work, which are used to indicate the quality/type of recent job-related outputs. An applicant for the position of a set designer for a theatrical event, for example, may be asked to supply photographs of his or her previous work.
- If appropriate, interview information can be supplemented with observations from simulations to predict *future behaviour*. If the position is for a sponsorship manager, for example, applicants can be asked to develop a sponsorship proposal and demonstrate how they would present this proposal to a potential sponsor. Another common approach, according to Noe et al. (2003), is to ask managerial applicants to respond to memos that typify problems that are commonly encountered. This will provide the potential employer with insights into the problem solving abilities of applicants, and how they are likely to respond to the challenges offered by the position.

Interviews are likely to be the most common means of selection used by event organisations, so it is worthwhile spending some time looking at how best to employ this approach. A well-designed set of interview questions will enable an assessment of the strengths and weaknesses of applicants to be made, and assist in matching them to the needs of the position.

Interviews

According to Noe et al. (2003), research clearly indicates that the interviewing process should be undertaken using a structured approach so all relevant information can be covered and candidates can be directly compared. Mullins (2005) suggests using a checklist of key matters to be covered in the interviews. A sample checklist for a paid position associated with an event is shown in figure 8.7.

Checklists should also be used if interviews are to be conducted for volunteers. Responses from volunteers may be sought to questions regarding the relationship between the volunteer's background/experience and the position(s) sought, reasons for seeking to become involved with the event, the level of understanding about the demands/requirements of the position(s) (such as time and training), and whether applicants have a physical or medical condition that may have an impact on the types of position for which they can be considered (keeping equal employment opportunity legislation in mind). Such checklists will enable the volunteer(s) to be matched with the position(s) that best suit their interests and abilities, resulting in better outcomes for the host organisation and increased volunteer satisfaction and retention.

INTERVIEWER'S CHECKLIST

Position title: ________________ Candidate's name: ______________________

Date: ________

Interviewees: ____

Interview

1 Qualifications held
2 Employment history
3 Extent to which applicant meets essential criteria for the position
4 Extent to which applicant meets desirable criteria for the position
5 Organisational fit
   (a) To what extent will the position result in personal satisfaction for the applicant?
   (b) To what extent does the applicant identify with the organisation's values and culture?
   (c) Can the applicant's remuneration expectations be met?

Assessment

Summary rating of applicant based on the above criteria. A simple scale of 'all, most, some, none' may be used for criteria 3 and 4. Additionally, some relevant summary comments may be made on each applicant.

Action

Follow-up action to be taken with applicant — for example:

- Advise if successful/unsuccessful.
- Place on eligibility list.
- Background/reference check.
- Arrange pre-employment medical check.

FIGURE 8.7 Sample interviewer's checklist

Applicant responses flowing from the interview process need to be assessed in some way against the key criteria for the position. One common means of doing this is a rating scale (for example, 1 to 5). When viewed collectively, the ratings given to individual items lead to an overall assessment of the applicant in terms of how he or she fits with the job, the event organisation and its future directions.

Interviews may be conducted on a one-on-one basis or via a panel of two or more interviewers. The latter has some advantages in that it assists in overcoming any idiosyncratic biases that individual interviewers may have, allows all interviewers to evaluate the applicant at the same time and on the same questions and answers, and facilitates the discussion of the pros and cons of individual applicants.

Once the preferred applicant(s) has been identified, the next step is to make a formal offer of appointment, by mail or otherwise. In the case of paid event staff, the short-term nature of many events means any offer of employment is for a specific contracted period. The employment contract generally states what activities are to be performed, salary/wage levels, and the rights and obligations of the employer and employee (see figure 8.8). In the case of volunteers, a simple letter of appointment, accompanied by details regarding the position, may be all that is necessary. It is also appropriate to consider supplying volunteers with a statement about their rights and those of the event organisation regarding their involvement in the event (see figure 8.9). Once an offer has been made and accepted, unsuccessful applicants should be informed as soon as possible.

FIGURE 8.8 General components of an employment contract

- A statement of job titles and duties
- The date of employment commencement
- Rate of pay, allowances, overtime, bonuses (and any associated conditions), method and timing of payment
- Hours of work including breaks
- Holiday arrangements/entitlement
- Sickness procedure (including sick pay, notification of illness)
- Length of notice due to and from the employee
- Grievance procedure
- Disciplinary procedure
- Work rules
- Arrangements for terminating employment
- Arrangements for union membership (if applicable)
- Special terms relating to confidentiality, rights to patents and designs, exclusivity of service, and restrictions on trade after termination of employment (for example, cannot work for a direct competitor within six months)
- Employer's right to vary terms and conditions subject to proper notification

FIGURE 8.9 Organisational and volunteer rights and responsibilities

MIDSUMMA FESTIVAL VOLUNTEER AGREEMENT

Midsumma's commitments

In order to enhance your experience, Midsumma will:

- provide your with orientation and induction
- ensure you have fun and meet people
- provide you with a healthy and safe workplace
- provide insurance coverage for you, while acting as a Midsumma Volunteer
- define your roles and develop clear job descriptions
- provide appropriate levels of support and management for you
- ensure your work complements but does not undermine the work of core staff
- respect you as a valuable team member
- acknowledge and value your contributions
- reserve the right to select the people who will represent Midsumma as Midsumma Volunteers as appropriate for the organisation, and to assign particular duties as felt appropriate
- provide clear conflict resolution processes.

Volunteer's commitments

In order to enhance the festival, Volunteers will:

- start at the scheduled time, and be dressed and groomed appropriately
- carry out specific duties to the best of their ability
- respect the authority of, and decisions made by, Midsumma Board members and staff
- contribute to the continuous improvement of the festival
- be honest and reliable
- adhere to and follow policy, procedure and guidelines.

FIGURE 8.9 *(continued)*

THE SPECIFICS

Punctuality

We request that Volunteers are punctual. If an unforeseen situation arises whereby a Volunteer will be late please contact the Event Team Leader, Volunteer Manager or Operations Coordinator so that other arrangements can be made.

Attendance

To ensure the smooth running of Midsumma events, volunteers are requested to notify the Volunteer Coordinator or Volunteer Operations Assistant as soon as possible if they are unable to attend their shift, to enable us to organise a replacement.

If a Volunteer does not attend an event at their arranged time without providing notice, the Volunteer Coordinator will discuss this matter with the volunteer at the earliest opportunity to ascertain appropriate steps to be taken.

Sign on / off sheets

Please ensure you sign on at the start of shifts, and sign off at the end. This is important for insurance purposes, and to assist Midsumma Festival in collecting statistical data in support of funding applications.

Etiquette

All Volunteers are representatives of Midsumma Festival and as such must be professional, courteous and respectful to the public at all times. All Volunteers agree to abide by all policies and procedures as issued from time to time.

Dress must be appropriate for the task you are undertaking, generally neat jeans and the Midsumma T-shirt.

The use of alcohol and drugs are prohibited while working your shift. Any Volunteer found to be under the influence will be retired for the duration of the event and disciplinary action may be taken.

Confidentiality

Occasionally Volunteers will be privy to confidential information of the festival. Volunteers must not divulge this information to other parties under any circumstances, either during the term of volunteering or after ceasing as a Volunteer.

Privacy statement

By registration, you agree to us collecting the personal information you provide. This information will generally be used solely by Midsumma Festival Inc. for the purposes of ensuring that we assign you to an appropriate volunteer position, for contacting you regarding events during the Festival, and maintaining health and safety records for all volunteers. We may give this information to third parties, but only where we are required by law to do so. You have the right to request details, or amend any personal information that Midsumma holds about you by contacting Midsumma Festival Inc. at any time.

Media

Volunteers are not authorised to speak to the media on Midsumma's behalf. Any requests by the media must be directed to staff. You will be notified of the appropriate staff members at the induction day.

FIGURE 8.9 *(continued)*

Health and safety

Midsumma is committed to providing a safe working environment for all its volunteers and will provide relevant induction sessions in relation to event specific health and safety issues. Volunteers are obligated to act responsibly with regards to health and safety as outlined in the Victorian Occupational Health and Safety Act 2004 and associated regulations.

Conflict resolution

The Midsumma Board are committed to resolving any conflict to the satisfaction of all parties. Please direct any conflicts to the Volunteer Coordinator or Team Leader in the first instance. If the conflict involves this person, please direct the issue to a staff or Board member. The issues, discussions and resolution achieved will be recorded in writing and a letter confirming the outcome of the meeting will be sent to all parties involved.

Termination

Where the conduct or behaviour of a volunteer places the health or safety of another person at risk or results in any illegal activity, that volunteer's involvement in the Festival may be immediately terminated by the Volunteer Coordinator, Midsumma staff or any other Board member.

Paid employment

Volunteer work for Midsumma Festival is not a prerequisite for paid employment and volunteering does not guarantee a paid position.

Source: Midsumma Festival 2010.

Induction

Once appointees (paid or voluntary) commence with an event organisation, a structured induction program designed to begin the process of 'bonding' the individual to the event organisation needs to be conducted. Getz (2005, p. 226) suggests a range of actions be taken as part of an effective induction program.

- Provide basic information about the event (mission, objectives, stakeholders, budget, locations, program details).
- Conduct tours of venues, suppliers, offices and any other relevant locations.
- Make introductions to other staff and volunteers.
- Give an introduction to the organisational culture, history and working arrangements.
- Overview training programs (both general and position specific).

In addition to these actions, it is sound practice to discuss the job description with the individual to ensure he or she has a clear understanding of matters such as responsibilities, performance expectations, approaches to performance evaluation, and reporting relationships. At this time other matters associated with the terms and conditions of employment should also be discussed/reiterated, including probationary periods, grievance procedures, absenteeism, sickness, dress code, security, holiday/leave benefits, superannuation, salary and overtime rates, and other benefits such as car parking and meals. One means of ensuring mutual understanding of these matters is to have the staff member or volunteer read and sign a contractual agreement. Figure 8.10 provides a template that can be used for drafting a contract or agreement with event volunteers.

VOLUNTEER AGREEMENT

This agreement indicates the significance of the relationship between ____________________ (organisation) and our Volunteers. The intent of this agreement is to set out the conditions of your involvement in the ____________________ Volunteer Program and of ____________________ (organisation) obligations to you.

1 ________________________________ (Organisation)
We, ____________________, agree to accept the services of ____________________ (volunteer) in the role of ______________________________, beginning ____________________, and extending until ____________________.

We commit to the following:

- To provide adequate information, training, and assistance so that the Volunteer is able to meet the responsibilities of their role.
- To ensure supervision and support to the Volunteer and to provide feedback on their performance.
- To respect the skills, dignity and individual needs of the Volunteer, and to work with them flexibly to meet individual requirements.
- To be receptive to any comments from the Volunteer regarding ways in which we might better accomplish our goals.
- To treat each Volunteer as a partner with the ________________ Volunteer Coordinator and staff, in accomplishing ______________________ goals.
- To provide safe workplaces and practices as well as appropriate insurance including public liability and personal accident insurance coverage during all rostered hours of work and for travel directly to and from the workplace.

2 ____________________________________ (Volunteer)
I, ______________________________, as a Volunteer, agree to commit to the following:

- To perform my Volunteer duties to the best of my ability.
- To adhere to the core values, policies and procedures, of ____________________ (organisation) including record keeping requirements.
- To meet time and duty commitments, or to provide adequate notice so that alternate arrangements can be made.
- To act at all times as a member of the team responsible for delivering the ____________________ program.
- To adhere to the ____________________ Confidentiality Agreement.

All work produced whilst working for______________________, or using ____________________ resources remains the property of ____________________. ______________________ (organisation) undertakes to fairly acknowledge and recognise the work of individual paid and volunteer staff.

3 AGREED TO:
Volunteer Signature: ____________________ Date: ________________
Volunteer Coordinator: ____________________ Date: ________________

This form is to be completed in duplicate with the copy being given to the Volunteer and the original filed in the Volunteer's personnel record at __________________________ (organisation).

FIGURE 8.10 Sample volunteer contract

Source: Volunteering Queensland 2010.

The induction process can also be facilitated by the development of an induction kit for distribution to each new staff member or volunteer. Such a kit might contain:

- an annual report
- a message from the organising committee chairperson/chief executive officer welcoming staff and volunteers
- a statement of event mission/vision, goals and objectives
- an organisational chart
- a name badge
- a staff list (including contact details)
- a uniform (whether a T-shirt or something more formal)
- a list of sponsors
- a list of stakeholders
- any other appropriate items — for example, occupational, health and safety information.

A central outcome of the induction process should be a group of volunteers and staff who are committed to the event, enthusiastic and knowledgeable about their role in it, and aware of what part their job plays in the totality of the event. It also serves to orient the volunteers and staff members to the culture of the organisation, providing them an introduction to its work practices and environment. This will assist in making them more comfortable, and hasten their adaptation to the work/team environment.

Training and professional development

According to Stone (2007), training and professional development are both concerned with changing the behaviour and job performance of staff and volunteers. Training focuses on providing specific job skills/knowledge that will allow people to perform a job or to improve their performance in it. Professional development, on the other hand, is concerned with the acquisition of new skills, knowledge and attitudes that will prepare individuals for future job responsibilities.

Both training and professional development are significant in driving the success of an event, acting to underpin its effective delivery. For small and mid-sized events, much training is on-the-job, with existing staff and experienced volunteers acting as advice givers. This approach, while cheap and largely effective, has limitations. The major one is that it is not often preceded by an assessment of the event's precise training needs and how best to meet them within resource limitations.

A formal approach to training needs assessment serves to determine whether training taking place is adequate and whether any training needs are not being met. Additionally, such an assessment generates suggestions about how to improve training provided by the event. These suggestions may include:

- sending, or requesting stakeholder/government support to send, staff/volunteers on training programs dealing with specific areas or identified training needs (for example, risk management, event marketing and sponsorship)
- identifying individuals associated with the event who would be willing to volunteer to conduct training sessions
- commissioning consultants/external bodies to undertake specific training
- encouraging staff/volunteers to undertake event-specific training programs (now provided by some public and private colleges, universities and event industry associations — see figure 8.11) in return for certain benefits (for example, higher salaries, appointment to positions of greater responsibility/satisfaction).

EXECUTIVE CERTIFICATE IN EVENT MANAGEMENT

The Executive Certificate presents a comprehensive overview of the industry and addresses key event management processes associated with the creation, conduct and delivery of corporate, public and private events. Public events include festivals (music, film, arts, cultural), street parades, fairs and sporting events. Corporate events comprise product launches, functions, fund-raising events, conferences etc. Private events are those such as weddings and parties. Since its commencement in 1966, the Executive Certificate has featured many of Australia's leading industry professionals as guest speakers. The program is offered in Sydney and Melbourne, as well as in the UK, Singapore, New Zealand, Malaysia and Macau.

The focus of the course is on developing an understanding of the overall development and delivery of various forms of events. The course is comprised of two distinct units — Event Management and Marketing and Event Operations.

FIGURE 8.11 Training program offered by the Australian Centre for Event Management, University of Technology, Sydney

Source: Australian Centre for Event Management 2010.

When trying to identify what training is required to facilitate the effective delivery of an event, the central consideration is to determine the gap between the current performance of staff and volunteers and their desired performance. This can be achieved by:

- performance appraisals of existing staff/volunteers (what training staff identify as being required to make them more effective)
- analysis of job requirements (what skills the job description identifies)
- survey of personnel (what skills staff state they need).

The types of training provided by events will vary; however, it is not uncommon for them to provide a level of general training for all staff in areas such as occupational health and safety and first aid, as well as training designed to provide position-specific skills and knowledge.

Supervision and evaluation

As a general rule, the bigger and more complex the event, the greater the need is for staff and volunteers to perform a supervisory function. This function may be exercised through a variety of means, including having would-be supervisors understudy an existing supervisor, developing a mentoring system or encouraging staff to undertake appropriate professional development programs.

One of the key tasks of supervisors and managers is that of performance appraisal. This task involves evaluating performance, communicating that evaluation and establishing a plan for improvement. The ultimate outcomes of this process are a better event and more competent staff and volunteers. Stone (2007) proposes a dynamic performance appraisal program (see figure 8.12) based on goal establishment, performance feedback and performance improvement.

According to Stone (2007), goals should be mutually arrived at by a supervisor and a volunteer or staff member. These goals, while specific to the particular job, are likely to relate to matters such as technical skills and knowledge, problem solving/creativity, planning and organising, interpersonal skills, decision making, commitment to quality and safety, the achievement of designated results, attitudes and personality traits, reliability/punctuality, and professional development. It is important that measurements of progress towards goals are established, otherwise there is little point in setting goals in the first place. A person charged with overseeing waste management for an event, for example, may be assessed in terms of the percentage of material recycled from the event, levels of contamination in waste, the percentage of attendees (as determined by survey) that understood directions regarding the placement of waste in containers, and the level of complaints regarding matters such as full bins. Other areas for assessment may include those associated with personal development (enrolment and completion of a specific course), interpersonal relationships (opinions of supervisors/co-workers) and problem solving/creativity (approaches employed to respond to the unexpected).

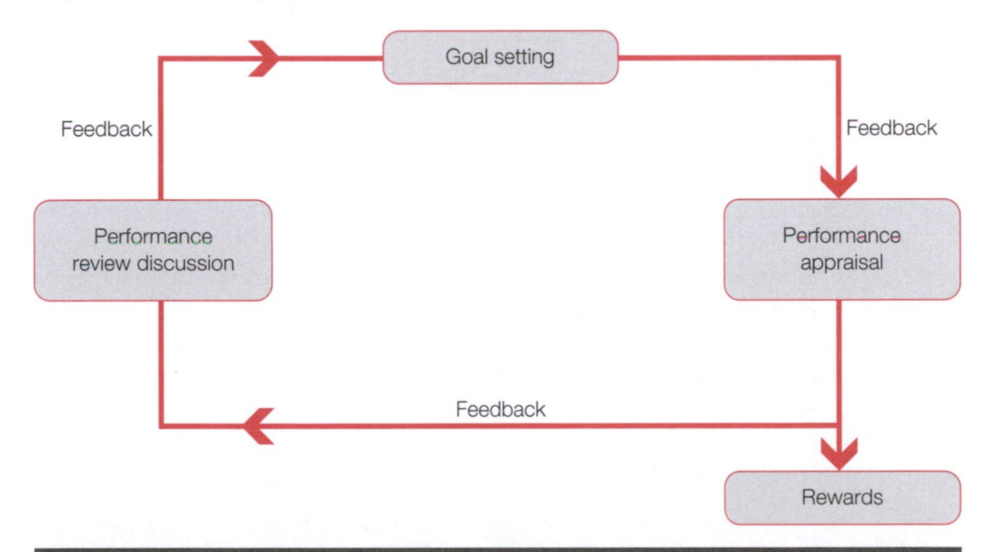

FIGURE 8.12 Dynamic performance appraisal program

Source: Stone 2007.

Performance, in terms of progress towards the established goals, can be assessed in a variety of ways, including performance scales. According to Wood et al. (2004), irrespective of what assessment measures are used, responses to the following questions must underpin any efforts in this area: What does the job require? What does the employee/volunteer need to do to perform effectively in this position? What evidence from how work is undertaken would indicate effective performance? What does the assessment of evidence of performance indicate about future actions required?

Once an appraisal has been conducted, there should be a follow-up review discussion in which the supervisor/manager and the staff member mutually review job responsibilities, examine how these responsibilities have been performed, explore how performance can be improved, and review and revise the staff members/volunteers short-term and long-term goals. The interview process should be a positive experience for both parties. To this end, it is worthwhile considering providing training to the managers/supervisors involved in this process so they adhere to certain basic practices such as preparing for the interview by reviewing job descriptions, reviewing previous assessments, being constructive not destructive, and encouraging discussion.

Integral to the appraisal system are rewards that paid staff receive in the form of salaries, bonuses, profit sharing, promotion to other jobs or other events, and benefits such as cars and equipment use (for example, laptop computers). Options also exist to reward volunteers for their efforts. These include:

- training in new skills
- free merchandise (for example, clothing, badges, event posters)
- hospitality in the form of opening and closing parties, free meals/drinks
- certificates of appreciation
- provision of a meeting space on festival site, e.g. Volunteers Lounge
- gifts of sponsor products
- opportunities to meet with celebrities, sporting stars and other VIPs
- promotion to more interesting volunteer positions with each year of service
- public acknowledgement through the media and at the event
- free tickets/event registration.

The 'flip side' to rewards — that is, discipline — also requires managerial consideration. It is useful to have in place specific policies and practices that reflect the seriousness of different behaviour/actions, and these should be communicated to all staff (paid and voluntary). These policies and practices are likely to begin with some form of admonishment and end with dismissal. Many of the approaches to disciplining paid employees (such as removing access to overtime) are not applicable to volunteers. Instead, approaches that may be applied to volunteers include re-assignment, withholding of rewards/benefits and suspension from holding a position as a volunteer.

Termination, outplacement and re-enlistment

Whether employing staff on contract or as permanent employees, event managers are occasionally faced with the need to terminate the services of an individual. This action may be necessary in instances where an employee breaches the employment contract (for example, repeatedly arriving at the workplace intoxicated) or continually exhibits unsatisfactory performance. This need may also arise when economic or commercial circumstances of the organisation conducting the event require it to shed staff (such as when there is insufficient revenue due to poor ticket sales).

Various legal issues surrounding termination need to be understood by those involved in event management. In Australia, these issues relate to unfair or unlawful dismissal/termination, and are spelt out in the *Fair Work (Registered Organisations) Act 2009* (Cwlth). As most events have less than fifteen employees they are not 'captured' by the unfair dismissal requirements of this legislation; however, they must still ensure that they adhere to its requirements concerning unlawful termination. These requirements concern the illegal nature of dismissal for reasons related to such matters as race, colour, sex, sexual preference, age, physical or mental disability, marital status and family responsibilities. It should also be noted that on occasions events will need to 'dismiss' volunteers. In this regard Getz (2005) suggests a variety of approaches. These include making all volunteer appointments for fixed terms (with volunteers needing to re-apply and being subjected to screening each time the event is conducted) and using job descriptions and performance appraisals to underpin any 'dismissal' action.

Outplacement is the process of assisting terminated employees (or indeed volunteers), or even those who choose to leave the event organisation voluntarily, to find other employment. By performing this function the event organisation is providing a benefit to employees for past service, as well as maintaining and enhancing its image as a responsible employer. Even volunteers who are no longer needed can be helped into other positions by being put in contact with volunteer agencies or other events.

With recurring events, such as annual festivals, opportunities often exist to re-enlist for paid or voluntary positions. Many staff from the Sydney and Athens Summer Olympic Games, for example, took up positions within the organisation responsible for the Beijing Olympics. To maintain contact with potential volunteers and past staff between events, a variety of approaches can be employed, including newsletters (see, for example, the Illawarra Folk Festival website, www.illawarrafolkclub.org.au), social events, the offer of benefits for re-enlistment, and personal contact by telephone between events.

Event managers should also keep in mind that staff will often leave of their own accord. The involvement of such staff in exit interviews can provide valuable information that could be used to finetune one or more aspects of an event's human resource management process. A study of volunteers at a jazz festival (Elstad 2003), for example, found the main reasons (in order) that volunteers quit were:

1. their overall workload
2. a lack of appreciation of their contribution
3. problems with how the festival was organised
4. disagreement with changing goals or ideology
5. wanting more free time for other activities
6. a lack of a 'sense of community' among volunteers
7. family responsibilities
8. the festival becoming too large
9. the inability to make decisions regarding their own position
10. a dislike for some of their responsibilities
11. lack of remuneration
12. moving out of the festival's geographic area.

Evaluation of process and outcomes

As with all management processes, a periodic review is necessary to determine how well, or otherwise, the human resource management process is working. To conduct such a review, it is necessary to obtain feedback from relevant supervisory/management staff, organising committee members, and paid and voluntary staff. Such a review might examine aspects such as the staff induction process, adequacy of training and supervision, regularity and effectiveness of work reviews, work conditions and salaries. It might also examine issues such as staff satisfaction levels and the retention rate of staff/volunteers. In visitor surveys of the event, it might be worthwhile to canvass the opinions of visitors on issues such as staff/volunteer friendliness, helpfulness, and adequacy of access to staff ranging from information and ticketing to attending to their special needs at the event. It might also be worthwhile to survey volunteers in order to discover what motivated them to volunteer, what the experience was like for them, and their suggestions for improvement of the volunteer process. As part of its review process, the Festival of Trees in Montana, for example, uses a questionnaire to obtain feedback from volunteers (see figure 8.13). A specific time should then be set aside, perhaps as part of a larger review of the event, to examine the extent to which the process as a whole (and its various elements) achieved its original objectives. Once the review is complete, revisions can be made to the process for subsequent events.

FESTIVAL OF TREES VOLUNTEER SURVEY 2009

First Name

Last Name

Where you volunteered

What motivated you to be a volunteer for the Festival of Trees?

What did you like best about volunteering at the Festival of Trees?

What do you think can be changed or improved? Do you have any suggestions?

What was your experience working with the Intermountain staff?

How would you rate your overall experience volunteering at the Festival of Trees?

- Select -

Can we contact you to volunteer for upcoming events? (Please provide name/phone)

Do you know of someone who would like a personal tour of the Intermountain Children's Home and Services campus? (please provide name/phone)

Additional comments

Submit Cancel

FIGURE 8.13 Example of a volunteer survey

Source: Festival of Trees 2009.

MOTIVATING STAFF AND VOLUNTEERS

Motivation is a key, if implicit, component of the human resource management process. It is what commits people to a course of action, enthuses and energises them, and enables them to achieve goals, whether the goals are their own or their organisation's goals. The ability to motivate other staff members is a fundamental component of the event manager's repertoire of skills. Without appropriate motivation, paid employees and volunteers can lack enthusiasm for achieving the event's corporate goals and delivering quality service, or can show a lack of concern for the welfare of their co-workers or event participants.

In the context of volunteers, pure altruism (an unselfish regard for, or devotion to, the welfare of others) may be an important motive for seeking to assist in the delivery of events. Although this proposition is supported by Flashman and Quick (1985), the great bulk of work done on motivation stresses that people, while they may assert they are acting for altruistic reasons, are actually motivated by a combination of external and internal factors, most of which have little to do with altruism. As Moore (1985, p. 1) points out, 'volunteers clearly expect to obtain some reward for their participation and performance'.

Researchers from a variety of disciplines have done much work over many years on what motivates people, particularly in the workplace. Perhaps the most relevant and useful of these studies within the context of festivals and events are content theories and process theories.

Content theories

Content theories concentrate on what things initially motivate people to act in a certain way. As Mullins (2005, p. 480) points out, they 'are concerned with identifying people's needs and their relative strengths, and the goals they pursue in order to satisfy these needs'. Figure 8.14 represents the essential nature of theories of this type.

Content theories assert that a person has a need — a feeling of deprivation — which then drives the person towards an action that can satisfy that need. Maslow's (1954) hierarchy of needs, illustrated in figure 8.15, popularised the idea that needs are the basis of motivation.

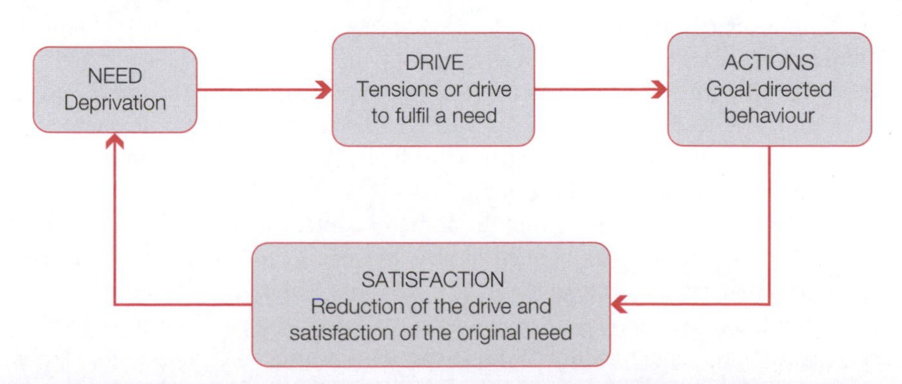

FIGURE 8.14 The basis of content theories of motivation

Source: Peach and Murrell 1995.

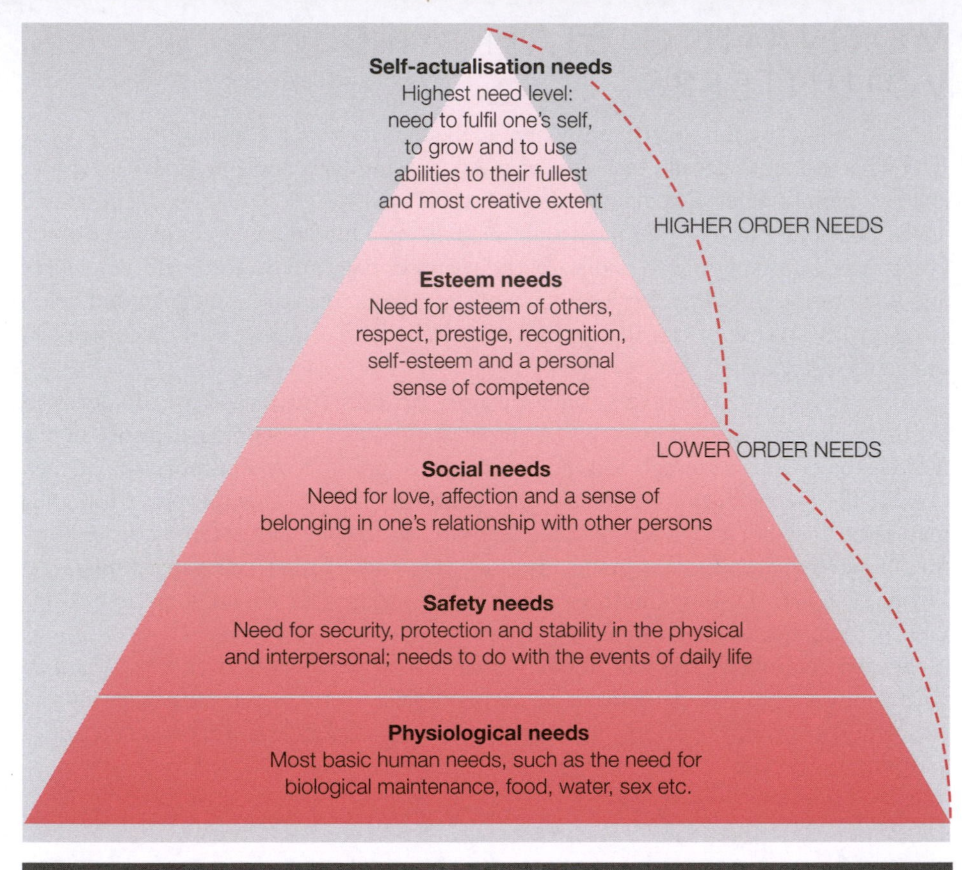

FIGURE 8.15 Maslow's hierarchy of needs

Source: Wood et al. 2004.

In essence, Maslow's theory proposes that lower order needs must be satisfied before people are motivated to satisfy the next, higher need. That is, people who are trying to satisfy physiological needs of hunger and thirst have no interest in satisfying the need for safety until their physiological needs are satisfied. The first three needs are perceived as deficiencies; they must be satisfied to fulfil a lack of something. In contrast, satisfaction of the two higher needs is necessary for an individual to grow emotionally and psychologically.

Although little empirical evidence exists to support Maslow's theory, it can give insights into the needs people may be seeking to fulfil through employment. Some research, for example, indicates a tendency for higher level needs to dominate as individuals move up the managerial hierarchy.

Another researcher who falls within the ambit of content theory is Herzberg (1968). He argues that some elements, which he calls hygiene factors, do not of themselves motivate or satisfy people. Among these factors are pay levels, policies and procedures, working conditions and job security. However, the absence or perceived reduction in these items can stimulate hostility or dissatisfaction towards an organisation. Herzberg further argues that other factors, which he calls motivators, of themselves lead to goal-directed behaviour. These elements include achievement, recognition and interesting work. Herzberg's theory is illustrated in figure 8.16.

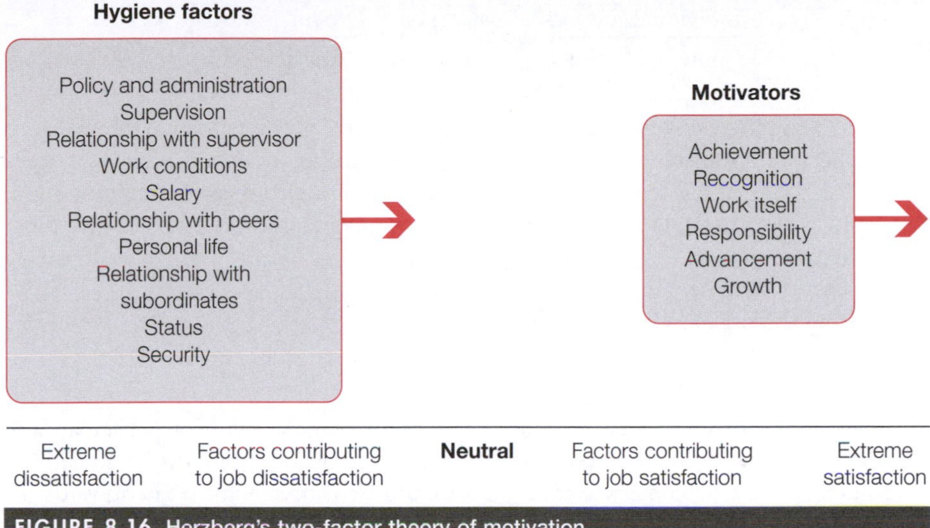

FIGURE 8.16 Herzberg's two-factor theory of motivation

Source: Based on Herzberg 1968.

Herzberg's theory suggests event managers can motivate staff and volunteers by:

- instituting processes of recognising achievement
- empowering staff so they can take responsibility for the outcomes of their part of the event
- providing opportunities for them to grow in skills, experience and expertise.

It also suggests event managers need to be conscious of certain hygiene factors that can act as demotivators. These might include attitudes of supervisors, working conditions such as the length of meal/coffee breaks and hours of work, quality of food provided, the status of one job compared with another (for example, waste management officer versus publicity coordinator), and policies such as the type/quality of uniforms provided to staff versus volunteers.

Content theories, such as those of Herzberg and Maslow, provide event managers with some understanding of work-related factors that initiate motivation; they also focus attention on the importance of employee needs and their satisfaction. They do not, however, explain particularly well why a person chooses certain types of behaviour to satisfy their needs (Wood et al. 2004). Process theories, the subject of the next section, take up this challenge.

Process theories

Representative of process theories of motivation are Adams's (1965) equity theory and Vroom's (1964) expectancy theory.

Equity theory

Equity theory is based on the reasonable premise that all employees (or, for that matter, volunteers) expect to be treated fairly. This being the case, if one employee or volunteer perceives a discrepancy in the outcomes that he or she receives (for example, pay or type of work allocated) compared with those of other employees or volunteers, that employee or volunteer will be motivated to do more (or less) work (Wood et al. 2004). This situation is represented in the following equation.

$$\frac{\text{Individual rewards}}{\text{Individual inputs}} \overset{\textit{comparison}}{\leftrightarrow} \frac{\text{Others' rewards}}{\text{Others' inputs}}$$

What an employee or volunteer perceives as fair in terms of compensation (monetary or non-monetary) is subjective. The best way of maintaining an awareness of what an individual is thinking in this regard is to develop and maintain open lines of communication. If inequity is perceived and goes unnoticed, a number of outcomes are possible, including:

- a reduction in effort
- pressure to increase remuneration
- exit from the organisation.

Expectancy theory

Expectancy theory holds that an individual's motivation to act in a particular way comes from a belief that a particular outcome will result from doing something (expectancy). This outcome will result in a reward (instrumentality). The rewards for accomplishing this outcome are sufficiently attractive/desirable to justify the effort put into doing it (valence). Motivation, under this theory (in its most simplistic form), can therefore be expressed as:

$$\text{motivation} = \text{expectancy} \times \text{instrumentality} \times \text{valence}.$$

This being the case, whenever one of the elements in this equation approaches zero, the motivational value of a particular decision is dramatically reduced. Event managers need to be aware of this and, therefore, try to maximise all three motivational components. In other words, there must be a clear payoff if employees and volunteers are to perform at a high level. To understand what this payoff needs to be for each staff member and volunteer is difficult; however, the chances of doing so are greatly increased if lines of communication are kept open and if a genuine effort is made to understand each individual.

As an example of how expectancy theory works, take the situation of people who decide to work voluntarily on their local community festival. They may have certain expectations such as:

- by working on the event they will gain certain new skills
- these new skills in turn will enhance their future employability, thus creating an *instrumentality*
- the jobs for which they will be able to apply with these new skills are ones that they would find rewarding, thus generating a high level of valence (*or attraction*) to the volunteer positions on offer.

While the focus in this section has been on the individual, it should not be forgotten that as events often involve a number of functional area 'teams', rewards for collective performance need also to be considered.

BUILDING EFFECTIVE STAFF AND VOLUNTEER TEAMS

As noted at the outset of the chapter, event organisations often come together quickly and exist only for relatively short periods of time. This being the case, one of the greatest challenges faced by an event manager is creating effective 'team(s)' capable of achieving an event's objectives. In the case of small-scale events, such as corporate product launches or hospitality-based events, the event manager will often create a single team comprising members of their own company's staff and those of a range of suppliers (the venue, A/V hire firms, caterers, etc.). To develop a sense of 'team' within such a group, the event manager will often rely solely upon one or more 'team' briefings/meetings, supported by detailed event production schedules indicating the roles to be performed by all involved. What simplifies this process in many instances is the ongoing (as opposed to one-off) use by event managers of a given set of contractors, who, over time, come to increasingly understand how best to integrate their activities with those of the event production firm. In the case of larger events where there are many function-based teams, and where the teams that are created exist for longer periods, creating effective teams becomes a more complex issue. In this regard, event managers need to give significant thought to such matters as:

- clearly establishing team tasks
- choosing team members with due regard to personality traits, skills/knowledge and availability (for the period of the event)
- providing adequate support in the form of training, information, resources, opportunities for team building, and designing processes to monitor team performance and provide feedback (Mullins 2005).

Most events are conscious of the significance of the creation of effective teams to their success, with some developing creative responses to facilitate their formation. The Manchester Commonwealth Games, for example, in their efforts to integrate volunteers and paid staff conducted a pre-event 'celebration'. This event, attended by The Earl and Countess of Wessex and hosted by a well-known television presenter, included motivational videos, live sketches, singing and other entertainment. Staff and volunteers attending this function were seated by the venue team and were greeted by their respective venue's management as part of the event's overall efforts at strengthening team bonds. Among other things, this event also sought to:

- inspire and motivate staff
- transfer key messages about what to expect and what was expected of staff and volunteers
- educate staff and volunteers about the global nature of the event and participating nations.

Writing in the context of volunteers in general, McDuff (1995, pp. 208–10), proposes a 14-point formula for effective team building and maintenance. Many of these points (noted following) can be said to apply equally to teams of paid staff.

1. *Teams are a manageable size.* Most effective teams are between two and 25 people, with the majority fewer than ten.
2. *People are appropriately selected to serve on a team.* Care and attention is paid to selecting people with the right combination of skills, personality, communication styles and ability to perform, thereby improving the chances of the team being successful.
3. *Team leaders are trained.* Leaders who find it difficult to delegate and want to do everything themselves make poor leaders. Try to ensure team leaders have training in supervision skills.
4. *Teams are trained to execute their tasks.* It is unrealistic to expect teams to perform effectively without appropriate training. The training should include the team's role in the activity and how that role contributes to the activity's overall success.
5. *Volunteers and staff are supported by the organisation.* Teams must feel that the administration is there to support their endeavours, not to hinder them.
6. *Teams have objectives.* The purpose of the team is spelt out in measurable objectives. Having a plan to achieve those objectives helps build trust.

7. *Volunteers and staff trust and support one another.* People trust each other when they share positive experiences. When each team is aware of the organisation's objectives and how its role helps to achieve those objectives, it trusts co-workers and supports their efforts.
8. *Communication between volunteers and the event organisation is both vertical and horizontal.* Communication, which means sending 'meanings' and understandings between people, is a process involving an active and continuous use of active listening, the use of feedback to clarify meaning, the reading of body language, and the use of symbols that communicate meaning. Communication travels in all directions — up and down the reporting line, and between teams and work groups. Working together is facilitated by good communication.
9. *The organisational structure promotes communication between volunteers and staff.* The organisation's structure, policies and operating programs permit and encourage all members of the organisation to communicate with their co-workers, their managers and members of other departments. This helps build an atmosphere of cooperation and harmony in the pursuit of common objectives.
10. *Volunteers and staff have real responsibility.* A currently fashionable concept of management is 'empowerment'. This means giving staff authority to make decisions about their work and its outcomes. Take, for example, a group of volunteers having the somewhat mundane task of making sandwiches. If they are empowered with the authority to decide what sandwiches to make, how to make them and what to charge, their enthusiasm for the task will probably be enhanced and there will be a corresponding improvement in outcomes.
11. *Volunteers and staff have fun while accomplishing tasks.* Managers should strive to engender an atmosphere of humour, fun and affection among co-workers within the culture of the organisation. Such actions as ceremonies to acknowledge exemplary contributions to the event, wrap-up parties and load-in celebrations can facilitate this atmosphere.
12. *There is recognition of the contributions of volunteers and staff.* Paid staff should express formal and informal appreciation of the work of volunteers, and volunteers should publicly recognise and appreciate the work of the paid staff. This mutual appreciation should be consistent, public and visible.
13. *Volunteers and staff celebrate their success.* Spontaneous celebrations with food, drink, friendship and frivolity should be encouraged by management of the event, to celebrate achievement of objectives. The event manager should allocate a budgeted amount for these occasions.
14. *The entire organisation promotes and encourages the wellbeing of volunteer teams.* Everyone in the organisation sees himself or herself as part of a partnership and actively promotes such relationships.

Once teams are in place and operating effectively, the event manager should monitor their performance and productivity by observing their activities and maintaining appropriate communication with team leaders and members. If deficiencies are noticed during the monitoring procedure, then appropriate action can be taken in terms of training, team structure changes or the refinement of operating procedures in a climate of mutual trust.

LEGAL OBLIGATIONS

Event managers need to be mindful of laws and statutes that have an impact on the employee and employer relationship, some of which have previously been noted in this chapter. Areas covered by these laws and statutes include occupational health and safety, discrimination, employee dismissal, salaries/wages, and working conditions (for example, holiday and long service leave, superannuation and workers compensation). As this area of the law is dynamic in nature, it is necessary for event organisations to remain abreast of any developments by contacting such bodies as:

- Worksafe Australia (for occupational health and safety matters)
- the Australian Human Rights Commission (for discrimination matters)
- state/territory and national bodies charged with overseeing industrial relations legislation (dismissal matters, wages and working conditions).

Event organisations, along with their employees, also have rights and responsibilities under common law that they must exercise when they enter into an employment contract. For employers, these include:

- pay correct wages
- reimburse employees for work-related expenses
- ensure a safe working environment suitable for the performance of the employee's duties
- not act in a way that may seriously damage an employee's reputation or to cause mental distress or humiliation
- not act in a way that will damage the trust and confidence necessary for an employment relationship
- not to provide a false or misleading reference (should one be provided)
- forward PAYE tax instalments to the Australian Taxation Office
- make appropriate payment under the Superannuation Guarantee legislation.

The rights and responsibilities for employees include:

- to obey the lawful and reasonable instructions of the employer
- to exercise due care in the performance of the work and to do it competently
- to account to the employer for all moneys and property received while employed
- to make available to the employer any process or product invented by the employee in the course of employment
- to disclose to the employer information received by the employee relevant to the employer's business
- to be faithful to the employer's interests; for example, by not passing on to a competitor information about the employer's business or denigrating the employer's products and services (Office of Industrial Relations, Department of Commerce, 2007).

In the context of volunteers, common law precedents also provide rights to damages if negligence can be shown on behalf of an event organiser.

SUMMARY

Event managers should approach the task of human resource management not as a series of separate activities, but as an integrated process involving a number of related steps, taking the event organisation's mission, strategies and goals as their starting points. These steps have been identified in this chapter as: (1) the human resource strategy and objectives; (2) policies and procedures; (3) recruitment; (4) training and professional development; (5) supervision and evaluation; (6) termination, outplacement and re-enlistment; and (7) evaluation and feedback. Each of these stages in the human resource management process, it has been argued here, have application in the context of both paid and volunteer staff, as well as to events of varying size and type. This chapter has also dealt with the issue of motivation, examining two broad theoretical perspectives on the matter, process and content theories. The final sections of this chapter dealt with mechanisms for developing task teams to conduct events, and with the legal considerations associated with human resource management.

QUESTIONS

1. Interview the organiser of an event of your choice and ask him or her what legal/statutory requirements have an impact on human resource management processes and practices.
2. In the context of a specific event, identify the policies and procedures regarding human resource management. Collect examples of forms and other material that support them.
3. Develop a job specification for a management position within a special event of your choice.
4. Construct an interview checklist for candidates seeking a management position within a special event of your choice.
5. Discuss two theories of motivation and indicate how an event manager might draw on these theories to motivate their paid and volunteer staff.
6. Identify an event that makes significant use of volunteers and critically assess its approach to recruiting, selecting, managing and motivating this component of its workforce.
7. Propose an induction program for paid staff entering into the employ of a large-scale sports event.
8. Identify a post event volunteer survey that has been conducted for an event, and discuss how the results of the survey might help to improve the future volunteer policies and processes of the event.
9. Interview the members of an event team, and compare the characteristics of the team with McDuff's 14 point formula for effective team building and maintenance described in the chapter.
10. In general terms, what responsibilities does an event organisation have to its employees under occupational health and safety legislation?

case study

THE PEOPLE MATRIX OF THE WOODFORD FOLK FESTIVAL

Building a passionate team

The internationally acclaimed Woodford Folk Festival (established in 1986) is one of Australia's biggest and longest-running cultural events. The Festival is produced by a not-for-profit incorporated association, the Queensland Folk Federation Inc. (QFF). The Festival, which runs over six days and nights and attracts an aggregate audience of around 120 000 patrons, is organised and managed by over 3000 volunteers with a core of 25 full-time paid staff.

The enormity of the human resources task undertaken in producing the Festival can be appreciated by examining its organisational structure. The task of recruiting, communicating with, resourcing, training, motivating, supervising and recognising this team of passionate and dedicated people is something we have spent many years developing and improving. The success of our mission can be measured by our team member retention rate and we believe it is also reflected in our patron visitation return rate: average volunteer return rate — 60 per cent; department head retention rate — 90 per cent; average patron return rate — 65 per cent.

'Engage passionate people' is one of the best pieces of business advice we have received. The Woodford Folk Festival has never been short of passionate people; the key to the success of our human resources philosophy has been in empowering those people, and recognising, rewarding and maintaining their energy, year to year.

The Woodford Folk Festival is a multi-artform community celebration. Our challenge is to build a temporary township to house and service a population of over 23 000 people for six days and nights. In addition to this, over 3000 artists are scheduled to perform across 22 stages (performing on average three shows each). This organisational feat is accomplished by 25 permanent staff, 240 (mostly volunteer) department heads and 'key offsiders', 200 contractors and 2800 volunteers (undertaking over 280 unique roles). The strength and success of the Festival lies in our ability to regroup this team year after year, while maintaining their energy and passion for the Festival.

The seven critical areas we identify and address in striving for high volunteer satisfaction and retention levels are:

- *Recruitment*. We ensure that the volunteer undertaking the job has been correctly selected for the position (for example, a 'people person' is in a public relations position).
- *Communication*. We ensure that the person knows exactly what the job entails (for example, a clear and detailed job description, including expected hours, is available).
- *Resourcing*. We ensure that the person is given the relevant resources to undertake the role (for example, appropriate equipment).
- *Training*. We ensure that appropriate training is delivered for the position (for example, inductions in specific tasks such as Responsible Service of Alcohol).
- *Motivation*. We ensure that the volunteer is motivated to do well (for example, we aim to match the values of the person with the values of the organisation).
- *Supervision*. We ensure that the person is given supervision and feedback on their work and has clear a communication path for problem solving.
- *Recognition*. We ensure that people are appropriately recognised for their contributions.

Delivering these seven fundamental elements in job fulfillment to 2800 volunteers is a challenging task. Achieving an appropriate ratio of supervisors (Festival department heads and key offsiders) to volunteers is critical to achieving success in job satisfaction. The perfect ratio for us is between ten and 12 volunteers to each department head. We have found more than 12 volunteers per department head results in a depersonalised environment where it is harder to deliver each of the fundamental elements listed. We apply the same ratio (1:12) between area managers and department heads and measure the success of our management of department heads by their retention rate, which sits at over 90 per cent annually.

The organisational structure of the Festival (as a business of the QFF) provides some insight into how the task of maintaining a group of dedicated staff and volunteers each year is accomplished. The structure consists of a series of layers as shown in figure 8.17.

At the centre of this concentric structure are the grassroots members of the Queensland Folk Federation (QFF) who annually appoint a Management Committee, which has statutory and fiduciary responsibility for the organisation and its activities. From here each new layer is appointed by the former layer; for example, the executive director appoints the general manager who in turn engages

the permanent staff and appoints a team of 25 Festival area managers and so on. The concentric structure highlights the flatness of our organisation (for example, the lack of unnecessary hierarchy or middle management) and the chain of communication.

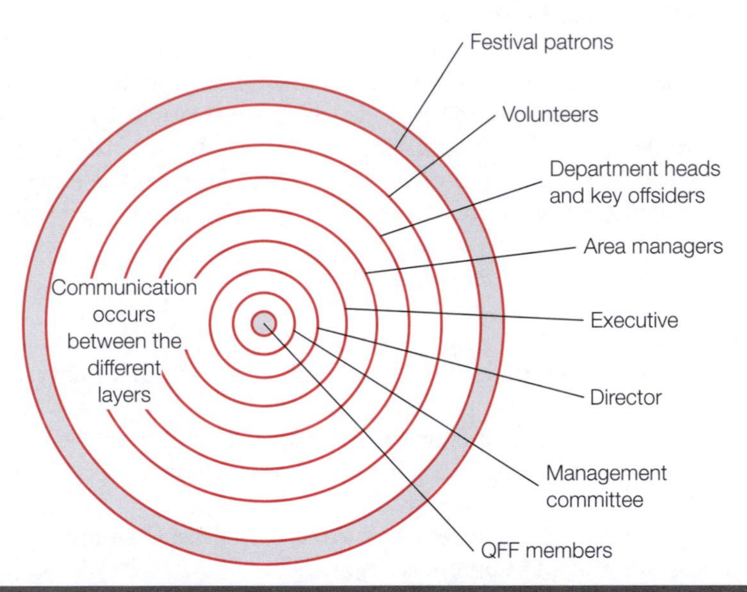

FIGURE 8.17 Organisational structure of the Festival

The management of the Woodford Folk Festival is divided into many small departments (this number reaching 180 departments in 2009) and a department head is appointed to each area. Key offsiders are appointed to assist managers of departments with over 12 members. Area managers (generally full-time staff members) work with department heads to facilitate the supply of services and resources needed to undertake their roles. A permanent full-time volunteers' manager supports department heads in recruiting and managing their team of volunteers to deliver their department's services at the Festival.

The success of this system is in large part due to the autonomy each Festival department enjoys. Department heads are given a high level of discretion and independence to plan and carry out their work. In our experience this autonomy empowers the department head to build a team and create a culture within their department. It also enables individuals to engage their personal management attributes in order to achieve greater department success and job fulfillment. Over the years, departments have developed unique identities within the greater Festival team. This is most clearly evident in the humorous naming of most Festival departments; for example the toilet cleaning department is called the 'Intergalactic S-Bend Warriors', the fencers are 'The Ministry of Da Fence', the crew that pick up cigarette butts are 'The Buttaneers'. And while there is no uniform for volunteers, many departments also identify themselves by wearing particular colours or by costuming; for example, 'Infology' team members wear purple clothing during their shifts and the 'Buttaneers' dress as pirates. It's this sense of fun and ownership that greatly contributes to volunteers' sense of belonging and their experiencing the Festival as a 'home'. Critically, almost 100 per cent of QFF paid staff began their career

as a volunteer at the Woodford Folk Festival. Succession planning is also essential to the Woodford people matrix. Department heads are empowered to appoint their own key offsiders (who are generally sourced from returning volunteers) and are encouraged to identify and train their replacement.

The result for the QFF and the Festival is a consistent preservation of corporate knowledge through very high staff retention. Recognition of individuals' contributions (both paid and volunteer) to our organisation and the Festival can be both complex and simple. It is complex in that the recognition should be relevant, timely and attractive, and simple in that a personal 'thank you' from the right person at the right time can convey sincere appreciation. In exchange for their time, Woodford Folk Festival volunteers receive a Festival entry ticket, a distinctive handmade volunteer medallion, an invitation to the volunteers' party, access during the Festival to a volunteers' lounge with complimentary facilities and a certificate of appreciation.

In 2008 we introduced the Woodford Organisers Conference (The Big Chat) — a weekend of reporting, training, networking and entertainment specifically developed for our 240 department heads and key offsiders. The conference weekend is one of the most useful tools for building capacity within the organising group by creating awareness across departments, increasing confidence and validating the skills set of individual department heads. Most importantly, it takes place in a social setting where people come together and work as a community.

Our human resource philosophy is further supported by systems including our online volunteer management tool. This tool, called 'VENUS', enables department heads to undertake volunteer management online and streamlines the business/data reporting end of management with the object of releasing valuable time for personal interaction. It also enables volunteers to move between departments in a common system. The system is used by both volunteers and department heads for applications, screening, role description, organisational and safety inductions, rostering, ticketing and agreements, contact detail management and communication history, reassignments and evaluations.

The success of our human resources philosophy, together with an organisational structure that enables people to move organically through the layers, has proved highly successful for the Woodford Folk Festival. Visitors to the Festival are often heard asking 'who runs this place?' One hundred and eighty departments work together side-by-side to deliver services to what is ultimately a township with a daily population of 20 000–30 000 people. This people culture is the foundation of the organisation and its ongoing health is central to all current and future successes.

Prepared by Amanda Jakes, General Manager Queensland Folk Federation and Deputy Festival Director, Woodford Folk Festival

Questions

1 What do you think are the main reasons for the success of the human resources strategy of the Woodford Festival?

2 What are some of the advantages of the flat management style employed by the Festival?

3 What are some of the ways in which the Festival motivates and rewards its volunteers?

REFERENCES

Adams, JS 1965, 'Inequity in social exchange', in *Advances in experimental social psychology*, ed. L Berkowitz, Academic Press, New York.

American Liver Foundation 2009, 'Houston Event Manager Job Description', www.liverfoundation.org.

Armstrong, M 1999, *A handbook of human resource management practice*, 7th edn, Kogan Page, London.

Australian Centre for Event Management 2010, 'UTS: Executive Education Executive Certificate (Event Management)' brochure, www.acem.uts.edu.au.

Beardwell, I & Holden, L 2001, *Human resource management: a contemporary perspective*, 3rd edn, Pearson Education, London.

Cherry Creek Arts Festival 2010, '2009 Volunteer Information', www.cherryarts.org.

Clark, R 2000, *Australian human resources management*, 3rd edn, McGraw-Hill, Sydney.

Crompton, R, Morrissey, B & Nankervis, A 2002, *Effective recruitment and selection practices*, 3rd edn, CCH Australia, Sydney.

Elstad, B 2003, 'Continuance commitment and reasons to quit: a study of volunteers at a jazz festival', *Event Management*, vol. 8, pp. 99–108.

Festival of Trees 2009, 'Festival of Trees - Calling All Angels Volunteer Survey', www.intermountain.org.

Flashman, R & Quick, S 1985, 'Altruism is not dead: a specific analysis of volunteer motivation', in *Motivating volunteers*, ed. L Moore, Vancouver Volunteer Centre, Vancouver.

Getz, D 2005, *Event management and event tourism*, 2nd edn, Cognizant Communication Corporation, New York.

Great Lakes Folk Festival 2008, 'Volunteer job descriptions 2008', www.greatlakesfolkfest.net.

Hanlon, C & Cuskelly, G 2002, 'Pulsating major sport event organisations: a framework for inducting managerial personnel', *Event Management*, vol. 7, pp. 231–43.

Hanlon, C & Jago, L 2000, 'Pulsating sporting events', *Events beyond 2000 — setting the agenda*, Proceedings of the Conference on Event Evaluation, Research and Education, eds J Allen, R Harris, LK Jago & AJ Veal, Australian Centre for Event Management, Sydney, pp. 93–104.

Herzberg, F 1968, 'One more time: how do you motivate employees?', *Harvard Business Review*, vol. 46, no. 1, pp. 361–7.

Manchester Commonwealth Games 2003, 'Manchester 2002 The XVII Commonwealth Games — Post Games Report', vol. 3, www.gameslegacy.com, p. 10.

Maslow, A 1954, *Motivation and personality*, Harper & Row, New York.

McCurley, S & Lynch, R 1998, *Essential volunteer management*, 2nd edn, Directory of Social Change, London.

McDuff, N 1995, 'Episodic volunteering', in *The volunteer management handbook*, ed. T Connors, John Wiley & Sons, New York.

Melbourne Commonwealth Games 2006, 'Melbourne 2006 workforce privacy policy', www.melbourne2006.com.au.

Midsumma Festival 2010, 'Midsumma Festival Volunteer Agreement', www.midsumma.org.au.

Moore, L 1985, *Motivating volunteers*, Vancouver Volunteer Centre, Vancouver.

Mullins, LJ 2005, *Management and organisational behaviour*, 6th edn, Financial Times/Pitman Publishing, London.

National Folk Festival 2010, 2010 Volunteer Application Form, www.folkfestival.asn.au.

Noe, R, Hollenbeck, J, Gerhart, B & Wright, P 2003, *Resource management*, 4th edn, McGraw-Hill, New York.

Office of Industrial Relations, Department of Commerce 2007, 'Rights and responsibilities', www.industrialrelations.nsw.gov.au.

Peach, E & Murrell, K 1995 'Reward and recognition systems for volunteers', in *The volunteer management handbook*, ed. T Connors, John Wiley & Sons, New York.

Stone, R 2007, *Human resource management*, 6th edn, John Wiley & Sons Australia, Brisbane.

Volunteering Queensland 2010, 'Volunteer Agreement', www.volqld.org.au.

Vroom, V 1964, *Work and motivation*, John Wiley & Sons, New York.

Wood, J, Chapman, J, Fromholtz, M, Morrison, V, Wallace, J, Zeffane, R, Schermerhorn, J, Hunt, J & Osborn, R 2004, *Organisational behaviour: a global perspective*, 3rd edn, John Wiley & Sons Australia, Brisbane.

MARKETING PLANNING FOR EVENTS

LEARNING OBJECTIVES

After studying this chapter, you should be able to:

1. describe how the marketing concept can be applied to festivals and special events
2. understand how event consumers can be segmented into markets
3. understand the consumer decision process for festivals and events
4. apply the principles of services marketing in creating marketing strategies and tactics for events and festivals
5. plan the event 'service–product' experience, including its programming and packaging
6. develop event pricing strategies or other entry options for special events
7. create strategies for place/distribution, physical setting and event processes that respond to consumer needs
8. apply the knowledge generated into an effective and efficient marketing plan.

INTRODUCTION

This chapter examines a strategic approach to festival and event marketing planning, and how the event manager carries out all of the marketing planning activities necessary to achieve the event's objectives, congruent with the event's corporate strategic plan. To begin, it is useful to explore the concept of marketing as an event management function.

WHAT IS MARKETING?

In simple terms, marketing is concerned with satisfying consumer needs and wants by exchanging goods, services or ideas for something of value. More often, consumers are not just purchasing products, but buying experiences (as they do with events and festivals), or adopting new ideas — for example, participation in extreme sports or new theatre forms, such as Chinese Opera or Japanese Noh theatre. Consumers might offer their dollars in exchange for a concert experience, but for some types of marketing exchanges — for example, community festivals — the time of the consumer to attend may be the only exchange. Alternatively, it can be viewed as a management philosophy, where the organisation exists to satisfy its identified consumer needs while achieving its various objectives. That is, the organisation's operations are centred on the satisfaction of identified consumer needs.

Miller and Layton (2000, p. 7) suggest that marketing 'consists of all activities designed to generate and facilitate any exchange intended to satisfy human needs and wants'. Miller and Layton go further and offer a 'micro' definition of marketing in a business context, which is applicable to event management: 'marketing is a total system of business activities designed to plan, price, promote and distribute products, services and ideas to target markets in order to achieve an organisation's goals and objectives' (p. 9). This definition recognises the essential nature of marketing and is used as the framework for this chapter's discussion of marketing planning for festivals and events. It is of interest to note that Hoyle (2009), in a book titled *Event marketing*, does not attempt to define what is meant by the term, and Getz (2007), in his multifaceted text *Event studies* that covers virtually all aspects of event management and its associated disciplines, does not define event marketing, and gives the topic only a few pages in a 440 page book. However, Davidson and Rogers (2006), in their text on the marketing of destinations and venues for conferences and other business events, use the British Chartered Institute of Marketing's definition: 'marketing is the management process responsible for identifying, anticipating and satisfying customer needs, profitability'. This definition is similar to the marketing philosophy discussed previously and forms the basis for the definition of event marketing to follow.

While it is agreed that the consumer is the primary focus of marketing, changes over time have reshaped somewhat the marketing function for events. These changes are:

- the increasing importance of stakeholders — for example, the community, government, investors/sponsors, media and suppliers of public services, such as the police and the ambulance service who can be as influential as consumers in affecting the success and survival of an organisation
- advances in technology such as the internet, and the consequent use of information and communication technologies (ICT), that affect the marketing of services, including events, especially their promotion and distribution
- the phenomenon of globalisation, particularly in the developed world, which has created global opportunities to enter new markets — for example, the touring and staging of events in offshore locations, and the ability to efficiently and effectively distribute event services to a global market.

As a result of these changes, marketers of events and festivals have the benefit of new knowledge in services marketing, stakeholder management, customer relationship management (CRM) and e-marketing to help shape their strategies.

There is another definition of the phrase 'event marketing' that could confuse readers, which is the use of events to promote a product or service to a defined target market. An example of this common occurrence is a breakfast cereal company using surf carnivals to promote their products. This chapter, however, is concerned with the actions taken by the event manager or marketer to achieve the event's marketing objectives, such as attendee satisfaction, revenue or participation numbers.

Therefore, event marketing can be defined as the process by which event managers and marketers gain an understanding of their potential consumers' characteristics and needs in order to produce, price, promote and distribute an event experience that meets both these needs and the financial or social objectives of the special event.

The following list shows the marketing activities that an event marketing manager may undertake to produce a successful festival or special event.

- Identify a target market whose needs can be satisfied by the event.
- Analyse the needs of the target market to establish the design of the event experience and the way in which it will be delivered in order to satisfy these identified needs.
- Predict how many people will attend the event and the times that different groups or market segments will attend.
- Research any competing events that could satisfy similar needs to devise a unique selling proposition (USP) for the event that enables it to be differentiated from similar leisure activities.
- Estimate the price or value that visitors are willing to exchange to attend an event — for example, ticket price or donation.
- Decide on type and quantity of promotional activity (otherwise known as integrated marketing communication), including the media mix (the various types of communication with the target market, such as print, television, radio and internet) and messages that will reach the audiences of the event.
- Consider how the choice and design of venue(s) and the methods of ticket distribution fit with the needs of attendees.
- Establish the metrics to judge the success of the event in achieving its marketing objectives.

All of these activities, fundamental for a successful event, are part of the marketing function. This chapter explores how event marketing managers seek insights into consumers of their festival/event and the event marketing environment before developing their marketing strategies and plans. In other words, the methods by which event managers then apply theories of marketing, including services marketing theories and customer relationship management (CRM), to develop their event marketing approach are examined.

The need for marketing

Some critics of marketing argue that some cultural festivals and events should not be concerned with target markets and satisfying market needs, but should simply focus on innovation, creativity and the dissemination of new art forms. The argument is that consumers' needs are based on what they know, so consumers are less likely to embrace innovative or avant-garde cultural experiences. Dickman (1997, p. 685) highlights the reluctance of some administrators 'to even use the word [marketing], believing that it suggested 'selling out' artistic principles in favour of finding the lowest common denominator'.

This view erroneously assumes that marketers, by adopting a consumer focus, respond only to the expressed needs of event visitors. In reality, sound marketing research can unveil the latent needs of consumers that only innovative events can satisfy. Often, a distrust of marketing is based on a misunderstanding of marketing principles and techniques. This attitude can be self-defeating for the following reasons.

- The use of marketing principles and techniques gives event managers a framework for decision making that should result in events that not only reflect innovation and creativity, but cater for market segments that seek novelty or the excitement of something new.
- Sponsoring bodies need reassurance that their sponsorship is linking their brand with their target markets. Sound marketing practices give marketers the ability to convince sponsors that a festival or event is the right marketing investment for them.
- All three levels of government (local, state and national) financially assist many festivals and events. Governments usually fund only those events whose management can demonstrate some expertise in marketing planning and management.
- Event stakeholders, such as the community, environmentalists, providers of public services such as the police, political leaders and consumers, are critical in today's societal marketing approach. A societal marketing approach (Kotler, Bowen & Makens 1999) emphasises the importance of society's wellbeing alongside satisfaction of the needs and wants of event or festival markets.
- Consumers, particularly those who reside in major cities, have an enormous range of leisure activities on which to spend their disposable income. This means a festival or special event, as a leisure activity, will attract only those who expect to satisfy at least one of their perceived needs.

All festival and event managers, therefore, can benefit from an understanding of marketing techniques and having some experience in using those techniques to satisfy the identified needs of a target market. Failure to understand the role of marketing, including its societal perspective, can lead to dissatisfied consumers and a weak relationship with stakeholders who can strongly influence an event's long-term survival, and, of course, to the failure of the event to reach its objectives.

Events as 'service experiences'

The marketing concept is just as applicable to a leisure service such as an event as it is to any other product. Consumers are exposed to many well-known brand names in leisure services that have been marketing success stories, and some of these are special events; for example, Sydney's Royal Easter Show, the Edinburgh Tattoo, the Melbourne Cup and Adelaide's Festival of Arts.

Events as services differ from products in that they must be experienced to consume them — the production, delivery and consumption of an event are *inseparable*, happening simultaneously in most cases. Given this immediacy of service consumption, the way in which an event is experienced can vary daily or each year the event or festival is staged. The challenge for event managers and marketers is to try to manage these, smooth out any *variations in quality* and ensure that there is an immediate recovery where poor service occurs. Because people are central to the delivery of most services (including the staff or vendors at an event, as well as its visitors), managing the quality of an event experience depends on managing its human resource delivery and the behaviour of its consumers — that is, people who attend an event affect the level of enjoyment of the other consumers, or, in other words, people are part of the product (experience). This is an important element in the selection of target markets, as if two incompatible groups are placed together at an event it will usually result in dissatisfaction for all.

Another key difference of services like events is that they are *intangible* and, unlike a product, cannot be owned. While sports equipment has physical qualities (it can be examined for its style, shape, texture and colour), sporting events or festivals have only experiential qualities. There is nothing tangible to be picked up, touched, felt or tried before purchasing tickets or after the event (other than event merchandise or mementos that can jog the memory of the event experience). Event marketers add some tangibility via event merchandise, promotional posters, event programs or compact discs of the artists' work or the conference proceedings, but the primary purchase is an intangible experience. The marketer has the challenge, therefore, of providing potential visitors with advance clues about the nature of the event experience.

It is generally agreed (see for example, Lovelock et al. 2004) that the intangibility of services makes them much harder to evaluate than goods, and this is also true for events. Many special events also have some *credence qualities* — characteristics that consumers don't have enough knowledge or experience to understand or evaluate. For certain types of event, real-time interpretation (surtitles at the opera or expert commentary at a sports game) and post-experience interpretation (views expressed by commentators or critics) enhance the consumer's total experience.

For marketers, a further challenge is the *perishability* of the event experience — for example, seats unsold at today's football game or tonight's concert will not be available for sale again. While an unsold product can be stored, today's unused opportunities for festival attendance cannot. Events are delivered in real time. If the weather is poor on the day of the festival, unsold tickets cannot be retrieved, and food and beverage sales for that day are lost. This means event demand and supply and the factors that may affect it must be well understood, so seats, food and beverage, and other vital supplies to an event are not wasted.

The five key characteristics of services discussed here — inseparability, variations in quality, intangibility, credence and perishability — each have implications for an event's services marketing mix, discussed later in this chapter.

The connection between event marketing and management

As the marketing function does not exist in a managerial vacuum, there is a need to understand the tight links between an event's marketing, and the overall management of the event. An event's management plan must be congruent with its marketing plan and vice versa. All plans have one function — to achieve the event's objectives by focusing on its target market's needs. Figure 9.1 illustrates this.

The role of strategic marketing planning

Before describing the strategic marketing planning process, it is useful to think about what 'strategy' means. In the world of business and in event management and marketing, strategy can be interpreted as how an organisation (or event) marshals and uses its resources to achieve its organisational objectives, within its ever-changing political, economic, competitive, socio-cultural and technological environments. Chapter 4 on event planning outlines this process. In this chapter the strategic planning process is linked to the marketing function to show the framework in which event managers develop marketing objectives and strategies to satisfy consumer needs. Strategies are:

- *longer-term, rather than short-term.* Once a marketing strategy is decided, it can be wasteful of resources and disruptive to an event to change the strategic direction. Careful thought is required before deciding on what marketing strategies to use to achieve event objectives.

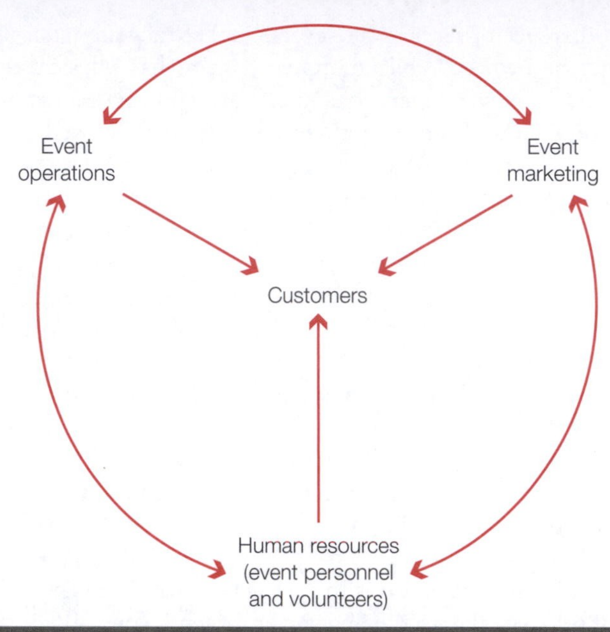

FIGURE 9.1 The event services trinity

- *not another word for tactics*. Strategy is the broad overall direction that an event takes to achieve its objectives, while tactics are the detailed manoeuvres or programs that carry out the strategy. Tactics can be changed as market conditions change, but the overall direction — the strategy — remains constant (at least for the planning period).
- *based on careful analysis of internal resources available to the event and external environments*. It is not a hasty reaction to changes in the market.
- *essential to survival*. Well-considered marketing strategies enable event managers to achieve the objectives of their event.

While the logic of deciding on a long-term strategy appears sound, festivals and events, like other organisations, vary in the extent to which their strategies are deliberate or emergent processes (Mintzberg 1994). In particular, festivals that begin their life as community celebrations run by local volunteers are less likely to have a deliberate strategy selection process. It is unlikely that the Birdsville Races in outback Queensland, for example, commenced with a formal marketing vision and process that led to the strong brand image that the event enjoys today. It can be wrong, therefore, to assume failure will result from implicit (rather than explicit) strategies or those that simply emerge from the hundreds of decisions made by organisers in staging an event. However, a holistic vision of an event's direction and the fit between the marketing strategy and vision is a desirable starting point. The following definition reflects the essence of the strategy concept for the practising events marketer: 'Strategic event marketing is the process by which an event organisation aligns the marketing resources available to the event organisation with the environments in which they occur, in order to fulfil the needs of event consumers and to achieve the event's objectives'.

Based on this definition, the starting points for any strategic marketing planning process should be the long-term mission or vision of the event organisers and its objectives, which is usually arrived at during an event's corporate strategic planning process. Figure 9.2 shows the forces that influence these platforms of the strategic marketing process.

FIGURE 9.2 Constructing the mission

The mission is defined, according to Johnson et al. (2005, p. 13) as 'the overall purpose of the organisation, which ... is in line with the values and expectations of major stakeholders, and concerned with the scope and boundaries of the organisation'. It answers the question, 'What are we here for?', and is the starting point for all planning activities.

As figure 9.2 demonstrates, both the stakeholders of the event and the personal values of its organisers are critical influences. The mission of the Woodford Folk Festival, now internationally recognised for its success, mirrors that of its founding body, the Queensland Folk Federation. Their mission is to 'stimulate, facilitate and foster the preservation and promotion of folk culture for the common good'.

The vision and values of the Queensland Folk Festival and the festival's director, Bill Hauritz, have had a profound effect on all aspects of the Woodford Folk Festival, including its marketing. Other events present more of an event-focused mission — for example, Brisbane's Out of the Box Festival of Early Childhood offers a festival with a mission to enrich the cultural lives of children, their communities and the city of Brisbane. Some events and festivals also state the philosophical principles that underpin their mission and guide event management and marketing. Out of the Box organisers express philosophies that recognise children as cultural contributors, children's individuality and diversity, and children's aesthetic, learning and care. In effect, an event's philosophies and mission statement are an important foundation for the marketing approach that best reflects the interests of its stakeholders and achieves its marketing objectives.

Stages in the strategic marketing planning process for events are: research and analysis of the internal, macro and micro environment, including the competitive, political, economic, social and technological (C-PEST) forces; research into the demographics and psychology of possible event consumers; segmentation of consumers into target market segments, and targeting and positioning by integrated marketing communications; the setting of marketing objectives; and decision making about generic marketing strategies and the event's services marketing mix. Figure 9.3 shows a recommended framework for developing the event marketing strategy.

EVENT MARKETING RESEARCH

Before the marketing strategy is developed, research is usually conducted at the macro level, to understand external forces that may affect the event and its markets; and the micro level, to gain insight into the event's resources and strategic capability. A range of event marketing information can be obtained from both primary and secondary sources to guide the marketing planning process.

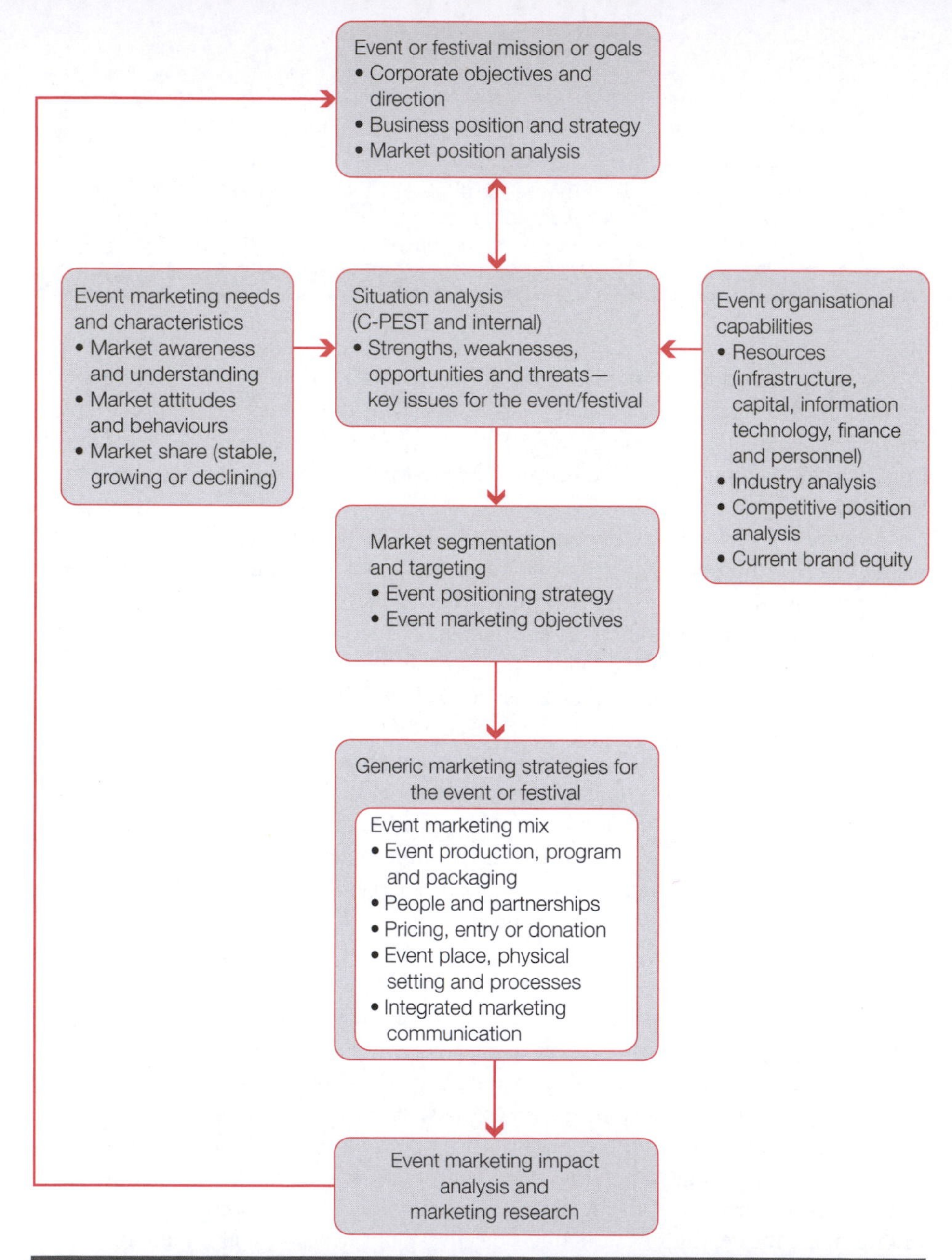

FIGURE 9.3 The strategic event marketing process

To begin, a search of secondary data on macro-level trends affecting leisure consumption and the competitive environment for events can be drawn from online and offline sources. Some useful information sources are:

- government statistics and reports (national and state statistics on the consumption of festivals and events, arts and sport)
- media coverage (about the events sector and particular events or festivals in the region)

- industry newsletters such as the international *Special Events* website (www.specialevents.com.au)
- historical and current data from other events, festivals and event organisers. A content analysis of the websites of festivals, events and event production agencies can be a valuable research technique. For example, David Grant Special Events, one of the largest special events producers based in Australia, has a website that displays innovative event activities (www.dgse.com.au) developed by his team.

A greater depth of understanding of macro-level issues, such as event funding by federal, state or local governments and the sponsorship environment; the seasonal saturation of events; the potential for oversupply of particular types of event; and new technologies for event delivery, can also be obtained through in-depth interviews with opinion leaders — for example, longstanding event directors or producers, public sector event agencies and academics, if they are willing to talk. Careful observation of the marketing of other events can give useful insights into these topics.

At the micro level, event marketers can use a mix of research techniques to gain insights into consumer segmentation and targeting. Past event reports that show vendor participation, event visitation, situational issues influencing past attendance and event satisfaction are useful resources, but are not always available. Often, established members of the event organising body (including volunteers) become a rich source of data about the event's consumption trends. More specific insights into existing event consumers can be reliably obtained from a mix of qualitative research (either in-depth interviews or a series of focus groups with eight to ten people in each of the different segments of the market) and quantitative research (on-site intercept surveys or post-event research). For intercept surveys, that are commonly undertaken at entry or exit points of the event, to be statistically valid a randomly selected sample of at least 200 attendees is recommended. In this context, 'random' means all event attendees have an equal chance of being selected for the survey. As they exit the event, for example, every tenth customer could be asked to participate.

Data related to the visitors' demographics, motives, satisfaction and intention to revisit the event (where applicable) are generally sought. The data analysis can be manually performed for a small-scale survey that seeks only descriptive data about event consumers. However, a statistical software package such as SPSS offers a deeper understanding of relationships between variables such as attendance motives and satisfaction. Data mining (analysis of data already stored by the event organisation from previous events) is another useful tool to establish demographics and motivations of consumers. However, do not succumb to paralysis through analysis. Market research is an aid to competent event marketing as it enables event marketers to better understand their consumers, and the environments in which they operate, but it does not replace it.

Analysing event environments

Strategic marketing is a planning tool based on thorough analyses. The marketer's own sense of judgement is not enough to make good strategic decisions (Rao and Steckel 1998). Astute marketing decisions emerge from a thorough analysis of competitor activities, the political, economic, socio-cultural and technological environments (C-PEST) in which the event occurs, and a rigorous analysis of the event organisation's internal resources to establish the organisation's strategic capability. In other words, what the event organisation is capable of with its available resources. This topic is touched on in chapter 4, and is fully explained here, as it is a fundamental component of the strategic planning process.

event profile

THE RE-BRANDING OF SYDNEY'S ROYAL EASTER SHOW

The Royal Agricultural Society of New South Wales has produced Sydney's Royal Easter Show for more than 120 years. In 1998 the show moved from its traditional venue at the Sydney Showgrounds at Moore Park, an inner city suburb of Sydney, to a custom-built site at Homebush in the geographic centre of Sydney, where it attracted a record crowd of 1.26 million, higher than the previous record crowd of 1.23 million set in 1947. The Moore Park site became the site of Fox Studios and its associated leisure precinct.

It took more than 50 years and a move to a site that became a venue for the Sydney Olympics 2000 for the attendance record to be broken. This is an obvious symptom of an event product not adapting to socio-cultural and demographic environmental changes. The rural population of New South Wales has been in relative decline since the 1940s, with a concurrent increase in the urban population, which led to a decline in interest in the traditional show activities of agricultural produce displays and show bags. To counter this declining interest, the show was re-branded in 2000 as the 'Great Australian Muster', to give it a fresh identity and reinforce it as a uniquely Australian event.

The elements that now make up the show include: *Celebrate Australia*, which is a celebration of Australia's bush heritage featuring bush skills put to the test in a Stockmen's Challenge; an International Rodeo Challenge; *The Man from Snowy River*, which is an action-packed re-enactment of the famous poem by Banjo Patterson; the *Hell West and Crooked Outback Stunt Show*, which is a high-energy, action-packed 30-minute show of stunts featuring fights, falls, fire, music and explosions; and the International Test Wood Chopping competition. These elements convey to the ever-growing urban population of Sydney their image of an idealised rural life where the pioneers of Australia battled the physical environment to produce the rugged Australian of myth and legend.

Event marketing is concerned with identifying consumer needs and then satisfying them within the boundaries of the organisation's mission. The marketers of the Royal Easter Show realised that the socio-cultural and demographic environments of Australia have changed, so they altered their product (a leisure experience) to reflect these changes.

The C-PEST analysis

Figure 9.4 depicts each of the analyses contained in the C-PEST framework. Note that the global entertainment environment is included because changes in the world of artistic or sporting endeavour need careful monitoring by event and festival managers. Such trend analyses are done for a good reason: to establish opportunities and threats for the festival/event and its management. Using this process, organisers can shape marketing strategies to capitalise on emerging entertainment opportunities and neutralise threats.

In conducting environmental analyses, it is easy to become overwhelmed by potential influences on the effective marketing of the event or festival. Stick to what is most critical to the event or festival in developing its marketing strategy in the current environment. To illustrate the C-PEST framework, the various environments of the Sydney Festival are used. Now over 30 years old, the Sydney Festival is a three-week celebration of dance, theatre, visual arts, opera and music, which energises the city's business district each summer.

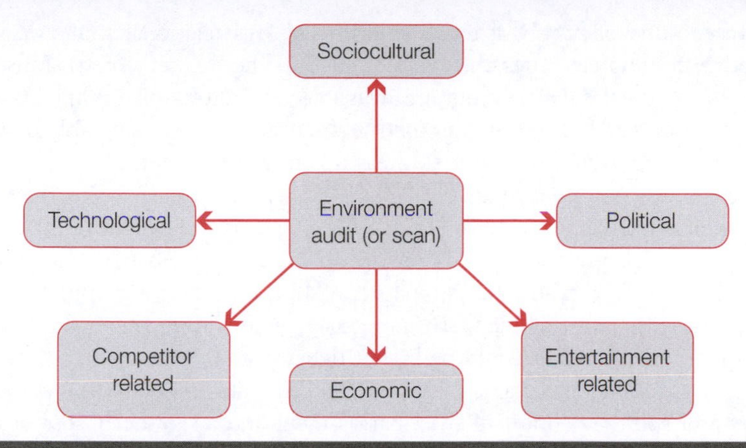

FIGURE 9.4 Components of the environment analysis

Competitive analysis

In describing competitor analysis and strategy, Porter's (1980) seminal work identified five elements that affect competition within an industry (see also figure 9.5). This analytical tool is used to understand both industry-level and company-level competition, and it can also guide festival and event managers in their marketing decision making.

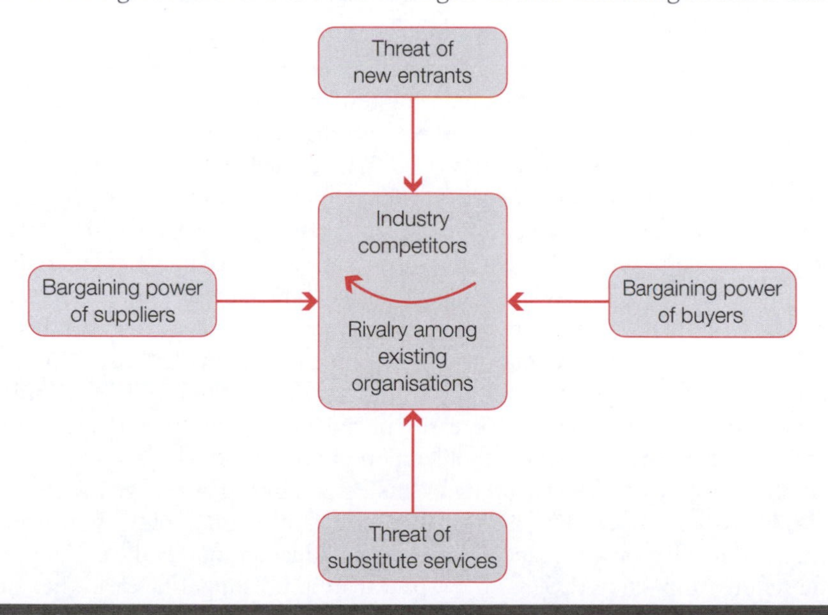

FIGURE 9.5 The five competitive forces

Source: Porter 1990.

To begin, festival or event *suppliers* are the venues, artists and physical resources (such as lighting and staging) needed to produce an event. Unless other artistic festivals occurring at the same time depend on these suppliers, no major difficulties usually emerge with event supply. However, given that the mission of the Sydney Festival is to provide the best of Australian and world talent for its audience, the organisers will liaise with suppliers of highly-valued artists who have the power to increase talent costs or specify the conditions under which the artists will perform. Here, a relational strategy of building long-term alliances with agents and other festivals is important to ensure a continuity of supply at reasonable prices. This relational strategy could also be applied in forging close ties with venues such as the Sydney Opera House, so the best venues for the festival's events are available and affordable. While some event suppliers such as venues and entertainment agents can wield considerable power, relationship marketing strategies help to address this power imbalance.

Because the *buyers* of the Sydney Festival are large in number, little power is concentrated in their hands as individuals. Their only power is their price sensitivity to the festival's offerings. Given the festival's mission of producing 'Australia's largest annual cultural celebrations with an international reputation for modern, popular and intelligent programming' (www.sydneyfestival.org.au), by providing the best international entertainment, an end result could be higher ticket prices. If consumers decide a particular offering does not give value for money, and they stay away in droves, the festival organisers and sponsors could suffer embarrassment and a significant loss of revenue. Consequently, the role of the marketer is to carefully identify (through observation, experience and market research) the price level at which this sensitivity could arise.

A threat of *new entrants* exists if there is some potential for market share to be lost to another festival offering similar experiences. Australian history is littered with festivals that no longer exist. Sydney's Waratah Festival, for example, was once a festival highlight for Australia's biggest city. Now, it is a fading memory for Sydney's older residents. If there are low barriers to new entrants, this can be a real threat to the festival's viability. However, festivals such as the Sydney Festival depend on government and other sponsors for much of their funding, so the barriers to entry are quite high. These entry barriers remain high while major sponsors (including state government and corporate partners) are satisfied with the results of the festival — that is, so long as the sponsoring bodies' objectives are met and the organisers' strategy for sponsorship management ensures their business results are achieved.

The notion of *substitutes* for an event or festival is based on the marketing premise that consumers are purchasing not a service, but a package of benefits — in this case, an array of stimulating entertainment. If a substitute experience provides entertainment that is more satisfying or just as satisfying in the same timeframe at a lower cost, then the threat of substitution becomes very real. A commonly cited strategy to avoid this threat is to offer a unique event experience to a well-defined target market that is not readily substituted. For the Sydney Festival, the scale and sophistication of festival programming mean the festival would not be easily or quickly replaced by another event on the city's calendar. Yet, the ongoing proliferation of events and festivals, and the 'copycatting' that typifies services (including events), is a growing challenge for event marketers. 'Me too' events occurring on a smaller scale at other times of the year may have little short-term effect on attendance. However, a gradual dilution of the existing event's unique selling proposition (USP — the aspect that best distinguishes it in the marketplace) is one potential outcome of new entrants with similar event offerings. It is these four elements that impact on the fifth element — industry competitors — and allow event marketers to gauge how intense competition will be for their event.

Political environment

All three levels of government can be active players in producing and sponsoring events and offering event development grants. For the Sydney Festival, both the New South Wales Government and Sydney City Council have played an active role in sponsorship and supply of venues. Strategies to maintain this involvement are necessary, especially if a change of government or minister occurs. As well as identifying the nature of government support, organisers need to take steps to understand new legislation or changes in the regulatory environment that affect event delivery — for example, rising public liability costs and regulations related to racing, gaming, lotteries. And, of course, if the politicians who fund the Sydney Festival believe that the electorate perceives the festival as a waste of public money that merely panders to an urban elite, their support of the festival would quickly vanish.

Economic environment

Some issues that have an impact on event marketing planning are the strength of the economy, foreign exchange rates, interest rates, employment rates, growth in household disposable incomes, and the government's fiscal policy (taxation, for example). The value of the Australian dollar compared to the currency of other nations, can raise or lower the cost of attracting foreign artists to the Sydney Festival. Methods of combating economic challenges that affect the festival's mission are subject to continual review by the event management. For example, if the Australian dollar suddenly devalued (as happened in the first part of this decade) the cost of international artists would increase. Therefore, the product strategy might change to focus more on Australian-based artists. Fortunately, in the latter part of the early twenty-first century, the value of the Australian dollar is at a near all time high with respect to the US dollar and the British pound, which makes payment of visiting artists much less.

Socio-cultural environment

Factors of a social or cultural nature that affect event marketing strategies are the size and variety of cultural/subcultural groups in the event's target market; changes in lifestyle, including work–leisure patterns; changing demography; changes in entertainment demand; and changes in education levels and household structures. Organisers of the Sydney Festival might observe that women aged 18–30 years are more outwardly mobile, less tied to child rearing than ever before, and have more time and income to participate in events. A slightly higher proportion of females than males has been shown among attendees at various festivals — for example, attendance at classical music festivals is usually skewed towards females.

Technological environment

Changes in technology present both opportunities and challenges for event organisers. In particular, the use of the world wide web, e-marketing (including e-newsletters) and a mix of online and offline event participation is now prevalent and is discussed in depth in chapter 10. The event website serves as a diverse branding tool for festivals and events, with opportunities for consumer interaction with event performers/players, up-to-the-minute event results and replays, and online recognition of event sponsors. For the annual Sydney Festival, organisers use web pages to show sneak previews of the upcoming events, promote major sponsors, advise on festival policies for receiving new submissions to its program, and provide current news about event personnel. In analysing the technological environment, event marketers should evaluate the advantages and disadvantages of all forms of technology.

Direct marketing via SMS messaging on mobile phones, for example, has become a popular event marketing tool, both before and during events. For those events with few resources and no permanent staff, the ability to build and maintain an effective website and stay abreast of new technology can be daunting. Yet, the failure to update a festival website on a regular basis or respond to online enquiries in a timely fashion can devalue the brand in the eyes of event visitors and sponsors. Marketers analysing their technological environment should note any opportunities for low-cost technical support that could be available to their event or festival. And, of course, the internet provides much efficiency by using electronic distribution of tickets to an event. The Sydney Festival is now also using social networking sites such as Twitter, Facebook, Flickr and YouTube to spread the word about different aspects of the festival.

The activity that takes place on social networking sites can be monitored by a process known as 'buzz tracking'. For a fee, a company monitors blogs to ascertain how and in what way a product such as an event is being discussed. With more than 30 million blogs now in existence and numbers doubling each year (McDermott 2006), this form of communication can create a positive or negative buzz about an event of which an event manager should be aware. Another is the concept of co-creation (Rice 2007), where consumers communicate electronically with event management to help create the event product by means of their input. It is not commonly used now, but it might have a major influence on future events. Good (2009) has a complete description of the various programs that can track this activity.

Entertainment environment

Entertainment is characterised by constant change as new ways of expression are developed, whether through new artistic forms or new types of sporting endeavour. The festival or event director generally tries to offer new experiences to consumers, to balance the familiar and novel event components. Trend analysis in the entertainment environment can be done via desk research and travel to centres of artistic innovation or places where emerging sports are practised (certainly a fun part of the job). While most events and festival organisers do not take an annual 'ideas tour' to exotic places to construct their marketing plan, they actively observe entertainment trends all year around. A good understanding of event innovations is also gained from reading professional and popular journals, networking with industry colleagues and travelling to trade fairs and exhibitions. Again, a key purpose of this analysis is to align the event's marketing strategies with opportunities and strengths, and to minimise the impacts of any threats and weaknesses. The board of directors of a major event like the Sydney Festival ensure that it keeps its freshness by changing the executive director occasionally.

Marketing internal resource analysis

Another essential step in developing a marketing plan is an assessment of the event's internal resources. Classic economists categorise the resources available to an entrepreneur as land, labour and capital. In event or festival organisations, the resources needed to effectively produce an event are human, physical and financial.

Human resources

The event marketer analyses the number and type of staff and volunteers available, the particular skill sets required to produce the event, the costs of employing people, and innovative ways in which people can contribute to the event's success. An analysis of the Sydney Festival would show that the festival's directors have been individuals with a high profile since the festival's inception. As a result, a lynchpin of the marketing communication strategy is the use of the director as the public face of the festival, who features strongly in media releases and interviews. Promoting a festival through its senior producers/directors and organised word of mouth by staff and volunteers can also minimise the cost of an event's marketing communication campaign. The Woodford Folk Festival is an example of a festival that, in its early days, capitalised almost entirely on word-of-mouth marketing through its volunteers to build a loyal body of event goers.

Physical resources

For an event, physical resources can include ownership of a venue (although this is rare, it is done by the Woodford Folk Festival). More often, they include computer hardware and software, desktop publishing equipment, access to venues at competitive rates and the use of conference rooms in buildings of some significance. The use of event management software capable of supplying timely data on all aspects of the festival is an example of physical resource strength. It is fair to assume community goodwill towards the Sydney Festival has become a valued resource.

Financial resources

Without access to suitable finance, no event marketing strategy can be put into place. Current access to funds or a demonstrated ability to acquire capital is an obvious strength for any event. This access includes the ongoing involvement of government and corporate sponsorship. With the direct involvement of the NSW Government, the patronage of the governor, the inclusion of the Sydney City Council on the festival board, and its corporate sponsors, the Sydney Festival enjoys a stable resource base. Adequate financial resources or backing for events and festivals often simultaneously depends on the strengths of its partnerships (a key reason for this element featuring in the event marketing mix). The adequacy or otherwise of financial resources has a significant impact on the marketing strategies and tactics available to the marketer.

The SWOT analysis

Once the C-PEST and the internal resource audit are completed, an analysis of strengths, weaknesses, opportunities and threats (SWOT) can be conducted. This summary of the critical issues identified through the C-PEST and internal resources analyses (Johnson et al. 2005) enables the event marketer to take advantage of the event's opportunities and strengths, improve weaknesses, negate threats and, just as importantly, have a solid foundation for establishing marketing objectives and strategies for the event. This task is made easier if all the data collected are summarised into no more than ten bullet points for each section of the SWOT analysis.

The event consumer's decision-making process

Understanding the consumer decision-making process for events and festivals is aided by the following PIECE acronym:

- *problem recognition* — the difference between someone's existing state and their desired state relative to leisure consumption
- *information search* — an internal and/or external search; limited or extensive search processes for leisure (including event) solutions
- *evaluation and selection* of leisure alternatives
- *choosing whether to attend* an event and which optional purchases to make at the event or festival
- *evaluation* of the post-event experience.

Reflecting this PIECE process, the consumer identifies a need that may be satisfied by attending an event or other leisure experience, searches for information about such an experience in different media (the internet, entertainment section of newspapers, the radio, magazines, friends and relatives), and then evaluates the alternatives available. Potential consumers examine how the leisure experience compares with a list of the attributes they most desire. Event goers may want to enhance family ties, so attend a local community festival that all members of the family can enjoy. Alternatively, they may be looking for a novel or innovative event to satisfy their curiosity. After experiencing (or 'consuming') the event, they re-evaluate the experience for its quality of service and its capacity to satisfy their identified needs.

Problem recognition

For would-be event or festival consumers, problem recognition means a difference exists between what they would like to experience and what they have to satisfy that need (Neal, Quester & Hawkins 2002). The central starting point for this problem recognition is the existence of one or more needs that may be satisfied by attending a festival or event. Events and festivals fulfil physiological needs (exercise, relaxation, sexual engagement), interpersonal needs (social interaction) and/or personal needs (enhanced knowledge, new experiences, fulfilment of fantasies) (Getz 1991, 1997). How quickly consumers decide whether to attend an event partly depends on their event purchase involvement — that is, the level of interest in the purchase process, once it has been triggered (Neal, Quester and Hawkins 2002). Some events are spontaneous, low-involvement decisions. For example, a person may visit their local shopping centre on the weekend, notice a small, cultural festival in progress in the recreation centre and wander over to join in. In contrast, attending events such as the World Cup in South Africa in 2010 or visiting London to experience Wimbledon's tennis championship are high-involvement decisions.

Information search

Before looking for information, most consumers try to determine (1) the relevant criteria on which to base their decision — the nature of event performers, the location, other attractions in the area, the ticket price and so on — and (2) the extent to which the event will satisfy their needs. As they compare different leisure experiences, event consumers engage in both external and internal searches for information.

External influences

Among the *external* influences on the potential event goer are various social factors. These factors are described below in the context of event participation.

- *Family and household influences*, such as the desires of children, often influence the leisure behaviour of parents. The need for family cohesion and building familial ties is a strong leisure motivator for many people. It explains the enormous numbers of children and exhausted parents who congregate at the show bag pavilions of agricultural shows around Australia. Many festivals focus on children's entertainment for this reason.
- *Referent groups* are those groups that influence the behaviour of individuals. Groups in close contact with individuals (peers, family, colleagues and neighbours) are known as primary referent groups. Those who have less frequent contact are secondary referent groups. Most people tend to seek the approval of members of their referent groups. If attendance at a particular festival is perceived to be acceptable and desirable, then group members are more likely to attend. Showing examples of a typical referent group (for example, a nuclear family or a group of young people) enjoying themselves at a festival can be a persuasive communication strategy when those groups represent the festival's target market.
- *Opinion formers or opinion leaders* are those people within any group whose views about events and leisure experiences are sought and widely accepted. These opinion leaders are often media, theatrical or sports personalities (including critics and

commentators) who are highly rewarded for their endorsement of products and leisure services. Often, the views of critics and commentators have a strong impact on attendance in sport and the arts.

The adoption of new leisure services tends to follow a normal distribution curve. Innovators (generally opinion leaders within a group) are the first to try the experience. Early adopters, who are a little more careful about adopting the innovation, follow them and act as opinion leaders for the majority. Laggards are the last to try something new; some may be loyal attendees of very mature events or events that are close to decline. It is logical that the marketing of new festivals or events begins by targeting the opinion formers or innovators within the market.

- *Culture* consists of the 'knowledge, beliefs, art, morals, laws, customs and any other capabilities and habits acquired as a member of society' (Neal, Quester and Hawkins 2002, p. 22), or, more simply, a historically derived design for living shared by a discrete group of people. Australia is an example of a culturally diverse country in which indigenous people and various ethnic groups with different designs for living co-exist, usually harmoniously, with the predominant Anglo-Celtic Australian culture. A consumer's cultural background can affect their buying habits, leisure needs, attitudes and values.

  Culture has a profound influence on the design, marketing and consumption of events and festivals. In effect, events are simultaneously a celebration and a consumption experience that reflect the consumers' way of life. A growth of interest in events as diverse as the Chinese New Year Festival in Bourke Street, Melbourne, the Panyiri (Greek) Festival in Brisbane and the Laura Aboriginal Dance and Cultural Festival in North Queensland demonstrate the influence of, and interest in, cultures different from the predominant Anglo-Celtic Australian culture.

An external search involving reference groups or other sources becomes especially important when event or festival attendance requires an extended decision-making process. Going to the Football World Cup, for example, is a high-involvement, extended decision, and event goers will seek advice from websites, travel agents and other sources. Participating in some cultural events, such as the Birdsville Races, could involve extended decision making because it requires travelling to an isolated township.

Internal influences

A range of *internal influences* also affects consumer decision making about events. These influences include *perception* (how we select and process information), *learning and memory*, *motives*, *personality traits* and *consumer attitudes*. If, for example, consumers have an existing preference (attitude) that steers them towards a classical music event, then they would deliberately select information about such events. Similarly, if consumers have information stored in their memory that helps to resolve a need (a mental picture of spectacular fireworks at Sydney's New Year's Eve celebrations), then that event could quickly become the single, most satisfactory solution to their entertainment needs on a given weekend in Sydney.

Personality, or an individual's characteristic traits that affect behaviour, is another influence on event or festival decisions (Stanton, Miller and Layton 1994). People can be introverted/extroverted, shy/self-confident, aggressive/retiring and dynamic/sluggish. Although the effects of personality on consumer choice are difficult to measure, it can be assumed that festivals that celebrate adventure or sporting prowess will attract participants with 'outgoing' personalities. An awareness of particular personality characteristics among event consumers can help marketers to fine-tune their marketing strategies.

Among all of the internal influences, most can be classified as Neal, Quester and Hawkins (2002, p. 19) opine: 'in developed economies, most consumer behaviour is guided by psychological motives'. A body of empirical research on motives for event and festival attendance has emerged since the 1990s. Three theories of event attendance motives, as summarised by Axelsen and Arcodia (2004), are:

1. the *needs achievement hierarchy* — a theory based on Maslow's original hierarchy, whereby motives change as each level of need, from the physiological through to self-actualisation, is satisfied
2. *'push' and 'pull' motives* — a theory that push factors (for example, social interaction, escapism, novelty, curiosity) propel consumers towards an event, while pull factors (for example, aspects of events, such as a style of music, the venue, wine and gourmet food) draw consumers to an event
3. *intrinsic motives* for leisure — a theory related to 'push' and 'pull' motives that consumers seek change from routine (escape) and intrinsic personal and interpersonal rewards from visiting/travelling to other environments. Examples of these rewards might be the increased sense of endurance and friendships formed during a historic horse-riding event (as described by Mannell and Iso-Ahola 1987).

A set of common motives (defined as the strength of the drive to satisfy the identified need) for attending festivals has been cited in a wide range of studies (see, for example, Backman et al. 1995; Crompton and McKay 1997; Uysal, Gahan and Martin 1993). A summary of motives for festival attendance that consistently emerge are:

- *socialisation or external interaction* — meeting new people, being with friends and socialising in a known group
- *family togetherness* — seeking the opportunity to be with friends and relatives and doing things together to create greater family cohesion
- *escape from everyday life, as well as recovering equilibrium* — getting away from the usual demands of life, having a change from daily routine and recovering from life's stresses
- *learning about or exploring other cultures* — gaining knowledge about different cultural practices and celebrations
- *excitement/thrills* — doing something because it is stimulating and exciting
- *event novelty/ability to regress* — experiencing new and different things and/or attending a festival that is unique.

This list tends to reflect Axelsen and Arcodia's (2004) three theories of event motives. These motives have been found in most festival studies and also among visitors to events and exhibitions. Both special event and gallery visitors during the Asia–Pacific Triennial Art Exhibition (staged at the Queensland Art Gallery every three years), for example, seek social interaction, novelty and relaxation through their attendance (Axelsen and Arcodia 2004). The order of importance given to different attendance motives appears to vary according to the type of festival or event. Visitors to a specialised festival, such as a hot air balloon festival, have been shown to be highly motivated by a desire to socialise with people sharing the same interest (Mohr et al. 1993), while people attending a community festival have been shown to be motivated by 'escape' from day-to-day life (Uysal, Gahan and Martin 1993).

Evaluating alternatives and making event choices

It is fair to assume that consumers rarely weigh up whether they will attend more than one or two events on a given day. Instead, they are likely to choose between an event/festival or the cinema; a private party or an entirely different leisure activity. For everyday products and services, evaluative criteria are often *price*, *brand image* and the *contents* of the market offer.

Events offering a leisure experience that consumers have not previously attended are quite hard to evaluate, and they experience some uncertainty due to the financial, social, psychological, sensory, performance and time-related risks involved (Lovelock, Patterson and Walker 2004). Even if a festival has free entry, there are travel costs, childcare and other costs involved. Socially, consumers may think about the types of people they will encounter at an event, and the psychological costs and benefits of those encounters. They also evaluate the time that it will take to attend the event, and sensory risks such as their ability to see the stage or hear the music with clarity. The choice of whether to attend sports events can be linked to the stadium atmosphere, layout and facilities, and the fans of the other team, rather than team performance.

Any number of values may be applied in making different event consumption choices. Functional values, such as perception of an event's price–quality relationship and ease of access, may dominate. Alternatively, emotional values may be more influential (the likely effects of a festival experience on mood). Other conditional values for a festival may be whether there is convenient transport, acceptable food and beverage or nearby suitable accommodation.

Post-event evaluation

Once consumers have attended an event, they generally start to compare what they expected with what they experienced. Consumer expectations arise from a combination of marketing communications (promotional activities) of the event or festival organiser, word of mouth from friends and family, previous experience with this or similar events, and the event's brand image. The exercise of comparing consumer's expectations with actual experiences of services is now commonplace. However, even when markets are tightly segmented into a group of people with a common characteristic, members of the same group can have different perceptions of the benefits they receive. Two close friends may attend Byron Bay's Splendour in the Grass event: one may rate all of the event services very highly, yet the other may not be as enthusiastic, despite having experienced the same service. The relationship between event goers' satisfaction, their perceptions of service quality and their intentions to revisit is very important to marketers who want to build a loyal visitor market.

Event satisfaction, service quality, repeat visits

Because leisure services are intangible, inseparable, variable and perishable, defining and maintaining service quality is difficult, as is identifying and recovering from services failures. From the viewpoint of a festival or event consumer, quality service occurs when expectations of the event match perceptions of the service experienced. Understanding perceived service quality is thus a primary goal of marketers. Both existing and potential attendees can have a perception of event quality (formed from experience of the event, word of mouth and/or other marketing communication). However, perceptions of the event itself are based on the *technical* (performance outcomes) and *functional* (process related) qualities of the experience (Gronroos 1990). Other external factors — for example, wet weather and personal factors such as an argument with a partner during the event — also affect consumer perceptions.

Because it is harder to evaluate 'technical' quality (such as the musical performance at the festival, or the performance of a sporting team), much of the focus in measuring perceived service quality is on functional aspects, or ways in which service is delivered. For this reason, the five main dimensions of service quality in the commonly used SERVQUAL questionnaire (Parasuraman, Zeithaml and Berry 1988) mostly reflect functional service aspects:

1. *assurance* — staff and/or volunteers give the appearance of being knowledgeable, helpful and courteous, and event consumers are assured of their wellbeing
2. *empathy* — the event staff and/or volunteers seem to understand the consumers' needs and deliver caring attention
3. *responsiveness* — the staff and volunteers are responsive to the needs of the consumer
4. *reliability* — everything happens at the event in the way the marketing communication has promised
5. *tangibles* — the physical appearance of the event equipment, artists' costume/presentation and the physical setting meet visitor expectations.

Using these five dimensions, the SERVQUAL questionnaire measures the difference between visitor expectations and perceptions of a festival or event. When the visitors' perceptions of their event experience match or exceed their expectations, a quality experience has been delivered, and the outcome is satisfied attendees who could decide to go to the event next time it is held.

Event satisfaction is related to perceived service quality, but it is experience dependent. Satisfaction can be measured only among existing visitors to the event. Because the event experience is heterogeneous, not every customer will be satisfied all the time. To maintain a competitive position, however, the event marketer should aim to achieve more than a basic level of satisfaction. A sense of delight or extreme satisfaction among event visitors is the ideal outcome (Lovelock, Patterson and Walker 2004). To this end, one objective in an event's strategic marketing should involve visitor satisfaction — for example, '95 per cent of event participants will give a satisfied or higher rating of the event'. Figure 9.6 shows how consumer dissatisfaction can occur based on some perceived gap in festival or event quality.

FIGURE 9.6 Quality – the fit between customer expectations and perceptions

Source: Morgan 1996, p. 159.

Given the difficulty in understanding consumer expectations (with there being no clear set of expectations for each service setting), it is often argued that a 'perceptions only' measure of satisfaction (one that excludes expectations) is more useful. For festivals, various writers suggest consumer 'perceptions' are better indicators of the link between quality, visitor satisfaction and intentions to revisit (see, for example, Baker and Crompton 2000; Thrane 2002). Because musical performance has been highlighted as an important determinant of quality at a music festival (Saleh and Ryan, 1993; Thrane 2002), the use of the SERVQUAL approach alone is probably not the marketer's best approach to research. Thrane (2002), however, also notes that aspects of quality measured by SERVQUAL do contribute to jazz festival patrons' satisfaction and intentions to revisit. A research instrument that adequately investigates both festival 'performance' and 'process' should be considered, therefore, in evaluating festival and event marketing strategies.

Table 9.1 summarises the mental process that potential event attendees go through when deciding to attend an event and the aspects determining their satisfaction with the experience, and then provides the resulting marketing strategic decisions that need to be made. These steps are discussed in depth in the next section.

TABLE 9.1 Event consumer decision-making process and the implications for marketing planning

Stage in the decision-making process	Implications for marketing strategies	Marketing decisions
Recognition of the need, such as novelty, social interaction, excitement	Selection of appropriate target market segments — marketer must know what needs can be satisfied	Target market — mass or focused
Search for information	Marketing communications options	Internet, direct email, paid advertising, publicity, posters
Evaluation of alternatives	Event product, promotional messages — does the event product satisfy the needs of the target market?	Product development? Promotion messages?
Choice of place of purchase	Ease of purchase	Internet, ticketing agency, at venue, post office mail, email
Evaluation of leisure experience	Service quality standards	Measurement of consumer satisfaction — how experience will be rigorously evaluated

STEPS IN THE MARKETING PLANNING PROCESS

Marketing planning involves distinct steps that event managers must understand to create a successful marketing plan. These steps include segmenting the market, targeting and positioning, setting measurable marketing objectives, choosing generic marketing strategies, and designing an effective marketing mix.

Segmenting and targeting the event market

Most events do not appeal to everybody, so it is essential to identify those consumer segments whose needs most closely match the event experience. The market segments chosen should be:

- *measurable* — that is, the characteristics of the segment (socioeconomic status, gender, age and so on) must be accessible to the event marketer
- *substantial enough in size* to be worth targeting
- *accessible* by normal marketing communication channels
- *actionable* by the event organiser, given the marketing budget and other resources (Morgan 1996).

The segmentation process uses the concept of the buyer decision-making process as a guide. The Sydney Festival, for example, has an extensive product range, categorised into music, dance, visual arts, family, theatre and cinema, free outdoor activity and opera/musical theatre. Each of these categories has different offerings, appealing to the buyer behaviour of different submarkets. The visual arts category alone features about 12 different offerings. By thinking about the potential visitors to the visual arts exhibits, the festival organisers can develop a mental snapshot of the overall target market for the visual arts category and events within it. Actual segmentation of the markets could be based on geography, demography (including the visitors' life cycle phase) and/or behaviour (lifestyles, benefits sought and attendance profile — that is, first-timers or repeat visitors).

Geographic segmentation based on the place of residence of event visitors is a commonly used method. Many community festivals are dominated by local visitors or day-trippers from the immediate state or region. For example, the McLaren Vale Sea and Vine Festival in South Australia drew 91 per cent of its audience from South Australia in 2006, with only small proportions from interstate (8 per cent) and overseas (1 per cent). For this reason, managers of community festivals often decide to focus on local residents as their major geographic segment. A key determinant of geographic segmentation is the potential 'drawing power' of the event as a tourist attraction. An event such as a capital city agricultural show (for example, the Ekka in Brisbane or the Royal Easter Show in Sydney) has drawing power for a state-wide geographic market, but only a minor interstate market. Although many event organisers have visions of creating tourist demand, few events develop the brand equity and 'pull' characteristics to succeed as independent tourist attractions. Many more events could succeed in attracting tourists if organisers improved their skills in packaging and marketing the event alongside other regional tourist experiences. If an event demonstrates its ability to attract geographically dispersed markets — for example, Melbourne's Australian Football League's Grand Final — then the potential geographic spread could be:

- local residents of the Melbourne metropolitan area
- day visitors from outside the metropolitan area
- intrastate domestic tourists
- interstate domestic tourists
- international inbound tourists.

However, it is a rare event that can attract such widely dispersed market segments. Major international sports events such as the Olympic Games or a FIFA World Cup are probably the only events that have such a widespread pulling power.

Demographic segmentation relies on the characteristics of people, such as age, gender, occupation, income, education and cultural group. The lifecycle phase of visitors is a further means of demographic segmentation, as is a socioeconomic scale based on occupation (usually of the major income generator in family units). Table 9.2 details this scale in an event context.

TABLE 9.2 A classification of socioeconomic market segments for events

Group	Socio-economic group	Occupational examples	Types of event group likely to attend	Approximate share of population (%)
A	Upper middle class	Higher managerial or administrative, professional: lawyers, doctors, dentists, captains of industry, senior public servants, senior military officers, professors	Cultural events such as fundraisers for the opera, classical music festivals	2
B	Middle class	Intermediate managerial, administrative or professional: university lecturers, head teachers, pharmacists, middle managers, journalists, architects	Cultural events (but purchasing cheaper seats), food and beverage festivals, historical festivals, arts and crafts festivals, community festivals	15
C	Lower middle class	Supervisory, clerical, junior managerial or administrative: clerks, sales representatives, nurses, teachers, shop managers	Most popular cultural events, some sports events, community festivals	20
D	Skilled working class	Skilled blue collar workers: builders, fitters, waterside workers, police constables, self-employed tradespersons	Motor vehicle festivals, sports events, community festivals	20
E	Working class	Semiskilled and unskilled workers: builder's labourers, factory workers, cleaners, delivery drivers	Some sports festivals, ethnic festivals	30
F	Social security	Those at the lowest level of subsistence: pensioners, casual and part-time workers	Very little, except occasionally free community events	13

Source: Adapted from Thompson and Hickey 2005.

Media buyers in advertising agencies first used these classifications because they tend to be quite good predictors of reading and viewing habits. In general, As and Bs read broadsheet newspapers such as the *Australian*, the *Sydney Morning Herald* and the *Age* in Melbourne, whereas Cs, Ds and Es read the tabloid press, such as Sydney's *Daily*

Telegraph and Melbourne's *Herald Sun*. However, these classifications are not always an accurate guide to income, because many Cs earn considerable incomes. The essential difference between As, Bs, Cs and the other categories is in the level of education. For directors of festivals and events that include cultural elements, their target market is usually an educated one (usually university graduates).

Other demographic variables are gender and age. The baby boomers, born between 1946 and 1960, are the largest and most affluent of the age demographics. Many are in the empty nester part of the family life cycle and most have reduced their mortgage repayments to negligible amounts. They therefore usually have considerable disposable income to spend on leisure experiences. Generation X, born between 1961 and 1980, is a growing market segment, among which food and wine festivals have become a popular leisure experience (with women marginally outnumbering men). Targeting the media-savvy, Generation X market, which is not at all homogeneous (singles, couples with and without children), requires a different approach. Depending on the event, several different generations may be targeted, with event program elements designed to cater for each age segment. Generation Y, born after 1981, is naturally the target market for most popular music and adventure events.

Marketers sometimes employ a combination of age and lifestyle segmentation. 'Full nesters' are the target market for events that feature entertainment for both children and adults, whereas 'AB empty nesters' are the perfect market for cultural festivals featuring quality food and drink, and arias from well-loved operas. However, care should be taken not to resort to age stereotypes. Many baby boomers are fit, active and interested in all types of culture (popular and contemporary, as well as high-culture festivals such as classical music or theatre). It could be argued that the most successful community festivals are those that are as inclusive as possible, rather than focusing on just one age group, but, of course, most baby boomers would feel positively ill at ease at a hip hop concert.

Psychographic segmentation, or dividing a market according to its lifestyle and values, is another useful marketing planning technique. The Roy Morgan Research Centre's research of Australian values and lifestyles has segmented consumers based on shared values and attitudes — for example, visible achievers, those who are socially aware and young optimists (Stanton, Miller and Layton 1994). However, like personality segmentation, psychographic market segmentation has serious limitations for an event marketer. It is difficult to accurately measure the size of lifestyle segments in a quantitative manner, which breaks one of the cardinal rules for market segmentation — that segments must be measurable in order to judge if it is worthwhile to target that segment. Nevertheless, this type of segmentation offers a better understanding of the types of experience that different 'lifestyle' groups seek from their leisure experience. For example, the 'surfer' lifestyle segment is attracted to events sharing their ethos and perspective on life. Any special event sponsored by Quicksilver is sure to be designed to appeal to this lifestyle segment.

Positioning the event

How to position an event in the mindset of the market is an important strategic decision. Positioning describes how target market segments perceive the company's offer in relation to competing brands (Pride 2006, p. 130). Event positioning can be achieved in at least nine different ways:

1. *the existing reputation or image of the event* — for example, the Olympic Games and other longstanding events such as a football world cup
2. *the charisma of a director or leader* — for example, the Sydney Festival's director, currently Lindy Hume, part of whose role is to generate positive publicity about the event to position the event in the perceptions of its consumers

3. *a focus on event programming* — for example, Ten Days on the Island in Tasmania, which is a festival programmed and positioned around the 'island' concept, where the artists originate from islands such as Iceland
4. *a focus on performers* — for example, major sports (such as football and golf) and theatre that highlight the players/performers (such as the 2009 Australian Masters golf tournament that featured Tiger Woods, and consequently drew much larger spectator numbers and television audiences)
5. *an emphasis on location or venue and its facilities* — for example, Wimbledon, which is now synonymous with world-standard tennis, or the Melbourne Cricket Ground (MCG), synonymous with Australian sport
6. *event users* — for example, Australian Rules Football fans attending the grand final at the MCG
7. *price or quality* — for example, a free civic concert series such as those that are part of the Sydney Festival's concerts in the park series, versus an operatic performance by the world's three best tenors
8. *the purpose or application of the event* — for example, Mercedes Australian Fashion Week, which is positioned by its showcasing the best of Australian fashion design, both in Sydney and Melbourne, while at the same time introducing the work of new designers to potential buyers. It positions itself as an industry-only event, made accessible to buyers, the fashion media and other fashion industry representatives
9. *the event category or 'product' class* — for example, fashion events, food and wine festivals, and concerts.

Once decisions have been made about the event's segmentation, targeting and positioning, a platform is available to decide on event marketing objectives, strategies and tactics.

Developing event marketing objectives

Any successful development of a marketing plan is based on sound marketing objectives. Cravens, Merrilees and Walker (2000, p. 272) make this important point: 'For marketing to be a beneficial business discipline, its expected results must be defined and measurable'. Masterman and Wood (2006) take the view that objectives are the keystone of the marketing plan as they set the boundaries and direction for the plan and are necessary to communicate the plan to others. Event marketing objectives can be profit oriented where the objective of the event is to maximise the return on investment in the event. Alternatively, an event marketer may want to use market-oriented objectives such as increasing market share of the leisure/festival market or to increase the geographic scope of attendees. Other types of event marketing objectives are to attract more participants, to improve the consumer satisfaction rating, to decrease the number of complaints from stakeholders or to increase revenues from food and beverage sales. What is essential is the marketing objective is measurable. That is, the achievement, or otherwise, of the objective can be empirically measured (Strauss et al. 2003). Hypothetical examples of marketing objectives for an event, such as the Perth International Arts Festival, might be to:

- increase box office receipts in 2011 by 10 per cent (market share growth objective)
- increase the number of acts by 10 per cent (event growth objective)
- increase the percentage of seats sold in all ticketed events to 80 per cent in 2011 (efficiency objective)
- retain 90 per cent of sponsors for 2011 (effectiveness objective)
- increase publicity generated in print and electronic media by a further 10 per cent for 2011 (efficiency objective).

It is important to stress again how marketing objectives, like all objectives, must be measurable and not expressed in vague terms that make measurement impossible. While many managers are tempted to state general aims rather than set objectives (making it harder to be accountable for whether event objectives have been achieved), this temptation must be resisted. Clearly defined and measurable objectives give the marketer the *ends*, while strategies and their supporting tactics are the *means* to those ends.

The dimensions of the marketing objective have an impact on the choice of marketing strategies. Consider the hypothetical objective for the Perth International Arts Festival of increasing box office receipts by 10 per cent in 2011. This increase is a substantial amount, much higher than the inflation rate, which implies that a business objective of the festival is to grow substantially each year to satisfy the entertainment and cultural demands of a more diverse audience base. The objective and the strategies to achieve it are chosen, therefore, only after careful analysis of the market needs, organisational capabilities and opportunities.

Choosing generic marketing strategies and tactics for events

Before events marketers begin the more precise task of deciding on marketing elements such as the program, the ticket price and other variables, they should reflect on their overall strategies for the event's future. Is there a plan to grow or expand the event and/or its markets? Or is there a plan to consolidate the current program and further penetrate existing markets? Any number of strategic options are available to the event/festival, depending on its resources, its competition and its objectives. (Chapter 4 explains a range of these strategies.)

Porter's (1998) application of generic strategies and the potential use of strategies of growth, integration and diversification are useful here as they affect events marketing. First, Porter (1998) suggests most organisations have a choice of *differentiation*, *focus* or *cost leadership* strategies For the event marketer, decisions on these strategies are based on whether the aim is for the event to hold a leadership position in a region or city's leisure market or to have a narrower, yet well-defined market scope. The Brisbane Festival appears to have established a leadership position, with brand equity in diverse market segments and some economies of scale and efficiency in its management (including its branding and communication strategies). In contrast, the Australian Gospel Music Festival draws a more specialised audience with a focus strategy, servicing a particular segment — that is, Christian music lovers — with a high-quality performance. A differentiation strategy means creating something that is perceived to be quite unique across the event/festival sector. Salient examples of events that employ this strategy are the Birdsville Races, which differentiates itself by its location as probably Queensland's most isolated race meeting, and Sydney's Sculpture by the Sea festival, which differentiates itself from other art festivals by its venue — the walk between two neighbouring Sydney beaches, Bondi and Tamarama.

Other marketing strategy options arise from the overall event strategies of intensive *growth*, *integration* and *diversification*. Perhaps the most commonly cited tool in deciding on growth strategies is the product–market matrix (Ansoff 1957, cited in Kotler, Bowen and Makens 1999) shown in figure 9.7.

An event that has a well-designed program, but is not yet drawing large numbers, could consider a market penetration strategy — that is, concentrating on attracting more people from the same target market. If organisers consider that the event could reach a different target market without changing its program, a market development strategy could be used. Finally, if consumer satisfaction studies show the event is not satisfying its current visitor needs, new and different program elements could be needed.

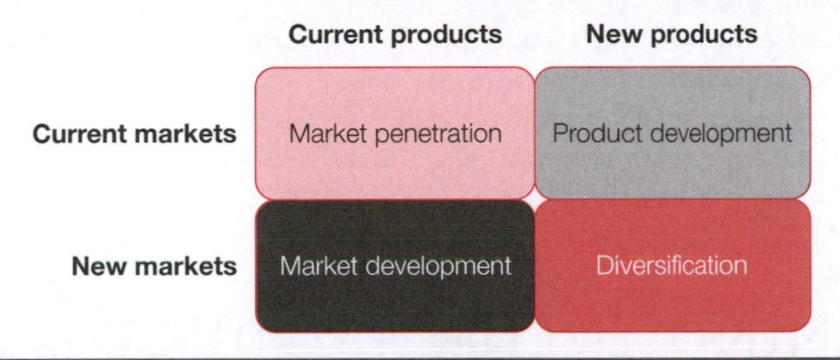

FIGURE 9.7 Ansoff's product–market matrix

Source: Ansoff 1957.

The Sydney Festival's introduction of a range of activities in Parramatta, a western suburb of Sydney, is an example of market development, in that it took the existing product of a cultural festival to a new market in Western Sydney. Another example of market development is its series of free family concerts in a park at Darling Harbour that introduces children to the wonderful world of serious music. A successful example of product development is its *Movies in the Overflow* program, which uses a Sydney Olympic Park venue to show free movies, sponsored by Channel 9.

Integration strategies also present marketing opportunities for events. An event producer may decide to formally integrate with a venue provider (a festival that goes under the wing of a cultural centre) or integrate with other events or festivals. More commonly, a festival may tour to other parts of Australia international acts, thereby reducing the overhead costs of the acts. It has been suggested that integration strategies have become more common in recent years among those events unable to cover excessive public liability fees. However, integration is also an opportunistic strategy: finding an event that complements the existing program and bringing new partnerships to a larger festival can be very attractive.

Diversification strategies can lead the marketer to add new events or support services to its stable of entertainment, or go into complementary businesses. A festival may develop an innovative range of merchandise for its existing market or it may market its software for visitor relationship management to other festivals. Such strategic options represent an important framework for deciding on the event's marketing mix, which is discussed next. This set of alternative strategies gives the event marketer a structure in which to think clearly about how to achieve the event's objectives, and the most effective means to do this

Selecting the event's 'services marketing' mix

Variations on the marketing mix have been made since the original four Ps of marketing were proposed by Professor Eugene McCarthy in 1960. This chapter uses an adaptation of Getz's (1997) event marketing mix to present ten closely related components of event marketing. While each element is of considerable strategic and planning importance, it is relatively easy to group them, as shown as follows:

- the event *product experience* (the core service), its *programming* (different event components, their quality or style) and its *packaging* (a mix of opportunities within the event or marketing of the event with other external attractions, accommodation and transport to the event)

- the *place* (location(s) where the event is held and how its tickets are distributed), its *physical setting* (the venue layout relative to consumer needs) and on-site event *processes* (queuing and so on)
- *people* (cast, audience, hosts and guests) and *partnerships* (stakeholders such as sponsors and media)
- *price*, or the exchange of value to experience the event
- *promotion* or *integrated marketing communication* (media and messages employed to build relationships with the event markets and audiences) (Getz 1997), which is discussed in some depth in the next chapter.

PLANNING EVENT 'PRODUCT' EXPERIENCES

Festivals and events, as service product experiences, contain three elements (Lovelock, Patterson and Walker 2004):

1. the *core* service and benefits that the customer experiences — for example, a performing arts or sports event
2. the *tangible 'expected'* product — for example, the venue and seating, pricing, essential services and access, food and beverages
3. the *augmented* product or additional features that differentiate an event from its competitors — for example, the quality of the artists or performers, service quality, the type of visitors, different modes of transport, and event merchandise available for sale to the event consumer.

As suggested earlier, an important characteristic of the marketing of leisure services is that people are also part of the product. In other words, much of the visitors' satisfaction comes from their interactions with other people attending the event. This means event marketers need to ensure (1) visitor segments within their audience are compatible and (2) there is an ease of interaction among people on-site that is facilitated by the event's elements.

Developing the event

The 'product' of an event is the set of intangible leisure experiences and tangible goods designed to satisfy the needs of the event market. The development of an event or festival can be easily modelled on the processes used to plan, create and deliver services as shown in figure 9.8.

The product life cycle concept suggests most events travel through the stages of introduction, growth and maturity to eventual decline or rejuvenation in a new form. Although there is no predictable pattern of life cycle transition for most products and services, many examples of events can be found that appear to have experienced all life cycle phases. Attendance at Australia Day festivals, for example, has waxed and waned as the 'product' has been changed (or rejuvenated) to reflect changing community needs. Once, only hundreds attended the celebrations staged for this day; now, with a rejuvenation of the Australia Day celebration 'product', attendances are again healthy. To avoid a decline stage, event managers need to closely monitor public acceptance of the content of their event product, to ensure it is still congruent with the leisure and emotional needs of contemporary society.

The creation of new service experiences usually ranges from major service innovations through to simple changes in the style of service delivery (Lovelock, Patterson and Walker 2004). These are evident in the special event and festival sector.

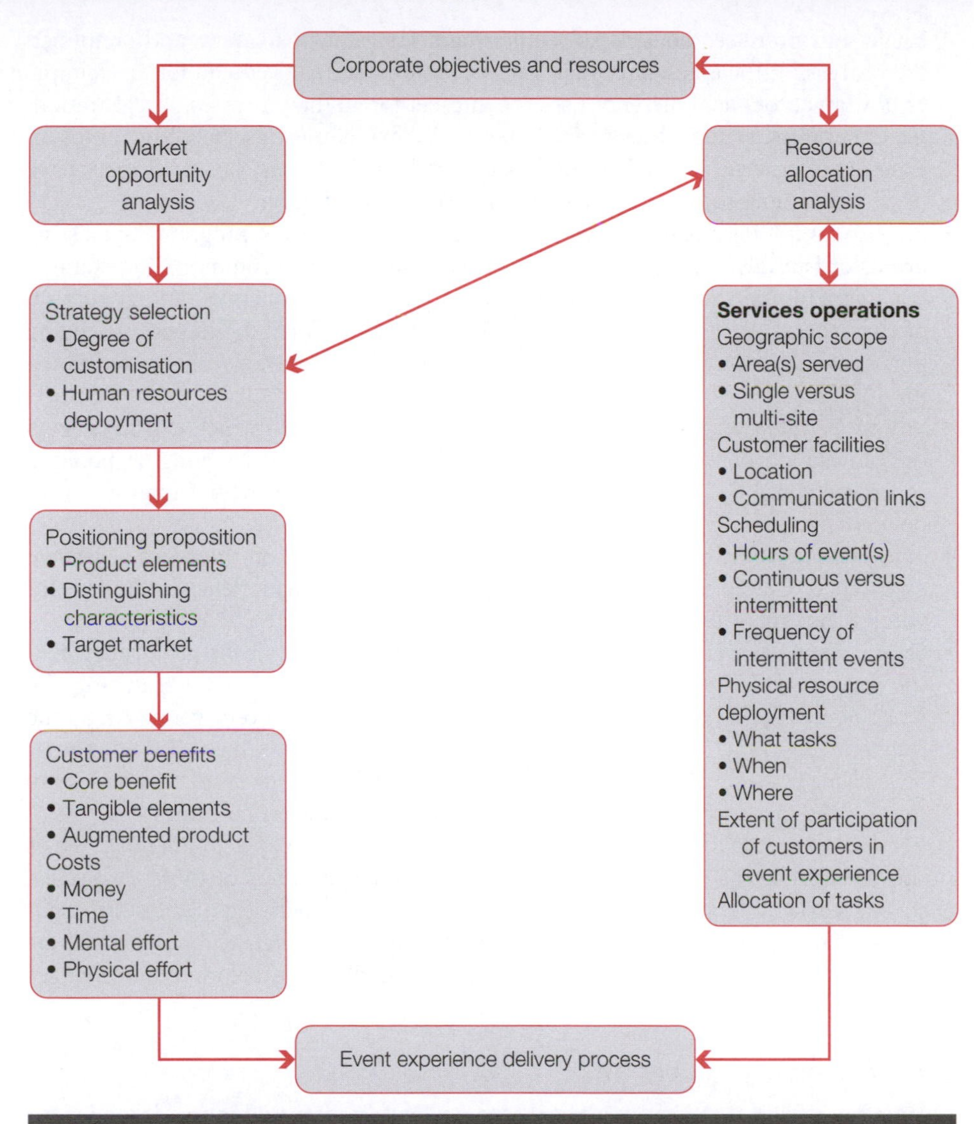

FIGURE 9.8 The process of creating an event 'product'

Source: Adapted from Lovelock et al. 2007, p. 184.

- *Major event innovations* — producing new events or festivals for previously undefined markets. Extreme sports events may represent one such innovation that emerged in the 1990s. In the first decade of the 21st century major sports events captured the imagination of the Australian people with the success of the 2000 Olympics, the Rugby World Cup in 2003 the Melbourne Commonwealth Games of 2006, and there is now talk among Australian premiers of bidding to host the Football World Cup in 2018 or 2022. However, major event innovations are extremely hard to identify in an already crowded and innovative events sector, in which a wide variety of events serve existing, rather than new, leisure segments.
- *Major process innovations* — use of new processes to deliver events in new ways with added consumer benefits. The internet has played a central role in innovating event marketing — for example, tickets for virtually all events can now be purchased online. More significantly, the use of the internet for promotion and distribution of

events has produced considerable efficiencies for event marketers, and simplified the process for the event consumer. See www.cauthe2007.uts.edu.au for an example of how an academic conference uses the internet for all the processes of registration, paper submission and paper reviewing, or www.manlymusicalsociety.com.au for an example of how an amateur musical society such as the Manly Musical Society have used their online presence to facilitate their ticket distribution.

- *Product (event) line extensions* — additions to the current event programs of existing events or festivals. This form of product development is very common. For example State agricultural shows invariably offer each year new products on an agricultural or rural theme. In 2010 the Sydney Royal Easter show offered the racing and diving pigs show, and Noddy the world's tallest horse — all extensions of the traditional product range.
- *Process (event delivery) extensions* — adjustments to the way in which existing events or festivals are delivered. The use of internet ticketing agencies and the booking of festival space by food and beverage vendors, for example, have enhanced event delivery processes.
- *Supplementary service innovations* — extra services that build on the event or festival experience. Examples are on-site childcare facilities, automatic teller machines and wireless hot spots at event sites or conference venues.
- *Service improvements* — modest changes that improve the event performance or the way in which it is delivered. Examples are a fashion festival featuring the work of a wider array of designers, and easier access to the event venue by public transport.
- *Style changes* — simple forms of product development for an event. Examples are improved seating arrangements, a new festival logo and better costumes.

For any event, the decision to undertake any of the 'product' development strategies proposed must be based on market research. Although it is not possible to pre-test events as market offerings, new concepts or style changes (such as a new festival logo) are readily tested in the target market using qualitative research techniques such as focus groups. Some form of event concept testing is desirable before major changes are made.

Programming the event

A critical aspect of the event product that is not widely discussed is the development of an attractive event program. For event managers, it is important to have an event portfolio that reflects (1) the mission, (2) the desired level of quality that satisfies artistic and market criteria, and (3) the revenue or profit objectives of event managers. The nature and range of market segments, and the ability to create thematic links between program elements are further considerations. Often, organisers need to balance the personal or artistic vision of event directors with the realities of market success criteria and the costs involved. The event program may also reflect media broadcasting requirements, the availability of desired performers or players, and the practicalities of staging the event concept. In addition, the event manager must consider the programming of competing events, the event's life cycle phase (for example, more mature events may require some innovative programming to survive) and the duration of the event.

An admirable example of event programming is the Tasmanian Ten Days on the Island festival created by Australian artistic director Robyn Archer. This festival gained its thematic cohesion by capitalising on Tasmania's island status and linking each event to an island theme — Iceland, Shetland, Newfoundland, Guernsey, Denmark,

Japan, Hawaii, Sherbro Island, East Timor, Reunion Island and Aotearoa/New Zealand (www.tendaysontheisland.org). Reflecting on their event programming experience at a Dublin discussion forum (Theatre Shop Conference 2002), Archer and several other producers pointed to at least four key elements in programming success:

1. *The need for a distinguishing core concept or theme in the program.* What is it that is presented that actually has meaning to the audience? The Stompem Ground event in Broome, Western Australia, celebrates Aboriginal musicians and bands that are out of the mainstream, some of whom are brilliant but unknown. Its program is of great import in providing a platform for new and existing Aboriginal artists.
2. *The need to marry the event program with its physical environment or site.* What kinds of performances will really be spectacular in this setting? What kinds of performers and stage structures (existing and created) will shine in this environment? The Perth International Arts Festival enhanced its 2006 program by staging events that focused on the culture of the local Aboriginal people under the trees in Kings Park, and the Opera of Samson and Delilah under the stars in the Supreme Court Gardens. Of course, Perth has a climate that has virtually no summer rain, thereby removing the risk of using outdoor venues.
3. *The role and operational approach of the artistic director/producer.* The producers are both program gatekeepers (selecting event participants from proposals submitted by performers) and poachers (travelling around to pick the best performers, just as sports clubs send out their talent scouts to sign talented athletes).
4. *Established criteria for program content.* Criteria include the compatibility of performers to a festival's market, the history of this type of performance at other events, and a performance's technical quality. Some producers of bigger festivals have a rule about (1) how many times an overseas act has performed within the country, and (2) a desired ratio of innovation and tradition in their event portfolio.

Programming is both an art and a science. The event manager considers the artistic, entertainment, educational or sport-related criteria that an event should achieve, as well as its marketing criteria. However, as with all successful entertainment, an intangible 'wow' factor also differentiates the truly successful event program.

Packaging the event

Packaging is perhaps an underdeveloped element of the event marketing mix. Avenues for packaging include the opportunity to package different types of entertainment, food and beverage, and merchandise as a single market offer (a service bundle), and the opportunity to package the event with accommodation, transport and other attractions in the nearby region (a holiday package). Some special events fail to exploit packaging opportunities that can be an effective means of better positioning the festival in its current markets and to engage in market development by attracting tourists. In contrast, motor racing events such as the SuperGP and the Clipsal 500 in Adelaide draw interstate and overseas tourists, demonstrating some sophistication with packaging. The ability to package an event goes back to its 'drawing power' discussed earlier. However, in the performing arts and sport, special package deals for existing subscribers or members represent another viable marketing of the package concept. Academic or professional conferences usually package the conference, accommodation, entertainment, and post- and pre-conference tours into one easy-to-book package. However, it is interesting to note that the Sydney Festival has no packages on offer to international or domestic tourists.

PEOPLE AND PARTNERSHIPS

The principles of relationship marketing and management of key stakeholders and consumers now pervade the marketing literature (see, for example, Masterman & Wood 2006). Many festivals and events start their lives on the basis of 'relationships and goodwill' between a dedicated group of people, so it is not unusual to find that successful events have solid partnerships and strong links with loyal supporters (attendees, volunteers, government and corporate representatives). For many festivals and special events, a 'sense of sharing a common vision' often pervades the atmosphere, with a loose alliance between the types of people who produce the event and those who enjoy it. With large-scale events, it is hard to create that same sense of belonging, but strategies dedicated to building relationships with volunteers, sponsors and visitors are common. Partnerships can be critical in attracting the resources to plan, manage and evaluate the event's marketing strategies.

Stakeholders are not just event staff and volunteers and event attendees, but also the wider residential community and providers of public services to the event such as the police service. Community consultation and relationship building should be marketing concerns for an event from its inception. While organisers of the Gold Coast SuperGP worked to overcome negative reactions by local residents, Melbourne's Formula 1 Qantas Australian Grand Prix (formerly Melbourne's Formula One Grand Prix) is an example of an event that retains a longstanding group of protestors campaigning for the restoration of the Albert Park race venue as public parkland. From a brand equity perspective, events need ambassadors internally and externally to fully capitalise on their competitive potential.

All event marketing communications (also known as promotion) should, if possible, foster relationships with its various stakeholders. Table 9.3 shows how to maintain cordial relationships with stakeholders and consumers through various stages of the relationship.

TABLE 9.3 Maintaining cordial relationships with stakeholders and consumers

Relationship stage	Communication objective	Communication emphasis for a large festival
Prospect Pre-relationship	Build awareness, initiate contact	Mass media with direct response Sales promotions
Repeat consumer Long term relationship	Encourage feedback, two-way dialogue	Post purchase follow-up via email
Key stakeholder Habitual relationship	Build trust through regular personalised communication	Direct mail (e)
Supporter Up sell commitment	Encourage and reward commitment	Personal selling Corporate hospitality
Advocate Encourages others	Encourage and reward advocacy	Personal communication Invitations to special events
Partner Exchanges of mutual value (sponsorship)	Regular exchanges allowing for high levels of mutual involvement	Involvement in internal activites of event organisation
Lapsed consumer	Encourage feedback and renewed interest	E-communication to discover why

Source: Adapted from Masterman & Wood 2006.

PRICING

Given the diversity of leisure experiences offered to consumers, price can be a key influence on event demand. Contrasts in pricing strategy exist according to the type of event and its target markets. A mass-market event, such as an agricultural show, must keep its price at a level of affordability for its customers — middle income, middle Australia. On the other hand, a fundraising event for the Sydney Theatre Company can ask a much higher price because its target market is much smaller (AB segments who are company subscribers), with the ability to pay for a high-price, high-quality experience. A high price can also project quality (or 'value for money') to potential consumers and influence their decision to purchase.

While many special events are ticketed, a large number of festivals do not charge an entrance fee, and some simply seek a gold coin donation. However, a 'free' event still presents costs to the consumer such as:

- time costs (opportunity to do other things with that leisure time)
- psychic costs (social and emotional costs of attendance, mental effort to engage in the social interaction required)
- physical costs (the effort to travel to and then consume the leisure experience)
- sensory costs (unpleasant environment and unnecessary loud noise).

The production of a free event usually has costs associated with it and these must be covered by some means other than an admission fee, such as sponsorship of some sort or government funding.

Other key influences on ticket price or entry fees are competing leisure opportunities and perceived value. The concept of 'net value' or the sum of all perceived benefits (gross value) minus the sum of all the perceived costs (monetary and others) is useful for event marketers. The greater the positive difference between perceived benefits and costs, the greater the net value to the consumer.

With special events such as the Sydney Theatre Company fundraiser, potential consumers compare the perceived benefits — dinner, drinks, entertainment, parking, opportunities to socialise, prestige, opportunity to rub shoulders with the rich and famous, and the novelty of an unusual night out — with the perceived costs. These costs could include money, time, the physical effort involved in getting to the venue, psychic costs (related to social interaction) and sensory costs (such as going out on a rainy night). If the organiser has adequately positioned the event and communicated its benefits, the target market is likely to perceive a positive net value and purchase tickets.

In establishing the pricing strategy for an event, an organiser will account for two cost categories:

1. *fixed costs* — those costs that do not vary with the volume of visitors (for example, venue rental, interest charged on loans, lighting and power costs, promotion, the cost of volunteers' uniforms, and artists' fees)
2. *variable costs* — those costs that vary with the number of visitors to the event (for example, the cost of plastic wine glasses at a festival, catering costs at a product launch, and the cost of staff needed to serve attendees). However, the great majority of costs of an event are fixed, which of course leaves the event manager with little wriggle room if things do not go according to the marketing plan.

As well as analysing these costs, the event manager should investigate the price of competing leisure experiences. If a similar leisure experience has a price of $\$x$, the three choices are:

1. match and charge the price $\$x$
2. adopt a cost leadership strategy and charge $\$x - 25$ per cent

3. adopt a differentiation strategy and use a price of $\$x + y$ per cent, and use marketing communications to promote the exceptional value of the event.

Pricing strategies used to achieve event objectives may be revenue oriented, operations oriented or market based. A revenue-oriented strategy is designed to maximise revenue by charging the highest price that the target market will pay. The Sydney Theatre Company's fundraiser is an example of a revenue-oriented pricing strategy. An operations-oriented pricing strategy seeks to balance supply and demand by introducing cheaper prices for times of low demand and higher prices at times of higher demand. Agricultural shows often use an operations-oriented pricing strategy. Finally, a market-oriented strategy uses differential pricing, which may be linked to alternative event packages. A clear link between packaging and pricing exists where a three-day music festival charges one price for those who participate for all three days (the fanatics), a day price to capture the first-timers or 'dabblers', and another price to see the headline act and enjoy a gourmet dinner package.

Key questions that the event marketer must resolve in determining the pricing strategy relate to both pricing levels and methods of payment. Figure 9.9 summarises the decisions to be made by the marketer, along with some of the strategic options available.

FIGURE 9.9 Pricing decisions for events marketers

How much should be charged?
- What costs must be covered?
- How sensitive are customers to different prices?
- What are leisure competitors' prices?
- What levels of discounts to selected target markets are appropriate?
- Should psychological pricing (for example, $10.95 instead of $11) be used?

What should be the basis of pricing?
- Should each element be billed separately?
- Should one admission fee be charged?
- Should consumers be charged for resources consumed?
- Should a single price for a bundled package be charged?

Who shall collect payment?
- The event organisation?
- A ticketing intermediary?
- Direct to event's bank account via a debit/credit card when tickets booked online?

Where should payment be made?
- At the event?
- At a ticketing organisation?
- At the customer's home or office by using the internet or telephone?

When should payment be made?
- When tickets are given out?
- On the day of the event?

How should payment be made?
- Cash — exact change?
- Credit card — via the internet? (now easy to use and very efficient as the consumer does the data entry)
- Credit card via the telephone?

FIGURE 9.9 *(continued)*

- Using PayPal (www.paypal.com.au), which simplifies accepting credit cards online
- Electronic funds transfer at point of sale (EFTPOS)?
- Token donation?

Source: Adapted from Lovelock, Patterson and Walker 2007, p. 258.

EVENT 'PLACE', PHYSICAL SETTING AND PROCESSES

'Place' refers to both the site where the event takes place (the venue) and the place at which consumers can purchase tickets to the event. Other decisions with marketing implications are (1) the design of the event setting, and (2) the processes used to deliver and experience the event.

The choice of a single venue or multiple sites for sports or cultural events should be made in the context of the event's overall strategy — for example, a strategy of market penetration or expansion. Increasingly, event marketers are recognising that market expansion can be achieved by taking their events to new locations. In 2007 Opera in the Vineyards featured some of the world's best opera singers performing in the wine areas of the Mornington Peninsula and the Hunter Valley (www.4di.com.au), an example of an innovative use of 'place' to add to an event's sense of occasion. A community festival such as the Sydney Italian Festival chose Stanley Street, East Sydney, the original Little Italy, as their original venue. This association with the history of Sydney enhanced the event experience of consumers as they learnt how Italian culture had shaped this part of the city, while enjoying the cultural delights of Italy. The festival has now moved to Leichhardt, the suburb in which many Italian migrants lived in during the 1950s and 1960s (www.sydneyitalianfestival.com.au).

The physical setting, as noted in the discussion of programming, is crucial for consumer satisfaction. Most services marketers include it as a key element in the marketing mix, alongside processes of service delivery.

In deciding the most appropriate place(s) for ticket distribution, organisers may question whether to use a ticketing agency. Ticketing agencies widen the distribution network, ease the consumer's purchase process and speed up the entry of customers to a venue. While they also facilitate credit card purchases and telephone bookings, charges are incurred by both the event organiser and the customer, which can be costly to both. The benefits of using a ticket agency depend on the type of event, the availability of other ticket distribution options (such as the box office of a small theatre company and/or direct mail), the willingness of the target market to pay for a ticketing service, and the service's relative affordability.

Selling tickets via a ticketing agency has some advantages for the event producer. Ticket sales can be monitored, and the data collected can guide decisions on the level of marketing communication expenditure needed to attract the targeted visitor numbers. The security problems inherent in accepting cash at the door or gate are also alleviated. Because customers pay in advance, the cash flow to the event producer occurs well before the staging of the event, with obvious financial advantages for the event organiser.

However, the use of the internet as a distribution medium for events is now widespread, with the key advantages of online ticket sales being:

- *speed* — consumers can purchase tickets without leaving their home, queuing or waiting for a phone operator to become available.
- *consumer ease* — consumers can view the different experiences offered by the event or festival in their own time, selecting the events or shows that best suit their pocket and time constraints, and the tickets delivered to their email address, complete with bar code.
- *revenue* — ticket revenue comes from the buyer's credit card, which facilitates security and ease of collection.
- *up-to-date technology* — more and more consumers expect leisure services to be available for purchase on the internet. An online presence is critical in establishing an event or festival brand.
- *cost* — the event only pays a small merchant fee to the credit card company or to PayPal, and the consumer pays no fee at all.
- *distribution* — the tickets are sent as an email to the consumer at practically no cost, but very conveniently for the consumer.

The Melbourne International Comedy Festival, a multi-venue, multi-show festival, is one of many events that employ online ticket distribution using a ticketing agency, Ticketmaster Australia, which also manages the Comedy Festival box office, online and telephone purchase of tickets. Because it is a multi-venue festival, the ability for consumers to print their tickets after online payment is not universal, which means at many venues, including the Melbourne Town Hall, patrons have to collect their tickets at the venue rather than having the convenience of printing them on their printer.

Events and festivals rarely have their own online booking system that can accept bookings and credit card details electronically at no charge to the consumer. However, advances in technology such as PayPal are likely to result in increased efficiencies in online distribution over time. In 2006 the Melbourne Commonwealth Games used an online booking facility from their website, as do many sports events. It is interesting to note, however, that some festivals, such as the Port Fairy Folk Festival, still stick with the old technology of snail mail — even in 2010. Because of its popularity, the Port Fairy Folk Festival requires potential attendees to register by mail, phone or email for a mail-out of tickets. Imagine the efficiencies for all stakeholders if they progressed to a simple e-commerce model such as that used by the Manly Musical Society.

An example of a festival that has recently commenced using its website to distribute its tickets to its consumers is the Woodford Folk Festival (http://woodfordfolkfestival.com). It is also significant that many other aspects of the festival production, such as registering to perform, to sell merchandise, and to become a volunteer, have all migrated to its website.

Another exemplar of e-distribution of event tickets is the Manly Musical Society. It produces two or three shows a year — mainly operetta. It uses an e-commerce website to distribute its tickets and control its inventory that is simple to use use, both for the consumer and the Society (www.manlymusicalsociety.com). The e-commerce system they use is relatively cheap to produce and very efficient, and it is much cheaper than using a ticketing agency or a box office. It also automatically delivers the revenue from the tickets to their bank account; easy, effective and efficient. The Manly Musical Society e-commerce ticketing system is explored in the following event profile.

Apart from ticketing, other operational processes have an immediate impact on the experience of event consumers. Visitors evaluate security checks on entry to the event, queuing for food and beverages, and the speed of access to services such as the car park and toilets. While later chapters address many of these event 'processes', the marketing implications of a smooth integration of 'front stage' and 'backstage' happenings at an event cannot be underestimated. The physical environment and processes that happen in that physical space directly contribute to the event's brand image.

event profile

MANLY MUSICAL SOCIETY

The Manly Musical Society is a recently formed not-for-profit organisation on the Northern Beaches of Sydney. They are a youth-based community group that provides an opportunity for local up and coming talent to perform musical theatre productions for the benefit of the public (www.manlymusicalsociety.com, 2009).

It staged its first production (*The Pirates of Penzance*) in November 2009. After producing a small but informative website, the society decided to incorporate 21st century technology into the site and to use e-commerce to sell tickets to their production at the Star of the Sea Theatre.

Management contracted Seat Advisor Australia, a box office software company based in Victoria, to install an e-commerce system into their website. Their main product SABO (Seat Advisor Box Office) is a box office software and venue management system, which offers the following benefits to event managers and marketers. The system:

- allows venues to keep their ticketing in-house
- is capable of handling 5000 to 10 million tickets per year
- is suitable for sports teams, theatres, cinemas, stadiums, event venues, theme parks, universities, horse racing, universities, casinos and more
- operates at a lower cost with no upfront costs
- offers a complete internet-based ticketing solution including box office, telephone and internet ticket sales, subscriptions, web presence and marketing
- offers a real-time unified inventory across all sales channels
- has colour-coded interactive SeatMaps with the ability for users to select the seat(s) of their choice with a click of the mouse
- allows customers to see their view from seat to centre stage/stadium when buying
- allows sophisticated database management
- includes patron preference tracking for marketing
- facilitates detailed sales and financial reporting.

(Seat Advisor Australia 2009)

The cost to the Manly Musical Society was a very small fee per ticket to SABO and a small credit card fee per booking. Compare this with the cost of maintaining a physical box office or a using a ticketing agency with the attendant problems of cost and managerial time, and consider the advantages to the consumer of no fee, seat selection and tickets delivered by email. It is clear that this system or a similar one will be used by event producers in the twenty-first century as the advantages to both event producer and consumer are marked.

The Manly Musical Society has since moved to a larger theatre — the Glen Street — and now use their in-house box office facilities. Nevertheless, the process offered by SABO is well worth investigating for any event producer looking for an effective and efficient method of ticket distribution.

THE MARKETING PLAN

The final step in the marketing planning process is to put all the thinking as outlined in this chapter into a coherent plan that is the basis for the revenue and marketing expenditure budget. Marketing plans can come in various construction formats, but the simplest and most effective is that proposed by McDonald (2002). It would usually include all the steps and content shown in figure 9.10 and gives guidance to how the marketing of the event is articulated to other stakeholders.

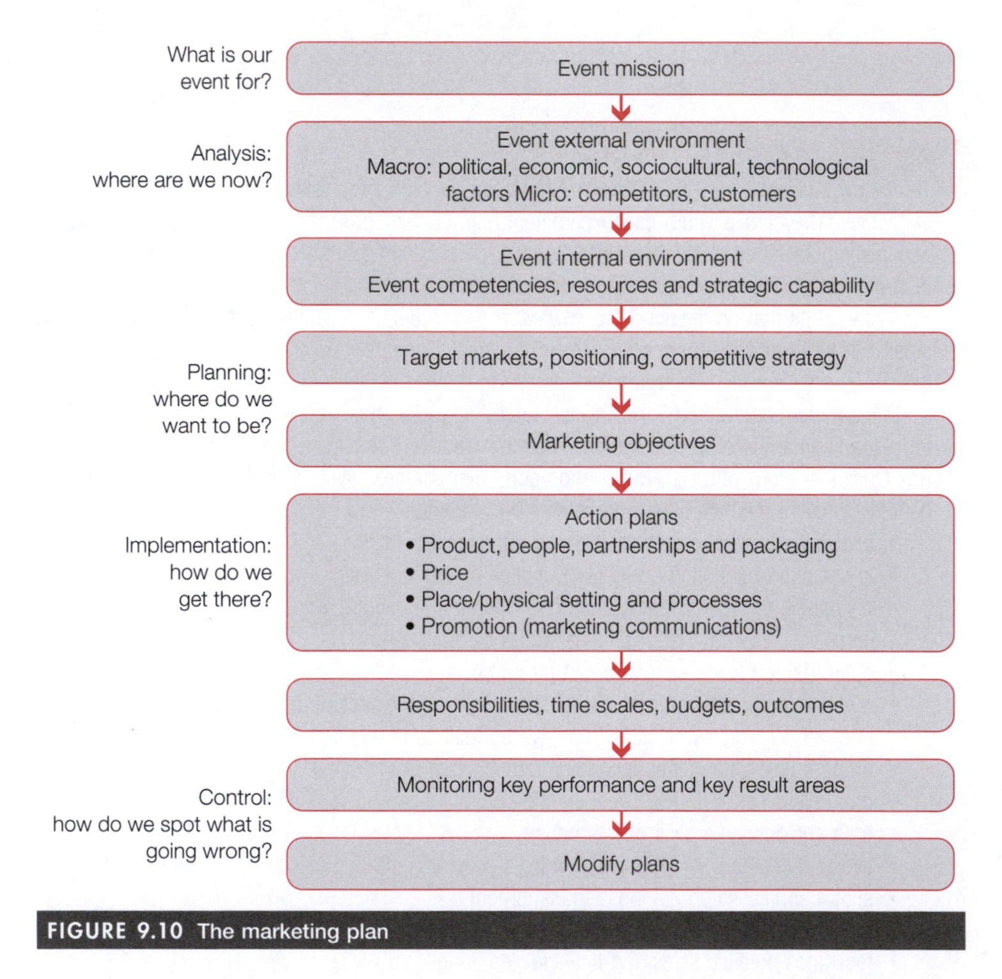

FIGURE 9.10 The marketing plan

The next chapter discusses one of the major aspects of the marketing plan, and one that generally takes most of the budget: the integrated marketing communications (IMC) of the event or the promotion (P). When the marketing plan is constructed, naturally the promotion is included in the plan.

SUMMARY

A common misconception of many in the festival and event area is that marketing means nothing more than 'event promotion'. As this chapter has shown, marketing is a clear, structured and coherent way of thinking about managing an event or festival to achieve objectives related to market/stakeholder awareness, event attendance, satisfaction and either profits or increased understanding of a cause.

The core of event marketing is the focus on existing and potential leisure consumers — in this case, the event attendees. Successful marketing flows from a complete understanding of these consumers — who they are, where they live and the leisure needs they seek to satisfy. This understanding comes from primary and secondary market research and two-way communication with event stakeholders and consumers. From this knowledge, event organisers can develop strategies and tactics that span the event product (including its programming and packaging), its place (venues, the physical setting and ticket outlets), its delivery processes, its people and partnerships, and integrated marketing communication.

QUESTIONS

1. Do you agree with the definition of marketing used in this chapter? How can it be improved?
2. Why should an event manager segment a market? What are the advantages?
3. Outline five key motives for attending a community festival. Why should event managers focus on these motives, rather than the motives of the festival organisers?
4. Identify the key steps in the consumer decision process. Offer examples of how each step affects the event consumer.
5. Given that the Manly Musical Society (see event profile on page 293) does not wish to make enormous profits and their cast and musicians are not paid, what do you think would be a fair price to pay for a ticket to one of their productions, that covers their costs and produces a surplus to fund their next production? Five shows including a matinee would be scheduled.
6. What are the advantages of conducting research into event consumers? Are there any negatives in this process?
7. Give three examples of product development that the Manly Musical Society could effectively undertake.
8. Compare and contrast the distribution tactics of the Port Fairy Folk Festival and the Manly Musical Society. Why do you think the Port Fairy Folk Festival uses these distribution methods? Could they make their distribution more effective and efficient? What would be the obstacles to this?

case study

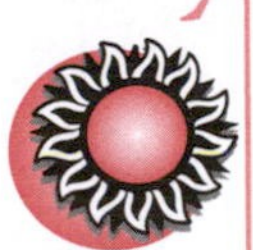

LAN BRAZILIAN FESTA AT THE ME BANK STARLIGHT CINEMA

'Outdoor cinemas are an outstanding summer entertainment experience and are fast becoming a regular social fixture for many moviegoers looking for a unique, relaxed and memorable occasion' (Val Morgan Cinema Network 2010). Open-air cinemas are a marvellous opportunity for people to relax, drink wine and enjoy the beautiful summer night, while watching cinema that interests them.

Starlight Cinema is an outdoor cinema located in North Sydney that has been in operation since 2004. Every summer patrons enjoy cinema on the verdant grass of the heritage North Sydney Oval. The latest film releases are presented on a 16 m × 8 m screen, for an average of 400 attendees per screening. The venue has a maximum capacity in outdoor cinema mode of 1800 attendees.

Starlight Cinema is a viable and proven entertainment concept, which was perfect to extend into a cultural festival. The marketing of the Brazilian Festa at Starlight Cinema is explored in this case study.

Cultural event

Culture is a profound influence on events and festivals, and there is growing interest in cultural events representing multicultural Australia, among the predominant culture of Anglo-Celtic Australians.

The Brazilian community in Sydney

Brazilian immigration to Australia started in 1970. The first Brazilians were relatively unskilled and mainly found employment in labouring and factory work. Around 1990 another wave of immigration from Brazil started, but this time the migrant community was composed mainly of young, educated professionals, who already spoke English and were looking for a better quality of life:

> According to the 2006 census, there were 7490 Brazilians in Australia, and almost half of them (3175) lived in Sydney. Although the census data shows that the community is increasing (in 2001 there were 4713 and in 1996 there were 3359) these numbers underestimate the true number. For instance, according to the Australian Bureau of Statistics, in 2005 there were 7100 Brazilian students in Australia. But even this number should be seen as too low. Australian Education International, a government agency, noted that between July 2004 and July 2006, the number of Brazilians on student visas in Australian programmes grew by 109 per cent. According to AEI, Brazil had the potential to become Australia's largest source of international student enrolments outside Asia during 2007 (Rocha, 2008).

The Brazilian Community is small, but makes a lot of noise in Sydney. There are Brazilian products, several restaurants, capoeira classes (an art form incorporating dance, martial arts and physical fitness) and several music shows.

Establishing and satisfying consumers' needs

The Brazilian Community in Sydney and the Starlight Cinema audiences were surveyed and researched, using both quantitative and qualitative methods, to indentify some of the target market's needs. At the time of the proposed special event, there was no Brazilian film festival or any other film event that showcased Brazilian films, and it was difficult to find screenings of Brazilian films as part of any other film festival in Sydney. Research revealed that the Starlight Cinema audience was looking for special events and different features in the Starlight Cinema program. The findings established that a market existed for a special cultural event and the Brazilian Festa at Starlight Cinema was conceived. The marketing aspects of the event are now described.

Target audience

- Brazilian residents in Sydney
- Brazilian students living in Sydney
- Brazilians who want to remember their culture
- Brazilians who want to showcase their culture to Australian friends
- Australians who appreciate South American culture
- Starlight Cinema audience
- Locals from Sydney's North Shore who appreciate the artistic aspects of other cultures.

Brazilian Festa age group

From the research into the target market it was found that the age demographics were:

- 19–25 years (7 per cent)
- 26–35 years (44 per cent)
- 36–45 years (27 per cent)
- 46–55 years (20 per cent)
- over 55 (2 per cent).

Brazilian Festa event concept — satisfying the market's needs

Brazil is seen around the world as having a culture that likes to party, play music and celebrate. Building on that image, the concept of the event was to create a 'Festa' (Portuguese for party or festival) bringing all the energy of Brazil to the North Sydney Oval, and finishing the event with a one-off screening of a Brazilian film. Starlight Cinema usually opens the doors at 7.00 pm, but, for the Brazilian Festa, the gates opened at 3.00 pm and a program of activities was designed to satisfy the needs of the community, including food stalls and music performances, as well as workshops and activities where consumers could learn about and experience the features of Brazilian culture that most appealed to them. The Festa also gave the Brazilian community an opportunity to satisfy a need to publicly revel in the Brazilian culture that they had left at home.

Positioning the event

Brazilian Festa was positioned in two ways. For the Brazilian community, the focus was on the film, particularly the unique opportunity of a Brazilian film screening in an outdoor cinema. For the Australian consumer, the focus of the event was the Brazilian 'festa' atmosphere and the opportunity to experience aspects of Brazilian culture.

Motivations

Research undertaken after the event showed that the audience was motivated to attend the event primarily by a desire to be entertained by performances, rather than to partake in a 'hands-on experience', followed by a need to learn more about Brazilian culture. This demonstrates that the audience is, first, looking for an escape from their everyday life and to be entertained, and, second, interested in learning about or exploring other cultures, which confirms the motivation theories about cultural events found in the event literature.

Event objectives

As this was the first time the event had been produced, the objectives were not great. The financial objective was to break-even. The marketing objective was to create an awareness of Brazil in the media. This was measured by receiving a half-page article in the *Sydney Morning Herald* and at least two articles in the Sydney Brazilian publication. The audience objective was 50 per cent Brazilians, 50 per cent non-Brazilians. Post-event research showed the audience was composed of 40 per cent Brazilians, 60 per cent and non-Brazilians. All other objectives for the event were achieved.

Challenges of programming a community culture event

One of the challenges of creating a community cultural event for the first time is to present a program that balances the 'pre-images' of a country, which are elements

that non-members of the community expect to experience, with what the various target markets expect of the event. For example, the Brazilian community do not generally want to see another capoeira or samba show, but the non-Brazilian consumers attend the event expecting these elements.

Furthermore, the Brazilian community is divided into residents and students who seek different experiences from an event. Residents attend for the Brazilian culture and students for the party.

The Brazilian Festa programming was created keeping in mind the balance between the two target markets' expectations. One of the surprises of the first Festa was that it attracted families, even though the program was not designed for children. As most of the families pre-booked their tickets, however, the organisers had the time to create suitable activities. This demonstrates just how flexible event marketers and organisers sometimes have to be.

Pricing

The first event experienced pricing and ticket selling problems. As the Brazilian Festa was designed to be a cultural event based on community involvement, management decided to set the same price for online sales and gate sales on the day, with the aim of providing everybody with the same purchasing opportunity. Patrons, therefore, did not have any incentive to buy prior to the event, which resulted in half the tickets being sold on the day. This created uncertainty for the organisers who needed to ensure there was an audience for performers and purchasers for the food outlets. The lesson learnt was to offer an incentive for online, pre-event purchase.

Promotion

Brazilian Festa was part of the Starlight Cinema's promotional plan. However, to achieve the event's objectives, additional targeted promotion was necessary. To reach the Brazilian community, the event was promoted using extensive e-marketing, including Facebook and Orkut. The event was also promoted utilising the event organiser's relationship with the Brazilian community's network and the support of the main Brazilian associations in Sydney, both of which had the distinct advantage of being at no cost.

Results

The first Brazilian Festa at Starlight Cinema was a successful event where all objectives were achieved. The event made a profit and more than 850 people attended the event, which is more than double the average audience at Starlight Cinema.

It was an extraordinary journey for the event producer, made possible by the development of many relationships, including a strong partnership with Starlight Cinema. The success of this partnership opens the way for more special events at Starlight Cinema in the future. Seventy-five per cent of attendees thought the event was good value for money and 82 per cent of the attendees said they would return for a possible event next year.

Case prepared by Flavia Fontes Laranjo, Festa Event Management, Producer Brazilian Festa

Questions

1 What was the marketing strategy used by Brazilian Festa? Why?

2 What other pricing strategy could Brazilian Festa have used?

3 How could network relationships be used to promote the event?

4 What type of qualitative and quantitative market research could the event producers undertake to establish needs and motivations of potential event consumers?

5 Describe how an effective and efficient distribution strategy could be implemented for the Brazilian Festa.

case study

THE GROWTH AND DEVELOPMENT OF THE MIDDLE EAST INTERNATIONAL FILM FESTIVAL, ABU DHABI

Abu Dhabi is one of seven Sheikhdoms (Emirates) of the United Arab Emirates (UAE). According to the 2005 census, Abu Dhabi's population was approximately 825 000 from a UAE population of 4.1 million, where 79.9 per cent of the population is non-national (EIU 2006). The rapid increase in the expatriate population over the past four decades of accelerated economic development helped to serve UAE's modernisation process and develop its tourism industry. Like other Arabian countries of the Gulf region, UAE's rapid economic development since the 1970s is due largely to huge oil reserves and its subsequent exportation, and it has attracted global attention as it was perceived to have adopted a successful strategy for sustained economic growth. Recently the region has tried to diversify its economy away from its oil reserves and has highlighted tourism as one of the key areas of growth. Since the early 1990s the UAEs, and especially Dubai's, tourism growth has been the outcome of a series of planned investments, iconic product developments (for example, Burj Al Arab, Burj Khalifa and Palm Jumeirah) and marketing strategies. Academics interested in the field of tourism have studied Dubai as a strong exemplar of tourism development (Henderson 2006; Sharpley 2008). Abu Dhabi, however, has adopted a different model of tourism development, away from the boosterism and 'bigger is better' philosophy of Dubai. It has tried to focus on more sustained and gradual development with an emphasis on preserving and conserving both the natural and cultural environment. Paul Gudgin, former Edinburgh Fringe festival director, during a recent visit to the region, described how Abu Dhabi is trying to position itself as the 'Cultural Capital of the Gulf.'

Developing Abu Dhabi's festival and event product

Destinations all over the world have realised the importance of festivals and events in driving tourist traffic. In times of increased global competition, economic difficulties and pressure on the tourist dollar, festivals and events can act as a key differentiator and offer added value and a 'reason to visit'. Events are a growing worldwide phenomenon and, in the UAE alone, there is an increasing number and range of festivals and events being delivered. The region has also witnessed exceptional growth in the development and expansion of high-profile events, especially in four key areas: (1) Concerts — for example, Coldplay, Andrea Botticelli and Beyonce, (2) Conferences — for example, GCC Sports Development Conference, Global Travel and Tourism Summit, and the Middle East Oil and Gas Conference,

(3) Festivals and Exhibitions — for example, Arabian Travel Market, Dubai Air Show and WOMAD, and (4) Sport Events — for example, Etihad Formula 1 Grand Prix, Dubai World Cup and Rugby 7s with recent announcements of plans for the region to bid to host the 2020 Olympics. New infrastructure developments such as Dubai Festival City, Abu Dhabi National Exhibition Centre (ADNEC), Yas Island and the proposed Saadiyat Island Cultural District (which will host Abu Dhabi's Guggenhiem and Louvre museums) were partly established to elevate the region's global reputation in creating and delivering 'flagship events'.

Bringing film to the region — the Middle East International Film Festival

The Middle East International Film Festival (MEIFF) was established in October 2007 by the Abu Dhabi Authority for Culture and Heritage (ADACH) and is a critical component of Brand Abu Dhabi. ADACH is the government institution in charge of conserving and promoting the heritage and culture of Abu Dhabi, aspiring to harness the pride of Abu Dhabi's people by developing the Emirate as a capital of art and culture. It aims to commit resources to the preservation of cultural treasures as well as the development of international art, music, literature and cinema. This vision is reflected in MEIFF's mission to:

- celebrate cinema in all its forms by creating a vibrant forum for storytellers from the Middle East and around the world
- affirm the key place Abu Dhabi holds as an emerging cultural centre and to foster the growth of its local film community.

Management structure and operations

The inaugural festival, which only ran for five days, was hosted in the prestigious five-star Emirates Palace Hotel, and, although funded primarily through ADACH, was managed by a local film production company with the majority of the specialised labour, including the festival director, being brought in from other key international film festivals. A key part of the program in the first year was the Abu Dhabi Film Financing Circle (FFC) offering an arena where global financiers, executives and filmmakers could meet and collaborate on film funds and co-productions. The festival also launched the Black Pearl Awards across a range of categories, offering the highest prize money of any film festival, and Variety's highly relevant Middle East Filmmaker of the Year award. Regional talent was also developed through the amalgamation of the Emirates Film Competition with the festival. MEIFF 2007 was successful in introducing the region to uncensored, independent film, forging links with the international film festival community and attempting to develop the local cinematic audience. Key issues, however, were the lack of an online box office system and database and, because of the festival's infancy and short planning cycle, attracting international media, film talent and a local audience.

The second year of the festival witnessed an increase in its length from five days to ten days, delivering a larger program of films and events. The management structure stayed the same although, to attempt to bring a more regional focus, the directorship of the festival was handed over to a local production company. Key innovations for this festival were:

- the introduction of an online booking system.
- The adoption of 'datakal' film database management system

- an increase in the number of venues to use the two multiplex cinemas, conveniently located in shopping malls, with shuttle buses provided from the Emirates Palace
- The inclusion of a 'How to Festival' section in the program to educate people about ticket sales and the festival program
- increased focus on Middle Eastern film in the program
- the introduction of a series of popular cultural initiatives, which attracted international media interest
  - Cinema Verite to celebrate socially conscious cinema, attracting key celebrities such as Jane Fonda and Susan Sarandon
  - Muslims on Screen and Television (MOST) initiative to improve the images of Muslims in Hollywood
- an increase in delegate numbers and ticket sales
- training and development opportunities in the Emirate through the locale of a New York Film Institute campus on site
- outreach activities developed with schools, universities and community groups.

Although the second edition of the festival succeeded in further consolidating Abu Dhabi's vision of becoming a centre for film production and raising awareness of Middle Eastern film, it continued to suffer from low ticket sales and a short lead in time to the festival in terms of planning and organisation.

The third edition of the festival, which came to a close on 17 October 2009, was the first under new executive director Peter Scarlet, fresh from New York's Tribeca Film Festival and a specialist in Middle Eastern film, and marked some significant developments. The move to a more strategically managed festival with its own full-time, permanent staff was a significant one offering more stability for the festival and looking to develop a locally-based and focused staffing structure. Foremost among the changes implemented was the new format of the feature competition sections: one for fiction films and one for documentaries, and half of each comprised of films from the Middle East. As Scarlet noted, 'the filmmakers who served on our juries, the journalists and industry figures who traveled here, and the members of our local audience were unanimous about the strength of our program, especially the strength of the selections of films from this region'. The festival received 1193 submissions from 80 countries, showed 128 films from 49 countries (see table 9.4) and saw attendance at screenings double 2008's numbers, to reach more than 31 000 people.

TABLE 9.4 Comparison — total number of films

Year	Number of films	Countries
2007	80	36
2008	151	36
2009*	128	49

*Middle Eastern films — 45 per cent of the total number of films

Other key innovations included:

- a series of masterclasses looking at the relationship between film and music composition and including musicians such as Richard Horowitz, who composed the score for Bertolucci's 'The Sheltering Sky'

- a series of 'In conversation with ... ' events with Oscar®-nominated actress Naomi Watts, fashion designer Jason Wu and Oscar®-winner A. R. Rahman
- the introduction of the MEIFF Tent, fully equipped with an 85-seat cinema, refreshment and hospitality spaces and private VIP area, which served to act as a focal point for the festival bringing together festival delegates, public, media and celebrities
- a Family Gala Day to support the screening of the festival's key family film — Shorts — and a masterclass aimed at introducing children to the world of filmmaking
- the FFC, which, after being taken out of the festival and moved to another location across the city in 2008, was brought back into the festival and supported by the recently established Abu Dhabi Film Commission
- (as in previous years) the welcoming of major stars from Hollywood, Bollywood and the Middle East, including two-time Oscar®-winner Hilary Swank, Demi Moore, Eva Mendes, Orlando Bloom, Freida Pinto, Zayed Khan, Lara Dutta, Akshay Kumar, Hend Sabry and Sawsan Badr, helping to raise the profile of the festival and increase media interest and awareness.

Again the festival faced a series of challenges, most notably in recruiting and training suitable, experienced staff and volunteers, again dealing with a short festival lead time and a need to level capacity and manage demand, particularly for the gala screenings.

TABLE 9.5 Films at the festival 2007–2009

Type of film	Number of films 2009	Countries 2009	Number of films 2008	Countries 2008	Number of films 2007	Countries 2007
Feature films	72	40	81	32	41	27
Short films	56	29	70	26	39	23
Total	128	49	151	36	80	36

MEIFF Festival Lifecycle

MEIFF provides a good example of how festivals grow and develop along the Festival and Event Product Lifecycle and the challenges that they face.

Beverland, Hoffman and Rasmusssen (2001) have traced the evolution of events in the Australasian wine sector since the 1980s through six stages: (1) conception, (2) launch, (3) growth, (4) consolidation, (5) decline and (6) revival. This model can also be applied to cultural events and festivals. At each stage of development, strategic management and marketing challenges exist that require strategic responses by festival and event managers. For example, during the conception stage, garnering local support and building a strong product is the dominant problem requiring clear aims for festival's to gain support among relevant stakeholders. During the launch stage, developing awareness is the dominant problem and a strong media campaign is critical. Remaining focused, maintaining funding and sponsors, and building recognition of the festival is found to be the dominant problem in the growth stage, requiring a wider range of offerings to retain the interest of loyal customers. Similarly, maintaining the focus on loyal festival visitors is the dominant problem for

festivals that have reached this stage of maturity and gained popular appeal. At this point, a number of festivals begin to reduce their offerings and limit ticket sales in order to maintain a focus.

This model can also be applied to MEIFF, as shown in figure 9.11.

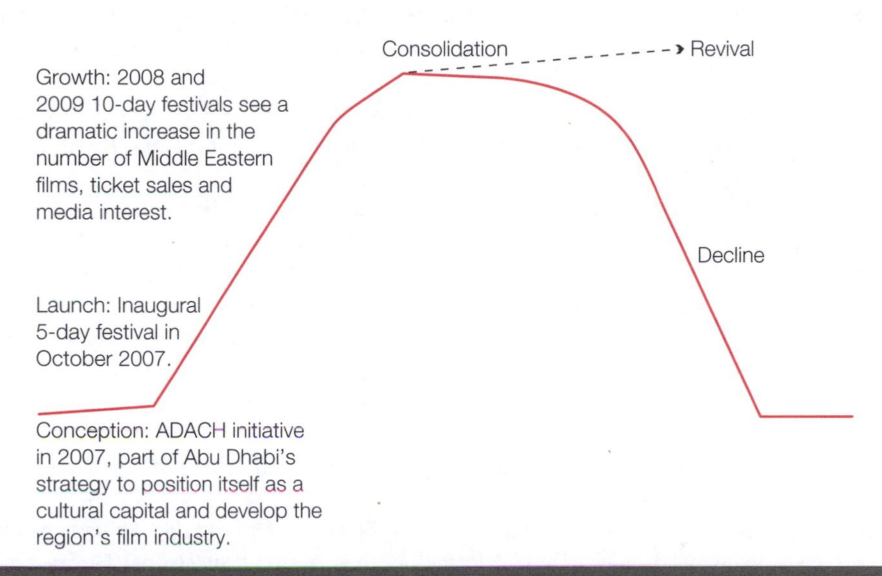

FIGURE 9.11 The Festival and Event Product Life Cycle

Conclusion

The Middle East International Film Festival is an excellent case study illustrating the growth and development of a cultural festival as it progresses through the Festival and Event Life Cycle. Although there is increasing competition in the region with the Dubai International Film Festival and recently established Doha Tribeca Film Festival, the Abu Dhabi festival has worked hard to deliver a unique and authentic product and to build up the necessary infrastructure, media and industry interest, and staffing base to support its future growth.

Prepared by Jane Ali-Knight, Edinburgh Napier University

Acknowledgements to Peter Scarlet, Executive Director, Kellen Quinn, Deputy Director and all the staff at MEIFF for their kind support when putting this case study together.

Questions

1 How does the launch and introduction of the MEIFF differ from standard marketing practice?

2 Given the festival's mission, could the product elements be improved? If so, how and why?

3 The life of the festival is dependent on what? How can the festival manager ensure that this support continues?

4 What is the purpose of the festival tent? Are there other ways of achieving this?

REFERENCES

Ansoff, I 1957, 'Strategies for diversification', *Harvard Business Review*, September–October, pp. 113–24.

Axelsen, M & Arcodia, C 2004, 'Motivations for attending the Asia–Pacific Triennial Art Exhibition', Paper presented at the 14th International Research Conference of the Council for Australian University Tourism and Hospitality Education, 10–13 February, Brisbane.

Backman, KF, Backman, SJ, Muzaffer, U & Sunshine, K 1995, 'Event tourism: an examination of motivations and activities', *Festival Management and Event Tourism*, vol. 3, no. 1, pp. 26–34.

Baker, DA & Crompton, JL 2000, 'Quality, satisfaction, and behavioural intentions', *Annals of Tourism Research*, vol. 27, no. 3, pp. 785–804.

Beverland, M. Hoffman, D. and Rasmusssen, M. 2001, 'The evolution of events in the Australasian wine sector', *Tourism Recreation Research,* vol. 26, no. 2.

Cravens, D, Merrilees, B & Walker, R 2000, *Strategic marketing management for the Pacific region*, McGraw-Hill, Sydney.

Crompton, J & McKay, S 1997, 'Motives of visitors attending festival events', *Annals of Tourism Research*, vol. 24, no. 2, pp. 425–39.

Davidson, R, & Rogers T, 2006, *Marketing destinations and venues for conferences, conventions, and business events,* Elsevier, Oxford..

Dickman, S 1997, 'Issues in arts marketing', in *Making it happen: the cultural and entertainment industries handbook*, ed. R Rentchler, Centre for Professional Development, Melbourne.

Euromonitor International 2008, 'Travel and tourism in the United Arab Emirates (October)', London Euromonitor International Plc., www.euromonitor.com.

Getz, D 1991, *Festivals, special events and tourism*, Van Nostrand Reinhold, New York.

—— 1997, *Event management and event tourism*, Cognizant Communications, New York.

—— 2007, *Event Studies: Theory, research and policy for planned events,* Elsevier, Oxford

Good, R 2009, 'Buzz Tracking And Social Media Monitoring: Best Tools To Do Ego Searching And Find Out Who Is Talking About Me — Mini-Guide', www.masternewmedia.org; Gronroos, C 1990, *Services Marketing and Management*, Lexington Books, Lexington, Massachusetts.

Henderson, JC 2006a, 'Tourism in Dubai: overcoming barriers to destination development', *International Journal of Tourism Research* 8, pp. 87–99.

—— 2006b, 'Destination development: Singapore and Dubai compared', *Journal of Travel and Tourism Marketing* 20 (3/4), pp. 33–45.

Hoyle, L 2009, *Event marketing,* John Wiley and Sons, New York.

Johnson, G, Scholes, K & Whittington, R 2005, *Exploring corporate strategy*, 7th edn, Pearson Education, Harlow, Essex.

Kotler, P, Bowen, J & Makens, J 1999, *Marketing for hospitality and tourism*, 2nd edn, Prentice Hall International, Upper Sadler River, New Jersey.

Lovelock, C, Patterson, P & Walker, R 2004, *Services marketing*, 3rd edn, Pearson Education Australia, Sydney.

—— 2007, *Services Marketing*, 4th edn, Pearson Education Australia, Sydney.

Mannell, R & Iso-Ahola, S 1987, 'Psychological nature of leisure and tourism experience', *Annals of Tourism Research*, vol. 14, no. 3, pp. 314–29.

Masterman, G & Wood, E, 2006 *Innovative marketing communications,* Elsevier, Oxford.

McCarthy, EJ 1960 (1st ed.), *Basic marketing: a managerial approach*, 13th edn, Irwin, Homewood Il, 2001.

McDermott, S 2006, *Why track blogs?*, http://www.attentio.com/blog/2006/02/19/24/.

McDonald, M 2002, *Marketing plans: how to prepare them, how to use them*, Butterworth Heinemann, Oxford.

Melbourne International Comedy Festival, www.comedyfestival.com.au.

Miller, K & Layton, R 2000, *Fundamentals of marketing*, 4th edn, McGraw-Hill, Sydney.

Mintzberg, H 1994, *The rise and fall of strategic planning*, Prentice Hall, New York.

Mohr, K, Backman, K, Gahan, L & Backman, S 1993, 'An investigation of festival motivations and event satisfaction by visitor type', *Festival Management and Event Tourism*, vol. 1, pp. 89–97.

Morgan, M 1996, *Marketing for leisure and tourism*, Prentice Hall, London.

Neal, C, Quester, P & Hawkins, H 2002, *Consumer behaviour*, 3rd edn, McGraw-Hill, Sydney.

Out of the Box Festival of Early Childhood (Brisbane), www.outoftheboxfestival.com.au.

Parasuraman, A, Zeithaml, V & Berry, L 1988, 'SERVQUAL: a multiple-item scale for measuring consumers' perceptions of service quality', *Journal of Retailing*, vol. 64, no. 1, pp. 22–37.

Porter, M 1980, *Competitive strategy*, Free Press, New York.

Porter, M 1990, *Competitive advantage of nations*, Free Press, New York.

Pride, W 2006, *Marketing: core concepts and applications*, John Wiley & Sons Australia, Brisbane, p. 130.

Rao, V & Steckel, J 1998, *Analysis for strategic marketing*, Addison-Wesley, Reading, Massachusetts.

Rice, J 2007, *Co-creation*, http://brand.blogs.com/mantra/2006/05/cocreation.html.

Saleh, F & Ryan, C 1993, 'Jazz and knitwear: factors that attract tourists to festivals', *Tourism management*, August, pp. 289–97.

Seat Advisor Australia 2009, Product overview, www.seatadvisor.com.au.

Sharpley, R 2008, 'Planning for tourism: the case of Dubai', *Tourism and Hospitality Planning and Development*, vol. 5, no. 1, pp. 13–30.

Stanton, W, Miller, K & Layton, R 1994, *Fundamentals of marketing*, 3rd edn, McGraw-Hill, Sydney.

Strauss, J, El-Ansary, A & Frost, R 2003, *E-marketing*, 3rd edn, Pearson Education, New Jersey.

Sydney Festival, *Festival history*, www.sydneyfestival.org.au.

Theatre Shop Conference 2002, 'Panel discussion: programming criteria used by international festivals', www.fuel4arts.com.

Thompson, W & Hickey, J 2005, *Society in focus*, 5th edn, Allyn and Bacon, New Jersey.

Thrane, C 2002, 'Music quality, satisfaction and behavioural intentions within a jazz festival context', *Event Management: an International Journal*, vol. 7, no. 3, pp. 143–50.

Uysal, M, Gahan, L & Martin, B 1993, 'An examination of event motivations', *Festival Management and Event Tourism*, vol. 1, pp. 5–10.

Woodford Folk Festival 2006, www.woodfordfolkfestival.com.

PROMOTION: INTEGRATED MARKETING COMMUNICATION FOR EVENTS

LEARNING OBJECTIVES

After studying this chapter, you should be able to:

1. define integrated marketing communications
2. describe the purpose of integrated marketing communications for event management
3. describe the constituent elements of these communications
4. efficiently and effectively apply these elements to the promotion of special events.

INTRODUCTION

While the term integrated marketing communications has long been found in the marketing literature (see for example James 1972; Shaw et al. 1981; Barry 1986; Linton and Morely 1995 Belch; and Belch 2004, Nowak & Phelps 2005), its first use in the area of a leisure activity (tourism) was probably that of McDonnell (1999) who used the case of Australian leisure travel to Fiji and Bali to demonstrate how integrated marketing communications help achieve a tourist destination's marketing objectives. He proposed the intefrag marketing continuum, which posited that the closer an organisation's marketing was to the integrated end of the continuum (and further away from the fragmented end, hence 'intefrag') the more effective it would be. As with tourism products and other leisure services, so with festivals and special events. The more integrated the marketing communication, the more effective it will be in achieving an event's marketing objectives because potential consumers see and hear uniform, consistent messages, imagery and activities produced to satisfy needs that motivate them to attend the event.

Smith and Taylor (2004) define the communications mix as consisting of:

- personal selling
- advertising
- sales promotion
- direct mail
- publicity
- sponsorship
- exhibitions
- packaging
- merchandising
- word of mouth
- corporate identity.

With the possible exception of exhibitions, all of these elements can be effectively used by marketers of special events. They state that integrated simply means that a *unified* message is consistently reinforced, when any or all of these communication techniques are used.

From another viewpoint, the American Association of Advertising Agencies defines integrated marketing communications (AAAA 1989) as:

> a concept of marketing communications planning that recognizes the added value of a comprehensive plan that evaluates the strategic roles of a variety of communication disciplines – general advertising, direct response, sales promotion, public relations – and combines these disciplines to provide clarity, consistency, and maximum communication impact.

Moreover, the Institute for Integrated Marketing Communications (IIMC 2006) defined IMC as involving:

> the coordination of various promotional elements and other marketing activities that communicate with a firm's customers. IMC focuses on the synergistic role of advertising, sales promotions, direct marketing, internet and interactive marketing, public relations and personal selling in the communications program.

Yet another view of IMC is that of Shimp (2003), who considers 'all sources of contact that a consumer has [with the event] as potential delivery channels for messages and makes use of all communication methods that are relevant to consumers'. The underlying premise of Shimp's view is, of course, that all sources of contact are consistent messages, constantly reinforced with similar meanings. Though none of these definitions mention the various methods of using the internet as a promotional medium (social networking sites, websites and ticket distribution sites), it also applies to this medium.

From these definitions it can be seen that for marketing communications to be properly integrated they must have the qualities of being unified and consistent with all aspects of the event's marketing mix and clear in their message, which results from a coordinated management process. This is reinforced by Linton and

Morley's (1995) claim that the advantages of integration (IMC) are consistency of message, more effective use of media, improved marketing precision, cost savings, creative integrity and operational efficiency – all laudable aims. Another change brought about by the application of IMC, as Nowak and Phelps (2005) identified, is that the boundaries between the different types of promotion, as previously listed, are vanishing.

Masterman and Wood (2006) have a useful table that compares traditional marketing communications processes with IMCs, which summarises the advantages of using IMC in an event's promotion plan (see table 10.1).

TABLE 10.1 Comparing traditional and integrated marketing communications mixes

Traditional Marketing Communications mix	Integrated Marketing Communications mix
Each type of promotion has separate function; fragmentation of messages and imagery and therefore brand image occurs	All types integrated into one strategy; synergy occurs between various types (for example, advertising and sales promotion)
Process starts with the event and its products	Process starts with event customer needs and how the event can satisfy these
Fragmented communication programs	Unified, consistent programs
Short-term objectives for each promotion campaign	Relationship and brand-building objectives
Mass audiences	Targeted to event consumers and stakeholders
Each type of promotion has specialist practitioners	Integrated campaign coordinated by a marketer

Source: Adapted from Masterman & Wood 2006.

APPLICATION OF IMC

As with all marketing techniques, IMC applications for events and festivals are based on knowledge about consumers and potential consumers; that is, the target market. How an event manages its relationships with this target market drives its brand value (Duncan 2002). An event brand such as the Sydney Gay and Lesbian Mardi Gras is 'an integrated bundle of information and experiences that distinguish [it]' (Duncan 2002, p. 13) from competing leisure experiences. Figure 10.1 offers an insight into the IMC process for an event, and the range of traditional and non-traditional media that help to create its brand relationships — that is, the image of the event that is projected to consumers and other stakeholders.

Branding for an event is much more than a physical identity or symbol, such as the five interlocking rings of the Olympics. The Olympics' brand is based on consumer perceptions, how they relate to that event and what it promises, as well as the physical logo and other symbolism (for example, the Olympic torch). However, intelligent, integrated and consistent use of the brand helps the event manager to make an intangible phenomenon more tangible for event consumers, as the 100 years of use of the Olympic symbols and imagery have exemplified.

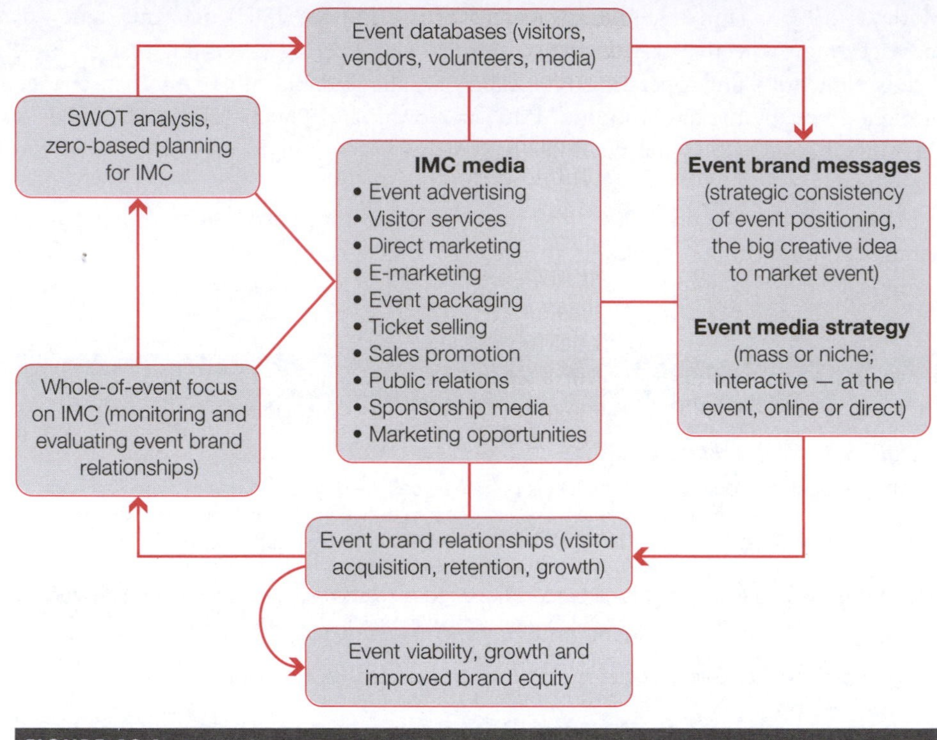

FIGURE 10.1 The IMC process model for events

Source: Based on information from Duncan 2002, p. 9.

In developing an IMC strategy, an event manager should understand there are four sources of brand messages, or marketing communications, as in this case they are synonymous (Duncan 2002):

1. *planned messages* (media releases, personal selling by the box office and/or ticket agency, advertising, e-newsletters, websites — in other words, all the planned promotional activities)
2. *unplanned messages* (unexpected positive or negative impressions formed by word of mouth, media coverage, complaints)
3. *product messages* (implied messages of information about the event — program, pricing, venue)
4. *service messages* (the nature of contact with festival or event staff or volunteers, the quality of event transport and other support services).

Given these message types, the event brand is shaped by more than its planned promotional tools; instead, there are many influences on the event and its brand, some of which are obviously more manageable than others.

Mirroring the strategy process, the development of an IMC plan hinges on an effective SWOT/C-PEST analysis, plus competitor, consumer and stakeholder research. The information from the analysis and research provides the platform for deciding whether objectives and strategies for the IMC campaign should be informational, transformational (attitudinal), behavioural or relational in their focus. Figure 10.2 shows how these different approaches correspond with the 'think, feel, act' model of consumer behaviour. However, for most community and social events, the majority of messages will be informational.

FIGURE 10.2 Event message objectives and strategies

Source: Adapted from Duncan 2002, p. 320.

ESTABLISHING THE IMC BUDGET

The quip 'I know that half of my advertising is wasted, but I don't know which half' is usually attributed to Lord Leverhume, the English industrialist and soap manufacturer, and the addition of 'and I don't know if that is half enough or twice too much' is attributed to the American department store magnate John Wanamaker (Kotler et al. 2006). So it can be seen that allocating the most efficient amount of resources for an integrated marketing communication plan is no easy task. Kotler et al. (2006) advise of four methods to establish a budget for this activity:

1. top down — what the event can afford
2. top down — percentage of sales method
3. top down — competitive parity method
4. objective and task method.

The first three methods are referred to as top down because management fixes an amount to be spent on promotion, without considering what its outcomes are to be, and imposes this promotion budget on the marketer.

What the event can afford

Most community festivals and amateur sports events have limited resources to produce the event, and the amount to spend on IMC can be rigorously debated among the executive. Such debate transpires probably because most people consider themselves to be experts on 'advertising' and therefore assert they know how much should or should not be spent. A figure is then decided based on what is thought can be afforded, not based on what is needed to achieve the event's marketing objectives. If an event is new or is being relaunched it will need more resources (financial and human) than an event that is well established in a target market. In this case what is thought can be afforded may well be far short of the resources required to communicate the event's need-satisfying properties to its target market. This method is what Belch and Belch (2004) refer to as the top-down method, where the board or top management sets a spending limit and the event marketer then constructs an integrated marketing communications plan that may or may not achieve the event's marketing objectives using the resources allocated. It also applies to smaller community festivals and events where the board or festival coordinator makes a decision on the spend when constructing a budget.

Percentage of sales method

This method is commonly used in the marketing of fast-moving consumer goods, where the budget for promotion is set at *x* per cent of the forecast revenue. It has the claimed advantage of providing stability to the event as the resources allocated to promotion should be commensurate with the return. However, it is clear that this method is based on the false premise of sales cause promotion rather than promotion causes sales.

Competitive parity method

This method establishes what other similar events spend on IMC and then bases promotional spend on this figure, and is based on the premise that if the norm for that sector is used, the event is adhering to the collective wisdom of the sector. This, of course, begs the question of whether the collective wisdom is correct. Every event has different characteristics and the IMC resources required can differ greatly. The disadvantage of the three top-down approaches (affordable, percentage of sales and competitive parity) is that they are not linked to any promotional objectives and the ways in which these objectives are achieved.

Objective and task method

The objective and task method consists of three sequential steps (Belch and Belch 2004):

- establish IMC objectives
- determine specific tasks to achieve these objectives
- calculate approximate cost of tasks.

This is the most rational of the three methods, and is supported by Masterman & Wood (2006 p: 275) who state 'that it is inherently the most logical approach'. It is also the most difficult as it requires estimates of the sales effect of a given expenditure. However, the objective and task method is certainly the most rigorous and effective of budgeting methods.

The budget then is the total of these costs, which is the method of budget construction that can help achieve an event's overall objectives. Figure 10.3 shows how this is done for a local community festival; by using this rational and logical method, the marketing communication objectives of an event can be met at reasonable cost.

Setting the integrated marketing communications (IMC) budget is usually one of the hardest tasks that the event marketer faces, particularly if the event is new and there is no precedent for revenues and ticket sales. However, by sticking to the objective and task method of IMC budget construction, the event marketer will be able to establish, by a process of elimination, communication methods that are unfeasible due to their cost, the most efficient (minimising inputs of cash, maximising outputs of target market reach and frequency) and effective (reaching the objective of the integrated marketing communication program) promotional plan.

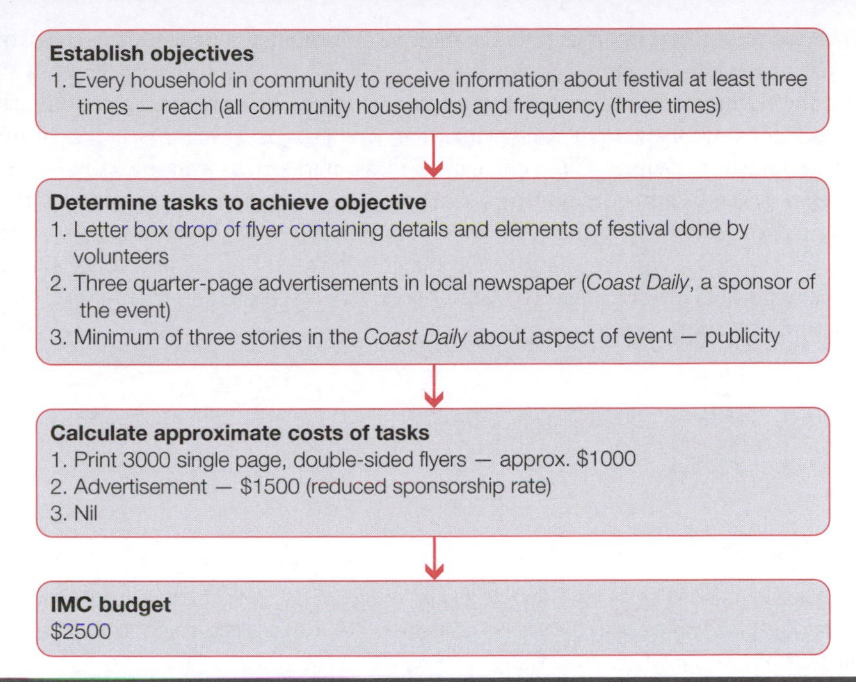

FIGURE 10.3 Objective and task budget setting for a community festival

ELEMENTS OF IMC

Importantly, consumers do not react to marketing messages in any set order — they may feel, then act (local festival attendance) and later reflect on the experience, or they may go through a sequential process of 'think, feel and act' (such as a decision to visit France to attend the next Rugby World Cup, a decision that has financial implications and therefore takes a great deal of thought, discussion and reflection). It is important to consider these different decision-making patterns of market segments when deciding how to set out the objectives of a promotional IMC campaign.

The IMC strategy reflects the thrust of the chosen objectives and uses both message and media strategies to fulfil them. To illustrate, a community festival may have an objective of increasing attendance from a somewhat uninvolved market segment, such as families with children under thirteen. Their message strategy would be developed with reference to a psychological appeal — for example, motivators such as the enhancement of bonds between parents and children or the role of the festival in cultural education of their children. Planning the IMC campaign requires 'one voice, one look' (Duncan 2002) — that is, all direct marketing, advertising, publicity and event packaging must convey the same message and look in its communication.

For the community festival, the media strategy involves choosing how the mix of planned advertising, e-marketing, publicity and/or other media will be used to best convey the message about the festival attendance of the target market in the most effective (achieving the IMC campaign's objectives) and most efficient (using the minimum of resources) manner. As shown in figure 10.1 the IMC mix can include a wide range of marketing communication functions. A public relations strategy could use a celebrity local artist that is part of the festival who could, during an interview with the local newspaper, discuss how attendance can facilitate a child's learning about their artistic culture. This could then be followed by a direct mail campaign to local residents and an email newsletter to a database of prior consumers featuring the same local artist discussing the same benefits.

Given the numerous marketing communication tools to include in an IMC mix, the event marketer must have familiarity with their strengths and weaknesses, including their budgetary implications. An event with a mass market (for example, the Sydney Royal Easter Show or a major sporting event) may use television advertising as a promotional device, whereas planned IMC for a community festival is more likely to concentrate on organised word of mouth, local media publicity and community service announcements as figure 10.3 shows. A brief review of the more commonly used marketing communication media is offered here.

event profile

SCOTLAND ISLAND FESTIVAL

Scotland Island is an island located in Pittwater, an inlet of Broken Bay in the far north of Sydney's metropolitan area, and was probably the second geographic feature in Australia named by Governor Phillip in 1788, Pittwater itself being the first.

Today, apart from the virtually uninhabited and much smaller islands in Sydney Harbour, there is probably no settled island so convenient to a large city in Australia. At its closest point it is only about 400 metres from the mainland at Church Point, but the moat of surrounding water ensures a healthy and relaxing freedom from motor traffic, pollution and city noise.

There are about 1000 people, 350 houses, a kindergarten and a handsome community hall set against the background of a community park. The tranquillity of the island attracts a concentration of talented people — artists, writers, photographers, singers, musicians, sculptors and poets — who find the experience of 'escaping from the madding crowd' encouragingly creative. It is this community that hosts biannually in the spring the Scotland Island Festival, which celebrates and recognises the variety of creative and artistic talent in its community members.

The festival has a standard flat management structure, with an overall festival coordinator and coordinators for the various festival programs (arts, film, writers' and kids' festivals and the Scotland Island Fair day), who report to the festival coordinator. Other office bearers are responsible for entertainment, sponsorship and publicity, and, of course, there is a treasurer. It is interesting to note that most of these volunteers are female.

The promotion budget for the festival was arrived at using the objective and task method, which kept it to an affordable amount. The promotional objective was to reach the target market — residents of the northern beaches of Sydney interested in artistic activities — at least three times, which assisted in attaining one of the objectives of the festival, to attract 3000 attendees.

Various tactics were employed to achieve this objective:

- use of an interactive website (level 4 on figure 10.6) that
  - allowed past and potential users to input their ideas on what the festival should contain (an example of co-creation)
  - gave all details of the festival events and their venues
  - enabled attendees to purchase tickets to the ticketed events using a credit card or PayPal
  - enabled interested people to volunteer for the festival
  - enabled visitors to read the results of the publicity campaign (the site www.scotlandislandfestival.org.au was produced by Girl Zed Productions)

- 5000 festival programs printed by a sponsor were distributed throughout the market area by sponsors and volunteers
- 1000 flyers for each program event were distributed in a similar manner
- 300 posters placed in businesses and community centres in the Pittwater area
- publicity — press releases to the local media, the *Manly Daily* and *Pittwater Life*, an example of which is shown below.

FILMMAKERS GET PROFESSIONAL HELP

Twelve young people from Scotland Island have taken the opportunity to have the films they're making for H_2O 360 Film Festival edited by a professional.

Experienced feature film editor, former islander and now Bayview resident Tim Wellburn was willing to share his knowledge and skills to assist these budding filmmakers with their projects.

'I've been working in the industry for 40 years and I've taken so much from it . . . it was lovely to give something back,' he said.

H_2O 360 is Scotland Island's own film festival and screening of entries will be held in November.

It's open to Australians living on islands and/or remote communities.

Scotland Island resident Sarah Bookey, 13, is taking part in H_2O 360 with a documentary on the festival.

'Tim edited the footage I'd shot,' she said. 'I didn't know how to edit before that.'

Wellburn said the young moviemakers showed a lot of promise.

FIGURE 10.4 Press release

Source: The Manly Daily 2006, 'Filmmakers get professional help', August 11, p. 27, www.scotlandislandfestival.org.

This campaign was integrated by using similar fonts and iconography on the website, flyers, posters and the flyers that are illustrated in the exhibit's heading.

The integrated marketing communication campaign was successful as the attendance objectives were met. In previous years, the infrastructure of the island was strained by the number of people who attended, but this was alleviated by extra ferries and a park and ride facilty. The difficulty the organisers had this year was volunteer burnout caused by the success of the festival and its size, given the isolation of the festival site.

Grateful thanks to Festival Coordinator Denise Catt for her help.

Advertising

Advertising is any form of non-personal promotion paid for by the event organisation. Radio, television, newspapers, magazines, websites, social networking sites (Facebook, MySpace Twitter, Flickr, YouTube and many others) mobile phones (cell phones), outdoor advertising (billboards, bus shelters and toilets) and mobile platforms such as buses and taxis are all media for advertising. For most events and festivals, the expense of mainstream media (capital city television, newspapers and radio) cannot be economically justified. Media partnerships such as a community festival's sponsorship by a television channel or newspaper can help to resolve this issue. However, the creative process of producing the messages can also be expensive, especially if done by an advertising agency. In creating advertising campaigns for events and festivals, it is necessary to:

- provide tangible clues to counteract the intangible nature of the event — that is, show the artistic event or sports players in action, the event logo, the spectacle of the fireworks and so on
- seek continuity over time by using recognisable symbols, spokespersons, trademarks or music — for example, football codes often use the tunes of famous artists, such as *We are the champions* by Queen
- promise what is possible to foster realistic expectations — for example, show real-time action (it is necessary to take care with promises about ticket availability because they can become contentious)
- make the service more tangible and recognisable by showing members of the target market enjoying the event — for example, the roar and spectacle of a grand final crowd at the football can be very persuasive to the target market of a football event.

The metric usually applied to advertising effectiveness is reach and frequency — the number of people in the target market that the promotional message has reached and how many times they have received the promotional message. Farris et al. (2006) consider as a general rule that four exposures (frequency) to a message are necessary for it to be effective. However, the important element of this is to budget correctly. There is not much use reaching 10 000 consumers once, when it would be more effective to reach 1000 consumers four times, by judicious selection of the promotion medium.

Public relations (publicity)

Public relations (publicity) is used to build mutually beneficial relationships with stakeholders and consumers. It uses a wide range of tools, including publicity, special promotional events, community consultation, e-publications and traditional newsletters. While all activities incur costs, media publicity is often favoured by festival organisers because it provides unpaid space in the media that reaches the event's market. An advantage to festival and event directors and marketers is that people generally enjoy reading about sport, the arts and entertainment. However, marketers must be aware that the media will use a story only if it has news value (a unique angle or item of information of interest to readers, viewers or listeners). Journalists also carefully assess the structure and style of media releases and the credibility of their source. The event profile demonstrates the advantages of this promotional method.

An interesting example of the use of publicity was the actor Russell Crowe, who is part owner of the South Sydney Rabbitohs National Rugby League franchise, handing out 1000 free tickets to a home game in a Sydney suburb. This action received a front-page story with photo in the Sydney tabloid *The Daily Telegraph* and gained the club publicity.

Sales promotion

Sales promotion consists of those activities that use incentives or discounts to increase sales or attendance. Examples of sales promotion are family days at city shows or exhibitions, offering group discounts or a free ticket for one child. Alternatively, consumers may be offered free merchandise (T-shirts and posters) when purchasing several tickets or more. An example is the Royal Easter Show offering a vacation care program where children on school holidays will be safely entertained by the enjoyment of the Show activities. Another example is the *Tix for Next to Nix* program at the Sydney Festival. This involves releasing a limited number of tickets (the number depending upon how popular the show is — the more popular the show, the fewer the number of tickets) at a downtown booth on the day of the performance for $25, which is usually a sizeable discount, but has the big advantage of clearing unsold tickets and avoiding the problem of perishability (Sydney Festival 2010).

Direct marketing

Direct marketing communicates one-on-one with existing festival or event goers via postal mail, the telephone or by email. It relies on organisers developing a list of people who previously attended the event (or similar events) and obtaining information about their demographic profile and preferences. Incentives for consumers to provide information may include entry in a competition or the receipt of next year's event program. Organisers can purchase lists of potential event consumers — those who fit the demographic profile — from direct marketing agencies. However, a key consideration in collecting information to build a database is the need to gain consumer permission and to respect consumer privacy. An understanding of current regulations about direct marketing (including the use of e-newsletters) is now mandatory. With the now almost total penetration of home computers in Australia, the use of email for these direct marketing activities is far more efficient. For example, Strauss *et al.* (2006) show in table 10.2 the cost efficiencies to be gained by using email, rather than postal mail. The task for the event marketer is to assemble a reliable email list of the target market, which is generally built up over time by collecting data from existing event goers. Anderson (2002) reports a trial by an American company that used 50 per cent email and 50 per cent direct mail for a lead generation campaign, which found the cost-per-lead for direct mail was $4026.00 versus $44.80 for email. With an 890 per cent difference in cost between the two strategies, email campaigns are far more efficient, and should be part of all event marketers' repertoire.

TABLE 10.2 Metrics for electronic and postal mail

Activity	Email	Postal mail
Delivery cost per thousand	$30	$500
Creative costs to develop	$1000	$17 000
Click through rate	10 per cent	N/A
Customer conversion rate	5 per cent	3 per cent
Execution time	3 weeks	3 months
Response time	48 hours	3 weeks

Source: Jupiter Communications.

Another effective method of collecting this data is to have a 'contact us' section on the event's website. Australia's probably best known folk music festival, the Woodford Folk Festival (www.woodfordfolkfestival.com), for example, has this feature. The event can build a database of all who made an enquiry by email, which means that they are part of its target market. This then gives an event a most efficient resource that can be used to transmit integrated marketing communications, as table 10.2 shows.

Online presence

The event website is another integrated marketing communication resource that, if used successfully, is a most effective and efficient method of communicating with its target market. The event website construction is usually best outsourced to a professional website designer; however, the event manager must know how to brief the web designer. Figure 10.5 shows the steps in website construction that form the basis of the brief to be given to the designer.

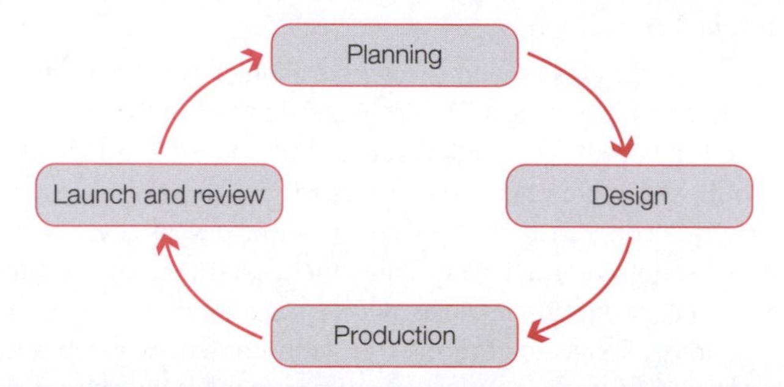

FIGURE 10.5 A model of the website construction process

Planning consists of establishing the purpose or function of the site, which can be to:

- offer information about the event to potential consumers; that is, to have an online brochure — brochureware
- provide a forum where potential consumers can interact with the site by asking questions of event staff via a contact us page, provision of a frequently asked questions (FAQ) page, provision of a full calendar of event elements — interact using Web 2.0 techniques
- provide a platform where consumers can make transactions by purchasing tickets using a credit card and then have the tickets emailed to them — transact
- have all aspects of the event management, marketing and production integrated into the website — integration.

The website of the Sydney Festival (www.sydneyfestival.org.au) is an excellent example of an effective and efficient site.

Figure 10.6 shows the choices and the nexus between investment and internet-based interaction.

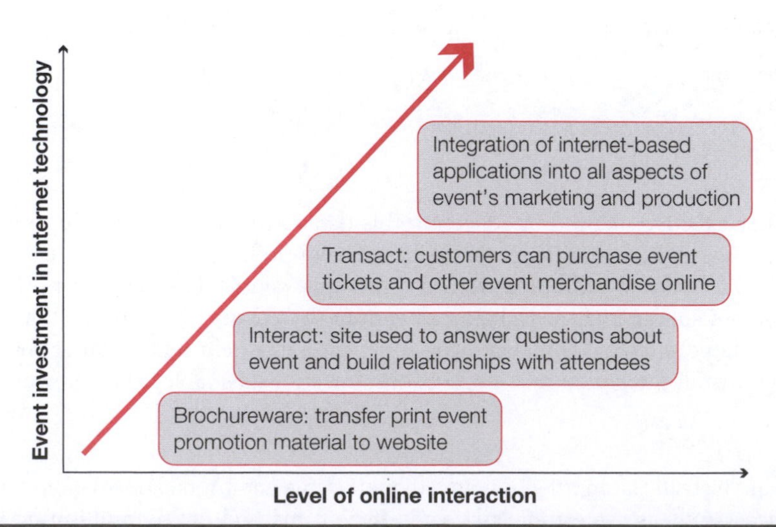

FIGURE 10.6 Types of internet-based marketing for events

Source: Adapted from O'Connor and Galvin 1997.

The function of the website depends on the type of event. For example a simple community cultural event needs only a brochure website, such as www.communitybuilders.nsw.gov.au/events. A larger community festival may decide on an interactive site; for example, www.sydneyitalianfestival.com.au. A large music festival could decide on a transaction site (www.woodfordfolkfestival.com). An academic or professional conference may choose an integration style, such as www.cauthe2007.uts.edu.au, where site delegates can register and pay for the conference, book accommodation and travel, submit academic papers and plan their program.

Once the website's function and objectives have been agreed, the next step is to decide on content and look, which of course has to be integrated and consistent with all other marketing communications that the event uses.

Website design

The key to the success of a website, no matter what function is chosen, is to ensure that the site is simple and easy to use — in other words, that it is user friendly. After the function is chosen, the design or look of the web pages containing the text graphics and other media are selected. They have to be consistent and integrated with all other marketing communications used by the event. While a site might need only a low-level interactivity to suit an event's needs, it still needs to be integrated with the other non-online communications.

An online search for advice on web design for the neophyte designer will produce millions of hits. In addition, there are thousands of published texts available on the subject of web design and creation. Two sites that specialise in sites for special events are www.dotorgwebworks.org/portfolio-events.htm and www.f8media.com. Another useful Australian site that offers advice on website construction is www.melbourneit.com.au/cc/website-design.

The basic website design principles are as follows:

- determine the basic layout of the site so that the various pages are linked in a coherent manner
- ensure that the content imagery is consistent with and integrated with any offline marketing communications and consistent throughout the site
- make sure that the site is easy to read by using an appropriate font and lots of white space. Use dot points rather than continuous text, and simple colour schemes rather than complex and garish (www.oakbankracingclub.com.au is a good example of these attributes).
- use an easy to understand navigation system (framed or unframed). Use either a side bar or navigation system along the top or bottom of the page, so that viewers know where they are and how to get to the pages they want.
- determine the copy and supporting graphics before posting to the site to ensure that they can achieve the site's objectives and adhere to the IMC standard
- don't make the text too complex or dense — no viewer enjoys ploughing through hectares of text, except perhaps academics. Lots of white space is easy on the eye and attractive to the viewer.
- don't use capital text in the copy as it implies SHOUTING
- while many texts suggest the use of thumbnail graphics linked to a larger version of the image, the speed of most browsers makes this usually unnecessary for most event websites, especially with the increasing use of broadband connection. However, if a site contains many graphics, the page will certainly load faster with thumbnails. The

spread of broadband connections means that many sites now effectively utilise flash animation.
- ensure that the home page (the first page in the site) can load quickly and is displayed on one or a maximum of two pages
- provide a clearly signposted 'contact us' page
- give details of the site's privacy policy to engender confidence in users
- for transaction sites, provide details of the security system used to ensure that users feel confident about using a credit card for purchases
- use a URL that is easy to remember, such as www.oakbankracingclub.com.au
- use the web page production program's default colours unless there is an aesthetic reason to vary them. For example, web surfers are used to and comfortable with blue for unvisited links, which then change to a darker colour such as purple to indicate a visited link.

Once the site has been produced it is then launched into cyber space. The launch process is relatively simple: a URL (uniform resource locater) is obtained from a domain name registrar such as www.auda.org.au and then loaded to a web server. The site can then be registered with search engines (such as Google) so that users will be able to locate it.

Part of the IMC for an event that uses a website is to promote the site at every opportunity. For example, all offline marketing communications such as advertisements, flyers, posters, press releases and event stationery need to highlight the address (URL) of the site, to encourage consumers to visit the site to use e-commerce to purchase tickets. Arrange for the event site to be linked with complementary sites that can encourage visitors to the site — for example, the regional tourism site. Other possible sites to link with would be national bodies of the particular artistic or sporting endeavour with which the event is involved and banner ads from event sponsors.

PERSONAL SELLING

Personal selling is defined by McCarthy & Perreault (1987) as direct face-to-face communication between a seller and a potential consumer. This form of promotion can occur in the event marketing process when the marketer explains the event and its need-satisfying attributes to either representatives of potential customers or to those customers direct.

Personal selling involves a lecture or presentation to a target market – for example a representative of a community festival addressing a high school assembly or a Rotary Club meeting; or the chief executive of a festival addressing a luncheon of corporate leaders; or a sales person following leads generated from a event's website of people interested in attending an expensive and exclusive fund raising event.

However, the key to efficient use of this method is to understand the costs involved. It is usually by far the most expensive of all promotional activities in terms of consumers reached. Therefore, it should be used only when a personal communication is deemed to be the most effective and efficient method of communicating the event's benefits.

It is usually considerably more expensive than other promotional activities in terms of consumers reached. Table 10.3 summarises into a promotional plan the various forms that IMC can take in the special event context, using an international football (soccer) game produced by Football Federation Australia (FFA) as the example.

TABLE 10.3 Sample promotional plan

Type of IMC	Reach	Frequency	Timing	Channel
Personal selling: Briefing of all FFA staff as to reason for and significance of the game by CEO	100% of involved staff	Once initially with monthly follow-ups	Game minus 6 months	Staff meeting
Briefing of stakeholders: stadium, suppliers, governments	All			Luncheon
Public relations: briefing of football (soccer) journalists (all media) by CEO	100%	At least four briefings	Game minus month 6, 4, 2 and 1 week	Media release and briefing
Media kit	All sports journalists who cover football	Twice	Game minus 6 months and an update minus 1 month	Sent to all by courier
E: Website	All interested consumers	Ongoing: all IMC features URL	Game minus 6 months	E-commerce site with full description of game, players, facilities, controversies; constantly updated. All promotion methods emphasise URL of website.
Direct mail: email sent to all consumers on FFA's membership list giving all game's details	All on list	Three times	Game minus 6, 3 and 1 month	Email
Sales promotion: if ticket sales below expectations announce family package. Details given at all FFA league games in host city	All target market	Two times	Game minus 1 month (if needed)	Media release, email and website
Advertising: Local radio stations	Use of stations that give access to required demographic	Three times	Game minus one month (if needed)	Radio advertising

It can be seen from table 10.3 that the promotional spend for even quite a large event (50 000 spectators) can be done quite cheaply, and therefore efficiently, by using e-marketing and public relations techniques.

SUMMARY

With the addition of the website to the event marketers' toolkit, it is possible to have a fully integrated marketing communications program that satisfies an event's marketing objectives at a relatively limited cost, provided that all marketing communications are consistent, integrated with all other communications from the event so that they are unified and consistent with all aspects of the event's marketing mix, and clear in their message. This outcome results from a coordinated management process that ensures the event's marketing communications are at the integrated end of the intefrag continuum, rather than the fragmented undesirable end.

This chapter shows why integrated marketing communications is a significant aspect of event marketing, the methods that can be used to achieve integrated marketing communications and the advantages of using internet-based marketing communications. Without effective integrated marketing communications, a special event will struggle to achieve its objectives, so the techniques discussed in this chapter make up an essential part of the event managers' toolkit.

QUESTIONS

1 Give an example of an event's marketing communications. Place it on the intefrag continuum and explain why it is at that position.
2 Give an example of an event that uses an integrated website in its operations. Describe how, by using a website, this event achieved marketing efficiencies and increased its effectiveness.
3 What is the major difficulty in using an email campaign to promote a new event? How can this problem be rectified?
4 Using the format of table 10.3, construct a promotional plan for an event of your choice.
5 Explain how personal selling would or would not be used in an event of your choice.

case study

SYDNEY'S ROYAL EASTER SHOW

This case study discusses the effectiveness of publicity and public relations when they are used skilfully.

Sydney's Royal Easter Show (subtitled 'Experience the Real Australia') is a major event that attracts hundreds of thousands of Sydney residents and visitors during its 14-day run. It was the 2006 winner of the Australian Tourism Award and Tourism NSW Award for Major Festivals and Events. While its main function is to highlight the contribution agriculture makes to the state of New South Wales, shows such as this also have an entertainment function.

During the 1950s and 1960s, sideshow alley was a prominent feature of agricultural shows and a must-see for many show visitors. It contained tents with acts of various styles of freakishness such as the bearded lady and the half man–half woman, or two-headed pigs and, long before the days of sexual liberty, strip shows

of a constrained type. However, during the 1970s this type of entertainment fell out of favour and was replaced with new thrill rides mainly for teenagers, usually imported from the United States.

In 2007 the Royal Easter Show brought back the sideshow, branding it the Psycho Sideshow of Anarchy featuring acts such as a sword swallowing space cowboy and midget belly dancer Tiny Rima (Lewis 2007). The sideshow is held in the Big Top tent that has three astonishing shows daily and a Tiny Top that seats thirty-six patrons for more specialised acts.

This innovation was publicised by means of a media release (shown in figure 10.7), which resulted in a page 3 feature story in the *Sydney Morning Herald* that featured colour photos of the various acts, a sympathetic story of the elements of the event, and time, cost and content information useful to visitors to the Show.

This excellent result came from the cardinal rule of publicity — the story has to be new and be of interest to the readers, listeners or viewers of the medium.

FIGURE 10.7 Media Release from RAS

SNEAK A PEAK AT THE REAL AUSTRALIA

The 2007 sydney royal easter show gets ready for action

A cast of furry farmyard animals, extreme performers and bizarre sideshow characters proved they are ready for action today at the dress rehearsal for the 2007 Sydney Royal Easter Show.

Australia's biggest annual celebration is full to the brim with agriculture, entertainment and fun, and ready for the gates to open at 9.30am on Thursday 5 April.

John Aitken General Manager Events & Marketing for the Royal Agricultural Society of NSW (RAS), says the 2007 Show is about discovering the real Australia.

'The Show offers a unique experience for Showgoers to interact with so many elements of the real Australia,' Mr Aitken said. 'We are showcasing the nation's rich agricultural heritage with some of the best Aussie entertainment, exhibitions and animal competitions.'

'In 2007, we have a renewed focus on agricultural education with even more interactive exhibits allowing city Showgoers to see, hear, touch and even take home a little bit of an Australian farm.'

'The Show will also revisit its bizarre sideshow past in the Psycho Sideshow of Anarchy as daring performers defy the confines of reality each day in The Big Top Amphitheatre and the Tiny Top Tent.'

'On top of that the Show celebrates two big anniversaries: ten years at Sydney Olympic Park and 100 years of the Grand Parade,' Mr Aitken said.

Showgoers will have the opportunity to interact with more animals than ever before with the expansion of old favourites the Dairy Farmers Farmyard & Animal Nursery and *Sunday Telegraph* Animal Walk.

The new pavilion, The Food Farm will teach city Showgoers about how food gets from the paddock to the plate with the 'Where does our food come from?' exhibition.

The entertainment again reaches dizzy heights with the new Aquaworld high dive show and Xtreme Korruption rocking NAB Arena twice daily with extreme freestyle motocross tricks and the mistress of the extreme, Lady Cannonball.

FIGURE 10.7 *(continued)*

Australia's oldest music festival is back on the scene bringing over 170 music acts to Showgoers over 14 days at two music venues: The VB Shed and the Next G Xtreme Arena. With You Am I, Something for Kate, Ash Grunwald, the Mess Hall, Josh Pyke, and Angus and Julia Stone the Show boasts a line-up to rival Australia's leading festivals.

Showgoers can view the Show and much of Sydney in air-conditioned gondolas with music and tinted windows on the 47 m tall SkyView Wheel.

For those looking for a more extreme experience the Carnival is the place to be. Newcomers the Power Surge and Raupen Bahn will make their mark alongside old Show favourites the Slingshot and Gravitron.

'Our entertainment line-up has something for every age and taste, and we want everyone to come along and experience and celebrate the real Australia with the best Show ever,' Mr Aitken said.

'All we are waiting for now are is the final bump-in of our 8000 exhibitors, with their 15 000 animal exhibits.'

. To plan your day, purchase tickets or vote for your favourite showbag, visit www.eastershow.com.au

Come and experience the real Australia at the 2007 Sydney Royal Easter Show
5 April to 18 April 2007
Winner of the Qantas Australian Tourism Award — Major Festival and Events

Source: Royal Agricultural Society 2007, 'Sneak a peak at the real Australia', 3 April, www.eastershow.com.au.

Questions

1 How can the press release from the Royal Agricultural Society be improved?

2 Why does the release mention the name of Mr Aitken, who is not the author of the release? What are the advantages of doing this?

REFERENCES

American Association of Advertising Agencies, www.aaaa.org.

American Marketing Association 2007, *Dictionary of marketing terms*, www.marketing-power.com.

Anderson, H 2002, 'E-mail v Direct mail: a head to head test', *Click Z Stats,* available at www.clickz.com/1465331.

Barry, T 1986, *Marketing — an integrated approach*, The Dryden Press, Chicago.

Belch, G & Belch, M 2004, *Advertising and promotion: an integrated marketing communications perspective*, 6th edn, McGraw-Hill, Boston.

Duncan, T 2002, *IMC: using advertising and promotion to build brands*, McGraw-Hill Irwin, New York.

Farris, P, Bendle, N, Pfeifer, P & Reibstein, D 2006, *Marketing metrics: 50+ metrics every executive should master*, Pearson Education, New Jersey.

IMC 2006, *Centre for integrated marketing communications*, imc.sdsu.edu.

James, B 1972, *Integrated marketing*, Penguin, Hammondsworth.

Kotler, P, Bowen, J & Makens, J 2006, *Marketing for hospitality and tourism*, Pearson Education International, New Jersey.

Lewis, D 2007, 'Freak Storm: sideshow alley to shake up the Show', *Sydney Morning Herald*, 4 April, p. 3.

Linton, I & Morley, K 1995, *Integrated marketing communications*, Butterworth Heinemann, Oxford.

Manly Daily 2006, 'Filmmakers get professional help', 11 August.

Masterman, G & Wood, E 2006, *Innovative marketing communications: strategies for the events industry,* Elsevier, Oxford.

McCarthy, EJ & Perreault, WD 1987, *Basic marketing: a managerial approach*, 9th edn, Irwin, Homewoud, IL, p. 744.

McDonnell, I 1999, 'The intefrag marketing continuum: a tool for tourism marketers', *Journal of Travel and Tourism Marketing*, vol. 8, no. 1.

Nowak, J & Phelps, J 2005, 'Conceptualising the integrated marketing communications phenomenon: an examination of its impact on advertising practices' in *A Reader in Marketing Communications,* Kitchen et al. Eds.), Routledge, New York.

O'Connor, J & Galvin, E 1997, *Marketing and information technology: the strategy, application and implementation of IT in marketing*, Pearson Education, Harlow, UK.

Shaw, R, Seminik, R & Williams, R 1981, *Marketing — an integrated analytical approach*, South Western Publishing, Cincinnati.

Shimp 2003, *Advertising, promotion and supplemental aspects of integrated marketing communication*, 6th edn, Thomson, Ohio.

Smith, J & Taylor, J 2004, *Marketing communications: an integrated approach*, 4th ed., Kogan Page, London.

Strauss, J, El-Ansary, A & Frost, R 2006, *E-marketing*, 4th edn, Pearson Education International, New Jersey, p. 341.

Sydney Festival 2010, Tix for Next to Nix, www.sydneyfestival.org.au.

11

SPONSORSHIP OF SPECIAL EVENTS

LEARNING OBJECTIVES

After studying this chapter, you should be able to:

1. understand the use of sponsorship in the context of festivals and special events
2. describe trends that have led to the growth of sponsorship as a marketing communication medium in the private and public sector
3. summarise the benefits that event managers can attract from reciprocal partnerships with sponsors
4. identify the key sponsorship benefits sought by events and sponsoring bodies
5. explain the importance of sponsorship 'leveraging'
6. understand the need for sponsorship policies to guide decision making by events and their sponsors
7. outline the sequential stages in developing and implementing an event sponsorship strategy
8. develop strategies and tactics to manage event–sponsor relationships and achieve positive and enduring relationships with sponsors.

INTRODUCTION

Sponsorship, either provided as cash or in-kind support such as products or services (often called 'contra') to a festival or special event, is central to the revenue and resources of new and continuing events. Event managers and marketers are usually actively engaged in tasks such as identifying potential sponsors, preparing sponsorship proposals and managing their ongoing relationships with sponsors, as event sponsorship is a large part of modern event management.

This chapter begins with a discussion of the role and growth of sponsorship as a marketing communication medium. It also explores the benefits that events and their sponsors seek, before explaining the policies, strategies and actions needed for successful event and festival sponsorship.

Interestingly, it is certainly not a modern concept as probably the first recorded instance of sponsorship was undertaken by the Medici family who ruled Florence from 1434 to 1637. Cosimo the Elder (1389–1464) and particularly his grandson Lorenzo the Magnificent (1449–92) sponsored graphic artists, sculptors and poets such as da Vinci, Donatello and Botticelli, who helped Florence to be at the centre of the artistic Renaissance period. It is reasonable to assume that they sponsored these artists for the same reason that the NSW and Australian governments sponsor Sydney's Museum of Contemporary Art — to generate goodwill towards them from a target market, to generate awareness and acceptance of their policies and to entertain their constituents and other stakeholders with hospitality centred on these artistic endeavours.

WHAT IS SPONSORSHIP?

Sponsorship has become a critical element in the integrated marketing communication mix (discussed in chapter 10) of many private and public sector organisations. Among the different types of marketing communication (for example, public relations, advertising, personal selling, sales promotions and direct marketing), sponsorship is said to be one of the most powerful media now used to communicate and form relationships with stakeholders and target markets (Grey and Skildum-Reid 2003).

Although sponsorship may be attached to social causes and broadcast media such as television programs as well as special events (De Pelsmacker, Geuens and Van den Bergh 2004), just about every public event is now sponsored in some way (Kover 2001). With the emphasis now on 'connecting with' rather than 'talking at' the marketplace, event and festival sponsorship can be an ideal way for marketers to create brand interaction with consumers and stakeholders.

The well-known American sponsorship consultancy IEG defines sponsorship as 'a cash and/or in-kind fee paid to a property (typically a sports, entertainment, event, or organisation) in return for the exploitable commercial potential associated with that property' (in Cornwell et al. 2005). They also state that sponsorship spending by companies in North America fell slightly in 2009 (by 0.8 per cent), but still amounted to a spend of $16.51 billion. This amount can be compared with a spend of $10.2 billion in 2003 and $13.4 billion in 2006. (IEG 2006; IEG 2009). However, the global spend on sponsorship grew to a new record of $44 billion, a 2.1 per cent increase over 2008 (IEG 2009) and they forecast that spending on sponsorship in the Asia–Pacific region will grow by 4 per cent in 2010 to $10.4 billion.

Sponsorship is a strategic marketing investment by the sponsor, not a donation (philanthropy) or a grant (a one-off type of assistance), which means events and festivals management must view sponsorships as working business partnerships between the sponsor and the sponsee (the event or property, as the modern marketing lexicon calls it). Sponsors are investors who expect to see a direct impact on their brand value (enhanced awareness and imagery) as well as the potential for increased sales. In the case of public sector sponsors, some kind of social marketing result is usually sought (for example, a greater awareness of water conservation or the dangers of drink driving). Heineken sought brand exclusivity for its beer and increased sales through its Rugby World Cup 2003 sponsorship, and Kia seeks heightened brand awareness and product features of its cars as a result of its sponsorship of the Australian Open tennis. An interesting example of contra used in sponsorship is Triple J and the pay TV channel V's sponsorship of the Big Day Out. The sponsor receives greater brand recognition and the event receives promotion on the radio and cable TV media, to which their target market listens. The important aspect of these sponsorship examples is that the sponsor seeks a return on their investment that is superior to the returns from an investment in other forms of promotion, or is complementary to their other marketing communications.

Creating a successful event that can generate cash or contra from sponsors means establishing a reciprocal relationship between the organisation providing the sponsorship (corporate, media and/or government) and the event. However, it also means an emotional connection must be made with those consumers targeted by both the event and its sponsors. This three-way relationship that underpins the success of sponsorship is illustrated in figure 11.1. Sponsors use events to emotionally tie their product or service to a market segment that identifies with the event and consequently identifies with the sponsor's product.

The chapter now discusses a number of trends, including the need for more innovative and flexible marketing media, which underpin the rising popularity of sponsorship.

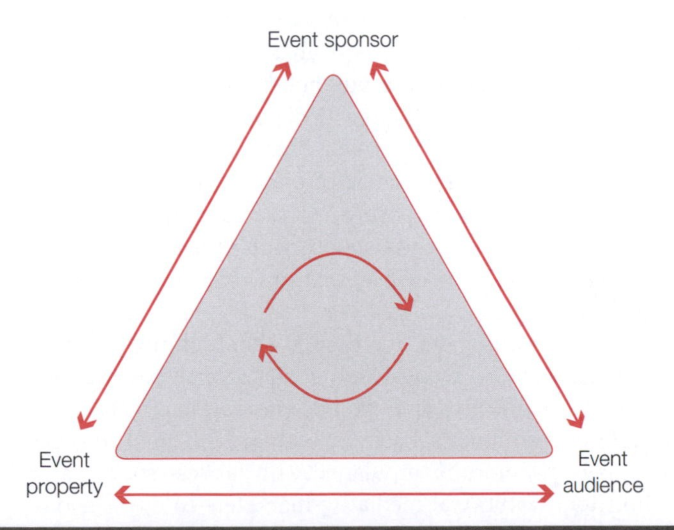

FIGURE 11.1 The trinity of sponsor, event and audiences

Source: Adapted from Fit Sponsorship, www.fitsponsorship.com

TRENDS INFLUENCING THE GROWTH OF SPONSORSHIP

The worldwide interest in sponsorship as a form of integrated marketing communication originates from a range of socio-cultural and business (including marketing and media) trends.

Firstly, a growth in the popularity of events and festivals as leisure experiences has paralleled recognition that festivals and events offer unique social environments to connect with discrete market segments. Creative sponsorship can reach consumers in environments in which they are having a good time and so they are more likely to accept a well-considered marketing message. There is also evidence (Crimmins and Horn 1996; McDaniel 1999; Schrieber 1994), that committed and loyal fans of a musical group or sport will attach themselves to those brands that support their interest; for example, Uncle Toby's, Billabong and Toyota are companies that have gained significant brand equity and consequent sales from Australian sports sponsorships. Similarly, Virgin Mobile, as a major festival sponsor in the United Kingdom, considers that 'festivals offer a fantastic opportunity for brands to get close to consumers when they are excited and passionate. It's by harnessing that passion and adding to that experience that you benefit' (*New Media Age* 2003). International companies operating in Australia also view sponsorship as an effective method to connect with their Australian market. For example, renowned Australian events such as the Australian Open Tennis tournament were sponsored in 2007 by a Korean car company, a multinational beauty care company, and an American finance company — and the Korean car company was still the major sponsor in 2010. These companies must believe that their target market both watches tennis and will feel emotionally closer to their product as a result of their sponsorship.

The previous examples are typical of companies expanding into international markets using event sponsorship to create brand awareness in their new markets. Another Australian example is Vodafone, which used its sponsorship of the Australian Rugby Union team events to launch its brand in Australia. The 3 Network used a sponsorship of Cricket Australia's international events in a similar fashion. The growth of sponsorship can also be attributed to changes in marketing itself — with the shift away from simple transactions to relationship building between the firm and its customers. New trends in marketing communication media give event sponsors the chance to interact directly with their markets to create a brand relationship. Simultaneous brand exposure can be achieved through a range of on-site communication and alternative media. Sponsors are getting extra exposure, for example, as a result of live streaming events onto the internet, text messages, sponsorship of live sites away from the event and giant screens at festivals that display text and photo messages from the crowd responding to billboard ads.

Sponsorship is also gaining an increasing share of most marketers' toolkits because consumers are more cynical about traditional advertising. Sponsorship is perceived to be a more effective and efficient promotional method. When sponsorship is perceived to be a commercial activity with some benefit to society, consumers view advertising as being more manipulative with far less social value (Meenaghan 2001b). The shift from traditional media by marketers to event sponsorship is also a result of:

- the rising costs of media space and the perceived reduced effectiveness of advertising — many consumers now simultaneously use multiple media, such as television, the internet, mobiles and text messaging, and social networking sites
- a growth in the overall number of media outlets (including pay and digital television channels, digital radio stations, specialist magazines, direct mail pieces and the internet) with media advertising becoming extremely cluttered (De Pelsmacker, Geuens and Van den Bergh 2004)
- the expansion of pay and free to air television channels (satellite, cable, and digital) and their subsequent need for program material. Events, especially sports events,

have thus had more opportunity to be televised, enhancing exposure opportunities available to event sponsors.
- the globalisation and commercialisation of sport (Hinch and Higham 2004) as both amateur and professional sports offer more opportunities for organisations to engage in sponsorship of events that have huge television audiences
- a proliferation of brands, products and services offered by fewer manufacturers/providers (Duncan 2002). Companies, therefore, may choose to improve their relationships with their distributors with event-related entertainment and hospitality.
- the relative inability of mass media to target a desired particular market segment, making the promotion not as effective as more tightly targeted promotions.

Sponsorship, especially through events and festivals, has been able to exploit these trends because it communicates in experiential environments, rather than via static media. The state of the economy can also influence the sponsorship environment, as generally a firm's promotional budget is reduced during periods of reduced economic activity. As well, the number of events and individuals seeking sponsorship compared with the sponsorship dollars available in Australia can sometimes be a challenge for the event manager to access new partnerships. Other potential influences on the event manager's ability to attract sponsorship are:
- changing expenditure patterns among marketers; for example, possible increased interest in radio and television program sponsorship and cause-related projects
- an increased diversity in the types of industries, firms and agencies using sponsorship (ranging from local florist shops to national financial institutions)
- a demand for more sophisticated (and innovative) sponsorships, tailored to a sponsor's needs, which produce a behavioural result (sponsorships that 'make the phones ring')
- the growing attachment of sponsors to events with broadcast coverage — events that are not televised or streamed to the audience via other channels are less attractive to corporate sponsors because the sponsors receive less exposure (De Pelsmacker, Geuens and Van den Bergh 2004)
- the increasing use of social networking sites (such as YouTube) in sponsorship activity; events using co-sponsorship (for example, the Festival of Running joining forces with a Football Australia A league team to promote its festival); and an increase in eco-friendly green activities (IEG 2010)
- the introduction sponsorship advisory companies into Australia that mirror IEG in the USA, whose role is to facilitate and broker relationships between an event (or property as they are known as in the American marketing lexicon) and potential sponsors. An Australian example is Fit Sponsorship Marketing (www.fitsponsorship.com) who specialise in working with rights holders (the event) in three areas: building capacity to attract and maintain corporate partners; helping find meaningful partners; and assisting in developing and servicing partners' needs. ArtsHub, a website that acts as a directory for companies operating in the arts sector, list several marketing organisations that can provide a similar service (www.artshub.com.au), and the Australian Business Arts Foundation brings together arts and business managers (www.abaf.org.au).

All of these environmental trends underline the need for event managers to ensure their preliminary research and SWOT and PEST analyses include a comprehensive analysis of the sponsorship environment. Part of ensuring the success of the event's sponsorship strategy is in knowing the range of benefits available to sponsor partners — not just the benefits to be accrued by the event or festival.

SPONSORSHIP BENEFITS FOR EVENTS AND SPONSORS

Sponsorships of events and festivals (the property) by corporations, media and government are based on a thorough assessment of the benefits to be derived. Event managers must therefore obtain a good understanding of the full suite of potential benefits that a sponsorship will bring to their event/festival and their sponsors so they can customise their strategies. Figure 11.2 shows the exchange relationship between events/festivals and the sponsorship partners first identified by Crompton (1994).

Before embarking on a sponsorship strategy, the event manager should consider the sponsor–partnering benefits for the event and whether the event or festival is 'sponsorship ready'. That is, the event manager must be in a position to be able to supply appropriate benefits to the sponsor, which as many large firms' websites show, they must have before they will even consider a sponsorship proposal.

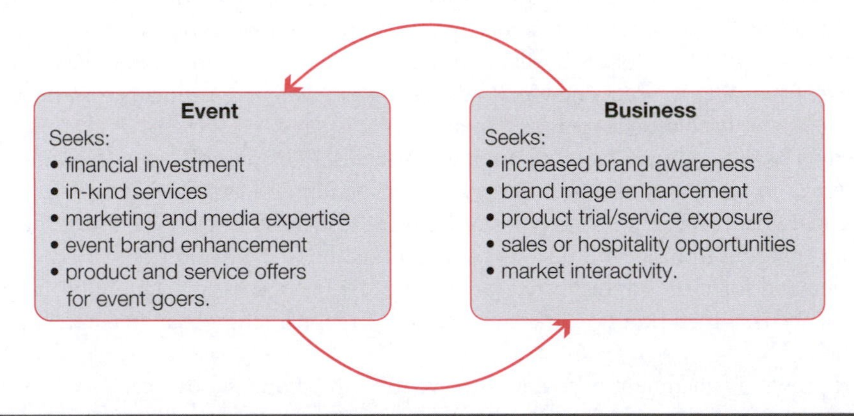

FIGURE 11.2 Exchange relationship in event sponsorship

Source: Crompton 1994.

How events can benefit from sponsorship

For many events and festivals, sponsorship through cash and/or contra (sponsorship paid for in services supplied by the sponsor, such as air travel or hotel rooms if the sponsor is an airline or hotel chain) brings a valuable opportunity for long-term business partnerships. In Australia, this is exemplified by Kia's long-term sponsorship of the Australian Open, and the 3 mobile telephone network's similar sponsorship of the Australian Cricket test team, both of which introduced the sponsors' products into the mass Australian market. For the event or festival, sponsorship is therefore much more than a means of boosting revenues, as it must also meet the needs and objectives of its sponsors.

Despite the obvious advantages of sponsorship, not all events and festivals understand the management implications of attracting business partners. Many event managers assume sponsorship is an appropriate source of income for their event, but confuse it with philanthropy. Geldard and Sinclair (2004) identify these questions that an event manager should ask before seeking sponsorship as a revenue stream:

- *Does the event have sufficient rights or benefits that can be offered to sponsors?* Organisations must be able to recognise the potential of the event to achieve their marketing objectives, such as image enhancement or the development of stronger relationships with suppliers/buyers. If the desired benefits are not present, an event manager would be wasting his or her time in seeking income from this source.

A better alternative in some instances may be to seek a donation, which, by its nature, does not require strategic marketing benefits to be given in return. It is not uncommon for corporations, particularly large corporations, to provide a philanthropic allocation of funds specifically for this purpose. Commonly, these funds are made available to events of a community or charitable nature.

- *Are the event's stakeholders likely to approve of commercial sponsorship?* It is not hard to imagine situations where some members of a particular association or the potential event audience might view commercial sponsorship negatively. A conservation body seeking sponsorship for its annual conference, for example, could find that its membership is against commercial involvement and at best, extremely selective about the companies with whom they will associate. In effect, broad support among the event's internal stakeholders is essential for sponsorship to be successful.
- *Is the target market of the event congruent with the target market of the sponsor?* In order for the sponsorship to be able to deliver benefits to a sponsor, the target markets must be congruent. For example, Uncle Toby's breakfast cereal and the surfing Ironman competition's markets (children and young adults and their mothers) were congruent, which meant that Uncle Toby's brand received the important marketing benefit of association with a respected group of athletes, whose performances were admired by its target market. But, as a general rule, events that appeal to mass markets, also appeal to producers of products that sell to a mass market, which is a reason why Coca-Cola sponsors many events.
- *Are there some companies that are simply not suitable as sponsors?* Event managers need to identify organisations that are inappropriate as sponsorship partners. A charity event aimed at raising funds for a children's hospital or another health-related cause, for example, is unlikely to accept sponsorship from fast food or alcoholic beverage companies.
- *Does the event have the resources and skills to market and manage sponsorship?* A considerable amount of time and effort is required to research, develop and market sponsorships to potential sponsor targets. Furthermore, sponsorship must be managed after the contract is finalised to ensure all promises made in the proposal are fulfilled. This involves allocating staff and other resources to building and sustaining the sponsor relationship.

Sponsors' benefits — links with the consumer response

The sponsor's investment in assisting a sport or art form event occurs because it is believed to create goodwill towards the sponsor's brand or product/service among attendees (Meenaghan 2001a; Crimmins and Horn 1996).

From the somewhat limited research undertaken it appears that sponsorship does stimulate goodwill (a positive attitude), which in turn influences consumer relationships with sponsors' brands (see, for example, Rifon et al. 2004 and Roy and Cornwell 2003). For example, Performance Research (2001) has reported that over half of those with an interest in the arts said that they would almost always buy a product that sponsored cultural events (Dolphin 2003). Figure 11.3 shows how sponsorship effects narrow at an individual event/activity level. It also demonstrates how the intensity of goodwill towards the sponsor moves in parallel with the intensity of fan or event consumer involvement.

Figure 11.3 also shows that the more actively engaged a person is with the sponsored event, the stronger the link between the sponsor's brand and the event (De Pelsmacker, Geuens and Van den Bergh 2004). This is a good reason why many companies sponsor festivals or sports events that have loyal and dedicated audiences.

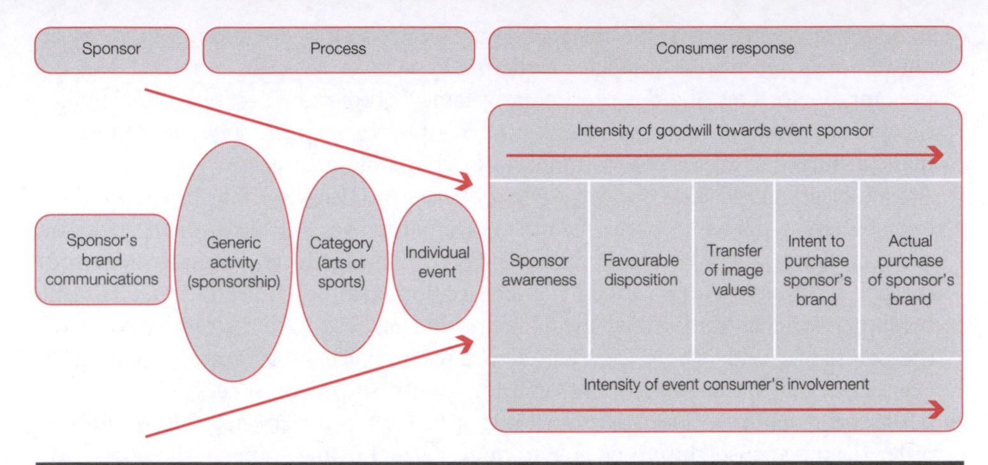

FIGURE 11.3 The sponsorship effects process

Source: Adapted from Meenaghan 2001a, p. 115.

Based on consumer behaviour theories, various writers on sponsorship (De Pelsmacker, Geuens and Van den Bergh 2004; Geldard and Sinclair 2002; Meenaghan 2001b) highlight an array of marketing benefits of event and festival sponsorship gained by corporate sponsors. These benefits are:

- *Access to specific niche/target markets.* The Council for Australian University Tourism and Hospitality Education (CAUTHE) holds an annual conference for tourism academics that provides an opportunity for book publishers who have titles in that area to access those who prescribe textbooks to their students. Other such events supply an effective and efficient medium for a firm to communicate with its potential consumers.
- *Corporate brand image creation/enhancement.* For major service providers like banks and telephony companies, the lack of a tangible product complicates the task of brand imaging. Sponsorship of festivals and events is therefore a valuable form of corporate image enhancement, which is illustrated by the Commonwealth Bank of Australia and the mobile phone company 3's sponsorship of Cricket Australia's Tests and one-day series in 2009–10.
- *Building brand awareness for an organisation and its services/products.* The 3 Network, a mobile phone company, built its brand awareness and product features by sponsoring Cricket Australia's Ashes cricket test series in 2009. Because mobile telephony is now a mass market, it can effectively use a sports event that is watched by a mass market — everyone from the Prime Minister to school children — all of whom are potential mobile phone users.
- *Influencing consumer attitudes about a product or service brand.* Some companies use sponsorship as a strategy to change consumer perceptions about a longstanding brand. Suncorp's Rugby World Cup sponsorship goal was to build credibility for the bank's GIO brand outside its home state of Queensland (Ferguson 2004). Consumer surprise about the link between an older brand such as GIO and the Rugby World Cup was welcomed by Suncorp as the first step towards repositioning GIO in the mindset of consumers in Australia's southern states.
- *Associating a product or service with a particular lifestyle.* A sponsor in 2007 of one of Australia's leading youth music festivals, the Big Day Out in Sydney, was New South

Wales Health, a governmental body, with a pertinent message on drug use aimed at the event's target market.

- *Improving relationships with distribution channel members.* A corporation may be seeking to develop stronger relationships with agents or firms that currently distribute its products, or to establish new distribution outlets. For well over ten years Qantas was a major sponsor of the Australian Grand Prix. One of the many ways in which Qantas used this sponsorship was as an incentive for its agency distribution network. Travel agents who met specified targets were invited to the event as guests of the sponsor and entertained royally in the sponsor's box.
- *Achieving product sales and merchandising opportunities.* The Big Day Out gave a water company and Lipton opportunities to both promote their product as a non-alcoholic alternative drink (Tooheys Extra Dry, Smirnoff Vodka, Jim Beam and Jaegermeister were the other beverage sponsors) and give away samples of the different flavours of the iced tea and water.
- *Demonstrating product attributes.* Festivals and events can be used by sponsors to demonstrate new products or technology. For example, the National General Assembly of Local Government was sponsored in 2006 and 2007 by Australia Post Billpay, which demonstrated how its technology made the payment of local government rates more effective and efficient.
- *Providing employee rewards and recognition.* Organisations often perceive the sponsorship of a sports or cultural event as a way of giving their employees access to a corporate box and/or tickets to reward or motivate them. For example, part sponsorship of the international 20/20 cricket games may include a certain number of tickets to these events, which the company can use to reward staff or distributors such as retailers in each of the cities where the games are played.
- *Creating goodwill and a climate of consent for an organisation's activities.* Companies as diverse as airlines, mining organisations, energy providers, banks and pharmaceutical manufacturers all support charity events to create an image in the community of being good corporate citizens. The Qantas community website (http://www.qantas.com.au/travel/airlines/community-support/global/en) lists the many sporting, cultural and community organisations that Qantas sponsors. This is done mainly to create goodwill between the Australian community and its national carrier, and generate positive political images of a company that relies on the support of the Australian government and citizens. Gwinner (2005) points out that if, without the sponsor, a sports event may not happen, or the standard of the athletes may not be as high, or that ticket prices may be more expensive, considerable goodwill is generated for the sponsor from the attendees of the event.
- *Entertaining key clients with corporate hospitality.* Corporate hospitality is an important drawcard for sponsors, especially those with business-to-business clients. Every major sports or cultural event is replete with corporate boxes, where the sponsoring organisation has opportunities to entertain key clients in an informal and enjoyable environment. Where working relationships are quite intense, corporate hospitality events can break down the barriers and create social bonds that forge a better relationship between suppliers and clients.

In looking at the many benefits derived by sponsors, it should also be remembered that public sector bodies (for example, local councils, state government health departments, authorities/commissions and agencies) often use sponsorship as a marketing communications tool. Many of the benefits illustrated in the corporate context are equally applicable to them. Most public sector agencies now employ marketing strategies to generate awareness of their products/services or issues and to influence community behaviour (for example, safe driving or water conservation), in addition to using event sponsorship to drive economic activity in the region or state. This public sector strategy is exemplified by the major event corporations funded by state governments in Australia's states and territories. In the 2007 New South Wales election campaign, then premier Iemma announced the formation of a New South Wales major events corporation to replace the existing major events board and the appointment of former Football Australia supremo John O'Neill to advise on its formation and subsequent activities (Clennell 2007).

Events and festivals may stimulate economic development in a regional area (for example, the Australasian Country Music Festival in Tamworth, New South Wales, or the Elvis Festival in Parkes, New South Wales) and also create a greater sense of identity or cohesion and enhance the facilities available to local residents. To attract sponsorship, event organisers must think about how they can provide at least several of the benefits identified here.

event profile

FUJITSU AND V8

In the late 1980s, Fujitsu's parent company refocused its business objectives around its key strengths in research and manufacturing in two main product categories — air conditioning and plasma display devices. The aim was to market leading products of a world-class standard. Fujitsu is now the number one supplier of air conditioning within Australia and regarded as the industry benchmark for plasma display technology products for picture quality and performance.

Fujitsu saw opportunities to further enhance brand awareness through associating itself in positive ways with other leaders in their respective fields. Successful businesses recognise the importance of brand differentiation, or making the brand stand out in the minds of consumers in ways that support the creation of strong consumer/brand relationships.

Fujitsu explored sponsorship as one way of broadening its marketing activities through finding additional ways to make the brand stand out from competitors. V8 Supercar racing was identified as a sport that was enjoying increasing popularity as a fast-paced, action-packed sport popular among a broad range of spectators and viewers. Marketers refer to this as identifying a broad consumer demographic. Strong growth in spectator and viewer numbers marks the sport as a 'winner', consistent with Fujitsu's desire to position its products as winners in their markets.

Fujitsu decided to associate itself with V8 Supercar racing through providing sponsorship of:

- the Fujitsu V8 Supercar Series, a series of V8 car races held around Australia.
- a V8 Supercar racing team, the Fujitsu Racing Team.
- Fujitsu General has also been appointed the 'Official Plasma Screen of the V8 Supercar Series'.

Fujitsu began its initial involvement with V8 Supercar racing through supporting an independent entrant — a privateer — in the Development series. This series of motor races runs across the country between March and December and provides young, talented V8 Supercar drivers the opportunity to improve and sharpen their skills, and the chance to break into the main Championship Series.

Fujitsu now sponsors the Development Series, called the Fujitsu V8 Supercar Series. It also sponsors a racing team — Fujitsu Racing.

The sport has grown rapidly over the past fifteen years and is now almost a year-round sport providing strong appeal to Fujitsu marketers. It is a good fit for them as one of their marketing aims is to change consumer mindsets around air conditioning as a year-round solution. Fujitsu identified these marketing opportunities from the partnership:

- increase in brand exposure to a very wide consumer demographic
- the sport attracts a wide range of people in its audience
- specific, direct involvement with the sport
- Fujitsu is able to develop much closer customer relationships
- Fujitsu is able to provide unique on-track experiences and corporate hospitality over longer periods.

V8 Supercars benefit from this partnership through:

- having plasma screens supplied to the official hospitality areas and in other areas
- these are perfect for showing the fast-paced action
- increased interest in the sport
- more people at the sport through the corporate hospitality Fujitsu provides
- obtaining greater synergies
- being affiliated with a high-tech sponsor raises the profile of the sport.

A different form of sponsorship

A key sponsorship benefit relates to the positive public relations that can be generated through sponsoring high profile not-for-profit organisations. Fujitsu has partnered with the Sporting Chance Cancer Foundation which was formed in 1998 by former Australian Cricket Captain Mark Taylor, Rugby League legend Reg Gasnier, Olympian Raelene Boyle and Triple Brownlow Medallist Bob Skilton.

Fujitsu benefits from this type of sponsorship through the promotional opportunities offered from their association as a principal sponsor of a key program — additional home care for cancer patients.

Sponsorship arrangements differ from those with V8 Supercars. In this example, Fujitsu donates a fixed dollar amount from the sale of each air conditioning unit which equates to hundreds of thousands of dollars, providing the Foundation with access to funds for specific programs.

Intelligent sponsorship for Fujitsu involves far more than putting its name on V8 Supercars or becoming associated with the Sporting Chance Cancer Foundation. Fujitsu has entered into partnerships with these organisations in ways designed to support its corporate strategy of building its brand and creating greater brand awareness.

Excerpt from The Australian Financial Review Case Studies with Business News.
Permission given by Australian Business Case Studies Pty Ltd.

Sponsorship leveraging — adding value to the investment

To fully capitalise on a sponsorship investment, corporate and government agencies usually develop a leveraging strategy or a range of marketing activities that extend the sponsorship benefits well beyond the event or festival's promised offer. The 2003 Sponsorship Decision Makers Survey found that more than 50 per cent of Australian sponsors are now spending at a ratio of around 2:1 on leveraging their sponsorships (Sponsorship Insights and the Australasian Sponsorship Marketing Association 2003). The average spend of Australian sponsors on leveraging is slightly higher than their counterparts in the USA. Nevertheless, Adidas, as an official sponsor of the FIFA 2002 World Cup, reportedly budgeted around $88 million to exploit its sponsorship, with the cost of official sponsorships being somewhere between $20 million and 28 million (Pickett 2002).

A topical example of sponsorship leveraging is the activities surrounding the mobile telephony 3 network's sponsorship of Australian test cricket. 3 did this by:

- giving 3 customers the opportunity to watch all the matches live on their iPhone — a technological marvel

- giving 3 customers access to *The Pitch*, a TV cricket show made specifically for mobile TV — another technological marvel
- the use of Australian cricket greats Brett Lee and Adam Gilchrist in promotional activity, including TV advertisements
- the use of members of the Australian cricket team in a 3 mobile Men of Cricket calendar, used to raise money for the McGrath Foundation

The fit between sponsor and sponsee

Cornwell et al.'s (2006) work shows that the greater the fit between sponsor and sponsee (the event) the more effective the sponsorship will be for both parties. Fit has been defined as relevance, complementality, or compatibility in the sponsorship literature (Rifon et al. 2004; Johar and Pham 1999), but another definition is the extent of the congruence between the sponsor's products and markets and the event's. Sponsorship consultant Colterman (2009) is of the view that 'fit' has these three dimensions:

1. The audience for the event and the sponsor's products are congruent.
2. The timing of the event fits the sponsor's schedule — for example, an event before Christmas suits, or fits, a department store's promotion schedule.
3. The nature of the 'property' (the event) has congruence with the current aims of the sponsor — for example, a sponsor who needs their 'green' credentials burnished may sponsor an 'eco' event.

Figure 11.4 shows the different *elements* and consequent *results* of the 'fit' phenomenon.

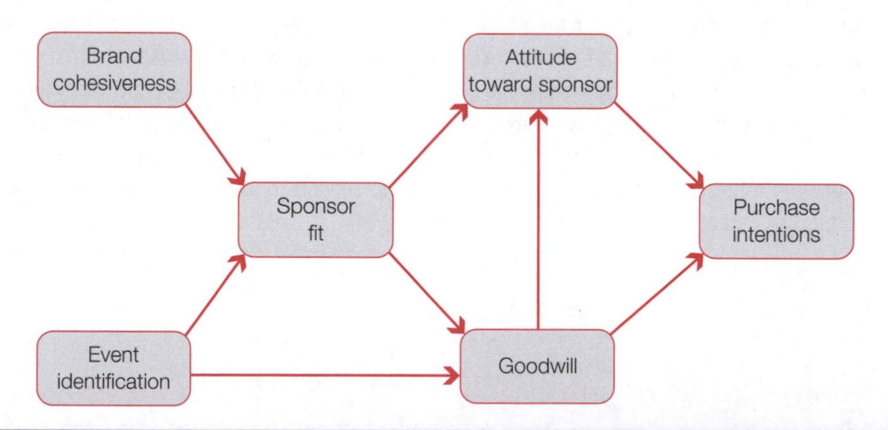

FIGURE 11.4 The effect of excellent sponsor fit

Source: Gwinner and Bennet 2007.

- Brand cohesiveness: brands that have a clear and distinct image. Qantas is an example of such a brand in the Australian marketplace.
- Event identification: how essential and important is the event to its audience. For the 18–25-year-old-music-loving demographic, the Big Day Out is an event with which it identifies strongly.
- Sponsor fit: how relevant to and compatible with the event market are the sponsor's products. Qantas's long running sponsorship of the Australian Grand Prix is an example of fit as both the event and Qantas are international and high tech.
- Attitude towards the sponsor: this is the favourable disposition that the event market has to the sponsor's product(s). Pay television Channel V's sponsorship of the Big

Day Out would increase the favourable disposition towards this music channel from the event's audience.

- Goodwill: when a sponsor takes actions that facilitate the event market's enjoyment of the event, goodwill is generated towards the sponsor. Radio station Triple J's sponsorship of the Big Day Out caused the audience to consider the station partly responsible for enabling the event to occur with the line-up of artists, which generated goodwill to the sponsor.
- Purchase intentions: the primary reason business sponsors invest in events — if purchase intention changes, the sponsorship is effective.

Gwinner and Bennet's (2007) study of the audience of an action sports event in the United States showed that 'those who perceive fit between an event's image and the sponsoring brand exhibit a significantly better attitude toward the sponsoring brand than those who perceive less fit between the two properties'. They also found that goodwill to the sponsor's brand(s) is influenced by fit. Another of their study's findings was that perceived fit positively impacted on purchase intentions through both the attitude toward the sponsor and goodwill elements shown in figure 11.4.

The lesson for event managers is to approach those organisations whose products have congruence with the perceptions of the event's market. In that way the benefits of the sponsorship are enhanced for the sponsor, which ensures both parties to the sponsorship achieve their objectives — the classic win–win situation.

THE VALUE OF SPONSORSHIP POLICY

Just as most corporations and government agencies will establish procedures and policies to guide their decision making, Grey and Skildum-Reid (2003) strongly recommend that all events seeking sponsorship design a sponsorship policy. They suggest that it should state:

- the event's history of sponsorship and its approach to it, including some definition of what constitutes sponsorship versus grants and donations
- the event's objectives, processes and procedures for seeking sponsorship
- the rules for entering into sponsorship and the kinds of companies that 'fit' the event
- the uniform approach adopted in seeking sponsorship, including whether all proposals are to follow a particular format and whether each sponsorship is required to have a management plan developed for it
- the levels of accountability and responsibility, such as who in the organisation can approve the sponsorship, who is responsible for its outcome, and who is the sponsor liaison person in the organisation
- the time at which the policy will be subject to review and evaluation.

It is noticeable that many sponsors now have a page on their corporate website that lists their sponsorship policy and what an event seeking sponsorship must produce (see, for example, Yarra Trams, www.yarratrams.com.au). It is wise for an event to review the requirements of potential sponsors to ensure that these are included in their sponsorship policy.

For most events and festivals, involving the senior management of the event as well as staff in the drafting of the sponsorship policy is a wise idea. Having a sense of ownership of the sponsorship policy becomes important if there are conflicts or disputes over decisions about sponsors. For larger events and festivals, the policy would also be presented to and approved by a board of directors.

STAGES IN DEVELOPING THE EVENT SPONSORSHIP STRATEGY

Developing an event sponsorship strategy is a distinct task. Remember that it will have an interactive relationship with the event's marketing strategy because, whether it is venue design, ticketing, integrated marketing communications or even the program itself, the sponsor's identification needs to be integrated in as many aspects of the event as is feasible.

A strategy means establishing the objectives of the event and ways to achieve them, which also applies to the event's sponsorship. For event managers, this involves thinking about event/festival consumers and the fit they might have with corporate brands. It also involves thinking about the attributes and values of the event and companies that might share those values; the mix of sponsors who together might create a close-knit sponsor family; and brainstorming the kinds of partnerships that will grow the event — in other words, enhancing the fit between sponsor and sponsee (the event property).

Profiling the event audience

The first step in sponsorship strategy development is to consider again the target markets of the event or festival. Market segmentation techniques are a sound basis for establishing fit between potential sponsors and the consumers who frequent your event. Like all forms of integrated marketing communication, event sponsorship is most successful as a marketing medium when there is a solid database that profiles existing visitors and members/subscribers and their preferences. Sponsors will look for a reliable picture (demographics, socioeconomic status, psychographics) of the event audience to ensure there is market congruence and that an investment in the event will help achieve their own marketing objectives efficiently.

Establishing what the event can offer potential sponsors

Despite the variation in the size and scope of different events and festivals, some common assets (defined as benefits that the property can offer the sponsor) include:

- the agreement to purchase product/services from a sponsor (for example, alcohol, transport, food)
- event naming rights
- exclusivity (the capacity to lock out competition within a brand category)
- business and sponsor networking opportunities
- merchandising rights
- media exposure, including advertising opportunities during the event
- venue signage
- joint advertising with sponsors
- the capacity to demonstrate their product or technology at the event
- corporate hospitality services
- tickets for the sponsor's use.

For a smaller property, the process will be less complex than with larger event organisations. A professional football team in a major league, for example, may have more than 100 saleable benefits over a series of games. A local festival staged annually has an inventory that is much easier to manage. Yet, with a little creativity, the festival or event marketer can also create new sponsor benefits. Apart from identifying benefits like signage not previously used for branding within the festival (for example, brand exposure at the front of a concert stage), some tailor-made assets for sponsors can be devised. A sports team can offer its best-known player consuming a sponsor's product, or a music property can offer an opportunity to go back stage to meet the performers.

It is safe to assume that many small- to medium-sized events and festivals with few if any sponsorship management staff will have untapped resources. However, in identifying and expanding the event's sponsor benefit register, careful consideration must also be given to the time and personnel needed to effectively manage and market those sponsor benefits.

Building the event sponsorship list

In designing a sponsorship strategy, event managers will usually work out how a list of potential sponsors can be established, given the bundles of property (festival or event) assets that are available for purchase. Geldard and Sinclair (2004) identify strategies for this, such as sole sponsorship, hierarchical packages (for example, tiers of gold, silver, bronze), a pyramid structure (whereby each sponsor level below the principal sponsor jointly spends the amount invested by the top sponsor with proportional benefits), a level playing field (all sponsors negotiate and leverage their own benefits), or an *ad hoc* approach where the property's assets are negotiated on what the market will bear.

Although sole sponsorship of a regional festival may have the advantage of 'keeping it simple', the festival's survival is threatened if the sole sponsor is lost. For this reason, many properties with a limited array of assets choose a tiered approach (different levels of dollar investment for set benefit packages). However, as Grey and Skildum-Reid (2003, p. 97) point out, 'most events/festivals end up formulating their packages so that all of the levels get access to the best benefits, with the lower levels simply getting less of the supporting benefits'. For this reason, many events and teams, including the Brisbane Broncos, now tailor their benefit packages for each sponsor using only broad categories, such as major media, corporate and support sponsors.

Using this approach, the sponsors are usually grouped according to their *type* (for example, naming rights, presenting sponsorship of a section, event, entry, team or particular day, preferred suppliers) and their *exclusivity* (among sponsors at any level, among sponsors at or below a given level, as a supplier or seller at the event or within event-driven marketing collateral) (Grey and Skildum-Reid 2003). The purchase of other event assets such as merchandising rights, licences and endorsements, hospitality, signage and database access by sponsors, to name just a few, can serve to further differentiate the event sponsor packages.

The use of tailor-made sponsorship packages rather than using a template that is sent to all and sundry is recommended for a number of reasons (Welsh 2003):

- Packaged event properties are rarely a perfect fit for potential sponsors — most are either too broad or too narrow in their consumer reach and the rights available may be either more or less than the sponsor wants.
- Sponsors are often seeking more control over their sponsorship and its potential leveraging than packaged strategies offer — the simple transactional nature of buyer–seller arrangements is being replaced by partnerships and, in some cases, the sponsor clearly has leadership in driving the relationship.
- Poor sponsorship packaging by events and festivals can lead to a greater instance of *ambush marketing* in certain industry/product categories (for example, banking and finance), or attempts by non-sponsoring companies to capitalise on an event's image and prestige by implying that they are sponsors (IEG Network 1997).

- Multiple layers of sponsorship introduced by events can cause confusion among audiences and sponsors — as the different sponsorship categories become more prolific, there is more potential for a loss of control by event organisers and sponsor conflicts (Shani and Sandler 1998).

In light of these challenges, the appeal of determining sponsor partnerships on a case-by-case basis (with all sponsors informed of this practice) is growing.

Matching event benefits with potential sponsors

Once the approach to building a potential sponsorship list is determined, the process of identifying the right sponsor(s) begins. As noted, a first criterion is to find those organisations that want to communicate with the same audience (or a significant component of it), or who have a specific issue (market, image, or penetration of a segment, for example) that sponsorship of the event may assist in solving. Various research techniques to identify potential sponsors can be used, such as carefully monitoring the business environment, networking, reading the financial and business press, and making thoughtful observation of market changes. Which organisations are looking to enter new markets in the event's region? Which companies appear to have attributes and values that match those of the event/festival?

An apposite example of a festival offering potential sponsors a list of event benefits is the Sydney Festival. It received sponsorship support in 2010 from the New South Wales Government, the City of Sydney and, principal sponsor, the ANZ Bank (Sydney Festival 2010). All three principal sponsors believed that the festival offered the opportunity to communicate with an audience that is important to them, as did the long list of other sponsors of the Sydney Festival.

The Sydney Festival lists these event benefits that it can deliver to potential sponsors (Sydney Festival 2010b):

- A loyal, educated audience
- Acknowledgement across an extensive marketing campaign
- Broad media coverage
- Exceptional corporate hospitality
- Creative promotions, product placement and sampling opportunities
- Access to very influential corporate and government stakeholders
- Positive brand alignment
- Sophisticated measurement and research tools.

They go on to assert that 'in short, we are a sophisticated business solution, and our award-winning business development team is committed to helping you achieve solid returns on any investment in the Festival' (Sydney Festival 2010).

By monitoring the business environment, an event manager can actively identify any government agencies or business firms that are seeking to reposition themselves, regain market acceptance or introduce new products or services. Once identified, and depending on the nature of the event, such organisations can become a sponsorship target. An organiser of a garden festival, for example, may notice that a horticultural company has just launched a new range of fertilisers. This development could be a sponsorship opportunity if the company can be convinced that the event draws the right consumer audience to increase awareness and sales of its new product line.

As Cowan (2006) points out, sponsorship of arts events has the following benefits for sponsors.

- It has the ability to attract key decision makers to the event. Many people in executive positions are interested in the arts and women executives are more likely to accept an invitation.

- The arts and the organisations that sponsor them find favour with politicians, as government support for artistic endeavours attests.
- Research by Brown and Dancin (1997) supports Cowan's claim that the goodwill created is much greater if the audience believes that the sponsor is making a particular contribution that enables the event to occur, rather than merely supporting an event that would have happened without the sponsorship.
- Many events, particularly creative arts events, generate media attention because they fulfil the first criterion for news — they are new — so a sponsor can be associated with good news stories.
- The twenty-first century will see companies valued because of their innovation and creativity; therefore, associating via sponsorship with innovative and creative arts events may help give them an image of innovation and being leading edge in technological innovation.

Once potential sponsors are identified, a more detailed examination of their business and marketing objectives and the types of assets that will meet their needs can be completed. Additional information that might be sought includes the types of event the organisation is willing to sponsor, whether the organisation is tied to particular causes (for example, charities) and the time in their planning cycle when they allocate their sponsorship budget (sponsorship proposals should be submitted to them some months before this time). Information such as this last item is likely to require a direct inquiry to the company's marketing personnel.

The sponsorship pitch

Once the potential sponsor(s) have been listed, the next challenge for the event manager is to determine the marketing or management person who will be the sponsorship decision maker within the targeted company. In small companies, this person is likely to be the chief executive officer (CEO) or managing director. In companies of moderate size, the marketing or public relations manager may make such decisions, while in large corporations, a dedicated sponsorship section could exist within the marketing, public relations or corporate affairs areas, as exists for Qantas, Telstra, Australia Post, Toyota and other major sponsors of Australian events.

Before developing any written proposal, it is customary to write a brief introductory letter to profile your event and the sponsorship opportunity. Some large corporations now have a website in which the event property can give details of the sponsorship opportunities that the company wants in a sponsorship, so decision making rests not on a personal whim, but on agreed criteria. Because of the efficiencies inherent in this, it is likely that all major sponsors of Australian events will eventually use this method.

There are many benefits in becoming acquainted with the company before preparing a proposal, simply because of the need to fully understand their product/brand attributes, their business objectives, their competition, how they use their current sponsorships and other promotional media and the ways in which sponsorship proposals need to be structured to satisfy their needs. Most major companies are inundated with sponsorship offers, so generally a request for the sponsorship proposal to be in writing will be made to weed out the tyre kickers.

The most successful sponsorship approach is one where the property has put a lot of effort into planning before approaching the sponsor (much like applying for a job). Certainly the more preparation and planning to better understand the organisation's culture and marketing objectives that is done beforehand, the more successful the proposal will be (Harrison 2004).

Preparing and presenting sponsorship proposals

A formal proposal document is commonly how sponsorship is negotiated and partnerships are formed. In broad terms, Geldard and Sinclair (2004) suggest that the sponsorship proposal should address the following questions:

- what is the organisation being asked to sponsor?
- what will the organisation receive for its sponsorship?
- what is it going to cost?

The length and level of detail a proposal uses to answer these questions depends on the value and cost of the sponsor partnership. However, a comprehensive treatment of these areas would mean the proposal would include:

- an overview of the event, including (as applicable) its mission/goals, history, location, current and past sponsors, program/duration, staff, past or anticipated level of media coverage, past or predicted attendance levels, and actual or predicted attendee profile (for example, age, income, sex, occupation)
- the sponsorship package on offer and its associated cost. In pricing the sponsorship, it should be remembered that marketers have a range of alternative promotional media such as advertising, direct marketing and other tools that could achieve similar outcomes (depending on the sponsor's marketing objectives), so the sponsorship should not cost more than other types of promotion reaching a similar volume of their target market.
- the proposed duration of the sponsorship agreement
- the strategic fit between the proposal and the business and marketing needs of the organisation. Discussion here will be based on research conducted using the sources noted earlier.
- the event's contact details for the company's response and follow-up negotiation.

Most sponsors of large events require at least a 12-month timeframe to maximise their sponsorship and around two years for a major sponsorship — for example, a Rugby World Cup. Sponsorships for events scheduled less than six months from the time of the initial approach have far less opportunity to be successfully leveraged by marketing personnel.

The failure rate with sponsorship proposals suggests that much more needs to be understood by event managers about their preparation. Ukman (1995) has some sage advice in these six attributes of a successful proposal:

1. *Sell benefits, not features*. Many proposals describe the features of the event, such as the artistic merit of the festival, rather than the event's marketing assets and sponsor benefits. Sponsors buy marketing communication platforms so that they can reach their stakeholders and market(s) to form relationships or sell products or services.
2. *Address the sponsor's needs, not those of the event*. Many proposals emphasise the event's need for money, rather than the sponsor's needs such as market access, corporate hospitality or a better understanding of a new brand. Remember, event sponsorships should be seen as partnerships, not a means to patch holes in the event budget (Harrison 2004).
3. *Tailor the proposal to the business category*. As noted, each of the event's benefits will have a different level of importance to each potential sponsor. An insurance company, for example, might be interested in an event's database, while a soft drink marketer is likely to be more concerned with on-site sales opportunities. A tailored strategy should be worked out based on some research and discussions among interested event personnel before constructing the sponsorship proposal.

4. *Include promotional extensions*. The two major sources of sponsor benefits are addressed here. First, there are the benefits being purchased; for example, identification in marketing material and on-site signage that come with the sponsorship and only require action on the part of the event manager. The second set of benefits emerges from the sponsor's event leveraging, such as trade, retail and sales extensions. Particular leveraging activities might include competitions, redemption offers (for example, free ticket offers for the customers of a sponsor's wholesalers) and hospitality. It is not enough to give sponsors a checklist of the direct benefits of the assets being purchased — a proposal should include the 'exploitation or leveraging menu' showing them how to leverage their investment.
5. *Minimise risk*. Risk can be reduced through indicating some guaranteed marketing activities (including media space reach and frequency) in the package, listing reputable co-sponsors and showing the steps that will be taken to minimise the risk of ambush marketing by other companies. A clear indication of how the event or festival will service the sponsorship should also be given prominence in the proposal.
6. *Include added value*. The proposal should be presented in terms of its total impact on achieving results for the sponsor, rather than focusing on one aspect such as media. Generally, sponsors will be looking for an array of those benefits highlighted earlier in the chapter — how the sponsorship will build relationships internally with staff, ways in which it will facilitate networking with other sponsors or potential business partners, and how it can build sales among consumer and business audiences.

Given that many of the organisations targeted by events as potential sponsors receive large numbers of proposals each week, an effort should be made to ensure the proposal provides sufficient information on which a decision can be made. If the organisation has published guidelines for sponsorship seekers to follow, it should be evident from the contents page and a quick scan of the proposal that these matters have been addressed. Some attempt to make a proposal stand out can also be useful. A food and wine festival may print a brief version of the proposal on a good bottle of wine, for example, as well as submitting the fuller version. But be aware that glossy, printed proposals and presentations are usually not well accepted, because they do not suggest that the event is offering a customised partnership (Grey and Skildum-Reid 2003).

Time is increasingly crucial in business. If a proposal is too long, has not been based on sound research, does not contain adequate information or it leaves out key elements (such as event contact details), the chances of the proposal being discarded are high. As a general rule, the length of a sponsorship proposal should be commensurate with the amount of money sought and must be as succinct as possible. If the dollar value of the sponsorship is substantial and the proposal is over five pages (more than ten pages could be too long), an executive summary should give a snapshot of its key elements along with a contents page.

Undertaking the sponsorship screening process

Commonly, organisations apply a screening process to sponsorship proposals as they seek to determine which relevant benefits are present. An understanding of this screening process is useful to the event manager as it assists in crafting sponsorship proposals. The framework for understanding the screening process developed by Crompton (1993) remains one of the most comprehensive developed to date. The framework adopts the acronym CEDAREEE to identify the major elements of the sponsorship screening process employed by corporations and it summarises nicely what has been already said in this chapter. The acronym is derived from:

- **C**ustomer audience
- **E**xposure potential
- **D**istribution channel audience
- **A**dvantage over competitors
- **R**esource investment involvement required
- **E**vent's characteristics
- **E**vent organisation's reputation
- **E**ntertainment and hospitality opportunities.

While not all of these criteria are applicable to every sponsorship proposal, it is a most effective checklist for the sponsorship proposer to evaluate the sponsorship offer to ensure that all aspects of sponsorship have been thought of, and that all the benefits of the sponsorship offer have been developed and described to the potential sponsor.

An organisation that has received a sponsorship proposal will act in several possible ways. After scanning the proposal, its management and/or marketing personnel may:

- bin it
- request further information
- seek to negotiate in an attempt to have the sponsorship offering improved to meet its needs
- accept the proposal as presented (it is more likely though that some adaptations will occur through negotiation).

Once sent, it is a useful practice to follow up sponsorship proposals within a reasonable period (for example, two weeks afterwards) to determine its status (for example, yet to be considered, under review or rejected). On occasions, the proposed sponsorship package may be of interest to the organisation, but they may wish to 'customise' it further. If this is the case, both the event and potential sponsor can negotiate to move the sponsorship towards a more mutually beneficial offer. Event managers should have a clear understanding of the minimum payment they are prepared to accept for the event sponsorship benefits on offer — to what extent can the event move in its negotiations to create a 'win–win' situation (particularly if multiple sponsors are being sought)? At this stage, it is vitally important not to undervalue the event's benefits — a sponsorship sold below its potential market value will eventually need a price correction, which creates tension with event partners.

An effective method of calculating the worth of an event sponsorship is to calculate the cost of communicating with the target market using other media, such as print. If the cost of newspaper advertisements that reach a target market of 10 000, with a frequency of three times is $x, the value of an event sponsorship that reaches the same size target market should not be less than $x, given all the other advantages that come to a sponsor with a good 'fit' with an event.

Negotiating event sponsorship contracts

It is standard business practice to commit the sponsorship agreement to paper to avoid misunderstandings about the event property's assets and benefits being offered, their costs, payment terms and the responsibilities of both parties. Where the contract was once just a reference for event organisers and sponsors, in the case of major sponsorship deals, the contract now establishes the ground rules for the ongoing working relationship between the sponsorship partners. Chapter 17 offers some more general guidelines about event contracts. With large-scale events, a contract is essential to ensure the obligations of both the event organiser and sponsor are met and that category exclusivity for the sponsor is protected to discourage ambushers. Closer event–sponsor relationships may technically be easier to establish in smaller-scale events and festivals, but the business practicalities of having a contract (approved by the lawyers of both parties) make a lot of sense. If a prolonged period of negotiation is needed for a sponsorship (this is usual for a very large event sponsorship property), having a legal letter of agreement to confirm that the sponsorship will go ahead is important.

To help plan the content of an event sponsorship contract, various sponsorship agreement pro formas are available, which can help draft the document for discussion with the sponsor and legal advisers. Some community organisations such as the English Community Rugby movement (www.community-rugby.com) offer sponsorship pro formas on their websites. Entering the words sponsorship agreement into a Google search engine provides event managers of smaller festivals and special events with many examples of sponsorship agreements that can be adapted to suit their needs.

Grey and Skildum-Reid (2003) offer excellent support materials of this nature in their toolkit. The content of a contract usually includes:

- the objectives and responsibilities of both parties
- benefits to be obtained by the event and the sponsor
- termination conditions
- ambush marketing protection
- details of media, branding and leveraging
- the promised exclusivity
- marketing and sponsor servicing
- insurance and indemnity requirements.

For small events and festivals, the scope and depth of the contract will be reduced (and the cost of legal advice is a key consideration), but often some in-kind (contra) support from a legal service could be obtained by a local community festival.

MANAGING SPONSORSHIPS

Once sponsorship has been secured, it must be effectively managed in order to ensure the benefits that were promised are delivered. Indeed, this is usually a requirement that is spelt out in some depth in sponsorship contracts for large events. However, a sponsorship management plan is essential for successful special event and festival management. This allows the event to successfully manage the sponsor's marketing needs listed in the sponsorship agreement and to build a quality, long-lasting relationship with its sponsors.

Effective management of sponsorship agreements involves everything from maintaining harmonious relationships between a sponsor's staff and people within the event/festival to ensuring sponsor's signage is kept in pristine condition. However, there should be no doubt about the level of attention that a sponsor likes or expects if the front-end negotiations have been well managed.

Effective relationships between events and sponsors (like any other relationship) are built on a strong foundation of communication, commitment and trust. If a sponsor believes that its sponsorship has been effective — that is, achieved the marketing and business objectives of the sponsorship — there is every likelihood that it will renew the sponsorship for another year. As has been stated before, the longer a sponsorship lasts, the better it is for both parties. Ford's former long-term sponsorship of the Australian Tennis Open is an example of how a sponsor's name can become synonymous with the event itself, thereby delivering branding benefits to the sponsor. Farrelly and Quester's (2003) research shows a link between having a market orientation (a customer-focused approach to doing business) and building commitment, satisfaction and trust between the sponsor partners.

It appears that sponsors who don't see their event partner as being particularly 'market/consumer-oriented' often engage in less joint marketing activities with that event. As a result, it is important to establish effective communication with sponsors so that they see the event manager as a serious marketer who will look for joint leveraging opportunities. Both the sponsor and the event need to have a reasonably equal input to how the sponsorship can be used to achieve its full potential. Perceptions by the sponsor of an equitable contribution to the relationship could lead it to look for a more customer-oriented event (Farrelly and Quester 2003) in its next sponsorship round.

Techniques for effective sponsorship management

A number of suggestions and techniques (based on Geldard and Sinclair 2004) can be adopted to ensure positive and enduring relations are developed with sponsors:

- *One contact*. One person from the event organisation needs to be appointed as the contact point for the sponsor. That person must be readily available (a mobile phone number helps), have the authority to make decisions regarding the event and be able to forge harmonious relationships with the sponsor's staff.
- *Understand the sponsor*. A recommended method of maintaining harmonious relationships is to get to know the sponsor's organisation, its mission, its staff, its products and its marketing strategies. By doing this, it becomes easier to understand the needs of the sponsor and how those needs can be satisfied.
- *Motivate an event organisation's staff about the sponsorship*. Keeping staff informed of the sponsorship contract, the objectives of the sponsorship and how the sponsor's needs are to be satisfied will help ensure the sponsorship will work smoothly and to the benefit of both parties.
- *Use of celebrities associated with the event*. If the event includes the use of artistic, sporting or theatrical celebrities, ensure sponsors have an opportunity to meet them in a social setting. Most people enjoy immensely the opportunity to tell anecdotes about their brush with the famous.
- *Acknowledge the sponsor at every opportunity*. Use all available media to acknowledge the sponsor's assistance. Media that can be used include the public address system at a local festival, newsletters, media releases, annual reports and staff briefings.
- *Sponsorship launch*. Have a sponsorship launch to tell the target market about the organisations and agencies that will sponsor the event or festival. The style of the launch depends on the type of sponsorship and the creativity of the event director. Finding an innovative angle to draw media coverage is valuable.
- *Media monitoring*. Monitor the media for all stories and commentary about the event or festival that include mention of the sponsor (a media monitoring firm may be contracted to perform this task). This shows the sponsor that the event takes a serious interest in the sponsorship and is alert to the benefits the sponsor is receiving.
- *Principal sponsor*. If the event has many sponsors, ensure the logo of the principal sponsor (that is, the sponsor who has paid the most) is seen on everything to do with the event, including stationery, uniforms, flags, newsletters, stages and so on. Usually, this requirement will be spelt out in legal agreements, but it is important to add value for the principal sponsor wherever it is possible.
- *Naming rights*. If the event has given naming rights to a sponsor, it has an obligation to ensure these rights are used in all communications employed by the event organisation. This includes making every endeavour to ensure the media are aware of, and

adhere to, the sponsored name of the event. Sometimes this is difficult, but it must be attempted so the event holds up its side of the deal.

- *Professionalism*. Even though volunteers may be involved in the management of many events, this does not mean that staff can act like amateurs. Sponsors expect to be treated efficiently and effectively, with their reasonable demands met in a speedy manner. Sponsorship is a partnership and loyalty to that partnership is often repaid with an ongoing investment.
- *Undersell and over-deliver*. Do not promise what cannot be delivered. Be cautious in formulating the proposal and then ensure the expectations raised by the sponsorship agreement are met and, ideally, exceeded.
- *Protect the sponsor from ambush marketing*. Avoid wherever possible giving opportunities for ambush marketing by the sponsor's competitors; that is, a competitor undertakes promotional activities around the event without paying sponsorship fees. The classic Australian example is the 2000 Olympics, in which Ansett, then one of the two Australian domestic airlines, was the official airline sponsor, but because of Qantas' promotional activity surrounding its slogan — The Spirit of Australia — being similar to the slogan of the Sydney 2000 Olympics — Share the Spirit — many thought that Qantas was the sponsor. Unfortunately Ansett became bankrupt shortly after the Games.

There is plenty of evidence of events that have found innovative ways to 'go that extra mile' with their sponsorship relationships. An artistic director of the Melbourne Festival once visited the workplace of one of the sponsors to talk about the creative processes and how these processes could assist the company and its staff with product development and organisational change (Harrison 2004). Often, it takes only a little imagination to think of ways in which to prove to sponsors that the event or festival is an active business and marketing partner.

Sponsorship management plans to service sponsors

Once the sponsorship contract has been signed, it is good practice to construct a sponsorship management plan (or action plan) to operationalise the agreement. At its most basic, this plan should identify what objectives the sponsorship will achieve for the sponsor, the benefits that have been promised, costs associated with providing specified benefits, review and evaluation approaches and the timeline for activities that need to be conducted to deliver on the sponsorship. These activities are discussed below.

Objectives associated with any given event sponsorship will be tailored to the needs of that partnership, but they should be specific to the sponsorship, measurable in that the success or otherwise of the sponsorship can be established, agreed to by the person responsible for carrying out the plan, realistic in that while perhaps challenging, the objectives can be achieved under normal circumstances, and have a timeframe in which the objectives have to be achieved. The sponsor's key objective in the TAC (Transport Accident Commission) Wangaratta Jazz Festival, for example, was to create awareness of the message 'If you drink, then drive, you're a bloody idiot' (Australian Business Arts Foundation 2004). The sponsor also had some sub-objectives related to forging community relationships. The event organiser, together with the sponsor, set out some specific performance measures in the event's management plan for later evaluation. Such measures included the minimum number of promotional spots on television and radio featuring recognition of the TAC and its social marketing message. In other words, the event organiser turned an ephemeral statement into a measurable objective.

All benefits and associated actions need to be clearly identified, along with the target group(s) to be reached and costs (financial or otherwise) that are associated with them.

These costs might include signage manufacture and erection (although these are usually supplied by the sponsor), supporting advertisements, promotional material, prize money, sponsor hospitality costs, professional fees, labour costs associated with hosting sponsors on-site, tickets, postage and preparation of an evaluation report. A budget needs to present all costs and show those costs in the context of the overall value of the sponsorship. Figure 11.5 provides a checklist of items to be included in a sponsorship budget (see chapter 7 for more information on preparing budgets). It should also be remembered that sponsorship (both in-kind and cash) attracts GST and this tax must be factored into any bottom line calculations. However, in many cases, particularly smaller events such as conferences or community festivals, the benefits that accrue to the sponsor cost the event practically nothing, except for the management time of ensuring what was promised is delivered. The sponsor supplies the promotional material, such as banners, signage and artwork for advertisements and other costs are absorbed into the administration of the event. Nevertheless, it is good practice to isolate costs associated with the sponsorship to establish the net benefit to the event the sponsorship generates.

Items that will incur cash outlays or person hours to support the sponsorship	Cost ($)
❑ Event programs	
❑ Additional printing	
❑ Signage production	
❑ Signage erection	
❑ Support advertising	
❑ Hospitality — food and beverage	
❑ Telephone, internet and fax	
❑ Public relations support	
❑ Tickets for sponsors	
❑ VIP parking passes	
❑ Cost of selling sponsorship (staff time at $ per hour)	
❑ Cost of servicing sponsorship (staff time at $ per hour)	
❑ Legal costs	
❑ Travel costs	
❑ Taxis and other transport	
❑ Evaluation research/report	
❑ Media monitoring	
Total costs	
Profit margin	
Minimum sponsorship sale price	

FIGURE 11.5 Items that can be included in a sponsorship budget

A list of the *actions* necessary to fulfil the sponsorship should be made, specifying what is to be done, when it is to be completed and who is responsible. Mapping out all of the management and marketing activities on a spreadsheet or other form of graphic display such as a Gantt chart is a useful management aid.

An *evaluation and review* process needs to be built into the sponsorship management plan. The review process should be ongoing and act to identify and address any problems that could affect sponsorship outcomes. Evaluation is concerned with providing a clear understanding of how the sponsorship performed against the objectives that were set for it. Evaluation seeks to answer questions such as: Did the promised media coverage eventuate? Did the attendee profile of the event reflect the market profile described in the sponsorship proposal? What was the overall quality of the sponsorship's delivery and management? Evaluation also gives the partners the chance to finetune the sponsorship arrangements, so both parties are well placed to renew the partnership in subsequent years.

In general terms, the development of the sponsorship action plan can be a creative and rewarding task that simply serves to communicate to the sponsor that its investment is being managed professionally.

MEASURING AND EVALUATING THE SPONSORSHIP

A shared responsibility of the property and its sponsor is the measurement of the overall impact of the partnership. There are two components to measurement and evaluation: first, the evaluation of the effectiveness of the partnership and how the sponsor and event have contributed to it and, second, the measurement of the consumer-related marketing objectives set by the sponsor. Kolah (2007) stresses this point by stating that an important aspect of sponsorship evaluation is to 'measure, measure, measure'. The tricky aspect is *what* to measure. For example, it is meaningless to measure the impact of an event on brand recognition of a brand such as Coca-Cola or Qantas, the two best-known brands in Australia. Measurement is enhanced if the sponsor's objectives are clear, and expressed in such a way that measurement can take place, and the target market is defined in precise terms. Therefore any measurement must be directed at the sponsor's objectives and the impact on that precisely defined target market.

Some of the factors that complicate the measurement of sponsorship are that brand marketers often use a number of media, including sponsorship, to create brand relationships and there are often carry-over effects of previous media and marketing expenditure on brand awareness and image (De Pelsmacker, Geuens and Van den Bergh 2004). Of particular importance in sponsorship measurement is the use of audience research that measures unaided and aided recognition of the event sponsor's name (sponsor awareness), attitudes towards the sponsor and any actions/behaviours that the sponsorship has caused in its target audience (this could be a signed contract on an important deal for a business-to-business bank client, or a driver who has reduced their driving speed as a result of the sponsor's event messages).

While there is a need for more formal research (and publicly available findings) about the effects of sponsorship, it is clear that some sponsors of high-dollar event properties are becoming very rigorous about their measurement of the value of sponsorship.

Given the ubiquity of e-marketing, Cohen (2005) suggests these opportune techniques for the measurement of e-activity generated by sponsorship of an event.

- Provided the sponsor has an email database of its customers (as it should), it can survey a sample of them pre- and post-event to measure changes in brand awareness, sponsorship association, brand favourability and intent to purchase.
- If the sponsorship includes an advertisement on the event's website (as it should) the click-through rate (CTR) can easily be measured by the event. This is the ratio between the number of visitors to the event's website and the number who clicked on the sponsor's ad, which would take them to the sponsor's website. Obviously the higher the ratio, the better for the sponsor.
- If a viral marketing campaign is used as part of the sponsorship leverage strategy (forward to a friend links that incorporate some aspect of the event sponsorship), the number of times this occurs can be measured.

- Count visits to web pages in the sponsor's website that feature event-related activities, such as contests, opportunities to win tickets and chances to meet the event celebrities.

Overall, it is clear that there is a marked contrast in the effort and expenditure devoted to measuring sponsorship effects across different events and festivals and among sponsors themselves. What is clear is that marketing budgets and sponsorship expenditure are subject to tighter scrutiny as competition for funds increases. It is timely, therefore, for all events and festivals and sponsorship managers (who also compete for dollars in their companies) to review their measurement tools.

SUMMARY

Sponsorship is now an often used component of the marketing communication media of most corporations and public sector organisations. Influences on sponsorship growth worldwide can be found in the business and marketing environment and in the diversity of consumer and stakeholder benefits that sponsorships create.

From the property's perspective, sponsorship often (but not always) represents a significant potential revenue source. Yet, sponsorships are business partnerships that offer resources beyond money. To succeed in attracting and keeping the sponsorship dollar, event organisers must thoughtfully develop policies and plans that maximise all the benefits associated with the event to achieve maximum outcomes for the sponsor, which will enable the sponsorship to continue over some years, rather than being a one-off.

The sponsorship proposal must be based on comprehensive research of the benefits that the event generates for potential sponsors. In this way, the reciprocal arrangement that is sponsorship is maintained. Event managers need to formalise and manage their agreements so that commitments made to sponsors are met.

This chapter has provided critical insights into how to construct sponsorship benefit packages and then manage their implementation in order to exceed sponsors' expectations. Never forget that sponsorship is a reciprocal arrangement between two parties, each of which require their needs to be met.

QUESTIONS

1 What is the difference between looking at event sponsorships as philanthropy rather than as a business relationship?
2 What is the significance of understanding Crompton's exchange relationship model for effective sponsorship management.
3 Describe the benefits sponsorship can offer a potential sponsor in contrast to other forms of marketing communications.
4 Sponsorship may not be appropriate for all events. Why is this?
5 Why are precise details of the property's target market important, if not vital, for a sponsorship proposal?
6 Identify a festival or event of interest to you and state the steps that you would follow in identifying potential sponsors for this event.
7 What methods are available for calculating the price to charge for a particular sponsorship proposal?
8 Select an event and establish the actions it takes to manage the sponsorships associated with the event.
9 What sorts of additional benefits could a three-day rock festival property offer potential sponsors in addition to the standard naming rights and brand exposure?

case study

NSW FIRE BRIGADES AND MCDONALD'S

Great partnerships come from a complementary, synergistic 'fit'. The best examples are where one partner's scarcity is the other's abundance.

NSW Fire Brigades (NSWFB) is one of the largest fire services in the world, certainly the biggest in Australia, covering over 90 per cent of the population of NSW. They are also one of the most trusted community brands in the state, having traded top billing on and off with their counterparts, the Ambulance Service of NSW, over many years.

This community trust has been built on decades of service excellence, or 'good deed', as a peak emergency response organisation. The Brigades would not claim to have ever harnessed, let alone exploited, this brand value through strategic marketing. Unlike corporate 'for profit' organisations, it is simply not their way, nor is it their skill, but they still have it in abundance.

However, their forward vision is to substantially build their fire prevention program, which they believe will vastly reduce the need for emergency response. Their intent is to do this through greatly enhanced education, communication and marketing programs throughout the state; a major challenge when 95 per cent of the organisation is made up of fire fighters, not marketers and communicators.

For over three decades McDonald's has serviced the community of NSW, employing nearly half of their national workforce of 56 000 people in that state. During this time McDonald's has become institutionalised in the daily lives of the Australian community.

Not without its detractors and its own challenges, McDonald's has proven to be a fierce competitor, proud innovator and astute marketer. The way McDonald's has embedded itself into Australian family culture is unrivalled and undeniable. With nearly 300 restaurants in NSW alone, McDonald's can clearly lay claim to being the genuine community hub of most suburbs and towns in the state. They are unquestionably outstanding marketers and communicators both within and outside their organisation.

McDonald's and the NSWFB have much in common. Both are major employers in the state of NSW, have a similar number of outlets in the suburbs and regions, and they share a major constituency — families.

Both organisations value the importance of community cohesion and, in many ways, they represent two of the core elements that bookend a community. After all, a town would not be complete without a fire station or a Maccas!

Equally, both organisations have clearly demonstrated their concern and support for the safety and prosperity of families in NSW; McDonald's through its long list of community responsibility programs and the NSWFB via its growing safety and prevention initiatives. Therefore, each can offer other elements or expertise that will vastly enhance the other's communication to that all-important shared audience.

McDonald's can offer the NSWFB its marketing wherewithal and position as a local community hub, while the NSWFB can offer McDonald's leverage from a most trusted community brand to help soften the commercial aspects of McDonald's and to heighten its community responsibility credentials.

So, how does it work?

The Brigades has a partnership structure based on a model known as the FIT Pillar & Beam™ *Brand Lead Partnership Approach*. Its feature is that partners are first and foremost aligned via their brands rather than an asset; that is, an event, program or activity (see figure 11.6). So, Brand alignment is the reason for the partnership, and assets can become the celebration and communication of it.

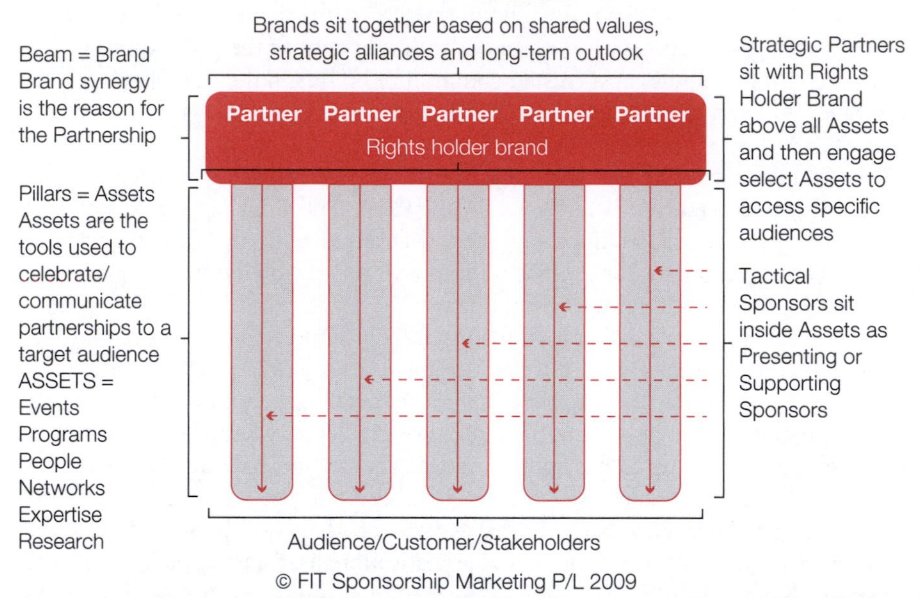

FIGURE 11.6 FIT Pillar & Beam™ Brand Lead Partnership approach

In the past the Brigades would have courted and attracted tactical 'sponsors' for their assets, such as Fire Prevention Week. Sponsors would have a presence within that week alone, then perhaps never be seen again.

However, Strategic Community Partners of the Brigades, such as McDonald's, now have a year-round connection based on a central, high-level alignment with the Brigades' brand. McDonald's has every right to talk about this partnership whenever they wish, within due approvals processes. It is not restricted to the timing or nature of a particular activity, so it can build a strong, year-round communications program to demonstrate its community support credentials.

This also benefits the Brigades, because it keeps the theme of fire safety front and centre in the eyes and minds of the general public throughout the year, but via a different communications channel than normal, therefore attracting new audiences for their all-important messages.

Once the overall brand connection has been established and communicated, the partners can jointly determine more specific agendas, which can have mutual benefit; that is, what assets can be leveraged.

For example, the Brigade Kids program has seen McDonald's invest in producing tens of thousands of educational CDs to encourage kids to become more aware of fire safety in the home. The Brigades return investment was in having fire fighters and fire equipment visit almost every McDonald's store in NSW on McDonald's Fire Brigades Kids Day. Families had the opportunity to look over a fire engine, learn about fire prevention, pick up a free Brigade Kids CD and enjoy a McDonald's lunch.

This particular leverage example demonstrates several things about an outstanding, best-practice partnership where everyone wins:

- McDonald's enhance their community goodwill credentials and gain a number of reasons for families to visit a McDonald's store.
- The Brigades get a powerful education tool produced and distributed for free.
- The public get free family entertainment and essential safety education.

Each party has committed what they have in abundance: McDonald's their marketing and distribution resources, and the Brigades their credentials, personnel and expertise.

Case prepared by Bruce McKaskill, MEntrep/Innov (SUT 2000), Managing Director, FIT Sponsorship Marketing Pty Ltd.

Questions

1 Explain the Pillar & Beam concept of brand partnership in your own words.

2 How can this concept be helpful in applying sponsorship to an event?

3 How does this brand partnership with the Fire Brigades of NSW help McDonald's?

4 How can the Pillar & Beam concept be applied to the sponsorship of a major sporting event?

REFERENCES

Australian Business Arts Foundation 2004, 'Business arts partnerships', February, www.fuel4arts.com.

Brown, TJ & Dancin, PA 1997, 'The company and the product: corporate associations and consumer product responses', *Journal of Marketing*, vol. 61, no. 1, pp. 68–84.

Clennell, A 2007, 'Former sports chief to push state into events big league', *Sydney Morning Herald*, 21 February, p. 7.

Cohen, H 2005, 'Not your grandfather's sponsorships', *ClickZ Experts*, www.clickz.com.

Colterman, B 2009, Why the Right Sponsor "Fit" is so Important, http://berniecolterman.wordpress.com/2009/09/08/why-the-right-sponsor-fit-is-so-important/.

Cornwell, T, Humphreys, M, Maguire, A, Weeks, C & Tellegen, C 2006, 'Sponsorship linked marketing: the role of articulation in memory', *Journal of Consumer Research*, vol. 33, pp. 312–21.

Cornwell, T, Weeks, C & Roy, D 2005, 'Sponsorship-linked marketing: opening the black box', *Journal of Advertising*, vol. 34, no. 2, pp. 21–43.

Cowan, D 2006, 'An evidence based case for arts sponsorship', *Arts and Business*, www.aandb.org.uk.

Crimmins, J & Horn, M 1996, 'Sponsorship: from management ego trip to marketing success', *Journal of Advertising Research*, vol. 36, no. 4, pp. 11–21.

Crompton, J 1993, 'Understanding a business organisation's approach to entering a sponsorship partnership', *Festival Management and Event Tourism*, vol. 1, pp. 98–109.

—— 1994, 'Benefits and risks associated with sponsorship of major events', *Festival Management and Event Tourism*, vol. 2, pp. 65–74.

De Pelsmacker, P, Geuens, M & Van den Bergh, J 2004, *Marketing communications — a European perspective*, 2nd edn, Prentice Hall Financial Times, Harlow, Essex.

Dolphin, R 2003, 'Sponsorship: perspectives on its strategic role', *Corporate Communications: an International Journal*, vol. 8, no. 3, pp. 173–86.

Duncan, T 2002, *IMC: using advertising and promotion to build brands*, McGraw-Hill Irwin, Boston.

Farrelly, F & Quester, P 2003, 'The effects of market orientation on trust and commitment — the case of the sponsorship business to business relationship', *European Journal of Marketing*, vol. 37, no. 3/4, pp. 530–53.

Ferguson, T 2004, Suncorp Sponsorship Manager, personal communication, 10 March.

Fit Sponsorship, www.fitsponsorship.com.

Geldard, E & Sinclair, L 2004, *The sponsorship manual*, 2nd edn, The Sponsorship Unit, Melbourne.

Grey, AM & Skildum-Reid, K 2003, *The sponsorship seeker's toolkit*, 2nd edn, McGraw-Hill, Sydney.

Gwinner, K 2005, 'Image transfer in global sport sponsorship: theoretical support and boundary conditions', in J Amis & B Cornwell (eds), *Global sport sponsorship*, pp. 191–206, Berg, New York.

Gwinner, K & Bennet, G 2007, 'The impact of brand cohesiveness and sport identification on brand fit in a sponsorship context', *Journal of Sports Management*, forthcoming.

Harrison, P 2004, 'Sponsorship — cutting through the hype', The Australia Council for the Arts, February www.fuel4arts.com.

Hinch, T & Higham, J 2004, 'Sport tourism development', in *Aspects of Tourism*, Channel View Publications, Clevedon, UK.

IEG Network 1997, 'Glossary: ambush marketing', www.sponsorship.com.

IEG (International Event Group) 2006, *IEG Sponsorship Report*, Chicago, Il.

IEG 2010, *IEG Sponsorship Report,* www.sponsorship.com.

IEG 2010, *Sponsorship.com trends,* www.sponsorship.com.

Johar, GV & Pham, MT 1999, 'Relatedness, prominence and constructive sponsor identification', *Journal of Marketing Research*, vol. 36, no. 3, pp. 299–312.

Kolah, A., (Ed.) 2007, *Sponsorship Works: a Brand Marketer's Casebook,* Sport Business Group, London, p. 43.

Kover, AJ 2001, 'The sponsorship issue', *Journal of Advertising Research*, February, p. 5.

Longridge, L 2004, 'Festival fund raising: noise', *Noise and the Australian Arts Council*, February, www.fuel4arts.com.

McDaniel, S 1999, 'An investigation of match-up effects in sport sponsorship advertising: the implications of consumer advertising schemas,' *Psychology and Marketing*, vol. 16, pp. 163–84.

Media 2004, 'Game, set and client match', 9 April (accessed via Factiva database, May 2004).

Meenaghan, T 2001a, 'Understanding sponsorship effects', *Psychology and Marketing*, vol. 18, no. 2, pp. 95–122.

—— 2001b, 'Sponsorship and advertising: a comparison of consumer perceptions', *Psychology and Marketing*, vol. 18, no. 2, pp. 191–215.

New Media Age 2003, 'Festivals — joining the throng', 31 July (accessed via Factiva database May 2004).

Performance Research 2001, *Independent studies*, Henley on Thames, England.

Pickett, B 2002, 'As Cingular Ads parody, not all sponsorships fit the brand-building bill', *National Hotel Executive*, September, www.prophet.com.

Rifon, N, Choi, S, Trimble, C & Li, H 2004, 'Congruence effects in sponsorship', *Journal of Advertising*, vol. 33, no. 1, 29–42.

Roy, D & Cornwell, T 2003, 'Brand equity's influence on responses to event sponsorships', *Journal of Product and Brand Management,* Vol. 12, no. 6, pp. 373–396.

Schrieber, A 1994, *Lifestyle and event marketing: building the new customer partnership*, McGraw-Hill, New York.

Shani, D & Sandler, D 1998, 'Ambush marketing: is confusion to blame for the flickering of the flame?', *Psychology and Marketing*, vol. 15, no. 4, pp. 367–83.

Sponsorship Insights and the Australasian Sponsorship Marketing Association 2003, 'Trends in sponsorship management: revelations from the 2003 Australasian Sponsorship Decision-Making Survey', www.asma.com.au.

Sydney Festival 2010a, 'Sydney festival 2007 facts and figures', www.sydneyfestival.org.au.

—— 2010b, 'Business benefits', www.sydneyfestival.org.au.

—— 2010c, 'Corporate and government stakeholders', www.sydneyfestival.org.au.

Telstra 2007, www.telstra.com.

Ukman, L 1995, 'Successful proposals', www.sponsorship.com.

Welsh, J 2003, *Reinventing sponsorship*, no. 2, Spring, pp. 1–2.

FURTHER READING

Anonymous 2003, 'Event sponsorship's fastest growing marketing medium (global sponsorships are expected to reach $26.2 billion in 2003)', *Business Line*, 21 August (accessed via Factiva database 2 May 2004).

Australasian Sponsorship Marketing Association 2001, 'Sponsorship case study: a closer look at the AFR 2001 National Sponsorship Awards Sponsorship Strategy Category Winner — Kellogg's Australia', *ASMA Sponsorship Report*, September, p. 4.

Ellery, S 2004, 'Hospitality — summer attractions', *PR Week*, 5 March (accessed via Factiva Database 2 May 2004).

National Bank 2004, 'Cirque du Soleil — our shared values', www.national.com.au.

Pearce, L 2003, 'Open seeks new sponsor after Heineken decision', *The Age*, 31 December.

Roy, D & Cornwell, TB 2004, 'The effects of consumer knowledge on responses to event sponsorships', *Psychology and Marketing*, vol. 21, no. 3, pp. 185–207.

Sigma 2004, 'People and community', www.sigmaco.com.au.

Sponsorship Research International 2000, *World-wide sponsorship market values*, London.

Wallis, N 2003, 'Analysis — festivals find their place in the sun', *Marketing Event*, 11 November.

SUSTAINABLE EVENT MANAGEMENT

LEARNING OBJECTIVES

After studying this chapter, you should be able to:

1. define the term sustainable development and its relevance to event production
2. discuss strategies and practical responses that events have employed and can employ in their efforts to become more environmentally sustainable
3. source information concerning the environmental management of events.

INTRODUCTION

Events, like most other areas of human endeavour, have increasingly responded to the challenge of sustainable development — 'meeting the needs of the present without compromising the ability of future generations to meet their own needs' (Our Common Future, 1987). Indeed, some events, such as the many environment-based festivals and expos, along with a number of large-scale sports events, have themselves become a vehicle for progressing their respective host community's efforts at sustainable development.

The events industry is changing rapidly in response to the demand for sustainable development. Audiences are more aware of sustainability issues and expect events to be produced responsibly. Additionally government agencies that regulate events and provide licences are placing increased environmental conditions on them, and clients and sponsors are increasingly demanding that their events, or the events they are involved with, are produced sustainably.

The resources used, waste produced, water consumed and greenhouse gases emitted as a result of event industry operations can be substantial. Events professionals and the industry as a whole have a responsibility to ensure their activities have minimal environmental impact. It is also important that events, whenever possible, create lasting positive environmental legacies for the communities that host them. If all event organisers keep sustainability at the heart of their planning, the industry can play a role in creating a sustainable future.

This chapter begins by providing an overview of the environmental impacts of events before moving on to discuss issues surrounding environmental best practice, certification and measurement. The final section provides an overview of the evolving response of the owners of the world's largest multi-sport event, the International Olympic Committee, to the challenge of sustianable event management. To demonstrate how a number of the practices discussed in this chapter can be employed in practice, several examples have been provided.

THE ENVIRONMENTAL IMPACTS OF EVENT PRODUCTION

The overarching environmental impacts of event production include:

- fossil fuel use due to transport and energy production
- emissions to air (greenhouse gases, pollution, particulates)
- water use, waste water production and chemical emissions to water
- materials and supplies purchasing, and consumption of non-renewable resources
- solid waste creation and disposal
- chemical use and disposal
- noise and light pollution
- habitat, biodiversity, and ecological impacts from activities in both the immediate surroundings and along the supply chain.

To reduce the environmental impact of your event, the following areas of operations need to be addressed:

- purchasing
- energy use
- waste management
- transport
- water management.

Sustainable purchasing in event planning

The impacts of purchasing and resource use are a major factor in the overall sustainability of an event. The principles of sustainable development suggest that in order to meet sustainability goals, the earth's resources must be used in moderation. This is often at odds with event production as an enormous amount of 'stuff' is needed to build and implement most events, and a lot of this has a once-only use.

The right choices in the daily purchasing and contracting decisions during the preproduction and planning phase of an event can lead to a considerable reduction in impact. The overarching concerns in procurement are the sourcing of materials, the manufacture of products, the distance freighted and the consequential waste that may be produced if disposal is necessary.

Using recycled or recyclable materials, re-using equipment and materials, and repurposing rather than discarding are all ways to reduce the environmental impacts of event procurement. 'Closed loop' systems are the aim — where one material feeds into the production of another. This can be either within your event, or through external processing by third parties. Choosing organic, buying fair trade, buying locally and using products with low carbon footprints are also steps to be taken.

One of the by-products of consumption is waste. And waste equals climate change. The climate change potential of a one-way system of resource use, manufacture, transport, product consumption and disposal is immense. The demand for more material means more mining, more transport and more land clearing, all of which contribute to climate change.

The materials and supplies purchased, especially those with one-way and short-lived expected use, affect the potential for a sustainable event. Consider the environmental and social impacts of purchasing, such as:

- the product's life cycle from extraction or growing of raw materials through to manufacture
- the impact on the community of growing, extraction and manufacture (social, economic and environmental)
- the distance raw materials and products travel to get to the end user
- fair payment and conditions for workers and producers
- if purchases for the event will unnecessarily deplete natural resources and cause pollution
- 'green-washing'. Investigate claims such as 'eco', 'natural', 'biological' and 'green'. Ask questions if claims are vague or have no certification.

FIGURE 12.1 Green purchasing checklist

The questions to ask when making a purchasing decision are:

- ❑ What is the product made from? Does it include recycled materials or sustainably produced materials?
- ❑ Where did the product come from?
- ❑ Who made the product?
- ❑ What does it come packaged in? Will the manufacture take packaging back?
- ❑ Is the product re-usable or more durable than alternatives?
- ❑ Is any special handling in the disposal necessary?
- ❑ Does the product conserve energy or water?

FIGURE 12.1 *(continued)*

- ❑ Does the product meet the relevant eco labelling certification?
- ❑ How will it be disposed of and what is the end-of-life plan for the product?
- ❑ Can it be recycled, reused, composted or returned to the manufacturer?

Purchasing policy

Writing a green purchasing policy will be useful for events or events companies or departments that have a high changeover of staff. By establishing this policy the event can ensure that environmentally preferable purchasing always occurs. Consider the following policy issues:

- *Commitment and overall goals.* Articulate the commitment to sustainable purchasing, quantifiable goals and intentions on buying reusable, refillable, durable and repairable products.
- *Energy and emissions.* Detail intention regarding energy sources, energy efficient electronic equipment, vehicle choices, travel policy, offsetting, lighting, heating and cooling.
- *Water.* Include details on aspects such as water efficiency products and procedures, refillable versus bottled water, policies on dust suppression or misting stations, auto shut off taps, flushing versus waterless toilets and urinals, and composting toilet requirements.
- *Toxins and pollutants.* Detail cleaning products, paints, varnishes, toilet treatment products, printing inks, pest control and other products that may be used in producing the event, which will make their way into water ways, onto the ground, into storm water drains or in sewer systems.
- *Forest conservation.* Detail certification and sustainable purchasing for timber, paper products, coffee, tea and other rainforest crops. It may be appropriate also to include sources of biodiesel in case it was grown on felled forest land.
- *Recycling and re-use.* Detail the products and packaging used that should be made from recycled materials or that are reusable. Choose products that can be recycled, include details on 'end of life' handling and ensure this issue is considered in all purchasing decisions.
- *Biodegradability*. List products that will be disposed of through composting or biogas processes to ensure these are purchased over non-compostable alternatives.
- *Local supply and product miles.* Detail a commitment to buying local as a first choice, choosing local contractors and staff, and buying products made from materials sourced from and manufactured in your own country.
- *Fair trade and fair production.* Detail a commitment to buying products that pay fair wages, a fair price to growers and that are grown and manufactured in fair conditions.

Sustainable energy use in event production

Most events will use energy, either sourced from landline 'mains' or from mobile generators. The impacts of energy use and production are well known — fossil fuel use and resulting carbon emissions. Curbing energy impacts is possible through reducing the amount of energy used and through looking to renewable and sustainable energy supplies.

Reductions in demand can be achieved through using energy efficient equipment, carrying out equipment switch-off campaigns, plus careful planning and cabling distribution of mobile generators. Zero emissions power supply is also a possibility for events with mobile power requirements.

Shining a light on the issues surrounding climate change in the context of the event, demonstrating sustainable energy production and use in action and potentially influencing the audience are also opportunities to take. Demonstrating alternatives to traditional energy production by powering the event through sustainable biofuels, solar, wind, hydrogen fuel cell and even pedal power may also be possible.

It must be noted that, in relative terms, the carbon emissions caused by energy used at most events is far outweighed by carbon emissions as a result of audience and participants travelling to an event. Nonetheless, plugging in and powering up must be done sustainably and, in doing so, is a public and highly visible commitment to an event's sustainability.

For events held indoors, the biggest wins in reducing energy impacts are through choosing a 'sustainable' or certified energy efficient venue, by putting programs in place to reduce demand for power (particularly by third parties) and through requesting the venue uses a renewable energy supplier. It may also be possible to purchase renewable energy credits or similar 'green power' tariffs, if the venue itself is not signed up permanently to a renewable energy supply.

Sustainable mobile power supply

Many events will use mobile generators to supply power. Most generators run on mineral diesel, a non-renewable and polluting fuel. When looking to reduce energy demand on diesel generators, the only way this can really translate to reduced emissions is to reduce the size (kVA) of a generator or the actual number of generators used.

Rather than using mineral diesel, sustainably fuelled generators are available in many countries. Look for generators that use waste vegetable oil biodiesel or crop-grown biodiesel that are certified sustainable. Pay attention to the quality of biodiesel and ensure it meets ISO 14214, so that you don't get back-yard biodiesel and inferior performance. Pure vegetable oil generators may also be available.

Zero emissions power supply

Rather than replacing mineral diesel with biodiesel it may be possible in some instances to use truly green, zero emissions energy sources such as solar, wind, pedal, or hydrogen fuel cell.

Mobile solar power generators are usually trailer-mounted, and often come with energy efficient sound and lighting production. This is necessary as using high power-consuming lights and equipment will not be the best choice when using a solar generator. Wind power is more of a boutique solution, but one that has significant demonstration value. The same can be said for the use of hydrogen fuel cells. Demonstrating what is possible in alternative energy supply while actually powering the event on these solutions is an obvious double winner!

Pedal power may not be the solution for every event as conference attendees are not going to want to pedal while watching speakers; however, it is a great option for interactive displays in community and cultural events. Look for a pedal power enthusiast group and get it to provide power for a section of the event. Figure 12.2 provides an overall summary of ways to reduce energy use and emissions at your event.

- ❑ Lead by example; showcase sustainable energy production and conservation.
- ❑ Hold the event in a venue that is certified sustainable or low-energy consuming.
- ❑ Choose green energy tariffs or buy green power/renewable energy credits.
- ❑ Plan power to reduce the size and number of generators needed.
- ❑ Reduce demand for power through energy-efficient equipment and energy consumption habits.
- ❑ Use sustainable fuels or zero emissions power supply.
- ❑ Put quotas and restrictions on users (traders, exhibitors).
- ❑ Supply all power generators; don't allow traders to bring their own.
- ❑ Measure usage and set future energy consumption goals.
- ❑ Report results.

FIGURE 12.2 Green energy checklist

Sustainable waste management in event production

Waste creation is the most visible impact of almost every event; however, many systems have been established and proven to manage waste effectively — ensuring minimal waste ends up in landfill — and reduce the amount of waste produced in the first place.

No matter the event size, waste management strategies are often similar and moving an event towards *zero waste* should be the goal. Zero waste may seem impossible, but having this as an underlying premise will move an event quickly from a mountainous landfill footprint to maximum diversion. Thinking of ways to prevent waste being created and to predefine how every waste stream will be captured and processed is the key to success.

Reducing the amount of 'stuff' can also have a retrospective waste-reducing effect. For every tonne of end-of-life-cycle waste, approximately 71 tonnes of waste is produced during the original product's journey from raw material to manufacturing, distribution and sale (Ciplat, Lombardi, Platt, June 2008).

It should be noted that waste creation also has a direct climate change impact. There is embedded energy in every single item that ends up in landfill — a legacy of mining, growing, manufacture, transport, consumption and disposal. There is also a direct emissions factor applied to treatment of every tonne of waste. So for the total volume of waste put into landfill or incineration by an event, a CO_2 figure can also be calculated and should be added to the event's overall carbon calculations.

A number of governments and non-government organisations have acted in recent years to develop event-specific waste management programs. These programs are designed to educate event managers in connection with reducing event-related waste and maximising the recycling of the waste that is collected. The Sustainable Living Foundation of Victoria is an example of one such body that has been active in this area. Specifically, it has developed an extensive range of free online resources (see www.slf.org.au) dealing with sustainable event planning and delivery. Central among these resources is an action plan designed to guide event managers as they seek to engage with the issue of waste management (see figure 12.3).

FIGURE 12.3 Waste wise event action plan

GOALS	ACTIONS	
Getting commitment and/or improving on last year	Achieve a [XX]% recycling rate for recyclables (i.e.% of recyclables sent off for recycling instead of to landfill).	❑
	Achieve below [XX]% contamination in the recycling bins.	❑
	Introduce food composting to the event.	❑
Setting up bin systems that work	**Bins**	
	Find provider for bins for general waste and recycling	❑
	Find provider who will collect the waste and recycling	❑
	Find out where waste will be transported to	❑
	Determine number of bins required	❑
	Waste streams	
	Provide the following streams for patrons: General Waste, Commingle, Food Scraps, Paper and cardboard	❑
	Provide the following streams for stallholders & staff areas: General Waste, Commingle, Food Scraps, Paper and cardboard	❑
	Put in measures to ensure stallholders comply with your waste requirements *[Provide clear advice to vendors on their obligations. Stallholders can be required to pay a waste/clean up bond, repayable when satisfied that requirements were met.]*	❑
	Position bin stations be to encourage patrons to use them correctly *[For example, position the bins as stations, always place general waste bins side by side with recycling bins. Never place recycle bins alone, do not place them back to back or facing away from each other.]*	❑
	Create a plan for where recycling and rubbish bins will be located to reduce littering and overflowing *[For example, position the bins in areas of high traffic and usage e.g. near food stalls, busy walkways, exit/entry points, toilets/shower blocks and in main seating and activity areas. Also, written timetable for emptying bins, bin monitoring etc.)*	❑
	Bin caps	
	Determine the number of bin caps required	❑
	Determine where bin caps be sourced from	❑
	Determine processes before bin caps are returned *[For example, bin caps collected & cleaned prior to collection or drop off]*	❑
	Cigarette butts	
	Install butt bin infrastructure at strategic locations	❑
	Provide smokers with free personal ashtrays (These are best distributed upon entry / when wrist banding / at bars.	❑

FIGURE 12.3 *(continued)*

Green purchasing, minimising and recycling packaging	Provide incentives for stallholders to use environmentally friendly packaging options *[For example, make it a contractual expectation, send out Purchasing Environmentally document from the MWMG, refer stallholders to SLF Planner Directory, provide information]*	❑
	Provide incentives for stallholders to maximise their recycling *[For example, set up separate bins for stallholder waste and recycling. Provide compost facilities for back of house, consider using Wash Against Waste Trailer]*	❑
	Inform stallholders/caterers of plans to introduce recyclable packaging policy at future events *[For example, newsletters, send outs]*	❑
	Have extra bin infrastructure arranged for back of house cardboard disposal *[For example, extra skips are often required specifically for stallholders]*	❑
Promoting your system	Raise awareness to patrons and staff that the event is waste-accountable *[For example, promotions of the event waste system will be placed on posters, websites and newsletters]*	❑
	Position any banners to gain maximum exposure *[For example, entry/exit points]*	❑
	Frequently remind patrons to dispose of their recyclables and waste correctly *[For example, check signage is on all bin caps, regular announcements over the PA system, posters, volunteers etc.]*	❑
Monitoring and reporting	Have measures to estimate waste stream volumes & contamination levels *[For example, waste audits will be conducted by event organiser. You can visually assess a sample of the bins – you don't need to look in every one!]*	❑
	Contract your waste contractor to provide data and/or a report on waste volumes, issues and areas for improvement	
	Produce an internal and/or public report on your waste management *[This is a good way of monitoring your progress]*	❑

Source: Sustainable Events Planner—www.slf.org.au/eventplanner

Large events will likely have a waste management company to plan and carry out waste operations. Making sure they are directed in sustainable practices or choosing a contractor that can supply sustainable solutions is important.

There are several questions that need to be considered when planning waste solutions:

- What waste treatment facilities exist locally and what processes do they use?
- What types of waste will be generated at the event?
- How can the types of waste generated be influenced or regulated?

- What processes can be put in place at the event to move it towards zero waste given the answers to the above three questions?

Figure 12.4 shows a waste management checklist.

Local facilities

- ❑ What facilities are there for processing waste locally and what will they accept for recycling?
- ❑ Can biodegradable waste be sent to local composting or biogas facilities?

Waste prevention

- ❑ Identify what waste could be produced and devise alternatives to prevent it.
- ❑ Regulate traders and contractors on what they can bring to the event.
- ❑ Consider re-usable food service ware. If you have to go disposable, make it biodegradable.
- ❑ Don't over-order supplies or over-cater for food.
- ❑ Envisage the end life of everything purchased to produce the event and all the products sold. Where could the waste end up, and how can it be recycled, composted or re-purposed?

Waste operations

- ❑ Can the waste team and audience easily access the bins?
- ❑ Group the bins; make sure there is always at least one of each option — recycle, general, compost — even double up on compost or recycle if these will produce more volume.
- ❑ Use bin tops or eye-level signage
- ❑ Get the audience involved in actively separating waste.
- ❑ Offer incentives or rewards for recycling. Put deposits on cups or bottles.
- ❑ Have recycling volunteers promoting your program and standing guard over the bins.
- ❑ Place appropriate bins and skips for materials such as timber, metal, film and plastic for production waste.
- ❑ Service food traders with compost and recycling, and set up cardboard bays for other traders.
- ❑ Get your teams involved in minimising waste production. Set targets and offer incentives.
- ❑ Pack up, store and re-use everything possible.
- ❑ Identify what could be salvaged for re-use and set up systems to capture salvageable goods.

FIGURE 12.4 Sustainable transport checklist

Types of waste produced at an event

Before devising sustainable waste solutions, the types of waste produced must be identified. Events will produce waste through production processes and through the audience or participant's involvement. At many events waste created from food and beverage activities is a major component of resulting volume. By controlling what food and drink is sold at the event, restricting what people can bring, and managing the interface between exhibitors and the audience will enable control over the waste generated.

Event production waste can include timber offcuts, plastic pallet wrap, cardboard boxes, scrap metal, plumber's piping, electrical cabling, batteries, plastic sheeting, e-waste, used liquid receptacles, and liquid/chemical/paint wastes.

Waste created by the audience or participants can include drink cans, plastic and glass bottles, paper, shopping bags, food packaging, cups, food, plus incidental items the audience or participants bring or need for specific event activities.

It is important to identify waste that may be created, specific to the event, to be able to adequately manage it. Think about what sponsors, traders, exhibitors, workshop creators, performers, athletes, spectators or fans may bring.

Waste prevention

If what type of waste could be created can be predicted, it is possible to put procedures and regulations in place to minimise or prevent it occurring in the first place. Interventions to prevent waste being created can include:

- Hire, don't buy.
- Have a 'No Plastic Bag' policy. Encourage traders to sell or give away re-usable shopping bags.
- Have a water bottle-free event. Use refillable cups and bottles only.
- Restrict single-serve sachets and straws, and discourage individually pre-wrapped food items.
- Use biodegradable takeaway food packaging only and collect it for composting. (Tip — don't allow pizza boxes!)
- Restrict handouts of brochures, showbags, sample sizes and freebie promotional items.
- Go electronic. Send programs via bluetooth or supply materials on a thumb drive.
- Use a paperless ticketing and registration system.
- Create vendor and sponsor contracts. Write restrictions into contracts and look to include clean pitch bonds, refundable post event.

Bin logistics and signage

Apart from identifying what could be recycled, composted or sent to landfill, it is important to put some thought into bin placements and signage. Easy access to bins, enough volume and frequency of placement of the bins, having them emptied so they don't overflow and putting clear and relevant signage on bins at eye level are essential. Also important is to always group the bins. If there is a recycling bin sitting alone without a general waste bin beside it, it will become contaminated with non-recyclables.

Recycling

Involving the audience in the separation of waste at an event will help to achieve the twin aims of encouraging the audience to get into the recycling habit and doing some of the separation work for the waste team.

Recycling is expected by traders, participants and the audience at most events. Recycling paper, cardboard, plastic, glass, metals, timber and aluminium is common practice. Once separated from general waste, in most circumstances mixed recycled materials are taken to a materials recovery facility (MRF) where there are electronic and mechanical systems in place to separate all the recyclables into single types and contaminants picked out. Some MRFs are council run, others are privately owned, and the technology and investment in infrastructure varies, which means each MRF will have different lists of what can be recycled there. Some will take plastic drink bottles, but not milk bottles. Only some can take Tetrapak. Most MRFs don't want plastic bags, and require waste to be loose rather than bagged.

It is important to find out how waste will be treated and what can be accepted at the chosen processing facility, so that the waste can be managed at the event appropriately before being sent to the MRF. There is no use putting in the effort of recycling at the event if it is all rejected once it gets to the MRF.

Biodegradable waste

Events with takeaway food services will have the potential to create a large volume of biodegradable waste. Apart from plates, bowls, cutlery and cups, there will also be catering kitchen waste and food scraps.

To capture and treat this waste appropriately a third bin is needed for the biodegradable food packaging, food scraps and catering waste. If biodegradable waste makes its way to landfill it will create methane — a greenhouse gas many times more potent than CO_2. The aim is to collect biodegradable waste and send it for composting or conversion into biogas, depending on facilities available nearby the event.

Don't leave it to the waste contractor to work out where biodegradable waste will end up. Insist on knowing where it will be processed, what level of contamination is acceptable, what the actual process the waste will go through, and what will be done with the compost on completion.

Salvage and re-purposing

By introducing salvage, re-use and re-purposing to an event, resources will be conserved and greenhouse gases avoided. It will also make a positive impact on an event's sustainability profile. Less new materials will need to be purchased and less waste will be produced, saving money.

It is important to pre-identify what items could be salvaged, to already have a home in mind for these items, and to put a system in place to ensure they are captured for salvage and not put in garbage skips. Setting up a salvage bay at the event is a good idea, along with partnering with a re-use centre to manage it and take the salvaged items away.

Waste volunteers

To reduce contamination of the recycling and compost bins and to have a point of interaction and eco-education with the audience, consider recruiting green or recycling volunteers. If an event has access to volunteers and stations them near the sets of bins, the quality of separation will drastically increase and almost guarantee no contamination in waste bins.

Recycle stations & incentives

To increase the profile of the event's waste and recycling activities, setting up a special waste station and incentivising the audience to participate will elicit a good result. Deposits can be charged on all drinks sold and refunds given when bottles, cans or cups are returned. Campers at festivals can be rewarded for bringing back bags of separated recycling.

event profile

SPLENDOUR IN THE GRASS 2009

Splendour In the Grass is an annual alternative arts and music event that has taken place at on the outskirts of Byron Bay, NSW, each July since 2001. As well as the latest and best in music from Australia and overseas, the festival features creative arts and performance, workshops, crafts and cuisine. In 2009 the two-day event attracted 17 500 people and sold out in 90 minutes.

Many who attend choose to immerse themselves in the full 'Splendour experience' by taking advantage of the on-site camping adjacent to the festival site. Some 2500 campers set up their tents directly outside the festival gates and quickly establish their own Splendour village for the weekend.

Splendour In the Grass has a long history of managing greenhouse gas emissions associated with the production of the festival and those of its patrons. Over the past five years Splendour In the Grass has calculated its 'internal' emissions, covering artist and crew transport, production, venue electricity and its diesel generators. Patrons were also given the opportunity to offset emissions over the duration of the event by way of purchasing a Carbon Offset Ticket. Patrons who purchased a Carbon Offset Ticket had their average daily emissions offset (154kg/patron across the duration of the event) through investment in accredited and independently verified wind farm generation. In 2009 the audience offset a massive 630 tonnes of carbon and invested $28 637 in renewable clean wind farm energy.

Apart from the Carbon Offset Ticket, Splendour In the Grass made a commitment to better tackle solid waste generation and developed and implemented a unique container recycling system. Previously the event had utilised the standard public place two-bin system (one for general waste and one for recyclables); however, due to issues of cross contamination, recycling rates were not as high as hoped.

Waste diversion program

Splendour In the Grass has always started at the top of the waste hierarchy by avoiding, where possible, the generation of waste in the first instance. Programs such as banning certain types of material and packaging on site have proved to be very effective in avoiding specific waste streams. When analysing where big reductions in waste generation could be made it was evident that there was need for a system that could boost recycling rates to around the 80 per cent mark.

As such, Splendour In the Grass implemented a container recycling system that placed an economic value on all drink containers (water bottles, soft drinks and alcoholic beverages). The system worked by patrons taking their empty drink container to a recycling centre where they were given a $1 drink ticket in return, that could be used towards the purchase of their next drink (be it bottled water, soft drink, energy drink or alcohol).

Four dedicated recycling stations were set up across the festival and the system was promoted through:

- the festival website and newsletters (over 45 000 subscribers)
- the event program
- signage across the site (including behind bars)
- dedicated press releases
- on-site art installations

- messaging via big screens adjacent to main stages
- word of mouth via the festival's Eco Cops (undergraduate environmental science students who spread the word about the event's environmental initiatives).

The results

The Container Recycling System was a huge success with patrons returning more than a quarter of a million water, soft drink, energy drink and alcoholic beverage containers for recycling. The benefits to the environment included:

- over 50 cubic metres of landfill space saved
- over four tonnes of aluminium and PET plastic recycled
- over 20 tonnes of bauxite avoided by recycling aluminium
- energy savings from recycling cans equivalent to running 660 000 television sets for one hour
- an overall recycling rate of 80.3 per cent.

And of course the site never looked better.

Sustainable transport solutions in event production

Moving people, supplies, equipment and waste to and from an event will most likely be the largest carbon impacts for any event. Transport of those attending the event will be the single largest impact. Fuel costs, where transport is a large variable expense, are helping to realise freighting efficiencies. However, when it comes to audiences, the convenience of driving often outweighs the cost or environmental considerations of travelling by public transport.

The success of public transport campaigns for any event relies on the ease, regularity, convenience and smooth running of the systems put in place. Sometimes this is out of the control of the event organiser, who needs to rely on existing networks and infrastructure. They can ensure, however, that links are set up between transport hubs and the event location, and that they incentivise the uptake of public transport over driving.

Innovations in sustainable transport solutions are increasingly apparent, with new technology offering drastic emissions reductions, fuel efficiency improvements and sustainable solutions for alternative fuels. Advances in vehicle technology has also meant hybrids and electrically powered vehicles are increasingly finding their way onto public roads. It is possible to include some of these solutions and innovations in the event, particularly with sponsorship alignments and for on-site vehicles.

A number of events, both large and small, are engaging with a range of initiatives designed to encourage communities to use more sustainable modes of transport. Many of these initiatives are in evidence in the TravelSmart special events planning resource kit found on their website, www.travelsmart.gov.au. (TravelSmart Australia 2007). Figure 12.5 provides a checklist on planning sustainable transport solutions for an event.

FIGURE 12.5 Sustainable transport checklist

- ❑ Analyse audience transport habits to create the best transport plan to encourage public transport uptake.
- ❑ Hold the event near a public transport hub.
- ❑ Provide free and conveniently timed shuttle buses to 'join the dots', with capacity to meet demand and ensure minimal waiting.
- ❑ Promote the existence of public transport options by providing timetabling and location details.

FIGURE 12.5 *(continued)*

- ❑ Offer rewards or incentives to those that use public transport.
- ❑ Bundle ticket sales with public transport options.
- ❑ Set up and promote car share options.
- ❑ Require that car parks are booked in advance and charge a fee to discourage driving. Patrons who do choose to drive will either need to pay the fee or find alternative parking nearby, which will add to local congestion.
- ❑ Plan deliveries and encourage load sharing by contractors.
- ❑ Buy locally and use local contractors, staff, talent and participants to minimise 'product miles'.
- ❑ Offer the audience the opportunity to offset their travel to the event through an add-on to ticket purchases.
- ❑ Consider offsetting all measurable transport of staff, crew and performers.

Sustainable water and sanitation for event production

Conserving water and managing waste water is the responsibility of every event manager. Sensitivity to water scarcity and conservation and respecting local water protocols are especially important if the event is in a rural area where the livelihood of the local population depends on adequate water supply. An event simply can't enter a local community and use up this most precious resource.

The main concerns for sustainable water management at an event are:

- water conservation
- emissions to water
- waste water management.

Management of various stages of water need to be considered, from fresh drinking water supply to handling sewage.

Clean water may be supplied to the event by tankers, through the mains water supply, or harvested at the event and stored in tanks. Water is used and waste water produced by catering and food stalls, cleaning, toilets and showers, handwash facilities, standpipes and free drinking taps, laundry, misting stations, dust settling, grounds preparation and gardens.

Events held in existing venues will not have control over implementing new water systems; however, choosing the right venue in the first instance is something that can be controlled. Regardless of the venue, implementing a water conservation campaign by layering a messaging program over existing infrastructure will be effective.

Outdoor events where water systems exist or need to be put in place have more options to reduce water consumption. Mechanical intervention to reduce water pressure, auto shut-off taps and low flow taps are examples of what can be done. Figure 12.6 details sustainable water management options.

FIGURE 12.6 Sustainable water management checklist

Water conservation

- ❑ Ensure water-saving devices are on taps, hoses, showers and drinking water standpipes.
- ❑ Reduce water usage through 'water wise' grounds preparation and gardening.
- ❑ Use dust suppressant additives to reduce water volume used on dampening dust.
- ❑ Capture water and store in rain water tanks.
- ❑ Use waterless urinals and toilets.

FIGURE 12.6 *(continued)*

- ❑ Reduce water pressure.
- ❑ Supply water-free hand sanitiser
- ❑ Conduct water conservation messaging.

Waste-water management

- ❑ Capture and treat grey water using soak-aways, reed bed or mechanical filtering to treat grey water.
- ❑ Re-use grey water on site for non-contact uses.

Emissions to water

- ❑ Use chemical-free cleaning products.
- ❑ Use biological toilet treatment products.
- ❑ Use non-toxic paints.

Audience messaging

- ❑ Conduct a water conservation campaign to encourage water saving by the audience.
- ❑ Include free water bottle refill stations.

Managing waste water sustainably

Waste water may be disposed of down the sink and into the sewer system or pumped into tanker trucks and transported away. Some waste water can make its way straight into the ground water using soak-aways. How waste water is managed is a primary environmental concern and will impact on the event's sustainability results.

Grey water is the waste water from showers or other washing operations. It is free of organic matter, and can be used for non-contact purposes such as toilet flushing and irrigation. Black water is sewage and catering sullage. Catering waste can be treated as grey water if any solid matter is caught through straining and water is filtered.

Emissions to water

Whichever way waste water is disposed of, cleaning products, paint residue, toilet treatment products and other chemicals have the potential for a hazardous environmental impact. Chemical-free waste water should be the goal.

When water is disposed of directly onto land, any chemicals present in the grey water will produce toxic residue that will remain in the soil and eventually make its way into waterways. Waste water disposed down roadside drains can make its way directly to water ways and oceans, depending on the local drainage system. Chemicals commonly used in toilets will disturb the natural processes in sewerage treatment plants, where biological, not chemical, treatment is used. The better option is to use biological treatment products, or use waterless toilets (composting) and waterless urinals.

Managing grey water

Events not connected to municipal sewer lines will need to pump waste water into tanker trucks and transport it to treatment plants along with event sewage, or alternatively to work out a way to dispose of grey water on site. The most sustainable option for grey water is to treat and recycle it onsite — which has the twin outcomes of reducing the requirement for fresh water and reducing the transport impact of trucking it away. If grey water is to be dealt with on site, it can be done through soakaways, or through treating grey water and re-using it at the event or on the land.

Local government and environmental agency regulations place restrictions on the collection of grey water and its disposal proximity to waterways, to ensure contaminants are filtered through the soil before entering the water course. It should be noted that protecting the riparian zone, the area that acts as an interface between dry land and a stream or river, is also vital. The plants that live in this zone protect soil erosion, holding banks in place.

Sustainable toilet options

The threat of having to go into a portable toilet cubicle can deter people from using facilities at an event at all. However, there are sustainable alternatives to chemical toilets. The use of waterless portable compost toilets, pioneered in Australia, is spreading across the world. Many music events in Australia have permanently installed these toilets; for example, the Meredith Music Festival and the Falls Festival, both in Victoria. The benefit of using this type of toilet is that it reduces transportable sewage by up to 80 per cent as waste is composted in situ. Reductions in water usage are also considerable.

Full-flush portable toilets should be avoided, as should those using chemical treatment products. Biological treatment products should be readily available and are much kinder to sewage treatment facilities.

SUSTAINABILITY POLICY FOR EVENTS MANAGEMENT

A sustainability policy will help to focus the greening efforts of the event production team. It is also a good document to release publicly, to have available for student enquiries, and to give to new contractors and staff. A sustainability policy should include discussion on:

- the commitment of the event to sustainability, resourcing and staff
- the consultation process, training of staff and education of key stakeholders
- the statement of objectives
- the key sustainability indicators the event's performance will be measured against.

It should include an overview on the key areas of energy use, transport, water and effluent management, resource consumption and waste management, plus other impacts such as light and sound pollution, ecological, heritage and conservation.

The sustainability policy should detail how the event will comply with targets, what auditing will be undertaken and how monitoring and review will take place. General observations could also be included such as government or industry policies or protocols that must be met, or that might impact on future operations. Include any codes of best practice, standards or certifications that are planned.

BEST PRACTICE, CERTIFICATION, MEASUREMENT

Without measurement, the ability to manage is hindered, which applies to the sustainability outcomes of an event. The impacts should be measured and protocols to do so are in discussion at a global level to define agreed industry measures.

The Global Reporting Initiative[1] is undergoing an Event Sector Supplement, which will detail how events can publically report on sustainability performance.

---

1. Global Reporting Initiative details what should be publically reported on for a company's sustainability impacts and legacies.

Measuring environmental impacts of event production

To assess how an event is performing against its environmental goals, it is important to measure, metrically, various impacts. These can be seen as the event's 'Key Sustainability Indicators'. The following is an example of the quantitative performance measures that can be used to assess the event's impacts, and, importantly, to set goals from year to year.

- Waste
  - weight of general waste (plus CO_2 emissions from treatment of waste)
  - weight of recycled waste (zero emissions)
  - weight of compostable waste (zero emissions)
  - weight of salvaged waste (zero emissions)
- Energy
  - landline power: kilowatt hours of grid power (converted to CO_2 emissions)
  - mobile power generators: litres of diesel
  - zero emissions power: kilowatt hours
- Water
  - clean water — total volume.
  - clean water harvested onsite — total volume
  - grey water — total volume.
  - sewage/sullage — total volume
  - all converted to CO_2 emissions from production and treatment processing
- Transport

  Production transport:
  - pre-event — the total distance and mode of travel for production staff in pre-event planning
  - site transport — the distance travelled at the event for onsite transport
  - crew transport — the distance travelled by crew to get to the event
  - all converted to CO_2 emissions

  Participant/spectator transport:
  - mode of transport — percentages of audience taking each mode of transport
  - average distance travelled — by each mode
  - all converted to CO_2 emissions

  Artist transport:
  - air — total distance travelled by air for all performers
  - ground — total distance and mode of travel for all performers at the event
  - all converted to CO_2 emissions.

Sustainable event industry organisations

Event industry groups with an environmental focus have emerged in recent years, which have also served to push events down the sustainability path. A Greener Festival, for example, is an organisation committed to assisting music and arts-based events and festivals in their efforts to green their operations. It does this by providing information and educational resources and by facilitating the sharing of ideas among event managers (www.agreenerfestival.com 2009). The Green Meetings Industry Council is another such organisation, which focuses on the conference and meetings sector in the US. The Council for Responsible Sport resources those producing sporting events and even offers a certification. The Sustainable Event Alliance is an international network of practitioners and stakeholders for producing events sustainably and serves to focus the industry and facilitate the creation of solutions.

At the level of event industry associations, a stronger emphasis is also being placed on the delivery of green events. The International Festivals and Events Association, for example, has, for a number of years, acted to acknowledge the environmental achievements of its members through its annual industry awards.

Green event certification and guidelines

The events industry has, in the past few years, seen the emergence of certifications to assess the performance of events on sustainability or environmental credentials. The British Standard BS 8901:2009 Sustainable Events Management System provides guidance for an overarching management system in event production. This standard is being used as the basis for a new international standard, the ISO 20121 Events Sustainability Management System. The various national standards bodies across the globe are cooperating in the creation of this new standard, launching in 2012, which will be used worldwide.

There are a range of other certification schemes also in development, or currently in use. The organisations involved include: A Greener Festival (UK); EcoLogo (North America) The Council for Responsible Sport (US); The Green Meetings Council (US). There is also movement in the development of an operational certification and a green event eco-label in Australia. Guidelines are sometimes developed in conjunction with various interest groups, such as Greenpeace (see figure 12.7).

FIGURE 12.7 The Greenpeace Olympic environmental guidelines: guiding environmental principles

GUIDING ENVIRONMENTAL PRINCIPLES

If followed carefully, the principles below will ensure that future Olympic Games and other major events have minimal environmental impact.

1 **Environmental sustainability**
It is vital to ensure that current exploitation of ecosystem resources, including extraction of raw materials, consumption of energy, manufacture and use of chemicals and disposal of wastes, does not compromise the viability of future generations and their access to natural resources and ecosystem services. A truly sustainable project ensures that:
- Substances such as fossil fuels do not systematically increase in the ecosphere
- Synthetic substances do not systematically increase in the ecosphere
- The bases for productivity and diversity of life are not systematically depleted
- Resources are used fairly and efficiently in order to meet human need.

2 **Precautionary principle**
This should be the overarching guide to decision making even in the absence of certainty regarding the potential impacts of all processes, materials and systems for hosting Olympic Games and other events. In practical terms, the implementation of the precautionary principle implies that:
- Action must be taken to avoid harm, or the threat of harm, before it occurs, even when firm evidence of cause and effect relationships is unavailable.
- Since all processes, materials and systems have environmental impacts they must be regulated accordingly until sufficient evidence becomes available that there is no potential risk to ecosystems or human health.
- High quality scientific information should form a central component of mechanisms for early detection of environmental threats.

FIGURE 12.7 *(continued)*

- A progressive, ever-improving approach which reduces environmental impacts should be adopted by all Olympic host cities or events.

3 **A preventative approach**
It is cheaper and more effective to prevent environmental damage than to attempt to manage it. Prevention requires thinking through the development process to prevent environmental impacts. Early planning is critical to a successful integrated environmental approach.

4 **Integrated and holistic approach**
Establish an approach centred around all potential environmental impacts from the start. This approach recognises that most of our environmental problems — for example, climate change, toxic pollution, loss of biodiversity — are caused by the way and rate at which we produce and consume resources. Adopt an integrated approach to environmental resource use and consumption addressing the full life cycle of the project including all material, water and energy flows, and the economic impact.

5 **Specific and measurable environmental goals**
Set specific environmental goals to fulfil these environmental guidelines at the outset of Olympic or other projects. Ensure that these goals are real, measurable and achievable and make them publicly available.

6 **Community, NGO and public involvement**
Consistent and high level consultation with community, environmental and social groups and the public is essential from the start. Establish a clear process for conflict resolution.

7 **Senior environmental management**
Place the management of environmental issues at a senior level within the overall management structure of the project. Environmental issues must be an integral part of any large scale event. Environmental teams and input from all levels of the project are vital for success.

8 **Environmental reporting and independent auditing**
Independent auditing of environmental information on all aspects of a development project is essential to ensure credibility. Make this information available to the public.

9 **Public education and training**
Plan and budget early to provide public education materials about the environmental aspects of your project. Ensure staff, suppliers, providers, sponsors and media understand the environmental initiatives of the project and why they were undertaken.

Source: Greenpeace 2003.

SUSTAINABLE EVENTS

While it is difficult to generalise about how events have approached the challenges posed by the concept of sustainable development, it can nonetheless be observed that a number of individual events have sought to engage directly with it. Many events are producing their events sustainably and are talking about it on their websites and in their promotional material. The recently formed Sustainable Event Alliance is evidence that the field of sustainable event management is evolving quickly.

Of particular note are major sports events such as the FIFA World Cup, the Commonwealth Games and the Olympic Games that have lead the way in exceptional sustainable event management practices. Of the major events that take place internationally, it is the Olympic Games (summer and winter) that, arguably, have the most developed approach to the challenges sustainable production poses. In seeking insights into how events might respond to sustainable development, it is useful then to overview how the Olympic Games' engagement with sustainability (which flowed from broader international efforts in this area) has evolved over time, the practices its 'owners' (the International Olympic Committee) employ in seeking to engage with sustainable development, and some of the issues it faces in trying to obtain worthwhile sustainability outcomes in its host cities/countries.

The Olympic Games and sustainable development

The International Olympic Committee (IOC) was initially slow to acknowledge the need to embrace environmental considerations in the planning and delivery of the summer and winter Olympic Games. Almost 20 years went by from the time (1974) the citizens of Denver, Colorado, rejected (by referendum) on environmental grounds the IOC's offer to conduct the Winter Olympic Games (Lenskyj 1998, p. 343), before the environment began to feature as a significant consideration in Games planning and delivery. The first major step in this direction was the signing of the Earth Pledge in 1992. This document emerged out of the Earth Summit in Rio de Janeiro in 1992 and was signed at the Games of that same year (XXV Olympiad in Barcelona, Spain) by all International Sporting Federations, National Olympic Committees and the IOC (Oittinen 2003). It required that signatories both acknowledge the importance of the environment to humanity's future and committed them to act in ways that would protect it (Planet Drum 2004a).

The next major environmental step by the IOC occurred after, what had been until that point, the most environmentally friendly Olympic Games, the Winter Games in Lillehammer, Norway, in 1994. It involved the signing by the IOC of a cooperation agreement with the United Nations Environment Programme (UNEP) designed to facilitate the leveraging of future Games for environmental awareness raising and education purposes (UNEP 2004). Under this agreement, the IOC's responsibilities extended to the:

- conduct of regional seminars with the intent of familiarising National Olympic Committees (NOCs) as regards environmental matters. Additionally, the NOCs were to be encouraged to create their own sport and environment commissions.
- creation of specialist and volunteer networks, comprising high-profile sports people that can serve as models for responsible conduct vis-a-vis the environment (IOC 2004a, p. 1).

In later years this relationship progressed to providing assistance to bidding cities in completing the environmental aspect of their bid documents, and memorandums of understanding between the UNEP and Olympic host cities (commencing with Athens in 2004) (G-ForSE 2004). It should be noted that the Olympics, while the first, is not the only event that UNEP has signed agreements with. UNEP worked with the recent (2006) FIFA World Cup, for example, to assist it in its efforts at integrating environmental considerations into its planning and projects (FIFA 2006).

The IOC's progress down the path of sustainable development continued with its Centennial Olympic Congress in 1994. At this meeting the environment was proposed as the third 'pillar' of Olympism (the others being sport and culture) and the environment and sport were discussed in a dedicated conference session. This session generated five conclusions and recommendations that subsequently have impacted directly, or indirectly, on the involvement of the Olympic Movement in sustainable development. Specifically, these conclusions and recommendations were:

- incorporation of concern for the environment as a prominent feature of the Olympic Charter
- extending the Olympic Movement's concern for the environment beyond merely the period of the Games itself. To facilitate this it was recommended that a Sport and Environment Commission be established.

- adoption of an environmental educational policy
- acting to ensure sport took place in a way consistent with sustainable development practices
- incorporation of the environment as a major criterion in the selection of Olympic Games host cities (Neeb n.d., p. 165).

The year after the Centennial Congress, the IOC acted to convene, in association with the UNEP, the first World Conference on Sport and the Environment (WCSE), an event that has been conducted biannually since. At this event a number of actions were taken, including the endorsement of the Congress's decision to make the environment the third pillar of Olympism and its recommendation to create a Sport and Environment Commission (SEC). The IOC acted to create an SEC that same year, charging it with advising the IOC Executive Board on the policy to be adopted by the IOC and the Olympic Movement as regards protection of the environment. The SEC's role also extended to a range of actions/directions, specifically to:

- have the whole Olympic movement embrace environmental considerations
- strengthen environmental guidelines for host cities
- create educational material concerning sport and the environment
- sponsor conferences and seminars concerning the environment
- sponsor a national clean-up day with NOCs from around the world
- work with other sport and environment organisations in promoting environmental issues
- utilise national and international athletes as environmental ambassadors
- establish the environment as a major issue for the Olympic Movement by working with the media (Neeb n.d., p. 166).

The increased focus of the Olympic Movement on the environment saw its charter amended in 1996 at the 105th IOC Session in Atlanta, USA, to formally acknowledge this change. Rule 2, paragraph 10 was inserted. It states that:

> the IOC sees that the Olympic Games are held in conditions which demonstrate a responsible concern for environmental issues and encourages the Olympic Movement to demonstrate a responsible concern for environmental issues, takes measures to reflect such concern in its activities and educates all those connected with the Olympic Movement as to the importance of sustainable development (IOC 2004b, p. 1).

The IOC's next major environment-related action was the decision to alter the criteria for bidding cities to embrace environmental considerations. This resulted in candidates for the 2002 Winter Olympic Games being the first to respond to bid criteria that included environmental considerations. These criteria have been developed and refined over time, with the current version having been developed in 2004.

The Olympic Movement continued to engage with the environment through its SEC and its WCSEs through the late 1990s and into the new millennium. Prior to the third WCSE in 1999, the IOC moved to adopt its own version of Agenda 21. This decision was endorsed at the Conference and a statement (the Rio Statement) was made as to how the Olympic Movement, and the sports community, should pursue this agenda (Athens Environmental Foundation 2004).

The efforts by the IOC to pursue a sustainable development agenda have been aided by the independent desire of some host cities to minimise environmental impacts of summer or winter Olympic Games and to generate a positive environmental legacy from it. For example, in the absence of any formal environmental guidelines from the IOC, the organisers of the 1994 Lillehammer Winter Olympic Games undertook a range of actions that resulted in this event being described as the first 'Green' Olympic

Games (Neeb n.d., p. 160). While the IOC developed environmental guidelines for bidding cities after these Games, the lead time of seven years involved in the selection process meant that such considerations did not formally come into play until the 2002 Winter Olympic Games (Neeb n.d.). The 1996 Atlanta Olympic Games and the 1998 Winter Nagano Games, therefore, were not under any specific requirement to act in this area, although they did commit to some environmental actions in their bid documents. The subsequent performance of these cities, however, as regards the environment did not approach that of Lillehammer. Indeed, the Nagano Games came in for particularly strong criticism by some environmental groups (Planet Drum 2004b).

The 2000 Olympic Games in Sydney were also awarded prior to the formal requirement to include within bid documents an environmental component. Nonetheless, the organisers of this event included as part of their successful bid document a set of environmental guidelines based on Agenda 21, a document that had already been embraced in Australia through its National Ecologically Sustainable Development policies. These guidelines primarily focused upon:

- planning and construction of Olympic facilities
- energy conservation
- water conservation
- waste avoidance and minimisation
- air, water and soil quality
- protecting natural and cultural environments
- merchandising
- ticketing
- catering
- waste management
- transport
- noise control (Sydney 2000).

The implementation of these guidelines resulted in the Sydney Olympics being acknowledged by the Chairman of the Earth Council, Maurice Strong, as the 'greenest or most sustainable Games ever' (cited in Campbell 2001, p. 1).

The Games that followed Sydney, Salt Lake City, Athens and Turin, were all subject to a bidding criteria inclusive of an environmental component. However, they appear not to have surpassed Sydney's efforts in this area, with Athens, for example, receiving a score of .8 out of a possible five for its environment program by the World Wide Fund for Nature (2004, p. 2). Such a poor result raises several issues for the 'owners' of large-scale 'mobile' events, such as the Olympics, which seek to engage directly with sustainable development (SD), but that must rely on the successful bidding city/country for their delivery. These issues relate to an event owner's capacity to control how an event is delivered once it has been awarded, and the linkage between a host city or country's ability to deliver on SD commitments and its overall level of support for and engagement with the concept.

While the IOC has made a meaningful effort over a more than ten-year period to embrace the concept of sustainable development, other large-scale events have only recently begun to take up the green challenge. The 2006 FIFA World Cup, for example, was the first time this event sought to incorporate environmental considerations into its preparation and staging, setting measurable environmental targets in the areas of water, waste, energy and mobility (FIFA 2006). The same can be said for the Commonwealth Games, which, while making some efforts in Manchester in 2002 to embrace environmental considerations, engaged more fully with the concept of SD in Melbourne in 2006 where it took place under a sustainable development framework (Office of Commonwealth Games Coordination n.d.).

SUMMARY

This chapter provided an overview of the environmental impacts of event production. Additionally, it sought to engender an appreciation of the current state of play with regard to best practice approaches to environmental management both through general discussion and the provision of detailed case study examples. Developments in the areas of 'Green' event certification and the measurement of event environmental impacts were also identified and described. The final part of this chapter examined the evolving efforts of one event owner, the International Olympic Committee, as it sought to engage with the concept of sustainable development.

QUESTIONS

1. How can the concept of sustainable development be applied to the event industry?
2. Briefly discuss the path followed by the Olympic Games in its efforts to engage with the concept of sustainable development.
3. How has increasing consumer awareness of environmental issues impacted on the conduct of events?
4. What types of solutions might be available to events seeking to reduce their environmental impact?
5. Briefly discuss how waste associated with food preparation and consumption at events can be minimised.
6. Select an event that has made a significant effort to engage with the concept of sustainable event production and identify and discuss the practices it employed for this purpose.
7. Identify two non-sporting events that have developed environmental policies. Briefly indicate the core aspects of these policies.
8. Describe the importance and stages of a sustainable event management system, as well as the tools that can be used to implement such a system.
9. What role does the United Nations Environment Programme now play in the delivery of environmentally friendly events?
10. Access the Sustainable Event Alliance website, www.sustainable-event-alliance.com, and briefly state the types of information available on it that might assist an event manager in producing events that are more environmentally friendly.

case study

WOMADELAIDE

WOMADelaide is an annual three-day, ticketed outdoor festival of music, arts and dance presented and managed by independent arts and events producer Arts Projects Australia. The 2005 festival, held on 4–6 March, attracted over 65 000 people and comprised more than 300 artists from 22 countries.

Since 1992 when WOMADelaide began, all waste materials generated by visitors and caterers at the event had been sent to landfill. In 2001 an on-site recycling system was introduced for use by event visitors.

The 2005 event was supported by Zero Waste SA through the Zero Waste Events Program. The Program offered the opportunity and funding to take a more holistic approach to waste management and reduction by implementing initiatives to reduce waste produced at all areas of the event. In addition, the event organisers and Zero Waste SA saw minimising waste at such a high profile event as an excellent opportunity to increase the community's environmental awareness.

WOMADelaide 2005 saw the start of a three-year waste minimisation program. The focus of the first year of the program was to highlight public education, provide a snapshot of the waste disposed of at the event and concentrate on minimising waste in the visitor areas. Years 2 and 3 (2006, 2007) saw the focus change to minimising waste in the catering areas of the event and to achieving zero waste.

Zero Waste SA provided funding for a waste audit team, bin caps, advertising, signage and reporting on the success of the waste minimisation initiatives in place at the event.

Waste minimisation initiatives

Several initiatives were employed at the 2005 event, in particular to minimise waste generated by event visitors. In the lead up to WOMADelaide 2005, visitors were informed of the initiatives in place through advertisements and information in *Eco Voice Magazine*, *The Advertiser* newspaper, the event website and programs and radio interviews.

At the event, visitors were requested to separate their biodegradable waste from recyclable drink containers at one of 114 easy-to-use, brightly coloured bin stations located throughout Botanic Park. No general waste bins were provided and regular stage announcements were made at the six stages around the Park reminding visitors to dispose of their waste appropriately and to take any general waste away with them.

Event sponsors, artists, stallholders and personnel received briefings on the waste minimisation initiatives in place and food vendors were contracted to provide only biodegradable crockery and cutlery and clear cornstarch glasses.

Plastic bags and promotional items such as balloons, magnets and foam hands were not permitted to be given out at the event. In the catering areas, bins were provided for biodegradable waste and cardboard and paper were collected for recycling.

Results from the event

Excellent results were seen at the 2005 event and event organisers received comments that WOMADelaide 2005 was the cleanest event to date at that time. Out of a total of 20.77 tonnes of waste generated, 68.9 per cent was diverted from landfill, as shown in table 12.1. A total of 35.4 per cent was sent for recycling and 33.5 per cent to a composting trial commissioned by Zero Waste SA. The composting trial provided information about how best to compost the biodegradable waste stream generated at WOMADelaide. The information also provided a methodology that enabled commercial composters to meet EPA licence conditions to accept event waste on an on-going basis. The WOMADelaide waste takes approximately 12 weeks to biodegrade. Observations showed that the waste degraded well.

The reaction to the waste minimisation initiatives at the event was very positive. Observations of event visitors showed 86 per cent used the bin stations correctly and the waste audit showed very low contamination in biodegradable bins in the visitor areas with 93.8 per cent of waste disposed of correctly (see figure 12.8).

TABLE 12.1 Waste recycled, composted and sent to landfill at 2005 WOMADelaide

Type of waste	Number of units	Weight (tonnes)	Percentage of total
Wine bottles	5083	3.0	
PET bottles	10 970	0.37	
Other recyclables	4704	0.53	
Cardboard	n/a	1.25	
Clay pots (La Compagnie Carabosse)	n/a	2.2	
Total material recycled		**7.35**	**35.4**
Total biodegradable material sent to composting trial		**6.96**	**33.5**
Total waste sent to landfill		**6.46**	**31.1**
Total waste material generated at event		**20.77**	**100**

Source: Zero Waste South Australia 2005.

Improvements to the initiatives were identified for WOMADelaide 2006. This event was Year 2 of the waste minimisation program and saw improved recycling facilities in the catering areas of the event with dedicated personnel provided to assist. From 2005 onwards, non-complying vendors have been banned from catering at WOMADelaide events. Resource recovery increased backstage with the provision of cardboard and paper skips in these areas.

Funding was also received from the South Australian Jurisdictional Recycling Group under the National Packaging Covenant, a cooperative approach between industry and government.

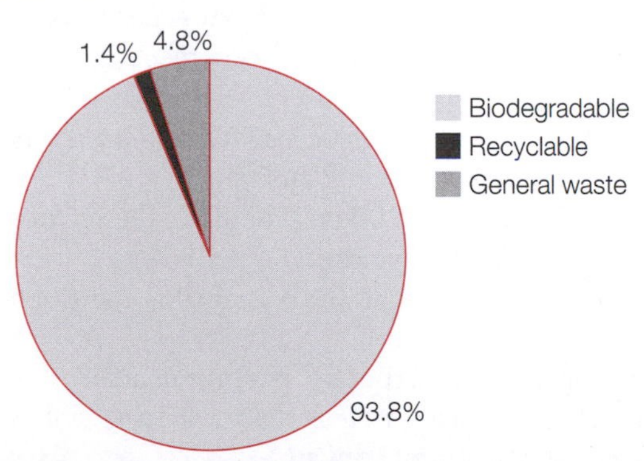

FIGURE 12.8 Recyclable general waste audit of event visitor biodegradable bins

Questions

1 Identify and briefly discuss each of the initiatives employed at WOMADelaide to minimise waste generated by event visitors.

2 In general terms, what were the key outcomes of WOMADelaide's waste minimisation efforts?

3 What areas of their waste management practices have WOMADelaide identified where improvements might be made?

REFERENCES

AGreenerFestival.com 2009, 'Welcome to AGreenerFestival', www.agreenerfestival.com.

Athens Environmental Foundation 2004, 'World conference on sport and the environment at Nagano 2001', www.athensenvironmental.org.

British Standards, BS 8901: 2009 www.bsigroup.com.

Campbell, N 2001, 'Future legacies — OCA's environmental initiatives', *Proceedings from the seminar 'Passing the torch: sustainable development lessons and legacies from the 2000 Sydney Olympic Games'*, Macquarie University Graduate School of Environment, 9 March 2001. Retrieved 19 February 2005 from CD *Sustainable development principles in action: learning from the Sydney 2000 experience*, Green and Gold Inc.

Ciplat, Lombardi, Platt, June 2008. 'Stop Trashing the Climate, p. 4. www.stoptrashingtheclimate.org, accessed October 2008. Originally sourced from Brenda Platt and Neil Seldman, Institute for Local Self-Reliance, Wasting and Recycling in the U.S. 2000, GrassRoots Recycling Network, 2000, p. 13. Based on data reported in Office of Technology Assessment, Managing Industrial Solid Wastes from manufacturing, mining, oil, and gas production, and utility coal combustion (OTA-BP-O-82), February 1992, pp. 7, 10.

Council for Responsible Sport, www.resport.org.

EcoLogo Events, www.ecologo.org.

Environment News Service 2004, 'WWF gives Athens Olympics no green medals', www.ens-newswire.com.

Falls Festival, www.fallsfestival.com.au.

FIFA 2006, 'Green Goal[a]: The OC and United Nations Environment Programme (UNEP) sign historic partnership agreement', *www.fifa.com*.

G-ForSE 2004, 'Athens — UNEP sign MOU', www.g-forse.com.

Green Games Watch 2000 2004, 'About us', www.nccnsw.org.au.

Green Meetings Industry Council 2007, 'Green meetings good for business', www.greenmeetings.info.

Greenpeace 2003, *The Greenpeace Olympic environmental guidelines —— a guideline for sustainable events*, www.greenpeace.org/australia/.

International Olympic Committee 2004a, 'The IOC, the environment and sustainable development', multimedia.olympic.org.

—— 2004b, 'Factsheet: environment and sustainable development', *Olympic charter*, http://multimedia.olympic.org.

Lenskyj, H 1998, 'Sport and corporate environmentalism: the case of the 2000 Olympics', *International Review for the Sociology of Sport*, vol. 33, no. 4, pp. 341–54.

Meredith Music Festival, www.mmf.com.au.

Neeb, S n.d., 'Green Games — the environmental efforts of the International Olympic Committee and the Lillehammer Olympic Organising Committee', in M Moragas, C Kennet and N Puig (eds), *The legacy of the Olympic Games 1984–2000*, IOC Olympic Museum and Studies Centre and the Olympic Studies Centre of the Autonomous University of Barcelona, Lausanne, pp. 159–83.

Office of Commonwealth Games Coordination (n.d.), *2006 Environment Strategy*, www.dvc.vic.gov.au.

Oittinen, A 2003, *The Olympic Movement and the Olympic Games, an environmental perspective*, www.ioa.org.gr.

Planet Drum 2004a, 'Environmental greenwashing of the 2002 Winter Olympic Games', www.planetdrum.org.

—— 2004b, 'Environmental recommendations go unheeded by Olympics organizers', www.planetdrum.org.

Sustainable Event Alliance, www.sustainable-event-alliance.com.

Sustainability Victoria 2006, *Waste Wise Events Toolkit*, Melbourne, www.sustainability.vic.gov.au.

Sydney 2000, *Environmental Guidelines. Sustainable Development Principles in Action: Learning from the Sydney 2000 Experience*, CD-ROM resource, Green and Gold Inc.

TravelSmart Australia 2007, www.travelsmart.gov.au.

United Nations 1992, *United Nations Conference on Environment and Development*, www.un.org.

United Nations Education, Scientific and Cultural Organisation, *Sustainable development — an evolving concept*, portal.unesco.org.

United Nations Environment Programme 2004, 'Agreement to Boost Environmental Awareness at Summer Olympics'. www.unep.org.

World Wide Fund for Nature 2004, *Environmental assessment of the Athens 2004 Olympic Games*, www.panda.org.

Zero Waste South Australia 2005, *Case study: WOMADelaide*, www.zerowaste.sa.gov.au.

EVENT TOURISM PLANNING

LEARNING OBJECTIVES

After studying this chapter, you should be able to:

1. describe 'event tourism' and the destination approach to event tourism planning
2. conduct an event tourism situational analysis to create a foundation for goal setting and strategic decision making
3. describe the range of goals that a destination might seek to progress through an event tourism strategy
4. list and describe organisations that might play a role in a destination's efforts at event tourism development
5. describe generic strategy options available to organisations seeking to develop event tourism for a destination
6. list and discuss approaches to the implementation and evaluation of event tourism strategies
7. discuss the potential event tourism has to generate positive outcomes in small communities and how event managers can remove or mitigate any negative impacts that occur.

INTRODUCTION

This chapter will explore the relationship between events and tourism from the viewpoint of destinations (cities, towns, regions, states or countries) seeking to develop and implement strategies to increase visitation. The chapter begins with an overview of event tourism, before moving on to propose and discuss a strategic approach to event tourism planning. This approach involves: conduct of a detailed situational analysis; the creation of event tourism goals; the establishment of an organisational structure through which event tourism goals can be progressed; and the development, implementation and evaluation of an event tourism strategy. It is argued in this chapter that the value of this process lies in its capacity to generate a coordinated strategic approach to a destination's overall event tourism efforts. The final part of this chapter seeks to redress the tendency in dealing with event tourism to focus on cities, states and countries. It does this by briefly examining the significant, positive role that event tourism can play in the context of small communities.

DEVELOPING DESTINATION-BASED EVENT TOURISM STRATEGIES

Government support at all levels has been integral to the expansion of event tourism. Not only have governments invested in the creation of specialist bodies charged with event tourism development, but many have also funded, or contributed significantly to, event-specific infrastructure, such as convention and exhibition centres and stadiums. The Asia–Pacific region, for example, has experienced significant investment in business tourism infrastructure by national and provincial governments (Kelly 2003). In the specific case of China, for example, there was only one convention and exhibition centre larger than 50 000 square metres in 1992. By 2003 this number had risen to 16 (Kaye 2005).

The willingness of governments to support event tourism through policy initiatives, financial support and legislation is increasingly evident. The 2006 Victorian *10 Year Tourism and Events Strategy*, for example, outlines a range of initiatives across some 14 policy areas that are designed to ensure the competitiveness of that state's event industry into the future. This same document also notes the decision by the Victorian Government to construct a new, 5000 seat, $370 million convention centre, the Melbourne Convention and Exhibition Centre, which opened in 2009 (Victorian Government 2006).

Responsibility for progressing event tourism efforts varies from destination to destination. In smaller destinations, such as towns and regional centres, involvement may be limited to organisations such as tourism promotional bodies, local councils and chambers of commerce. Larger destinations (cities, states, countries) are likely to have an expanded range of organisations involved in the event tourism area, including convention and exhibition centres, tourism commissions/departments, major event agencies, convention and visitor bureaus, government departments involved in areas such as sport and the arts, and specialist event organising companies.

THE EVENT TOURISM STRATEGIC PLANNING PROCESS

A strategic approach to a destination's event tourism development efforts offers significant benefits. These benefits lie primarily in the areas of coordination and in the building of an event tourism capacity that represents the best strategic fit with the area's overall tourism efforts, and its current and projected business environment. This approach is presented in figure 13.1 as a series of sequential steps, each of which is discussed in this section.

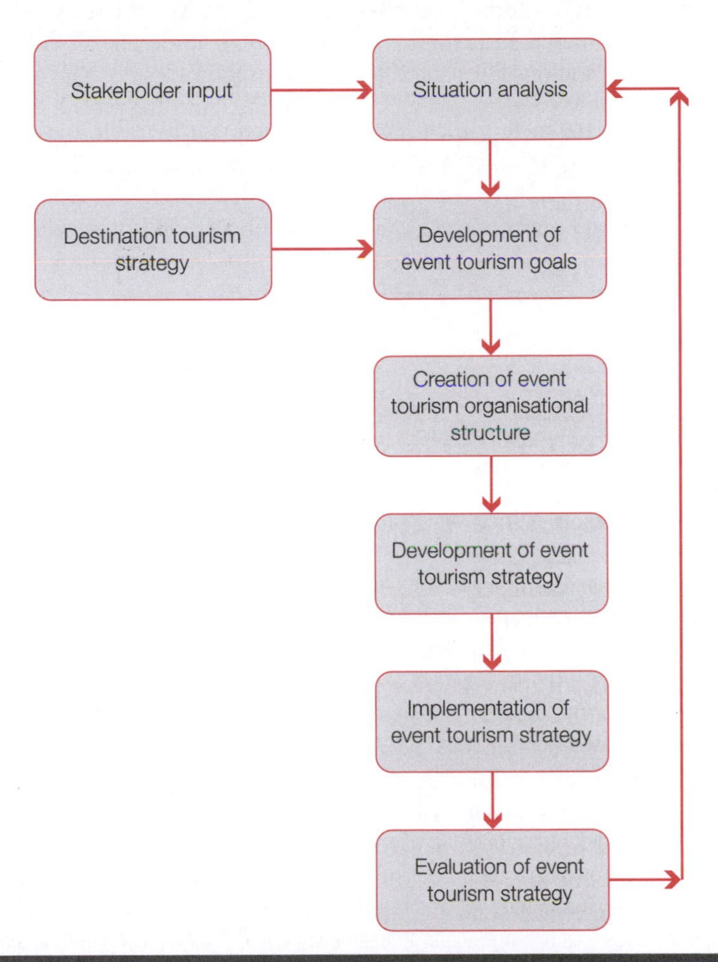

FIGURE 13.1 Event tourism strategic planning process

The timeframe in which event tourism strategic plans operate will vary from destination to destination, but five- to 15-year planning horizons are not uncommon. Events Tasmania, for example, employs a ten-year rolling events plan (Events Tasmania 2006a), EventScotland's major events strategy spans the period 2003–15 and, as noted previously, the Victorian government's event tourism strategy extends over a ten-year period.

SITUATIONAL ANALYSIS

A detailed situational analysis should underpin the decisions made on what event tourism goals to set for a destination. This analysis should reflect the various perspectives of key stakeholders in the event area, such as tourism bodies, the destination's community, and government agencies associated with areas such as the arts and sport, and major event organisers. In preparing the major events strategy for Scotland, for example, the consultancy company charged with this task (Objective Performance

Limited) spent 18 months engaged in research, including interviewing more than 80 individuals and organisations involved in major events in Scotland and internationally (Scottish Executive 2002). In the case of the Victorian Government's event tourism strategy, more than 70 formal submissions were received in response to an initial discussion paper and a further 50 interviews were undertaken with industry and government organisations (Victorian Government 2006, p. 43). The South Australian government used two events — the Adelaide Fringe and the world music and dance festival, Womadelaide — as test cases to establish whether the state's premier arts event — the Adelaide Festival of Arts — could move from biennial to annual (see the following event profile).

event profile

SOUTH AUSTRALIAN FESTIVALS: TWICE THE IMPACT OR HALF THE AUDIENCE?

Background

In January 2009 the 'South Australian Tourism Plan 2009–2014' was announced by the state Premier Mike Rann. The plan outlines a targeted increase in visitor expenditure from $3.5 billion in 2002 to $6.3 billion in 2014. The plan identifies festivals and events as a strategy in the key focus area of 'leverage'. That strategy — 'grow new and existing festivals and events to act as a hook to visit South Australia and grow its image' — is an example of event tourism as destination marketing and destination brand development (SATC 2009). Prior to 2009 the importance of festivals and events to the community was acknowledged, but there was no clear statement regarding the part that event tourism might play in the state's tourism plan.

Following a bidding war in 1996, the resulting loss of the Australian Formula 1 Grand Prix to Melbourne, Victoria, after eleven highly successful events staged in Adelaide, was felt deeply by the South Australian community. Advisory groups were established to work with the South Australian Tourism Commission and Events SA (then called Australian Major Events) to find new events for the state. The Grand Prix was replaced by the V8 Super Cars race in 1999, the Tour Down Under professional cycling race in the same year, and the Adelaide International Film Festival in 2002. There was a push to develop a year-round calendar of events, as the Adelaide Festival, WOMADelaide and the Adelaide Fringe were each scheduled around the likelihood of better weather, leading to a heavy concentration of festivals and events in the month of March (known locally as 'Mad March').

Of concern to the government, however, was the biennial nature of the three iconic arts events for the state. The Adelaide Festival and the Adelaide Fringe had run in even-numbered years since the 1960s, and WOMADelaide had run since its inception, initially as a part of the 1992 Adelaide Festival, in the alternate, odd-numbered years.

The response

As a response to a perceived threat that one of Adelaide's events might again be 'poached' by another Australian state, the premier announced additional funding to support WOMADelaide in becoming an annual event from 2004. There was concern that this might lead to twice the number of events with half the quality and half the audience, but the 2004 event was as successful as any held in previous years. Indeed, the event's duration increased from three to four days in 2010, and announced record ticket sales, even though some of the days were rain affected.

The Adelaide Fringe, buoyed by the success of WOMADelaide, was supported by the South Australian Government to move to become an annual event from 2007. Again this was met with concern among arts industry commentators and practitioners, who worried that there might be some diminution of quality or that sponsors may not be found to support the event on an annual basis. There was also concern that the Fringe would now be annual while its natural 'running mate' the Adelaide Festival was still biennial.

The 2007 Adelaide Fringe was heralded as a critical and box office success and subsequent festivals have shown a steady increase in audience numbers and ticket sales. In 2010 the Premier announced that the government would support the Adelaide Festival being run annually from 2012.

Outcomes

Although South Australia is a much smaller market than the other states of Australia, and there is strong competition from festivals in Brisbane, Sydney, Melbourne and Perth, the South Australian festivals continue to attract and build audiences. The events calendar is now more consistent and Events SA and the South Australian Tourism Commission continue to look for and to develop festivals and events across the whole year.

The initial success of this event tourism strategy is known in terms of data concerning audience numbers and ticket sales. The real indicator of the strategy's success, however, will only be known once data concerning the numbers of visitors to the state for these festivals and events — and their reason for visiting — is available.

A strengths, weaknesses, opportunities and threats (SWOT) analysis (see chapter 4) is a useful way of assessing the situation that a destination faces in its efforts to develop event tourism. Figure 13.2 lists a range of factors that might feature in such an analysis.

FIGURE 13.2 Possible factors for inclusion in a destination's event tourism SWOT analysis

STRENGTHS/WEAKNESSES

Existing stock of events

- Type
- Quality
- Uniqueness/competitive advantage
- Number
- Duration/timing (for example, whether most events are scheduled at a particular time of the year, such as summer, and whether this clustering is advantageous or disadvantageous from a tourism perspective)
- Current financial situation
- Image/reputation (particularly in visitor markets) of individual events
- Level of current demand from regional, intrastate, interstate and overseas visitor markets
- Level of understanding (developed through market research) of the needs of visitor markets
- Current economic, social and environmental impacts
- Existing links between events and the destination's tourism industry (for example, level of packaging evident and level of partnering with tourism industry marketing bodies)
- Stage of individual events in terms of their 'product' life cycle
- Evidence of long-term strategic planning

FIGURE 13.2 *(continued)*

Venues/sites/facilities/supporting services

- Number, type, quality and capacity of venues/outdoor event sites
- Capacity of local suppliers (for example, equipment hire, food and beverage services) to support various types of event
- Stock of supporting local tourism services (for example, accommodation suppliers, transport suppliers, tour operators)

Human resources

- Level/type of destination event venue/event management expertise
- Capacity of a community to provide volunteers to support event delivery
- Range/type of event-related training conducted in the area, or accessible to people from the area

Stage of event sector development

- Existence of organisations such as event industry associations, convention and visitors bureaus and major event agencies

Destination location relative to major tourist markets

- Travel time and costs
- Types and frequency of public transport to and from the area

Degree of political support

- Level of available funding for event tourism
- Level of/potential for legislative support
- Level of coordination/cooperation between local, state and national governments (and associated agencies) in the event area

Level of community support

- Prevailing community perspectives on the economic, environmental and social impacts of events
- Level of anticipated local patronage for events (necessary to underpin the economics of many events)
- Level of willingness of the community to absorb short-term negatives, such as crowding and traffic congestion
- Willingness of the community to support events via volunteering and the provision of home hosting services, etc.

OPPORTUNITIES/THREATS

Potential for partnering with selected organisations to progress one or more event tourism goals

- Possible partnering bodies include:
  - Government departments
  - Cultural organisations
  - Tourism bodies
  - Chambers of commerce
  - Tourism businesses (to package events)
  - Environmental groups (to minimise impacts/maximise environmental outcomes)

FIGURE 13.2 *(continued)*

Level and type of competition from events in other destinations

- Direct competition from similar events
- Indirect competition from dissimilar events taking place within the same time period as the existing/planned events

Market tastes/preferences for events

- Ability of an area to respond to changing market needs through existing and new events
- Impact on existing/planned events of changes in such areas as family structures, community age profiles, patterns of work/retirement and attitudes to health, etc.

Availability of external funds

- Capacity to attract government grants or loans
- Likelihood of attracting sponsorship

Potential to link events with overall destination branding efforts

- Strength and nature of existing destination brand (for example, the Mudgee region of New South Wales uses events to reinforce its image as a producer of quality food and wine – see discussion later in this chapter)

Local cultural/environmental attributes that have the potential to be leveraged for event purposes

- Capacity of an area's flora or fauna, Indigenous culture, history, ethnicity, architecture, local agricultural pursuits, etc. to be embraced within an event context

Presence of local chapters/bodies with affiliations to parent organisations that regularly conduct events

- Capacity of local sporting/business/cultural bodies to bid for and host events owned by their respective parent bodies; for example, national/international conventions, annual industry trade fairs and state/national/international annual sporting competitions

Environmental and social impacts

- Capacity of a destination to absorb event tourism impacts without negative environmental or community outcomes. Potential problem areas associated with events include waste generation, anti-social behaviour, crowding and the inability of local area infrastructure to cope with large, temporary population increases
- Existing community perspectives on the environmental and social impacts of events

General economic conditions

- Employment levels
- Interest rates
- Inflation
- Consumer confidence levels

Other

- Changes in weather patterns due to global warming
- Security and health issues (for example, terrorism, bird flu)
- Political climate (for example, the extent to which events involving particular groups or nations will be supported by key stakeholders, such as state or national governments).

DEVELOPMENT OF EVENT TOURISM GOALS

The role event tourism is required to play in a destination's tourism development efforts will vary according to the overall tourism strategy that is being pursued. An understanding of this strategy is important as it provides, for example, the basis for establishing event tourist visitation targets, as well as insights into destination branding and positioning efforts that an event strategy may be required to support. While each destination's event tourism goals will differ, common considerations in setting such goals can be identified. These are discussed below.

Leveraging events for economic gain

A key consideration in any event tourism strategy is the potential for events to bring 'new' money into a destination from outside visitors (see chapter 2). A major research study of the summer and winter festivals in Edinburgh, Scotland, for example, produced the following key findings in this regard:

- 65% of all visitors to Edinburgh said the Festivals were their sole reason or a very important reason for visiting Edinburgh
- 70% of people attending Edinburgh Festivals came from outside of the city, with 15% coming from countries outside the UK
- £76 million [~A$190 million] was spent by festival visitors with accommodation providers in Scotland, with £49 million [~A$122 million] of this being in Edinburgh itself.
- 70% of hotel occupancy in some months could be attributed directly to festival activity (Edinburgh Fringe Festival 2006)

Even in developing countries, events can generate significant tourist demand (and therefore export income). In the Caribbean, for example, peaks in visitation in many countries often coincide with an event (Nurse 2003).

Geographic dispersal of economic benefits flowing from tourism

When the destinations seeking to engage in event tourism are large geographic entities, such as states or countries, it is not uncommon for them to use events as a means of encouraging travel to areas outside major tourism centres. One of the key reasons for the South Australian state government's support of the Barossa Under The Stars event was that it was expected that it would draw interstate visitors to the capital city of Adelaide — and then beyond — to the winery region of the Barossa (see the 'Barossa Under The Stars' case study, pages 413–415). In this way the economic benefits from visitation are more widely spread.

Destination branding

A destination's 'brand' can be thought of as the overall impression, association or feeling that its name and associated symbols generate in the minds of consumers. Events are an opportunity to assist in creating, changing or reinforcing such brands. According to a study by Jago et al. (2003), efforts at using events for destination branding purposes depend greatly on local community support and on the cultural and strategic fit between the destination and the event(s) conducted there. This study also found, in the context of individual events, that event differentiation, the longevity/tradition associated with an event, cooperative planning by key players and media support were central factors in the successful integration of individual events into a destination's overall branding efforts.

The Australasian Country Music Festival, Australia's largest country music event, is an excellent example of how an event can be used for destination branding purposes. This event has been extensively leveraged to create a 'brand' for the town of Tamworth where, arguably, none existed before. The town is now firmly established as 'Australia's country music capital', a position it has sought to strengthen via a variety of means. These means have included developing a 'Roll of Renown' to tribute country music artists, building a guitar-shaped tourist information centre and swimming pool, constructing a 20-metre high 'Golden Guitar' at one entrance to the town, establishing an interpretive centre that overviews the evolution of country music in Australia and erecting memorials to country artists (Harris and Allen 2002).

Another example of 'identity' creation through events can be observed in the Scone district of New South Wales. This area brands itself as the horse capital of Australia and conducts multiple events to reinforce this position, such as rodeos, horse races, long-distance charity rides, as well as its major event, the Scone Horse Festival.

Many other examples of branding through events can be identified. The general category of food and/or wine festivals, for example, performs this function for a number of destinations, reinforcing to the broader market the destination's status in connection with these products. Take, for example, the Mudgee Wine and Food Festivals. These events involve selected winemakers and food producers from the Mudgee region of New South Wales showcasing their products at several Sydney (the region's major market) locations through the year.

Another aspect of the link between events and destination branding is the use of events by tourism marketing bodies as integral parts of broad 'theme' years. These themes can be used for marketing business event destinations, developing existing events or to reinforce key themes associated with their general tourism product. The goal of the German National Tourist Board's themed year in 2003, 'Germany — routes to success: trade fairs, congresses, conferences and more', was to consolidate and develop Germany's market position as an international destination for trade fairs, congresses and conferences (Germany National Tourist Board 2004). Australia's Northern Territory conducted a 'Year of the Outback' in both 2002 and 2006. During these themed years a number of new events were created, or existing events modified, to embrace the outback theme (Australian Outback Development Consortium Limited 2006). Auckland used events to focus on four key themes identified as core to its tourism strengths:

- maritime
- cultural and ethnic diversity
- artistic and creative
- active outdoor and sporting (Auckland City 2010).

Destination marketing

Associated with the issue of destination branding is the more general one of destination promotion. Destinations often use events to progress their overall tourism promotional efforts. Smith and Jenner (1998), for example, point to the dramatic rise in visitation to Atlanta, Georgia (a 78 per cent rise in overseas visitors and a 35 per cent rise in domestic visitors) over the three-year period following its announcement in 1990 as the site of the 1996 Olympics. They attribute this increase, in part, to the publicity that Atlanta was able to obtain as a result of hosting the Olympics. Such tourism-related outcomes are common in the context of mega-events, with De Groote (2005) providing a more extensive listing of such benefits in the context of the subsequent summer 2000 Olympic Games in Sydney, including:

- acceleration of Australia's tourism marketing efforts by ten years. This outcome was in large measure due to the generation of an additional A$3.8 billion in publicity for Australia between 1997 and 2000, with a further A$300 million in additional advertising exposure coming from partnerships with major Olympic sponsors such as Visa, McDonald's, Kodak and Coca-Cola.
- increase in international visitation (by 10.9 per cent in 2000 to almost five million visitors). This outcome was in part due to post-Games tactical programs conducted by the Australian Tourist Commission (now Tourism Australia), which saw some 90 campaigns launched involving 200 industry partners worth a total of A$45 million. These programs were intended to convert interest and awareness into actual visitation.
- rising interest in Australia and Sydney as a destination by potential travellers and as a location for the conduct of conferences. This interest was in part due to a campaign by the Australian Tourist Commission, which saw some 100 business events conducted off the back of the event.
- high level of intended return visitation, with an estimated 88 per cent of the 110 000 international visitors who came to Australia for the Olympics indicating that they were likely to return to Sydney as a tourist.

The 2008 Beijing Olympics generated similar levels of interest among its estimated 4.7 billion global audience due to the positive images seen at the event (Nielsen 2008).

Creating off-season demand for tourism industry services

Events have the capacity to be scheduled in periods of low tourism demand, thereby evening out seasonal tourism flows. Skiing centres, for example, often use events as a means of generating demand during non-winter periods. Events can also be used as a means of extending the tourist season by conducting them just before or just after the high-season period. In connection with the use of events for this purpose, this can serve to move market perceptions of a destination from that of a single-season-only location to one providing year-round leisure opportunities.

Enhancing visitor experiences

Events add to the range of experiences a destination can offer, and thus increase its capacity to attract and/or hold visitors for longer periods of time (Getz 2005). In this regard, destinations often seek to add to their stock of existing events. These offerings, in turn, are communicated to their potential visitor markets by such means as web-based event calendars (see figure 13.3).

FIGURE 13.3 Eventscorp Events Calendar 2010 (April)

Fremantle Street Arts Festival	3–5 April	Fremantle	Experience the skill and outrageous behaviour of the world's best buskers as they perform street theatre acts in the vibrant port city of Fremantle.

FIGURE 13.3 *(continued)*

Margaret River Wine Region Festival	8–12 April	Margaret River	Graze your way through over 50 of the regions best wineries and eateries at the Vintage Festival at Leeuwin Estate, sample fresh local produce from Busselton to Augusta, enjoy the vibes of the vintage street fiesta and discover Australia's finest wine region.
Quit Forest Rally	16–18 April	Busselton & Nannup	Head to Busselton's Barnard Park to witness Australia's best off road rally drivers at the Quit Forest Rally, the second round of the Australian Rally Championship. Transforming Nannup into the service park as the rally action thrills spectators on surrounding gravel stages.
Red Bull Air Race	17–18 April	Perth	The Red Bull Air Race World Championship features the world's best race pilots in a motor sports competition that combines speed, precision and skill. Using the fastest, most agile and lightweight racing planes, pilots navigate a low-level aerial track made up of air-filled pylons, flying at speeds reaching 370 km/h (230 mph) while withstanding forces of up to 12G. Get tickets to enjoy a premium event experience.
Busselton Festival of Triathlon	30 April–2 May		Busselton has triathlon fever that inspires thousands. Be a part of this festival that features a children's triathlon, family entertainment and the challenging Half Ironman, a qualifying event for Ironman Australia.

Eventscorp is the Western Australian Government's events agency whose objective is to identify, develop and deliver world class events that promote and enrich Western Australia.

Source: Eventscorp 2010, 2010 Events Calendar, www.westernaustralia.com

Catalyst for expansion and/or improvement of infrastructure

Events can provide a significant spur to both public and private investment in a destination. Many writers (for example, Getz 2005; Carlsen and Millan 2002; Ritchie 2000; Selwood and Jones 1993; and Hiller and Moylan 1999) have highlighted the role that particularly large-scale events can play in urban renewal, and in the subsequent development of a destination's attractiveness and capacity as a tourist destination.

Investment by the private sector in restaurants and tourist accommodation, for example, is often central to this process, and may sometimes extend to the building of large-scale infrastructure items. The main stadium for the Sydney 2000 Olympic Games, Stadium Australia (now ANZ Stadium), was developed and is owned by private sector interests. Even at the level of small-scale community-based events, significant positive changes to the physical aspects of a destination can result from the conduct of events intended to stimulate tourist visitation.

Progression of a destination's social, cultural and/or environmental agenda

A range of agendas may be pursued through the conduct of events — tourism development is but one of these. These other agendas may serve to condition how event tourism is approached, or may be independent of such considerations.

The pursuit of broader outcomes can be observed in the context of the Manchester Commonwealth Games, for example. This event was leveraged by the city's council as a catalyst for educational, skill-building and health improvement programs, as well as a means of creating awareness and understanding of the various communities (from Commonwealth countries) that live in the Manchester area (Carlsen and Millan 2002). Environmental agendas can also be progressed through events. The Sydney 2000 Olympics sought to be labelled the 'Green Games'. Among its many achievements in this regard was the clean-up of an area (Homebush Bay) that was highly contaminated with industrial waste. This area later became the main Olympic site (Harris and Huyskins 2002). Both the 2000 Sydney and 2008 Beijing Olympics ran substantial cultural programs alongside the sporting programs for the event. Sydney staged four festivals as part of the Olympic Arts Festival program, while Beijing staged five Olympic Cultural Festivals as an integral part of the overall legacy planning for the event. For the 2012 Olympic Games, London, the London Organising Committee has also committed to using the event for urban renewal purposes. Its new Olympic Park will act to transform the surrounding east London neighbourhoods, which include some of the poorest and most physically deprived areas of the United Kingdom, into a vibrant new urban city quarter (London Organising Committee for the Olympic Games 2006).

MEASURING PROGRESS TOWARDS EVENT TOURISM GOALS

Whatever event tourism goals are set by a destination, specific benchmarks need to be established to assess progress towards those goals. For example, in its 2006–10 strategic plan, Tasmania's major event agency, Events Tasmania, established performance objectives in areas such as event visitor numbers and their yield, winter/shoulder events conducted, the potential for event leveraging, the frequency of the event (that is, 'one-off', annual or biennial) and what the media impact of the event might be (Events Tasmania 2010a and 2006a).

Other areas of a purely tourist nature, where goals might be set and progress measured, include tourist income generated from events, changes in length of tourist stays, use levels of tourism services (particularly accommodation), the extent of geographic spread of tourism flowing from the conduct of events, the volume of event-related media coverage received by a destination, and changes in destination market position/image resulting from the conduct of events.

CREATION OF AN EVENT TOURISM ORGANISATIONAL STRUCTURE

To progress a destination's event tourism goals, it is necessary to allocate responsibility for achieving these to one or more organisations. In the case of towns or regions, such responsibilities often lie with the same body charged with overall tourism development. In the case of cities, states or countries, multiple organisations may be involved, such as bodies responsible for festivals, business tourism, major events and overall tourism development (see table 13.1). In the Australian state of Victoria, for example, four significant organisations with major roles in event tourism development can be identified:

1. Victorian Events Industry Council (VEIC). This body is a subset of and is managed by the Tourism Alliance Victoria and is 'a peak industry policy council of associations, corporate businesses and government agencies representing event organisers, venues, suppliers and service providers for Melbourne and regional Victoria.' The VEIC represents these stakeholder interests to Federal, State and local government and agencies, media, and other industry sectors (Victorian Events Industry Council 2010).
2. Tourism Victoria (the state's tourism commission) provides assistance to event organisers and local government to increase visitor numbers, length of stay and visitor yield at events. The aim of this assistance is to 'enhance the event's tourism marketing strategy as well as to assist with event delivery and development' (Tourism Victoria 2010).
3. The Victorian Major Events Company is a state funded organisation that acts to target and attract major international events that can serve to provide substantial economic impact and/or international profile for Melbourne and Victoria (Victorian Major Events Company 2006).
4. The Melbourne Convention and Visitors Bureau's primary role is to work with organisations such as large corporations and industry associations to secure the rights to host international and national business events in Melbourne and Victoria. Funding for the organisation comes from the state government and the private sector (via sponsorship, cooperative promotions and membership fees) (Melbourne Convention and Visitors Bureau 2010a).

In addition to these bodies, local and regional tourism bodies and some government departments, such as Arts Victoria and Sport and Recreation Victoria, also play a role in event tourism development in Victoria.

The existence of multiple bodies charged with event tourism development at a destination creates the potential for a loss of focus on its overall event tourism goals, as well as a less coordinated approach to their achievement. For these reasons, there is a strong case for the creation of a single body, either within an existing organisation, or in the form of a new organisation with a charter to coordinate, assist and, if necessary, 'push' organisations towards the achievement of broader whole-of-destination event tourism goals. The government event advisory boards noted previously can also perform this function providing their charter extends to such matters as facilitating cooperation within the event field, strengthening information flows, linkages and networks.

TABLE 13.1 Major event tourism organisations

Organisation type	Description
Government event advisory boards	Bodies such as these can be found in several states in Australia (for example, NSW Major Events Board). The purpose of these bodies, while there is some variation, is essentially one of providing the government of the day with event-related strategic and policy advice, as well as encouraging greater statewide coordination in the event sector.
Major event agencies	These bodies are commonly state or country based. Their roles vary depending on their charter. In some instances, they may be involved only in seeking to attract large-scale events through the bidding process (for example, Victorian Major Events Company). In other instances, they may also have responsibility for creating new events and developing existing events (Those agencies with a broader charter may also be charged with overall responsibility for facilitating the development of event tourism in a destination.
Government tourism organisations	These organisations, at local, regional, state and national levels, may perform a variety of event tourism development roles. In some cases, they may be responsible for developing and implementing a whole-of-destination event tourism strategy, in others their role may be more limited, such as acting only to promote destination event experiences to tourist markets. At the level of individual events, it is not uncommon for these organisations to act to provide such services as marketing and operational advice/assistance, assistance in obtaining necessary permissions/licences, and funding via competitive grants.
Business event agencies	Often government sponsored bodies, these agencies act to develop and support business events within a destination. These organisations are commonly called convention and visitors bureaus or convention and exhibition bureaus.

In the absence of a single overseeing body, alternative mechanisms can be used to bring about a degree of coordination and cooperation within the event sector. These mechanisms include shared board memberships between key event tourism bodies, clearly defined organisational missions to prevent overlapping efforts, regular 'round table' meetings between key organisations, and conditions on funding that require broader event tourism goals to be addressed by bodies involved in the area. The State Government of New South Wales' requirement that the Sydney Convention and Visitors Bureau (SCVB) create a new division (the New South Wales Convention Bureau) to progress its goal of spreading the economic benefits of tourism into regional areas, is an example of this last point (Sydney Convention and Visitors Bureau 2002).

DEVELOPMENT OF AN EVENT TOURISM STRATEGY

In terms of general strategic options available to a town, city, region, state or country's event tourism body, several possibilities can be identified. These strategies concern the development of existing events, bidding to attract existing (mobile) events, and the creation of new events. These three broad strategic options are not mutually exclusive; for example, event tourism bodies in any one destination may employ composite strategies involving several or all of these options to achieve their destination's event tourism goals. Whatever strategy is selected, it needs to reflect the insights gained from the preceding situational analysis.

Existing event development

A range of possible approaches to using existing events to advance a destination's event tourism efforts can be identified. One option is to identify one or several events that have the capacity to be developed as major attractions for an area ('hallmark' events), with a view to using them as the foundation for image-building efforts. The previously cited example of the Australasian Country Music Festival at Tamworth is indicative of how events can be used in this way. A variant on this approach is to develop a single hallmark event that can then be supported by a range of similarly themed events. The Scone example discussed earlier (with its 'hallmark' Scone Horse Festival and associated smaller scale horse-based events) is reflective of such a strategy. It may also be possible to merge existing smaller events to create one or several larger events, or to incorporate smaller events into larger events to add to their uniqueness and subsequent tourism appeal. Yet another approach is to develop one or several hallmark events, while at the same time maintaining a mix of small-scale events scheduled throughout the year, as a means of generating year-long appeal for a destination.

Event bidding

Many events are 'mobile' in the sense that they move regularly between different destinations. Some sports events (for example, state/national/international sporting competitions) and many business events (for example, association/corporate conferences and exhibitions) fall into this category. Some types of event tourism organisations (namely, national or state-based major event agencies, and convention and visitor bureaus) have been specifically established for the purpose of attracting new events to a destination via the bidding process. Organisations charged with this task need to be able to firstly identify mobile events — a task that convention and visitor bureaus often undertake by maintaining representatives in other states and overseas, and by directly communicating with meeting, incentive and exhibition planners. To attract such events, it is necessary to prepare a formal bid (see chapter 4) that makes a persuasive case as to why an event should be conducted in a specific destination. Before doing so, however, it is necessary to ensure a sound match exists between the event being sought and an area's capacity to host it. Regarding its bidding efforts, the Victorian Major Events Company (2006) notes:

> A decision to bid to host an event is only made after an exhaustive assessment of the event's history and projected feasibility within Melbourne and Victoria. Such assessment includes consultation and cooperation with venues, sporting associations, local government, sponsors, the sporting public, media and various State Government Departments including the Office of Premier and Cabinet, Tourism Victoria, Parks Victoria, Sport and Recreation Victoria and Business Victoria.

New event creation

New event creation should be based around the activities and themes identified in a prior situational analysis as providing substantial scope for the development of tourist markets. It should also be the case that new events, as Tourism Victoria (2006) points out, are capable of being integrated into the overall tourism product mix of a destination. Exactly what new events are created will vary with the strategic needs of each destination, with the range of generic options including active participant-based events, spectator-based sport events, and religious events, events with environmental/cultural/heritage themes, music-based events, special interest events and business events. As with the development of existing events, event tourism organisations need to be mindful of the need to ensure new events are adequately resourced if they are to have the best chance of long-term survival. This being the case, it may be desirable for organisations involved in event tourism to limit their support to only a few new events.

General considerations in event tourism strategy selection

In making decisions about what event tourism strategy to pursue, it can be useful to think in terms of what 'portfolio' (or mix) of events (for example, festivals, sporting competitions, business events) is likely to deliver the required benefits for a destination from event tourism. A useful first step in this regard is to rate events (existing, new and events for which bids are proposed), using available data and professional judgement, against established criteria. A simple 1 (low) to 5 (high) rating system (see figure 13.4) could be employed for this purpose. If appropriate, a weighting could also be applied to each criterion, so the final numeric value associated with each event would be a product of the extent to which it was viewed as meeting each criterion, multiplied by the importance of that criterion.

Event name	Criterion 1	Criterion 2	Criterion 3	Criterion 4	Total
A	1	2	3	4	10
B	1	4	5	5	15
C	2	4	3	1	10

FIGURE 13.4 Event rating scale

It is also useful to view events in the context of a particular destination in a hierarchical manner. Using this approach, events with high tourism value and the capacity to progress many of an event tourism body's goals would appear at the top, while those with lower tourism value and limited ability to progress its goals would be placed at the bottom. Such a hierarchy is commonly represented as a pyramid, as per the Events Tasmania hierarchical model of events (see figure 13.5). By representing the current stock of events in this way, insights also emerge about where 'gaps' may be in an area's event portfolio and what possible roles an event tourism body may play for events at different locations within the hierarchy (see the note in figure 13.5).

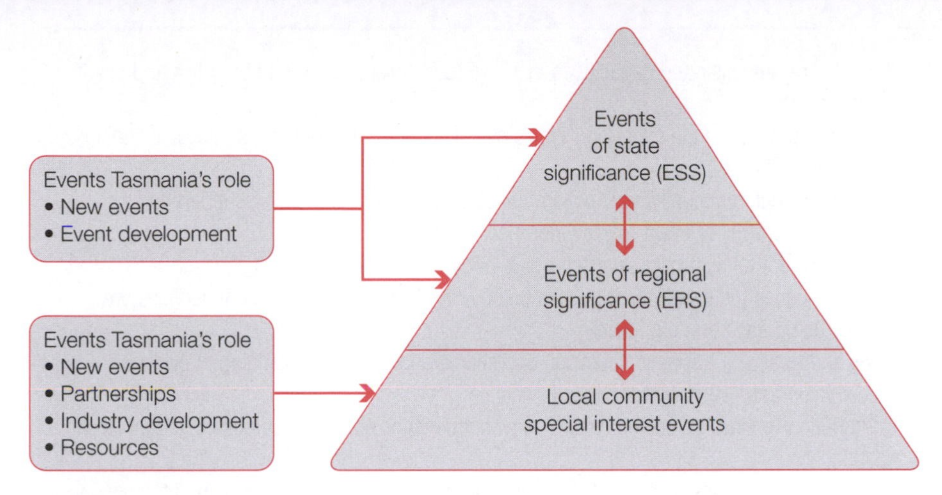

ESS/ERS support

• Funding programs • Strategic planning and marketing • Research and evaluation • Targeting funds/grants — agreements, performance bench marking • Event experience design and event programming • Resource leverage — sponsorship, industry • Facilitate linkages

Local community special interest events

• Regional events coordinators • Forums, training • Resources • Website references and research information • Training opportunities

FIGURE 13.5 Events Tasmania hierarchical model of events

Source: Events Tasmania 2006a, p. 4.

IMPLEMENTATION OF AN EVENT TOURISM STRATEGY

Once an event strategy has been selected, the next step is for the organisation(s) concerned to implement it by undertaking actions appropriate to its/their charter. This being the case, such actions may vary, from the provision of advice and marketing support to the actual development and conduct of new events. The following section seeks to identify, and broadly categorise, the full range of actions that organisations directly involved in event tourism development may engage.

Financial support

Financial support may be provided in the form of grants, sponsorship and equity.

Grants

Grants are a common means of providing support for events that are deemed to have tourism potential. Tourism New South Wales, for example, operates a Regional Flagship Events program that provides either one-off $10 000 grants, or for events with stronger tourism potential, $20 000 a year for three years (Tourism New South Wales 2006). Most other Australian states and territories operate similar systems. Queensland Events, for example, operates a granting system in partnership with local councils and regional tourist organisations (Queensland Events 2010a). Some local and city councils have also moved to create event tourism grant schemes (for example, Richmond Valley Council in northern New South Wales, Hobart City Council and Brisbane City Council). These grants are commonly based on a range of criteria, such as those in figure 13.6.

- Potential, or demonstrated capacity, to increase tourist visitation, yield per visitor and length of visitor stay
- Relationship between the event and area's overall tourism development strategy, including its branding efforts
- Level of evident community/local government/business/tourism industry support and associated capacity of event to grow and become self-funding
- Event's current tourism packaging efforts or potential for tourism packaging
- Timing — does the event occur outside peak visitor seasons when tourism services are already being used at a high level?
- Level and quality of business, financial, operational and marketing planning in evidence
- Media value associated with the event
- Contribution to strategic social, cultural, environmental or economic outcomes sought by the destination
- Existence of processes designed to evaluate the event, particularly its tourism outcomes

FIGURE 13.6 Common grant selection criteria employed by event tourism organisations

Grants may also be provided by event tourism bodies in the form of seed money to allow new events to be established, or for specific purposes, such as the conduct of a feasibility study to determine the viability of a proposed event. Grants can also be used as a form of incentive to conduct an event in a specific destination. Events Tasmania, for example, operates a touring events grants scheme that provides grants from $1000 to $12 500 to special interest groups, associations and clubs based on the length of stay and the number of interstate and overseas visitors involved (Events Tasmania 2010b). Through Sport and Recreation Tasmania (a government department), the Tasmanian Government also provides funding support for organisations conducting national sporting championships when certain conditions are met (Sport and Recreation Tasmania 2006).

Sponsorship

Some event tourism organisations and/or national/state/local governments act to directly sponsor events as a way of financially assisting them, and/or as a way of leveraging the opportunity presented by the event to progress their destination branding efforts or broader development agenda. Brisbane City Council, for example, will consider sponsoring events (on an application basis) that progress its *Living in Brisbane 2026 vision* (Brisbane City Council 2010).

Equity

To facilitate the conduct of an event, a tourism event organisation may act to directly invest in it. The IndyCar race, for example, was an event that took place on the Gold Coast in Queensland in a traditionally off-peak period for tourism services, and was operated by IndyCar Australia. The company was jointly owned by the State of Queensland (through Queensland Events) and the private sector organisation International Management Group (IMG) (Office of the Information Commissioner 1995). The event ended in 2008 after eighteen years amidst some controversy, and how the Queensland Government now feels about this form of direct investment is unknown.

Ownership

Some event tourism bodies develop and produce events to stimulate visitation to their destination. They act in this way for a variety of reasons, including to ensure their charter is progressed without the need to rely on the private sector (which may be unwilling to take on the financial risk involved in event creation and delivery) and to overcome a lack of local event management expertise. Queensland Events, for example, operates a subsidiary company, Queensland Events Gold Coast, that owns and operates two events — the Gold Coast Airport Marathon and the Pan Pacific Masters Games (Queensland Events 2010b). Other event tourism bodies in Australia have also acted to establish and develop new events, including Events Tasmania, Australian Capital Territory Tourism and Northern Territory Major Events.

Bid development and bid support services

As previously noted, bidding is the major focus of some forms of event tourism organisations. Such organisations act to research, develop and make bids, and/or work with bidding bodies (such as sporting bodies or professional associations) to facilitate the making of a bid. Once a bid is won, event tourism organisations commonly play little, if any, further role other than perhaps assisting to stimulate event attendance or to assist with the creation of an organising committee. Occasionally, however, these bodies will assist with the management and operations of the events they attract.

Event sector development services

Event sector development services include research, training and education, and the establishment of partnerships and networks.

Research

Some tourism event organisations commission or undertake research on a range of event-related matters as a way of gaining information that will aid the development of individual events or the sector in general. Matters explored include trends in event visitor markets, developments in competitor destinations, visitor perceptions of the quality of event experiences (particularly those supported by the event organisation concerned), event sector stakeholder viewpoints, event economic impacts, and overall sector management practices. Regarding this last point, research can be insightful in assisting event agencies to develop programs designed to build the events sector. Evidence for this can be found in Goh's (2003) study, which highlighted weaknesses in this area in the context of Irish festivals, specifically:

- 47 per cent of festivals have no data on their audiences
- 59 per cent of festivals do not provide training for their volunteers
- 23 per cent of festivals have no presence on the World Wide Web
- 58 per cent of festivals have no strategic plan.

Events Tasmania is an excellent example of an organisation that places a high value on research, undertaking studies to determine, for instance, specific event market segments, projected event consumer behaviour, economic yield and expenditure. It also encourages event organisers to integrate a research strategy into their long-term planning to assist them in making more informed decisions in connection with their future strategic directions. It is also the case that event organisers seeking government assistance need to undertake market research in support of their proposals. Additionally, Events Tasmania maintains a watching brief on developments in the area of event management research so as to identify and incorporate such developments within the Tasmanian event sector (Events Tasmania 2006).

Training and education

To promote best practice and continuous improvement, and by doing so assist in creating events that are sustainable in the longer term, some event tourism organisations undertake — or commission outside bodies to undertake — training in areas such as event project management, event marketing and general industry best practice. A number also maintain a resource base (electronic and/or print based) on which event organisers can draw for educational/training purposes, while some conduct industry events, such as conferences (for example, Event Tasmania's annual Xchange conference), to facilitate the sharing of event industry-specific knowledge.

Partnerships and networks

A range of opportunities exist for event tourism organisations to facilitate the development of cooperation and the building of networks within the event sector, and between the event sector and outside bodies. The grants process, for example, can be used to encourage linkages with organisations that have the potential to enhance the attractiveness of events to visitor markets, or that can provide access to these markets. This can be done by explicitly favouring applications that demonstrate links with, for example, tourism bodies and cultural institutions, such as museums, heritage organisations, art galleries and community arts organisations. Other ways in which such links can be established include purposefully arranging formal and informal meetings and functions involving members of the events industry, tourism organisations and the general business community. Once networks are established, they can serve a variety of purposes, such as facilitating the sharing of information and expertise, expanding access to sponsorship opportunities and developing partnerships (both within and external to the event sector) that will assist in further developing tourist markets.

Event tourism organisations may also find they have much to gain by communicating their strategies to a range of public and private sector organisations, thus encouraging dialogue that may lead to the identification of opportunities to progress a common agenda. Government departments associated with the arts, sport and state development, for example, may all see opportunities to further their goals through an association with one or more event tourism bodies.

Coordination

Event tourism bodies can play a range of coordination roles. These roles include developing an event calendar to reduce event clashes (see figure 13.3) and providing a 'one stop shop' at which event organisers can obtain relevant permissions and clarify government policies and procedures of relevance. Given that a range of government organisations may be involved in the delivery of any one event, event tourism organisations can also act to establish coordination and consultation protocols between different government units and agencies, as well as assisting events to 'navigate' their way through legislative and compliance issues. Auckland City Council, for example, in acknowledgement of the significance of this function to the development of its events sector, has proposed a range of actions as part of its events strategy, specifically:

- Establish a senior cross-organisational team to manage the council's involvement in events in the city:
  Members of this team would act as the first point of contact for any new ideas, event proposals or major issues. There would be collaboration with Tourism Auckland, the

Inter Agency Events Group (central government), Auckland Regional Council, other local authorities and the Auckland events sector. For instance, this could be for coordinating the timing of events, audience catchments, public transport, complementary funding, marketing, promotion, and new events.

- Build on the one-stop-shop approach for the council's facilitation of events.
  A relationship manager would be the key point of contact for any council business with the event organiser, including regulatory processes, funding and other forms of support.
- Develop processes to assist event organisers to bid for major events such as international sports events.
- Review the decision-making processes to enable more timely decisions about funding for an event.
- Build the council's knowledge and understanding of events through networking, research and evaluation.
  This would include researching global event trends and best practice, international acts scheduled to visit Australasia, cutting-edge ideas for events, feasibility studies, economic impact assessment, customer satisfaction surveys and post-event evaluations based on clear performance criteria. It would also include networking with the events sector, including people aspiring to join the industry (Auckland City Council 2005).

Event/destination promotion services

To assist organisations (such as sporting bodies and professional associations) in their efforts to stimulate market interest in their events, event tourism organisations, depending on their charter, may provide a range of assistance in the marketing area. Such assistance may extend from the provision of marketing collateral (see figure 13.7) to the creation of comprehensive supporting promotional plans (see figure 13.8). Additionally, such organisations may seek to facilitate the conduct of events by, for example:

- providing information to organisations seeking to conduct events on a destination's event-related facilities and services
- hosting familiarisation tours and site visits by event organising committees
- assisting with the preparation of event programs and pre- and post-event tours
- acting as a liaison between government and civic authorities.

In the Australian context it is noteworthy that Tourism Australia (the federal government statutory authority responsible for international and domestic tourism marketing) has established a separate body (Business Events Australia — BEA) to market Australia as a business and major events destination.

FIGURE 13.7 Promotional collateral — Melbourne Convention + Visitors Bureau

The Melbourne Convention + Visitors Bureau (MCVB) publishes an annual *Melbourne Planner's Guide* which is the flagship publication for Melbourne's Business Events Industry, providing Meeting Planners and Event Organisers essential information on premier venues, accommodation, products and services, as well as touring and leisure program ideas.

MELBOURNE PROMOTIONAL TOOLKIT

MCVB has a wealth of resources to assist Event and Conference Organisers in securing an event and boosting delegate numbers.

FIGURE 13.7 *(continued)*

From brochures, maps and spectacular visual tools, to a handy gifts and merchandise shop, utilise MCVB's toolkit to generate interest and bookings for your Melbourne event.

OFFICIAL MELBOURNE VISITORS GUIDE

The *Official Melbourne Visitors Guide* is designed to provide visitors to the city with a comprehensive understanding of the things to see and do.

The *Guide* is produced quarterly and showcases the four distinct seasons of Melbourne.

OFFICIAL MELBOURNE VISITORS MAP

This brochure covers both the inner city and immediate surrounds, detailing Melbourne's train and tram services and providing grid references to major attractions and accommodation around Melbourne.

MELBOURNE PROMOTIONAL DVD

This footage highlights the key strengths that Melbourne has to offer for your next Business Event. Available in DVD format.

ORDER GIFTS AND MERCHANDISE

Entice your decision-makers or inspire your delegates with some exciting Melbourne, Victorian and Australian merchandise.

MCVB has a range of promotional material, gifts, and brochures available to assist Meeting Planners, and to encourage delegates to make the most of their time in the city and surrounding areas. These include:

- Posters
- Postcards
- DVDs
- Clip-on koalas
- Melbourne books
- Pins
- Lanyards
- Bags

Melbourne Convention + Visitors Bureau (MCVB), www.mcvb.com.au.

Source: Melbourne Convention + Visitors Bureau 2010.

FIGURE 13.8 Tourism Australia promotion plan for the 2006 Ashes cricket tour

BACKGROUND

Tourism Australia developed an events marketing program in conjunction with Cricket Australia around the 3 mobile Ashes series, the 2006/07 *3-Mobile Ashes Series*, to leverage off the publicity surrounding the event in the United Kingdom and to increase awareness of Australia as a holiday destination. The program involved a mix of activities including viral and online marketing, a visiting journalist program, the release of tourism products and guidebooks, and trade engagement.

Tourism Australia also worked with the Department of Industry and Tourism Resources and Cricket Australia on a research study on the economic impact of the Ashes program.

The Hon Fran Bailey MP officially launched the Ashes Events marketing program on 17 November 2006.

FIGURE 13.8 *(continued)*

MARKETING ACTIVITIES

Viral activity

A viral campaign was developed, featuring video messages between Shane Warne and Phil Tufnell. The first video phone message, filmed by Shane Warne in Melbourne, featured Shane Warne taunting his old sparring partner about the forthcoming Ashes series. Tufnell responded with his own video message and a typically defiant response, by simply saying, 'Don't worry about where I am, Shane. Ask yourself how the bloody hell you're going to get the Ashes back?'

While working in Australia, Phil Tufnell also created a series of firsthand experience blogs of his experience in Australia. In these, he reviewed and previewed each of the Test matches.

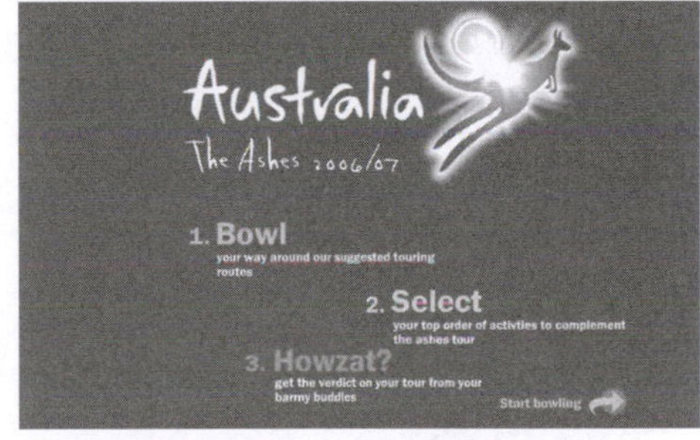

ONLINE

Tourism Australia built Ashes-specific event content on all English editions of the consumer website — www.australia.com. A dedicated 'Ashes OzPlanner' was created to help consumers develop an itinerary around the Ashes series and is featured on the UK edition of www.australia.com.

The 'Ashes OzPlanner' included ten suggested touring routes for fans, such as the Ashes Mega Tour, West Coast Overs and Tail Enders. Fans could access the planner at www.australia.com/ashes. The planner included information about such things as places to stay and things to see and do, as well as information on local watering holes where our great food and wine could be enjoyed.

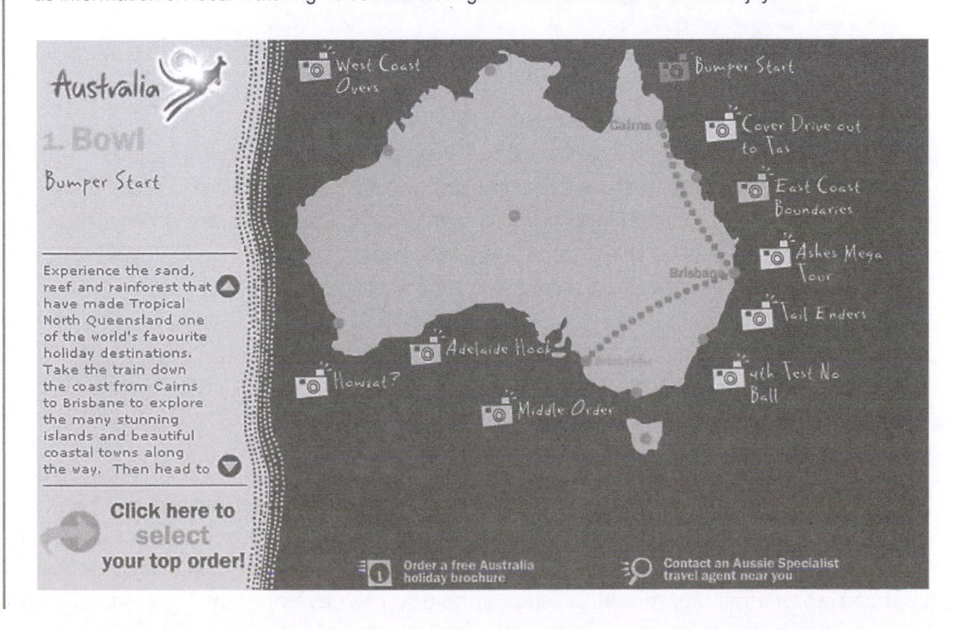

FIGURE 13.8 *(continued)*

CONSUMER BOOKLETS

Tourism Australia developed *The Cricket Fan's Guide to Australia*, experience-led consumer booklets. A total of 50 000 copies of the booklet were produced and distributed throughout Travelex retail outlets in Australia and through the Heathrow Airport in London to customers in the process of converting British pounds into Australian dollars. The booklets included information about activities travellers could experience around the Test Match destinations.

VISITING JOURNALIST PROGRAM (VJP)

A dedicated program was developed around the Ashes for UK journalists. Tourism Australia organised tours of Australia, before or after the match, in order to expose visiting journalists to various aspects of Australian landscape, culture and lifestyle. These tours were designed to generate positive stories of a wide range of Australian experiences in the UK media. This was a great opportunity for the media to share a slice of the great Australian outdoor lifestyle with millions of Brits back home.

Source: Tourism Australia 2006b.

Other

Other roles that event tourism organisations may play include: assisting in the development of business, marketing and risk management plans; providing advice on the negotiation of television rights and merchandising strategies; and lobbying on behalf of the sector on matters relating to new infrastructure development.

EVALUATION OF AN EVENT TOURISM STRATEGY

Evaluation is fundamental to the success of any strategy. At the destination level, the broad goals that have been set for event tourism, and the objectives associated with those goals, will form the basis of any evaluation that takes place. The collection and interpretation of information is central to this process, with data on visitor flows associated with event tourism being of particular importance. In the context of business tourism in Australia, for example, data are available from a variety of sources, including Tourism Australia, state tourist commissions and city-based convention and visitor bureaus. International bodies, such as the International Congress and Convention Association (ICCA) and the International Meetings Industry Association (IMIA), also conduct research that relates to Australia's comparative performance in this area. Tourism Australia (2006a), for example, provides the assessment (drawing on ICCA research) given in figure 13.9 of Australia's business-related event performance.

FIGURE 13.9 Australia's business-related event performance

In terms of association meetings per country, Australia was in fourteenth place in the global rankings in 2008, after being in eighth position in 2005. The USA was ranked number one, followed by Germany, Spain, France, the United Kingdom and Italy. In 2008 Australia had a market share of 3.0 per cent comparative to all other countries, an increase from 2.9 per cent in 2004. Australia's market share peaked in 2000 with 4.2 per cent.

In terms of meetings per country in 2008, Australia dropped to third from its 2006 position of number one in the Asia Pacific region, holding 182 international meetings. In 2008 Japan was ranked first, followed by China, Australia, Korea, Singapore, Thailand, India, Malaysia, Chinese Taipei and Hong Kong.

In terms of market share, Europe was number one in 2008 with almost 56 per cent of the meetings market, compared to all other regions. Australia's market share dropped from 3.6 per cent in 2005 to 3.0 per cent in 2008. Asia Pacific and Middle East has the second largest market share with 18.6 per cent in 2008 — the highest percentage for this region of the past ten years. North America's market share decreased gradually over the past decade from 14 per cent in 1996, to 10.6 per cent in 2005, but increased to 11.4 per cent by 2008 Latin America's market share increased to a record percentage of 9.2 per cent in 2008 which is the highest of the past ten years.

Sydney jumped the rankings in 2005 to achieve equal 17th in the world for the number of meetings, up from equal 27th in 2004, but fell to 24th by 2008. Melbourne has also dropped its ranking to 39th in the world in 2008, down from 22nd in 2005. The next highest ranked Australian cities in 2008 were Adelaide and Brisbane in 86th position. In 2005 Cairns was in equal 63rd place, a drop from 54th place in 2004. By 2008 Cairns had dropped to 128th position, equal with Perth. In 2008 Sydney was ranked 7th place for number of meetings per city when compared with other cities in the Asia–Pacific and Middle East regions. Melbourne follows in 11th position. Adelaide and Brisbane were ranked equal 16th with Adelaide up from 29th and Brisbane up one from 17th in 2005. Cairns and Perth are both ranked 20th and the Gold Coast equal 25th, up ten positions since 2005.

Australia is ranked 16th in the world for the estimated total number of participants attending international meetings in 2005 (83 334 participants), a decrease from 93 309 participants in 2004. In 1996, the figure for Australia was 94 593 participants. The number of meeting participants peaked in 2000, with 143 799 participants. In the Asia Pacific and Middle East region, Australia is in 2nd position in terms of estimated total number of participants attending international meetings. Japan was ranked second in the region.

FIGURE 13.9 *(continued)*

The average number of participants per meeting in 2008 was 638, up by 20 from 2007, but down from the peak in 2000, with the average number of participants per meeting then at 843. The average number of participants per event was highest in North America, with 1027participants in 2008.

Source: 'The International Association Meetings Market 1999–2008'; statistics report published by ICCA, the International Congress and Convention Association, www.iccaworld.com

In addition to whole-of-destination assessments of event tourism performance in the context of specific types of event, or events in general, each organisation involved in an area's event tourism development should have its own goals. To conform to the basic model of event tourism strategic planning used in this chapter, these goals should link directly to the destination's overall event tourism goals. Such individual assessments should also serve to 'build' towards an overall picture of a destination's event tourism performance, which can then be used to form the basis for future strategic decisions regarding event tourism development.

TOURISM EVENTS AND REGIONAL DEVELOPMENT

While the focus of discussion regarding event tourism is often on cities, states or countries, many regions and towns have acknowledged the benefits that can potentially flow from event tourism and have actively sought to engage in it. Local government in many regional areas is actively showing support for such efforts, being keen for communities to reap the economic and other benefits associated with events. Richmond Valley Council in northern New South Wales (Richmond Valley Council 2006) and Wagga City Council (Wagga City Council 2006) are but two examples of local government areas that have in the last few years established their own system of 'tourism event' grants.

SUMMARY

For destinations ranging in size from small towns to countries, event tourism is increasingly becoming a key aspect of their overall tourism development efforts. In this chapter, a basic event tourism strategic planning model has been proposed that seeks to bring a measure of structure and discipline to this process. The first step in the model is a detailed situational analysis, which leads to the establishment of event tourism goals. These goals are then progressed through an organisational structure created for this purpose. Ideally, such a structure would involve the creation of a single organisation with responsibility for the area, or the allocation of such responsibility to an existing body. In the absence of such an organisation, other options, such as regular meetings between key bodies in the area, can be used with similar intent. Once a structure is in place, strategic options need to be considered. Such options centre on using existing events, bidding and/or the creation of new events.

In pursuit of the selected strategy, a destination may engage in a range of actions including the provision of financial support, promotional assistance and general efforts directed at sector development. How successful these practices are in progressing a destination's event tourism strategy and its associated goals needs to be assessed at both the destination level and the level of those organisations with a major input into the event tourism development process. Information gained from this process can then be used to refine future event tourism development efforts.

QUESTIONS

1. Discuss the value of having a clear understanding of a destination's overall tourism strategy before embarking on the process of creating an event tourism strategy.
2. List and discuss three goals that a destination may seek to progress through the development of an event tourism strategy.
3. What types of non-tourism goals might a destination seek to achieve by expanding its focus on event tourism?
4. In the absence of a single body with responsibility for directing a destination's event tourism efforts, what approaches might be used to ensure a coordinated response to this task?
5. Briefly discuss the three broad strategic options available to destinations seeking to expand visitation through the use of events.
6. Briefly explain the strategic value to destinations of establishing objective criteria upon which to rate their events.
7. What types of action might bodies with a major involvement in event tourism consider taking to develop the event sector in their destination?
8. Briefly discuss how events can play a role in branding a destination.
9. Draw a basic event tourism strategic planning model. Briefly describe each step in this model.
10. Discuss the various forms that grants from event tourism bodies can take.

case study

BAROSSA UNDER THE STARS MUSIC CONCERT

Background

Barossa Under The Stars (BUTS) was originally conceived in 1996 as a music concert in the Barossa Valley wine-growing region of South Australia, to promote the region as a tourist destination to intrastate, interstate and international visitors. The concerts were also staged to provide international entertainment to the local community (and, consequently, to the event's South Australian, national and international attendees).

Local Barossan identities were looking for an event that would provide an activity to be held in the alternate years to the Barossa Vintage Festival, increase media exposure for the Barossa region, provide international quality events in the region for the local community, and increase accommodation occupancy rates.

Target markets

The organisers had originally identified five discrete market segments for the event:

1. *Baby Boomers* — 50 (plus) year-old males and females who were wine drinkers
2. *Generation X-ers* — 18–24 year-old males and females who were beer and spirit drinkers
3. *The Barossan community* — the 'local' audience
4. *People from metropolitan Adelaide and regions surrounding the Barossa Valley* — the 'state' audience
5. *People from interstate* — the 'national' audience.

Stakeholders

The two major stakeholders were the Barossa Wine and Tourism Association (BWTA) and the commercial promoter Adrian Bohm Presents. The BWTA was a representative body for the winemakers, tourism operators, accommodation and other businesses in the region, as well as the local community, and was funded by subscription from them (largely the winemaker members of the organisation) and by grants from the South Australian Tourism Commission.

Event concept

An event that had attracted the attention of the original BUTS working party, and that had been staged successfully for many years, was an outdoor music concert at Leeuwin Estate Winery in Margaret River, Western Australia. The event had consistently sold out tickets up to its capacity, regardless of the entertainment program or the artists involved in the annual event. Leeuwin had held other events and concerts throughout the year just as successfully. The Leeuwin Estate event was adopted as the model for the Barossan event.

Situational analysis

At that time, there were no winery-based concerts of this scale held in South Australia and only two outside the state: one at Leeuwin Estate winery at Margaret River, Western Australia, and the other at Orlando Wyndham winery in the Hunter Valley, New South Wales. There had been the successful staging of musical concerts of a smaller scale in the Barossa that were part of the Barossa Vintage and Barossa Music Festivals. These concerts had occurred at a variety of outdoor venues and inside the wineries themselves. There was a strong culture, developed by the Barossa Vintage Festival over the decades, of support for and attendance by the local community at concerts and events.

There was no agreement from the BUTS organising committee on why the Leeuwin Estate event is as successful as it is. It is approximately three hours' drive from Perth, the capital city of Western Australia, whereas the Barossa site is just under one hour's drive from Adelaide. The Leeuwin Estate site has a capacity of almost 7000. This is matched by each of the three venues used in the Barossa. Transport to the Barossa event is mainly by private vehicle, with a total of 35 coaches being used for the 2006 event. Leeuwin used over 100 coaches at their 1997 event. The Barossa event has between 500–750 VIPs at each event; Leeuwin had 1100 in 1997. The Barossa event has approximately 2000 regulars (based on direct mailing lists), or 25 per cent; the Leeuwin event has 5000 regulars each year, or just over 70 per cent.

It is clear that the Leeuwin event has some considerable advantages over the Barossa event. It has been running for 21 years, uninterrupted, at the same venue. It has strong, consistent management and a clear, single direction that it pursues. In contrast, BUTS has relied on the collective experience of the individuals involved and has not been able to establish itself as a 'heritage' event; rather, it has survived on a year-by-year basis. The event remains vulnerable to the vagaries of an international agents' marketplace, rather than capitalising on the intrinsic worth of the event. The event has not been able to capture the ongoing commitment of a core loyal audience to the extent that the Leeuwin Estate event has.

Outcomes

The four stated objectives of the event from its inception were to:

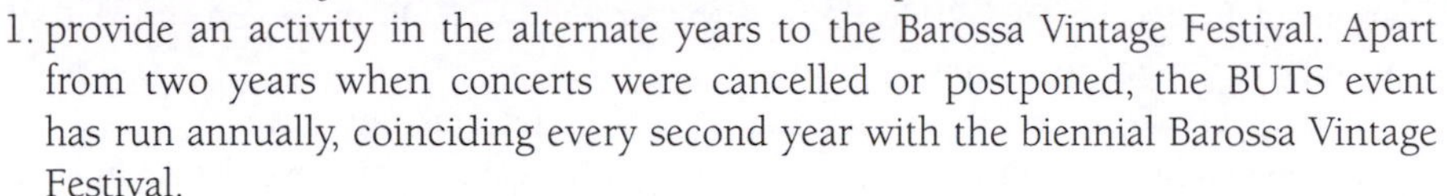

1. provide an activity in the alternate years to the Barossa Vintage Festival. Apart from two years when concerts were cancelled or postponed, the BUTS event has run annually, coinciding every second year with the biennial Barossa Vintage Festival.
2. increase media exposure in the Adelaide metropolitan market. Although the event does generate media coverage beyond the paid campaigns, there is no data on the extent of that media coverage, of its reach into any particular target market or of its effectiveness. The extent of media exposure in the Adelaide metropolitan market is therefore unknown. The media coverage often gives more prominence to the artist, rather than the region or venue.
3. provide international quality events in the region for the local community. Each of the main acts (apart from the biggest seller, Australian John Farnham) would be considered 'international' and at least some of the audience is local in origin. There is no audience data to indicate what proportion of those attending is either from the local community or outside the local region, interstate or international visitors.
4. increase accommodation occupancy rates in the region. The amount of available accommodation has certainly increased, particularly with the opening of the Barossa Novotel Resort. Although exact occupancy rates are unknown, it is clear that accommodation is impossible to obtain the Saturday night of the event (suggesting 100 per cent occupancy) and there are normally strong bookings for the nights immediately prior to and following the event.

Prepared by Steve Brown, former event manager, Barossa Under The Stars 1997–1999 and 2003–2005.

Questions

1 Undertake a situational analysis for the event and identify the goals that could be set for the event based on your analysis.

2 Identify ways in which the Barossa Under The Stars event could be used to generate positive outcomes for the Barossan community.

3 Describe how you would evaluate the event to provide evidence of its contribution to the positive outcomes identified in question 2.

REFERENCES

Auckland City Council 2005, 'Auckland City Events Strategy', www.aucklandcity.govt.nz.

Australian Outback Development Consortium Limited 2006, 'Year of the Outback', www.outbackinfront.com.

Brisbane City Council 2010, 'Living in Brisbane 2026 Vision Documents', www.brisbane.qld.gov.au.

Carlsen, J & Millan, A 2002, 'The links between mega-events and urban development; the case of the Manchester 2002 Commonwealth Games', in *Proceedings of the Events and Place Making Conference*, eds L Jago, M Deery, R Harris, A Hede, J Allen, Australian Centre for Event Management, University of Technology, Sydney.

De Groote, P 2005, 'Economic and tourism aspects of the Olympic Games', *Tourism Review*, vol. 60, no. 1, pp. 12–19.

Edinburgh Fringe Festival 2006, 'About the Fringe — 2004 economic impact study results', www.edfringe.com.

Eventscorp 2010, '2010 Events Calendar', www.westernaustralia.com

Events Tasmania 2006, 'Role of research in events Tasmania', www.eventstasmania.com.

—— 2010a, 'Funding Support for Major Events', www.eventstasmania.com.

—— 2010b, 'Touring Grant', www.eventstasmania.com.

Germany National Tourist Board 2004, www.germany-extranet.net.

Getz, D 2005, *Event management and event tourism*, 2nd edn, Cognizant Communication, New York.

Goh, F 2003, 'Irish festivals, Irish life: the facts and how to use them', presentation at the 2003 Irish Festivals Association Conference, www.aoifeonline.com.

Harris, R & Allen, J 2002, *Regional event management handbook*, Australian Centre for Event Management, University of Technology, Sydney.

Harris, R & Huyskens, M 2002, 'Public events: can they make a contribution to ecologically sustainable development?', www.business.uts.edu.au.

Hiller, H & Moylan, D 1999, 'Mega-events and community obsolesence: redevelopment versus rehabilitation in Victoria Park East', *Canadian Journal of Urban Research*, vol. 8, no. 1, pp. 47–81.

ICCA 2009, 'Statistics Report 1999–2008' www.iccaworld.com.

Jago, L, Chalip, L, Brown, G, Mules, T & Ali, S 2003, 'Building events into destination branding: insights from experts', *Event Management*, vol. 8, pp. 3–14.

Kaye, A 2005, 'China's convention and exhibition center boom', *Journal of Convention & Event Tourism*, vol. 7, no. 1, pp. 5–22.

Kelly, M 2003, 'Feature article', *Venue Managers Association News*, 22 November.

London Organising Committee for the Olympic Games 2006, 'World experts back London 2012 plans for first sustainable Olympic Games in countdown to World Environment Day', www.london2012.com.

Melbourne Convention + Visitors Bureau, 'Melbourne Promotional Toolkit', www.mcvb.com.au.

Mudgee Wine, '2006 Mudgee Food and Wine Fair', www.mudgeewine.com.au.

Nielsen 2008, 'China becomes a more compelling international tourist destination, thanks to Olympic Games', http://blog.nielsen.com.

Nurse, K 2003, 'Festival tourism in the Caribbean: an economic impact assessment', in *Proceedings of the Fifth Annual Caribbean Conference on Sustainable Tourism Development*, Caribbean Tourism Organisation.

Office of the Information Commissioner 1995, 'Decision no. 96018', www.oic.qld.gov.au.

Queensland Events 2010a, 'Regional Events Development Program', www.queenslandevents.com.au.

Queensland Events 2010b, 'Queensland Event Corporation', www.queenslandevents.com.au.

Richmond Valley Council 2006, *Tourism event funding application*, Lismore, New South Wales.

Ritchie, B 2000, 'Turning 16 days into 16 years through Olympic legacies', *Event Management*, vol. 6, pp. 155–65.

SATC 2009, 'South Australian Tourism Plan 2009–2014', South Australian Tourism Commission, www.tourism.sa.gov.au.

Scottish Executive 2002, 'Scotland's major events strategy 2003–2015: competing on an international stage', www.scotland.gov.uk.

Selwood, HJ & Jones, R 1993, 'The America's Cup in retrospect: the aftershock in Fremantle', in *Leisure and Tourism: Social and Environmental Change: Papers from the World Leisure and Recreation Association Congress*, eds AJ Veal, P Jonson & G Cushman, Centre for Leisure and Tourism Studies, University of Technology, Sydney, pp. 656–60.

Smith, A & Jenner, P 1998, 'The impact of festivals and special events on tourism', *Travel and Tourism Analyst*, vol. 4, pp. 73–91.

Sport and Recreation Tasmania 2006, '2006–07 National Championship Program', www.development.tas.gov.au.

Stadium Australia Group 2006, 'Invester relations', www.anzstadium.com.au.

Sydney Convention and Visitors Bureau 2002, *Annual Report 2001–02*, Sydney.

Tourism Australia 2006a 'Business fast facts — ICCA data, statistics report — International Association Meetings Market 1996–2005', www.tourism.australia.com.

—— 2006b, '3 Mobile Ashes Series', www.tourism.australia.com.

Tourism New South Wales 2006, 'Regional flagship events program', http://corporate.tourism.nsw.gov.au.

Tourism Victoria 2006, *Annual Report 2005–06*, Melbourne.

—— 2010, www.tourism.vic.gov.au.

Victorian Events Industry Council 2010, 'About', www.veeci.org.au.

Victorian Major Events Company 2010, 'Mission', www.vmec.com.au.

Wagga City Council 2006, 'Event promotion grants', www.wagga.nsw.gov.au.

PART 3

EVENT OPERATIONS AND EVALUATION

This part of the book looks at how choice of venue, theme and elements such as safety have a bearing on the successful staging of events. The following chapter relates to how the science of logistics can be adopted to manage events. The final chapter in this section describes the critical role of evaluation in the event management process and the range of techniques available to effectively conduct this.

14

STAGING EVENTS

LEARNING OBJECTIVES

After studying this chapter, you should be able to:

1. analyse the staging of an event according to its constituent elements
2. demonstrate how these elements relate to each other and to the theme of the event
3. understand the safety elements of each aspect of staging
4. identify the relative importance of the staging elements for different types of event
5. use the tools of staging.

INTRODUCTION

The term 'staging' originates from the presentation of plays at the theatre. It refers to bringing together all of the elements of a theatrical production for its presentation on a stage. Most events that use this term take place at a single venue and require organisation similar to that of a theatrical production. However, whereas a play can take place over a season, a special event may take place in one night. Examples of this type of event are product launches, company parties and celebrations, awards ceremonies, conference events, concerts, large weddings, corporate dinners, and opening and closing events.

Staging can also refer to the organisation of a venue within a much larger festival. A large festival may have performance areas positioned around a site. Each of these venues may have a range of events with a distinct theme. At the Sydney Royal Easter Show, there are a number of performance areas, each with its own style. Because it is part of a much larger event, one performance area or event has to fit in with the overall planning of the complete event and with the festival programming and logistics. However, each performance area is to some extent its own kingdom, with its own micro-logistics, management, staff and individual character. One stage of Sydney's Royal Easter Show had the theme 'world music and dance', for example. The venue had its own event director, stage manager, and light and sound technicians. Although it was part of the overall theme of the Royal Easter Show, it was allowed a certain amount of autonomy by the Easter Show Entertainment Director.

The main concerns of staging are as follows:

- theming and event design
- programming
- choice of venue
- audience and guests
- stage
- power, lights and sound
- audiovisuals and special effects
- decoration and props
- catering
- performers
- crew
- hospitality
- the production schedule
- recording the event
- contingencies.

Of course there are other areas of event management that are part of staging, such as risk, logistics and finance. This chapter analyses the staging of an event according to these elements. It demonstrates how these elements revolve around a central event theme. The type of event will determine how important each of these elements is to the others. However, common to the staging of different events are the tools: the stage plan, the contact and responsibility list, and the production schedule.

THEMING AND EVENT DESIGN

When staging an event, the major artistic and creative decision to be made is that of determining the theme. The theme of an event differentiates it from other events. In the corporate area, the client may determine the theme of the event. The client holding a corporate party or product launch may want, for example, mediaeval Europe as the theme, or Australiana, complete with native animals and bush band. Outside the corporate arena, the theme for one of the stages at a festival may be blues music, debating or a children's circus. Whatever the nature of the event, once the theme is established, the elements of the event must be designed to fit in with the theme. This is straightforward when it comes to deciding on the entertainment and catering. With the mediaeval corporate party, the entertainment may include jongleurs and jugglers, and the catering may be spit roasts and wine. However, audiovisuals may need a lot of thought to enhance the theme; the sound and lights must complement the entertainment or they may not fit in with the period theme. Figure 14.1 is a breakdown of the elements of staging, and it emphasises the central role of the theme of the event.

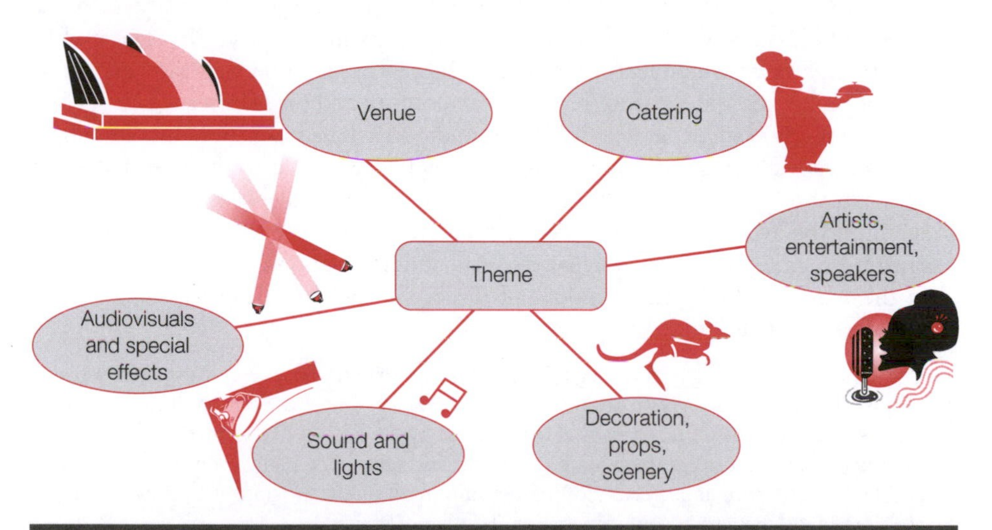

FIGURE 14.1 The elements of staging revolve around the theme

Many event organisers and academics stress the importance of the theme. Don Getz, in his seminal work on event studies, states that the theme gives 'meaning to an event.' (Getz 2005, p. 223) The Community Chest Maynardville Carnival organisers in South Africa, Greg Damster and Wren Dry (Tassiopoulos 2005, p. 399) advise:

> A theme is essential for any event as it creates cohesion... The main attraction of your event must be inline with your theme. This must be the pivotal with the programme and smaller events revolving around this.

PROGRAMMING

The program of the event is the flow of the performers, speakers, catering and the other elements of the event over time. It is the 'what's on' of the event. The program creates the core event experience for the attendee. Ultimately the event experience for the attendee and the sponsors rests on the success of the program. Silvers (2004, p. 271) describes its importance:

> An event experience must be choreographed and blocked out as carefully as any dance or play. The professional event coordinator crafts a plan that takes the attendee or guest through a structured progression of various sights, sounds, tastes, textures, smells, highs, lows, climaxes, diversions, and discoveries that delivers the intended impact and message of the event.

The program contains the schedule of performance. As with all the elements of staging, programming is both an art and a science. The program of the event depends on:

- the expectations of the audience
- the constraints of the venue and infrastructure
- the culture of the client and main sponsors
- the availability of elements of the staging and their relationship to each other
- the logistics
- the creative intent of the event team.

It is similar to the order in a street parade — the timeline or schedule of the program is set out in a linear fashion. Far from this being a simple example, a parade is multifaceted and there is little the event manager can do to change it once it starts moving. Consider the music: the brass band cannot be performing near the highland pipe band; they perform at slightly different beats. An event program also has a rhythm all of its own. The mix of entertainment, catering and speeches has to be well thought out so the event builds and the audience has times of intensity and times of rest. A New Year's Eve program, for example, gradually lifts the audience to the moment before midnight.

A large festival's program is a complex of activities. Many festivals use a form of a Gantt chart to map the various attractions and to help the audience navigate the event program. If the event is broadcast, the event program may have to be in sync with the television programming. This is a major consideration for sports events.

In the words of Colin Slater (2005) of the event company Sing Australia (in the Australian Capital Territory):

> The program on the night must begin by establishing the atmosphere . . . You don't want to boss the audience — give them time to settle in. Then we get the MC to introduce the night so the purpose of the event is clearly known by all. Also, I like to involve the audience before they eat to get them all to loosen up and relax. The night should start bright and happy and have its plateaus, so it is not full-on all night. Program it to finish on an absolute high whether they are dancing or clapping or singing.

The program will create the 'wow', surprise and 'specialness' of the event. For many special events this is the key to a memorable experience. In the corporate product launch, for example, the wow is sometimes known as the reveal; that is, when the product comes into view of the attendees. In some countries, events and festivals are starting to age and corporate special events have trouble thinking of new ideas. The festivals will stay with a similar program as this is the safest option. As the event consultant, Tracey Hull (2009) points out:

> The development of an event is essential over time. There needs to be room for the innovative cutting edge to come into an event program. We don't want the event to become the same old, same old. We have to remember that innovation is vital to the life of an event.

Innovation and creative thinking are vital to the sustainability of festivals and special events. Not only do they make the program more interesting for the attendees and the staff, thinking creatively about a program can significantly reduce the cost of promotion and attract new sponsors. Uniqueness attracts the press, which in turn attracts sponsors who want press coverage for their brand.

CHOICE OF VENUE

The choice of venue is a crucial decision that will ultimately determine many of the elements of staging. Figure 14.2 lists the major factors in the choice of a venue. The venue may be an obvious part of the theme of the event. A corporate party that takes place in a zoo is using the venue as part of the event experience. However, many events take place within 'four walls and a roof', the venue being chosen for other factors. It can be regarded as an empty canvas on which the event is 'painted'. Figure 14.3 demonstrates the variety of venues that have been used for events.

- Matching the venue with the theme of the event
- Matching the size of the venue to the size of the event
- Venue configuration, including sight lines and seating configuration
- History of events at that venue, including the venue's reputation
- Availability
- What the venue can provide
- Transport to, from and around the venue; parking
- Access for audience, equipment, performers, VIPs, staff and the disabled
- Toilets and other amenities
- Catering equipment and preferred caterers
- Power (amount available and outlets) and lights
- Communication, including telephone
- Climate, including microclimate and ventilation
- Emergency plans and exits

FIGURE 14.2 Factors to consider in venue selection

- Wetlands, caves, extinct volcanoes, beaches, rainforest clearings
- School halls, town halls, shopping malls
- Theatres, picture theatres, art galleries
- Factory floors, empty factories, disused mines, current mines
- Harbours, boats, ships, islands, foreshores
- Avenues, streets, roads, bridges and freeways
- Rooftops, car parks, railway sheds
- Shearing sheds, vineyards, farmyards
- Back yards, front yards, the whole house
- Foyers, stages, loading docks
- Churches, both consecrated and deconsecrated
- Conference centres, entertainment centres, function centres and sports centres.

FIGURE 14.3 Variety of event sites

The list illustrates that almost any area can be the site of a special event. In some of these cases, such as extinct volcanoes and caves, the uniqueness of the venue adds to the 'specialness' of the event. The event manager must be aware of the advantages and disadvantages of using purpose-built sites such as conference centres or a hotel function room. The main advantage of such sites is that they allow control of a greater number of environmental variables such as the temperature of the room, audience entrances and exits, and the light and sound. This control enables the event team to compel the audience to completely focus on the stage. The layout of most function rooms follows a similar pattern, thereby giving event staff familiarity with the type and use of the facilities. The familiarity, however, can be a disadvantage as the attendees may be tired with the same type of venue. The advantages of an unusual (or non-purpose) site are its uniqueness and the surprise this gives to the attendees. The site becomes part of the event.

As Warren Fahey (2005) of Larrikin comments:

> When we advised people on weddings we always preferred the 'backyard wedding'. It's more Australian, more of a celebration and the families can inject more of their own personality into this special event. They don't have to move out after a few hours to let in the next wedding.

When the audience and the performers mix together, and where they and the venue become the entertainment package, the delineation between stage and auditorium is no longer appropriate. In these situations, the traditional roles of stage manager and event manager become blurred.

A special event that uses a purpose-built venue, such as an entertainment centre, will find that much of the infrastructure is in place. However, because so many factors in an event depend on the venue or site, an inspection is absolutely necessary. If time permits, the event manager should attend a function at the venue to observe how the facilities are used during an event. There are many tips to testing a facility while on site, such as placing a long-distance telephone call, trying the food and staying in the approved accommodation.

Two documents that are a good starting point for making an informed choice about the venue are the venue map and the list of facilities. It is good practice for the event manager to meet the venue management before committing to hire the venue. The principal purpose of this meeting is to check the accuracy of the two documents, because the map, the list of facilities and the photographs can be out of date or aimed at promoting the venue rather than imparting detailed information. The photograph of the venue, for example, may be taken with a wide-angle lens so all the facilities are included. Such a photograph may not give a realistic view of the site if it is being used for event design. Also, these meetings are part of the occupational health and safety consultation process and proper notes need to be kept. Chapter 18 describes the importance of consultation with the suppliers and other stakeholders of the event risk management.

Using an internet search engine is often the first action in the investigation of a suitable venue. Some websites display a choice of venues once certain information (such as size of audience, approximate location and type of event) has been entered. The major hotels, convention and exhibition centres, universities and purpose-built venues have websites to enable the matching of event requirements to venue characteristics. However, this method has the same limitations as those of using photos and brochures to assess a venue. The websites are a tool for selling the venue, not a technical description. In addition, many suitable venues may not have an internet presence. An internet search will show only venues that expect to host events. If the event is truly special, the event venue may be part of that theme. A car park or a rainforest, for example, will not appear in a search for event venues.

AUDIENCE AND GUESTS

The larger issues of audience (customer) logistics are described in chapter 15. The event staging considerations concerning the audience are:

- position of entrances and exits
- arrival times — dump or trickle

- seating and sight lines
- facilities.

Goldblatt (2005) emphasises the importance of the entrance and reception area of an event in establishing the event theme, and suggests the organiser should look at it from the guest's point of view. It is in this area that appropriate signage and meeting and greeting become important to the flow of 'traffic' and to the wellbeing of the guests. An example of a carefully planned entrance area was at a recent folk festival, where the children's area was entered through the mouth of a large papier-mâché dragon.

Once the guests have entered the event area, problems can occur that are specific to the type of event. In the case of conferences, audiences immediately head for the back rows. Interestingly, the opposite problem occurs at sports events, where the front rows are rushed as soon as the gates open. The solution, therefore, is in the type of admission — for example, organisers can adopt reserved seating methods, using ticket numbers or roped-off sections and a designated seating plan. This will allow the crowd to be evenly distributed in the venue. The style of seating can be chosen to suit the event; theatre, classroom and banquet-type seating are three examples. Ultimately, the seating plan has to consider:

- the type of seating — fixed or movable
- standing room, if necessary
- the size of the audience
- the method of audience arrival
- safety factors, including emergency exits and fire regulations
- the placement and size of the aisles
- sight lines to the performances, speakers or audiovisual displays
- disabled access
- catering needs.

The facilities provided for the guests will depend on the type of event. Referring to figure 14.4, the corporate event will focus on particular audience facilities as they relate to hospitality and catering, whereas a festival event will concentrate on audience facilities as they relate to entertainment. There are no chairs, for example, for the audience in some of the Port Fairy Folk Festival performance areas, but the nature of the festival means spectators are happy to bring their own chairs or sit on the ground. At the other end of the spectrum, a conference dinner will have high-quality furnishings and facilities.

THE STAGE

A stage at an event is rarely the same as a theatrical stage complete with proscenium arch and auditorium. It can range from the back of a truck to a barge in a harbour. In event management, the term 'stage' can be applied to the general staging area and not just to a purpose-built stage. However, all stages require a stage map called the stage plan. The stage plan is simply a bird's-eye view of the performance area, showing the infrastructure, such as lighting fixtures, entrances, exits and power outlets. The stage plan is one of the staging tools (figure 14.11) and a communication device that enables the event to run smoothly. For large events, the stage plan is drawn in different ways for different people and supplied on a 'need-to-know basis'. A stage plan for the lighting technician, for example, would look different from the plan for the performers. The master stage plan contains all these different plans, each drawn on a separate layer of transparent paper. Other plans used in event design are the front elevation and side elevation. In contrast to the bird's-eye view of the stage plan, these plans show the staging area as a ground-level view from the front and side respectively. They assist in establishing the audience's sight lines — that is, the audience's view of the staging area and performers.

A large stage plan was used for a conference of the Société Internationale d'Urologie in Sydney. The 3000 guests were treated to three streams of entertainment that reflected modern Australia: 'multicultural', including a lion dance and Middle Eastern dancers; 'land and sea', including a large sailing boat and Aboriginal and Australiana entertainers; and 'cities', with fashion parades and modern dancers. The event manager was able to estimate the number of seated guests by using a protractor and drawing the 'table interference areas'. This is the size of the table plus the area around the table needed for the seating, service and crowd flow.

Roger Foley (2005), of Fogg Production, the creator of the Australian Multicultural Show, described the stage plan:

> The stage plan is 100 per cent accurate. I went to the building's architects to get an exact drawing and we used that as the master stage plan. The accuracy of having all the building's peculiarities on a plan allowed all the subcontractors to anticipate any problems in setting up. [There were] 1-metre markings on the building's circumference. All these little things enabled the whole show, including 13 stages and 21 food stalls, to be set up and bumped out in 24 hours. A stage plan for each of the individual stages was created by enlarging that section from the master plan and filling in the necessary information.

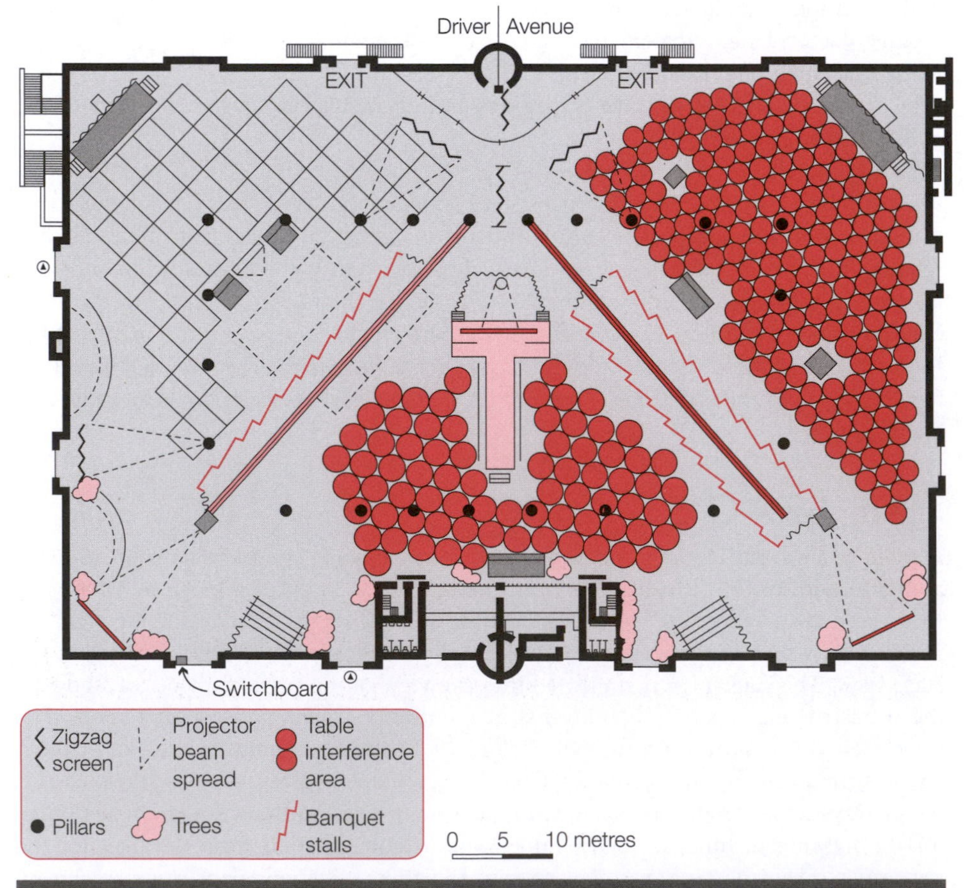

FIGURE 14.4 An example of a stage plan

When the staging of an event includes a large catering component, the stage plan is referred to as the venue layout or floor plan. This is the case in many corporate and conference events, for which hospitality and catering become a major part of the staging. Figure 14.5 illustrates how the focus on the staging elements changes according to the style of event.

The stage manager is the person in control of the performance and responsible for signalling the cues that coordinate the work of the performers. The scheduling of the event on a particular stage is generally the responsibility of the event manager. The stage manager makes sure this happens according to the plan. The public face of the event may be called the master of ceremonies (MC) or compere. The compere and the stage manager work closely together to ensure all goes according to the plan. The compere may also make public announcements, such as those about lost children and program changes.

The combination of electric wiring, hot lights, special effects and the fast movement of performers and staff in a small space that is perhaps two metres above ground level makes the risk management of the staging area particularly important. At the event, stage safety is generally the responsibility of the stage manager. Figure 14.6 lists key safety considerations.

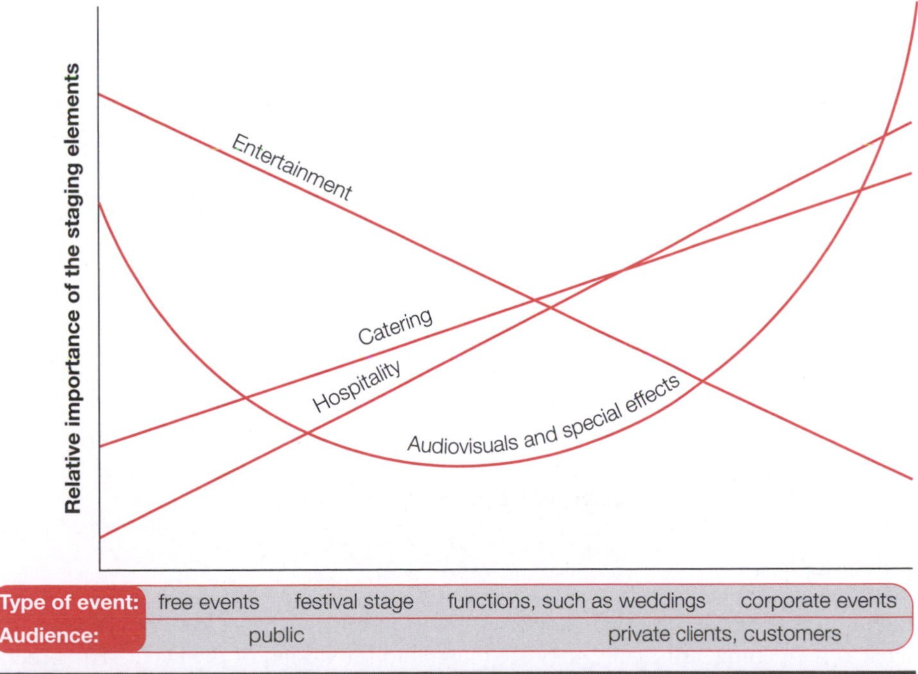

FIGURE 14.5 The relationship between types of event and the relative importance of the staging elements

Jamie McKew (2005) gives this advice for stage managers:

> Make sure you anticipate the many little things that can ruin an otherwise great concert experience. Watch out for distracting buzzes or cracks in the sound (e.g. from powerful fridges); settle out-of-control children or noisy audiences; ensure all small stage requirements are there (e.g. chair, stool, table, water); ensure you have competent MCs who are well prepared; stop delays before they start.

- There must be a well-constructed stage done professionally by a company with adequate insurance.
- There must be clear, well-lit access points to the stage.
- All protrusions and steps should be secured and clearly marked.
- Equipment and boxes should be placed out of the way and well marked.
- There should be work lights that provide white lighting before and after the event.
- All electric cabling must be secured and tagged.
- A first-aid kit and other emergency equipment should be at hand.
- There must be clear guidelines on who is in charge during an emergency and an evacuation plan.
- A list of all relevant contact numbers should be made.

FIGURE 14.6 Factors to consider in stage safety

The backstage area is a private room or tent near the performance area and is set aside for the performers and staff. It provides the crew with a place to relax and the performers with a place to prepare for the performance and wind down afterwards. It can be used for storage of equipment and for communication between the stage manager and performers, and it is where the food and drink are kept.

POWER

Staging of any event involves large numbers of people. To service this crowd, electricity is indispensable. It should never be taken for granted. Factors that need to be considered concerning power are as follows:

- the type of power — three phase or single phase
- the amount of power needed, particularly at peak times
- emergency power
- the position and number of power outlets
- the types of lead and the distance from the power source to the device
- the correct wiring of the venue, because old venues are often improperly earthed
- the incoming equipment's volt/amp rating
- safety factors, including the covering of leads and the possibility of electricity earth leakage as a result of rain
- local and state regulations regarding power.

LIGHTS

Lighting at a venue has two functions. Pragmatically, lights allow everyone to see what is happening; artistically, they are integral to the design of the event. The general venue or site lighting is important in that it allows all other aspects of staging to take place. For this reason, it is usually the first item on the checklist when organisers decide on a venue. Indoor lights include signage lights, such as exit and toilets, as well as those illuminating specific areas such as catering and ticket collection. Outside the venue, lighting is required for venue identification, safety, security and signs.

Once the general venue or site lighting is confirmed, lighting design needs to be considered. The questions to ask when considering lighting are both practical and aesthetic:

- Does the lighting fit in with and enhance the overall event theme?
- Can it be used for ambient lighting as well as performance lighting?

- Is there a back-up?
- What are the power requirements? (Lights can draw far more power than the sound system.)
- Will it interfere with the electrics of other systems? A dimmer board, for example, can create an audible buzz in the sound system.
- Does it come with a light operator — that is, the person responsible for the planning of the lighting with the lighting board?
- What light effects are needed (strobe, cross-fading)? Can the available lights do this?
- What equipment is needed (for example, trees and par cans)? Is there a place on the site or in the venue to erect it?
- How can the lighting assist in the safety and security of the event?

The lighting plot or lighting plan is a map of the venue that shows the type and position of the lighting. As Reid (1995) points out, the decisions that the event manager has to make when creating a lighting plan are:

- placement of the lights
- the type of lights, including floods and follow spots
- where the light should be pointed
- what colours to use.

event profile

INNOVATION AND FLEXIBILITY IN STAGING

As part of the 2009 Vivid Festival, the company Smart Light Sydney presented a series of light sculptures around the Quay and Rocks area of Sydney. The 25 installations were set so that the public could walk the area and experience the 'Light in all colours and forms, glowing, flashing, merging, transforming the city into a spectacular living canvas' (*The Truth Booth* 2010).

The organisers called for artists to propose their concepts. These ranged from submitting their previous work to highly innovative installations set up only for this event. The use of smart technology was a requirement to enter the event. Once approved, the artists were responsible for the delivery of their work. 'Of course there was a settling in period for these artists as they got used to the area and [the] technical resources.' (Thomas 2010)

One of the more innovative works was the projection of current weather patterns from around the world via the internet, onto the internal ceiling of a dome. The images were enhanced by the use of a fog machine, which gave the images depth. The images were made up of maps and graphs, as well as real-time sunsets and cloud formations from around the world. It was a highly innovative work and technically complex, which was not at first fully appreciated. The full scope of work involved in setting it up became more obvious when the artist arrived. However, the innovative nature of the work was important to the theme of the event and, although the artists were responsible for the delivery of their installation, the organisers realised they needed to be flexible.

> Once we fully understood the requirements of this installation, we went to the universities to see if they could help. They did. We were able to source IT technicians and the specialised computers needed. It turned into a fabulous and fascinating display.

Source: Thomas 2010, interview with Sharon Thomas, Smart Light Sydney, www.smartlightsydney.com

SOUND

The principal reason for having sound equipment at an event is so that all of the audience can clearly hear the music, speeches and audio effects. The sound system is also used to:

- communicate between the sound engineer and the stage manager (talkback or intercom)
- monitor the sound
- create a sound recording of the event
- broadcast the sound to other venues or through other media, including television, radio and the internet.

This means the type of equipment used needs to be designed according to:

- the type of sound to be amplified. This includes spoken word and music.
- the size and make up of the audience. An older audience, for example, may like the music at a different volume from that preferred by a younger audience.
- the acoustic properties of the room. Some venues have a bad echo problem, for example.
- the theme of the event. A sound system painted bright silver may look out of place at a black tie dinner.

The choice of size, type and location of the sound speakers at an event can make a difference to the guests' experience of the sound. Figure 14.7 shows two simplified plans for speaker positions at a venue. The speakers may all be next to the stage, which is common at music concerts, or distributed around the site. They may also be flown from supports above the audience. At a large site, with speakers widely distributed, the sound engineers need to account for the natural delay of sound travelling from the various speakers to the members of the audience.

For small events, a simple public address (PA) system may be used. This consists of a microphone, a microphone stand and one or two speakers. It is basically the same as a home stereo system with a microphone added and generally has only enough power to reach a small audience. The quality of sound produced makes such systems suitable for speeches only.

For larger events that have more complex sound requirements, a larger sound system is needed. This system would incorporate:

- microphones, which may include lapel microphones and radio microphones
- microphone stands

- cabling, including from the microphones to the mixing desk
- a mixing desk, which adjusts the quality and level of the sound coming from the microphones before it goes out the speakers
- an amplifier
- speakers, which can vary in size from bass speakers to treble speakers and which enhance the quality of the sound within a certain sound spectrum
- a sound engineer or sound technician, who looks after all aspects of the sound, particularly the sound quality that is heard by the audience
- back-up equipment, including spare leads and microphones.

The next step up from this type of system includes all of the above as well as:

- foldback speakers (also called monitors) that channel the sound back to the speakers or performers so they can hear themselves over the background sound
- a foldback mixing desk
- a foldback engineer who is responsible for the quality of sound going through the monitors.

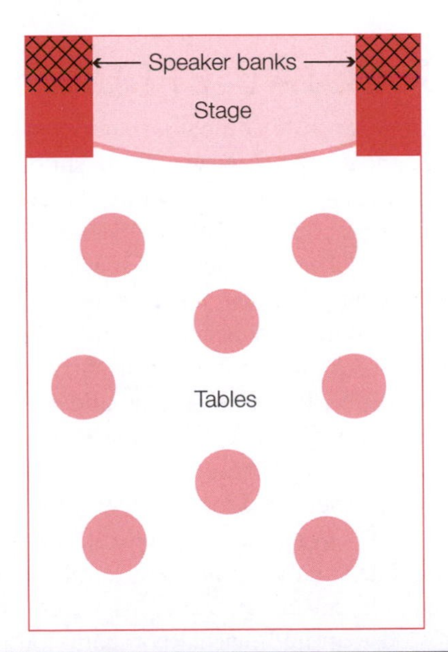

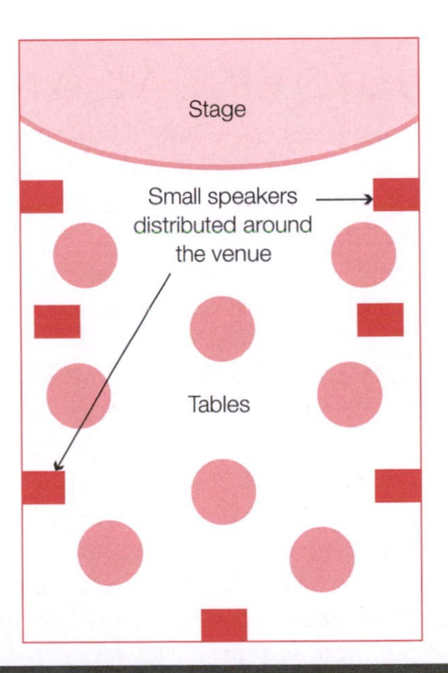

FIGURE 14.7 Two examples of audio speaker layout

If an event needs a sound system managed by a sound engineer, time must be allocated to tune the sound system. This means the acoustic qualities of the venue are taken into account by trying out the effect of various sound frequencies within the venue. This is the reason for the often-heard 'testing, one, two, one, two' as a sound system is being prepared. The sound engineer is also looking for any sound feedback problems. Feedback is an unwanted, often high-pitched sound that occurs when the sound coming out of the speakers is picked up by the microphones and comes out of the speakers again, thereby building on the original sound. To avoid the problem of feedback, microphones must be positioned so they face away from sound speakers. The tuning of a large sound system is one of the main reasons for having a sound check or run-through before an event. Figure 14.8 shows a simplified sound run-through.

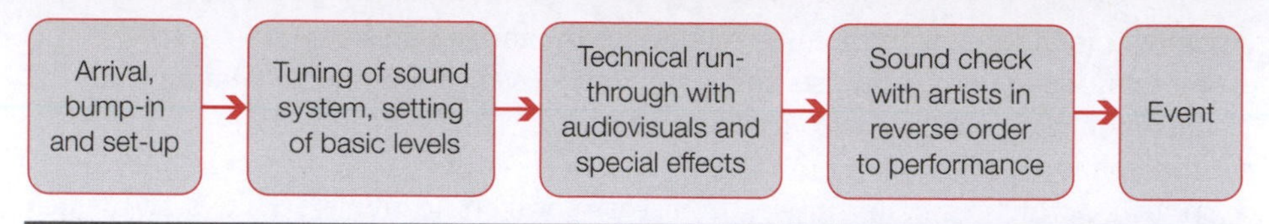

FIGURE 14.8 A simple flow chart for sound systems

Volume and sound leakage during an event can become a major problem. Local councils can close an event if there are too many complaints from residents. At some venues, for example, there are volume switches that automatically turn off the power if the sound level is too high. At multi-venue events, sound leakage between stages can be minimised by:

- thoughtful placement of the stages
- careful positioning of all sound speakers (including the monitors)
- constant monitoring of the volume level
- careful programming of the events on each stage in a way that avoids interference.

AUDIOVISUAL AND SPECIAL EFFECTS

Many event managers hire lighting and sound from separate companies and integrate these external services into the overall design of the event. However, some suppliers provide both lighting and sound equipment and act as consultants before the event. These audiovisual companies can supply a fully integrated system of film, video, slides and, often, special effects. However, most audiovisual companies are specialists in flat-screen presentations and the special effects area is often best left to specialists in each field. Pyrotechnics obviously require different skills and licences from those of ice sculptors, for example. Complex events that use a variety of special effects and audiovisuals require a coordinator who is familiar with the event theme and knows how to link all of the specialist areas. This coordinator is called the event producer. Although the terms 'event manager', 'stage manager' and 'event producer' are confusing, they are terms used in the industry. The position of event producer is created when many different specialists are involved in the event. Organisers of corporate events, including product launches and conferences, often subcontract the audiovisual elements, because the specialist knowledge required means an expert is needed to operate these systems effectively. The decision to use an audiovisual company for an event depends on:

- how the audiovisual presentation fits in with the overall event design
- the budget allocated to the event
- the skills of the audiovisual company, including its technical hardware, software and the abilities of the audiovisual producer and writer.

For large-budget events, the audiovisual company will act as a consultant, with the producer and writer researching and creating a detailed audiovisual script.

The event producer must know exactly what they are getting when hiring specialists. Fireworks, for example, must be individually listed, fully integrated into the event and not just left to the specialist. The timing of setting off the various devices must be exact, without any gaps.

According to Goldblatt (2005), special effects at an event are used to attract attention, generate excitement and sustain interest. In larger festivals, such as the opening of the Melbourne Festival on the Yarra River, the pyrotechnics become part of the overall logistics planning. Event managers and planners must fully realise the importance of event decoration, scenery and appropriate props as an enhancing tool for the staging of any event.

Because much of the audiovisual and special effects technology is highly complex, it is often 'pre-programmed'. This means that all lighting, audiovisual and sound 'pre-sets' (technical elements positioned before the event) — including the changing light and sound levels, and the cueing of video and slide presentations — can be programmed into the controlling computer. The computer control of much of the audiovisuals means the whole presentation can be fully integrated and set up well in advance. Because these aspects are pre-arranged, including all the cue times, few technicians are needed to control these operations during the event. The disadvantages, however, are that spontaneity can be taken from the event; and the more complex the technology, the more things can go wrong. Moreover, the technology becomes the master of the cue times and it is nearly impossible to take advantage of any unforeseen opportunities.

PROPS AND DECORATION

Some events are similar to operatic productions in their use of scenery, stage properties (props) and decoration. Skilled use of these elements can make the attendees feel as though they are in an imaginary world. The audience can often enhance this by dressing the part and becoming part of the entertainment. Themed parties, festivals and dinners are a significant part of the event industry. The way in which these staging elements are combined and their relative emphasis at the event often reflects the personal style of the event company. Malouf (1999) devotes more than two-thirds of her book to theming in events, particularly the use of flowers, lights and colour to create a sense of wonder. The South African company Party Design regards décor as the key to their success. They have a dedicated factory with more than 1000 employees devoted to the creation, design, manufacture, delivery, set-up and return of event décor.

The large sports events are now famous for their props. The fish sculptures of the Sydney Olympics were repeated at the Melbourne Commonwealth Games. Some of these props have been auctioned after the event to become sculptures in parks and offices.

CATERING

Catering can be the major element in staging, depending on the theme and nature of an event. Most purpose-built venues already have catering arrangements in place. Parliament House in Canberra, for example, contracts with catering companies. The conference dinners that take place in the Great Hall can use only the inhouse caterers. Figure 14.9 illustrates some of the many factors to be considered in catering.

The event producer Reno Dal (2005) makes the following points about aspects of catering:

> My rule for the staff-to-client ratio at a corporate function is:
> silver service, 1 to 10 ratio
> five-star service 1 to 25 ratio
> general catering 1 to 50 ratio.
>
> I emphasise that there should be 'waves of service'. This means that the main course and beverage arrive at the right time and then waiters leave the guests until the appropriate moment for the next course. I like to see each table as a stage, with the

placements presented in the same manner as a theatrical stage. The waiters become the performers dressed to the theme. The waiters love it — after all, it's a difficult job at the best of times.

INHOUSE OR CONTRACTED?

The advantage of inhouse catering is the knowledge of the venue. The advantages of contract catering are: (1) the event manager may have a special arrangement with the caterer that has been built up over time; (2) the event manager can choose all aspects of the catering; and (3) the catering can be tendered out and a competitive bid sought.

Quality control factors to consider

- Appropriateness and enhancement of the event theme
- Menu selection and design, including special diets and food displays
- Quality of staff and supervision
- Equipment, including style and quantity, and selection of inhouse or hired
- Cleanliness
- Cultural appropriateness — a major consideration in a culturally diverse society
- Staff-to-guest ratio

Costs

- Are there any guarantees, including those against loss and breakages?
- What are the payment terms?
- Who is responsible for licences and permits: the caterer, the venue or event management?
- What deposits and upfront fees are there?
- What is the per capita expenditure? Is each guest getting value commensurate with the client's expenditure?

Waste management

- Must occur before, during and after the event
- Must conform to health regulations and environmental concerns
- Must be appropriate to the event theme

FIGURE 14.9 Issues to be considered when arranging catering for an event

The consumption of alcoholic beverages at an event gives rise to many concerns for the event manager. These include the special training of staff, which party holds the licence (venue, event manager or client) and the legal age for consumption. The possible problems that arise from the sale of alcohol — for example, increased audience noise at the end of the event and general behavioural problems — can affect almost all aspects of the event. Due to the high risk in this area, one event company sends its entire staff to responsible service of alcohol (RSA) training. The decision on whether to allow the sale or consumption of alcohol can be crucial to the success of an event and needs careful thought.

The serving of alcohol can be negotiated with a caterer in a variety of ways. The drinks service can be from the bar or served at the table by the glass, bottle or jug. A caterer may offer a 'drinks package', which means the drinks are free for, say, the first hour of the catered event. A subtle result of this type of deal is that the guests may find it hard to find a drinks waiter in the first hour.

PERFORMERS

The 'talent' (as performers are often called) at an event can range from music groups to motivational speakers to specially commissioned shows. A performing group can form a major part of an event's design. As well as the cost of the performer, the major factors to consider when employing artists are listed below:

- *Contact* — the event's entertainment coordinator needs to establish contact only with the person responsible for the employment of the artist or artists. This could be the artist, an agent representing the artist, or the manager of a group. It is important to establish this line of authority at the beginning when working with the artists.
- *Staging requirements* — a rock band, for example, will have more complex sound requirements than those of a solo singer. These requirements are usually listed on a document called the spec (specification) sheet. Many groups will also have their own stage plan illustrating the area needed and their preferred configuration of the performance area.
- *Availability for rehearsal, media attention and performance* — the available times given by the artists' management should include the time needed for the artists to set up on stage as well as the time needed to vacate the stage or performance area. These are referred to as 'set-up' and 'pull-down' times. These times need to be considered when, for example, scheduling a series of rehearsals with a number of performing groups.
- *Accompanying personnel* — many artists travel with an entourage that can include technicians, cooks, stylists and bodyguards. It is important to establish their numbers and their roles and needs.
- *Contracts and legal requirements* — the agreement between the event manager and the performers is described in chapter 17. Particularly important to the staging are union minimum rates and conditions, the legal structure of the artists, and issues such as workers compensation, tax structure and public liability. Copyright is also important because its ownership can affect the use of the performance for broadcast and future promotions. The rider must be costed and understood. This aspect of contracts is covered in chapter 17.
- *Payment* — most performing groups work on the understanding that they will be paid immediately for their services. Except for 'headline' acts that have a company structure, the 30-, 60- or 90-day invoicing cycle is not appropriate for most performers, who rarely have the financial resources that would allow them to wait for payment.

Performers come from a variety of performance cultural backgrounds. This means different performers have different expectations about the facilities available for them and how they are to be treated. Theatre performers and concert musicians, for example, expect direct performance guidelines — conducting, scripting or a musical score. Street and outdoor festival performers, on the other hand, are used to less formal conditions and to improvising.

Supervision of performers in a small theatre is generally left to the assistant stage manager, whereas a festival stage may not have this luxury and the stage manager may be responsible. Regardless of who undertakes the supervision, it cannot be overlooked. The person responsible needs to make contact with the artists on arrival, give them the appropriate run sheets, introduce them to the relevant crew members and show them the location of the green room (the room in which performers and invited guests are entertained). At the end of the performance, the artists' supervisor needs to assist them in leaving the area.

THE CREW

The chapter on human resource management (chapter 8) discussed the role of staff and volunteers at an event. While a large festival or sporting event will usually rely on the work of volunteers, staging tends to be handled by professionals. Dealing with cueing, working with complex and potentially dangerous equipment and handling professional performers leaves little room for indecision and inexperience. Professionalism is essential when staging an event. The staging of a concert performance, for example, will need skilled sound engineers, roadies, security staff, stage crew, ticket sellers and even ushers. (The roadies are the skilled labourers who assist with the set-up and breakdown of the sound and lights.) The crew is selected by matching the tasks involved to the skills of each crew member and ensuring everyone can work together.

The briefing is the meeting, before the event, at which the crew members are given the briefs, or roles, that match their skills. The names and jobs of the crew members are kept on a contact and responsibility sheet.

Neil Cameron, the organiser of many events and lantern parades around Australia and overseas, stresses the importance of being 'brief' at the briefing. His events involve large numbers of performers moving near fire sculptures. These sculptures can be more than three storeys high and take weeks to build. He first briefs the support organisations, such as St John Ambulance and the fire brigade, and emphasises the importance of communication and chain of command. At the crew briefing, Neil is conscious of not overloading the leaders with too much information.

The event producer should also not forget that the crew comes with an enormous amount of experience in staging events. The crew can provide valuable input into the creation and design of the event. Interestingly, the changes in the event industry, particularly in the audiovisual area, are reflected in the make-up and number of crew members. As the industry developed, the event crew was often sourced from the casual labour available in the music industry, called the roadies. However, with the sophistication of the events, the modern crew is more likely to be specially trained and with trade and information technology skills.

HOSPITALITY

A major part of the package offered to sponsors is hospitality. What will the sponsors expect event management to provide for them and their guests? They may require tickets, food and beverages, souvenirs and gifts. The event may benefit in the long term by also offering hospitality to stakeholders, VIPs and others, including politicians, media units, media personalities, clients of the sponsor, potential sponsors, partners and local opinion leaders. Anyone offered hospitality is referred to as a guest of the event.

The invitation may be the guest's first impression of the event, so it needs to convey the theme of the event. It should create a desire to attend, as well as impart information. Figure 14.10 is a checklist for covering the various elements of hospitality.

In their classic work on sports events, Graham, Goldblatt and Delpy (1995, p. 84) describe the four stages for achieving success in the provision of hospitality to guests. Stage 1 is to know the guests' expectations. Stage 2 is to exceed the guests' expectations, particularly by providing extra amenities. Stage 3 is to be responsive to changes in the guests' needs during the event. Stage 4 is to evaluate the hospitality at the event so it can be improved next time.

Corporate sponsors may have a variety of reasons for attending the event and these reasons have to be considered in hospitality planning. The reasons include networking opportunities for business, an incentive for a high sales performance, an opportunity for entertaining possible clients, or just the creation of customer goodwill.

The hospitality experience is particularly important at corporate events. In one sense, such an event is centred around hospitality (figure 14.5). Being a private function, there is no public and the members of the audience are the guests. Most of the items on the hospitality checklist, from the invitations to the personal service, are applicable to staging these events. For the guests, the hospitality experience is fundamental to the event experience.

HOSPITALITY CHECKLIST

Invitations

- ☐ Is the design of a high quality and is it innovative?
- ☐ Does the method of delivery allow time to reply? Would hand delivery or email be appropriate?
- ☐ Does the content of the invitation include time, date, name of event, how to RSVP, directions, map and parking?
- ☐ Should promotional material be included with the invitation?
- ☐ Does there need to be a follow up call?

Transport

- ☐ Are there suitable cars and drivers with uniforms, ID and security clearance?
- ☐ Have alternative cars been requested?
- ☐ Is a police escort required?
- ☐ Is there a tracking system for the vehicles and identification signage?
- ☐ Are there refreshments for the VIPs in the cars?

Arrival

- ☐ Has timing been planned so guests arrive at the best moment?
- ☐ What are the parking arrangements?
- ☐ Who will do the meeting and greeting? Will there be someone to welcome them to the event?
- ☐ Have waiting times been reduced? Will guests receive a welcome cocktail while waiting to be booked into the accommodation, for example?
- ☐ How will the event staff recognise the VIPs? Do they need photos?

Amenities

- ☐ Is there to be a separate area for guests? This can be a marquee, corporate box (at a sports event) or a club room.
- ☐ What food and beverages will be provided? Is there a need for a special menu and personal service?
- ☐ Will there be special entertainment?
- ☐ Is there a separate, high-quality viewing area of the performance with good views and facilities?
- ☐ Has special communication, such as signage or an information desk, been provided?

Gifts

- ☐ Have tickets to the event, especially for clients, been organised?
- ☐ What souvenirs (programs, pins, T-shirts, compact discs) will there be?
- ☐ Will there be a chance for guests to meet the 'stars'?

Departure

- ☐ Has guest departure been timed so guests do not leave at the same time as the rest of the audience?

FIGURE 14.10 Looking after corporate sponsors and VIPs — a hospitality checklist

There are a number of systems to assist the event manager develop a quality hospitality experience for the guests. Getz (2005, p. 179) defines the dimensions of service as:

- tangibles — time, cleanliness
- reliability — such as consistency
- responsiveness — such as promptness
- assurance — such as courteousness
- empathy — such as individual attention.

Both Getz (2005), and Tum et al. (2006) describe the event or festival from the service perspective. The event team can use the tools of service mapping. The attendee's or customer's on-site experience is described in the form of a flow chart. Each of the customer actions, such as parking, buying the tickets and finding their seats, is assessed from the customer's point of view as a series of service experiences (see chapter 9). This enables the event to be audited and improved from the perspective of the attendee.

THE PRODUCTION SCHEDULE

The terms used in the staging of events come from both the theatre and film production. A rehearsal is a run-through of the event, reproducing the actual event as closely as possible. For the sake of 'getting it right on the night', there may also need to be a technical rehearsal and a dress rehearsal. A production meeting, on the other hand, is a get-together of those responsible for producing an event. It involves the stage manager and the event producer, representatives of the lighting and sound crew or audiovisual specialists, representatives of the performers and the master of ceremonies. It is held at the performance site or stage as near to the time of the event as possible. At this crucial meeting:

- final production schedule notes are compared
- possible last-minute production problems are brought up
- the flow of the event is summarised
- emergency procedures are reviewed
- the compere is introduced and familiarised with the production staff
- the communication system is tested.

The production schedule is the main document for staging. It is the master document from which other schedules, including the cue or prompt sheet and the run sheets, are created. Goldblatt (2005) describes it as the detailed listing of tasks, with specific start and stop times occurring from the set-up of the event's equipment (also known as 'bump-in') to the eventual removal of all the equipment ('bump-out' or 'load-out'). It is often a written form of the Gantt chart (chapter 6) with four columns: time, activity, location and responsibility. Production schedules can also contain a description of the relevant elements of the event. In the hotel venues it is also called the 'event order'. The more the event program relies on tight programming and the use of entertainers and audiovisuals, the more detailed is the production schedule. For highly produced events, such as national day celebrations with large budgets spread over a few hours, the operations manual is often called the production book.

Two particularly limited times on the schedule are the bump-in and bump-out times. The bump-in is the time when the necessary infrastructure can be brought in, unloaded and set up; the bump-out is the time when the equipment can be dismantled and removed. Although the venue or site may be available to receive the equipment at any time, many other factors set the bump-in time. The hiring cost and availability of equipment are two important limiting factors. In most cases, the larger items must arrive first. These may include fencing, tents, stage, food vans and extra toilets. Next could come the audiovisual equipment and, finally, the various decorations. Supervision of the arrival and set-up of the equipment can be crucial to minimising problems during the event. The contractor who delivers and assembles the equipment is often not the operator of the equipment. This can mean that once equipment is set up, it is impossible to change it without recalling the contractor.

Bump-out can be the most difficult time of an event, because the excitement is over, the staff are often tired and everyone is in a hurry to leave. Nevertheless, security and safety are important at this stage. The correct order of bump-out needs to be on a detailed schedule, which is often the reverse of the bump-in schedule. The last item on the checklist for the bump-out is the 'idiot check'. This refers to the check that is done after everything is cleared from the performance area, when some staff search for anything that may be left.

The run sheets are lists of the order of specific jobs at an event. The entertainers, for example, have one run sheet while the caterers have another. Often, the production schedule is a loose-leaf folder that includes all the run sheets. The cue sheets are a list of times that initiate a change of any kind during the event and describe what happens on that change. The stage manager and audiovisual controller use them.

RECORDING THE EVENT

By their nature, special events are ephemeral. A good quality recording of the event is essential for most event companies, because it demonstrates the ability of the organisation and can be used to promote the event company. It can also help in evaluating the event and, if necessary, in settling later disputes, whether of a legal or other nature. The event can be recorded on video, as a sound recording or as photographs. Any visual recording of the event requires planning. In particular, the correct lighting is needed for depth of field. The following factors need to be considered for video recording:

- What is it for — promotion, legal purposes or sale to the participants?
- What are the costs in terms of time and money?
- How will it affect the event? Will the video cameras be a nuisance? Will they need white lighting?
- What are the best vantage points?

Recording the event is not a decision that should be left until the last minute; it needs to be factored into the planning of the event. Copyright clearance, for example can be an issue long after the event. Once an event is played out, there is no going back.

CONTINGENCIES

As with large festivals and hallmark events, the staging of any event has to make allowances for what might go wrong. 'What if' sessions need to be implemented with the staff. A stage at a festival may face an electricity blackout; performers may not arrive; trouble may arrive instead. Micro-contingency plans thus need to be in place. All these must fit in with the overall festival risk management and emergency plans. Further, at corporate events in well-known venues, the venue will have its own emergency plan that needs to be given to all involved.

SUMMARY

The staging of an event can range from presenting a show of multicultural dancers and musicians at a stage in a local park, to the launch of the latest software product at the most expensive hotel in town. All events share common staging elements, including sound, lights, food and beverages, performers and special effects. All these elements need to create and enhance the event theme. The importance of each element depends on the type of event. To stage an event successfully, a number of tools are used: the production schedule, the stage plan and the contact and responsibility list, all of which are shown in figure 14.11.

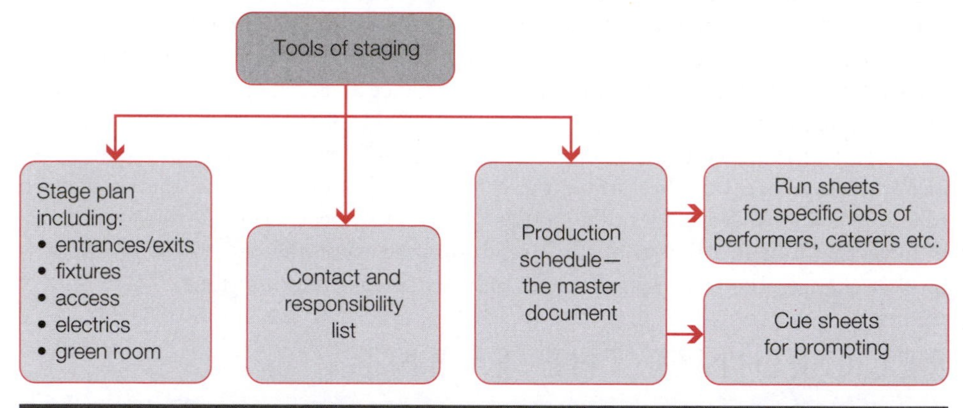

FIGURE 14.11 A summary of the tools necessary for staging an event

QUESTIONS

1. Discuss the relationship between the staging of a theatrical play and the staging of a special event. What are the similarities? What are the differences?
2. Many corporate events use a classic film, such as *The Godfather*, a book or a TV series as the theme for the event. Decide on five themes and list the elements of staging — venue, food, design, program, props, sound system, and entertainment — and their relationship to the theme.
3. The elements of the staging of an event vary in importance according to the type of events. Discuss this in relation to the events held at a university.
4. Using the list of event sites in figure 14.3 (page 425), produce a spreadsheet with the opportunities and risks each site would contain. Caves, for example, would have decoration opportunities and risks in the sound production, such as echo or a dead sound.
5. Compile a stage plan, contact responsibility list and production schedule with the relevant run sheets for:
   (a) a corporate party for the clients, staff and customers of a company
   (b) a fun run with entertainment
   (c) a large wedding
   (d) one of the stages for a city arts festival.
6. Discuss the constraints on programming the following events:
   (a) a large musical concert in a disused open-cut mine
   (b) an association award dinner
   (c) a multi-stage arts festival

(d) a rough-water swim
(e) a mining exhibition conference
(f) an air show
(g) a tax seminar for accountants.

7 What are the advantages for contracting one supplier for all the staging elements? What are the disadvantages?
8 Develop a program for a battle of the bands concert appealing to 18 year olds. Be aware of the artistic content, time between performers for setting up, stage placement of the bands, audience responses and the flow of the program.
9 Discuss whether the event manager needs to know the terminology of staging. What depth of technical knowledge should the event manager have?

case study

FESTIVAL OF THE OLIVE

Scope

Festival of the Olive is a two-day festival celebrating Australia's modern Mediterranean influences and its colonial past. One of the premier events in Western Sydney's cultural calendar, it presents an opportunity for a collaboration between olive growers, olive oil and food producers, olive industry bodies, Mediterranean Australians, culinary experts, performers and artists.

This biennial event, developed and produced by the Historic Houses Trust (HHT), regularly attracts crowds of 4000 visitors, with its primary objective being to showcase the historic Elizabeth Farm. Elizabeth Farm House was commenced in 1793 and contains part of the oldest surviving European building in Australia. It is a property owned and operated by the HHT, a state government organisation under the umbrella of Arts NSW, part of the Department of Arts, Sports and Recreation.

This case study examines the Festival of the Olive 2005, which took place on the weekend of 5 and 6 November from 10.00 am to 5.00 pm at Elizabeth Farm, Rosehill, New South Wales. Festival of the Olive had been held on this historic site on four previous occasions.

Rationale

While the olive is recognised as part of Australia's recent multicultural history, it also plays a part in our colonial past. Festival of the Olive is held at Elizabeth Farm because Australia's oldest surviving exotic tree is planted in its gardens. The tree, a European olive (*Olea europaea*), planted in 1805, continues to produce fruit today. Appropriately, Festival of the Olive 2005 also commemorated the two hundredth year of this planting.

Development stage 1

As event coordinator, I was presented with the production folders from previous incarnations of Festival of the Olive. These folders included debrief meeting minutes, allowing me to prepare a summary — basically a SWOT analysis — that charted the development, successes and failures of previous festivals. I then entered into discussions with the head of the public programs unit (PPU) of the HHT to

discuss my findings, proposed expenditure and vision for the festival. I then had two weeks to develop a festival proposal, which was presented at the first production meeting, held onsite at Elizabeth Farm.

This meeting, chaired by the head of PPU, was held three and a half months out from the festival and involved a wide range of HHT stakeholders: the curator/manager, chief guide, gardener and office manager of Elizabeth Farm; the HHT marketing manager and publicist; the retail manager; the sponsorship manager; and education unit representatives. At this meeting it was unanimously decided to keep the staging areas consistent with Festival of the Olive 2003, as it was deemed to have been a very successful use of a small site. This meant the site was broken into the following precincts:

- shuttle bus and ticketing entry point
- reserved parking area
- garden areas
- Elizabeth Farm House
- children's activity area
- stallholder areas
- main stage and viewing area
- food and beverage area
- talk and taste tent
- coolroom storage and service entry area
- Elizabeth Farm tearooms
- toilet areas
- garbage and cleaning supplies areas.

After presentation of the festival proposal, meeting attendees were invited to make suggestions on any aspects of the festival. The attendees made suggestions relating to keynote speakers/demonstrators, possible local content, catering and entertainment. This resulted in a broad range of diverse opinions, invaluable local knowledge and access to HHT corporate knowledge.

Festival management structure

At the first production meeting the festival's management structure was consolidated. As event coordinator, I had ultimate carriage of the project, with direction from the head of PPU. The marketing, retail, education and sponsorship units of the HHT were each given carriage of relevant aspects of the festival, with the next meeting as the deadline for their proposals. It was important to allow at least a month between each meeting as staff members were working on multiple projects at any given time. This way it could reasonably be assumed that there would be time to do what was undertaken and that each meeting constructively built towards the festival.

Festival development stage 2

During this time I began sourcing the festival's infrastructure — such as, stages, marquees, equipment hire, electrics providers, shuttle buses. I also started to negotiate with local community groups, organisations and businesses, caterers, stallholders and 'celebrity' chefs. My main hurdle during this development stage was finding an appropriate form of engagement with the local community.

Previously the festival had relied on the fundraising arm of a religious organisation to provide introductions into the local community. This group also coordinated and ran one of the primary catering stalls, which was seen as an appropriate

revenue profiling raising/cultural profiling opportunity by both parties. Unfortunately this association had not been maintained in the 'off' years when the festival was not held. As a result of changes in management and staff, links with the community group had disappeared.

While many long-term stakeholders questioned how the festival would continue without this association, it was also a chance to re-evaluate the notion of 'community involvement'. This became a necessity once I started talking with other local community groups.

I discovered that many of these groups were already involved in a 'spring/multicultural' fair, to occur on the same Saturday as our festival, presented by the local council. It seemed the council had used our 'off' year to establish a fair similar in content to the Festival of the Olive.

This discovery led to the realisation that Festival of the Olive could no longer be delivered on the goodwill of local community groups. In fact, despite the altruistic inferences of the festival's community event of the year award, I was of the opinion that Festival of the Olive should be developed and produced as a food festival whose inspiration was the local community's Mediterranean heritage. Thus the 'community' aspect of the festival could more suitably be seen in its ability to reflect the heritage of a section of the local community, and hence be relevant and popular within the local community.

After consultation with HHT festival stakeholders, we decided to consult and engage with businesses that presented aspects of Mediterranean cultural heritage on a commercial basis. This would allow the festival to present and reflect aspects of Mediterranean cultures with an approach that was more in keeping with a museum-curated approach. The festival's content, like Elizabeth Farm House, could then be more easily 'read' as an objective interpretive tool.

Programming the staging areas

There were three main staging areas scattered throughout the site: the main stage (musical and dance entertainments), the talk and taste tent (cooking demonstrations and olive oil tastings), and the Eastern garden (book readings and local primary school art display). These stages were programmed using a Gantt-type chart, with a view to minimising competing attractions in the three areas. Where possible, entertainment groups would play for at least two sets, giving visitors the chance to see them at least once. When there could only be one set — for example, an energy-sapping dance routine — nothing was programmed in the competing staging areas. Each area had a stage manager, MC and sound technician. All stage managers were communicating via radio to ensure that each stage's program stayed to time and, where necessary, accommodated and communicated slight changes to timings to facilitate the audience moving from one area to another.

All hired festival structures (marquees and stall tents) were white and unadorned, chosen to purposefully juxtapose, and hence highlight, the heritage environment. These structures were situated in a beautifully re-created 1830s garden; the only site dressing needed was potted Mediterranean plants. These were hired for the weekend and used to soften edges of event structures that appeared too brutal in the environment.

Each stage area was designed with its program requirements, ambience and audience sight-lines in mind. For example, in the talk and taste tent, theatrical lighting was used to ensure the chefs were illuminated to dramatic effect and the cooking

cart was elevated to make best use of the overhead mirror that allowed the audience a view of the chef's frenetic workbench. A team of well-trained staff was on hand to ensure the food sampling was orderly, food safety regulations were adhered to at all times and that the Q&A sessions ran smoothly.

Conclusion

Despite Festival of the Olive 2005 competing with three other major events — two offering free entry — it managed to achieve visitation and revenue targets. In terms of staging, as a result of the festival having been held on four previous occasions, its successful delivery was made much easier. It was primarily a case of an appropriately resourced research and development phase, with tight management controls implemented by the event coordinator, the head of PPU, stage managers and staff allocated to specific event operation roles.

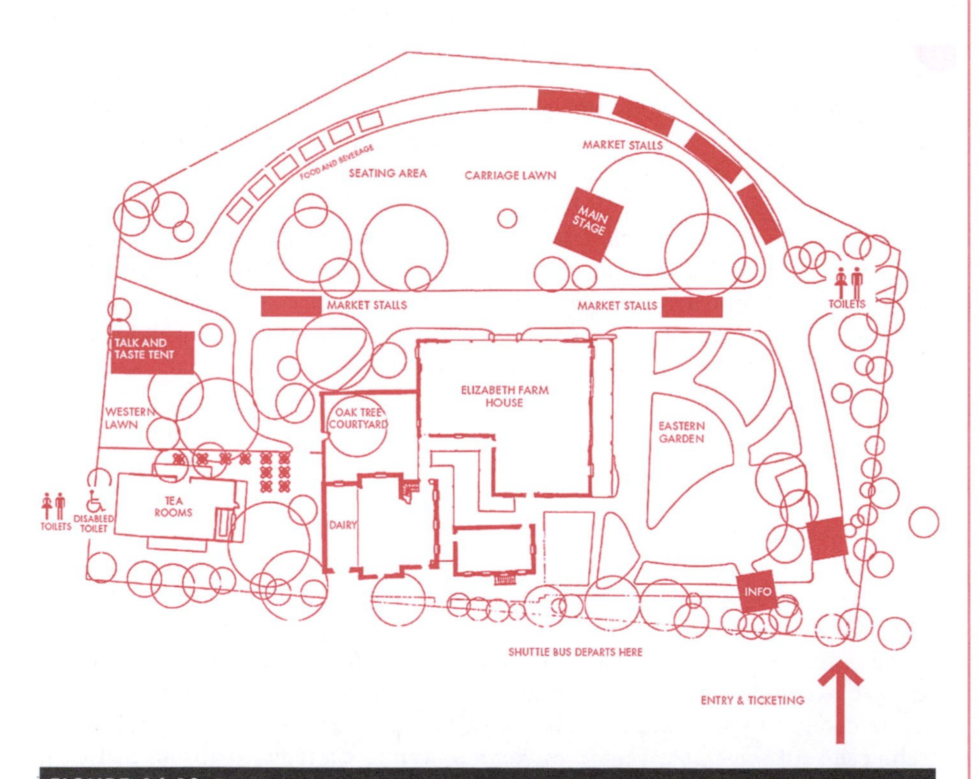

FIGURE 14.12 Festival of the Olive map

Mark Lillis, Historic Houses Trust

Questions

1 What are the characteristics of the theme of this event?

2 How does the theme reflect the requirements of the stakeholders and how did this change?

3 List the elements of staging.

4 Referring to chapter 6, what project management tools were used and why?

case study

AL MAHABBA AWARDS FESTIVAL 2008 ABU DHABI, UAE

Al Mahabba Awards Festival was created to inspire Muslims all over the world and reward artistic expressions of the Prophet Mohammed (pbuh). The Al Mahabba Awards, held from 24–26 April 2008 in Abu Dhabi, aspired to unite the Muslim community through their love for the Prophet. For the first time in international events history, the Al Mahabba Festival brought people from every continent together through two mutual expressions: the arts and religion.

Al Mahabba Awards started three years ago in response to a series of disrespectful cartoons depicting the Muslim Prophet Mohammed, published in a Danish newspaper. In the aftermath of the global uprising against the cartoons, a group of young Muslims decided to establish a festival to promote artistic expressions of love for the Prophet Mohammed. The first event, organised by the Al Tabah Foundation in Saudi Arabia, was held in Dubai in 2006 and, after much success, the second edition of the event was held in 2008 under the patronage of His Excellency Sheikh Mohammed bin Zayed Al Nahyan, Crown Prince of Abu Dhabi and Supreme Deputy Commander of the UAE Armed Forces, and under the honorary Chairmanship of HE Sheikh Abdullah bin Zayed Al Nahyan, Foreign Minister of the UAE.

Managing the event in the second year was production company Pyramedia, under the leadership of its CEO Nashwa Al Ruwaini. Pyramedia provided the Al Mahabba Awards with two venues: the Abu Dhabi Cultural Foundation and Al Raha Beach Theatre, in which all the events could be held over the three-day period, as well as extensive press and publicity, marketing, and production and post-production services. Stars from all over the world, including Native Deen, Zain Bhikha, Ehab Tawfik and Mohamed Henedi, came together to show their support for this festival as an example of unity among the international Muslim community, and because of their love of the arts and culture in representing the Prophet. Support from non-Muslims was also shown, with many of the participants joining the festival to demonstrate to the world the real aspects of Islam, and help change the misconceptions and negative images that exist around the world today.

The events of the festival included an opening ceremony welcoming the guests from all over the world, followed by a music concert featuring artists from as far away as the USA and as close as the UAE. Day two of the festival started with an Islamic Film Conference, with international film directors including Malek Akaad, son of the Hollywood producer of the 'Halloween' film series, and Bader Ben Hirsi, award-winning film director. This was intended to highlight the importance of using film and television to portray the Islamic world in a better light and combat the negative stereotypes that exist on the silver screen today. The day moved on with a Classical Concert and ended with a Scholar Conference about religion and art, which revealed the essence of art and literature in Islam and its existence since Islam's early days.

The third day began with a Women's Concert featuring female musical artists from around the world, and ended with the glamorous, Oscar-style awards ceremony, announcing winners in ten categories. The festival received submissions of

over 200 artistic pieces from 28 countries for nomination in the categories of songs, advertisements, documentaries, TV programs, films, books, photography, graphic arts, mass media and event of the year. A select few were chosen to take part in the world-class awards festival that provided the world with a chance, through modern media channels, to reflect on Islamic artistic works. The Al Mahabba Awards 2008 judging committee was headed by Dr Abdel Hakim Murad, a professor from Oxford University in the UK, and comprised a group of specialists in the fields of literature and the arts. The winners in each category were given their awards on the final day of the festival during an elaborate awards ceremony. In all, over the three days, 23 Nasheed bands and singers performed in the festival, expressing their love and respect for the Prophet through song. An exhibition featuring Islamic works of art was set up in the lobby of Al Raha Beach Theatre, for guests to browse the hundreds of works by Muslim artists across the world. In order to ensure maximum exposure for the festival, an extensive marketing and advertising campaign was undertaken in the UAE, with a particular focus in the UAE. Press worldwide, were also contacted and invited to attend the three-day festival. A press conference was held a week before the festival to introduce the aims and events of the festival to the press and public.

Pyramedia, with its specialist broadcasting team, filmed each event for broadcast on Al Resalah channel and the Poet channel, one of the leading channels associated with the highest rated TV shows in the region, 'The Million's' Poet' and 'Prince of Poets'. The channels are available on Nilesat and Arabsat to millions of viewers around the world. The stage at Al Raha Beach Theatre in Abu Dhabi, on which the majority of concerts and ceremonies were held, was built by the artist Mohamed Gomaa from Egypt, with an Islamic theme in mind, including wide arches and hanging lanterns. Each work of art displayed in the exhibition in the lobby of the theater was carefully hung on boards designed especially for the occasion. One of the greatest challenges for the festival was garnering the public's interest and encouraging them to attend. With a marketing and press campaign underway to ensure the maximum amount of people were aware of the events happening over the three days, every outlet emphasised that the entrance to all events was free, with 2000 seats available in the theatre. Each of the five ceremonies and concerts held had a full theatre, with men, women and children occupying every seat and even the aisles to witness the artistic show of love for the Prophet.

Questions

1 The case study uses the term 'Islamic theme'. Discuss what this means and how it frames the staging elements.

2 The program included many components such as poetry, film and music. Discuss why other aspects of events were not included — such as sport and product exhibitions.

3 Using a table with the elements of staging, compare this event to other events with a religious theme such as World Youth Day in Sydney, Australia, and the Indian Kumbh Mela festival on the Ganges.

4 Explain how the elements of staging — such as the program, lighting and stage setup — would be reconfigured to enable the broadcast of the event.

REFERENCES

Dal, R 2005, pers. comm.

Fahey, W 2005, pers. comm.

Getz, D 2005, *Event management and event tourism*, 2nd edn, Cognizant Communications, New York.

Goldblatt, J 2005, *Special events*, 4th edn, John Wiley & Sons, New York.

Graham, S, Goldblatt, J & Delpy, L 1995, *The ultimate guide to sports event management and marketing*, Richard Irwin, Chicago.

Hull, T 2009, pers. comm.

Malouf, L 1999, *Behind the scenes at special events*, John Wiley & Sons, New York.

Party Design, www.partydesign.co.za.

Reid, F 1995, *Staging handbook*, 2nd edn, A&C Black, London.

Silvers, JR 2004, *Professional event coordination*, John Wiley & Sons, New York.

Slater, C 2005, pers. comm.

Tassiopoulos, D 2005 *Event Management, a professional and developmental approach,* 2nd edn Juata Academic, Lansdowne.

The Truth Booth 2010, 'Festivals', http://thetruthbooth.com.au.

Tum, J, Norton, P & Wright, JN 2006, *Management of event operations*, Elsevier Event Management Series, London.

LOGISTICS

LEARNING OBJECTIVES

After studying this chapter, you should be able to:

1. define logistics management and describe its evolution
2. understand the concept of logistics management and its place in event management
3. construct a logistics plan for the supply of customers, event products and event facilities
4. use event logistics techniques and tools.

INTRODUCTION

This chapter adapts the science of business and military logistics to events. The management of an event is divided into supply, setting up and running the event on site, and the shutdown process of the event. Communication, transport, flow supply and linking the logistics with the overall event plan are the elements of event logistics treated in this chapter. Various checklists that can assist in the management of event logistics are outlined.

WHAT IS LOGISTICS?

> Logistics means having the right thing, at the right place, at the right time.
>
> *Logistics World*

The management science of logistics assists the event manager to identify the elements of special event and festival operations. Careful attention to event operations are vital to the success of an event. It is an area of high risk; crowd movements, staging, site familiarity, temporary structures and equipment are all factors that can combine to produce a volatile situation and that need to be highly prioritised in event operations. Although the term 'operations' is often used for events, the temporary nature of festival and special event operations gives the sourcing and movement of its elements a priority not found in day-to-day operations of a business. Movement of people and material is essential to all special event operations. Logistics is an analysis tool to manage an aspect of an event by subdividing the work into categories. Many people regard event management as what is happening during the event. This ignores the event set-up and shutdown. Logistics concerns the whole of operations. Unlike business logistics, event logistics takes place over a comparatively short time and there is rarely the time to improve it. The logistics has to be right the first time. The tools and techniques of logistics fit into a project approach to event management.

Placing the word 'logistics' into its historical context provides an understanding of its use in present event management. Logistics stems from the Greek word *logistikos*, 'skilled in calculating'. The ancient Romans used the term for the administration of their armies. The term evolved to refer to the practical art of the relocation of armies. Given the complexity of modern warfare, logistics became a science that included speed of operations, communications and maintenance of the armed forces. After World War II, modern businesses applied the experience and theory of logistics as they faced similar problems with transport and supply to those faced by the military.

The efficient movement of products has become a specialised study in the management discipline. Within large companies, especially international companies, a section can be devoted to coordinating the logistics requirements of each department. Logistics has become a discipline in its own right. This has led to consolidation into a separate independent function in companies, often called integrated logistics management. Logistics is the planning, implementing and control of the flow and storage of products, and the related information from production to the point of consumption, according to consumer requirements.

The value of a company's product or services can be improved by the efficient coordination of logistics in the company. In Australia, due to the special conditions and widespread distribution of customers, services and products, logistics takes on an importance not found in many other countries. Event logistics is part of the 'back-of-house' of an event. It is a supporting function of the event that goes unnoticed by most attendees, except when it doesn't work.

For a complete understanding of event logistics, this chapter is divided into sections dealing with the tasks of event logistics and the role of the logistics manager.

THE ELEMENTS OF EVENT LOGISTICS

The elements of event logistics can be organised into the logistics system shown in figure 15.1. This system is used to organise the logistic elements of an event.

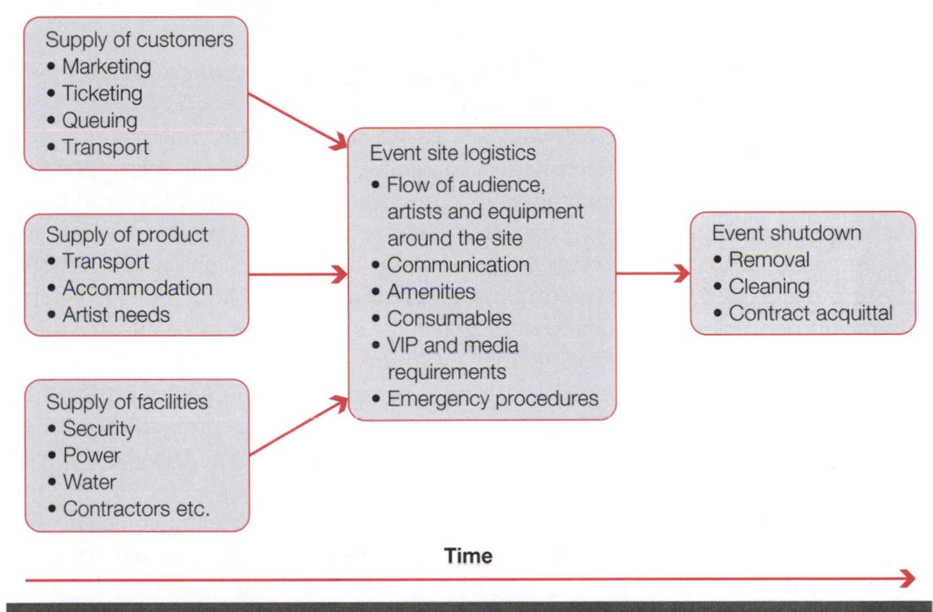

FIGURE 15.1 Elements of the logistics system

Whereas most logistics theory concerns the supply of products to customers, event logistics includes the efficient supply of the customer to the product, and the supply of facilities to and from the event site. In this sense, it has more in common with military logistics than modern business logistics. Business logistics is an ongoing activity and part of the continual management of a company. Military and event logistics often concern a specific project or campaign rather than continuing management. There is a defined preparation, lead-up, execution and shutdown. As well, issues such as inventory control and warehousing that are the basis of business logistics are not as important to a one-off event.

The areas of importance to event logistics can be categorised as follows:

- *Supply* — this is divided into the three areas of customer, product and facilities. Supply also includes the procurement of the goods and services.
- *Transport* — in Australia, the transport of goods and services can be a major cost to an event and requires special consideration.
- *Linking* — logistics is part of the overall planning of an event and is linked to all other areas. Logistics allows the event operations to be part of an integrated approach to event management. Logistics must be linked with marketing as marketing is a tool that sources and creates the flow of the attendees. Figure 15.2 illustrates a risk when logistics and marketing are not closely linked. With large multi-venue events, the logistics becomes so complex that an operations or logistics manager is often appointed. The logistics manager functions as part of the overall network management structure outlined in this chapter.

- *Flow control* — this refers to the flow of products, services and customers during the event.
- *Information networks* — the efficient flow of information during the event is generally a result of efficient planning of the information network. This concept is expanded in the section about on-site logistics.

All these areas need to be considered when creating a logistics plan. Even for small events, such as a wedding or a small product launch, a logistics plan must be incorporated in the overall event plan. For these types of event, logistics comes under the title 'staging', which is described in chapter 14.

Given that the major elements of logistics are supply and movement, logistics plays a large role in some types of event, including:

- events that have a large international component, such as major conferences, sports events and overseas corporate incentive programs. An example is the importance of logistics to the 2010 Commonwealth Games in New Delhi and the World Cup in South Africa. In both cases, completely new transport and security systems, and infrastructure had to be created to enable these events to occur. A new iTransie system was created for the FIFA Cup in Johannesburg and a colour-coded integrated transport network was implemented to enable the smooth flow of people, including coloured 'park and ride' tickets, entrance banners, volunteers' sashes and stickers on shuttles. In both New Delhi and Johannesburg security impinges on logistics. The organisers of the Commonwealth Games used the events prior to the Games, such as target shooting and hockey, to test their security systems and the ability of numerous agencies to work together.
- complex events in foreign countries, including trade exhibitions and conferences
- events that occur in remote locations and need most of the supporting resources transported to the site
- exhibitions of large or complex products, such as mining or agricultural exhibitions
- events that are moving, such as travelling exhibitions and races.

SUPPLY OF THE CUSTOMER

The customers of an event are those who pay for it. They can be the audience (concerts and festivals), spectators (sports) and the sponsors or clients (corporate events). The customers have expectations, including logistical aspects, which must be met for a successful outcome. The way in which the event is promoted will particularly influence their expectations.

Links with marketing and promotion

The supply of customers is ultimately the responsibility of marketing activities. The numbers, geographic spread and expectations of the customers affect the logistics planning. The targeting of specialist markets or widespread publicity of an event will require a logistics plan with very different priorities. The transport requirements of the customers vary according to the distance travelled — for example, the majority of the audience of the Port Fairy Folk Festival drives from Melbourne, so vehicle access and parking are a priority at the festival site. The WOMADelaide festival in Adelaide, with its nationwide publicity campaign, has a large interstate audience. This offers opportunities for special negotiations with the airlines and hotels.

If the publicity of an event is spread nationwide, the logistics will be different from those of a product launch that concerns only the staff and customers of a company. In this way, the logistics is closely linked to the marketing of an event.

Figure 15.2 illustrates one link between marketing and logistics.

In some countries, forgery of tickets for major events is a common problem. Part of the marketing plan for an event may involve the pre-sale of tickets. Selling tickets long before an event, however, allows the forger plenty of time to make false tickets. Improvements in copying and printing technology and the high price of tickets to major events have opened up this opportunity for crime. In a recent discussion about this problem in Kampala, Uganda, a number of event managers made the following observations. The consequences of ticket forgery are:

- loss of income
- security issues that arise from lack of control over who is entering the event site
- legal implications, such as non-compliance with the *Trade Practices Act*
- no control over numbers of attendees, with resulting capacity problems affecting such factors as electricity, food, toilets and parking
- loss of reputation for the event and the event company.

Possible solutions were brainstormed and compared with consideration to the resources needed to implement them. It was proposed that tickets could be individually named and numbered or barcoded, which would necessitate greater control at the entry point to the event when checking tickets, and may mean delays while all tickets are checked. This is the solution used by the travel industry to control and monitor overseas airline tickets, as well as using magnetic strips on tickets, which are difficult to forge. One solution proposed was to abolish tickets and instead make money from sponsorship and merchandise. Another was to make the tickets of a type and quality that would render forgery almost impossible and that would extend the time necessary to produce forgeries (the same solution as is used to produce banknotes). High quality printing can be difficult to copy; however, this solution would increase the operating cost of the event. Another idea was that unique tickets would only be available for purchase on site, thus restricting or even eliminating the time needed to create a forgery. Thinking outside the square of 'mechanical fixes', one event manager suggested it is a marketing, public relations and ethical issue (KIES 2009), and that event companies need to inform attendees that forgery is a crime and, ultimately, decreases the number of future events. This solution would involve a marketing plan and a communication strategy outlining the way an event team communicates to their future attendees.

One aspect to this problem that was unearthed during the discussion was the lack of real information about illegal tickets. The questions, 'How many tickets are forged?' and 'How are the tickets forged and distributed?' were not answered. The problem may be smaller — or larger — than previously imagined. With more accurate information, the event manager can estimate the resources needed to combat illegal copying.

FIGURE 15.2 Marketing and logistics: discussion on forgery

Ticketing

Ticketing is important to events whose primary income is from the entrance fee. Most corporate events, including office parties and product launches, and many public events are free. However, for other events, such as sports events, the extent of ticket sales can determine success or failure. Ticket distribution is regarded as the first major decision in event logistics.

The pricing and printing of the tickets is generally not a logistics area; however, ticket distribution, collection and security are of concern. In Australia, tickets for events can be sold through distributors such as Ticketek for a fee, or they can be sold by mail. The Port Fairy Folk Festival sells all its tickets at least four months in advance. Selling tickets at the gate gives rise to security problems in the collection, accounting and depositing of funds. The ticket collectors need training to deal with the public and to move the public efficiently through the entrance. The honesty of the staff may also be a security concern. Larger venues use an admission loss-prevention plan to minimise the possibility of theft.

It is not unusual in Australia to sell tickets through retail outlets such as Ticketek or Ticketmaster. One event used local tourism information centres as a distribution channel to sell tickets. Music concerts often use music stores to sell tickets as they have the equipment necessary for processing credit cards and handling cash. Inventory control and cash receipts are two areas that require special attention when using retail outlets for ticket distribution. Numbering of the tickets and individual letters of agreement with each outlet are the most efficient methods of control. The letter of agreement would include the range of ticket numbers, the level of the tickets (discount or full price) and the method of payment. Depending on the size of the event, the ticketing can be crucial to the event's success and can take up a significant amount of the event director's time. Figure 15.3 is a checklist of the logistics of ticketing an event.

An innovative method of ticketing for festivals is to use the hospital-style wristbands called crowd control bands. These are colour coded to indicate the level of the ticket — a day ticket, a weekend ticket or a special performer's ticket. The use of these wristbands introduces a visual method of control during a large event, because the sale of food and drinks is allowed only if the wristband is shown. In this way, the food vendors become part of the security for the event.

The internet is primarily used for the distribution of tickets for large events, concerts and conferences in many countries. This use of the internet illustrates the linking of logistics and marketing. Originally, events were marketed via this medium through advertisements on a website. The introduction of encrypted data enabled an increase in the privacy and security of online payment methods and ticket sales. The website collaborates with the existing ticketing system and also can be connected to travel agencies. Conference Bay has introduced a new system used for the ticketing of conferences, which involves internet bidding. Conferences register with the website and then users place their bid for a ticket. According to the Conference Bay website (www.conferencebay.com):

> Find an event you'd like to attend and make a bid. We contact the organiser and negotiate on your behalf. The more seats they have going spare, and the nearer the time to the event, the lower the price they're likely to accept!

The internet has introduced some unique risks in the sale of tickets. Aside from the obvious risk of security of the payment method, the online scalping of tickets on eBay is a risk. One legal challenge was a result of the Big Day Out promoters placing a warning on their tickets to dissuade scalping. eBay won the decision, arguing that this 'condition of sale' breached the *Trade Practices Act*. The Big Day Out was ordered to change the warning on the tickets.

Tickets can be sent to the purchaser's mobile phone via short message service (SMS). The use of barcoding enables events, such as exhibitions, to track their attendees via their mobile phone or portable digital assistant (PDA). The barcode is downloaded to the PDA or phone as an image file and scanned at the entrance and booths. The 2D codes or matrix codes, such as the Vodafone Load-a-Ticket, present new possibilities for ticketing as these codes are easier to read by scanners and cameras than barcodes, and contain more information.

Invitations are a form of ticketing used for corporate and private events. Many of the items on the ticketing checklist can be adapted for an invitation checklist. Although the costly collection of payment is not a problem inherent in using an invitation ticketing system, the timing and number of acceptances is of concern. Some corporate event managers invest many resources in ensuring they receive acceptances with enough time to plan the event. The acceptance rate — the number of acceptances divided by the number of invitations — can be as low as 5 per cent.

Does the artwork on the ticket contain the following?

- ☐ Number of the ticket
- ☐ Name of the event
- ☐ Date and time of the event
- ☐ Price and level of the ticket (discount, complimentary, full price, early bird)
- ☐ Seating number or designated area (ticket colouring can be used to show seating area)
- ☐ Disclaimer (in particular, this should list the responsibilities of the event promoter)
- ☐ Event information, such as a map, warnings and what to bring
- ☐ Artwork so the ticket could be used as a souvenir (part of the ticket could be kept by the patron)
- ☐ Contact details for information
- ☐ Security considerations, such as holograms to prevent copying
- ☐ Colour scheme, font and size suitable for reading and downloading from the event website

Printing schedule

- ☐ When will the tickets be ready?
- ☐ Will the tickets be delivered or do they have to be collected?
- ☐ If there is an error or a large demand for the tickets, will there be time for more to be printed?

Distribution

- ☐ What outlets will be used — retail, Ticketek (or similar), the internet, mail or at the gate?
- ☐ Has a letter of agreement with all distributors, setting out terms and conditions, been signed?
- ☐ What method of payment will be used (by both the ticket buyer to the distributor and in the final reconciliation) — credit card, cash, direct deposit?
- ☐ Are schedule of payment and reconciliation forms available?
- ☐ Does the schedule of communications referring to ticket sales indicate sales progress and whether more tickets are needed?

Collection of tickets

- ☐ How will the tickets be collected at the gate and transferred to a pass-out?
- ☐ How experienced are the personnel and how many will there be? When will they arrive and leave?
- ☐ Is a separate table for complimentary tickets needed at the ticket collection site?
- ☐ What security arrangements are in place for cash and personnel?
- ☐ How will the tickets be disposed of?

Reconciliation of number of tickets with revenue received

- ☐ What method of reconciliation will be used? Is an accountant being used?
- ☐ Is the reconciliation ongoing, at the conclusion of the event, or at the end of the month?
- ☐ Has a separate account been set up just for the event to assist the accountancy procedure?

FIGURE 15.3 Ticketing – logistics checklist

Queuing

Often, the first experience of a customer at an event is queuing for tickets or parking. Once inside the event, customers may be confronted with queues for food, toilets and seating. An important aspect of queue theory is the 'perceived waiting time'. This is the subjective time that the customers feel they have waited. There are many rules of thumb about diminishing the customers' perceived waiting time. In the catering industry, an informal rule is one food or beverage line for every 75 to 100 pax. Figure 15.4 lists some factors to consider in the logistics of queuing.

- How many queues and possible bottlenecks will there be?
- Has an adequate number of personnel greeters, crowd controllers, ticket collectors and security staff been allocated?
- Is signage (including the estimated waiting time) in place?
- When will the queues form? Will they form at once or over a period of time?
- How can the perceived waiting time be reduced (for example, queue entertainers)?
- What first aid, access and emergency procedures are in place?
- Are the lighting and sun and rain protection adequate?
- Are crowd-friendly barricades and partitions in place?

FIGURE 15.4 Queuing — factors to consider

At many large events, such as the Olympics, the perceived waiting time at the entrance queues is diminished by the use of entertainers. Exit queuing can be the last experience for the customer at an event and needs the close attention of the event manager. At Darling Harbour's New Year's Eve celebrations in Sydney, the authorities use 'staggered entertainment' to spread the exit time of the crowds. The perceived waiting time at a corporate event can be reduced by corralling the guests into one area while they wait for the opening or start of the event. This can be a cocktail bar area with pre-show entertainment.

The oversupply of customers at a commercial event can give rise to security and public safety problems that should be anticipated in the logistics plan. Only pre-sale tickets will indicate the exact number of the expected audience. When tickets are sold at the entrance to an event, the logistics plan has to include the possibility of too many people turning up on the day. Oversubscription may be pleasing for the event promoter, but can produce the logistical nightmare of what to do with the excess crowd.

Customer transport

Transport to a site is often the first physical commitment by the audience to an event. The method and timing of arrival — public or private transport — is important to the overall logistics plan. The terms used by event managers are 'dump', when the audience arrives almost at once, and 'trickle', when event goers arrive and leave over a longer period. Each of these needs a different logistics strategy. The first impression of the event by the audience can influence all subsequent experiences at the event. For this reason, it is the most visible side of logistics for customers. The arrival and departure are a part of the event hospitality experience. The first and last impression of an event will be the parking facilities and traffic control.

The selection of the event venue or site has to account for the availability and cost of transport to and from the site. As well, the transport to other facilities has to be considered. A venue that involves a 'long haul' will increase the overall costs of a conference or event, as well as adding to the organisational confusion. Lengthy travel can make the event seem less attractive to the delegates and, therefore, have an impact on attendee numbers.

For large events, festivals and parades, further logistics elements are introduced to the transport of the customer to the event. In particular, permission (council, main roads departments, police) and road closures need to be part of the logistics plan.

The significance of transport to the event stakeholders such as local authorities is illustrated by the publication of *Traffic management for special events* by the New South Wales government and *Managing travel for planned special events* by the US Department of Transportation. The New South Wales document defines events in terms of their impact on traffic:

> A special event (in traffic management terms) is any planned activity that is wholly or partly conducted on a road, requires multiple agency involvement, requires special traffic management arrangements, and may involve large numbers of participants and/or spectators. Examples are marathons, fun runs, cycling events, parades, marches and street market days. (RTA 2006, p. 9).

Most states in Australia require a traffic management plan to be submitted to the local council to gain their permission. The New South Wales guide maps out the processes the event organiser needs to follow to obtain approvals. First the event team must classify their event into one of four classes based on the event's impact on traffic and the surrounding area. This initial process is illustrated by figure 15.5. Each of the four classes of events branches to a different process. A Class 1 special event, for example, such as a major car race through the streets, would follow a process that includes such actions as preparing a detailed traffic management plan and advertising the traffic aspects of the event to the wider public.

An event plan based on the principles of project management, as described in chapter 6, will be able to absorb these processes with ease. This New South Wales guide is similar to those in many states around Australia and illustrates one of the many formal processes necessary to conduct an event.

An innovative way of solving many logistics problems (parking and so on) and enhancing the audience experience was used by the organisers of the Australian Music Festival in Glen Innes, New South Wales. The festival took place at the old Glen Innes railway station, and the audience arrived by steam train, the Great Northern, with the performers. By the time the passengers arrived from Central Station (Sydney) on the Great Northern train, the festival experience had already begun.

The Glen Innes festival also demonstrates how the transport arrangements for the customer (audience) can be linked to the transport of the product (musicians). This can be taken much further and include sponsorship deals with transport companies. In particular, the transport of equipment can be offset against the large number of tickets required to transport the audience. Australian domestic airlines often negotiate a discount for excess baggage charges incurred by performers if the event account is large enough.

The lack of transport facilities can be used as part of the event experience. As Nick Rigby (2005), Head Ranger at Cape Byron, New South Wales, describes:

> For our inaugural environmental heritage concert at the Pass we did not allow cars near the site as it would have spoilt the feeling of the evening. The audience had to park a

kilometre away and walk along the beach to the Pass. This little journey was part of the environmental experience. We had volunteers steering people in the right direction and welcoming them to Cape Byron. It was quite a sight, over a thousand adults and children strolling along the beach with their picnic 'Eskies' and blankets.

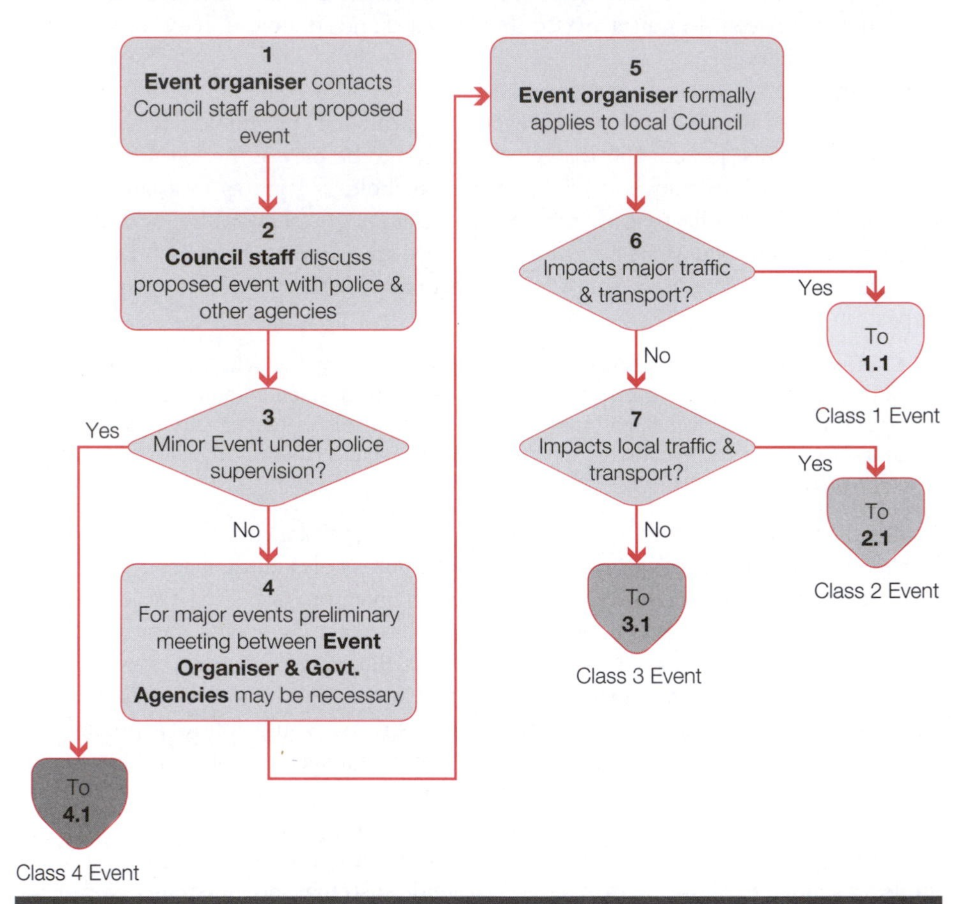

FIGURE 15.5 A sample of the special event transport management planning process

Source: RTA 2006, p. 20.

Figure 15.6 lists the elements of customer transport that need to be considered for an event.

FIGURE 15.6 Customer transport checklist

- ☐ Have the relevant authorities (for example, the local council, the police and the Department of Main Roads) been contacted for information and permission?
- ☐ What public transport is available? Are timetables available?
- ☐ Has a back-up transport system been organised (in case the original transport system fails)?
- ☐ Is the taxi service adequate and has it been informed of the event? (Informing the local taxi service is also a way of promoting the event.)
- ☐ What quality is the access area? Do weight and load restrictions apply? Are there other special conditions that must be considered (for example, underground sprinkler systems under the access area)?

FIGURE 15.6 *(continued)*

- ☐ Is there adequate provision for private buses (including an area large enough for their turning circle), driver hospitality and parking?
- ☐ Is there a parking area and will it be staffed by trained personnel?
- ☐ Is a towing and emergency service available if required?
- ☐ Has transport to and from the drop-off point been organised (for example, from the parking station to the site or venue entrance and back to the parking station)?
- ☐ At what rate are customers estimated to arrive (dump or trickle)?
- ☐ Is there adequate access and are there parking facilities for disabled customers?
- ☐ Are the drop-off and pick-up points adequately lit and signposted?

SUPPLY OF PRODUCT — PRODUCT PORTFOLIO

Any event can be seen as the presentation of a product. Most events have a variety of products and services — a product portfolio — that helps to create the event experience for the customer. The individual logistics requirements of the various products need to be integrated into a logistics plan.

For a large festival, the product portfolio may include more than 200 performing groups from around Australia and overseas. For a small conference, the product may be a speaker and video material. The product can also include the venue facilities, which is why the term 'the event experience' is used to cover all aspects of the customers' experience. It can include, for example, the audience itself and just catching up with friends, in which case the people become part of the product portfolio.

Transport

If the product portfolio includes products coming from overseas, the logistics problems can include issues such as carnet and customs clearance. A carnet is a licence issued by Customs that allows the movement of goods across an international border. A performing artist group coming into Australia is required to have clearance for all its equipment and needs to pay any taxes on goods that may be sold at the event, such as DVDs or compact discs.

A large account with an airline can allow the event manager an area of negotiation. An airline company may grant savings, discounts, free seats or free excess baggage in exchange for being the 'preferred airline' of the event.

The artistic director should forward the transport requirements for the performers to the logistics manager well before the event. This illustrates the linking of the functional areas of a large event.

Sonder, in his text on event production (2004), lists five cost items of transport issues under the revealing heading 'The high cost of entertainment'. One of these issues is the transport of the artists to the venue. Birch (2004, p. 191) in his informative description of his life in events, relates many stories of transporting artists. He describes one opera diva's refusal to take the artist shuttle bus to the performance at the opening of the Olympics as she was expecting a private limousine.

Importing groups from overseas or interstate provides the logistics manager with an opportunity to communicate with these groups. The 'meet and greet' at the airport and the journey to the site can be used to familiarise the talent with the event.

The artist's event or festival kit may, for example, include a site map, rehearsal times, accommodation details, the dressing room location, equipment storage and transport home details.

Accommodation

The accommodation requirements of the artists (such as performers, keynote speakers or competitors) must be treated separately from the accommodation of the audience. The aim of the event manager is to get the best out of the 'product'. Given that entertainers are there to work, their accommodation has to be treated as a way of increasing the value of the investment in entertainment. Substandard accommodation and long trips to the site are certain ways of reducing this value. Often, these requirements are not stated and need to be anticipated by the logistics manager.

Artists' needs on site

A range of artists' needs must be catered for, including transport on site, storage and movement of equipment, stage and backstage facilities, food and drink (often contained in the contract rider), sound and lights. All of these have a logistics element and are described in detail in chapter 14.

As with accommodation, an efficient event manager will anticipate the on-site needs of the artists. Often, this can only be learned from experience. The manager needs to be sensitive to requirements that are culturally based, such as food, dressing rooms (separate) and appropriate staff to assist the performer. The artist's requirements on site have a very strong sense of urgency. Often there is not a lot of time to adjust the food, costumes, dressing rooms or on-site transport if the artists are dissatisfied. These last minute changes can impinge on the production time of the event. Therefore understanding the artists' needs should be regarded as a critical task. The term 'artist' used in this section refers to speakers, MCs and sports personalities, as well as cultural artists such as musicians. They are also referred to as the 'talent'.

SUPPLY OF FACILITIES

The supply of the infrastructure to an event site introduces many of the concepts of business logistics. The storage of consumables (food and drink) and equipment, and the maintenance of equipment become particularly significant. For a small event taking place over an evening, the venue supplies most of the facilities. The catering, toilets and power, for example, can all be part of the hiring of the venue.

Figure 15.7 illustrates a common spreadsheet system for planning and monitoring the sourcing and payment of suppliers. Such a system enables the event team to simply display their good governance. As the event or festival grows, this spreadsheet can be scaled up.

Larger festivals or more innovative events require the sourcing of many of the facilities. Some of these facilities are discussed in detail in chapter 14. An inaugural outdoor festival needs to source almost all of the facilities. To find the best information about the availability and cost of facilities, the event manager should look for a project in the area that required similar facilities. Earth-moving equipment, toilets, generators, fencing and security, for example, are also used by construction and mining companies. Some facilities can be sourced through film production companies. Many of the other facilities, such as the marquees and stages, travel with festivals. Large tents and sound systems need to be booked in advance.

Register of suppliers and purchase order status 2011 festival

Item	Status	Quotes sought	Quotation received	Supplier	Contact details	Services/ goods to be supplied	Cost	Order number	Issued	Invoices	Amount
Copyright											
Catering for performers	Confirmed										
Children's rides											
Clean-up staff											
Entertainment	Confirmed										
Fireworks	Confirmed										
First aid											
Food stalls											
Garbage bins											
Generator	Confirmed										
Lighting towers	Confirmed										
Marquees etc.											
Parking	Contacted										
Portaloos											
Security											
Sound system	Confirmed										
Staging	Call for quotes										
Venue	Confirmed										

FIGURE 15.7 List of suppliers for a jazz festival

Innovative events, like a company-themed Christmas party in an abandoned car park, require a long lead time to source the facilities. It may take months to source unusual and rare props and venues, for example. These lead times can significantly affect the way in which the event is scheduled.

ON-SITE LOGISTICS

The site of an event may vary from an old woolshed for a bush dance to an underground car park for a Christmas party, to a 50-hectare site for a festival. Logistics considerations during the event become more complex with the size of the event. The flow of materials and people around the site and communication networks become the most important areas of logistics.

Flow

With larger festivals and events, the movement of the audience, volunteers, artists and equipment can take a larger part of the time and effort of the logistics manager than does the lead-up to the event. This is especially so when the site is complex or multi-venue and there is a large audience. A mistake made by people unfamiliar with events is to disregard what happens at various times on the event site or venue. For some events, the site is in constant motion, although this may not be obvious to the audience. During the lead-up to an event, subcontractors can take care of many elements of the logistics. The movement of the electricity generators to the site, for example, is the responsibility of the hire company. However, once the facilities are on site, the logistics manager is responsible for their positioning, movement and operation.

Something is being moved around on most event sites. The logistics must take into account the potential for flow of equipment and people during an emergency. The access roads through a large festival and during the event have to accommodate:

- artist and equipment transport
- garbage removal
- emergency fire and first-aid access and checking
- stall set-up, continual supply and removal
- security
- food and drink supplies
- staging equipment set-up, maintenance and removal
- site communication.

As illustrated by figure 15.8, even during a straightforward event, many factors of the traffic flow must be considered. The performers for an event need transport from their accommodation to the stage. Often, the performers go via the equipment storage area to the rehearsal rooms, then to the stage. At the conclusion of the performance, the performers return their equipment to storage, then retire for a well-earned rest in the green room. For a community festival with four stages, this to-ing and fro-ing can be quite complex.

At the same time as the performers are transported around the site, the media, audience and VIPs are on the move. Figure 15.8 does not show the movement of the food vendors' suppliers, water, security, ambulances and many more. When any one of the major venues empties, there is further movement around the site by the audience. This results in peak flow times when it may be impossible to move anything around the venue except the audience. These peaks and lows have to be anticipated in the overall event plan.

1. Performers and their support crew	Accommodation Equipment storage area Rehearsal area Stage Equipment storage area Social (green) room
2. Media	Accommodation — media centre Stages Social area
3. VIP	Accommodation Stages Special requests
4. Audience pick-up points	Specific venue

FIGURE 15.8 Some traffic patterns at a multi-staged music festival to be considered when planning

Each event contains surprising factors in traffic flow. For the Easter Show, which was formerly held at the old Sydney Showground, the narrow gate that allowed entrance to the performers was also the gate that was used for the various animals. Each day of the two-week show had a queue that contained a mix of school orchestras, dancers, bands, sound equipment, Brahman bulls, sheep trucks, camels and horses moving in both directions. This flow was coordinated by one gatekeeper.

Communication

On-site communication for the staff at a small event can be via the mobile phone or the loud hailer of the event manager. Given the complexity of larger events, however, the logistics plan must contain an on-site communications plot.

The communications plot includes fax, two-way radios, pagers, mobile phones, PDAs and landline extensions. It can also contain the title of each manager, as well as the complaints and neighbours hotline.

The communication of information during an event has to work seamlessly with the other functions of event management. In particular, the immediacy of the information is important. The information has to be highly targeted and timely enough for people to act on it. This immediacy of information is unique to events because they must meet a deadline and generally involve large numbers of people. For this reason, event management tends to involve a variety of communication methods and devices, including:

- *two-way radios* — very common at large events, where the channels are reserved for emergency and police
- *mobile phones and text messages* — although limited by capacity, possibly becoming overloaded in an emergency. For this reason, some large venues acquire additional coverage.
- *signage* — a common form of communication. Its placement and clarity are important issues (dealt with later in this chapter).

- *runners* — people whose job it is to physically take the information to the receiver. Runners are indispensable if there is a power failure. Some large public events have bicycles ready for this purpose.
- *news sheets* — paper news sheets used to inform the exhibitors of daily program changes and updates on the attendee numbers and types
- *loud hailer* — surprisingly useful devices at some events such as parades
- *a sound system* — useful for announcements. The event team should know how to use it correctly.
- *flags* — often used at sports events such as car racing
- *visual and audio cues* — used to communicate the start or finish of an action. Whistles, horns and flashing lights can all be used in this way. Artistic lighting can be used to move an audience around a venue.
- *closed circuit television and web cams* — used in venues such as exhibition and entertainment centres
- *short-range FM radios* — used to broadcast information during the event
- *WiFi and Bluetooth* — two technologies that are employed at some conferences and exhibitions to send and receive information such as last-minute news and attendee numbers. These can provide a comprehensive mobile network for immediate data transfer.
- *bulletin boards* — a humble and often effective way of contacting the volunteers and performers on site.

The movement around the event site or venue of equipment, suppliers and people — that is, the logistics during the event — needs an efficient communication system. For this reason, events often have levels of redundancy or back-ups for any one type of communication. The test of good communication planning is a power failure or emergency when the system will stop or be overloaded, and the event management team will be swamped with decisions to be made. Communication planning has to account for such a situation, so it must be a fundamental part of the project management and undergo a thorough risk assessment. A common experience is the lack of mobile phone connections over the New Year's Eve event celebrations when lines are swamped with calls.

On-site signage is an important part of communicating to the attendees of an event. It may be as simple as messages on a whiteboard in the volunteers' dining area, or it may involve large on-site maps showing the public the locations of facilities. Two important issues of on-site signage are position and clarity. A direction sign that is obscured by sponsors' messages, for example, diminishes its value to the event.

For large events, the signage may need a detailed plan. The issues to consider are:

- overall site placement of signs — at decision points and at danger spots, so they are integrated into the event
- the types of sign needed, such as directional, statutory (legal and warning signs), operational, facility and sponsor
- the sign literacy of the attendees — what sort of signs are they used to reading?
- the placement of signs — entrance, down the road, height
- the supply of signs, their physical maintenance and their removal
- the credibility of the signs — if a facility is moved, then the signs may need to be changed.

The most effective way of communicating with the audience at an event is to have the necessary information in the program. Figure 15.9 shows information for the audience for a small festival in northern New South Wales.

~FESTIVAL INFORMATION~

Staying at the festival Limited on-site camping is available at a flat rate of $10 per person. N.B. this fee is not for profit, it's to cover the costs of providing facilities.

Other accommodation There are three caravan parks in Lismore, delightful rural cabins, B&Bs, hotels, motels and backpacker accommodation. You can book your stay in or around Lismore through the Lismore Tourist Information Centre (no booking charge). Please tell them you are coming to the festival.

People with disabilities Facilities are provided for people with disabilities. If you have special needs please contact us first and we will do our best to help you.

Volunteers Our heartfelt thanks to all the wonderful folk who have given their time and energy to create this very special event.

This festival is run entirely by volunteers, who appreciate a helping hand! If you can put in a couple of hours to help it would be great, just check in at the festival office.

Festival workers put in even more time. If you would like to help with setting up or clean-up, etc., please call us.

The bars The festival is a licensed event, run strictly according to licensing regulations! Under 18s and anyone who seems intoxicated will not be served. No BYO. Photo ID required.

First aid The Red Cross will be on site throughout the festival.

Car parking We welcome back the **Tuncester Bush Fire Brigade** to take care of the car park.
(Donations to these two essential voluntary services would be appreciated.)

Lost and found care for children and things — located in the club house.

Tickets Please bring your ticket to exchange for a wristband which must be worn throughout the festival. Spot checks will happen!

We suggest you bring your own mug for soft drinks, etc. to save on disposables. Sunscreen and hats are strongly recommended and you may need a jumper for the cool spring nights.

The Lismore Folk Trust Inc.
A not-for-profit organisation run solely by volunteers, the Trust produces this annual festival, the Lismore Lantern Festival and other events throughout the year. Membership entitles you to concessions at all Folk Trust events, newsletters (vacancy for an editor!) and is essential support for the festival. You can find out more about the Trust, and how to join, at the festival office.

Proudly supporting Summerland House, Alstonville.

FIGURE 15.9 Festival information from the Northern Rivers Folk Festival program

Amenities and solid waste management

For large festivals and events, the logistics site map always includes the layout of the amenities. Figure 15.10 is an example of a large festival logistics site map that shows the layout of amenities.

Figure 15.10 shows a large scale view of the Deni — Play on the Plains Festival and World Record Ute Muster site map. The event has refined its set up over a number of years. Normally a site map shows the parking. However, at the muster the parking area is part of the event experience. It is in this area that the ute owners are able to show off their vehicles. At the same time, this area is the accommodation, as the ute owners and their friends camp next to their utes. The different coloured regions allow the event organisers to divide the 6000 utes and enable them to have a greater level of control.

Figure 15.11 is a close-up of the entertainment area for the festival. The circular arrangement of the stalls allows the audience to move around the site. The entertainment areas shown as the 'arena', bull ride, and carnival are around the outside of the field. This arrangement suits the type of crowd and the flow of the audience. At night the area marked stage becomes the focus of the crowd. Once the evening show has finished, the audience walks back to the accommodation.

FIGURE 15.10 Deni — Play on the Plains Festival and World Record Ute Muster logistics site map

DENILIQUIN PLAY ON THE PLAINS FESTIVAL
AND WORLD RECORD UTE MUSTER
TRADE SITE MAP
2005

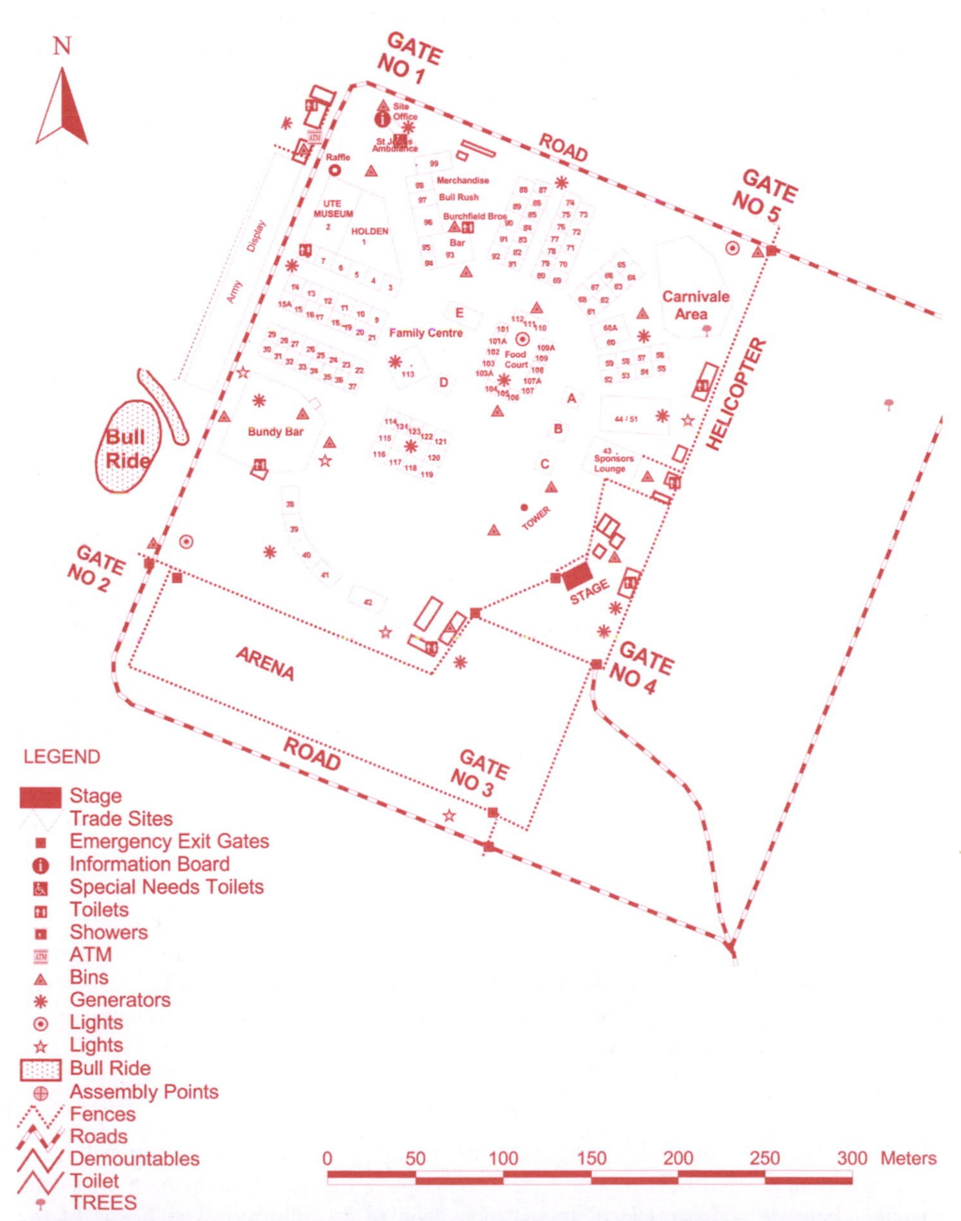

FIGURE 15.11 Close-up of the staging area of the Deni — Play on the Plains Festival and World Record Ute Muster

A change in the demographic attending means that forward planning of the site layout is imperative to accommodate the change. More families are attending, due to the marketing of the event. Over the past few years, the family camping area has almost doubled in size and is now nearly the same size as the ute camping area.

As one can see in this map, safety is a major concern to the event organisers. Many young people attend the event and there is alcohol for sale on site. However, the way the site is laid out contributes significantly to the minimum number of incidents over their years of operation.

The site map is an indispensable tool for the event manager and is described in more detail later in this chapter. The schedules for the maintenance and cleaning of the amenities are part of the plan. For smaller events, these areas may be the responsibility of the venue management and part of the hiring contract.

Responsibility for cleaning the site and restoring it to its original condition is of particular importance to an event manager, because it is generally tied to the nature of the event. An event in Sydney's Royal Botanic Gardens attracted a huge audience to a delicate area. The mere movement of the audience severely damaged the grass and resulted in the Gardens administration being suspicious of any further events in the area. If a national park is used as the site for an event, a review of environmental factors (REF) is mandatory. The REF is a list of criteria that the activity must meet to be permitted under various acts and regulations. These include the *National Parks and Wildlife Act 1974* (NSW), the *Endangered Fauna (Interim Protection) Act 1991* (NSW) and the *Threatened Species Conservation Act 1995* (NSW). The REF must also contain descriptions of the implications of the activity, the impact on the existing environment and land use, and the activity's significance to the local Aboriginal community.

Well-maintained toilets, particularly their number, accessibility and cleanliness, can be a very important issue for the audience. A rule of thumb for community festivals is one toilet for every 150 people. According to the *City of Ballarat Event Planning Guide*, the number varies according to factors such as gender, alcohol use and length of time of the event (Event Ballarat 2004). Respondents to the Port Fairy Folk Festival audience survey stressed that the state of the toilets was an important factor for return visits to the festival. The logistics manager has to be aware of 'peak flows' during an event, and of the consequences for vehicle transport of waste and the opening times of treatment plants.

The collection of solid waste can range from making sure the venue manager has enough bins, to calling for a tender and subcontracting the work. The number of bins, workers and shifts, the timelines for collection and the removal of skips should be contained in the logistics plan, because they interrelate with all of the other event functional areas. This is a further example of the linking of the elements of logistics. A plan for primary recycling (recycling at collection point) would include both the education of the public (signage) and the provision of special bins for different types of waste (aluminium, glass, paper).

Consumables — food and beverage

The logistics aspects of food and beverage on a large, multi-venue site primarily concern storage and distribution. Food stalls may be under the management of a stall manager because state and local regulations need to be followed. The needs of the operators of food stalls, including transport, gas, electricity and plumbing, are then sent to the logistics manager. The sale of alcoholic beverages particularly can present the logistics manager with security issues.

At a wine and food fair, the 'consumables' are the attraction. The collection of cash is often solved by the use of pre-sale tickets that are exchanged for food and wine samples. The tickets are bought at one place on the site, which reduces possible problems with security, cash collection and accounting.

Figure 15.12 lists some of the main factors to consider when including food and beverage outlets at an event. As well as feeding and watering the public, catering logistics includes the requirements of the staff, volunteers and performers. The catering area for the staff and performers, often called the green room, provides an opportunity to disseminate information to the event staff. At the Northern Rivers Folk Festival, a strategically placed, large whiteboard in the green room was used to communicate with volunteers.

Last, but not least, is the catering for sponsors and VIPs. This generally requires a separate plan to that for the general catering. In some festivals, a hospitality tent is set aside for special guests. This aspect of events is covered in chapter 14.

Due to the temporary nature of special events and festivals and the large number of inexperienced volunteers, food can be a high risk item in the event. In Australia it is recommended that the event organisers follow the Food Standards Code. The importance of correct storage was illustrated in 2002 at a community festival in Melbourne when 272 people were treated for food poisoning. The methodology of hazard analysis critical control point (HACCP) is being applied to large events. The hazards are identified in the preparation and delivery of food. Critical control points are instances in this process when the risk can be controlled. It is part of the general risk management methodology described in chapter 18.

- Have local and state liquor licences been granted?
- What selection criteria for stall applicants (including the design of the stall and menu requirements) will be used?
- What infrastructure will be needed (including plumbing, electrical and gas)?
- Does the contract include provisions for health regulations, gas supplies, insurance and worker's compensation?
- What position on the site will the stalls occupy?
- Have arrival, set-up, breakdown and leaving times been set?
- What cleaning arrangements have been made?
- Are the environmental impacts understood by the stallholders?
- Do stallholders understand the need for ongoing inspections, such as health, electricity, plumbing, garbage (including liquids) disposal and gas inspections?
- Are there any special security needs for which organisers must cater?
- How and when will payment for the stalls be made?
- Will the stallholders provide in-kind support for the event (including catering for VIPs, media and performers)?
- Are all staff trained in the responsible service of alcohol?

FIGURE 15.12 Food and beverage — factors to consider

Figure 15.13 illustrates the importance of food handling education for volunteers. Checklists such as this illustrate the micro-management needed in events, particularly when it comes to food.

VIP and media requirements

The effect on event logistics by media coverage of the event cannot be overestimated. Even direct radio broadcasts can disrupt the live performance of a show, both in the setting up and the actual broadcast. The recording or broadcasting of speeches or music often requires separate microphones or a line from the mixing desk and these arrangements cannot be left until just before the performance. Television cameras require special lighting, which often shines directly into the eyes of the audience. The movement of a production crew and television power requirements can be distracting to a live performance and need to be assessed before the event.

Checklist

It is very easy to forget to do things when you are busy trying to organise events. If you tick the boxes of this checklist for each activity you will be less likely to miss important jobs.

Event: .... Date:...

Have you . . .	**YES**	**NO**
• decided which activity on the decision path covers the event?	☐	☐
• notified your enforcement agency about the event?	☐	☐
• identified all volunteers participating in the event?	☐	☐
• provided volunteers with the appropriate information sheets?	☐	☐
• checked that handwashing facilities will be provided?	☐	☐
• checked that drinkable water will be available at the site or an adequate supply will be transported to the site?	☐	☐
• checked whether power or gas will be available (if needed)?	☐	☐
• determined how to dispose of waste water and rubbish?	☐	☐
• checked that premises and temporary stalls are clean and appropriate for the activity being undertaken?	☐	☐
• checked that adequate temperature control equipment will be available?	☐	☐
• checked that a thermometer will be available if potentially hazardous foods will be handled?	☐	☐

Talk to your local enforcement agency if you have any concerns.

If you have answered NO to any question, you need to consider what can be done to ensure that your charity or community organisation meets the Food Safety Standards.

FIGURE 15.13 Food safety checklist

Source: FANZ 2007.

Media organisations work on very short timelines and may upset the well-planned tempo of the event. However, the rewards in terms of promotion and event finance are so large that the media logistics can take precedence over most other aspects of the event. These decisions are often made by the event manager in consultation with event promoters and sponsors. This is an area that illustrates the need for flexible negotiations and assessment by the logistics/operations manager.

The requirements of VIP guests can include special security arrangements. Again, it is a matter of weighing up the benefits of having VIPs with the amount of extra resources that are needed. This, however, is not the logistics manager's area of concern; the event manager or event committee should deal with it. Once the VIPs have been invited, their needs have to take precedence over the public's needs.

Emergency procedures

Emergency procedures at an event can range from staff qualified in first aid, to using the St John Ambulance service, to the compilation of a comprehensive disaster plan. The location of first aid facilities should be indicated on the site map and all of the event staff should be aware of this location. Large events require an emergency access road that has to be kept clear. These issues are so important that a local council may immediately close down an event that does not comply with the regulations for emergencies. Festivals in the countryside can be at the mercy of natural disasters, including fires, storms and floods. Figure 15.14 is an example of an emergency response plan.

The event must have a formal, written emergency response plan, which should be developed with [Australian] standards. The plan should be provided to all event organisers, key stakeholders, police and emergency service personnel. The plan should:

- detail arrangements for on-site emergencies not requiring outside help
- specify arrangements to request further police and other emergency services assistance
- specify arrangements to hand over control to police and emergency services as required
- identify personnel who can authorise evacuation
- identify how the event will be interrupted
- provide a grid plan of the venue and all services
- identify access and evacuation routes
- identify evacuation areas for performers, employees and patrons
- establish an emergency control centre, which has back-up power and lighting
- provide details of coded messages to alert and stand down emergency service and security personnel
- identify the role event staff will take in supporting civilian services
- identify meeting points for emergency services
- identify triage and ambulance loading areas
- include details of hospitals prepared for a major incident
- identify access and egress routes, and the security of these routes
- provide details of a temporary mortuary facility.

Note: In any major incident, for the purposes of the law, the venue is considered a crime scene and thus under total control of the police.

FIGURE 15.14 An example of an emergency response plan

Source: Government of Victoria 2004.

Considerations for creating the plan include: under whose authority is the plan being prepared? What are the plan's aims and objectives? The emergency plan will influence the design of the site, particularly for large public events. Local councils require emergency access to all parts of the event. The access route must be the correct width for an emergency vehicle and kept clear at all times. A mistake in this area can result in the event being closed immediately.

Emergencies can happen at any time during the event and their occurrence will have an effect on the evacuation procedures. For major emergencies when the site needs to be cleared, the evaluation procedure is different for each of the following points in time:

- when the audience is arriving, before they have entered the venue or site. The logistics involved is concerned with stopping the inflow.
- when some of the audience is already in the venue and others are arriving. This is a complex period of two directions of flow: people who are arriving and haven't heard that the event has been cancelled, and those who are eager to leave.
- during the event, when most of the audience is on-site.

The disaster plan stresses the lines of authority and necessary procedures. These procedures include the partial evacuation of the festival site in the event of a disaster (particularly prolonged heavy rain). It notes that rescuers should concentrate on personnel in immediate danger when conducting an evacuation.

SHUTDOWN

Military logistics is divided into three phases:

1. deployment
2. combat
3. redeployment.

Redeployment, the complete movement of military forces and equipment to a different area, often takes the most effort and time. Similarly, the exiting of the people and removal and return of equipment that take place during an event can take a considerable amount of time and effort. In many cases, the amount of time and effort spent on the shutdown of an event are in direct proportion to the size of the event and its uniqueness. Repeated events, like many of the festivals mentioned in this chapter, have refined their shutdown schedule over many years. Shutdown can run quickly and smoothly. All the subcontractors know exactly how to get their equipment out and where they are placed in the order of removal. The event manager of a small event may only have to sweep the floor and turn off the lights.

Most difficulties arise in inaugural events, large events and multi-venue events. In these cases, logistics can be as important after the event as at any other time and the need for planning is most apparent. As illustrated in figure 15.15, the management of an event shutdown involves many elements. In project management terminology, this is called the asset handover and project closure. In event management, the most forgotten part is the closure of the project.

The tools of project management can be used to manage the shutdown process. The shutdown plan should include a work breakdown structure, a task/responsibility list and a schedule with a critical path and be subject to risk analysis. It forms part of the overall event project plan.

The on-site issues initially involve the crowd. Whether for a sports event, a conference or a concert, not much major work can be done until the crowd leaves. However, some tasks can be started, such as packing one stage while the crowd's attention is elsewhere. Crowd management at this time is vital because the event management is responsible for the crowd's safety as people leave the venue and make their way home. It is wise to include this issue in the risk management plan. If some members of the crowd want to 'party on', it is smart to plan for this intention well ahead of time so that it can be either countered or allowed to continue safely. Some of the local discos and hotels may welcome the increase in patrons, if told beforehand.

Crowd dispersal

- ☐ Exits/transport
- ☐ Safety
- ☐ Related to programming
- ☐ The dump and staggered entertainment

Equipment

- ☐ Bump-out schedule, including correct exits and loading docks
- ☐ Shutdown equipment using specialist staff (for example, computers)
- ☐ Clean and repair
- ☐ Store — number boxes and display contents list
- ☐ Sell or auction
- ☐ Small equipment and sign-off
- ☐ Schedule for dismantling barricades

Entertainment

- ☐ Farewell appropriately
- ☐ Payments — cash
- ☐ Thank-you letters/awards/ recommendations

Human resources

- ☐ The big 'thank you'
- ☐ Final payments
- ☐ Debrief and next year
- ☐ Reports
- ☐ Celebration party

Liability

- ☐ Records
- ☐ Descriptions
- ☐ Photo
- ☐ Video

On-site/staging area

- ☐ Cleaning
- ☐ Back to normal
- ☐ Environmental assessment
- ☐ Lost and found
- ☐ Idiot check
- ☐ Site/venue hand-over

Contractors

- ☐ Contract acquittal
- ☐ Thank you

Finance

- ☐ Pay the bills
- ☐ Finalise and audit accounts — best done as soon after the event as possible (the following day or week)
- ☐ Thank donor and sponsors

Marketing and promotion

- ☐ Collection of media clippings/video news
- ☐ Reviews of the event — use a service?
- ☐ Market research on community reaction

Sponsors and grants

- ☐ Acquit grants and complete reports — don't be placed on the D list of funding bodies!
- ☐ Meet sponsors and enthuse for next time

Government and politics

- ☐ Thanks to services
- ☐ Reports to council and other government organisations

Client

- ☐ Glossy report, video, photos
- ☐ Wrap-up and suggestions for next time

FIGURE 15.15 Event shutdown checklist

The site may look empty after the event, but the experienced event manager knows that the work has only just begun. The equipment needs to be collected, repaired and stored, or immediately returned to its owners. Small equipment such as hand-held radios are easily lost, so many events have a sign-on/sign-off policy for these items. With large crowds, you can almost guarantee there will be an assortment of lost items. A member of staff needs to walk the site to check whether anything has been left behind — called the 'idiot check' in the music industry. At this point, the event manager realises the value of a torch!

As the site is being shut down, it may also be prepared for the next event. This is a consideration for all the other resources. The equipment may be packed away so it can be easily found and used for the next event. Shutdown thus has a further element: preparation for the next event. Extensive site clean-up is also often required, as detailed in the following event profile.

event profile

CLEAN-UP

For the organisers of Sydney's annual Gay and Lesbian Mardi Gras, site clean-up is a major task. Hundreds of thousands of people line the streets to watch the Mardi Gras parade each February or early March, requiring significant crowd control measures and leaving a lot of rubbish behind when they leave.

Rubbish removal, particularly the removal of broken glass, is a significant problem. A study of the Sydney Mardi Gras found that one small section of the roadway took more than two hours to clean. To make matters worse, some local residents put their own household rubbish out on the street, including old fridges and lounge suites, believing that a general council clean-up was in progress and that it was a good opportunity to get rid of unwanted items. One year, more than 15 000 plastic milk crates were collected, requiring significant labour and time and three semi-trailers. Given the size of the crowds, crowd control barriers are used extensively. The collection of the barriers after the event is a major shutdown exercise, requiring 16 trucks and 63 staff in a closely controlled operation.

The clean-up staff are carefully coached on how to deal with the public. The intoxicated nature of many people in the crowd is just one of the problems.

Dennis Wheeler, Event project management system (CD-ROM)

The shutdown of an event is the prime security time. The mix of vehicles, movement of equipment and general feeling of relaxation provides a cover for theft. The smooth flow of traffic leaving an event at its conclusion must also be considered. Towing services and the police may need to be contacted.

Very large events may require the sale of facilities and equipment at a post-event auction. Some events in Australia find that it is more cost-effective to buy or make the necessary equipment and sell it after the event. Finally, it is often left to the person in charge of logistics to organise the final thank-you party for the volunteers and staff.

Back at the event office, there will be at least a few weeks of project closure. This will include acquitting all the contracts, paying the bills and collecting all the records of the event, media clippings and any incident report sheets. These records will assist when all the reports have to be prepared and any funding is acquitted.

Although the next step may not be the responsibility of the person in charge of logistics, the event logistics manager will have an important role. The event is not over until the management of the event has been assessed (chapter 6). The logistics plan is part of the overall event project plan, so has to be assessed for its effectiveness. It cannot be assessed unless there are written documents or files to compare against the reality of the event logistics. It will be difficult, if not impossible, to suggest real improvements for the next event without these. Too often, in the rush to the next event, the logistics problems are forgotten. The event management produces not just the event, but also a way in which to manage the event.

Checklists are an example of a logistics management system. They represent the micro-management of the event. In the past, many events would have discarded these checklists after the event, yet the checklist is a portable tool — for example, the ticket checklist is common to all events, so it can easily be adapted to a checklist for invitations to a charity event.

In placing the checklist as part of a project management system, O'Toole (2010) states:

> An example of an essential tool or technique that arises from the special circumstances of events (such as the overriding importance of the deadline, temporary organisation, unquantified objectives, the wow factor, variety of work cultures) is the common use of the checklist -also called a prompt list. The advantages of a using these lists are:
>
> - a common method easily understood by just about all staff and volunteers regardless of their experience
> - an effective way to control and monitor any of the event management processes
> - able to be changed quickly — created, added to, edited or deleted — according to the circumstances
> - they introduce management by project. Each task on the checklist is a microproject.
> - a recording of the event process on a micro scale. The checklist can be used in future events.

TECHNIQUES OF LOGISTICS MANAGEMENT

The tools used in business and military logistics can be successfully adapted to event logistics. Because an event takes place at a specific time and specific place, the tools of scheduling and mapping are used. The dynamic nature of events and the way that the functional areas are so closely linked mean a small change in one area can result in crucial changes throughout the event. The incorrect placement of an electric generator, for example, can lead to a mushrooming of problems. If the initial problem is not foreseen or immediately solved, it can grow to affect the whole event. This gives initial negotiations and ongoing assessment a special significance in event logistics. The logistics manager needs to be skilled in identifying possible problem areas and needs to know what is *not* on the list.

We will now consider the role of logistics managers and their relation to the other functional areas and managers of an event.

The event logistics manager

As mentioned throughout this chapter, the logistics manager has to be a procurer, negotiator, equipment and maintenance manager, personnel manager, map maker, project manager and party organiser. For a small event, logistics can be the direct responsibility of the event manager. Logistics becomes a separate area if the event is large and complex. Multi-venue and multi-day events usually require a separate logistics manager position.

Part of the role of the logistics manager is to efficiently link all areas of the event. Figure 15.16 shows the lines of communication between the logistics manager and other managers for a large, complex, multi-venue event. It is a network diagram because, although the event manager or director has ultimate authority, decision-making authority is usually devolved to the submanagers who work at the same level of authority and responsibility as the event manager.

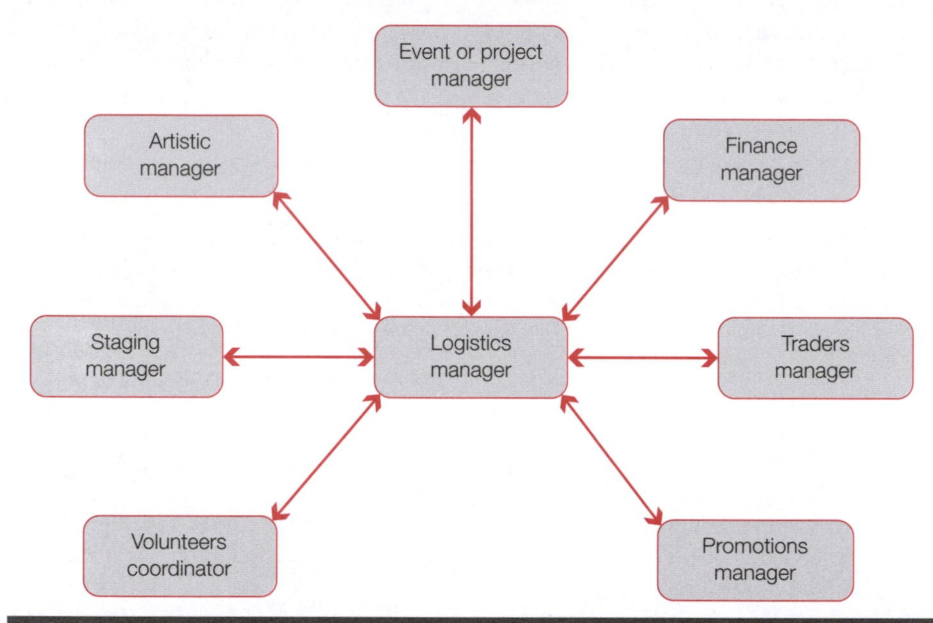

FIGURE 15.16 The lines of communication between the logistics manager and other managers for a multi-venue event

The information required by the logistics manager from the other festival managers is shown in table 15.1. Clear communication between managers in this network is also partly the responsibility of the logistics manager. Many of the tools and techniques of the logistics manager are discussed in chapter 9.

TABLE 15.1 Information required by the logistics manager from the other festival managers

Position	General role	Information sent to logistics manager
Artistic director	Selection of, and negotiation with, artists	Travel, accommodation, staging and equipment requirements
Staging manager	Selection of, and negotiation with, subcontractors	Sound, lights and backstage requirements and programming times
Finance director	Overseeing of budgets and contracts	How and when funds will be approved and released and the payment schedule
Volunteers coordinator	Recruitment and management of volunteers	Volunteers selected and their requirements (for example, parking, free tickets)
Promotions manager	Promotion during the event	Requirements of the media and VIPs
Traders manager	Selection of suitable traders	Requirements of the traders (for example, positioning, theming, electricity, water, licence agreements)

Figure 15.17 shows an example of a job advertisement for a project management position involving logistics.

FIGURE 15.17 A job advertisement for a position relating to event logistics

LOGISTICS OPERATIONS MANAGER

Overview

Rugby World Cup is the third largest sports event in the world. The inaugural tournament took place in 1987 and it is held every four years. In 2007 the tournament was held in France and enjoyed a cumulative worldwide audience of over three billion.

Rugby World Cup 2011 (RWC 2011) will take place in New Zealand over a seven week window in September and October 2011 with the Final held at Eden Park on Labour Day weekend 22–23 October, 2011.

As part of its '*Stadium of Four Million*' promise, RNZ 2011 is working with regions and communities throughout New Zealand to play host to the 20 teams. Thirteen venues have been chosen to host pool matches. The semi-finals, Bronze Final (play-off for third and fourth place) and the Final will be held in Auckland, with Wellington and Christchurch each hosting two quarter-final matches. The team bases were confirmed toward the end of 2009, with 23 cities and towns due to hold teams over the course of the Tournament.

RNZ 2011 now requires a **Logistics Operations Manager**, a unique opportunity to be part of the team that will shape and deliver New Zealand's largest ever sporting event.

The role

The Logistics Operations Manager will initially be working with management and functional areas to complete the freight and logistics delivery plan through a detailed scoping of requirements for venues, teams, training grounds, operation centres and other Tournament locations. Subsequently the role will involve the procurement of relevant suppliers whilst working alongside the legal and finance teams.

During Rugby World Cup 2011, the Logistics Operations Manager will manage a team of staff and volunteers to ensure effective operational delivery. This will include monitoring delivery standards of key suppliers, managing issues with key stakeholders and, where necessary, hands on problem solving. Finally, the role will put in place effective strategies for disposing of surplus equipment post-Tournament.

The successful candidate will have significant experience in a related role preferably within an international event operations or multi site logistical environment. Project management experience is essential, as is experience with contract management and working with a wide variety of stakeholders. Advanced computer skills, including knowledge of MS Project, is also required to be able to do the role effectively.

This is a chance to be involved with one of the largest sporting events that that New Zealand will ever see. If you have what it takes, we would like to hear from you.

Key results areas

	Expected performance outcomes
Freight	• Work with the relevant functional areas and management to scope and prepare the freight and logistics delivery plan for the Tournament • Coordinate the Freight RFP and appointment process including preparation of the RFP responses for the purpose of evaluation by the Senior Management team

FIGURE 15.17 *(continued)*

	Expected performance outcomes
Freight	• Manage the operational delivery of an appropriate strategy that provides for an effective and cost efficient against the freight delivery plan • Manage the operational planning and delivery of freight requirements • Manage any support provision with delivery stakeholders including border control agencies • Effectively link International to New Zealand to Hotel to Venue movements for Teams
Logistics	• Provide operational management and planning for logistics including: – Initiate a programme to scope, refine and place functional area and external stakeholder FF&E requirements accounting for budget and site (Venue) constraints – Plan and deliver the operational logistics strategy considering scale, time, manpower, stakeholder priorities and security requirements – Create an effective operational link between any appointed Freight provider and logistics teams – Establish contingency plans and risk mitigation strategies to ensure continuity of delivery during Tournament time – Plan post Tournament bump out and return/disposal of FF&E as appropriate • Manage support to/from external groups including Venues, Regional Groups, IMG and RWCL
Strategic direction, planning and budget	• Assist in the identification of key issues and relationships relevant in achieving strategic and operational goals • Assist in the preparation of the annual budget process • Monitor budget results on a monthly basis, comparing actual against budget and forecasts, noting major variances, supplying explanations and recommending corrective action
Business excellence	• Assist in the proposal and tendering processes to appoint key suppliers and in selecting providers for specialist pieces of work required • Ensure best practice processes are in place to support structures, strategies and operations to promote, manage and control the resources and activities of RNZ 2011 • Assist in the identification and implementation of all legal, statutory and contractual requirements for the organisation in order to achieve the objectives of the tournament • Display sound judgment and decision making capability • Contribute to the development of a culture of innovation, achievement and commitment to business outcomes
Staff management	• Provide support and direction for staff to enable them to achieve agreed KPIs • Ensure training and development initiatives are introduced which are relevant in improving performance and efficiency • Oversee the planning, execution and supervision of projects undertaken by the operations support

FIGURE 15.17 *(continued)*

General	• Provide high quality customer service to all parties, internal and external • Undertake other duties/Projects as determined by the Senior Management team to meet organisation objectives

Reporting relationships:

This job reports to: Hospitality and Logistics Manager
This job's direct reports are: Logistics Coordinators (to be appointed)

Key relationships will include:

Internal
VIP Manager
Accreditation Manager
Match Services Manager
Team Services Manager
Ticketing Manager
Finance Manager
Programme Manager
ICT Manager
Human Resources Manager

External
Stadia and Venues
Sponsors hospitality managers (IMG)
Related Sponsors (Heineken, MasterCard)
Suppliers
Community Representatives
Boarder control agencies

Attributes, qualifications and experiences considered desirable for the role

The following is a list of desirable attributes, qualifications, skills and experiences:

Qualifications and experience	• Tertiary qualification(s) preferred • At least 3 years experience in related environment • Relevant exposure to international sporting events and a range of international venues • Advanced knowledge of Microsoft Project, Word, Excel, PowerPoint • Good working knowledge of email systems, internet and other forms of technology • Project management experience • Experience working with a wide variety of stakeholders and the ability to communicate
Personal attributes	• Excellent people skills, able to adopt a variety of approaches to interact professionally with a variety of people and requests • Excellent organisational skills, able to juggle conflicting priorities professionally and cope effectively under pressure • Ability to work well within a team and build successful working relationships

FIGURE 15.17 *(continued)*

Personal attributes	• Strong customer service orientation • Willingness to take ownership and be held accountable • Ability to be an independent-thinker and contribute to the decision making process • Excellent communication skills, written and oral • Good sense of humour and high energy levels • Good initiative and flexibility • Sound business acumen • Ability to resolve problems with minimum impact • Awareness of confidential nature of material • Willingness to go the extra mile when required

Source: Rugby New Zealand 2011 Ltd.

Site or venue map

A map of the event site or venue is a necessary communication tool for the logistics manager. For small events, even a simple map can be an effective tool that obviates the need for explanations and can quickly identify possible problem areas. The map for larger festivals can be an aerial photograph with the logistic features drawn on it. For smaller events, it may be a sketch map that shows only the necessary information to the customer. The first questions to ask are 'What is the map for?' and 'Who will be reading it?'. A logistics site map contains very different information from that on the site map used for promotional purposes. The map needs to filter information that is of no interest to the logistics plan. Monmonier (1996, p. 25), in his highly respected work on mapping, summarises this concept:

> A good map tells a multitude of little white lies; it suppresses truth to help the user see what needs to be seen. Reality is three-dimensional, rich in detail, and far too factual to allow a complete yet uncluttered two-dimensional scale model. Indeed, a map that did not generalize would be useless. But the value of a map depends on how well its generalized geometry and generalized content reflect a chosen aspect of reality.

The three basic features of maps — scale, projection and the key (showing the symbols used) — have to be adapted to their target audience. Volunteers and subcontractors, for example, must be able to clearly read and understand it. The communication value of the site map also depends on where it is displayed. Some festivals draw the map on the back of the ticket or program.

The checklist for items to be included on a site map can be very detailed. Figure 15.18 shows a standard checklist of the logistics site map for a small festival.

For a recent event in outback New South Wales, a sketch map on the ticket showed how to find the site, parking and the location of facilities. Next to the map was a list detailing the behaviour expected of event participants. The festival site map could be used by volunteers, staff, performers and all other personnel at the event. For corporate events, a simple map of the venue at the entrance, showing the location of seating, toilets, food areas and the bar, can relieve the staff of having to answer a lot of questions!

- ☐ Scale and direction (north arrow)
- ☐ A list of symbols used on the map (key)
- ☐ Entrance and exits
- ☐ Roads and parking
- ☐ Administration centre
- ☐ Information booths
- ☐ First-aid and emergency road access
- ☐ Lost children area
- ☐ Electricity and water outlets
- ☐ Toilets
- ☐ Food and market stalls
- ☐ Tents and marquees
- ☐ Equipment storage areas
- ☐ Off-limit areas and danger spots (for example, creeks, blind corners)
- ☐ Green room
- ☐ Maintenance area
- ☐ Pathways
- ☐ Telephones
- ☐ Automatic teller machines
- ☐ Media area

FIGURE 15.18 Site map checklist

NEGOTIATION AND ASSESSMENT

No matter what the size of the event, mutual agreement on supply and conditions is vital. In particular, the special but changing nature of one-off events requires the logistics manager to master the techniques of dynamic negotiation. In his work on negotiation and contracts, Marsh (1984, p. 1) defines negotiation as:

> a dynamic process of adjustment by which two parties, each with their own objectives, confer together to reach a mutually satisfying agreement on a matter of common interest.

Logistical considerations need to be covered by the initial negotiations with subcontractors. Agreement on delivery and removal times are an indispensable part of the timelines, because they form the parameters of the critical path.

The management of special events in Australia is a dynamic industry. The special nature of many events means initial negotiations cannot cover many aspects. Decisions and agreements thus need to be continually reassessed. Both parties to the agreement have to realise that the agreement needs to be flexible. However, all possible problems have to be considered at the beginning and there are logistics tools to enable this to happen.

Having prepared the schedules and site map, an important tool to use is what Pagonis (1992, p. 194) describes as the skull session:

> Before implementing a particular plan, I usually try to bring together all of the involved parties for a collective dry run. The group includes representatives from all appropriate areas of the command, and the goal of the skull sessions is to identify and talk through all the unknown elements of the situation. We explore all possible problems that could emerge, and then try to come up with concrete solutions to those problems. Skull sessions reduce uncertainty, reinforce the interconnection of the different areas of specialisation, encourage collaborative problem solving, and raise the level of awareness as to possible disconnects [sic] in the theatre.

Goldblatt (1997) calls this gap analysis. Gap analysis is studying the plan to identify gaps that could lead to a weakening in the implementation of the logistics plan. Goldblatt recommends using a critical friend to review the plan to look for gaps in logical thinking.

The identification of risk areas, gaps and 'what ifs' is important in the creation of a contingency plan. At the Woodford Folk Festival, which takes place in the hottest months of the year in Queensland, the supply of water was identified as a priority area and a contingency plan was created for a viable alternative. This included having water carts on call and making sure the nearest water pipe was available to the general public.

CONTROL OF EVENTS LOGISTICS

The monitoring of the logistics plan is a vital part of the overall control of an event. An important part of the plan is the identification of milestones — times by which crucial tasks have to be completed. The Gantt chart (chapter 6) can be used to compare projected performance with actual performance by recording performance times on the chart as the tasks occur. It is a simple monitoring device.

The aim of the logistics manager is to create a plan to enable the logistics to flow without the need for active control. The use of qualified subcontractors with experience in events is the only way in which to make this happen. This is where the annual festival, with its established relationship with suppliers, has an advantage over the one-off, innovative event. The objective of the director of the Port Fairy Folk Festival, for example, was to enjoy the festival without having to intervene in any on-site problems!

EVALUATION OF LOGISTICS

The ultimate evaluation of the logistics plan is the success of the event and the easy flow of event supply and operations. However, the festival committee, the event director and/or the sponsors may require a more detailed evaluation. The main question to ask is whether the logistics met their objectives. If the objectives as set out in the plan are measurable, then this task is relatively straightforward. If the objectives require a qualitative approach, then the evaluation can become imprecise and open to many interpretations.

An evaluation enables the logistics manager to identify problem areas, thus enabling improvement and adding value to the next event (this topic is discussed further in chapter 16). Techniques used in evaluation are:

- quantitative — a comparison of performance against measurable objectives (sometimes called benchmarking)
- qualitative — discussion with stakeholders.

The term 'logistics audit' is used for a systematic and thorough analysis of the event logistics. Part of the audit concerns the expectations of the audience and whether they were satisfied.

For very large events, the evaluation of the logistics may be contained in the overall evaluation that is put out to tender. The Australian Department of Foreign Affairs and Trade launched a multidimensional promotion of Australia in India. It included a series of events throughout India, ranging from trade shows to cultural activities. The logistical problems of such a varied event spread over a large area in a foreign country with a huge population are many. The evaluation report on this promotion was mostly concerned with the business outcomes, but large sections were concerned with the logistics. The participants evaluated areas such as travel, communication and accommodation. Other areas of logistics were 'evaluated' by the event organisers as they were unseen by the participants and, therefore, deemed a success. As a result of the security measures put in place, for example, there were no terrorist activities during the promotion. (The day after the promotion finished, a train was blown up.)

THE LOGISTICS OR OPERATIONS PLAN

Whether the event is a school class reunion or a multi-venue festival, a written logistics plan needs to be part of the communication within the event. It could range from a one-page contact list with approximate arrival times, to a bound folder covering all areas. The folder for a large event would contain:

- a general contact list
- a site map
- schedules, including timelines and bar charts
- the emergency plan
- subcontractor details, including all time constraints
- on-site contacts, including security and volunteers
- evaluation sheets (sample questionnaires).

All of these elements have been described and discussed in this chapter. They can make up the event manual that is used to stage the event. The manual needs to be a concise document because it may need to be used in an emergency. An operation manual may be used only once, but it has to be able to withstand the rigours of the event. Some organisations, particularly in the exhibition industry, have a generic manual on their intranet that can be adapted for all their events in any part of the world.

Although we emphasise the importance of planning, over-planning can be a significant risk, particularly with the special event, because there is often a need to respond to and take opportunities when they arise. Artistry and innovation can easily be hampered by a purely mechanical approach to event creation. As pointed out in the Marine Corps' publication *Logistics* (1997):

> To deal with disorder, the logistics system must strive for balance. On the one hand, it must estimate requirements and distribute resources based on plans and projections; otherwise the needed support will never be available where and when it is required. On the other, a system that blindly follows schedules and procedures rapidly loses touch with operational realities and inhibits rather than enables effective action.

SUMMARY

Military logistics is as old as civilisation itself. Business logistics is a recent science. Event logistics has the advantage of building on these areas, using the tools of both and continually improving on them as the event industry in Australia grows. Event logistics provides a framework to manage the operations of the event.

The event logistics system can be broken down into the procuring and supply of customers, products and facilities. Once on site, the logistics system concerns the flow around the site, communication and requirements of the event. At the conclusion of the event, logistics relate to breaking down structures, cleaning and managing the evacuation of the site or venue.

For small events, logistics may be the responsibility of the event manager. However, for larger events, a logistics manager may be appointed. Their role within the overall event management was described earlier and their relationship with other managers is vital. The logistics of an event needs to be treated as any other area of management and have in-built evaluation and ongoing control. All of these elements are placed in a plan that is a part of the overall event plan.

Logistics is an invisible part of events. It enables customers to focus completely on the event without being distracted by unnecessary problems. It becomes visible only when it is looked for or when there is a problem. It enables the paying customer, the public, the client or the sponsor to realise and even exceed their expectations.

QUESTIONS

1 Logistics and operation are two terms that are often used together with reference to special events. Discuss the difference between them.
2 Checklists are used by most event teams. Compile a checklist for the following aspects of event management (the best way to do this is to imagine that someone else will be undertaking each task using the checklist):
   - registration
   - power
   - lighting
   - advertising
   - volunteers
   - site inspection (on the day of the event)
   - equipment needed (by the event organiser, on the day of the event)
   - parking
   - artists needs (such as accommodation and transport).
3 Set out an emergency plan for a small event.
4 List the logistics tasks for:
   (a) a graduation ceremony for 2000 people
   (b) the launch of a new property development in a foreign country
   (c) an environmental awareness concert.
5 Discuss the significance of a service road or cleared pathway at a public festival.
6 It is often remarked that the best logistics staff come from the military. What are the differences in military logistics and event logistics? What are the advantages of hiring staff with military experience?

case study

BREAKFAST ON THE BRIDGE: ON-THE-DAY LOGISTICS

Breakfast on the Bridge was a free public event that occurred on 25 October 2009 as part of the final weekend of a food and lifestyle themed festival called 'Crave Sydney'. The public was invited to share a picnic on the iconic Sydney Harbour Bridge. It was estimated that the event would cost approximately $1 million and generate more than $10 million worth of publicity for Sydney worldwide.

It may be described as a whimsical event — laying grass on a major bridge so that 6000 people could enjoy a breakfast; however, the event generated enormous positive community engagement and publicity for Sydney. At the event's media launch the then Premier of NSW, the honourable Nathan Rees, said the bridge was 'closed for traffic, open for breakfast'.

The event involved a number of concepts and logistical issues that are outlined in this case study.

The concept

The core of the event was the concept of a picnic. It was envisaged that people would arrive in family groups and with friends, and share a picnic on the grass with music and food, on the bridge that links the two sides of Sydney. The bridge is rarely closed to traffic and this occasion was a world first.

The grass

Originally the event was envisioned as a sit-down breakfast, similar to café style seating with tables, chairs and waiters. However, the logistical problems of doing this style of service could not be solved within the time window of the allowed 12 hours of bridge closure. The picnic concept was the next model to be considered. The creative director suggested it be held on real grass. Initially there was scepticism about whether this would work; in particular, the event team was concerned that the bridge is long, the grass could create problems by leaving dirt on the bridge deck, the time period allowed for the event was short and the physical access to the bridge is narrow. Despite these perceived challenges, the organisers decided to consult experts in the laying of turf.

The specialist turf company involved in World Youth Day had experience laying grass and flooring on a large scale, to a strict deadline. After examining the site, they convinced the event team that it could be done, estimating the amount of grass required and explaining how it could be laid to meet the deadlines. Tests were undertaken to ensure it would work. These included rolling out and rolling up smaller areas of grass (500 metres) in a car park. The effort and time taken was multiplied up to the full 10 500 square metres of grass. From these tests and formulas, the company identified that it would be quicker to use manual labour to roll up the turf at the conclusion of the event, within the allocated time of two hours. On the day the team used machines to lay the rolls of turf — starting at both ends of the bridge simultaneously and rolling inward — and manual labour to roll it up — starting from the centre and working outwards. After the event the grass was not wasted; it went to some of Sydney's parks and golf courses.

The site

The Sydney Harbour Bridge consists of eight lanes for traffic, two walkways and two train lines. The average number of vehicles to cross the bridge is approximately 180 000 per day. Although the event took place on a Sunday, it posed a disruption to regular traffic, so the logistical time frame was arranged to be as narrow as possible. Only six of the lanes were used for the picnic. Lane seven was used to house the services, facilities and temporary infrastructure, including grey portable toilets, the audio system, cabling, fencing and the food distribution on the day. The service lane had to be bumped in and set up as the turf was being laid on the six lanes. All of this had to be completed between midnight and 4 am. Lane eight was reserved for emergency access.

A major incident occurred at 3 am during the set up of the site. A speeding car pursued by police had broken through the barriers at the northern end of the bridge and drove through the site. It sped down the grassed lanes and contractors and other workers managed to get out of the way. It was eventually chased into Hyde Park at the southern end of the bridge, crashing down the stairs. The two occupants were arrested.

The crowds

The event site is 35 times longer than it is wide. Six thousand people had to be loaded into the space and it was crucial that they feel comfortable; if the crowd felt penned in, it would defeat the purpose of the picnic. The approximate schedule for managing the crowd was: open the bridge at 6.30 am, load the crowd by 7 am, picnic until 8.30 am, and exit the crowd by 9 am. Thereafter the schedule included removing the grass by 11 am – 12 pm and opening the road by 12 pm – 1 pm. The event team invested a lot of effort in planning the crowd management, developing scenarios and testing them. They had many meetings with internal staff, security and safety officials with crowd management qualifications. The creative director pressed for an elegant solution, befitting the design of the event. One of the proposals was that the crowd walk down the centre of the bridge and find a spot to picnic. However, it was thought that this would probably result in people stopping in the middle of the space and, as there was only one entrance to the bridge, it would produce problems with the flow of the people. The solution was to divide the site into 17 numbered areas called pods. As the people arrived they were given a white card with the number of their pod. The event had over 40 marshals dressed as cricket umpires and around 100 volunteers dressed in cricket uniforms, who ushered the people to their numbered area.

Managing the crowd's exit was achieved using broadcasted announcements by cricket star Richie Benaud over the sound system. On the day the exit of the crowd presented no problems. They started moving by 8.30 am and, as the project manager commented, 'We had happy music playing, they'd had a good time and they literally skipped off the site'.

The cows

One of the more unusual sights to greet the crowd was a number of dairy cows. This was part of the original concept of a regional themed fete at the entrance of the picnic ground. The event organisers had envisaged distributing food gifts from regional NSW to the crowd as they arrived, such as yoghurt, apples, bread and jam. The cows were intended to show people where the produce originated. At the planning meetings, however, it was decided that handing out products at the entrance would cause crowd flow problems, so the distribution points were repositioned and products were handed out once people were seated. The cows stayed and the oddness of it all — 'cows on the bridge' — created a lot of media interest.

The rain

On the day of the event, it rained heavily. At 11.30 am, after the crowd had left and the street sweepers were cleaning, and the rain helped to clean the bridge after the event.

Breakfast on the Bridge was a world first. No city in the world has closed its major bridge, laid it with fresh turf and hosted a breakfast. The combination of creative ideas and the restrictions on the logistics produced an event that generated media coverage around the world, including the front page of the national paper in the Kingdom of Saudi Arabia.

Alastair Lyall, Project Manager Special Events, Community Engagement and Events, NSW Premier's Department.

Questions

1 Why were the toilets painted grey?

2 Why were the volunteers and marshals dressed in cricket uniforms?

3 Why were machines used to lay the turf and people for the rolling up of the turf?

4 What other techniques could be used to move the crowd off the site?

REFERENCES

Birch, R 2004, *Master of ceremonies*, Allen & Unwin, Sydney.

Events Ballarat 2004, *City of Ballarat event planning guide*, 2nd edn, www.ballarat.vic.gov.au.

FSANZ 2007, 'Introduction to the New Food Safety Standards', Food Standards Australian New Zealand, July, www.foodstandards.gov.au.

Goldblatt, J 1997, *Special events: best practices in modern event management*, 2nd edn, Van Nostrand Reinhold, New Jersey.

Government of Victoria 2004, *Event management: planning guide for event managers in Victoria*, Melbourne.

KIES 2009, 'Workshop', Kampala International Events Summit, http://kies.co.ug.

Logistics World 2010, www.logisticsworld.com.

Marine Corps 1997, *Logistics*, doctrinal publication no. 4, www.doctrine.quantico.usmc.mil.

Marsh, PDV 1984, *Contract negotiation handbook*, 2nd edn, Gower Press, Aldershot, England.

Monmonier, M 1996, *How to lie with maps*, 2nd edn, University of Chicago Press, Chicago.

O'Toole, W 2010, EPMS CDROM 2nd edn, www.epms.net.

Pagonis, Lt General WG 1992, *Moving mountains: lessons in leadership and logistics from the Gulf War*, Harvard Business School Press, Boston.

Rigby, N 2005, pers. comm.

RTA 2006, *Guide to traffic and transport management for special events*, Version 3.4, New South Wales, www.rta.nsw.gov.au.

Rugby New Zealand 2011 Ltd 2010, 'Logistics operations manager position overview', www.rugbyworldcup.com.

Sonder, M 2004, *Event entertainment and production*, John Wiley & Sons, New York.

Tum, J, Norton, P & Wright, JN 2005, *Management of Event Operations* Elsevier, London.

US Department of Transportation 2003, *Managing travel for planned special events*, Federal Highway Administration, Washington.

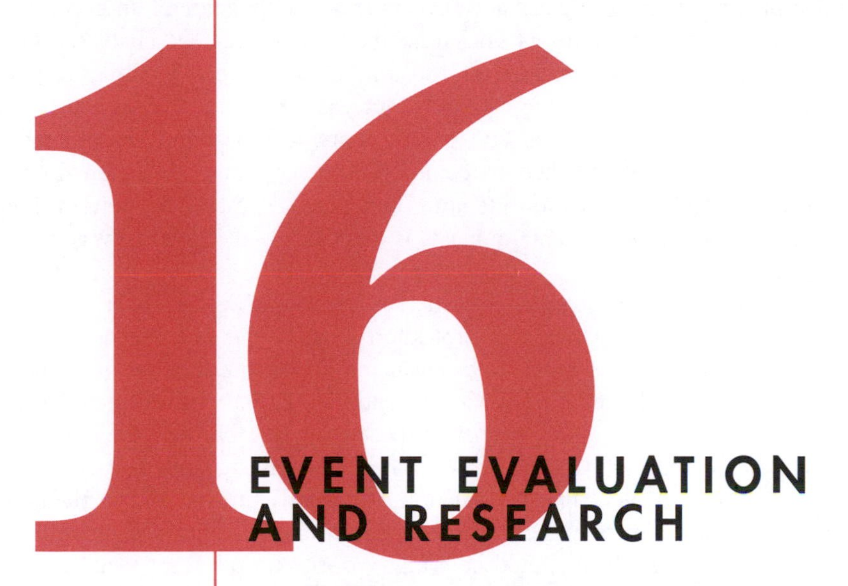

EVENT EVALUATION AND RESEARCH

LEARNING OBJECTIVES

After studying this chapter, you should be able to:

1. describe the role of evaluation in the event management process
2. discuss the nature and purpose of post-event evaluation
3. understand and discuss the evaluation needs of event stakeholders
4. identify and use a range of sources of data on events
5. create an evaluation plan for an event
6. apply a range of techniques, including the design of questionnaires and the conduct of surveys, in evaluating events
7. understand how to analyse data on events
8. prepare a final evaluation report
9. use event profiles to promote the outcomes of events
10. apply the knowledge gained by the post-event evaluation process to the planning of a future event.

INTRODUCTION

Event evaluation is critical to the event management process. It is the final step in the planning process, where the goals and objectives set at the start of an event are used as benchmarks to determine its final outcomes and success. It enables event managers to evaluate their own processes and to communicate event outcomes to key stakeholders. As events become more central to our economy and involve considerable investment by host organisations and governments, it is becoming increasingly important to accurately evaluate their outcomes. While economic evaluation dominates much of the field of evaluation literature and practice, the triple bottom line of economic, social and environmental impacts is increasingly recognised by governments and researchers alike.

Event management is still a young industry and is struggling in some areas to establish legitimacy and acceptance as a profession. One of the best means for the industry to gain credibility is for events to be evaluated honestly and critically, so their outcomes are known, their benefits acknowledged and their limitations accepted. However, event evaluation serves a much deeper purpose than just 'blowing the trumpet' for events. It is at the very heart of the process where insights are gained, lessons are learnt and events are perfected. Event evaluation, if properly utilised and applied, is the key to the continuous improvement of events and to the standing and reputation of the event industry. As such, it should be a high priority for all event managers to properly evaluate their events and to disseminate this evaluation to their stakeholders and interested groups. If done well, this will not only enhance the reputation of their events, but also their own reputation as professional event managers.

WHAT IS EVENT EVALUATION?

Event evaluation is the process of critically observing, measuring and monitoring the implementation of an event in order to assess its outcomes accurately. Evaluation is a continuous process that takes place throughout the life of an event. However, it has three key phases:

- pre-event evaluation, also known as feasibility studies, which takes place before the event in order to ascertain whether it is viable to stage it. This was discussed in chapter 5 under the heading of 'Evaluating the event concept'.
- the monitoring and control process, which takes place during the implementation of the event in order to ensure that it is on track and to take remedial action if required. This process was discussed in chapter 6 on project management and events.
- post-event evaluation, which focuses on the measurement of event outcomes and on ways in which the event can be improved.

This chapter will focus on the post-event evaluation phase and process.

EVENT IMPACTS AND EVALUATION

An important aspect of event evaluation is the calculation of event impacts, both positive and negative, short term and long term, on their stakeholders and the wider host community. This is particularly important for government stakeholders, who are interested in the bigger picture of the impacts of an event on the host city, state or nation, as was discussed in chapter 3. Such assessment will often focus on economic impacts, as governments and funding bodies require evidence of what the event has achieved in relation to the investment of taxpayers' funds. Governments also use such assessments to conduct a cost–benefit analysis in order to compare the outcomes of investment in events with other potential uses of resources. Economic impact studies are also used by governments to prioritise which events to support, as was discussed in the case of UK Sport in chapter 3.

Given this emphasis by government on the economic dimension of events, it is not surprising that the study of economic impacts dominates both evaluation practice and the academic literature on events (Raybould, Fredline, Jago and Deery 2005; Wood, Robinson and Thomas 2006). In a comprehensive review of the academic literature, Sherwood, Jago and Deery (2005) analysed the content of a total of 224 refereed journal articles and event-related conference papers. As might be expected, the most frequent focus was on economic impacts (28.1 per cent), followed by social impacts (19.6 per cent), event management (13.4 per cent) and tourism impacts (12.9 per cent). Only two articles in the study focused on the environmental components of events. The researchers noted a growing unease in host communities with this emphasis on economic evaluation, noting that the failure to adequately address social and environmental impacts may lead to a misrepresentation of the long-term contribution of events to the host community.

A counter-trend has been a growing emphasis on the wider social and cultural impacts of events, highlighting aspects such as social capital (Hilbers 2005), host community perceptions of event impacts (Fredline, Jago and Deery 2005), community engagement in events (Harris 2005) and methods of evaluating social impacts (Wood et al. 2006). Also, the increased awareness of climate change has been reflected in the conduct of events, as well as in the research area. Of the 43 research papers presented at the 2009 International Event Management Research Conference held at Surfers Paradise in Australia, 12 papers (28 per cent) were focused on environmental issues and sustainability, the other main areas being event management (28 per cent), community and culture (16 per cent), event audiences (14 per cent) and legacy (14 per cent). Raybould et al. (2005) have developed a holistic triple-bottom-line approach to the economic, social and environmental impacts of events. They identify key performance indicators in each of the three domains and suggest a technique for examining them holistically by providing a framework for dealing with the inevitable trade-off between positive and negative impacts within the three domains.

For economic impacts, they suggest using traditional indicators such as the net income as a ratio over the expenditure necessary to host the event, the financial yield of visitors and the net benefits per person of the event to the host community. For social impacts, they propose using a range of indicators such as the percentage of locals who attend, volunteer for or are employed by the event; the percentage of local businesses contracted to supply goods and services; the value of access to new facilities developed, or access to facilities denied to locals during the event; crime reported associated with the event; crowd management incidents; traffic counts or dollar value of time lost in traffic; and the quantity and quality of media exposure generated by the event. For environmental impacts, they suggest indicators such as the energy consumed at the venue and in transport to the event, water consumed at the event, waste water recycled, waste generated at the event and waste recycling.

Much work needs to be done to perfect indicators and measurement techniques for each of the three domains, and to find adequate means to document and record them. However, such approaches may ultimately provide a fuller and more accurate evaluation of the impacts of events on their communities.

POST-EVENT EVALUATION

Post-event evaluation is concerned primarily with measuring the success of an event in terms of its objectives by collecting and analysing relevant data from the event. It is also concerned with evaluating the process of organising the event, and feeding back lessons and observations learnt from this into the ongoing event management process. Post-event evaluation can also build up a picture of the event, facilitating the communication of its outcomes to key stakeholders. Van Der Wagen (2001), Shone and Parry (2004) and Silvers (2004) identify a number of important functions of post-event evaluation. These include:

- measurement of event outcomes
- creation of a demographic profile of the event audience
- identification of how the event can be improved
- enhancement of event reputation
- evaluation of event management process.

These functions are further elaborated in the following text.

Measurement of event outcomes

In the planning phase, key goals and objectives are identified in relation to the event. These become important benchmarks, sometimes known as key performance indicators (KPIs), which enable the success of the event to be measured in relation to its outcomes. For example, a community festival may set clear objectives in relation to the number of people attending, the level of audience satisfaction and the financial performance of the event. For major events, the event objectives and the means to measure them may be much more complex, involving benchmarks such as economic impacts, media coverage, tourism outcomes and sponsor benefits. For corporate events, important benchmarks might include levels of staff motivation, product awareness or sales generated. In each case, these are the agreed criteria by which the success of the event will be judged and the evaluation process will need to establish reliable ways to measure them and report back to stakeholders.

Creation of a demographic profile of the event audience

For future planning purposes, it will be useful to establish not only the number of people who attended the event, but also where they came from, how they heard about it and demographic details such as age range, gender, levels of education and income. Establishing an accurate demographic profile of the audience will enable marketing strategies to be refined and the spending of marketing funds to be better targeted.

Identification of how the event can be improved

Another important function of event evaluation is the identification of what worked and what did not, providing a sound basis for improved planning in the case of ongoing events. For example, the Parkes Elvis Festival in the central west of New South Wales conducts an annual survey of visitors to the festival in association with a university research partner. In addition to tourism and demographic information, the survey seeks to obtain opinions of visitors to the festival by asking them what they enjoyed most about the festival and what improvements could be made. The information gained from this study has led to improvements to the festival program and organisation, such as the extension of trading hours of outdoor activities, the upgrading of the festival parade, the improvement of signage and the inclusion of new activities in the program.

Enhancement of event reputation

Capturing and disseminating the achievements of an event can assist greatly in building its reputation and credibility. Thus some events make extensive use of their final reports to gain media exposure and support. This becomes critical when the reputation of an event has been damaged by negative publicity, as was the case when the AIGP withdrew from the Gold Coast Indy in 2009, and additional V8 Supercar races were scheduled to create the Nikon SuperGP event (Jabour 2009). Other events use the reporting of event outcomes to gain public acceptance, as the Sydney Gay and Lesbian Mardi Gras has done by issuing frequent reports of the economic impacts of the event. Governments also report regularly on the economic impacts of major events in order to gain political advantage by demonstrating the benefits of the events as a result of their investment and support.

Evaluation of event management processes

Another key purpose of post-event evaluation is to examine the processes used by the event manager in the planning and conduct of the event. By careful analysis of these processes the event manager will improve not only the outcomes of the event, but also their own skills and techniques in managing it, as was discussed in chapter 6. The use of computers allows the event manual to be reviewed, refined and used for the next incarnation of the event. Important questions to consider are whether the budget and resources were adequate, whether the critical path timeline was sufficient and whether key documents such as marketing, operations and risk management plans, policies and procedures and checklists can be revised and updated for future use. In this way, by evaluating the processes of organising the event, event managers can improve and refine their own professional skills and practices.

KNOWLEDGE MANAGEMENT

This refinement of the skills and practices of event management has led to the development of the field of event knowledge management. The staging of major events and conferences has now become so complex that event managers and organising bodies cannot afford to start from scratch in the planning of events. They must start from what has been learnt from the previous staging and history of the event and build on this to further develop the event's management practices and profile. Multi-sport events such as the Olympic and Commonwealth Games, and individual championships such as the FIFA World Cup and the FINA World Swimming Championships, have developed a formal process for the transfer of knowledge from one event to the next. The International Olympic Committee (IOC) has established the Olympic Games Knowledge Service in Lausanne, Switzerland, responsible for making the expertise gained from previous Olympic Games available to bidding cities and future Olympic host cities. The process was formalised by the payment of A$5 million to the Sydney Organising Committee for the Olympic Games (SOCOG) for the intellectual property of the Sydney Olympics (Halbwirth and Toohey 2005). This process of the transfer of knowledge takes place partly through the documentation of the event and partly through the skills and experience of key event personnel, who become highly sought after because of their successful track record in organising events. Thus many of the Australian personnel from the Sydney Olympic Games have played key roles in Olympics in Athens, Beijing and London; Commonwealth Games in Manchester and Delhi; and Asian Games in Doha and Guangzhou. Major corporate events and conferences now also formalise the transfer of knowledge process, with the development of standard procedures and manuals for their events in order to achieve consistency and to build a body of knowledge and best practice in relation to their events.

Post-event evaluation, then, serves a variety of purposes in relation to events. In addition to assessing event outcomes, it also feeds observations and information back into the event management cycle, leading to a process of continuous improvement (see figure 16.1).

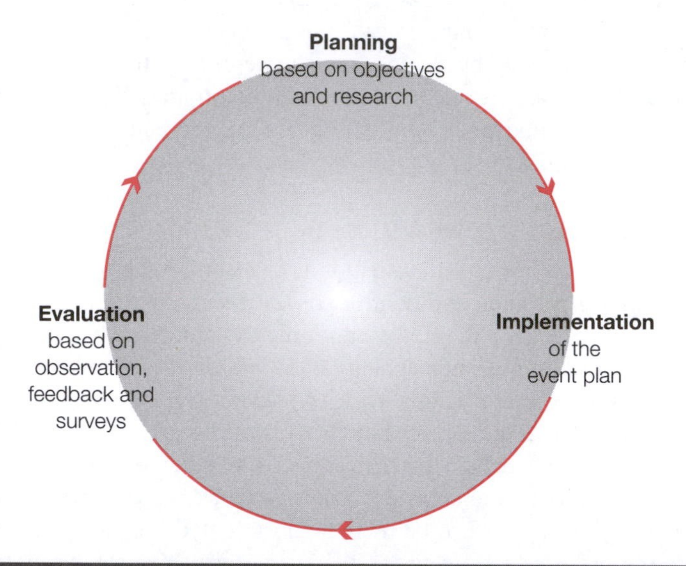

FIGURE 16.1 Evaluation and the event management process

THE EVENT EVALUATION PROCESS

The event evaluation process has five major stages:

- planning and identification of event data required
- data collection
- data analysis
- reporting
- dissemination.

The process must be planned from the outset of the event and will involve the commitment of resources including staff, time and budget. As the collection of data can be expensive, budget will sometimes be a limiting factor in the design of the event evaluation process.

Planning and identification of event data required

The first step is to define the purposes of the evaluation and therefore what data will need to be collected. From the purposes listed above, it is evident that there will often be a number of complementary agendas in relation to the needs of different stakeholders in events:

- The host organisation will want to know what the event achieved. Did the event come in on budget and on time? Did it achieve its objectives? How many people attended and were their expectations met?
- The event sponsor may have other measures. Was the level of awareness of the product or service increased? What penetration did the event advertising achieve?

What media coverage was generated? What was the demographic profile of the people who attended?

- Funding bodies will have grant acquittal procedures to observe and will usually require audited financial statements of income and expenditure, along with a report on the social, cultural or sporting outcomes of the event.
- Councils and government departments may want to know what the impact was on their local or state economies.
- Tourism bodies may want to know the number of visitors attracted to the area and what they spent, not only on the event, but also on travel, shopping and accommodation.

All of these complementary and overlapping agendas must be taken into account in determining the purposes of the evaluation.

Once the purposes of the evaluation have been defined, the data that need to be collected can be identified and listed. These can be grouped into matching areas or subsets; for example, one group of data may relate to attendance and demographic profile, another to audience response and satisfaction levels, another to media coverage and another to sponsor outcomes. The fuller and more specific the identification of data required, the easier it will be to plan the collection of the data.

Qualitative and quantitative data

It is important at this stage to distinguish between two different types of data, both of which will often be involved in the event evaluation process.

Qualitative data are based on individual perceptions and responses and are often obtained through informal and in-depth interviews, focus groups, staff feedback and participant observation. They can provide valuable insights, but are often anecdotal and lend themselves to narrative rather than statistical analysis.

By contrast, quantitative data are measurable and subject to statistical analysis. Data are often collected via methods such as box office receipts, financial records and surveys, and lend themselves to conclusions based on statistical analysis.

Both forms of data can play a valuable role in the event evaluation process, but their use will need to be carefully balanced in order to provide a total picture of the event.

Data collection

Each of the subsets listed above will now require consideration as to how the data are to be collected and analysed. Silvers (2004) and Veal (2006) suggest several main sources of data on events and these are discussed in the following text.

Event documentation

The process of organising the event will provide many opportunities for the collection of significant data.

- *Financial performance* — the event budget and final balance sheet will provide detailed information on income and expenditure, profit or loss of the event. This can be compared with previous costs of staging the event and may require interpretation with regard to variance; for example, downturns in the economy, or currency exchange fluctuations in relation to international events or visiting performers.
- *Paid attendance* — for a ticketed event, box office reports or participant registration lists will generally provide information with regard to event attendance. Ticket sales reports may provide other valuable information such as gender analysis and postcode breakdowns.

- *Crowd size* — for free entry events, police crowd estimates, public transport and car park figures can be helpful in calculating attendance numbers. Other tools such as judging the percentage of the venue filled in relation to its known capacity and photographic surveys taken at regular intervals can help to estimate attendance.
- *Demographic information* — if participants are required to fill in an event registration form, this can be designed so that valuable demographic information is captured, such as age, gender, point of origin and spending patterns.
- *Performance statistics* — an examination of contracts will reveal numbers of performers engaged in, say, a multi-site festival over several days.
- *Merchandise sales* — sales records will provide data on the sale of merchandise and the contribution of these sales to the income of the event.
- *Safety profiles* — accurate recording of occurrences such as first-aid treatments and on-site incidents will help to establish risk management and safety profiles of the event.

These are just some examples of the useful data that can be compiled from the event documentation in order to build up a picture of the event. Organisers of the Australian Masters Games, for example, are required to provide a detailed profile of the event, including the number of participants and their partners, the number and type of competitions/functions that were conducted, the marketing and risk management strategies employed, and detailed statements of income and expenditure. The profiles of previous events are of immense value to the organisers of future Games events.

Media monitoring

Media coverage is an important aspect of an event. This coverage can be either positive or negative, depending on the event outcomes, the impact on the community and the kind of relationship built up with the media. It is important to monitor and record this coverage as part of the event documentation. If the event is local, it may be possible to do this by keeping a file of newspaper articles and by listening and looking for radio and television interviews and news coverage. For larger events, it may be necessary to employ a professional media-monitoring organisation that can track media coverage from a variety of sources. They will usually provide copies of print media stories and transcripts of radio interviews and news coverage. Audiotapes and videotapes of electronic coverage can be obtained for an additional charge. This coverage provides an excellent record of the event and can be used effectively in profiling the event for potential sponsors and partners.

A further issue is content analysis of the media coverage, as this is not always positive. Negative media coverage can impact on the reputation of the event and by implication on stakeholders, such as host organisations and sponsors.

Some media monitors attempt to place a monetary value on positive media coverage, based on the cost of purchasing the equivalent amount of media space and/or time. Such valuations should be regarded as approximate only, but may provide a useful comparative assessment of media coverage. A media evaluation of Floriade 2007, conducted by Media Monitors (see the event profile on pages 504–507), valued the total media coverage of the event at $1 218 615 (Department of Territory and Municipal Services 2008).

Event observation

Another means of collecting data is by structured and detailed observation of the event. This may involve the event manager as well as staff, attendees and key stakeholders in the event.

Management observation

There is no substitute for direct observation of the event (sometimes called 'management by looking around'). Knowing the event and its objectives well, the event manager is in a good position to observe aspects such as general ambience, performance quality, audience response and crowd flow, which can make or break an event from the point of view of participants. They will also be well placed to observe the levels of performance of contractors and staff, and defects in site design or event operations, which may constitute important lessons to be learnt from the event.

Staff observation

Staff members are also in a good position to critically observe the event and their observations and reports may provide information on a number of important aspects of the event. However, staff will provide more accurate and useful data if they are trained to observe these issues and are given a proper reporting format; for example, checklists to evaluate items such as attendance figures, performance quality and audience reaction. Security staff may be required to report on crowd behaviour, incidents, disturbances and injuries.

Stakeholder observation

Other key players in an event, such as venue owners, councils, sponsors, vendors, police and first-aid officers, can often provide valuable feedback from their various perspectives.

- *Venue owners* may be able to compare the performance of the event with their normal venue patterns and comment usefully on matters such as attendance figures, parking, access, catering and facilities.
- *Police* may have observed aspects such as crowd behaviour, traffic flow and parking and may have constructive suggestions for future planning.
- *Councils* may be aware of disturbances to the local community or difficulties with street closures or compliance with health regulations.
- *Sponsors* may have observations based on their own attendance at the event, or may have done their own surveys of audience reaction, awareness levels and media coverage.
- *Vendors* may have information on the volume of sales or the waiting time in queues that will be valuable in planning future catering arrangements.
- *First-aid providers* may provide statistics on the number and seriousness of injuries such as cuts, abrasions or heat exhaustion that will assist in future planning of safety and risk management.

All of these key stakeholders may have observations on general planning issues such as signage, access, crowd management, communication and the provision of facilities that will have implications for improvement of the event. It is important that their observations are recorded and incorporated into the evaluation and planning stages of the event management process.

De-briefing meetings

A valuable opportunity for feedback on the event management process is provided by the de-brief meeting. This should be held as soon as practical after the event, while memory and impressions of the event are still fresh. Staff members, contractors, public authorities such as police and ambulance and other key stakeholders may be invited to the de-brief meeting. For larger events, the process might even be conducted as a series of meetings devoted to individual aspects of the event such as operations and marketing. Participants should be given notice of the meeting prior to the event, so that they are aware that their observations will be welcomed and noted. For the best results, an agenda should be prepared and circulated and the meeting should be carefully chaired and not allowed to ramble or descend into blame or recrimination. A well run de-brief meeting can make a major contribution to the understanding of what went well and what didn't, any significant risk factors that were revealed and any implications for the future improvement of the event.

Focus groups

Focus groups can provide a good opportunity to test participant reactions to an event and to obtain in-depth perceptions of particular stakeholder groups. They are normally directed discussions involving a small group of eight to 12 people with similar demographics, conducted by professional interviewers in a relaxed environment. The event manager or their representative may be an observer and is sometimes hidden by a two-way mirror so as not to intrude on the process. The focus group can provide a detailed, directed discussion and is a useful tool to explore participant attitudes, opinions and motivations.

Surveys

It would be ideal to seek the opinions and responses of all attendees of an event, but for most large events this task would be too costly and impractical. Survey techniques involve seeking the opinions and responses of a representative sample of total attendees in order to obtain vital and accurate data on the event. The better the design of the questionnaire form used and the more rigorous the survey process, the more accurate will be the results obtained.

Surveys can range from simple feedback forms targeting event partners and stakeholders to detailed audience or visitor surveys undertaken by trained personnel. The scale of the survey will depend on the needs and resources of the event. Simple feedback forms can usually be designed and distributed using the event's own internal resources. They may seek to record and quantify basic data, such as the expenditure of event partners, or feedback from local retailers and accommodation providers as to the effect of the event on their levels of business activity.

Surveys are used to ascertain reliable statistical information on audience profiles and opinions and visitor patterns and expenditure. They may be implemented by direct interviews with participants or may rely on participants filling in written questionnaires. They may be undertaken face-to-face, or by telephone, mail or email. Face-to-face interviews will usually generate a higher response rate, but techniques such as a competition with prizes as incentives for participation may improve the response rate of postal or email surveys.

Undertaking effective surveys requires expertise and considerable organisational resources. For event organisers with limited in-house experience and expertise, professional assistance can be called on for tasks, ranging from the design of questionnaire forms to the full implementation of the survey process. Professionally prepared generic templates and questionnaires are also available to assist the event manager in this process — see the model Attendee Survey in *Module 14: Event Management* (NSW Department of State and Regional Development 2009) and the *APEX post-event report template* (Convention Industry Council 2006).

In the case of repeat events, event organisers may wish to repeat the same survey each year in order to compare successive events and to establish trends, or they may want to embark on more ambitious research programs surveying different aspects of the event each year. Whatever the scale and approach that is decided on, experts such as Getz (2005), Jago and Dwyer (2006) and Veal (2006) agree on certain basic factors that should be kept in mind. These are:

- *purpose* — clearly identify the purpose and objectives of the survey. A clearly stated and defined purpose is most likely to lead to a well-targeted survey with effective results.
- *survey design* — keep it simple. If too much is attempted by the survey, there is a danger that focus will be lost and effectiveness reduced. Questions should be clear and unambiguous and should be tested by a pilot study before the actual survey.
- *language* — questions should use a suitable vocabulary and be grouped around topics. Avoid using 'leading' questions that encourage pre-conceived answers, and the use of biased or emotive language.
- *open versus closed questions* — an open question is one that invites the interview subject to answer without prompting a range of responses. A closed question is one where the interview subject is offered a range of answers to choose from, such as rating an item on a scale of 1–5 or on a range of poor to excellent. Open questions can provide a greater opportunity for the respondent to express their opinion, but are harder to quantify. Closed questions are more restricted, but lend themselves to easier coding and analysis. A good questionnaire form should seek an appropriate balance between open and closed questions.
- *size of sample* — the number of participants must be large enough to provide a representative sample of the audience. The sample size will depend on the variability in the population to be sampled, the level of precision required and the available budget. If in doubt, seek professional advice on the size of the sample.
- *randomness* — the methodology employed in the selection of participants must avoid biases of age, sex and ethnicity. A procedure such as selecting every tenth person who passes by a specified point may assist in providing a random selection. With multi-venue and multi-day events, care should also be taken that the survey process is spread evenly across venues and days of the event in order to provide a truly random sample of participants.
- *support data* — the calculation of some outcomes will depend on the collection of support data. The calculation of total visitor expenditure, for example, will require accurate data on the average expenditure of visitors as well as support data on the number of visitors to the event. Then the spending pattern revealed by the survey can be multiplied by the number of visitors to provide an estimate of the total visitor expenditure for the event.

Sample event participant questionnaire

Notice that in the sample questionnaire (see figure 16.2), the first nine questions have been coded so that responses can be readily analysed and the last three questions have been left open to enable respondents to express their opinions. The questionnaire has been designed to be delivered in interview format, though show cards could be used to display the range of choices for questions two to nine.

Secondary data

In addition to the data collected from the above sources, other data may be available, which were collected for some other (primary) purpose, but which may be useful in evaluating some aspect of the event. These are known as secondary data (Veal 2006).

Examples include:

- research bureaus
- web searches
- journal databases.

Hello. I am from the __________ festival. Could you spare a few minutes of your time to answer some questions to help us to improve the festival?

DEMOGRAPHIC

1. Gender: Male Female
2. Can you tell me which of the following age groups you belong to?
   Under 15 15–24 25–44 45–64 65+
3. Where are you from?
   Local (Go to Question 7)
   Elsewhere in the state Interstate Overseas (list country) ________________
4. Who are you travelling with today?
   Travelling alone Couple Family Friends or relatives
   Club, Society Business associates Other __________ specify
5. How many nights are you staying?
6. Where are you staying?
   Hotel/Motel B & B/Guest House Caravan Park/Camping With Friends/Relatives
   Other __________ specify

MARKETING

7. How did you first hear about the festival?
   Brochures/posters Newspaper Radio TV Visitor info centre Internet
   Word of mouth Other __________ specify

ACTIVITIES/BEHAVIOUR

8. How did you travel from your home or place of accommodation to the festival?
   Walked Car Public Transport Other __________ specify
9. What activities have you participated in at the festival?
   Concerts Food stalls Displays Craft tent Games Exhibition

ATTITUDE/MOTIVATION

10. What did you like most about the festival?
    ____
11. What aspects of the festival do you think could be improved?
    ____
12. Are there any additional comments that you wish to make about the festival?
    ____

Thank you for your time and I trust that you enjoy the rest of your time at the festival.

FIGURE 16.2 Event participant questionnaire

Sources: Veal 2006, NSW Department of State and Regional Development 2009.

Research bureaus

There are many public and privately-funded research organisations that will provide access to valuable data either free of charge or for a modest fee. The Australian Bureau of Statistics, for example, produces detailed information on a wide variety of topics, including Australian social trends, census statistics and how Australians spend their leisure time. Their directory of culture and leisure statistics provides useful information on topics such as attendance at cultural venues and events, attendance at arts festivals and children's participation in cultural and leisure activities. The Bureau of Tourism Research produces annual national and international visitor surveys, which provide accurate data on visitor patterns and expenditure on a wide range of activities, including travel, accommodation and attendance at festivals and events.

Web searches

A web search of similar events will produce a surprising amount of data, including how other event managers have approached the issues of event coordination and evaluation. Some will even include copies of their event reports, providing detailed information on event outcomes and impacts.

Resource centres and clearing houses

A number of websites act as clearing houses for the various websites and publications relevant to event management. Examples include Event Management — Resource Links (Australian Centre for Event Management 2010), and WorldofEvents.net based at Leeds Metropolitan University in the UK (www.worldofevents.net 2010), which bring together websites and documents of interest to event students and event management professionals.

Journal databases

Also found on the web are journal databases that will enable event managers to track down research articles in tourism marketing and event-specific journals, which can be of great assistance in researching and evaluating an event. Some of these articles may be accessed directly from the web or through public and university libraries. Articles can be found on a wide range of event issues, including marketing, sponsorship, audience motivation and satisfaction, impacts, risk management, operations and evaluation.

By undertaking a thorough scan of relevant secondary research, event managers can proceed from an informed and knowledgeable position in the creation and implementation of an event evaluation plan.

Data analysis

Much of the data from sources such as event documentation and observation listed above can be analysed manually in order to identify key event outcomes such as attendance and financial results. These data may need some degree of interpretation; for example, by comparing them with stated event objectives, or with similar data from previous events.

Data from surveys will need to be analysed in order to reveal useful statistics and trends. This can be done using a spreadsheet package such as Microsoft Excel, or the Statistical Package for the Social Sciences (SPSS) software package used widely by event and tourism academic researchers. This will enable the calculation of frequencies (for example, what percentage of respondents rated the event as poor, average, good, very good or excellent) and of means or averages of variables such as the average spend by visitors to the event. These packages also enable statistical information to be presented graphically; for example, the use of line graphs, bar charts or pie charts.

If open questions have been used in the survey, these will need to be coded or categorised so that their frequencies can be calculated. They may best be reported using a narrative rather than a statistical format.

Reporting

After the relevant data have been collated and analysed comes the task of writing and preparing the event report. The first consideration is for whom the report is intended. Reviewing the purposes of the evaluation discussed at the beginning of this chapter may prove useful. This may influence the style of writing, the amount of detail and the overall presentation of the report. In some cases a number of versions of the report may have to be prepared for different audiences, such as the host organisation, government, sponsors and the media, though the core of the report will remain constant. Veal (2006) distinguishes between the report as narrative, telling the story of the event and its achievements, and the report as record, creating a formal and definitive account of the event process and outcomes. The narrative will need to be largely descriptive, focusing on key points and interpreting the data to create a cohesive picture of the event. It may be argued that all evaluation is to some degree subjective, but nonetheless the writer should try to reflect the event as accurately as possible, quoting relevant data to support conclusions and assumptions. Quotations from attendees, media reports, photographs and copies of flyers, posters and programs may all help to communicate the flavour and atmosphere of the event.

The function of the report as the record of the event will lend itself to the use of statistics to create an accurate profile of the event, supported by appropriate detail through the use of such devices as tables and graphs. Any outcomes noted, such as economic or tourism impacts, should be supported by a description of the methodology used to evaluate them and the number of survey responses obtained.

Both the narrative and record functions of the event report combine to present a useful basis for reporting to stakeholders and for planning the next event.

Dissemination

The final step in the post-event evaluation process is to disseminate the event report to relevant stakeholder groups. This may be done by face-to-face meetings with key stakeholders such as the host organisation, government and sponsors, where the content of the report can be verbally communicated and discussed. For the host organisation this may represent an important closure and for sponsors it may give rise to a discussion on continued involvement with the event. It is worth considering additional formats of the report, for example a PowerPoint presentation may be prepared for face-to-face presentations, or a media release may be prepared to accompany distribution of the report to the media. If the event report is well written and carefully distributed, it can be an important tool for enhancing the reputation and future prospects of the event.

event profile

FLORIADE

This is an example of an event report compiled by the management of the Floriade national flower and garden festival held in Canberra in 2007, based on event documentation and research commissioned by the event. The strong theme of Aussie icons, myths and legends and professional marketing of the event produced outstanding results, which are documented in the report, a précis of which follows.

Floriade 2007 event report

Floriade, the largest festival of its kind in the southern hemisphere, is managed by Australian Capital Tourism and staged annually on the grounds of Commonwealth Park, Canberra. The theme for

Floriade 2007, staged from 15 September to 14 October, was *Aussie icons, myths & legends*. Over a million bulbs and annuals brought Commonwealth Park to life with blooms of gold, green and every colour in between, over the month-long spring festival.

Evaluation

Attendance

Total attendance at Floriade 2007 was 394 916 — representing a 5.3 per cent increase on the 2006 attendance figure — the highest attendance rate since records began.

Direct expenditure

Floriade 2007 contributed direct expenditure of $20.3 million to the Australian Capital Territory, which, while slightly less than the previous year's expenditure due to a drop in interstate overnight visitation, still demonstrates a significant return on investment to the ACT economy.

Attendees

A total of 109 080 interstate and international visitors came to Canberra specifically for Floriade, or extended their stay because of it. Of the total number of attendees, 46.1 per cent were from the ACT, 53.0 per cent were from interstate and 0.9 per cent were international visitors.

The majority of interstate attendees were from regional New South Wales and Sydney (37.9 per cent and 36.8 per cent of total interstate visitors), along with Queensland (9.3 per cent), Victoria (9.1 per cent) and South Australia (2.6 per cent).

The interstate market represents high value to the local economy, with 55.8 per cent staying overnight and 44.2 per cent visiting Floriade on a day trip.

International and interstate visitors to Floriade visited a variety of Canberra attractions during their trip, including restaurants/cafés (60.5 per cent), the Australian War Memorial (26.4 per cent), Parliament House (17.2 per cent), Nature Reserves/National Parks (14.6 per cent) and the National Museum of Australia (12.7 per cent).

Satisfaction

Attendees to Floriade were generally satisfied with the event, with 98.5 per cent being very satisfied or somewhat satisfied — up slightly from 97.1 per cent in 2006.

Celebrating success

Data from sources other than the official Floriade research indicated a very successful Floriade in 2007.

- 34 748 people visited the Canberra and Region Visitors Centre (CRVC) during Floriade.
- The CRVC recorded strong accommodation sales throughout September and October.
- The Floriade website recorded 64 036 visits during September and October (an increase of 22.5 per cent on 2006), and www.visitcanberra.com.au recorded almost 129 000 visits during the same period.
- Floriade 2007 enjoyed a strong October long weekend, with 72 859 attendees over three days.

Marketing

The *Aussie icons, myths & legends* marketing campaign was a nationally integrated program targeting Sydney, Brisbane, Adelaide, regional New South Wales and Canberra, and incorporating dynamic marketing partnerships.

- Publications included the 2007 Floriade poster, programs, newspaper inserts, website, Aussie Icons Trail maps, postcards and the Essential Guide to Floriade 2007 sold onsite.
- Advertising included television, radio, print advertising, e-marketing, ambient and outdoor advertising.
- A public relations campaign included the distribution of media kits to over 500 media outlets nationwide, high-profile television coverage in Australia, extensive local news coverage across all networks, international crews from Thailand and Hong Kong, an extensive Visiting Journalist Program, and the production of a promotional DVD. The campaign captured the highest ever volume of media coverage of Floriade.

- Promotional launches and events included a Sydney media launch at Taronga Zoo, a Floriade concept launch by seven-time world surfing champion Layne Beachley at the National Museum of Australia, and an opening launch by ACT Tourism Minister Andrew Barr.

Media evaluation

A media evaluation revealed that Floriade 2007 received extensive media coverage including 268 press articles, 710 broadcast summaries including radio and television, and 137 internet alerts between 8 February and 21 October 2007. A Media Analysis Report conducted by Media Monitors reported total media coverage worth $1 218 615, including print, television, radio and internet.

Sponsorship and partnerships

Sponsorship

Floriade 2007 received extensive sponsor support, with ten executive sponsors, 11 premier sponsors, 14 associate sponsors and 31 support sponsors.

Partnerships

Floriade worked with a variety of partners in order to implement the 2007 program. The Aussie Icons Trail, which aims to extend the experience of Floriade beyond the gates of Commonwealth Park, was a partnership with Australian Capital Tourism, and included 14 attractions and 3 travel providers. Apprentices, students, businesses, community groups and schools also contributed to the building, entertainment and running of the festival.

Floriade onsite

The gardens

Over a million tulips, bulbs and annuals in bloom depicted the theme *Aussie icons, myths & legends*, inspired by great Aussie inventions, sports, celebrities, history, flora and fauna.

Showcase Gardens

The Floriade showcase garden competition, designed to educate people about plant varieties, garden design and landscaping, required all entries to include elements of water-wise gardening. It attracted a record 17 entries from members of the landscaping industry and CIT students, competing to win a trip to the Ellerslie Flower Show in New Zealand.

Entertainment

Highlights of the diverse entertainment program included giant sand sculptures depicting the Australian War Memorial and Old Parliament House, a free public concert by Troy Cassar-Daley, the Telstra Road to Tamworth competition, a Patting Paddock for children with all sorts of spring baby animals, and a wide array of street theatre, buskers, community and school performers.

Beach Shacks and Surfboards for Sale

Fifteen beach shacks built by the CIT Building and Construction students were offered for sale, with another five auctioned on the final day of the event, along with three surfboards painted by local indigenous artist Duncan Smith.

Workshops, Demonstrations and Exhibitions

A varied program included the ActewAGL Look'n'Learn Marquee centre of education and learning, the Interflora Exhibition Marquee combining flowers and fashion, the Beanie Marquee from the Alice Springs Beanie Festival, a photographic exhibition *Celebrate, Inspire, Connect* by renowned photographer Steve Parish, and an array of stalls selling gardening goods, delicious produce, beautiful fashion and accessories.

Source: Department of Territory and Municipal Services 2008.

The following item from the Australian Broadcasting Commission website demonstrates how the above report on Floriade 2007 has been used to generate news media about the event.

Record crowd for Floriade 2007

Canberra's Floriade festival attracted the biggest crowd on record last year.

A report on the event says almost 395 000 visitors attended Floriade and the event contributed more than $20 million to the Canberra economy.

But Tourism Minister Andrew Barr says there was a reduction in the number of interstate visitors choosing to stay in Canberra overnight.

'One of the things that we're doing to address that is putting night time events on this year to provide an incentive for people to want to stay overnight to be able to participate in activities during the day but also into the night time as well,' he said.

'This year's event will include outdoor film screenings at night in a bid to encourage more visitors to stay in Canberra longer.'

Mr Barr says the Government will consider widening the festival to include several sites in Canberra.

'One is around Kingston foreshore Eastlake as part of the planning work that's being done in that precinct and the other one is the International Arboretum and I think that's a longer term opportunity to be able to expand the event there,' he said.

Source: Australian Broadcasting Commission 2008.

Encore Festival and Event Evaluation Kit

The *Encore festival and event evaluation kit* has been developed to facilitate the task of evaluating community events. It is produced and distributed by the Cooperative Research Centre for Sustainable Tourism. The kit provides a standardised, user-friendly, computerised tool for the evaluation of festivals and events. It consists of four key modules:

- demographic module
- economic module
- marketing module
- additional questions module.

Demographic module

This module enables the user to assess the demographic profile of festival and event attendees, competitors and exhibitors. Questions are chosen that relate to aspects such as gender, age, education and income. Once the data are collected and entered, a number of demographic-related reports can be produced automatically in tabular and graphic formats.

Economic module

This module calculates the direct in-scope expenditure that results from the event in a given region. This refers to the amount of new money attracted to the host region that would not have entered the region if the event had not been held. Direct in-scope expenditure can be fed directly into a computable general equilibrium (CGE) model or an input/output model to assess the flow-on effect on the local economy and produce an economic impact figure for the event. It is calculated by assessing:

- the expenditure of visitors from outside the region to the event
- the event-related income generated by the organisers from outside the region and spent within the region.

The region must first be clearly defined, usually as a city name or a regional description. The event expenditure of locals within the region will not be counted, as it is assumed that this money would have been spent on other goods or services had the event not been held.

The expenditure of visitors from outside the region whose primary purpose was not to attend the event is also excluded, as it is assumed that they would have visited the region even if the event had not been held. An exception would be if the event had caused them to extend their visit, in which case their expenditure for the extended period of their visit would be counted.

The event organiser may wish to collect these data for other purposes, but they are not included in the direct in-scope expenditure of the event.

Marketing module

This module enables users to assess marketing-related issues by asking event participants questions that identify their motives for attending the event, how they heard about it, what they liked and disliked, their levels of satisfaction and whether they are likely to return to the next event.

Additional questions module

This module enables users to frame their own questions and to collect data on specific elements that may be unique to a particular event. This option increases the flexibility of Encore and enables users to customise the evaluation to their own needs.

Tools within Encore

Encore includes three tools:

- a survey instrument to collect data from festival or event attendees. Once questions have been selected or new questions entered, Encore can automatically prepare and print a questionnaire based on these questions and a template for the data entry.
- a calculation of the level of in-scope expenditure attributed to the event
- a reporting tool, which presents the results of each of the visitor survey questions in both tabular and graphic form.

Using this fairly simple process (see figure 16.3), a comprehensive event evaluation can be conducted economically and effectively. Using Encore evaluation kit has the added value that it has been vetted by Australian state government treasuries, lending it a degree of universality and acceptance (Jago 2006).

FUTURE DEVELOPMENT OF ENCORE

At the time of writing the Sustainable Tourism Cooperative Research Centre (STCRC) is undertaking preliminary research to review and extend the capabilities of the Encore product. Encore is internationally recognised as providing quality data on the in-scope expenditure associated with events. However, with the growing prevalence of sustainability philosophies as a governing force behind event evaluation, moves are afoot to develop Encore into an adaptable tool, which can also measure the plethora of positive and negative social and environmental impacts of events.

Building on established social and environmental theories and methods, including ecological footprint analysis, carbon calculators, social impact scales, energy and waste audits, stakeholder concerns and psychological values testing, this review involves collaboration with actual Encore users to understand their experiences, thus allowing assessments of the tool's usability and relevance. On the basis of this review, recommendations will be made on possible product modifications, and base-line data will be provided, which will be used to develop revised Encore templates to meet the requirements of a range of users, from organisers of smaller events and festivals conducting a simple event evaluation, through to event organisers, state tourism organisations (STOs), national tourism organisations (NTOs) and government authorities conducting a comprehensive evaluation of medium-large events.

Source: Carmel Foley, University of Technology, Sydney, Katie Schlenker, University of Technology, Sydney, Stephen Schweinsberg, University of Technology, Sydney 2009.

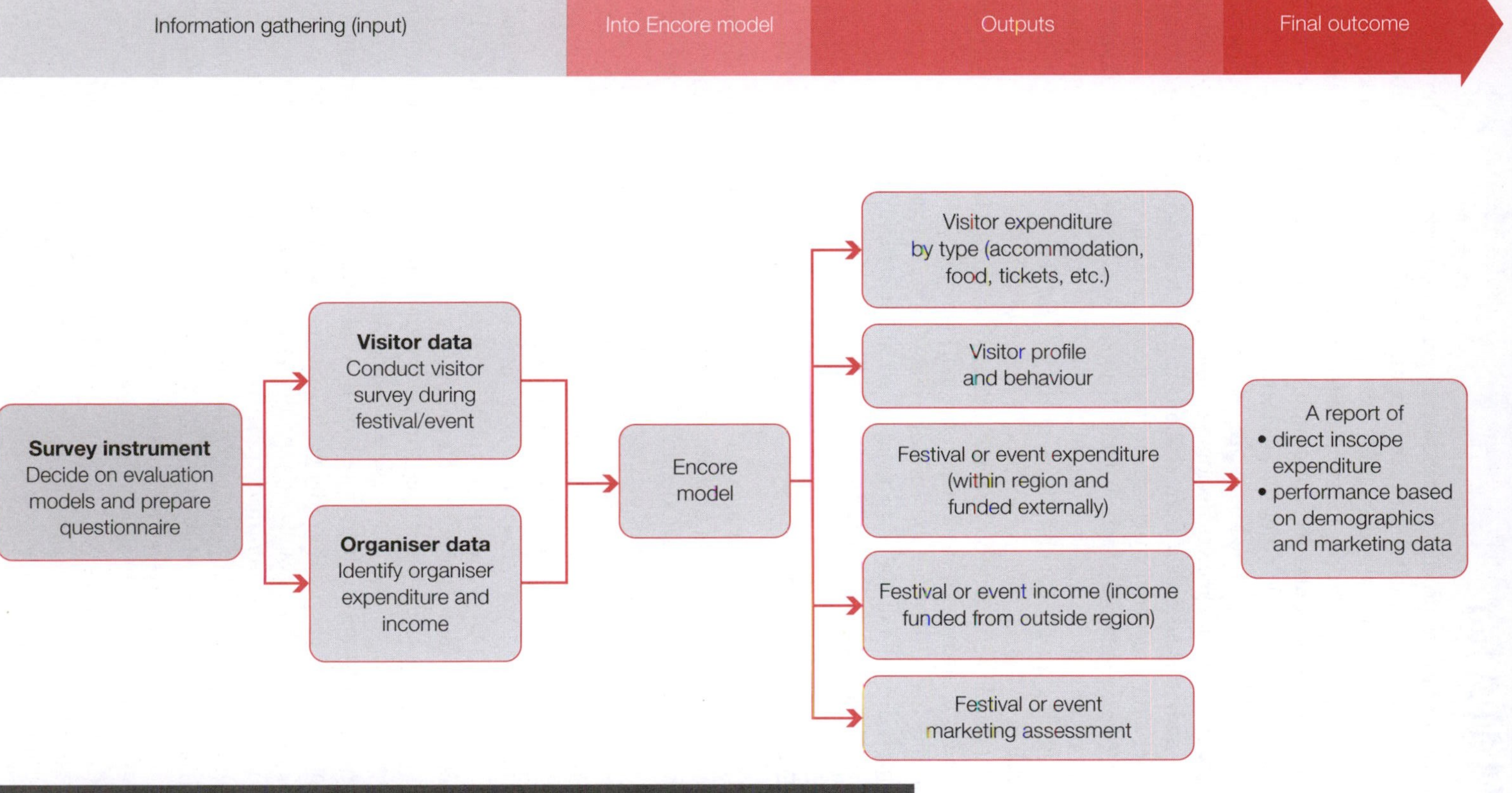

FIGURE 16.3 The festival/event evaluation process

Source: Jago 2006.

SUMMARY

Event evaluation is the process of measuring and assessing an event throughout the event management cycle. It has three phases, including feasibility studies, event monitoring and control, and post-event evaluation. Post-event evaluation serves a number of purposes, including measuring the success of the event in relation to its objectives, and analysing and reflecting on it in order to feed lessons learnt from the event back into the ongoing event management process.

Good evaluation is planned and implemented from the outset of the event management process. It involves deciding on the purpose of the evaluation, and then identifying and collecting data from a number of sources including event documentation, observation, de-brief meetings, focus groups and surveys. A good evaluation plan will strive to create the right balance between qualitative and quantitative data in order to provide a full and accurate picture of the event. Surveys are an important tool for providing quality data on the event and rely for their success on well-designed questionnaires and a rigorous survey process.

Once data have been gathered from all sources, an event evaluation report should be compiled and distributed to all stakeholders. This report should tell the story of the event and provide an accurate and enduring record of its outcomes and achievements. Once compiled, it should be distributed to all major stakeholders and can serve to enhance the future reputation and success of the event.

QUESTIONS

1. Identify a major event in your area with which you are familiar. Identify and list the purposes that the event might have in undertaking a post-event evaluation.
2. Identify a major event and then design an evaluation plan that will provide a profile of the event and form the basis of a report to key stakeholders.
3. Imagine that you are employing staff to work on a particular event. Design a report sheet for them to record their observations of the event. Decide what aspects you want them to observe and what benchmarks you want them to use.
4. Select an event that you are familiar with, and identify the stakeholders that you would invite to a final evaluation meeting. Write an agenda for the meeting that will encourage well-organised feedback on the event.
5. Source three corporate event survey forms from the internet. Compare and contrast these to decide which one you think is the best designed, and why.
6. Obtain copies of three evaluation reports from libraries, event organisations or the internet. Compare and contrast the methodology, style and format of these reports.
7. Choose one of the three evaluation reports that you have identified for the previous question, and, using the information contained in the report, draft a media release that outlines the outcomes of the event and the benefits to the local community.
8. Identify a high-profile event in your region and monitor as closely as you can the media coverage of the event, including print, radio and television coverage. Make a list of all of the media items that you were able to identify.

case study

TRIPLE-BOTTOM-LINE EVENT EVALUATION AND THE 2010 COUNTRYLINK PARKES ELVIS FESTIVAL

Introduction

This case study reports on a project by the School of Leisure Sport and Tourism (UTS) and the University of Queensland to conduct a triple-bottom-line event evaluation of the 2010 CountryLink Parkes Elvis Festival.

The CountryLink Parkes Elvis Festival

The CountryLink Parkes Elvis Festival is held annually in the town of Parkes, in the Central West of NSW. From its humble origins as a one-night community celebration of Elvis's birthday in 1993, the festival has now grown into a major tourism drawcard, attracting more than 10 000 people to Parkes and nearby centres every January. In 2009 the festival generated revenue in excess of $5 million. Currently the CountryLink Parkes Elvis Festival runs for five days and includes over 140 individual events. Festival events include: the Elvis Street Parade; the Back to the Altar with Elvis — Renewal of Wedding Vows service; the Elvis Gospel Church Service; and the 'The King's Castle', a display of the largest collection of items previously owned by Elvis in the southern hemisphere. The increasingly popular festival has attracted such sponsors as CountryLink, Coca Cola, ClubsNSW, Rex Regional Express and Andersen First National Real Estate, which has aided the festival's ongoing success.

Local businesses and the community at large are central to the sustainable management of the festival. The local organising committee that started the festival in 1993 continues to run the event in collaboration with the Parkes Shire Council. As the festival matured, the organising committee and Council appointed a part-time festival coordinator to help manage the event. Each year sees an increase in the number of businesses that decorate their shopfronts with Elvis paraphernalia and organise their own Elvis events. Many of the street buskers and the majority of volunteers for the event are drawn from the local community, and many residents open their doors to visitors by providing home hosting services. The growth of the festival has offered local organisers the opportunity to support and pursue joint marketing initiatives with other regional tourism attractions including the Parkes Radio Telescope ('The Dish') and the nearby Western Plains Zoo. The establishment of a permanent home for 'The Kings Castle' museum has ensured that Parkes can now market itself year round as the 'Elvis Capital of Australia'.

In terms of economic impacts the festival has gone from strength to strength in recent years. On the back of an 18.75 per cent increase in visitor numbers from 2008 to 2009, the following flow-on benefits were reported by Parkes Council:

- a $1.4 million increase in visitor expenditure from $3.6 million (2008) to $5 million (2009)
- an increase in average night stay from 3 nights (2008) to 3.5 nights (2009)
- a 350 per cent increase in advertising sales from $1206 (2008) to $4200 (2009).

Regional events such as the Parkes Elvis Festival have become important economic lifelines for rural areas that are struggling to weather the effects of declining

traditional industries and associated high levels of unemployment. But what of the social and environmental impacts that come with an increase in the size and profitability of an event like the CountryLink Parkes Elvis Festival? Will, for instance, an increase in the number of street stalls and pedestrian traffic result in carrying capacity issues in areas such as Parkes Railway Station (the arrival point for the Elvis Train from Sydney) and Cooke Park (the major outdoor venue for the festival)? The interest of the Parkes Elvis Festival organisers, in this and other issues, parallels a broader scholarly interest that has seen event evaluation and reporting shift from a predominantly economic focus to a more comprehensive understanding that encompasses the positive and negative social and environmental impacts of events on host areas (Fredline, Raybould, Jago, & Deery, 2005; Getz, 2008).

Triple-bottom-line evaluation of the festival

In a bid to assist organisers to understand the various economic, social and environmental impacts of their event, researchers designed a set of survey instruments to deliver a comprehensive triple-bottom-line evaluation of the 2010 CountryLink Parkes Elvis Festival. Data on the economic, social and environmental impacts of the event were gathered through a range of surveys, administered to festival organisers, attendees and local residents. The survey instruments are described below.

Economic impacts

Two surveys were administered to gather data necessary to estimate the direct inscope expenditure, or 'new money', coming into Parkes as a result of the festival. First, as part of a broader attendee survey — which gathered data on attendee demographics, travel characteristics, motivations for attendance, satisfaction and marketing data — attendees were asked to estimate their total expenditure in Parkes associated with their trip to the festival. This included expenditure in the following categories: event tickets; accommodation; meals, food and drinks; other entertainment costs; transport; personal services; and any other expenditure. Researchers surveyed a total of 371 festival attendees over a three–day period, on site during the festival, using a three–page written survey instrument. Second, organisers of the 2010 CountryLink Parkes Elvis Festival completed a survey, which gathered data on income and expenditure resulting from the festival, including the percentage breakdown for each income/expenditure category that was received from outside the Parkes region.

Social impacts

In order to gather residents' perceptions on the social impacts that may have resulted from the hosting of the 2010 CountryLink Parkes Elvis Festival, a phone survey of 403 local residents was administered approximately two weeks following the festival. The survey asked residents to comment on the occurrence of a range of social impacts, and how they feel about such outcomes, answering on a scale ranging from a very negative outcome through to a very positive outcome, with a neutral midpoint. Also included were some basic demographics and questions on the level of interest and involvement in the festival by residents, which can help to explain residents' perceptions.

Environmental impacts

Data were gathered using differing methods to enable the evaluation of the environmental impacts of the 2010 CountryLink Parkes Elvis Festival. First, festival organisers

completed an environmental impact checklist, which evaluates environmental performance in the areas of event planning, venue and site selection, promotions, merchandising and education, water, waste, energy, catering, accommodation, travel and transport. Second, included in the attendee survey were questions on mode of transport and distance travelled, which provides data needed for the calculation of the travel and transport impacts of the event.

Implications for the future

The benefit of conducting a triple-bottom-line evaluation is that event organisers are able to gain a more comprehensive understanding of the range of impacts resulting from the 2010 CountryLink Parkes Elvis Festival. Not only can they measure the economic contribution in terms of direct inscope expenditure, but these economic benefits can be assessed alongside the impacts of the festival on the host community and the environment. Measures of inscope expenditure confirm that the festival continues to inject substantial new money into the Parkes economy, as well as a significant flow-on effect to the economies in other parts of NSW.

The results of the community and attendee surveys indicated that visitors and residents alike are overwhelmingly positive in their assessment of the 2010 CountryLink Parkes Elvis Festival. In an unprompted question asking residents their overall impressions of the festival, words most commonly used were 'great', 'brilliant', 'fantastic', and 'fun'. Those residents who participated in the festival (for example, as a spectator or volunteer) derived huge pride and social satisfaction from it, and appear proud to play even a small role in making the festival what it has become today. Conversely, those who did not participate are more likely to 'tolerate' the event for the financial benefits it provides, while still enjoying the community pride that the festival creates. Knowledge of these perceptions is important to being able to continue to deliver a festival that provides positive social impacts for locals. In addition, the identification of perceived negative impacts has provided organisers with information that can feed into future event planning, in order to minimise or avoid negative impacts.

The results of the environmental impact survey indicate that festival organisers are making a concerted effort to contain negative impacts on the environment. The event venues are located within walking distance of much of the accommodation (such as camping grounds and motels). There is a festival bus provided for attendees residing outside of the town centre so that they do not need to bring their own vehicle to the event. Recycling systems for rubbish are in place. Public transport (including a special train from Sydney) brings a significant proportion of attendees to the festival. The survey has provided organisers with recommendations for further initiatives that could be implemented to further reduce the environmental impact of the event.

Importantly, festival organisers can use the baseline data from the 2010 evaluation as a point of comparison for evaluation in years to come. By using the same methods and survey instruments, organisers will be able to adopt a longitudinal perspective, allowing for changes in economic, social and environmental impacts to be charted over time. For example, changes in residents' perceptions of the social impacts can be benchmarked against previous findings to identify trends and to respond appropriately. Similarly, completion of the environmental impact checklist in future will enable organisers to see where improvements have been made in regards to the environmental impacts of the festival.

Social, environmental and economic impacts are important to calculating the overall success and outcomes of an event. It is counterproductive to concentrate on one of these (in many ways competing) dimensions to the exclusion of the others. Results of the 2010 CountryLink Parkes Elvis Festival indicate that organisers have achieved a good balance between economic, social and environmental impacts. Continued triple-bottom-line evaluation and thoughtful response to findings will ensure that this good balance is maintained.

References

Fredline, E., Raybould, M., Jago, L., & Deery, M. (2005). Triple Bottom Line Event Evaluation: A proposed framework for holistic event evaluation. In J. Allen (Ed.), *Proceedings of Third International Event Management Research Conference: The Impacts of Events*. Sydney: Australian Centre for Event Management, University of Technology, Sydney

Getz, D. (2008). Event Tourism: Definition, evolution, and research. *Tourism Management, 29*(3), 403–28.

Acknowledgements

The Sustainable Tourism Cooperative Research Centre, established and supported under the Australian Government's Cooperative Research Centre's Program, funded this research. The authors are very appreciative of the assistance and contribution provided by Kelly Hendry (Tourism Manager, Parkes Shire Council), Katrina Dwyer (Events Coordinator, Parkes Shire Council) and Ellie Ruffoni (Parkes Elvis Festival Coordinator). Information in this case study relating to the CountryLink Parkes Elvis Festival is drawn from a number of unpublished reports prepared by Parkes Shire Council. Also acknowledged is the work of Jetty Research, who assisted with the analysis of data and the preparation of reports to Council.

Case prepared by
Carmel Foley, University of Technology, Sydney
Katie Schlenker, University of Technology, Sydney
Stephen Schweinsberg, University of Technology, Sydney.

Questions

1 What is meant by 'triple bottom line evaluation', and why is it recommended that festivals adopt this approach?

2 What benefits might be obtained by the festival from the surveys conducted?

3 Why were two separate surveys needed in order to calculate the economic impacts of the festival?

REFERENCES

Australian Broadcasting Commission 2008, *Record Crowd for Floriade 2007*, ABC News, 17 March, www.abc.net.au.

Australian Centre for Event Management 2009, *Event Management — Resource Links*, http://business.uts.edu.au/acem.

Convention Industry Council 2006, *APEX post-event report template*, www.convention industry.org.

Department of Territory and Municipal Services 2008, *Floriade 2007 Event Report*, www.tams.act.gov.au.

Fredline L, Jago, L & Deery, M 2005, 'Host community perceptions of the impacts of events: a comparison of different themes in urban and regional communities', in *The impacts of events: proceedings of international event research conference held in Sydney in July 2005*, ed. J Allen, Australian Centre for Event Management, Sydney.

Getz, D 2005, *Event management and event tourism*, Cognizant Communication Corporation, New York.

Halbwirth, S & Toohey, K 2005, 'Sport event management and knowledge management: a useful partnership', in *The impacts of events: proceedings of international event research conference held in Sydney in July 2005*, ed. J Allen, Australian Centre for Event Management, Sydney.

Harris, R 2005, 'Approaches to community engagement by public events', in *The impacts of events: proceedings of international event research conference held in Sydney in July 2005*, ed. J Allen, Australian Centre for Event Management, Sydney.

Hilbers, J 2005, 'Research and evaluation of "Communities together" festivals and celebrations scheme 2002–04: building community capacity', in *The impacts of events: proceedings of international event research conference held in Sydney in July 2005*, ed. J Allen, Australian Centre for Event Management, Sydney.

Jabour, B 2009, 'Tony Cochrane delivers A1GP spray', www.goldcoast.com.au.

Jago, L 2006, *Encore festival and event evaluation kit*, draft document prepared for CRC for Sustainable Tourism, Melbourne.

Jago, L & Dwyer, L 2006, *Economic evaluation of special events: a practitioner's guide*, Common Ground Publishing, in association with Cooperative Research Centre for Sustainable Tourism, Melbourne.

NSW Department of State and Regional Development 2009, *Module 14: Event Management*, www.business.nsw.gov.au.

Raybould, M, Fredline L, Jago, L & Deery, M 2005, 'Triple bottom line event evaluation: a proposed framework for holistic event evaluation', in *The impacts of events: proceedings of international event research conference held in Sydney in July 2005*, ed. J Allen, Australian Centre for Event Management, Sydney.

Sherwood, P, Jago, L & Deery, M 2005, 'Unlocking the triple bottom line of special event evaluations: what are the key impacts?', in *The impacts of events: proceedings of international event research conference held in Sydney in July 2005*, ed. J Allen, Australian Centre for Event Management, Sydney.

Shone, A & Parry, B 2004, *Successful event management*, Thomson Learning, London.

Silvers, JR 2004, *Professional event coordination*, John Wiley & Sons Inc, Hoboken, New Jersey.

Van Der Wagen, L 2001, *Event management for tourism, cultural, business and sporting events*, Hospitality Press, Melbourne.

Veal, AJ 2006, *Research methods for leisure and tourism: a practical guide*, Pearson Education Limited, Harlow, England.

Wood, EH, Robinson, LS & Thomas, R 2006, 'Evaluating the social impacts of community and local government events: a practical overview of research methods and measurement tools', in *Events and festivals: education, impacts and experiences*, eds F Jordan & S Fleming, Leisure Studies Association, Eastbourne, UK.

www.worldofevents.net 2010, www.worldofevents.net.

PART 4

LEGAL, RISK AND OHS MANAGEMENT AND EVALUATION

This final part of the book looks at the legal factors that event managers need to be aware of, and how to identify, minimise and manage the risks inherent in an event.

LEGAL ISSUES OF EVENT MANAGEMENT

LEARNING OBJECTIVES

After studying this chapter, you should be able to:

1. explain the central role of event ownership in event management
2. identify and construct the necessary contracts for events and their components
3. understand and be able to comply with the variety of laws, licences and regulations governing event production
4. describe the necessity for and the process of insuring an event.

INTRODUCTION

Underpinning all aspects of an event is the legal framework that ensures all relevant parties are treated fairly and within any applicable law. To complicate matters, the laws relating to events and their management can vary slightly for each legal jurisdiction (city, state or country) in which the event occurs.

This chapter introduces the concepts of event ownership and the crucial duty of care of event management. It discusses the use of contracts (including insurance contracts) that document the relationship between the event and its various stakeholders. It is important, therefore, that event and festival management be familiar with key terms used in contracts. It then continues to discuss the various licences that event managers must obtain, and the duty of care that the event has to its stakeholders.

A key question in event organisation is that of ownership. The legal owner of an event can range from the event coordinator, the management committee, a separate legal entity or the sponsors. It is important to recognise that the ownership of the event entails legal responsibility and, therefore, liability. The members of an organising committee can be personally held responsible for their event. This is often expressed as 'jointly and severally liable'. The structure of the event administration must reflect this, and the status of various personnel, such as the event coordinator, the subcontractors and other stakeholders, must be clearly established at the outset. Likewise, sponsorship agreements will often have a clause as to the sponsor's liability and, therefore, the extent of their ownership of the event. All such issues need to be carefully addressed in the initial agreements and contracts.

The organising committee for a non-profit event can become a legal entity by forming an incorporated association. Such an association can enter into contracts and own property. The act of incorporating, under the relevant association incorporation Act in each state, means that the members have limited liability when the association incurs debts. However, this does not grant them complete exemption from all liability such as negligence and duty of care. By law, an association must have a constitution or a list of rules. Such documents state the procedures and powers of the association, including auditing and accounting matters, the powers of the governing body and winding-up procedures. In many cases, community and local festival events do not form a separate incorporated association as they are able to function under the legal umbrella of another body, such as a local council or social club. This gives the event organising committee considerable legal protection as well as access to administrative support. For a one-off event, this administrative support can save time and resources, because the administrative infrastructure, such as a fax machine, phone lines, secretarial help and legal and accounting advice, is already established.

An apposite event example of this is the annual conference hosted by the Council for Australian University Tourism and Hospitality Education (CAUTHE), which is an association that was incorporated in the state of New South Wales in 1996. The conference is hosted and convened by a different Australian university each year, but the legal ownership of the event lies with the association, CAUTHE, which has a constitution that covers the legal requirements mentioned above.

Establishing an appropriate legal structure for an event management company is a matter for legal advice. Several structures are possible for an event company, which could operate as a sole trader, a partnership or a company limited by liability. Each of these legal structures has different liability implications. Legal advice can determine the most appropriate structure for a particular circumstance.

CONTRACTS

Hill and Hill (2005) define a contract as 'an agreement with specific terms between two or more persons or entities in which there is a promise to do something in return for a valuable benefit known as consideration'. They continue by noting that 'since the law of contracts is at the heart of most business dealings, it is one of the three or four most significant areas of legal concern and can involve variations on circumstances and complexities'. They state that a contract contains the following elements:

- an offer
- an acceptance of that offer which results in a meeting of minds
- a promise to perform
- a valuable consideration (which can be a promise or payment in some form)
- a time or event when performance must be made (meet commitments)
- terms and conditions for performance, including fulfilling promises
- performance.

A contract can be either a written or an oral agreement. However, in the world of event management, an oral contract is of little use if problems occur in the future; therefore, it is appropriate to put all contractual agreements in writing. This may frequently take the form of a simple letter of agreement, not more than a page in length (see figure 17.1), which incorporates the elements mentioned. However, when large amounts of money and important responsibilities are involved, a formal contract drawn up by lawyers is often necessary.

As Goldblatt (1997) explains, a typical event industry contract will contain:

- the names of the contracting parties, their details and their trading names
- details of the service or product that is offered (for example, equipment, entertainment, use of land and expert advice)
- the terms of exchange for the service or product
- the method of solving any disagreements
- the signature of both parties indicating understanding of the terms of exchange and agreement to the conditions of the contract.

To make this mutual obligation perfectly clear to all parties, the contract would set out all key elements. These would consist of financial terms (including a payment schedule); a cancellation clause; delivery time; the rights and obligations of each party; and an exact description of the goods and services being exchanged.

FIGURE 17.1 An example of a letter of agreement

The South Australian Wooden Boat & Music Festival

Goolwa S.A. Saturday March 10th to Monday 12th 2007

Date:

To:

This is a letter of agreement between your act ....
(referred to as the Performer) and the 2007 Wooden Boat & Music Festival (referred to as the Festival).

The program currently has your performance scheduled at the following places and times: ....
....
....
....

FIGURE 17.1 *(continued)*

Performer(s) will receive complimentary weekend passes, which must be collected from the information booth just outside the main gate. After ticket collection someone from your group should register at the Folk Fed Reception area (at the Steamers Bar) at least 1 hour before your performance. Invoices and other paperwork can be organised at this time.

The full group will need to arrive at the specified stage at least 30 mins prior and communicate with both sound tech and MC.

The performance fee of $................................. will be paid by cheque within 21 days of the performance. To authorise payment we need a tax invoice to the 'SA Wooden Boat & Music Festival' and 'Statement by Supplier' if you (or your group) are not obliged to pay tax. These forms should be given to us during the Festival or mailed in advance. A copy of the 'Statement by Supplier' form is included.

A site map is also included. If you need to contact us on site the Folk Fed Site Coordinator phone is 0437 815 076.

Thanks for agreeing to be part of the Festival.

Signed (for the Festival)............................. Date: ....

Name: .... Position: ....

Signed (for the Performer) .... Date: ....

Name: .... Position: ....

Please fill in and return these forms ASAP.

The South Australian Wooden Boat & Music Festival

Standard Contract Conditions

Travel arrangements: which may be made by the Festival are final and the cost of changes not agreed to by the Festival shall be borne by the performer(s).

Outside performances: The performers shall not undertake any other engagements within 100 km of the Festival during the period one week before or after the event. This condition may be waived in writing by negotiation with the Festival.

Cancellation: If any performances by the performer(s) are cancelled or prevented for any reason, including, but not limited to, public calamity, strike, lockout, Act of God, or other reasons beyond the control of the Festival, the Festival shall not be liable to the Performer(s) for fees, costs, expenses or damages of any kind.

Deductions: The festival shall have the right to deduct or withhold from the Performer(s) any amounts required by law. The Festival does not take responsibility for payment of any tax amounts under superannuation guarantee legislation relating to artists' income from this engagement.

Publicity: The Performer(s) agree to allow short 'takes' of their performance to be photographed or otherwise recorded by the Festival or Festival approved media to assist in promotion of the Festival. The Performer(s) shall provide the Festival with appropriate promotional materials, photos, bios etc., to adequately promote the event and the Perfomer(s).

All notices: regarding this agreement shall be in writing and served by mail, email, or facsimile addressed to the parties at their respective addresses.

FIGURE 17.1 *(continued)*

In the event of a dispute: this agreement shall be governed by and construed in accordance with the laws of South Australia.

Alterations: to this agreement may not be made without written consent of both parties.

Signed (for the Festival)............................ Date: ....

Name: .... Position: ....

Signed (for the Performer) .... Date: ....

Name: .... Position: ....

Please fill in and return these forms ASAP.

Event management organisations may need a wide range of contracts to facilitate their operation. Some of these are shown in figure 17.2.

An event of medium size would require formal contracts covering the:

- event company or coordinator and the client
- entertainers
- venue
- suppliers (for example, security, audiovisual and caterers)
- sponsor(s).

For smaller events, these details may be arranged by letters of agreement.

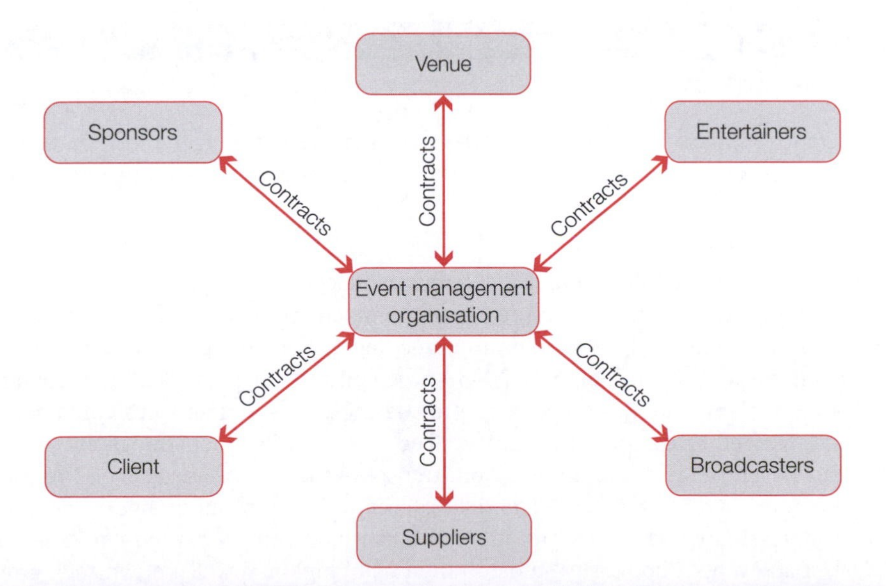

FIGURE 17.2 Contracts required by an event management organisation

Contract management

A contracts lays the foundation for event management as it specifies the goods and services to be supplied to the event. That is, it describes the standards of the goods and services that are to be delivered by the supplier. The process of managing contracts is illustrated in figure 17.3. A common misconception is that once a contract has been negotiated, it does not require further action. Event contracts need to be monitored and reviewed if necessary. Changing circumstances, a common feature of event management, can lead to contractual problems. In some areas of an event, particularly large sports events, this can lead to contracts being renegotiated.

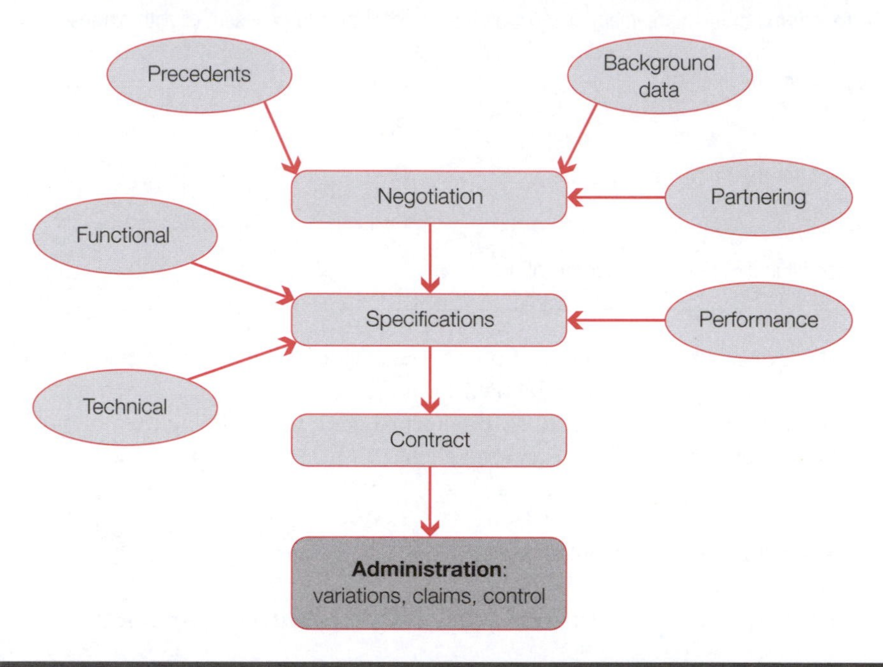

FIGURE 17.3 The contract management process

Source: O'Toole and Mikolaitis 2002.

Different contracts have different 'styles' and the event manager must be familiar with them. Some of the characteristics of these contracts are discussed below.

Entertainment

As well as the specifications for the entertainment contracted (for example, timing, artists, repertoire), a common feature of entertainment contracts is the 'rider', which comprises an amendment or addition to a document. For example, hiring a headline performer may necessitate signing a 20–30-page contract. The contract often contains a rider requiring the event company to provide the goods and services contained in the rider, as well as the performance fee. The rider can list such things as types of food and beverage, extra accommodation, transport and set-up assistance. The event company ignores this at its peril. The rider can be used by the entertainer's agent as a way of increasing the fee in real terms, which can have serious consequences for the budget of an event. A university student union that employs a well-known rock group at a minimal fee for a charity function, for example, would find its financial objectives greatly damaged by a rider stipulating the reimbursement of food, accommodation and transport costs for 30 people.

Another important clause in any entertainment contract is exclusivity. A headline act, for example, may be the major attraction for a music festival. If the act is also performing nearby this could easily detract from the appeal of the event. A clause to prevent this is inserted into the contract. It indicates that the performer cannot perform within a specified geographic area during the event or for a certain number of days prior to and after the event. The intricacies of entertainment contracts lead many texts to suggest that event managers obtain legal advice from lawyers specialising in entertainment law about contracts when planning a celebrity concert.

The contract must contain a clause that stipulates that the signatories have the right to sign on behalf of the contracting parties. An entertainment group may be represented by a number of agents. The agents therefore must have written proof that they exclusively represent the group for the event.

Venue

The venue contract can have specialist clauses, including indemnifying the venue against damage, personnel requirements and the provision of security staff. The venue contract usually contains these elements:

- *security deposit* — an amount, generally a percentage of the hiring fee, to be used for any additional work such as cleaning and repairs that result from the event
- *cancellation* — outlining the penalty for cancellation of the event and whether the hirer will receive a refund if the venue is re-hired at that time
- *access* — including the timing of the opening and closing of the doors and actual use of the entrance ways
- *late conclusion* — the penalty for the event going over time
- *house seats* — the free tickets reserved for venue management
- *additions or alterations* — possible changes to the internal structures of the venue
- *signage* — the signs of any sponsors and other advertising (venue management approval may be required for all promotional material)
- *cost* — the cost of hiring the venue for the required time. For events such as conferences held in hotels, the venue may charge on a per person per day fee basis that includes all food, beverage and venue hire, rather than separate rates for each element, which reduces the fixed costs of the conference and makes it easier for the event manager to match expenditure and revenue.

To avoid misunderstandings and potential unforeseen costs, it is prudent to ascertain exactly what facilities are included in the venue hire. Just because a piece of equipment was seen during a site inspection does not mean it is included in the venue hire cost.

Sponsor

The contract with the sponsor would include all that the sponsee promises to deliver — such as, naming rights, signage, celebrity involvement and media mentions — and the fee (consideration) given in return. Details of how the payment is made (cash or contra) and at what times would also usually be included in the contract. Geldard and Sinclair (1996) advise that among other things, the level of sponsor exclusivity during an event will need to be reflected in the contract between the event management and the sponsor. Possible sponsor levels are: sole sponsor, principal sponsor, major or minor sponsor and supplier. Details of what the event will do to inhibit ambush marketing can also be included. The contract would also describe hospitality rights, such as the number of complimentary tickets supplied to the sponsor, and the interaction rights of the sponsor in relation to the event (for example, the right to present the winner's trophy).

Broadcast

Broadcast contracts can be very complex due to the large amounts of money involved in broadcasting and the production of related merchandise, such as videos and sound recordings. The important clauses in a broadcast contract address the following key components:

- *territory or region* — the broadcast area (local, state or international) must be defined. If the contract states the region as 'world', the event company must be fully aware of the rights it is bestowing on the broadcaster and their potential value.
- *guarantees* — most important is the guarantee that the event company has the rights to sign for the whole event, because performers' copyright can preclude any broadcast without written permission from their record and publishing companies. Comedy acts and motivational speakers are particularly sensitive about broadcasts and recordings, and the contract may require explicit permission from them to broadcast their performance.
- *sponsorship* — this area can present problems when different levels of sponsorship are involved. Sometimes the rights of the event sponsor and the broadcaster's sponsors can clash, which can mean some delicate negotiations to resolve the difficulty. This is particularly applicable to sports events, where the match sponsor's products can clash with an individual team member's sponsorship.
- *repeats, extracts and sub-licences* — these determine the allowable number of broadcast repeats, whether the broadcaster is authorised to edit or take extracts from the broadcast and how such material can be used. The event company may sign with one broadcaster, only to find that the rights to cover the event have been sold on for a much larger figure to another broadcaster. In addition, a sub-licence clause may annul many of the other clauses in the contract. The sub-licensor may be able to use its own sponsors, which is problematic if they are in direct competition with the event sponsors.
- *merchandising* — the contract may contain a clause that mentions the rights to own products originating from the broadcast. The ownership and sale of such recordings can be a major revenue source for an event. A clause recently introduced in these sorts of contracts concerns future delivery systems. Multimedia uses, such as CD-ROMs, pay television and now the internet, are all relatively recent and new communications technologies continue to evolve. It is an error to sign away the future rights of an event when the contract contains terms or technologies that are unknown to the event company. It is therefore prudent to seek legal advice from an entertainment law firm.
- *access* — the physical access requirements of broadcasting must be part of the staging and logistic plan of the event. A broadcaster can easily disrupt an event by demanding to interview performers and celebrities. It is therefore necessary to specify how much access the broadcaster can have to the performers and at what times. In this way all stakeholders' needs can be met without disrupting the event.
- *credits* — this establishes, at the outset, the people and elements that will be listed in the titles and credits.

The broadcaster can offer all kinds of assistance to the event organisation. It has an interest in making the event presentable for television and therefore will often help decorate and light the venue. However, their level of assistance will depend on their stake in the event.

Suppliers

Events use many goods and services that are supplied by various providers. The quality and quantity of these goods and services must be specified in the contract. For example, the contract for the provider of security services would state the number of security personnel; their qualifications and certifications; the times that they would be in attendance at the event; and the roles that they would play in the event. Similarly, the contract for the supply of catering services would list the quantity and quality of the food and beverage, and the number, type and qualifications of the staff provided. This is a form of control discussed in a previous chapter.

CONSTRUCTING A CONTRACT

The process of constructing a contract is shown in figure 17.4. It comprises five key steps:

- *intention* — preliminary discussions between a potential supplier and event management to establish if the supplier's product's specifications and its price are suitable for the event
- *negotiation* — once a supplier has been deemed to be suitable, discussions take place on price and product enhancements until agreement has been reached to the satisfaction of both parties, which can be formalised in a summary known as a 'heads of agreement'
- *initial acceptance* — the supplier is then advised that their offer is provisionally accepted
- *agreement on terms* — further discussions may then take place on the fine detail of the agreement, including elements such as payment terms and discounts for meeting volume targets
- *signing* — once all details have been agreed upon they are incorporated in the contract, which is then signed by responsible officers of the supplier and event management.

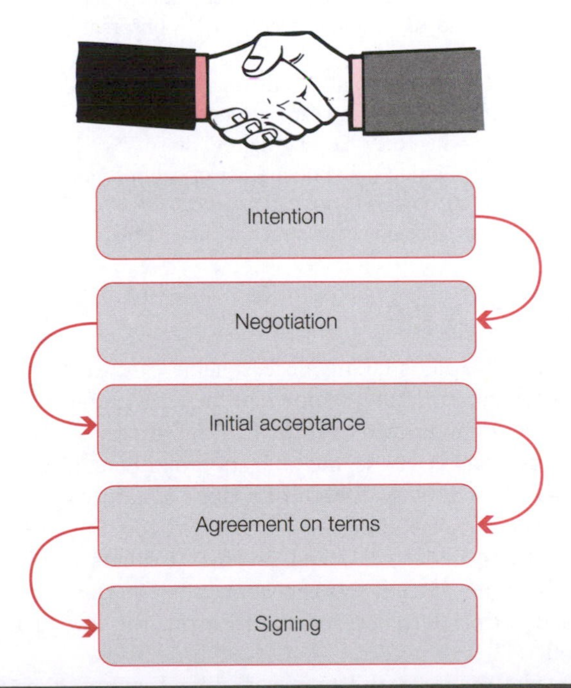

FIGURE 17.4 The process of constructing a contract

This process can be facilitated if the event management has standard contracts for specific services, where the name of the supplier and any special conditions can be inserted. This saves the event company going through unfamiliar contracts from sponsors, suppliers and entertainers, which can be very time consuming.

For large events and more complex contracts, a 'heads of agreement' is sent after the preliminary negotiations are completed. This is a summary of any important specific points, listing the precise service or product that is being provided. The contract can be renegotiated or terminated with the agreement of all parties. The final contract should contain a clause that allows both parties to use an arbitrator in the event of a disagreement.

TRADEMARKS AND LOGOS

Another kind of ownership issue for event management is the ownership of trademarks and logos. During the planning stages for the Sydney 2000 Olympics, a federal court order was granted to the Sydney Organising Committee for the Olympic Games preventing another party from using an image that was deemed to be too similar to their own logo. This illustrates the relevance of the ownership of event symbols.

The event company must also be aware of the risks of misrepresenting its event. When promoting an event, there can be a danger of exaggerating its benefits. Descriptions of the product must always be accurate, as disgruntled consumers may take legal action to gain punitive damages when they feel that advertising for an event has made false claims. The *Trade Practices Act* can be used to argue such cases:

> Part V of the *Trade Practices Act 1974* (Commonwealth) prohibits 'unfair practices' within the marketplace and has, in certain instances, been effectively used to protect those involved in events marketing.
>
> The sections most often relied on are section 52, which prohibits 'misleading or deceptive' conduct, and sections 53(c) and (d) which concern representations made by a corporation that it has, or its goods and services have, sponsorship approval or affiliation that it in fact does not have.
>
> These sections are of obvious benefit to individuals and associations alike as they provide the means by which effective action can be taken against those who wish to associate themselves with an event when they have no right to do so.
>
> Section 52 states 'a corporation shall not, in trade or commerce, engage in conduct that is misleading or deceptive or is likely to mislead or deceive.' Section 52 has often been used to restrain the unauthorised use of 'personalities' in advertising and marketing strategies.

DUTY OF CARE

A fundamental legal principle is taking all reasonable care to avoid acts or omissions that could injure a 'neighbour'. This is known in the legal literature as duty of care and is covered by an area of law known as torts. It is defined by the Legal Services Commission of South Australia (2010) as 'the obligation of a person to exercise reasonable care in the conduct of an activity. Breach of a duty of care which causes damage or loss to another may give rise to an action in tort.' A tort is a breach of duty owed to other people and imposed by law and, in this, it differs from the duties arising from contracts, which are agreed between contracting parties. Unlike criminal law, which is concerned with deterrence and punishment, the law of torts is concerned with compensation.

For event management, duty of care means taking actions that will prevent any foreseeable risk of injury to the people who are directly affected by, or involved in, the event. This would include event staff, volunteers, performers, the audience or spectators and the general public in the surrounding areas.

Another duty of care is to ensure that the noise from an event (particularly music events) does not impinge upon the amenity of the venue's neighbourhood. All states of Australia have an *Environmental Protection Act* (EPA) that governs the annoyance to residents caused by noise from music played at venues. For example, the Victorian *State Environment Protection Policy (Control of music noise from public premises) No. N-2* controls the timing and noise level of music coming from non-residential premises. This generally means that police have the power to instruct venues to abate noise after midnight. It behoves event managers to know how the EPA will impact upon their event and ensure that it adheres to EPA requirements. These requirements can usually be obtained from either the local council or the police.

The Australian Safety and Compensation Council has a strategy to improve the safety of workplaces, which encapsulates the concept of duty of care. Figure 17.5 illustrates how this strategy is operationalised. This aspect of duty of care is further explored in the following chapter on risk management.

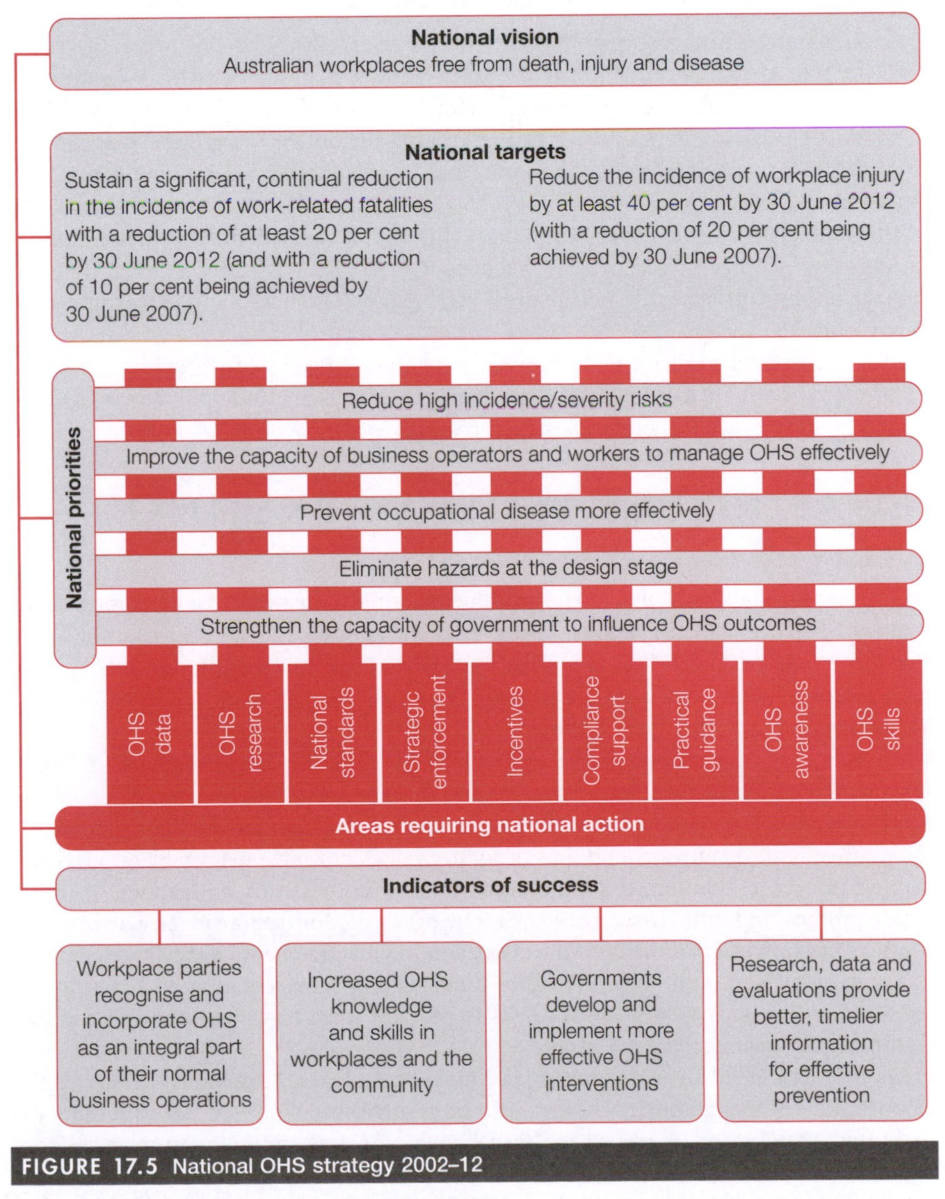

FIGURE 17.5 National OHS strategy 2002–12

Source: Australian Safety and Compensation Council 2007.

Thorpe et al. (2009, p. 130) in their book *Sports Law* give many examples of sports events being sued for lack of duty of care to either competitors or spectators. They include the case of *Harris v Bulldogs Rugby League Club* where Mr Harris was injured by a firework while viewing a match at the Sydney Showground, the home ground of the Sydney Bulldogs. Mr Harris was watching the game from a terraced area known as Bulldog Hill. Flares had been let off during the game, and about ten minutes before the match finished Mr. Harris was hit in the eye by a flare, and consequently lost his sight in that eye. He then sued the club for not taking adequate security measures. The club argued that they had employed Workforce International, who issued 80–90 staff to provide security to the venue, in addition to 47 police placed in and out of the stadium. All spectator's bags were searched before entering the ground. It was therefore found that the club had not breached its duty of care as it had provided adequate security measures.

Another interesting case reported by Thorpe et al. (2009) is one where a cricket ball, hit out of the ground during a match, struck a passerby, who subsequently sued the cricket club hosting the event. However, the claim was unsuccessful as it was held that while the possibility of a ball being hit out of the ground was foreseeable, the risk to passersby was so remote that a reasonable person would not have foreseen it.

The important lesson to be learnt from this is that provided appropriate duty of care is taken to protect competitors, spectators, staff and passersby is taken by event managers they will generally not be breaking the law. This can include warning signs of any potential risks.

All event managers need to be conscious of this obligation to provide a safe and healthy environment for their event participants, spectators and staff, to avoid damaging law suits as well as other consequences.

LEGAL ISSUES WITH MARKETING EVENTS

The major legal issue is that of misleading potential consumers or misrepresenting details of the event to consumers. However, Thorpe et al. (2009) do make the point that hyperbole or 'puffery' is not illegal; terms that are not measurable or objective such as 'game of the century', 'concert of a lifetime', 'see the world's best' are given a wide degree of latitude by the courts.

What is illegal is making misleading representations about elements of an event. This is defined by Section 51A of the *Trades Practices Act 1974* (TPA) as 'where a corporation makes a representation with respect to any future matter (including the doing of, or refusing to do any act) and the corporation does not have reasonable grounds for making the representation, the representation shall be taken as misleading'. In other words promoting Keith Urban as the headline act in a country music festival when no contract has been signed between the event and his management, and talks are only in a very early stage, could be construed as a misleading representation and contrary to Section 51A of the Act. Very similar laws in relation to persons are found in the Fair Trading Acts of each state of Australia.

Another case cited by Thorpe et al. (2009) is that of The Hospitality Group (THG) who produced hospitality packages including premium seats for the international rugby test matches to be played in 1999. Some of THG's promotional material contained these words: '10 reserved grandstand seats guaranteed in a block of 10 between the 22 metre lines for the 1999 Bledisloe Cup at Stadium Australia'. THG did not have any contractual arrangement with the Australian Rugby Union (ARU) or with any other body that guaranteed it seats at the test matches of that year. The courts found that THG was in breach of Section 51A as it could not provide any evidence that it could supply such seats.

Section 52 of the TPA refers to misleading and deceptive conduct and states: 'a corporation shall not, in trade or commerce, engage in conduct that is misleading or deceptive or is likely to mislead or deceive'. A corporation, in this case, would refer to the body producing the event. An example of enforcing this section of the Act is that of Tony Mundine, the then official heavyweight champion of Australia, who successfully restrained Layton Taylor Promotions Pty Ltd from advertising a match, in which Mundine was not boxing, as the Australian heavyweight title bout (Thorpe et al. 2009).

Section 53 of the TPA refers to false representations as to quality, sponsorship and approval. The pertinent issue for event managers is (c) represent the goods or services have sponsorship approval, performance characteristic, accessories, uses or benefits they do not have; and (d) represent that a corporation has a sponsorship, approval or affiliation that it does not have. An example given by Thorpe et al. (2009) is that of World Series Cricket whose advertising was stopped because it implied that it had sponsorship or approval from the Australian Cricket Board, which breached 53 (c).

Section 54 of the TPA refers to the promotional (or *make representations* in legalese) offers of gifts or prizes with an intention of not providing such prizes. For example, the producers of an Australia-wide musical event could promote it with an offer of a recording contract to the winners, but have no arrangements with a recording company to do so. The event would be in breach of Section 54 of the TPA.

Ambush marketing refers to the practice of appearing to be a sponsor of an event, when not being so. The first successful example of ambush marketing was at the 1984 Los Angeles Olympics when Nike booked every available billboard in Los Angeles before and during the Games, and placed pictures of competing United States athletes and the Nike swoosh, which had an effect of implying Nike was a sponsor of the US team. The problem was that Converse, not Nike, was the sponsor of the US team. It is therefore necessary for an event producer to try to find legal ways to stop the practice. The main weapon is to protect the intellectual property rights of the sponsor's logo, trademarks and theme. Alternatively they can claim misleading and deceptive behaviour under Part V of the TPA. The ambushed party can obtain an injunction to restrain the ambush behaviour and claim damages to compensate losses from the economic effects of the ambush.

Notwithstanding this it is strongly advisable to seek appropriate legal advice when event producer's actions may possibly be in breach of the Trade Practices Act.

INSURANCE

Central to any strategy of liability minimisation is obtaining appropriate insurance. Useful suggestions for obtaining appropriate insurance include the following:

- Allow enough time to investigate and arrange the correct insurance. This may include asking for quotes and professional advice. Finding the right insurance broker is the first priority.
- Make sure the event committee or company is fully covered for the whole time — that is, from the first meeting.
- Request all suppliers of products and services show they have liability cover.

- Be prepared to give the insurance broker all information concerning the event and the companies involved. They may require a list of possible hazards, such as pyrotechnics.
- Be prepared to record the details of any damage or injury. Photographs and videos are helpful.
- Keep all records, as a claimant has six years to formulate a claim.
- Do not accept the transfer of liability of the suppliers to the event management.
- Check what is included and excluded in the insurance document. Rain insurance, for example, is specific about the amount and time of the rain. Are the event volunteers covered by the insurance?
- Are additional stakeholders insured? These are companies or individuals covered by the insurance but are not the named insured. The sponsors and the venue, for example, may benefit from the insurance policy.

There are many kinds of event insurance. These include weather insurance; personal accident insurance for the volunteer workers; property insurance, including money; workers compensation insurance; public liability; and directors' and officers' liability. The choice of the particular insurance cover is dictated by the risk management strategy developed by event management.

The cost of premiums in all insurance areas is a burden on the event industry and to many community festivals. A number of strategies have been implemented to manage this situation:

- *bulk buying.* — a number of events and event companies could pool their insurance premiums and approach insurance brokers with a large pool of funds in order to negotiate bulk discounts.
- *analysing the activities of the event into levels of risk* — the high premium may be the result of one aspect of the event. By changing or eliminating this from the event program it may reduce the event risk seen by the insurance company.
- *creating a comprehensive risk management procedure* — many events that previously ignored risk management have turned to the formal risk management process. This is one positive outcome of the insurance issue. The risk management plan becomes a document used to communicate with the insurance company. Given the experience of insurance companies, it is wise to seek their input on this document.
- *capping liability* — some state governments have enacted maximum levels of payouts for damages sustained at an event. This allows insurance companies to predict their payments and, therefore, lower the premiums for public liability.
- *holding harmless clauses or forfeiting the right to sue* — the attendee signs a contract to the effect that they are voluntarily assuming the risk inherent in the event activity. This requires legal advice as there has not been a test case at the time of writing.

The Australian insurance broker Rural and General Insurance Brokers (RGIB) has a department that specialises in special event insurance. Its website, www.ruralandgeneral.com.au, has an online form that can help event managers and the insurance company decide what the appropriate level of insurance is for their event. By completing this form the event manager can anticipate the likely risks, eliminate them, and hence reduce the insurance premium.

Event managers are well advised to consult an insurance broker such as RGIB to ensure that they are not placing the event or themselves in a catastrophic situation where a claim can severely financially damage the event or themselves.

event profile

SO YOU THINK YOU HAVE INSURANCE!

Multi-sport is more than just sport. It's an adventure, a journey and a challenge that demands skill, experience, fitness and endurance. It's also eco-sport; taking advantage of the wonderful natural features of our land, with courses set over alpine moors, through majestic forests and down wild rivers. Cross-country skiing, whitewater kayaking, running and mountain biking are just some of the skills demanded to negotiate courses.

There are three major one day multi-sport events established in Tasmania — the Ben Lomond Descent, the Tasmanian Winter Challenge and the Mersey Forest Descent. The organisers of each are associated through canoeing and are the Tamar Canoe Club, the Tasmanian Board of Canoe Education and Canoe Tasmania respectively.

Operating on the basis of verbal advice obtained from the Australian Canoe Federation when the events were first established, it was assumed that each event had cover afforded through the policy of the ACF which extends to affiliated clubs and associations (an insurance levy is a component of affiliation costs).

In early 1988, the Tamar Canoe Club decided to organise a new multi-sport event in the Launceston area. They were aware that Australian Canoeing Inc.'s (formerly the ACF) insurer had recently changed and thought it best to check the extent of the cover provided for such an event under the new policy.

The reply received was that only canoe events were covered — multi-sport events were not. The Tamar Canoe Club was rightly concerned that such a change had occurred in the cover provided by the new policy and sought clarification from Australian Canoeing Inc. The reply was that multi-sport events were definitely not covered. Further, they had never been covered under previous policies. The original advice had obviously been incorrect. It was indeed fortunate that the events had no need to claim against the 'insurance'.

The lesson is clear — organisers of events should never assume that they have suitable insurance. Always check and, if possible, receive written confirmation from the insurer or their agent that cover is provided and it meets the event's requirements.

Footnote: At the start of 1999, Australian Canoeing Inc. engaged a new insurer. The new policy has some provision for multi-sport events, but not those which include XC skiing.

Source: Office of Sport and Recreation Tasmania 1999, A sporting chance: a risk management framework for the sport and recreation industry, OSRT, p. 9.32

REGULATIONS, LICENCES AND PERMITS

There are long lists of regulations that need to be adhered to when staging a simple event. Generally, the bigger and more innovative an event, the greater the number of regulations to which it must adhere, and these regulations may vary from state to state. To avoid inadvertently contravening any legal regulation that governs the conduct of events, it is necessary to conduct rigorous research to establish what needs to be done. Inquiries with events of a similar nature is a good place to start, and then with the police and local government officials.

It is the responsibility of event management to ascertain and comply with all pertinent rules and regulations. A street parade through Sydney, for example, can come under the control of various government authorities. The Paddington Festival Parade along Oxford Street required a series of long meetings with two local councils, police and traffic authorities. The event itself was over in two hours. In Victoria, a special licence is required to erect tents over a certain size. This includes tents that are used for only one night. Local noise regulations can change within the same city, within the jurisdiction of different councils. Event management must pay particular attention to workplace health and safety regulations.

Figure 17.6 describes some of the permits, licences, insurances and regulations with which a community festival taking place on the south coast of Victoria must comply. An event manager may need to seek legal advice to ensure all relevant regulations are taken into account.

Insurance

(a) Public liability insurance of $10 000 000; excess $500; property damage claims only

(b) Personal accident insurance covering 500 volunteers:
- $800 — weekly benefits
- $60 000 — death benefits

The policy also covers the committee, charitable and school organisations that provide the food stalls.

(c) Occasionally, special insurance is taken out to cover tents with specific risks — for example, a circus tent.

(d) Car parks are covered against damage to vehicles.

(e) Insurance against theft, fire and other damage to the equipment owned by the festival committee. Equipment includes storage sheds, staging, electrical equipment, tables and chairs.

Legislation to be aware of

1. *liquor licensing for alcohol*
2. *health* — food vans, smoking and toilets
3. *state building regulations* — tent construction and people in the arena. Tent construction workers must be licensed.
4. *Country Fire Authority* — fire reels, hoses and extinguishers
5. *licences governing security personnel*
6. *Police Act* — vehicle access along streets, crowd control
7. (a) *Local Government Act* — leasing of municipal property
   (b) *by-laws of the relevant shire council* — drinking alcohol in the streets, fence erection, signage, street closure, planning permits and stall permits
8. *Banking Act* — control of finances
9. *Insurance legislation*
10. *residential tenancies and caravan parks legislation* — accommodation of performers, ticket holders and guests
11. *Associations Incorporation Act* — governing the organising committee
12. *general contract law* — agreements with performers, printing and agreement with the Australasian Performing Rights Association (APRA)
13. *Environmental Protection Authority (EPA)* — noise levels

FIGURE 17.6 Sample legal requirements for a festival

Permits and licences allow special activities during an event such as the handling of food, pyrotechnics, the sale of liquor and road closures. They also cover the performances. The Australasian Performing Rights Association (APRA) issues licences for the performance of its members' works. APRA functions as a collection society, monitoring and collecting royalties on behalf of its members (music composers and their publishers). So when an event company decides to set fireworks to music, it is not just a matter of hiring a band, or playing recorded music. APRA's website, www.apra-amcos.com.au, hosts an online application form to enable the organisation to issue a permit to play the works listed on the form, and the fee applicable.

The Phonographic Performance Company of Australia (PPCA) performs a similar role in regard to the public performance of recorded music. As the PPCA (2007) says on its website:

> Under section 85(1) of the Copyright Act 1968 ('the Act'), the copyright in relation to a sound recording is the exclusive right to do all or any of the following acts:
>
> (a) to make a copy of the sound recording;
> (b) to cause the recording to be heard in public;
> (c) to communicate the recording to the public; and
> (d) to enter into a commercial rental arrangement in respect of the recording. (PPCA 2007)

For event management the relevant section refers to the recording to be heard in public, which means that if an event plans to play any recorded music at an event they must receive a licence from the PPCA and pay any fees. In regard to what is a 'public performance' it states:

> The courts have given some guidance; however, by making it clear that a performance can still be a 'public performance' even if:
>
> (a) the performance is given for free;
> (b) the audience is small;
> (c) there is no admission fee to hear or see the performance; or
> (d) the performance is confined to members of a club. (PPCA 2007)

An application form can be found on the PPCA's webite, www.ppca.com.au.

The Director of Licensing Services for APRA has these words of advice for event managers:

> Concerts, festivals, and any event where recorded or live copyright music is played or performed, require a license from APRA. In the first instance, the onus lies with the promoting entity to apply, and then enter into the relevant license agreement, although APRA may contact the organiser in the lead up to the event.
>
> Signed license agreements should be finalised two weeks prior to any event. Where APRA is unable to make satisfactory communication or obtain a license agreement within the specified timeframe the matter is referred to APRA's legal department, who will commence legal action to enforce APRA's rights. An event promoter may sign the requisite license agreement, but then fail to supply the supporting documentation such as box office statements, or pay the relevant license fees. APRA will move to obtain these documents and fees through legal processes.
>
> Obtaining a license that authorises the public performance of music at events is administratively simple, and the 1000 events that APRA has licensed around Australia in the last 12 months is testament to the co-operative, functional relationships that we enjoy with concert and event promoters. (Sarris 2007)

The two organisations' roles can be differentiated thus: PPCA represents copyright owners in sound recordings; a sound recording licence is required when recordings are publicly performed. APRA represents copyright owners in musical works (compositions and lyrics); a musical work licence is required whenever musical works are performed in public (Learson 2007). It is therefore a good idea for the event manager to check with APRA and PPCA if it is planned to play recorded or live music at the event to ensure that they are not contravening any performers' copyright.

The Australian government's Business Licence Information service (BLIS) also provides online assistance to facilitate permissions by event managers, at www.bli.net.au.

Many regulations, permits and licences change with each local government area and state, and new regulations and reinterpretations of the old rules are proclaimed regularly. For example, occupational health and safety (OHS) is a matter for state and territory governments. However, Safe Work Australia's role is to promote best practice in occupational health and safety to develop national OHS policy and guidelines, and to promote consistency in legislation produced by state and territory governments (Safe Work Australia 2010). This means that OHS regulations are now somewhat more uniform than they were. Each state has a department to regulate OHS; for example, WorkCover provides guidance in OHS matters in New South Wales (WorkCover NSW). However, in essence it is the responsibility of event management to provide a safe and healthy workplace to their staff and volunteers. If in doubt, consult the OHS department in the state in which the event is to be held. This topic is discussed further in chapter 18.

The *Public Halls Act* is administered by local councils and often its interpretation will vary from council to council. Their rulings are generally based on public safety, health and convenience. If an event is using a public hall as its venue it is advisable to ensure that it holds the appropriate licence. Local councils are also responsible for issuing entertainment licences and open air permits for events.

Even event accounting may need permits. An event company must register a business name before opening a bank account.

This complex area needs the close attention of event management, who must undertake detailed research into all regulations affecting their event and should allocate time to deal with the results of that research. Government agencies may take a long time to respond to requests. It is necessary, therefore, to begin seeking any permits and licences early and to factor delays and difficulties with obtaining them into the timeframe of the event planning process.

SUMMARY

Event managers have a responsibility to understand the legal requirements of event production. As well, they have a duty of care to all involved in the event. Any reasonably foreseen risks to stakeholders have to be eliminated or minimised to avoid legal liability. Therefore, minimising any legal liability is part of the job of event managers. This includes identifying the ownership of the event, careful structuring of the event management, taking out insurance, and adhering to all laws, rules and regulations pertaining to the event. Specific legal issues of concern to the event management team include licensing, contracting, trademarks and trade practices. Legal matters can be complex and can differ from state to state. It is recommended firstly that any event company seeks advice from the police and local government when unsure of the regulations surrounding event production in a particular area, and secondly from a law firm that has some expertise in contract and entertainment law.

QUESTIONS

1. What are the ramifications of the duty of care concept for event managers?
2. How would an event manager ensure that no duty of care breaches occurred?
3. Why do organisations such as APRA and PPCA exist?
4. What are the elements that should be found in a contract for the supply of entertainment at a celebratory dinner for 500 people?
5. Why should a community festival that takes place in a public park take out public liability insurance?
6. Give three examples of how the *Trade Practices Act* can impact on the management of special events.
7. What permits and licenses would be required for a country music festival held in a recreation reserve that featured local amateur talent performing many cover versions, and at which food and alcoholic beverages would be served?

case study

SOUTH AUSTRALIAN BREWING COMPANY PTY LTD V CARLTON & UNITED BREWERIES LTD (2001)

The Facts

The Australian Football League (AFL) promotes and organises the annual Australian Rules football competition (the competition). The competition consists of home and away matches (which are, in themselves, events) between the participant clubs of the AFL throughout Australia and a finals series. The Adelaide Football Club (known as the Crows) commenced playing in the AFL in 1991, while the Port Adelaide Football Club (Port) commenced AFL participation in 1997. Since Port commenced participating in the AFL, the two Adelaide-based clubs have been scheduled to play two football matches against each other in the course of the home and away series in Adelaide.

Both the applicant — the South Australian Brewing Company Pty Ltd (SAB) — and the respondent — Carlton and United Breweries Ltd (CUB) — are brewers, wholesalers and retailers of beer. At the time of the events — between 1997–2001 — SAB was a sponsor of the Crows and Port, while CUB was a sponsor of the AFL.

It is now part of the vernacular, at least within South Australia, that the two matches between AFC and PAFC at Football Park each season are 'Showdown' matches. Prior to this case, the Showdown matches have taken place on 20 April and 16 August 1997, 19 April and 9 August 1998, 2 May and 22 August 1999, 23 April and 6 August 2000, and 15 April 2001. They have been called successively the first to the ninth Showdowns or Showdown matches or Showdown 1–9. The match known as Showdown 10 was scheduled to take place on 5 August 2001.

The case concerns promotional activities undertaken by CUB in relation to the Showdown 7 and Showdown 9 matches, and partly undertaken and planned in relation to the Showdown 10 match; however, the latter issue is not relevant for current purposes.

SAB claims that the Showdown title for those football matches was developed and then promoted as a vehicle for the promotion of West End beer. The name 'Showdown' was to be used in relation to the bi-annual matches referred to, and the promotional and entertainment events associated with those matches. Both the Crows and Port had been consulted about and supported the proposal. SAB became the registered owner of trademark No 750487 from 8 December 1997 in the word mark SHOWDOWN in respect of 'sports events, live entertainment services being entertainment services provided in conjunction with sporting events being services in class 41' (the word mark). Since 1997 SAB has promoted each of those football matches as 'West End Showdown' matches.

In March and April 2000, in relation to the Showdown 7 match, CUB conducted a competition offering the chance to attend the Showdown 7 match 'in a VB box with 7 mates' for those who purchased a carton of CUB's Victoria Bitter beer. An eligible participant had to complete an entry form for the 'Experience Showdown 7' competition, and would then be put in the draw to select the winner. A similar competition was conducted in relation to the Showdown 9 match.

SAB alleged, amongst other matters, that the conduct of CUB in relation to the Showdowns 7 and 9 promotions had:

1 infringed the word mark (under the Trade Marks Act 1995 (Cth); and
2 contravened s 52 of the *Trade Practices Act 1974* (Cth) (the TP Act) by falsely representing to consumers that:
   (i) there is an association between the Showdown matches and CUB that CUB is 'a/the' brewing company that sponsors:
      (a) the AFC (Crows) and the PAFC (Port); and/or
      (b) the SANFL (of which SAB was the sponsor); and/or
      (c) the Showdown matches.

CUB claimed, as part of its defence, that the word 'Showdown' has a generic meaning to describe the bi-annual football matches between the Crows and Port conducted by the AFL, and that its use of that word is in that generic sense. It denied using the word as a trade mark. CUB thus disputed that, in relation to the Showdown 7 promotion and the Showdown 9 promotion, it had infringed the word mark.

In response to the alleged contraventions of s. 52 of the TP Act in relation to those promotions, CUB contended in general terms that it had not made the representations, and alternatively that to the extent that it had made any such representations, they were not misleading or deceptive and were not likely to mislead or deceive.

CUB also contended that SAB itself had misused the word 'Showdown', in effect, by seeking to appropriate to itself ownership of the bi-annual football matches between the Crows and Port when, in reality, they are 'owned' or prescribed by and under the control of the AFL. It also contended that SAB had made use of the Crows and Port logos, and photographs of the club captains, in certain of its promotional material when it was not entitled to do so. In effect, CUB asserted that SAB had deliberately and in a calculated manner sought to promote itself as having the right to stage the Showdown matches and to use the intellectual property of the AFL concerning the Crows and Port when it does not have such rights, and in effect to undermine the value of the rights which the AFL has granted to CUB.

Highlights of the judgement of Mansfield J. (SABC v CUB, 2001)

In the view of Mr Justice Mansfield, it is clear that the presentation of the bi-annual football matches between the Crows and Port as part of the AFL competition is made by the AFL, and that SAB has no role to play in the presentation of those football matches. The AFL conducts the competition, and its objects include the promotion throughout Australia of Australian Rules football. It has the objects *of controlling the program of matches for the competition*, and of controlling the activities of players and others in any activity associated with football, including promotional activities. Moreover, the AFL controls each club's playing apparel, and each club is given the right to use that club's playing apparel. The AFL retains the absolute and exclusive right to engage in sponsor advertising, including the use of any trade mark or logo, on any player. No club or player may display on any player any trade mark or logo or other advertising without the AFL's permission.

The infringement of the word mark

He continues by discussing Section 120(1) of the Trade Marks Act that provides that a person infringes a registered trade mark if that person uses as a trade mark a sign that is substantially identified with the trade mark in relation to goods or services in respect of which the trade mark is registered. CUB contended that its use of the word 'Showdown' in relation to the Showdown 7 promotion is not use of the word mark 'as a trade mark'. He found, and it is not really disputed by SAB, that the word 'Showdown' has a generic or vernacular use to refer to the Showdown matches, as well as its trade mark use by SAB.

He then goes on to consider, the question of whether CUB has used the word 'Showdown' in relation to the Showdown 7 promotion in a descriptive sense or as a mark. He decided that the answer to that question depends upon the nature and purpose of the impugned use, having regard to the context in which that use occurs. He considered that the particular form of presentation of the word 'Showdown' is in the context of drawing attention to an event, as it is used as part of the exhortation 'Experience Showdown' in the advertising material. The Showdown 7 promotion was to invite persons to attend a football match conducted by the AFL, which he found to be described generically by many in South Australia as a Showdown match.

He then declared that there is evidence that there is an association in the minds of a proportion of those in South Australia who are over 18 and buy or consume beer between the word 'Showdown' and SAB. SAB set out by its promotional and advertising material to engender such an association. The context in which the 'Showdown' expression was used by CUB in relation to the Showdown 7 promotion is that there was soon to be the Showdown 7 match. CUB wished to promote the sale of its Victoria Bitter beer product by that promotion, involving the competition described. For that purpose, which is of course an entirely proper purpose, it identified the event in respect of which the competition was conducted. It identified that event by the use of the 'Showdown'. The text of the advertisements is directed to the event, by the words 'Experience Showdown 7' and by the nature of the prize offered.

He then decided that the purpose and nature of the use of the word 'Showdown', having regard to the fact that the football match was by then commonly known as a Showdown, is simply to describe accurately the occasion of the football match. It was not to use that word as a trade mark. Accordingly, he did not consider that the word mark of SAB has been infringed by the use by CUB of the word 'Showdown' in relation to the Showdown 7 promotion.

The contravention of the TPA

In the judgement of Mr Justice Mansfield, the promotional and advertising material produced by CUB in relation to the Showdown 7 (and 9) promotion did not represent to consumers that the Showdown 7 (and 9) match, or Showdown matches, CUB is the brewing company that sponsors either the Crows or Port or the SANFL or the Showdown matches. The reference to 'the' brewing company in the allegation must indicate an assertion of a representation that, somehow, CUB is the exclusive brewing company sponsor of the clubs or of the SANFL or of the Showdown matches.

Consequently, he decided:

> that part of the Showdown 10 promotion which offers as a prize attendance at the Showdown 10 match in the "VB Superbox" does not convey that CUB has any particular sponsorship and promotional rights at Football Park than the capacity to offer the occupancy of a premier corporate box at the Showdown 10 match at which Victoria Bitter beer and other CUB products will be available for consumption. It is not therefore necessary to refer in any detail to the signage and other rights which CUB has in relation to Football Park for AFL matches played there under its arrangements with the AFL, and the AFL arrangements with the SANFL. I also do not consider that the use of "VB" as distinct from "CUB" or "Carlton and United" as the name of the box is misleading or deceptive or is likely to mislead or deceive. It is correct that the term "VB Superbox" is not the term by which CUB's corporate box in the Park Pavilions is known. But it is difficult to see how any member of the public might be relevantly misled or deceived by what is really a marketing description of a facility which CUB has the capacity to offer as a prize in the proposed competition. I think, in context, that the description used means no more than that CUB, as the promoter of that competition and as the supplier of Victoria Bitter beer, has the capacity to offer that prize. Accordingly, I reject that aspect of SAB's claim. (53 IPR 90, para. 124)

Lessons

This case makes clear that it is very difficult to establish any intellectual property rights in common everyday words. Even though SAB had registered a trade mark in the word SHOWDOWN, it was the stylised presentation of the word rather than the word itself that was protected.

The case also illustrates the importance of contractual arrangements in relation to intellectual property, sponsorship and events. Both SAB and CUB had contractual relationships in connection to the AFL competition — SAB with the two teams; CUB with the AFL. Notably the CUB contract with the AFL was the more significant, primarily because the AFL owned most of the intellectual property in connection with the teams, the competition and the sport. Event managers should therefore always be wary of just who owns what intellectual property when negotiating sponsorship of an event.

Finally, whenever dealing with these sections of the Trade Practices Act, it is always relevant to ask 'for who was the advertising intended?' Event managers will only be liable for breaches of the TPA if the section of the public (as reasonable men or women) for whom the advertising is intended could be mislead or deceived.

Another issue that arose in the case, which was not pertinent to the study above but is most relevant to event managers, was the approval of the use of survey evidence as admissible evidence. While there are some technical rules surrounding its admissibility, it is nonetheless important for event managers to note that they can use their research methods skills to enhance their legal arguments as well as their professional performance.

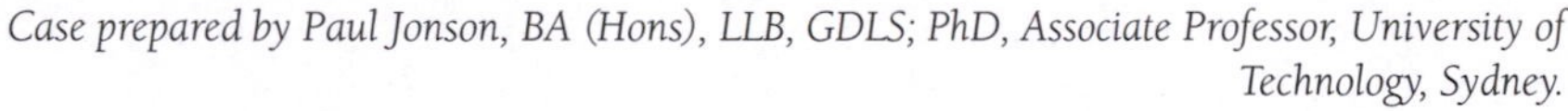

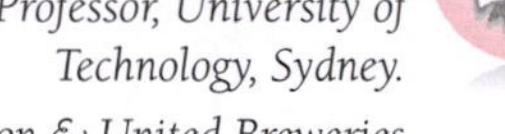

Case prepared by Paul Jonson, BA (Hons), LLB, GDLS; PhD, Associate Professor, University of Technology, Sydney.

This case is drawn from South Australian Brewing Company Pty Ltd v Carlton & United Breweries Ltd (2001) 53 IPR 90; [2001] FCA.

Questions

1 Was this, in effect, a successful attempt at ambush marketing by CUB? Explain your reasoning.

2 What, if anything, could you, as an event manager, have done to prevent the 'ambush'?

3 When organising an event, what intellectual property should you protect? How would you do it?

REFERENCES

Australian Safety and Compensation Council 2007, *National OH&S strategy 2002–2012*, www.safeworkaustralia.gov.au.

Fewell, M 1995 (ed.), *Sports law: a practical guide*, LBC Information Services, Sydney.

Geldard, E & Sinclair, L 1996, *The sponsorship manual*, The Sponsorship Unit, Olinda, Victoria.

Goldblatt, J 1997, *Special events: best practices in modern event management*, 2nd edn, Van Nostrand Reinhold, New Jersey.

Hill, G & Hill, K 2005, 'Contract', law.com dictionary, http://dictionary.law.com.

Learson, C 2007, pers. comm., 14 March.

Legal Services Commission of South Australia, 2010 *Law hand book glossary*, Government of South Australia, www.lawhandbook.sa.gov.au.

O'Toole, W & Mikolaitis, P 2002, *Corporate event project management*, John Wiley & Sons, New York.

PPCA 2007, 'Legal position available', www.ppca.com.au.

Rural and General Insurance Brokers, 'Public liability insurance for special event and public gathering insurance', www.ruralandgeneral.com.au.

Safe Work Australia 2010 *About Safe Work Australia*, www.safeworkaustralia.gov.au.

Sarris, A 2007, pers. comm., 14 March.

South Australian Brewing Company Pty Ltd v Carlton & United Breweries Ltd (2001) 53 IPR 90; [2001] FCA.

Thorpe, D., Buti, A., Davies, C., Fridman, S., & Jonson, P., 2009 *Sports Law*, Oxford University Press, Australia & New Zealand.

WorkCover NSW, www.workcover.nsw.gov.au.

RISK MANAGEMENT

LEARNING OBJECTIVES

After studying this chapter, you should be able to:

1. define risk and its relationship to the management of festivals and special events
2. understand the context of risk
3. use the tools of risk identification and identify the risks specific to events
4. understand the latest methodologies of risk management
5. understand the core concepts of occupational health and safety.

INTRODUCTION

The Event Management Body of Knowledge (EMBOK 2006) identifies risk management as one of the five knowledge domains necessary for the management of an event. With the growth of the festival and event sector around the world, governments and other key stakeholders realise that they are partially liable for the conduct of events. This is driving the adoption of a formalised risk management procedure for all events. As the number and size of events and festivals increases, so does the public awareness of any mishaps or disasters. Any mistakes made during the planning and execution of major public events such as the Olympics and the Grand Prix reach the press immediately. At the same time it is inevitable that the more events, the more mistakes. This is also driving the occupational health and safety Acts in each state. The planning of events and festivals can no longer be ignored by the authorities. They realise that an incident at an event is too often a result of incompetence in management; therefore, they want proof of management competency long before the festival starts.

A working definition of event risk is any future incident that will negatively influence the event. It could also be described simply as 'possible problems'. Note that this risk is not solely at the event itself. In many texts on events, risk is taken to mean direct safety risk or financial risk, but this definition ignores problems in other areas of event management that may harmfully influence the success of the event. Fraud, for example, is a risk that has surfaced at many events. Misrepresentation of the event by marketing or over-promotion is another risk. Each of these risks may result in safety and financial troubles at the event.

Risk, in the event context, may be formally defined as the likelihood and consequence of the special event or festival not fulfilling its objectives. Risk management can be defined as the process of identifying these problems, assessing them and dealing with them. Fortunately, risk management may also uncover opportunities. For example, the risk of rain at one festival created the opportunity to give away rain capes with the sponsor's logo on them. Similarly, it is common to see hats with logos being handed out at public events when it is a sunny day. In the past, the risk management may have been done in an informal manner; however, the current management environment demands that the process be formalised and documented. The event team must be able to show that risk management is being employed throughout the project. As the South Aftican risk management expert, Errol Ninow (Tassiopoulos 2009, p. 343), points out:

> Risk management is not a highly visible activity and most people are unaware that it has even taken place.

This chapter outlines the process of risk management. The process is made up of understanding the context of risk, risk identification, evaluation and control. This process can be applied to all the areas of event management.

RISK MANAGEMENT PROCESS

Special events are particularly susceptible to risks. A unique venue, large crowds, new staff and volunteers, movement of equipment and general excitement are all a recipe for potential hazards. The event manager who ignores advice on risk prevention is courting disaster and foreshortening his or her career in the event industry. The sensible assessment of potential hazards and preventive action is a part of the overall risk management.

Risk is not necessarily harmful. One reason, among many, that an event company wins the job of organising an event is that competing companies perceive the event to be too risky. The successful company can manage all the risks with its current resources. Risk is the basis of the entrepreneur's business. Without risk, there can be no competitive advantage. Without the appearance of risk, there can be no tightrope walking or extreme games. Part of what makes an event special is the uncertainty — it has not been done before.

The early versions of the Australia New Zealand Risk Management Standard (AS/NZS 4360: 1999) gave a clear definition of risk management:

> Risk management is the term applied to a logical and systematic method of establishing the context, identifying, analysing, evaluating, treating, monitoring and communicating risks associated with any activity, function or process in a way that will enable organisations to minimise losses and maximise opportunities. Risk management is as much about identifying opportunities as avoiding or mitigating losses.

The final word on risk management should be given to the new international standard on risk ISO 31000:

> Risk management should be embedded in all the organization's practices and processes in a way that it is relevant, effective and efficient. The risk management process should become part of, and not separate from, those organizational processes. (AS/NZS ISO 31000: 2009 P: 20)

Every part of event management has potential risks. Berlonghi (1990) in his original and groundbreaking work on event risk, categorises the main areas of risk as:

- *administration* — care must be taken to ensure contracts are in place and all permits and licences are secured
- *marketing and public relations* — the promotion section must be aware of the need for risk management. By their nature, marketeers are optimistic about the consequences of their actions and tend to ignore potential risks.
- *health and safety* — a large part of risk management concerns this area. Loss prevention plans and safety control plans are an important part of any risk management strategy. The risks associated with food concession, hygiene and sanitation require specific attention.
- *crowd management* — this includes risk management of crowd flow, alcohol sales and noise control (see chapter 15 on logistics)
- *security* — the security plan for an event involves careful risk management thinking
- *transport* — deliveries, parking and public transport contain many potential hazards that need to be addressed.

A good risk management strategy will also cover any other operational areas that are crucial to the event and that may need special security and safety precautions, such as ticket sales and other cash points and communications.

Risk management is an integral part of the larger picture of event strategic planning. The event portfolio or event program of a government or a company undergoes the risk management process. The likelihood and consequence of success or failure is a major consideration in the strategic planning. A portfolio of events and festivals will be subject to a comparison so that the level of support can be ascertained. A consideration in this comparison is the probability of success. Operational risk, such as a melee at a tennis match, will affect the reputation of the event and this may flow into the long-term planning of the event. These areas of strategic planning are described in chapter 4.

In chapter 6, the areas of event project management are introduced and risk is one of those areas, but it is not an isolated area. The risk management process cuts across all other knowledge areas. In any of the areas of knowledge and management, the risks must be identified and pre-empted and their management fully integrated into the event plan. By using a project management approach to the event, risk management becomes an underlying process that is employed continuously in every area of the management.

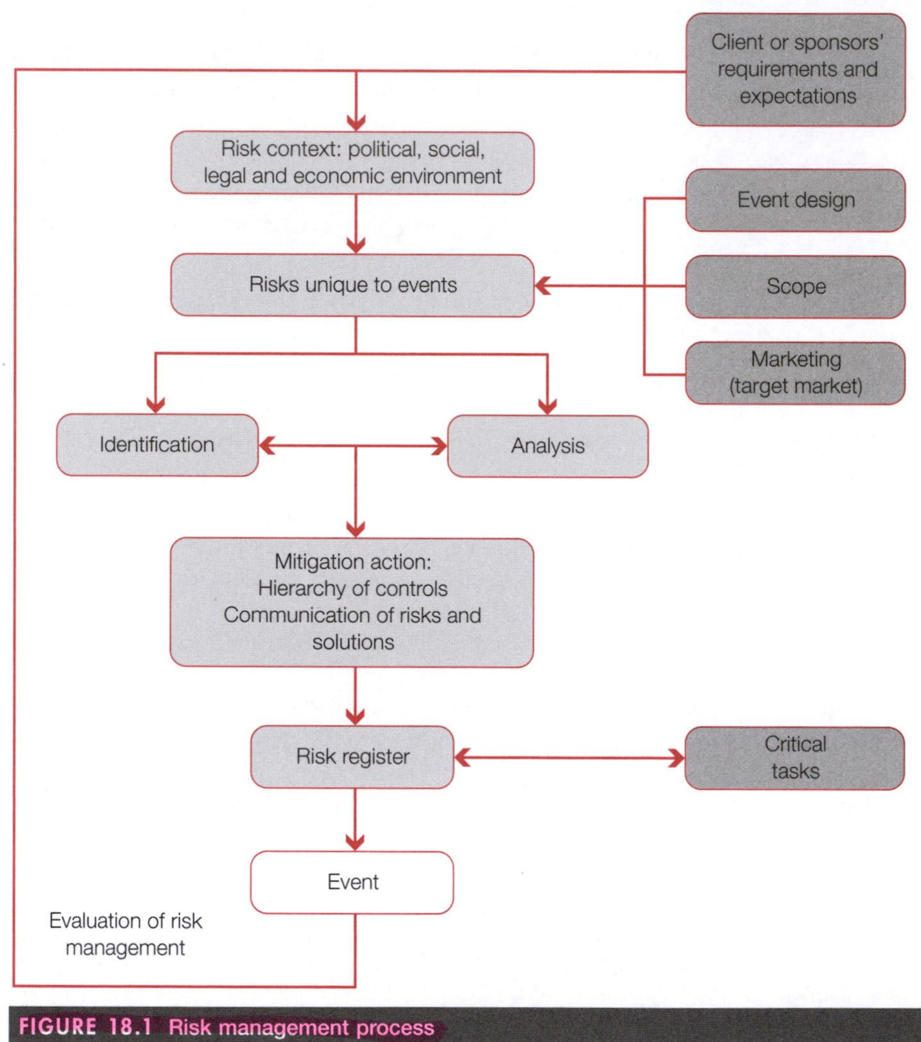

FIGURE 18.1 Risk management process

Source: O'Toole 2010.

Figure 18.1 shows the risk management process as explained in this chapter. It begins by the event team understanding the environment or context of risk. For example, a small rain storm in Dubai stopped all the traffic coming to an event, as the drivers were unfamiliar with driving through the puddles of water on the road. However, a similar downpour in London would have little effect on the traffic coming to the event. The context of risk is combined with the expectations of the stakeholders, the constraints of the other event plans and an understanding of risks that are unique to events. The risks are identified and analysed. Once the risks are understood, the action necessary to mitigate the risk is decided. The description of the risk, its analysis and the treatment form the risk register, from which arises critical tasks that become part of the event plan. Once the event occurs, the whole process is evaluated and used to assist the next risk management process. Although this diagram is structured as a flowchart, risk management does not follow such a simple step-by-step process. The event team must be aware of risk at all times. This chapter explains in detail these elements of the risk management process.

A simple example of this is as follows. A risk that is all too common in events is problems with the master of ceremonies (MC). The event team decides that the comedian who has been hired to be the MC could insult the sponsor. They know this because it has happened at other events and the sponsor has been in the press recently. This is the context of the risk. They analyse the risk and decide that it deserves attention. Next they must minimise the risk. The treatment options include such measures as:

- tell the comedian not to make jokes about the sponsor
- revoke the hiring and hire a professional MC
- tell the sponsor there may be jokes.

These options are placed in the risk register. Whichever treatment option is chosen, it will need to be put in action by the team. Therefore the risk register will create a task that is critical. The task of finding an alternative MC, for example, will then be put in the overall project or event plan.

Understanding context

The context of risk management includes the type of event, the management structure, the stakeholder analysis and the general risk environment. An example of the risk context is the threat made by the Shiv Sena group in India against the Australian cricket matches in India, as a result of the highly-publicised attacks on Indian students in Australia. Terrorism is a major concern for some events. The worldwide publicity that major events attract make them a target for political extremists. As well as Shiv Sena, an affiliate to the notorious Al-Qa'ida has threatened the Commonwealth Games in New Delhi. This has to be taken in the context of the attacks on the Sri Lankan cricket team in Islamabad, Pakistan, in March 2009, when eight people were killed. While the attacks on the World Trade Center and Pentagon in 2001 increased the perceived threat in countries previously thought safe from terrorism, it must be remembered that terrorism at events has been a concern since the Munich Olympics. In India, the terrorism threat and reality has been an ongoing concern since 1947. The 2001 attacks in the USA and the numerous violent incidents such as the bombs in Bali have increased the public perception in western countries of this risk. Some nations deal with terrorism as part of their day-to-day security.

The conclusion is that the surrounding environment, whether it is political, economic, social or cultural, has to be taken into account in the risk management process. The organisational cultures of the client and the event company are also part of the context to be considered. Some companies or organisations are highly risk averse and would prefer a predictable event that has been tried and tested for many years. These clients prefer the 'franchised' event.

A large part of the risk will originate with or involve the stakeholders. A comprehensive stakeholder analysis is a prerequisite for thorough risk management. The stakeholders may also provide the support to deal with the risks. The legislation on duty of care and public liability are further examples of the event environment that will impinge on the risk management process. The financial risk is an example of an ever-changing context. The currency exchange rate, the financial state of the sponsors, fraud and the demands of the shareholders are some of the external developments that can affect the financial viability of the event. A comprehensive risk assessment cannot be performed without understanding the context of the event, the risk environment, such as the incidents that have occurred in the past, and the stakeholders' requirements. One must remember this context is changing and therefore needs to be reassessed as the event management progresses. The introduction of the limits on liability in a number of states, such as the *Civil Liability Act 2003* in Queensland, is an example. The legal context and these Acts are dealt with in more detail in chapter 17.

Occupational health and safety (OHS) codes and guidelines are continually being updated and impinge on many aspects of the event risk management. Figure 18.2 illustrates a financial risk that arose due to the event environment. It shows that major changes can have quite conflicting effects on events.

There are various media reports on whether the global financial crisis has caused the cancellation of events or if the industry is unchanged. In an industry that depends on positive promotion and emphasising the benefits, it is notoriously difficult to obtain hard data. At this early stage, the available information is diverse, anecdotal and indirect, reporting such impacts as the cancellation of multi-million dollar, well-established conferences; a decline in travel and hotel occupancy; and numerous bankruptcies, all of which indicate the scope of the problem.

According to the China Council for the Promotion of International Trade there have been many cancellations. Outbound exhibitions have dropped by almost 5 per cent, which may seem insignificant; however, the number and size of exhibitions grew solidly in the preceding years. They report a reluctance of local companies to go to exhibitions overseas. At the same time the number of inbound exhibitions is dropping. Despite these factors, new exhibition spaces and already existing exhibition spaces are increasing rapidly; therefore 'it is predictable that there will be fierce competition among exhibition hall owners.'

There is a lack of real data for many countries; however, as the exhibition industry is highly linked around the world, it can be reasonably assumed that this is a world-wide problem. As expected, events with the closest links to certain types of industry are most affected.

One result of the crisis has been the formation of industry lobby groups such as the Meetings Mean Business group in the USA. One of their concerns is about the conditions placed by government on recipients of the Troubled Asset Relief Program (TARP). Also they are concerned that the new philosophy of accountability and limited executive payments will flow on to staff incentives; legitimate staff trips and hospitality at major events may be considered by the government and the public to be staff 'junkets'.

The public events industry seemingly had a mixed response to the financial crisis. Some countries' events seem to be greatly reduced and others to be growing. This may be best described as a readjustment period in the festival sector. On a positive note, the number of exhibitions and conferences with the topic 'the world financial crisis' has increased exponentially.

FIGURE 18.2 The effect of the global financial crisis on events

Sources: China's Foreign Trade 2009; De Lollis 2009, U.S. Travel Association 2009.

Figure 18.3 illustrates a risk due to the changing regulatory environment. The office party is almost seen as a fixed part of the corporate calendar. However, an unintended effect of the legislation is the cancellation of what some people might regard as a harmless pursuit. One event company, however, realised an opportunity. It was willing to organise and be responsible for office parties.

BOSSES PULL THE PLUG ON PARTIES

Bruised by the threat of lawsuits under discrimination and health and safety laws, employers are increasingly often dodging the responsibility of organising office Christmas parties.

The chief executive of the business lobby group Employers First, Garry Brack, painted a grim picture for employers hosting parties under occupational health and safety laws.

'These days you have got to provide a perfectly safe environment for your staff,' he said. 'Can you imagine that is sensible in any set of circumstances?'

Add booze to the mix and it becomes nearly impossible.

'You've got to make sure they don't drink too much; make sure they don't get hurt; make sure they get home safely. Have you got the cab driver's phone number?'

According to Mr Brack, to avoid a discrimination claim if a drunken staff member breaks the law an employer would have to organise training in the lead-up to the event and keep tabs on how much people were drinking at the party.

Despite the difficulties, many Australian employers are still sponsoring parties, defying a trend in Britain.

There, a survey of 3500 company bosses found four out of five would not organise a party in the run-up to Christmas.

Almost all of those questioned in the British survey said festive parties caused arguments among staff and often led to official complaints, and two-thirds said they had sacked a member of staff because of their behaviour.

FIGURE 18.3 A risk due to the changes in the regulatory environment

Source: O'Malley 2005.

Identifying risks

The next stage in the process is identifying the risks. Pre-empting problems requires skill, experience and knowledge. Something that appears safe to some of the event staff may contain hidden dangers. A sponsor's sign at an event may look securely mounted when examined by the marketing manager, but it will require the specialist knowledge of the stagehands to ensure it is secure. As the event manager cannot be an expert in every field, it is best to pool the experience of all the event staff and volunteers by convening a risk assessment meeting. The meeting should aim to gather risk management expertise. For large or complex events, an event risk consultant may be hired. The meeting is also an opportunity to train and motivate event staff in the awareness, minimisation and control of risks. Under the OHS Acts in each state and the national code the meeting with staff and their input is mandatory for a safe work environment. This is described in the section on consultation.

Identification techniques

Risk can arise anywhere in the management of events. It is essential that the event team has numerous techniques available to it. Several of these techniques, such as using the work breakdown structure and fault diagrams, were developed in project management and operation management. Some are common in the military and emergency services, such as scenario development.

Work breakdown structure

Breaking down into manageable parts the work necessary to create an event can greatly assist in the identification of risks. It provides a visual scheme as well as the categorisation of the event into units associated with specific skills and resources. An example of the work breakdown structure (WBS) is found in chapter 6. Isolating the event areas in this way gives a clear picture of the possible problems. One of the areas of the WBS for an award night, for example, is the work associated with the master of ceremonies (MC). This question has been posed at many event workshops: 'What could go wrong with the MC?'. Some of the problems identified by event managers' experience include the MC:

- being inebriated
- not turning up
- leaving early
- not reading the script
- using inappropriate language
- having a scruffy appearance
- believing they are the main act
- being unable to use a microphone
- insulting the sponsor.

This does not imply that these are common problems; however, an event manager would be foolish to ignore the experience of others.

The construction of a WBS assists another area of management, the creation of the risk management plan, illustrating the importance to event management of the project management system. Although the WBS is a necessary tool for risk management, it may not reveal the problems that result in a combination of risks. A problem with the ticketing of an event, for example, may not be severe on its own. If it is combined with the withdrawal of a major sponsor, the result may require the event to be cancelled.

Test events

Large sporting events often run smaller events to test the facilities, equipment and other resources. The Olympics test events were effectively used to iron out any problems before the main event. A test is a self-funded rehearsal. The pre-conference cocktail party, for example, is used to test some aspects of the conference. It can test the venue parking, caterer, sound system and type of performers. Many music festivals will run an opening concert on the night before the first day of the festival as a means of testing the equipment.

Classifying risk and SWOT

To assist risk analysis it is useful to have a classification system according to the origin of the risk. Internal risks arise in the event planning and implementation stage. They may also result from the inexperience of the event company. These risks are generally within the abilities of the event company to manage. External risks arise from outside the event organisation and may need a different control strategy. This technique focuses on mitigating the impact of the risk — dealing with the consequences. The impact of a star soccer player cancelling, for example, may be minimised by allowing free entry to the event. For this reason, the SWOT analysis is a risk identification technique. The strengths and weaknesses correspond to internal risks and the opportunities and threats correspond to external risks.

Fault diagram

Risks can also be discovered by looking at their impact and working backwards to the possible cause. This is called a result-to-cause method. A lack of ticket sales at an event, for example, would be a terrible result. The fault diagram method would go back from this risk through the various event aspects to postulate its cause. The list of causes is then used to manage the risk. Insufficient ticket sales may be traced back to problems in promotion such as wrong information in the press release or incorrect target market. It may be traced to problems in logistics such as incorrectly placed signage or parking problems. In each of the work breakdown categories there can be problems that would result in a lack of ticket sales. In the case of a recent Grand Prix, the event owners saw a competing event as the cause of low ticket sales.

Incident report

Almost all large public events have an incident report document. These may be included in the event manual and are to be filled out by the event staff when there is an incident. The incident data can then be used by agencies to give an event risk profile. The ambulance service has such data on medical incidents for events. This data is useful for estimating resources to allocate. By giving the ambulance service key characteristics of an event, such as audience number, alcohol availability, age group and type of event activity, they can predict the type of medical incidents most likely to occur.

Contingency plan

An outcome of the risk analysis may be a detailed plan of viable alternative integrated actions. The contingency plan contains the response to the impact of a risk and involves a decision procedure, chain of command and a set of related actions. An example of contingency planning is the planning for the Delhi Commonweatlh Games. This could pose a major problem for any event in the local area, particularly as there will be events such as weddings and religious celebrations happening the same time.

Scenario development and tabletop exercises

The use of a 'what if' session can uncover many risks. A scenario of problems is given to the event team and interested stakeholders. They work through the problems and present their responses. These responses are collated and discussed. These tabletop exercises are surprisingly effective. One tabletop exercise used the scenario of an expected fireworks display not happening at a major New Year's Eve event. All the agencies around the table then responded, describing the consequences as they saw it and their contingency plans. The problems included disappointed crowds, a rush for public transport and other crowd management issues. Would the event company be able to announce to a crowd of 500 000 what had happened? The fireworks went off as planned in the following year. Two years later, however, the fireworks did not occur due to a sudden increase in the wind. A number of agencies such as police, emergency services and railways were able to use their contingency plans. Major sponsors and government clients may send an event company a number of scenarios and ask for their response. This is a way of testing the competence of the event management.

Consultation

Part of each state's occupational health and safety code is the concept of consultation. The event management team is required to consult with the various suppliers on their safety plans for the event. It is slightly different for different regions; however, consultation can also be used to strengthen the risk identification and analysis. Suppliers have a wealth of information on what can go wrong. Consultation does not imply just asking questions, the event manager must provide relevant information so that the other party can give a considered opinion. This opinion must be taken into account in the planning of the event and risk management. Consultation is further explored in the section on Occupational Health and Safety.

The event and venue team

The importance of staff and volunteers to identifying risks cannot be underestimated. Kim Davis from the Queensland Performing Arts Centre (QPAC) recommends that the team have a strong 'situational awareness'. The event should be thoroughly researched. The demographics of the event must be understood. 'If the event attracts [people from] a range of demographics, how will each group interact or impact on each other?' The performers too — or the event attraction — will have certain expectations of their audience, which need to be understood. Davis also observes that 'no venue is an island — be aware of international and local issues and how these may impact on an event' (Davis 2009).

Accurate identification

An essential aspect of risk identification is the process of accurately describing the risks. The risk for an outdoor event is not 'weather'. A beautiful fine day is still 'weather'. Heat or rain may be the risk descriptor. However, this is still not accurate enough. Extreme heat or heavy rain before the event is closer to describing the actual risk. The process of describing the risk accurately also enables the event team to think the risk through.

A seemingly simple risk of rain is, in practice, quite complex.

For example, a film festival may go ahead 'rain, hail or shine'. But the question is 'how much rain and when?' The risk is not a light sprinkle or rain after the event. The risk analysis process demands that the risk is properly described. Note that the rain at one event may not be a disaster for an event company if they have distributed their risk by having events around the country. Lightning may pose a high risk as the consequence for an outdoor festival with large metal towers is serious.

Analysis and evaluation of the risk

It is obvious that there are an infinite number of things that can go wrong and a finite number that can go right. Identifying risk can open a Pandora's box of issues. Risk assessment meetings often reveal the 'prophets of doom' who can bring an overly pessimistic approach to the planning process. This is itself a risk that must be anticipated. The event team must have a method of organising the risks so they can be methodically managed. Once the risks are accurately described, they should be mapped according to:

- the likelihood of the incident occurring. Emergency Management Australia recommends that the risk is rated on a five-point scale from rare to almost certain. Rare means that the incident will occur only in exceptional circumstances; for example, an earthquake in Sydney. The other ratings are unlikely, possible, likely and almost certain. Rain at an event in Indonesia during the monsoon period would be rated as 'almost certain'.
- the consequence if the incident does occur. The five-point rating scale for the consequences are insignificant, minor, moderate, major and catastrophic. Insignificant, according to SAI Global, means that the incident would be dealt with by routine operations; for example, no injuries, no financial loss. Catastrophic means that the consequence would threaten the event and the event organisations; for example, death, huge financial loss (SAI Global 2006).

These are often called the dimensions of risk and provide the event team with a tool to rate the risks. A risk that is assessed as catastrophic and almost certain to happen will need immediate action. The Australia Standard describes this risk as 'extreme'. A risk that is unlikely and insignificant will not be afforded the same attention as risks of a higher rating. Other risk management models include the perception of the risk and its frequency as part of the risk assessment.

An accurate way of describing the risks is essential to clear communication. At one risk meeting, for example, the risk of providing incorrect information to the media was identified as likely and the consequence was moderate to major. It was assessed as needing attention and requiring a solution. At another meeting it was found that the decision to possibly cancel the event was being left to the event's general manager (GM). However, during the event, the GM would be in a high security area with politicians and difficult to contact. The risk of 'GM impossible to contact' was rated certain and catastrophic. The solution was simple: have security clearance for a 'runner' to be able to communicate between the event team and the GM.

A risk meeting with the staff and volunteers is often the only way to uncover many risks. It is important that the meeting be well chaired and focused, since the time needed for risk assessment must always be weighed against the limited time available for the overall event planning. An effective risk assessment meeting will produce a comprehensive and realistic analysis of the potential risks in a risk register. The risk register is the document output of the risk management process and is further explained in the documentation section later in this chapter.

Control

After the risks have been evaluated, the event management team needs to create mechanisms to control any problems that might arise. The decisions include:

- changing the likelihood that a problem will occur — this can include avoiding the problem by not proceeding with that aspect of the event. A water-ski event, for example, was unable to obtain insurance. The management identified the part of the event that was high risk, a high speed race, and cancelled it. This enabled the event to go ahead with the necessary level of insurance.
- changing the consequence if the problem does occur — such as contingency planning and disaster plans
- accepting the risk
- transferring the risk to another party.

Insurance is an example of changing the consequence by transferring the risk and accepting a smaller risk. The risk that is now accepted is:

- the insurance contract will be honoured (for example, the insurance company could go bankrupt)
- the event makes enough money to pay for the insurance.

The risk management process can be defined, therefore, as transferring the risks to a part of the event management that has the resources (including skills, experience and knowledge) to handle it. This is an important point because the risk is rarely, if ever, completely eliminated, except by cancelling the event. Once a risk has been identified and a solution planned, its likelihood of occurring and its consequences are reduced.

In his comprehensive manual on risk management for events, Berlonghi (1990) suggests the following risk control strategies:

- *cancel and avoid the risk* — if the risk is too great it may be necessary to cancel all or part of the event. Outdoor concerts that are part of a larger event are often cancelled if there is rain. The major risk is not audience discomfort, but the danger of electrocution.
- *diminish* the risk — risks that cannot be avoided need to be minimised. To eliminate all possible security risks at an event, for example, may require every patron to be searched. This solution is obviously unworkable at a majority of events. Instead, a risk minimisation strategy will need to be developed; for example, installing metal detectors or stationing security guards in a more visible position.
- *reduce the severity of risks that do eventuate* — a major part of safety planning is preparing quick and efficient responses to foreseeable problems. Training staff in

elementary first aid can reduce the severity of an accident. The event manager cannot eliminate natural disasters, but can prepare a plan to contain the effects.
- *devise back-ups and alternatives* — when something goes wrong, the situation can be saved by having an alternative plan in place. In case the juggler does not turn up to a children's party, for example, the host can organise party games to entertain the children. On a larger scale, back-up generators are a must at big outdoor events in case of a major power failure.
- *distribute the risk* — if the risk can be spread across different areas, its impact will be reduced if something does go wrong. One such strategy is to widely spread the cash-taking areas, such as ticket booths, so that any theft is contained and does not threaten the complete event income. This does not eliminate the risk, it transfers it to an area that can be managed by the event company, such as security and supervision. Having a variety of sponsors is another way to distribute risk. If one sponsor pulls out, the others can be approached to increase their involvement.
- *transfer the risk* — risk can be transferred to other groups responsible for an event's components. Subcontractors may be required to share the liability of an event. Their contracts generally contain a clause to the effect that they are responsible for the safety of their equipment and the actions of their staff during the event. In Australia, most performing groups are required to have public liability insurance before they can take part in an event.

A more formal system, the hierarchy of controls, has been developed in the OHS standards. According to the OHS Practical Solutions Database (Australian Safety and Compensation Council) this hierarchy provides an order of control measure for risks:

1. Elimination — controlling the hazard at source
2. Substitution — replacing the source of the risk with a safe one
3. Isolation or engineering — removing the link between the source of risk and the person
4. Administration — training, developing policies and procedures for safe work practices, creating a team spirit
5. Personal protective equipment — e.g. respirators, ear plugs.

When controlling risk the event team should start at the top of the hierarchy and, if that is not possible, move to the next level of control. The hierarchy of controls is a framework that enables the event team to systematically work through the risks. However, event risk management can be far more complex as some risks require a number of these controls to be used.

Mitigating actions

The following examples of mitigating actions are based on recommendations of the Federal Emergency Management Agency (2000).

At every event, people will leave some items unattended. Event officials must decide beforehand how to handle unattended packages and have a written plan for all personnel to follow. The issues to consider include: Who will respond? Are dogs trained to identify explosives available? Will the area be evacuated?

Concealment areas are areas where persons may hide or where someone may hide packages or other weapons. The best way to avoid problems in these areas is to map the event venue and identify the areas that could be used as hiding spots. Venue staff can assist in this matter.

Venue and security personnel should work together to conduct a security sweep of the venue. A few areas to address in advance are: How often is security going to go through the event site? What are they looking for? How do they handle incidents? Who is going to do the sweep? Once a sweep of the area has been done the area must be secured.

Each of these mitigating actions, in addition to Berlonghi's strategies, can be reduced to the management of two risk dimensions: likelihood and consequence. A back-up generator is an example of reducing the consequence of a blackout. Checking the capacity of the electricity supply is an example of reducing the likelihood of a power failure.

Risk communication

Effective risk communication includes the following:

- *understanding the terminology of risk* — the risk needs to be accurately described and understood by all event staff and volunteers.
- *open communication channels* — it is a well-known problem at events that staff are hesitant to tell event management that a task has not been completed. If they identify problems there must be a way that this can be communicated to the event management in a timely manner. The State Emergency Service uses a system of team leaders. It is part of the leaders' role to collect this data.
- *informal methods of communication* — management theorists, such as Peter Drucker (1973), stress how important these informal methods are to the success of a company. This is true for events. The dinners, chats over coffee or just a friendly talk can greatly assist the communication process. Walking the site is a time-honoured way to find out what is going on.

The formal process of communicating risk includes the distribution of the risk plan. It is the output or deliverable of the risk management process. The plan contains a list of identified risks, their assessment, the plan of action, who is responsible and the timeline for implementation. In the fluid event management environment, a fixed plan may be quickly out of date. A risk management plan of a parade, for example, will have to be revised if there are any additions to the parade, such as horses. For this reason, it is recommended by most project management texts that a live risk register be established. The risk register is a plan that is constantly updated and revised. As new risks are identified they are added to the register. The register has a number of functions:

1. It is a live management tool.
2. It can be used to track risks so they are not forgotten.
3. It is proof of actions for a work-in-progress report.
4. It can be used after the event to help prove competent management.
5. It can be used for the next event to assist risk identification and planning.
6. It can have various levels of access to allow staff and senior management a role in risk management.
7. It can communicate the main issues, simply and clearly.

A live risk register can be put on the intranet or internet and is therefore accessible to all members of the event team. It can be printed at any time and placed in a report to the various stakeholders. The risk register therefore provides a snapshot for the event management process.

Further risk management methodologies

Principles of safe design

As the generic risk management methodology spread to different industry sectors, it became obvious that many problems were related to how the asset or end product of a project was initially designed.

The Australian New Zealand Standard (Standards Australia 2004, p. 13) states:

> Management of risk is an integral part of good management. It is an iterative process of continuous improvement that is best embedded into existing practices or business processes.

This suggests that risk management pervades all areas of the event initiation, planning and implementation. The Australian Safety and Compensation Council (2006, p. 6) has applied this to the design stage of a project:

> A safe design approach begins in the conceptual and planning phases with an emphasis on making choices about design, materials used and methods of manufacture or construction to enhance the safety of the finished product.

They describe five principles of safe design, which can be applied to the design of an event, namely:

1. Person with control — person who makes the key event management decisions
2. Product life cycle — safe design encompasses all aspects of the event including the after-event outcomes
3. Systematic risk management — using the identification/assess/control process
4. Safe design knowledge and capability — the event team should be trained and competent
5. Information transfer — the event team needs an effective and timely communication and documentation system for the risk management.

Each of these principles is employed over the phases from pre-design to design completion shown in figure 18.4. The risk management process of context, identify, analyse, evaluate, control is juxtaposed with the design process. The design process is common in many areas of event management such as staging, theming, programming, marketing and site choice and layout. The figure illustrates how the risk can be embedded in these areas.

An important part of the safe design methodology is the concept of downstream problems that result from upstream risk. It is an excellent metaphor to help the event team realise the consequence of mistakes or seemingly small faults early in the planning of an event. A forgotten phone call to a supplier early in the planning can result in all kinds of problems at the event. Every member of the event team — from the person doing the photocopying to the event director — is responsible for the success of the event. A volunteer who moves a race marker to allow a car to park prior to a marathon race can inadvertently invalidate the whole race. Consider the chain of events: the race marker was returned to a slightly different spot. The race went around that marker quite a few times, significantly shortening the race. All the competitors came in with new 'personal bests' until they realised something was wrong. The shortened race meant that the results were invalid to the world marathon officials. The competitors entered this race as it was a qualifying race for world championships. Therefore all their months of practice were to no avail. This all occurred because a volunteer wanted to help a motorist.

Hazard analysis and critical control points (HACCP)

A specific application of the generic risk standard to a part of the event industry is found in the food industry. The hazard analysis and critical control points (HACCP) is a methodology that includes consulting, documentation, implementation and internal auditing for the food industry and hospitals. It is important to consider the HACCP methodology as the event caterers will be familiar with it and it illustrates how these tools are used. Food is a major source of risk at events. Some regions in Australia require a special temporary off-site food premises registration form to be completed to allow food to be sold at community events. The risk can take many forms. It may be an obvious risk such as the cleanliness of the facilities or a secondary risk arising from a problem in another area of the event management. An example of an often-overlooked secondary risk is the risk of a blackout or power outage. Most event managers would identify the consequence as the sound system not running, lights not working and the elevator stopping mid-floor and trapping people. However, there is also the loss of temperature control for the food. The consequence of an increase or drop in the temperature for food can be classified as major. This simple example illustrates that the food risk management must be linked with the overall event risk management.

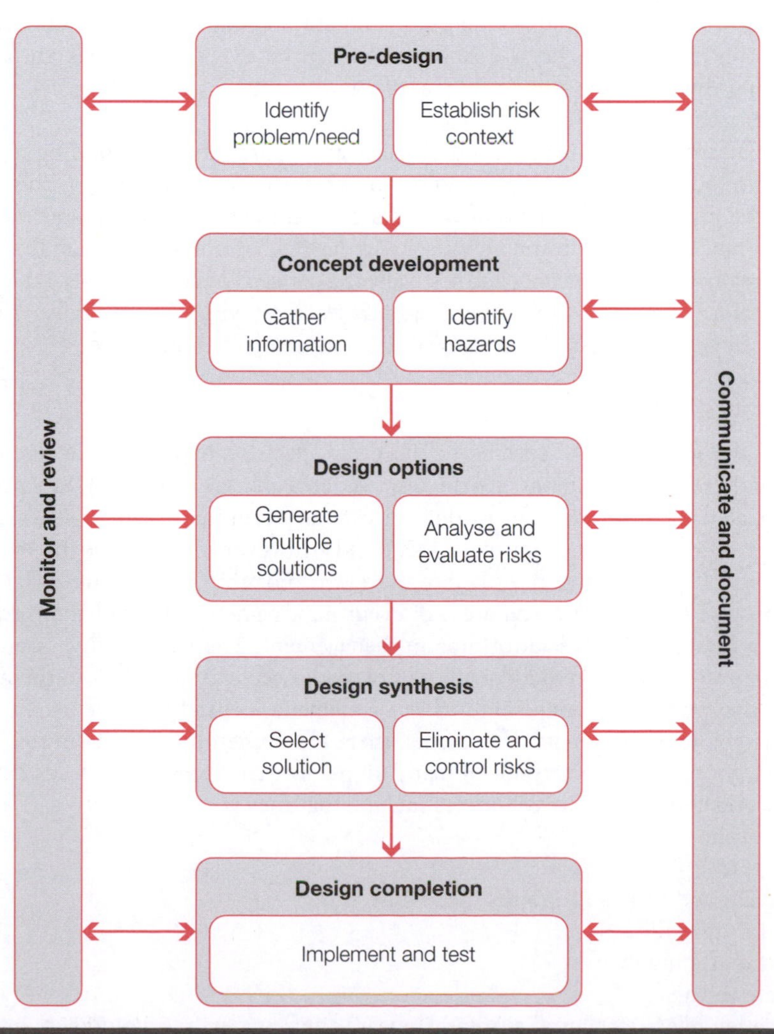

FIGURE 18.4 The risk management process from the design perspective

Source: Australian Safety and Compensation Council 2006, p. 19.

The HACCP system consists of the following seven principles (US Food and Drug Administration 2001):

1. Conduct a hazard analysis.
2. Determine the critical control points (CCPs).
3. Establish critical limit(s).
4. Establish a system to monitor control of the CCP.
5. Establish the corrective action to be taken when monitoring indicates that a particular CCP is not under control.
6. Establish procedures for verification to confirm that the HACCP system is working effectively.
7. Establish documentation concerning all procedures and records appropriate to these principles and their application.

Although these principles were developed for the food industry, the concept of CCPs has application in the wider event context. O'Toole (2010), in describing the event project, identifies an 'exposure profile' in the timeline of the event project. The exposure profile identifies critical points over the project when the event team is most exposed to risk. An example is when the main entertainment act has been advertised but the contract has not been finalised. Experienced event companies are adept at minimising this exposure profile by identifying the critical points. They focus on the exposure profile and control the risks.

A similar approach to risk is found in vulnerability profiling and building resilience, which is found in the work of Salter (2005) on preparing for emergencies. This method stresses the process of risk planning, as distinct from the risk plan as a document, and the importance of the community's capacity to deal with hazards. Although this has not been formally applied to events and festivals, the concept of continuously building the capacity of a community to deal with hazards by identifying and minimising hazards through the active process of planning and self-assessment is attractive.

Specific event risks

Many of the risks that are specific to the event industry happen at the event itself. Issues with crowd movement are an obvious area of risk. The consequences of a crowd-related incident can lead to duty of care and criminal liability issues, so they are a high priority in the event manager's mind. However, the risks at the event may be a result of ignoring the risks before the event. For this reason, the risk management must be tracked across all areas of event management. Many of the risks at the event can be tracked to a lack of time in management. The lack of time is, in reality, an inability to scope or predict the amount of work necessary to carry out the management of the event. The conclusion is that a systematic method must be used.

Due to the temporary nature of events, there are numerous risks. Using volunteers at events, for example, can result in many kinds of risks. Some of the risks listed at a recent workshop relating to volunteers include that they:

- don't listen
- don't turn up
- complain and form sub-groups that 'white ant'
- can't be controlled
- have no accountability
- deplete the asset.

The latter refers to a problem with repeat events, when the volunteers are set in their ways and the event needs to change.

This discussion is not exhaustive. It highlights some of the areas specific to events.

Crowd management

Two terms often confused are crowd control and crowd management. As Abbott (2000, p. 105) points out:

> Crowd management and crowd control are two distinct but interrelated concepts. The former includes the facilitation, employment and movement of crowds, while the latter relates to the steps taken once the crowd has lost control.

The concept of crowd management is an example of pre-empting problems at the event by preparing the risk management before the event. Many crowd control issues arise from inadequate risk management by the event company. However, there can still be unforeseen risks with crowds.

There are many factors that impinge on the smooth management of crowds at an event. The first risk is correctly estimating the number of people who will attend the event. No matter how the site is designed, too many attendees can put enormous strain on the event resources. Even at free events, too few attendees can significantly affect the event objectives. The launch of the Paralympic mascots in the Sydney Domain attracted an audience of only 500 when the site was designed for thousands. It gave an empty look to the event site. Crowd risk management is also a function of the audience type and the audience's standard of behaviour. A family event will have different priorities in risk management compared with a rock festival. The expectations of the crowd can be managed if the right kind of information is sent out before the event.

Crowd management for large events has become a specialist field of study and there are a number of consultancies in this area. The crowd control issues are amply illustrated by the incidents at the large outdoor events such as the Big Day Out and the Haj. An excellent resource on the study of crowds is found at www.crowdsafe.com.

A comprehensive study of crowd behaviour published by Emergency Planning College in the UK gives the following advice:

Key advice for successful crowd management includes:

- Thorough planning and preparation, using a wide range of "what if...?" scenarios, including unexpected scenarios.
- Adoption of a system-wide approach.
- Coordination between all agencies involved.
- Utilisation of personnel who have plentiful first-hand knowledge, skills and experience in planning for and managing crowd events.
- Communication with the whole crowd – both audio and visual – particularly in emergency situations.
- Leadership and guidance to initiate crowd movement in emergencies.
- Acknowledgement that seemingly small problems occurring in combination can have a significant impact on event success.

(Emergency Planning College 2009, p. 5)

The behaviour of the people who attend the event is vital to its success and the source of its greatest risk. Incidents in the crowds can have catastrophic outcomes resulting in shutdown the event and can put the event company and the client under threat of criminal negligence charges.

Alcohol and drugs

Events can range from a family picnic with the audience sipping wine while watching a show, to a New Year's Eve mass gathering of youths and the heavy consumption of alcohol. Under the law, both events are treated the same. The Responsible Service of Alcohol provision in many countries is a method of reducing the likelihood of this risk. Some annual events have been cancelled due to the behaviour problems that arise from selling alcohol. The alcohol risk management procedures can permeate every aspect of some events, including limiting ticket sales, closing hotels early, increasing security and roping off areas.

For the New Year's Eve celebrations at Darling Harbour, the management also identified the major risks resulting from broken glass. In the past, the site needed a large and expensive clean-up after the event and the safety issue was paramount. After consultation with all of the stakeholders, their risk management procedure included:

- erecting a perimeter fence around the site
- allowing alcohol only in licensed premises
- having an alcohol-free and glass-free policy for all public areas
- rearranging the entertainment to appeal to families and senior citizens
- publicising the new policy in all advertisements.

A worthy mention is the risk of drugs at events. Many modern events, in particular rave parties, involve risks arising from drug use. Emergency and first-aid services are faced with the quandary of treating the problem and reporting the incident to police. Some rave or dance parties are secret — which is part of the allure — and first-aid services have to decide whether to inform the police of these parties and, therefore, risk the possibility of not being contracted again by the organisers. Another risk related to drug use is the presence of syringes and their safe handling by staff.

Communication

The risks involved in communication are varied as concern the event organisation and reporting any risks. Setting up a computer and filing system for the event office can prevent future problems. Easy access to relevant information is vital to good risk management. A standard, yet customised, reporting procedure can also reduce the risk of ineffective communication. Communication can include how the public is informed of the event, signage, and keeping attendees informed when they are at the event site. The event manual is an excellent communication device for the procedures, protocol and general event information for staff and volunteers. There can be a risk of too much data obscuring the important information; therefore, it needs to be highly focused.

Environment

The risk to the environment posed by modern businesses is of increasing concern to the general community. There are dangerous risks, such as pollution, spills and effluent leakage, and more indirect risks that can be minimised by waste recycling and water and energy conservation. The impacts and therefore the priorities for their control will vary over the event project life cycle.

Emergency

An awareness of the nearest emergency services and their working requirements is mandatory for the event management. Outside emergency services will be used if the situation is beyond the capabilities of the event staff and needs specialist attention. It is important to understand the chain of command when emergency services arrive.

They can be outside the control of the event management staff, who would act purely in an advisory capacity. Emergency services may be called in by any attendee at an event.

Preparing the attendee

Many of the problems at events can be minimised by preparing the people who come to the event. Part of an event will be the 'wow' or surprise and there is a tendency by the organisers to keep the event a mystery. However a responsible event team should be aware that many aspects of the event can be communicated to the audience long before they arrive. The UK website set up by the National Health Service (NHS 2008) in the UK is an excellent example. The pages on its Festival Safety Guide provides tips on safety issues for a person who will attends a festivals including what to pack, first aid, food safety and sun protection. The pages are written in as style that their intended audience understands and it includes video of attendees talking about what they bring to minimise problems as well as interviews with the safety staff.

event profile

CROWD CONTROL AT THE CHINESE OLYMPICS

The Beijing Olympics provided many stories of events management. The massive scale of the Olympics and its public relations potential for China created a high risk environment. As the story below illustrates the environment of the event, the social and historical culture in which it sits, influences the types of risks.

CROWD NIGHTMARE HAUNTS BEIJING OLYMPICS ORGANISERS

From spitting and booing to full-scale riots, Chinese fans loom as a potential public relations disaster for the Beijing Olympics.

Organisers have spent millions of US dollars on "civilising" their notoriously unruly spectators, fearing a repeat of rowdy scenes that regularly mar football and basketball matches here.

'You cannot deny it — the difficult area in staging a civilised Olympics rests in the quality of the people,' senior Games organiser Zhang Faqiang told state media.

Leaving nothing to chance, officials have organised lessons in cheering, queuing and sportsmanship for home spectators, many of whom have little experience of such events.

But concern remains over possible flare-ups which would embarrass the hosts in front of a worldwide audience running into billions.

In June, angry fans turned on the national football team during their 1-0 defeat to Qatar, booing, hurling bottles and fighting in the latest of a series of unseemly incidents.

Back in 2004, hundreds of incensed supporters blockaded the Japanese team hotel in Beijing after their Asian Cup final victory over China, creating unwelcome headlines abroad.

Similar trouble erupted during this year's East Asian Cup when the crowd jeered and threw rubbish at the Japanese team, who were also abused during the 2007 Women's World Cup in China.

The chequered history prompted Japanese Prime Minister Yasuo Fukuda to urge Chinese fans, often resentful over Japan's invasion of the 1930s and 1940s, not to boo Olympic athletes from his country.

'Many Chinese people may cheer only for Chinese athletes. That would be all right,' Fukuda said in May, according to Japanese media.

'But if they criticise opponent nations and do something like booing against them, it will provoke antipathy among people of these nations.'

Crowd behaviour has even caused concern among Chinese Olympians, particularly after unsporting scenes at the 'Bird's Nest' Olympic Stadium.

Source: Harris 2008.

Review

Evaluating the successes and failures of the risk control strategy is central to the planning of future events. The event company must be a 'learning organisation'. The analysis of, and response to, feedback is essential to this process.

OCCUPATIONAL HEALTH AND SAFETY (OHS) AND EVENTS

The health and safety of the people at events is the highest priority for any event team. The risks in this part of the event management's responsibilities are enormous — both to the event and to all the key stakeholders. The results of an incident can reverberate around a country and affect future events and the whole event industry. In South Africa, the crowd crush at the Ellis Park Stadium in Johannesburg directly led to the introduction of the South African National Standard SANS 10366:2004 Health and Safety at Live Events and the Safety at Sports and Recreational Events Bill.

The regulations and legislation concerning occupational health and safety (OHS) in Australia are the responsibility of state and territory authorities. However, all states are signatory to the National OHS Strategy 2002–2012 that attempts to provide a national consistency to the OHS legislation in the states. This has evolved into a National code that is expected to be progressively adopted by the state governments.

According to WorkCover NSW; Adoption of the National Code is part of the move towards harmonisation. States and territories have amended their legislation to allow for the adoption of the National Code. National model OHS. The legislation is expected by December 2011. Although each of the states has differing Acts concerning OHS, the concepts of duty of care and consultation are fundamental to the state Acts and the National Code.

Consultation

Each state Act in Australia has a slightly different definition of the key term consultation. Each OHS Act agrees on the importance of consultation. According to WorkCover Victoria:

> Consultation is a two way conversation between employers and employees that involves:
>
> - Sharing information (information must be made available in a timely way and in a form that can be understood by employees);
> - Giving employees a reasonable opportunity to express their views (employees should be encouraged to play a part in the problem solving process); and
> - Taking those views into account (employees should help to shape decisions, not hear about them after they are made).

If there is more than one employer, they should work together to ensure they all meet their responsibilities.

The event team must consult with the event stakeholders such as the suppliers, volunteers and sponsors on event health and safety. Risk management must be an agenda item at all meetings.

For larger special events and festivals, WorkCover Victoria recommends that the event team develops an event safety policy. Figure 18.5 lists the suggested contents of a safety policy.

3.2 EVENT SAFETY POLICY

The event safety policy is a document that communicates the values, objectives and broad commitments of the event organiser to conducting a safe event. It represents a high level commitment by the event organiser that sets the tone for how, and to what degree, the system for managing safety will be supported.

3.2.1. What types of things should an event safety policy include?

Some suggested items and themes for inclusion in an event safety policy are:

- statements conveying management commitment;
- continual improvement of safety performance;
- working in consultation;
- objectives or targets for personal injury performance (e.g. number of medical treatments per 1000 spectators);
- compliance with Victorian OHS legislation;
- a commitment toward a high level of event security;
- a reference to the safety of participants, entertainers, members of the public, event staff and contractors;
- competent and trained staff; and
- signed by the CEO.

WorkSafe Victoria's website, www.worksafe.vic.gov.au, should be accessed for more information and future updates.

FIGURE 18.5 Event safety policy

Source: WorkSafe Victoria 2006, 'Advice for managing events safely', p. 11. www.worksafe.vic.gov.au

The New Zealand Ministry of Civil Defence and Emergency Management (2003) recommends that large events form a safety committee (see figure 18.6). This is a cross-functional committee with responsibilities for OHS in each of its departments.

The relevant OHS Acts vary around Australia and it is mandatory for an event team to understand the legislation and relevant codes and guidelines. The relevant Acts for event teams in South Australia are listed in figure 18.7 on the following page.

OHS Acts ensure a sustainable event industry and the national code. Other countries such as South Africa, New Zealand and the UK have very similar legislation for events. The core of all the OHS Acts is the risk management procedure as described in this chapter. When this is combined with the relevant codes, guidelines and legislation, it gives the event team a safety framework for events.

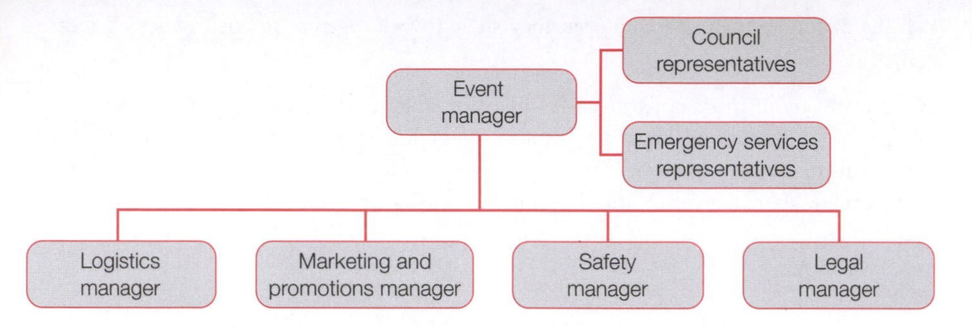

The responsibilities in each area are:

Logistics manager
- Emergency management
- Traffic management
- Site management
- Security management
- Communication and contacts
- Waste management
- Staff provisioning

Marketing and promotions manager
- Promotion
- Advertising
- Media releases

Safety manager
- Health and safety guidelines
- Water supply management
- Food management
- Public safety management
- Public health management
- Evacuation scheme
- Alcohol management plan

Legal manager
- Permits
- Consents
- Insurance
- Finance
- Contracts
- Other legal responsibilities

FIGURE 18.6 Recommended safety committee composition

Source: New Zealand Ministry of Civil Defence and Emergency Management 2003, pp. 18–19.

Development Act and regulations
Disability Discrimination Act
Dog and Cat Management Act
Environment Protection (Machine Noise) Policy
Environmental Protection Act
Equal Opportunity Act
Explosives Act
Food Act and regulations
Liquor Licensing Act
Local Government Act
Occupational Health, Safety and Welfare Act and regulations
Public and Environmental Health Act, Regulations and waste control regulations
Road Traffic Act
Summary Offences Act
Swimming Pools (Safety) Act

FIGURE 18.7 Relevant Acts for event teams in South Australia

SUMMARY

Risk management is a modern, formal process of identifying and managing risk. It is one of the functions of any event management and the process should be part of the event's everyday organisation. There are risks that are specific to particular events. To correctly identify these risks, knowledge of the unique risks is essential. The risk is more than risks at the event itself. The output of this process is a live risk register that shows the risks and their management schedule. As part of this risk strategy, the management has to understand its legal requirements. It has a duty of care to all involved in an event. Any reasonably foreseen risks have to be eliminated or minimised.

The safety of the event attendees is a prime concern for the event team. Any event comes under the various state-based OHS Acts. Risk management, duty of care and consultation are the three core elements of the methodology recommended in the OHS Acts. These combine with the codes, legislation and guidelines to provide the safety framework in which the event team must work.

QUESTIONS

1 List the risks to a regional festival arising from these areas:
   (a) local organising committee
   (b) sponsorship
   (c) volunteers
   (d) council politics
   (e) participants in a parade
   (f) computers
   (g) experience of organising group.
2 Are corporate special events covered by the risk policy of the venue or the client? Why?
3 Event management has been described as 'just solving problems'. Can risk management replace all the other methods of management, such as marketing, logistics and project management, to create an event?
4 Contrast the risks involved in staging an outdoor concert and those involved in producing an indoor food fair. What risk management strategy could be used to reduce or eliminate these risks?
5 What is the OHS Act in your state? What organisation penalises an event for not following the OHS Act?

case study

THE HAJJ OF 2009 AND THE H1N1 VIRUS

حدثنا عمرو بن علي حدثنا يحيى بن سعيد القطان حدثنا المغيرة بن أبي قرة السدوسي قال سمعت أنس بن مالك يقول
قال رجل يا رسول الله أعقلها وأتوكل أو أطلقها وأتوكل قال اعقلها وتوكل

A person asked the Prophet: 'Shall I bind my camel and put my trust in God or I unbind it and put my trust in God.'
The Prophet said: 'Keep it bound and put your trust in God.'

The yearly pilgrimage of nearly 3 million people of the Islamic faith from over 140 countries to the Kingdom of Saudi Arabia is one of the largest events in the world. It is expected of every Muslim to undertake the journey to Mecca if they can afford it and are able to physically complete it. It is one of the five 'pillars' or duties of Islam. The pilgrimage involves the movement of millions of people around the site to perform specific rituals. These include:

- Circling the Kaaba — a black stone cube set in the centre of the Mosque — seven times
- The search for water and drinking from the water of the Zamzam spring. The pilgrims re-enact the search for water by moving rapidly between two landmarks
- Prayer and contemplation on Mount Arafat
- Stoning the devil, whereby the pilgrims throw stones at a wall to symbolise the rejection of the Devil by the prophet Abraham.

The movement of the pilgrims and the action of thousands of people throwing stones at a wall have resulted in a number of major problems. In particular, the deaths due to the stampede on the bridge in 2006 motivated the Saudi government to hire a crowd management specialist company to advise on these issues. Other risks include the spread of fire from the cooking stoves to the highly flammable tents in the accommodation area of the valley of Mina. All these risks have been minimised by various means, although the movement of huge of crowds remains a constant management issue.

With the large numbers of people coming from many countries, the risks during the Haj are well publicised. In the past there have been serious incidents and disasters that can be summarised under three headings:

- Crowd management problems — including stampedes and riots
- Fire — the combination of cooking fires and tents has resulted in major tragedies
- Protests — the importance of the occasion combined with the attention the event gains around the world has led to a number of protests including the violent occupation of the Grand Mosque in 1979.

One of the recently recognised risks is the rapid spread of disease to the pilgrims and from them to their countries on their return. The Hajj brings people from developed, developing and underdeveloped countries. Some of these countries do not have effective public health programs. These pilgrims may not be vaccinated against numerous diseases. Khan (2003) points out that overcrowded

conditions are perfect for transmitting infections such as invasive meningococcal meningitis:

> Outbreaks of typhoid and cholera have also been recorded during Hajj. Although most early cases of meningitis were reported in pilgrims, the outbreaks quickly spread to their immediate contacts and then to those with no pilgrim contact, and cases were continued to be identified even 3 to 4 months after the Hajj, most likely as a result of pilgrims assimilating in the community and dispersing bacteria.

At that time, in 2003, it was quickly recognised that the Hajj could result in the worldwide spread of the meningococcal virus.

The year 2009 presented the Saudi Arabian authorities with the new risk of the spread of the H1N1 virus, causing the swine flu type A. Around the world the threat of an outbreak of swine flu led to numerous events and festivals being cancelled. The enormous number of people and the overcrowding at the Hajj created the right conditions for the spread of the flu. There have been a number of precedents for the spread of disease around the world as a result of the pilgrimage. As mentioned by Prof. Khan, the meningococcal meningitis spread rapidly to other countries after the pilgrims returned from Mecca. The Saudi government then made the meningitis vaccination mandatory and a requirement for obtaining a Hajj visa. This one requirement has helped control the international spread of the disease.

Similarly, there was a sudden increase in a particular strain of polio in 2005 that was traced to a tribe in Nigeria. Some of their members travelled to Mecca that year to perform the Hajj. Both the World Health Organization (WHO) and the Saudi Government took action. Until this outbreak, WHO had considered polio to be practically eradicated worldwide. The Saudi authorities made it mandatory for pilgrims from specific countries, such as India, Afghanistan, Nigeria, Pakistan and Sudan to be given an oral vaccine when they arrived at the ports in Saudi Arabia. Additionally, they recommended that pilgrims who had already been vaccinated have a booster vaccination six weeks prior to arrival.

The male pilgrims have their head shaved as part of the rites of the Hajj. The huge number of people and the short period of time make this a unique aspect of the event in the world. In the past, shaving the head was performed by anyone able to do it. The highly infectious and dangerous hepatitis B can be rapidly spread by the use of contaminated razor blades. The symptoms may not be obvious until well after it has been passed to a person. The Saudi authorities now have a licensing system for barbers, have set up barber chairs in the area and recommended that all Hajjees ask for a new blade (Saudi FETP).

One of the common illness is a respiratory infection known as the Hajj cough. It ranges from a mild cough to a major illness. According to the Saudi authorities, the spread of this respiratory infection can be minimised by simple precautions such as washing hands, covering coughs and sneezes and disposing of tissues correctly.

To minimise the likelihood and consequence of H1N1 and other infections, the Saudi Ministry of Health and the World Health Organization advised the elderly, children, pregnant women, and patients with chronic diseases to postpone their participation in the Hajj and Umrah in 2009 due to the risk of contracting the pandemic influenza during the pilgrimage. Nationals of all countries other than Saudi Arabia require special Hajj visas. The authorities have used the Hajj visa process to make the vaccination mandatory for a number of diseases. At the ports, all the passengers are screened as they arrive and placed in temporary quarantine areas if they are suspected of being infected.

Pilgrims are educated before, during and after the Hajj with brochures, websites, signage and advice on health issues. One site in the UK recommends that the pilgrims, prior to the Hajj, have a full medical and dental check-up six months before leaving. They also recommend the pilgrims wear good shoes or sandals as there is a large amount of walking, and to take a medical kit as access to medical equipment is limited by the huge number of people. At the same time, the provision of medical facilities and first aid areas on site has been upgraded.

Hajjees, upon their return home, are also encouraged to arrange for a screening stool culture and full blood count to ensure they haven't picked up any diseases or parasites.

The scale of the Hajj and the countries it draws from is unique in the world. It presents risks that may be minor for other events. The scale and consequence of these risks require government-level action. It could not be solved by the event team. The management of the risk brings into play the two types of medicine: preventive, to reduce the likelihood; and therapeutic, to reduce the consequence. The Saudi authorities have implemented measures at many levels. The education on the causes of the spread of the disease of the participants is a vital part of this risk minimisation. They used what was learned from other similar risks to contain the spread of the new world pandemic.

Sources: Saudi FETP, 'Head Shaving', Saudi Epidemiology Bulletin, www.fetp.edu.sa; Javed, N 2007, 'Hajj tests faith — and health', Toronto Star, 18 Dec., www.thestar.com; Khan MA '2003 Outbreaks of Meningococcal Meningitis during Hajj: changing face of an old enemy', Department of Medicine and Infectious Diseases, The Aga Khan University Hospital, Karachi. JPMA, vol. 53, no. 1, 2003.

Questions

1 List the risk identified in the case study and analyse them using likelihood and consequence.

2 The World Cup is another event that attracts large numbers of people from around the world. Which of the risks outlined in the case study would be prevalent at the World Cup? Discuss the difference using the measurement of the risks into their likelihood and consequence.

3 Of all the risks identified in the case study, which ones are a result of crowding and which ones are a result of people arriving from countries without a comprehensive vaccination system?

4 Discuss which of the risks can be minimised through education. How would demographic factors (such as language and country-of-origin) affect the success of such an education program?

REFERENCES

Abbott, J 2000, 'The importance of proper crowd management and crowd control in the special events industry', in Events beyond 2000: setting the agenda, proceedings of conference on event evaluation, research and education, eds J Allen, R Harris, LK Jago & AJ Veal, Australian Centre for Event Management, Sydney.

AFP 2009, 'Hu'll stop the rain on Mao parade', The Australian, 24 Sept.

AS/NZS ISO 31000:2009 Risk management — Principles and guidelines 2009 SAI Global Sydney Australia.

Australian Safety and Compensation Council 2006, *Guidance on the principles of safe design for work*, Commonwealth of Australia, Canberra.

Australian Safety and Compensation Council, 'Hierarchy of controls', OHS practical solutions database, www.ascc.gov.au.

Berlonghi, A 1990, *Special event risk management manual*, Bookmasters, Mansfield, Ohio.

Davis, K 2009, 'Adopting a consistent approach to induction and training', presentation at the 3rd Annual Safety and Security of Puyblic Events and Venues Conference.

China's Foreign Trade 2009, FOCUS — How is the financial crisis affecting China's Exhibition Industry?, 31 Mar., www.ccpit-cft.cn.

De Lollis, B 2009, 'Posh trips for jobs well-done are fading away', *USA Today*, 27 Feb., www.usatoday.com.

Drucker, P 1973, *Management*, Harper and Row, New York.

EMBOK 2006, *Event management body of knowledge*, www.embok.org.

Emergency Planning College, 2009, 'Understanding Crowd Behaviours: Guidance and Lessons Identifed', www.cabinetoffice.gov.uk/ukresilience.

Federal Emergency Management Agency 2000, *Special events contingency planning job aid manual*, Emergency Management Institute, Canberra.

Food and Drug Administration, *Hazard analysis and critical control point principles and application guidelines*, www.cfsan.fda.gov.

Harris, T 2008, 'Crowd nightmare haunts Beijing organisers', *The Sydney Morning Herald*, 4 July.

New Zealand Ministry of Civil Defence and Emergency Management 2003, *Safety planning guidelines for events*, Wellington, New Zealand.

NHS 2008, Festival Health, www.nhs.uk.

O'Malley, N 2005, 'Bosses pull the plug on parties', *The Sydney Morning Herald*, 1 November, www.smh.com.au

O'Toole W 2010, *Event project management system CDROM*, 2nd edn, Sydney, www.epms.net.

SAI Global 2006, *Risk management for events*, SAI Global Assurance Services, Sydney.

Salter, J 2005, 'Emergency planning capability assessment', *Civil care and security studies*, R Gerber & J Salter (eds), Kardoorair.

Silvers, JR 2008, *Risk management for meetings and events*, Elsevier Butterworth-Heinemann.

Standards Australia 2004, *AS/NZS 4360/2004*, Australian New Zealand Risk Management Standard, Canberra.

Tassiopoulos D, Editor 2009, *Events management; a developmental and managerial approach*, 3rd edition, Juta, South Africa.

US Food and Drug Administration 2001, *HACCP: a state of the art approach to food safety*, www.cfsan.fda.gov.

U.S. Travel Association 2009, 'About us', Meetings Mean Business, www.meetings meanbusiness.com.

Work Safe 2006, *Advice for managing events safely*, Victorian WorkCover Authority.

WorkCover NSW, 2009 *Making a difference* NSW Government Publication.

INDEX

3 Network 330, 332, 334, 337–8
4th World Congress of Asian Psychiatry (2011) 16
10 Days on the Island (Tasmania) 14, 286–7

Aboriginal Australians
- protests and boycotts of events 6
- reconciliation events 6, 62

accommodation 462
Adelaide Festival 7, 14, 65, 390–1
Adelaide Fringe Festival 390–1
advertising 315–16
adidas 337
Al Mahabba Awards Festival 2008 (Abu Dhabi) 447–8
alcohol consumption 559–60
ambush marketing 349
amenities 467–70
America's Cup defence
- Auckland (1999–2000, 2002–03) 40, 67
- Perth/Fremantle (1986-87) 8, 13, 40, 65

annual picnics 7
Ansett 349
Ansoff's product-market matrix 283
artists *see* performers
Arts Victoria 399
- Festivals DIY Kit 195, 196

arts/cultural festivals 7–8, 15
- *see also* specific festivals, e.g. Cherry Creek Arts Festival

Asia–Pacific Economic Cooperation forum (APEC) 32
association conferences 45
Athens Olympic Games (2004) 63, 378, 380
Atlanta Olympic Games (1996) 380, 395
Auckland City Council events strategy 406–7
auctions 208
audience
- accommodation 426–7
- demographic profile 494
- identifying 139
- preparing for risks of event 561
- profiling 340
- seating plans 427
- as stakeholders 134–5

audiovisual and special effects 434–5
Australasian Country Music Festival (Tamworth) 14, 63, 336, 395
Australasian Performing Rights Association (APRA) 535–6
Australia
- business-related event performance 411–12
- event timeline 4
- first festival celebrated by white colonists 6
- modern tradition of celebrations 6–8

Australia Day celebrations 131, 284
Australia Day Council 17
Australian Capital Territory (ACT), festival funding criteria 93–4
Australian Centre for Event Management (ACEM), education and training programs 24, 238
Australian Football League (AFL) 537–41
Australian Formula One Grand Prix
- in Adelaide 8, 62
- Auditor General's review of the economic evaluations 81–3
- background 78–80
- battle between the states over hosting 65
- economic evaluations 80–1
- in Melbourne 14, 49, 63
- Save Albert Park protest group 79–80, 288
- sponsorship 335, 338
- in Sydney 8

Australian Motorcycle Grand Prix (Phillip Island) 63
Australian Multicultural Show 428
Australian Music Festival (Glen Innes) 459
Australian Open Tennis Tournament 14, 74–5, 330, 332, 347
Australian Safety and Compensation Council 529

Barossa Under the Stars 394, 413–15
Beijing Olympic Games (2008) 62, 63, 64, 130, 398, 561–2
beverages, on-site logistics 470–1
Bicentenary celebrations 8–9, 39
bidding for events
- bid development 405
- bid support services 405
- bidding process 93, 137
- and event tourism strategy 401
- formation of bidding bodies 92

Big Day Out 15, 62, 131, 334, 335, 338–9, 456
Billabong 330
Birdsville Races 14, 262
Boat Show (Sydney) 17
bottom–up estimating 203
brand messages, sources of 310

branding 309, 394–5
Brazilian Festa at Starlight Cinema 295–8
break-even charts 197–8, 198
Breakfast on the Bridge (Sydney) 64, 486–8
Brisbane Commonwealth Games (1982) 8, 13
broadcast contracts 535–6
broadcast rights 207–8
budget construction 192–6
business events
  benefits to host cities 16–17
  and incentive travel 16
  performance in Australia 411–12
Business Licence Information Service (BLIS) 536
business opportunities 68
business outcomes, leveraging 68–9
Busselton Festival of Triathalon 397

C-PEST analysis 266–70
career opportunities in event industry 23
carnets 461
Caribbean Days Festival (North Vancouver) 106
Carnival, Rio de Janeiro 13
cash flow 199–201
catering 435–6
CEDAREEE framework 345–6
celebration spaces and precincts 39
Centennial Olympic Congress (1994) 378
Central Sydney Operations Group (CSOG) 34
Certified Special Events Professional (CSEP) 18
charity fundraising events 14–15
Chelsea Flower Show (Britain) 13
Cherry Creek Arts Festival, volunteer program 217–18
City of Ballarat Event Planning Guide 470
civic pride 7
Civil Liability Act 2003 (Qld) 548
climate change 129
combination strategy 109
Commonwealth Games *see* specific games, e.g. Manchester Commonwealth Games
Commonwealth Heads of Government Meeting (CHOGM) 32
communication
  integrated marketing 288
  on-site 465–7
  and risk management 555
community arts movement 8
Community Chest Maynardville Carnival 423
community engagement in special events, strategies for 49–51
community events
  Encore Festival and Event Evaluation Kit 507–8
  nature of 14–15, 47
  perspective of community members 48
community festivals movement 7
community perceptions of impacts of events 73–7
community sector
  community events 47
  major events 48–9
  ownership and control of events 64–5
  regional festivals 48
  special events 47–51
  strategies for community engagement 49–51
  types of events generated 128
competition, five competitive forces 267
competitive advantage
  provided by hallmark events 13–14
  provided by mega-events 12–13
competitive parity method 312
conferences and congresses 45
consolidation strategy 109
consumables, on-site logistics 470–1
content theories of motivation 243–5
contract management process 523–4
contracts
  broadcast contracts 535–6
  constructing 527–8
  defined 521
  entertainment contracts 524–5
  letters of agreements 521–3
  sponsor contracts 525
  suppliers contracts 526–7
  typical event industry contracts 521
  venue contracts 525
control systems 111
corporate sector
  association conferences 45
  corporate use of events 44
  external events 45
  internal events 44–5
  perspective on special events 43–6
  recognition of power of events 43–4
  return on investment 46
  types of events generated 128
cost centres, prioritising 205

costing
costing time 203–4
determining ticket prices 206
and estimating 201–9
financial reporting 208–9
and pricing 210–13, 289–90
sensitivity analysis 204
tips for increasing projected income 207–8
tips on reducing costs 204–5
Council for Australian University Tourism and Hospitality Education (CAUTHE) 520
Council for Responsible Sport 375
Cricket Australia 330, 332, 334
Croc Festival 138
crowd control 559, 561–2
crowd management 63, 474, 559
cultural events 14
customer transport 458–61
customers *see* supply of customers
Customs clearance 461

Darling Harbour Authority 63
Darling Harbour (Sydney) 9, 39, 65, 67, 458
Day of the Dead (Mexico) 13
De-briefing meetings 499–500
Delhi Commonwealth Games (2010) 547, 551
demographic segmentation 278–80
Deni — Play on the Plains Festival and World Record Ute Muster 467–8
design *see* event design
destination branding 394–5
destination marketing 14, 35, 395–6
destination promotion services 407–10
destination-based event tourism strategies, developing 388
direct marketing 317
disaster plans 474
drug use at events 559–60
duty of care 528–30

Earth Hour 10, 129
Earth Pledge 378
Earth Summit (Rio de Janeiro) 62, 378
East Coast Blues and Roots Music Festival (Byron Bay) 15, 64
economic environment of event 269
economic impact studies
conducting 71, 493
government use of 71–3
sources of impacts of an event 71
use of multiplier ratio 71
economic impacts of events
leveraging events for economic gain 394
and role of government 70–1
economic sustainability, and event management 10–11
Edinburgh Festival (Scotland) 7, 13, 36, 106, 394
Ellis Park Stadium disaster 562
email, for direct marketing 317
emergency procedures, on-site logistics 473–4
emergency response plans 473
emotive power of events 66
employment creation 69
Encore Festival and Event Evaluation Kit 507–8
energy use, in event production 362–3
entertainment contracts 524–5
entertainment environment of event 270
environmental analysis
competitive analysis 267–8
components of 267
economic environment 269
entertainment environment 270
political environment 268–9
socio-cultural environment 269
technological environment 269–70
environmental impacts of events
measuring 375
need for environmental impact assessment 66–7
need to modify or minimise impacts 67
operations areas to be addressed 360–75
Environmental Protection Acts 528–9
environmental sustainability, and event management 10–11, 377–80
EPARS (event, plan, archive and review system) 174, 175
equity, and events with tourism potential 404
equity theory of motivation 245–6
event audience *see* audience
event concept creation
choosing the event concept 140–1
choosing the venue 139–40
deciding the timing of the event 139
defining the purpose of the event 138–9
designing the event experience 141–2
identifying the event audience 139
summarising the process 141

event concept evaluation
financial screen 144
marketing screen 143
operations screen 143–4
event consumers decision-making process
evaluating alternatives and making event choices 274–5
external influences 272–3
implications for marketing planning 277
information search 272–4
internal influences 273–4
post-event evaluation 275
problem recognition 272
event corporations, establishment in late 1980s 9
event design
and event concept 141–2
principle of safe design 555–6
and project management 178
and theme 423
event documentation 497–8
event evaluation
defined 492
impact of events 492–3
and strategic planning 111–13
see also post-event evaluation
event evaluation process
data analysis 503
data collection 497–503
debriefing meetings 499–500
disseminating event report 504
Encore Festival and Event Evaluation Kit 507–8
event documentation 497–8
event observation 498–9
event participant questionnaires 501, 502
focus groups 500
identifying data required 496–7
journal databases 503
management observation 499
media monitoring 498
model 509
qualitative and quantitative data 497
reporting 504
research bureau data 502–3
resource centres and clearing houses 503
secondary data 501, 502–3
staff observation 499
stages 496
stakeholder observation 499
surveys 500–1
web searches 503
event experience, designing 141–2
event generators, and types of events 128
event impacts *see* impact of events
event industry
birth of 8–11
career opportunities 23
challenges facing new industry 10–11
contracts 521
corporate involvement 9–10
education and training programs 22–4
industry assocations 18–20
regulatory bodies 20
structure 17–20
event industry suppliers, roles 17
event insurance, types 532–3
event knowledge management 495–6
event logistics
control of 484
elements of 453–4
evaluation of the logistics plan 484
importance of checklists 477
logistics or operations plan 485
negotiation and assessment 483–4
on-site logistics 464–74
shutdown 474–7
supply of the customer 454–61
supply of facilities 462–4
supply of product 461–2
event management
connection with event marketing 261
and economic sustainability 10–11
energy use 362–3
and environmental sustainability 10, 360–80
limitation of project management approach 177–8
purchasing policy 361–2
sustainability policy 374
transport solutions 371–2
waste management 67–8, 364–71
water management and sanitation 372–4
Event Management Body of Knowledge (EMBOK) 21, 157, 174, 544
event management companies/organisations
contract management 523–4
establishment of organisational structure 95–107
legal structures 520
role of 17
types of contracts required 532
event management education and training
Australian Centre for Event Management (ACEM) 24

event management education
and training (*continued*)
knowledge and skills required by event managers 20–2
training delivery 22–3
event management organisations *see* event management companies/organisations
event management theory, convergence with project management theory 178
event market segmentation 278–80
event marketing
activities of marketing manager 259
changes in marketing function for events 258–9
connection with event management 261
defined 259
and events as 'service experiences' 260–1
legal issues 530–1
need for marketing 259–60
event marketing communications, relationships with stakeholders and consumers 288
event marketing planning process
choosing generic marketing strategies and tactics for events 282–3
developing event marketing objectives 281–2
the marketing plan 294
positioning the event 280–1
pricing strategy 289–91
segmenting and targeting the event market 278–80
selecting 'services marketing' mix 283–4
steps in 277–84
event marketing research
analysing event environments 265
C-PEST analysis 266–70
event consumer's decision-making process 271–5
event satisfaction, service quality, repeat visits 275–7
human resources 270–1
internal resource audit 270–1
PIECE process 271–5
sources of marketing information 263–5
SWOT analysis 271
event message objectives and strategies 311
event organisers, role of governments as producers or host organisations 35
event ownership 520
event planning
applying project management 156, 158
sustainable purchasing 361–2
use of spreadsheets 179–83
event 'product' experiences
developing the event 284–6
packaging the event 287
planning 284–7
process of creating an event 'product' 285
programming the event 286–7
event production
energy use 362–3
environmental impacts 360–74
measuring environmental impacts 375
transport solutions 371–2
waste management 364–71
water management and sanitation 372–4
event risk, defined 544
event satisfaction 275–7
event sector development services
partnerships and networks 406
research 405–6
training and education 406
event security *see* security at major events
event services trinity 262
event sponsorship strategy
building event sponsorship list 341–2
establishing what the event can offer potential sponsors 340–1
matching event benefits with potential sponsors 342–3
negotiating sponsorship contracts 346–7
preparing and presenting sponsorship proposals 344–6
profiling the audience 340
the sponsorship pitch 343–7
undertaking sponsorship screening process 345–6
event strategy
developed by governments 35–9
EventScotland example 36–9
Townsville City Council case study 52–6
event team, as a key stakeholder 134
event tourism goals
catalyst for expansion and/or improvement of infrastructure 398
creating off-season demand for tourism industry service 396
destination branding 394–5
enhancing visitor experiences 396
geographic dispersal of economic benefits 394
leveraging events for economic gain 394
measuring progress towards 398–9
progression of destination's social, cultural and/or environmental agenda 398

event tourism organisational structure, creation of 399–400
event tourism planning
creation of an organisational structure 399–400
destination-based strategies 388
development of goals 394–8
major event tourism organisations 400
and regional development 412
situational analysis 389–93
strategy development 401–3
SWOT analysis 391–3
event tourism strategic planning process 388–9
event tourism strategy
bidding for events 401
evaluation 411–12
general considerations 402–3
hierarchical model of events 402–3
new event creation 402
using existing events 401
event tourism strategy implementation
bid development and support services 405
coordination 406–7
event sector development services 405–6
event/destination promotion services 407–10
financial support 403–4
grants 403–4
ownership 405
event typology 128
event websites
and sales promotion 317–20
website construction process 318
website design 319–20
event/destination promotion services 407–10
Events Tasmania 405–6
hierarchical model of events 402
Eventscorp, Events Calendar 2010 396–7
EventScotland, events strategy 36–9
Executive Certificate in Event Management (at ACEM) 238
Exhibition and Event Association of Australasia (EEAA), objectives and functions 19–20
exhibitions, nature of 16–17
expectancy theory of motivation 246
Expo 88 (Brisbane) 8, 9, 13, 39, 67

Fair Work (Registered Organisations) Act 2009 (Cwlth) 240
feasibility analysis 92
feasibility studies 492
federal government, involvement in special events 32
Federation, celebration of 6–7, 39
Federation Square (Melbourne) 39
fee+ approach to pricing 213
'feel good' factor 62
Festival of the Olive 443–6
Festival of Trees, Volunteer Survey 241–2
festivals
Arts Victoria Festivals DIY Kit 195, 196
funding criteria in ACT 93–4
importance and nature of 15
legal requirements 534
FIFA World Cup
as a mega-event 12
security 63
sponsorship 337
and sustainability 380
film festivals 15
financial management of events
break-even charts 197–8
budget construction 192–6
cash flow 199–201
categories of costs 203
characteristics of 189
control and financial ratios 197–201
costing and estimating 201–9
costing time 203–4
financial reporting 208–9
fixed costs 201
forecasting finance and ROI 190–2
importance of 188
perceived value/cost pax 199
pricing 210–13
process from project management perspective 189–90
and project management 177
projected costs 202
ratio analysis 198–9
revenue sources 205–6
sensitivity analysis 204
tips for increasing projected income 207–8
tips on reducing costs 204–5
variable costs 201
financial ratios
and control 197–201
ratio analysis 198–9
financial reporting 208–9
financial screening of event concept 144
financial support, for event tourism strategy 403–4
fireworks 434, 530

Fisherman's Wharf, San Francisco 39
Floriade (Canberra) 15, 504–7
focus groups 500
food
  catering 435–6
  on-site logistics 470–1
food safety checklist 472
Food Standards Code 471
food and wine festival 15
Ford 347
forgery of tickets 455
4th World Congress of Asian Psychiatry (2011) 16
franchising events 138
Fremantle Street Arts Festival 396
Fringe Festival 209
Fujitsu 336–7
functional organisational structures 95–100
funding for events
  revenue sources 205–6
  role of governments 35

G20 Summit 32, 65
Gantt charts 166–8
gap analysis 463–4
geographic segmentation 278
GIO 334
Glasgow Commonwealth Games (2014) 36
Global Financial Crisis, effect on events 548
Global Reporting Initiative 374
globalisation, and maintenance of local cultures 129–31
goals and objectives of events 106–8
Gold Coast Indy motor race 68–9, 130, 404
government sector
  awareness of economic significance of events 70–1
  consent authorities and regulatory bodies for events 33–4
  creation of celebrations spaces and precincts 39
  development of event strategies 35–9, 70–1
  event organisation 35
  event/destination marketing 35
  funding for events 35
  involvement of different levels in events 32–3
  ownership/management of venues for events 33
  perspective on special events 32–43
  provision of services for events 34
  roles in special events 33–5
  types of events generated 128
  use of economic impact studies to assess funding of events 71–3
grants, to support events with tourism potential 403–4
Greek Orthodox Folk Dance Festival (San Francisco) 105
green energy checklist 364
green event certification and guidelines 376–7
Green Meetings Industry Council 375
green purchasing checklist 361–2
A Greener Festival 375
growth strategy 109

Ha'il Desert Festival (Saudi Arabia) 183–6
Haj of 2009, and the H1N1 virus 566–8
hallmark events
  defined 13–14
  and destination marketing 14
Harris v Bulldogs Rugby League Club 530
hazard analysis critical control point (HACCP) methodology 471, 556–8
Henley-On-Todd Dry River Boat Regatta (Alice Springs) 14
Herzberg's two-factor theory of motivation 245
H1N1 virus 566–8
hiring charges 205
Home Show (Sydney) 17
Homebake 15
Homecoming Scotland (2009) 36
'hoon effect' 62
hospitality
  checklist 439
  provision to VIPs/guests/sponsors 438–40
host communities
  creating a local atmosphere 130–1
  and forces of globalisation 129–30
  impact of technology 130
  involving 130–1
  receptiveness to events 129
host organisations, types of 127–9
human resource planning for events
  building effective staff and volunteer teams 246–8
  considerations 216
  legal obligations 248–9
  motivating staff and volunteers 243–6
  rights and responsibilities of employers and employees 249

human resource planning process for events
human resource strategy and objectives 218–24
steps in 216–17
human resource strategy and objectives
employment contracts 233
evaluation of process and outcomes 241–2
induction 235, 237
interviews 231–2
job analysis 220
job descriptions 220–3
job specification 223
policies and procedures 224–6
recruitment, selection and induction 226–31
staffing 219–20
strategy 219
supervision and evaluation 238–40
termination, outplacement and re-enlistment 240–1
training and professional development 237–8
Hutchison, Jon 10
Hyundai Hopman Cup, Perth 14

impact of events
balancing 60–70
community perceptions of 73–7
economic 70–2, 394
environmental impacts 66–8
evaluation 492–3
legacy of events 76
negative impacts 60–1
political impacts 65–6
positive impacts 60–1
social and cultural impacts 61–5, 493
tourism and economic impacts 70, 493
in-house events, sourcing 136
in-kind gifts 205
in-kind support and bartering 207
incentive travel, and business events 16
industry associations 18–20
training and certification programs 22
IndyCar Australia 404
Inner Harbor, Baltimore 39
insurance 531–3
integrated marketing communication (IMC)
advertising 315–16
applications for events and festivals 309–11
compared to traditional marketing communications processes 309
defined 308
elements of 313–20
establishing the budget 311–13
personal selling 320
process model for events 310
promotional plan 321
public relations (publicity) 316
sales promotion 316–20
intellectual property 495
International Association of Public Participation (IAP2) 49
International Climate Change Summit (Copenhagen) 10, 32, 65
International Congress and Convention Association (ICCA) 16
International Festivals and Events Association, affiliates in Beijing and Singapore 11
International Motor Show (Sydney) 17
International Music Festival (Canberra) 15
International Olympic Committee (IOC) 32, 76, 378–80, 495
International Special Events Society (ISES)
professional code of ethics 18–19
role and mission 18
standardisation of roles, titles, salaries and job descriptions 23
International Symposium on Hepatitis C Virus and Related Viruses (2011) 16
internet-based marketing for events 318
invitations 457

Johnnie Walker Classic golf tournament 14

Kentucky Derby (USA) 13
Kia 332
knowledge management 495–6

legacy of events
consideration during strategic planning 114
and event evaluation 76
legal issues
contracts 521–8
duty of care 528–30
insurance 531–3
legal requirements for a festival 534
regulations, licences and permits 533–6
related to marketing 530–1
trademarks and logos 528
legislation
relevant to events 534
relevant to OHS and event teams in South Australia 564
licences 533–6

lighting 430–2
Lions Club International Convention, Sydney (2010) 16
Lipton 335
local atmosphere, creating 130–1
local events, nature of 14–15
local governments, involvement in special events 32
logistics
defined 452
see also event logistics; on-site logistics
logistics management
importance of checklists 477
information needed by logistics manager from other festival managers 478
role of event logistics manager 477–82
site or venue maps 482–3
techniques of 477–83
logistics site maps 467–9
logos 528
London Olympic Games (2012) 42–3, 398
Los Angeles Olympic Games (1984) 8

McDonald's 353–5
'main-con' approach to pricing 213
major events
community perspective 48–9
defined 14
Manchester Commonwealth Games (2002) 380, 398
key stakeholders 135–6
and urban regeneration 40–2
workforce requirements 220
Manly Jazz Festival 67
Manly Musical Society 292, 293
Margaret River concerts 14
Margaret River Wine Region Festival 397
market segments for events 278–80
marketing
and logistics 454–5
nature of 258
and project management 177
see also event marketing
marketing screen, of event concept 143
Maslow's hierarchy of needs 244
media
role in events 132–3
as stakeholder in events 132–4
media coverage of events
broadcast contracts 535–6
broadcast rights 207–8
and event evaluation process 498
impact on on-site logistics 471–2
Meetings & Events Australia (MEA), aims and programs 19
meetings industry 16–17
mega-events
defined 12–13
legacy of 76
Melbourne Commonwealth Games (2006) 9, 11, 13, 14, 63, 68, 96, 98
workforce privacy policy 225–6
Melbourne Convention Centre + Visitor's Bureau 399, 407–8
Melbourne Cup 14
Melbourne Festival 14, 434
Melbourne International Comedy Festival 292
Melbourne International Jazz Festival 15
Melbourne Olympic Games (1956) 13, 132
Melbourne Writers Festival 15
merchandising 207
MICE (Meetings, Incentives, Conventions and Exhibitions) industry 16–17
Middle East International Film Festival (Abu Dhabi) 299–303
Midsumma Festival Volunteer Agreement 233–5
mission statements 103–6, 262–3
mobile phone applications 133
mobile power supplies 363
motivating staff and volunteers
content theories of motivation 243–5
equity theory 245–6
expectancy theory 246
process theories of motivation 245–6
Mount Isa Rodeo 15
Movember 14
Mudgee Wine and Food Festival 395
Mulga Bill Festival (Yeoval) 47
multi-organisational or network structures 101–2
Multicultural Festival 209
multiculturalism 8
multiplier ratios 71
music festivals 16, 131
musicians *see* performers

National Apology to Stolen Generation 65
National Business Events Study (NDES) 16
National Event Summit (2009) 142
National Folk Festival (Canberra) 105, 112–13
volunteer registration form 229–30
National Garden Festivals (UK) 40
national governments, involvement in special events 32

national parks 470
network structures 101–2
'new age movement' 8
New South Wales Health 334–5
Newcastle Foreshore Development 39
Northern Lights Festival Boreal (Sudbury, Ontario) 107
NSW Department of Environment and Climate Change 67
NSW Fire Brigades (NSWFB) 353–5
Nymagee Outback Music Festival 14

objective and task method, budgeting for promotions 312–13
occupational health and safety
  and events 562
  National Code 562
  national OHS strategy 2002–12 529, 562
  regulations 536
  safety committees 563–4
  state OHS Acts 562–3
Oktoberfest (Munich) 13
Olympic Games
  legacy of hosting 76
  as mega-events 12
  and national government involvement 32
  security 63
  and sustainable development 378–80
  see also International Olympic Committee; specific games, e.g. Sydney Olympic Games (2000)
Olympic Games Knowledge Service 495
on-site logistics
  amenities and solid waste management 467–70
  communication 465–7
  consumables — food and beverages 470–1
  emergency procedures 473–4
  flow of equipment and people 464–5
  VIP and media requirements 471–3
operational planning
  control systems 111
  event evaluation, shutdown and reporting 111–14
  Rugby World Cup (2003) case study 115–23
  series of plans required 110–11
  test events 111
  use of standing plans 111
operations plans 485
operations screen, event concept 143–4
Optus Festival Buddy 133
Oregon Shakespeare Festival 103, 104–5
organisational structures for event delivery
  establishment of 95
  functional structures 95–100
  multi-organisational or network structures 101–2
  program-based matrix structures 101
Out of the Box Festival of Early Childhood 263
ownership of events
  contracts 521–8
  and duty of care 528–30
  insurance 531–3
  legal issues with marketing of events 530–1
  regulations, licences and permits 533–6
  trademarks and logos 528
  types 520

parametric estimating 203
Parkes Elvis Festival 15, 132, 336, 511–14
participants *see* audience; performers
perceived value/cost pax 199
perceived waiting time 458
percentage of sales method, budgeting for promotions 312
performers
  accommodation 462
  employment and supervision 437
  needs on site 462
permits 533–6
personal selling 320
Philadelphia Folk Festival 96
Phonographic Performance Company of Australia (PPCA) 535–6
PIECE analysis 271–5
PIER (post implementation evaluation and review) 174
pitching for events 136–7, 147–50
political environment of event 268–9
political impacts of events 65–6
Port Fairy Folk Festival 96, 109, 131, 292, 454, 470
post-event evaluation
  creation of demographic profile of audience 494
  defined 492
  enhancement of event reputation 495
  of event management process 495
  identifying possible improvements 494
  and knowledge management 495–6
  measurement of event outcomes 494
power considerations 430

pre-event evaluation 492
pricing
decisions for event marketers 290–1
establishing a pricing strategy 289–90
importance of 'pricing right' 210–12
influences on 289
models 213
process theories of motivation 245–6
product life cycle concept 284
product portfolio, transport 461–2
production schedules 440–1
program-based matrix structures 101
programming of events 423–4
programs for events, consumer information 467
project evaluation 174–5
project management, operational planning 110–14
Project Management Body of Knowledge (PMBoK 2008™) 160
project management of events
advantages of 155
communication with stakeholders and event team 161
controlling the scope 160
design and quality 160
event phase 159
financing the event 160
focus of 154–5
human resources 161
implementation phase 158–9
initiation phase 158
knowledge areas 159–61
limitations of approach to event management 177–8
marketing 160
need for 154
phases of 157–62
planning phase 158
procurement 161
risk management 160
shutdown phase 159
stakeholder management 161
time management 160
project management systems and software 176–7
project management techniques
defining the project and scope of work 163–4
delegation and self-control 173
earned value 174
Gantt charts 166–8
identifying tasks and responsibilities 166
meetings 172
monitoring the project 172
network analysis and critical path 168–9
payback period and return on investment 171
project management triangle 169–70
quality 173
reports 172
resource analysis 165–6
responsibilities (from documents to deliverables) 170–1
scheduling 166–70
use in event management 162–3
work breakdown structure (WBS) 164–5
work in progress (WIP) reports 173–4
project management theory, convergence with event management theory 178
project managers
key competencies in events 161–2
role of 161
projected income, tips for increasing 207–8
promotional plan 321
promotions budget 311–13
Public Halls Act 536
public relations (publicity) 316
publicity, reducing costs 204
purchasing policy 361–2
purpose statements 103–6

Qantas 335, 338, 349
quality 173
Queensland Events 403
Queensland Music Festival 14, 15
queuing 458
Quit Forest Rally 397

raffles 208
ratio analysis 198–9
Reconciliation Week 6, 62
recording events 441
recycling 67
Red Bull Air Race 397
Red Nose Day 14
regional festivals
as community builders 48
economic impacts 69–70
nature of 15
regulations 533–6
regulatory bodies
and events industry 20
role of governments 33–4
regulatory environment, changes and risk management 548–9
Repco Rally Australia (2009) 64
reporting, event evaluation process 504

research bureau data 502–3
retrenchment strategy 109
return on investment (ROI), forecasting 190–2
revenue sources 205–6
review of environmental factors (REF) 470
risk, in an event context 544
risk identification techniques
- accurate description of risks 552
- classifying risk and SWOT 550
- consultation 551
- contingency plans 551
- event and venue team 552
- fault diagrams 550–1
- incident reports 551
- scenario development and tabletop exercises 551
- test events 550
- work breakdown structure 549–50

risk management
- defined 545
- main areas of risk 545
- and project management 160, 545–6
- specific event risks 558–61
- and strategic planning 545

risk management methodologies
- hazard analysis critical control points (HACCPs) 471, 566–8
- principles of safe design 555–6

risk management process
- analysis and evaluation of risk 552–3
- control 553–4
- from design perspective 557
- identifying risks 549, 549–52
- mitigating actions 554–5
- overview 544–7
- risk communication 555
- risk management methodologies 555–8
- understanding context 547–9

risk management strategy
- alcohol and drugs 559–60
- areas to cover 545
- communications 560
- crowd management 559
- emergency services 560–1
- environmental impacts 560
- preparing the attendee for the event 561

Roskilde Festival 96, 97
Rotary International Convention, Sydney (2014) 16
Royal Botanic Gardens (Sydney) 470
Royal Easter Show (Sydney) 266, 322–4
RSVP 26–8
Rugby World Cup (2003) 9, 11, 13, 63, 68, 334
- operational planning 115–23

Rural and General Insurance Brokers (RGIB) 532
Ryder Cup, Scotland (2014) 36

Safe Work Australia 536
safety *see* occupational health and safety
sales promotion
- direct marketing 317
- nature of 316–17
- online presence 317–20

San Jose Jewish Film Festival 103
sanitation at events 372–4
Save Albert Park protest group 79–80
scenario development and tabletop exercises 551
Schoolies Week (Gold Coast) 49, 63, 64
Scone Horse Festival 395, 401
scope definition 163–4
Scotland, government events strategy 36–9
Scotland Island festival 314–15
seating plans 427
security at major events
- during shutdown 476
- and threat of terrorism 63, 547

sensitivity analysis (costing) 204
service quality evaluation 275–7
Services for Australian Rural and Remote Allied Health Conference (2006) 105
shutdown
- management of 159
- on-site issues 474–6
- planning for 113–14
- project closure 476–7
- and security 476
- site clean-up 476

shutdown checklist 475
signage 465, 466
Sing Australia 424
site clean-up 476
site map checklist 483
site maps 467–8, 482–3
situation analysis 108, 388–93
social and cultural impacts of events
- community ownership and control of events 64–5
- crowd behaviour 63
- evaluating 493
- 'feel good' factor 62
- 'hoon effect' 62
- positive and negative impact 61–3

social media, role in events 133
socio-cultural environment of event 269
socioeconomic market segments for events 279
solid waste management 467–70
Sony Playstation 10th Anniversary Party 144–5
Sorry Day 62
sound systems 432–4
South Australian Brewing Company Pty Ltd v Carlton and United Breweries Ltd 537–41
South Australian Wooden Boat and Music Festival 521–3
South Bank Parklands (Brisbane) 9, 39, 67
Southbank precinct (Melbourne) 9, 39
special effects 434–5
special events
  as benchmarks for our lives 5
  categorisation of 12
  community perspective 47–51
  corporate perspective 43–6
  defined 11–12
  form and content 15–17
  government perspective 32–43
  as 'service experiences' 260–1, 284
  size 12–15
  types 12–17
spectators, as stakeholders 134–5
Splendour in the Grass 369–71
sponsor contracts 525
sponsors
  attracting 131
  benefits of event sponsorship 333–7
  fit with sponsees 338–9
  as partners in events 131–2
  use of events 329
sponsorship
  benefits for events 332–3
  benefits for sponsors 333–7
  of events with tourism potential 404
  exchange relationship in event sponsorship 332
  and fit between sponsor and sponsee 338–9
  measuring and evaluating 351–2
  role of 328–9
  three-way relationship underpinning success 329
  trends influencing growth of 329–31
  see also event sponsorship strategy
sponsorship contracts, negotiating 346–7
sponsorship leveraging 208, 337–8
sponsorship management
  need for effective management 347–8
  techniques for effective management 348–9
sponsorship management plan 349–51
sponsorship policy, value of 339
sponsorship proposals, preparing and presenting 344–6
sponsorship screening process 345–6
Sport and Environment Commission (SEC) 378–9
Sport and Recreation Victoria 399
sports events
  economic impact studies in UK 71–3
  importance and benefits of 15–16
  insurance 533
  and sustainability 377–80
sports sponsorships 330
spreadsheets, using to plan an event 179–83
stability strategy 109
stages
  relationship between type of event and staging elements 429
  safety considerations 430
  and stage plans 427–30
staggered entertainment 458
staging events
  accommodating audience and guests 426–7
  audiovisual and special effects 434–5
  catering 435–6
  contingencies 441
  employment and supervision of performers 437
  entry and exits 426–7
  lighting 430–2
  main concerns 422
  managing the crew 438
  power considerations 430
  the production schedule 440–1
  programming 423–4
  props and decoration 435
  provision of hospitality for guests/sponsors 438–40
  recording the event 441
  seating plans 427
  sound system 432–4
  the stage 427–30
  theming and event design 422–3
  tools of staging 442
  venue choice 424–6
stakeholder management 161

stakeholders
co-workers (event team) 134
in events 126
host community 129–31
and marketing communications 288
media 132–4
participants and spectators 134–5
relationship to events 127
sponsors 131–2
state governments
competition between states for events 9
involvement in special events 32
rivalry over hosting events 65
strategic event marketing process 264
strategic event planning process
concept or intent to bid 92
decision to proceed or cease 92
establishment of organisational structure 95–102
for existing events 114
feasibility analysis 92
formation of a bidding body and bid preparation 92–5
goals and objectives 106–8
identification of strategy options 108–10
legacy program 114
nature of 102–3
operational planning 110–14
purpose, vision and mission statements 103–6
situation analysis 108
steps 91
strategy evaluation and selection 110
strategic marketing process, role of 261–3
strategic planning process, explained 90–1
strategy evaluation and selection 110
strategy options, identification 108–10
Suncorp 334
suppliers contracts 526–7
supply of customers
customer transport 458–61
links with marketing and promotion 454–5
queuing 458
ticketing 455–7
supply of facilities 462–4
supply of product
accommodation 462
artists' needs on site 462
transport 461–2
surveys, event evaluation 500–1
sustainability
energy use 362–4
purchasing policy 361–2
transport solutions 371–2
waste management 364–71
water management and sanitation 372–4
sustainability policy for events management 374
Sustainable Event Alliance 375
sustainable event industry organisations 375–6
sustainable events
green event certification and guidelines 376–7
major sports events 377–8
Olympic Games 378–80
Sustainable Tourism Cooperative Research Centre (STCRC) 507
SWOT analysis 108
Sydney Biennale 15
Sydney Convention Centre and Visitors Bureau 400
Sydney Festival 14, 133, 318, 342
Sydney Gay and Lesbian Mardi Gras 9, 14, 15, 63, 104, 130
Sydney Olympic Games (2000) 9, 13, 63, 67, 68, 76, 101, 380, 396, 398, 495, 528
Sydney to Hobart Yacht Race (1998) 62

TAC 349
talent *see* artists
target markets 278–80
technological environment of event 269–70
10 Days on the Island (Tasmania) 14, 286–7
tendering for events 136–7
terrorism threat, security at major events 63, 547
tertiary education institutions, and event management education 22–3
test events 111, 550
The Hospitality Group (THG) 530–1
Theme Traders 147–50
themed years 395
themes, and event design 422–3
3 Network 330, 332, 334, 337–8
ticketing
determining ticket prices 206
forgery of tickets 455
invitations 457
logistics checklist 457
on-line ticket sales 292, 456
scalping 456
ticket distribution 455–7
ticket scaling 207
ticketing agencies 291, 456

timing of events, deciding 139
toilets 470
top–down estimating 203
total quality management (TQM) 173
Tour de France 13
tourism, and festivals 15
Tourism Australia, promotional plan for 2006 Ashes cricket tour 408–10
tourism and economic impact of events
  business opportunities 68
  employment creation 69
  leveraging the business outcomes of events 68–9
  in regional communities 69–70
Tourism New South Wales, Regional Flagship Events program 403
Tourism Victoria 399
Townsville City Council, events strategy 52–6
Toyota 330
Trade Practices Act 1974 (Cwlth) 455, 456, 528, 530–1, 537, 538, 540
trade promotion, and special events 32
trade site maps 469
trademarks 528
traffic management plans 459
Traffic management for special events (NSW government) 459
transport
  of customers 458–61
  of products 461–2
transport solutions 371–2
Tropfest 15, 132–3

UK
  economic impact studies of sporting events 71–3
  events associated with British royal family 65
  Scotland's events strategy 36–9
  use of events as tools for urban regeneration 40–3
Uncle Toby's 330, 333
under-pricing, cycle of 211
United Nations Environment Program (UNEP) 378–9
urban regeneration, resulting from event-based strategies 40–3

V8 Supercar racing 336–7
value pricing 213
value-added project manager approach to pricing 213
venue contracts 525
venue maps 482–3
venues
  choosing 139–40, 291–3, 424–6
  and event management 17–18
  governments as owner/manager of 33
  importance of physical setting 291
  variety of event sites 425
Victorian Events Industry Council (VEIC) 399
Victorian Major Events Company 399, 401
Virgin Mobile 330
virtual existence of events 133
vision statements 103–6
Vivid Festival 431–2
Vodafone 330
Volunteering Queensland 236
volunteers
  building effective teams 246–8
  Cherry Creek Arts Festival Volunteer Program 217–18
  Festival of Trees Volunteer Survey 241–2
  Midsumma Festival Volunteer Agreement 233–5
  motivating 243–6
  sample volunteer contract 236
  use of 177
  using to reduce costs 205
  Volunteering Queensland 236
  waste volunteers 369

Walk Against Want 14
Wangaratta Jazz Festival 15, 33, 349
waste management
  bin logistics and signage 368
  biodegradable waste 369
  in event production 67, 364–7
  recycle stations & incentives 369
  recycling 368
  salvage and re-purposing 369
  solid waste management 467–70
  types of waste produced at an event 367–8
  Waste Wise Event Action Plan 365–6
waste prevention 368
waste volunteers 369
water management
  emissions to water 373
  grey water 373
  main concerns at an event 372
  sanitation 374
  and sustainability 373
water management checklist 372–3
waterfront precincts 39

websites *see* event websites
Weipa Crocodile Festival 62
Winter Olympic Games
  Lillehammer (1994) 378, 379
  Nagano (1998) 132, 380
Wolfe Island Scene of the Crime Festival 103–4
WOMADelaide 381–3, 390, 454
Woodford Folk Festival 15, 109, 131, 292, 317, 483
  human resources policy 250–3
  mission 263
word-of-mouth advertising 131, 270
WorkSafe Victoria, event safety policy 563
World Fairs, as mega-events 12
World Masters Games — Melbourne (2002) 9
World Masters Games — Sydney (2009) 76–7
World Swimming Championships, Melbourne (2007) 14, 68
World of WearableArt event 99–100
World Youth Day, Sydney (2008) 9, 13
'wow factor' 178

YouTube 133

zero emissions power supplies 363